Lecture Notes in Computer Science   13095

More information about this subseries at http://www.springer.com/series/7409

Constantine Stephanidis ·
Masaaki Kurosu · Jessie Y. C. Chen ·
Gino Fragomeni · Norbert Streitz ·
Shin'ichi Konomi · Helmut Degen ·
Stavroula Ntoa (Eds.)

HCI International 2021 - Late Breaking Papers

Multimodality, eXtended Reality, and Artificial Intelligence

23rd HCI International Conference, HCII 2021
Virtual Event, July 24–29, 2021
Proceedings

Springer

Editors
Constantine Stephanidis
University of Creteand Foundation
for Research and Technology – Hellas
(FORTH)
Heraklion, Crete, Greece

Jessie Y. C. Chen
U.S. Army Research Laboratory
Aberdeen Proving Ground, MD, USA

Norbert Streitz 🅐
Smart Future Initiative
Frankfurt am Main, Hessen, Germany

Helmut Degen
Siemens (United States)
Princeton, NJ, USA

Masaaki Kurosu
The Open University of Japan
Chiba, Japan

Gino Fragomeni
U.S. Army Combat Capabilities
Development Command Soldier Center
Orlando, FL, USA

Shin'ichi Konomi
Faculty of Arts and Science
Kyushu University
Fukuoka, Japan

Stavroula Ntoa
Foundation for Research and Technology –
Hellas (FORTH)
Heraklion, Crete, Greece

ISSN 0302-9743   ISSN 1611-3349   (electronic)
Lecture Notes in Computer Science
ISBN 978-3-030-90962-8   ISBN 978-3-030-90963-5   (eBook)
https://doi.org/10.1007/978-3-030-90963-5

LNCS Sublibrary: SL3 – Information Systems and Applications, incl. Internet/Web, and HCI

This Springer imprint is published by the registered company Springer Nature Switzerland AG
The registered company address is: Gewerbestrasse 11, 6330 Cham, Switzerland

Foreword

Human-Computer Interaction (HCI) is acquiring an ever-increasing scientific and industrial importance, and having more impact on people's everyday life, as an ever-growing number of human activities are progressively moving from the physical to the digital world. This process, which has been ongoing for some time now, has been dramatically accelerated by the COVID-19 pandemic. The HCI International (HCII) conference series, held yearly, aims to respond to the compelling need to advance the exchange of knowledge and research and development efforts on the human aspects of design and use of computing systems.

The 23rd International Conference on Human-Computer Interaction, HCI International 2021 (HCII 2021), was planned to be held at the Washington Hilton Hotel, Washington DC, USA, during July 24–29, 2021. Due to the COVID-19 pandemic and with everyone's health and safety in mind, HCII 2021 was organized and run as a virtual conference. It incorporated the 21 thematic areas and affiliated conferences listed on the following page.

A total of 5222 individuals from academia, research institutes, industry, and governmental agencies from 81 countries submitted contributions, and 1276 papers and 241 posters were included in the volumes of the proceedings that were published before the start of the conference. Additionally, 174 papers and 146 posters are included in the volumes of the proceedings published after the conference, as "Late Breaking Work" (papers and posters). The contributions thoroughly cover the entire field of HCI, addressing major advances in knowledge and effective use of computers in a variety of application areas. These papers provide academics, researchers, engineers, scientists, practitioners, and students with state-of-the-art information on the most recent advances in HCI. The volumes constituting the full set of the HCII 2021 conference proceedings are listed in the following pages.

I would like to thank the Program Board Chairs and the members of the Program Boards of all thematic areas and affiliated conferences for their contribution towards the highest scientific quality and overall success of the HCI International 2021 conference.

This conference would not have been possible without the continuous and unwavering support and advice of Gavriel Salvendy, founder, General Chair Emeritus, and Scientific Advisor. For his outstanding efforts, I would like to express my appreciation to Abbas Moallem, Communications Chair and Editor of HCI International News.

July 2021   Constantine Stephanidis

HCI International 2021 Thematic Areas and Affiliated Conferences

Thematic Areas

- HCI: Human-Computer Interaction
- HIMI: Human Interface and the Management of Information

Affiliated Conferences

- EPCE: 18th International Conference on Engineering Psychology and Cognitive Ergonomics
- UAHCI: 15th International Conference on Universal Access in Human-Computer Interaction
- VAMR: 13th International Conference on Virtual, Augmented and Mixed Reality
- CCD: 13th International Conference on Cross-Cultural Design
- SCSM: 13th International Conference on Social Computing and Social Media
- AC: 15th International Conference on Augmented Cognition
- DHM: 12th International Conference on Digital Human Modeling and Applications in Health, Safety, Ergonomics and Risk Management
- DUXU: 10th International Conference on Design, User Experience, and Usability
- DAPI: 9th International Conference on Distributed, Ambient and Pervasive Interactions
- HCIBGO: 8th International Conference on HCI in Business, Government and Organizations
- LCT: 8th International Conference on Learning and Collaboration Technologies
- ITAP: 7th International Conference on Human Aspects of IT for the Aged Population
- HCI-CPT: 3rd International Conference on HCI for Cybersecurity, Privacy and Trust
- HCI-Games: 3rd International Conference on HCI in Games
- MobiTAS: 3rd International Conference on HCI in Mobility, Transport and Automotive Systems
- AIS: 3rd International Conference on Adaptive Instructional Systems
- C&C: 9th International Conference on Culture and Computing
- MOBILE: 2nd International Conference on Design, Operation and Evaluation of Mobile Communications
- AI-HCI: 2nd International Conference on Artificial Intelligence in HCI

Conference Proceedings – Full List of Volumes

38. CCIS 1420, HCI International 2021 Posters - Part II, edited by Constantine Stephanidis, Margherita Antona, and Stavroula Ntoa

39. CCIS 1421, HCI International 2021 Posters - Part III, edited by Constantine Stephanidis, Margherita Antona, and Stavroula Ntoa

40. LNCS 13094, HCI International 2021 - Late Breaking Papers: Design and User Experience, edited by Constantine Stephanidis, Marcelo M. Soares, Elizabeth Rosenzweig, Aaron Marcus, Sakae Yamamoto, Hirohiko Mori, P. L. Patrick Rau, Gabriele Meiselwitz, Xiaowen Fang, and Abbas Moallem

41. LNCS 13095, HCI International 2021 - Late Breaking Papers: Multimodality, eXtended Reality, and Artificial Intelligence, edited by Constantine Stephanidis, Masaaki Kurosu, Jessie Y. C. Chen, Gino Fragomeni, Norbert Streitz, Shin'ichi Konomi, Helmut Degen, and Stavroula Ntoa

42. LNCS 13096, HCI International 2021 - Late Breaking Papers: Cognition, Inclusion, Learning, and Culture, edited by Constantine Stephanidis, Don Harris, Wen-Chin Li, Dylan D. Schmorrow, Cali M. Fidopiastis, Margherita Antona, Qin Gao, Jia Zhou, Panayiotis Zaphiris, Andri Ioannou, Robert A. Sottilare, Jessica Schwarz, and Matthias Rauterberg

43. LNCS 13097, HCI International 2021 - Late Breaking Papers: HCI Applications in Health, Transport, and Industry, edited by Constantine Stephanidis, Vincent G. Duffy, Heidi Krömker, Fiona Fui-Hoon Nah, Keng Siau, Gavriel Salvendy, and June Wei

44. CCIS 1498, HCI International 2021 - Late Breaking Posters (Part I), edited by Constantine Stephanidis, Margherita Antona, and Stavroula Ntoa

45. CCIS 1499, HCI International 2021 - Late Breaking Posters (Part II), edited by Constantine Stephanidis, Margherita Antona, and Stavroula Ntoa

http://2021.hci.international/proceedings

HCI International 2021 (HCII 2021)

The full list with the Program Board Chairs and the members of the Program Boards of all thematic areas and affiliated conferences is available online:

http://www.hci.international/board-members-2021.php

HCI International 2022

The 24th International Conference on Human-Computer Interaction, HCI International 2022, will be held jointly with the affiliated conferences at the Gothia Towers Hotel and Swedish Exhibition & Congress Centre, Gothenburg, Sweden, June 26 – July 1, 2022. It will cover a broad spectrum of themes related to Human-Computer Interaction, including theoretical issues, methods, tools, processes, and case studies in HCI design, as well as novel interaction techniques, interfaces, and applications. The proceedings will be published by Springer. More information will be available on the conference website: http://2022.hci.international/.

General Chair
Prof. Constantine Stephanidis
University of Crete and ICS-FORTH
Heraklion, Crete, Greece
Email: general_chair@hcii2022.org

http://2022.hci.international/

Contents

Multimodal Interaction

Towards Effective Odor Diffusion with Fuzzy Logic in an Olfactory Interface for a Serious Game

Miguel Garcia-Ruiz[1]([⊠]), Bill Kapralos[2], and Genaro Rebolledo-Mendez[3]

[1] Algoma University, Ontario P6A2G4 Sault Ste. Marie, Canada
miguel.garcia@algomau.ca
[2] Ontario Tech University, Oshawa, Ontario L1G OC5, Canada
bill.kapralos@uoit.ca
[3] Monterrey Institute of Technology, 64849 Monterrey, Nuevo Leon, Mexico
g.rebolledo@tec.mx

Abstract. The real world is multisensory and our experiences in this world are constructed by the stimulation of all our senses including visual, auditory, touch, olfactory, and taste. However, virtual environments including virtual simulations and serious games, and the human-computer interface more generally, have focused on the visual and auditory senses. Simulating the other senses such as the sense of smell (olfaction) can be beneficial for supporting learning. In this paper we present a simple and cost-effective olfactory interface constructed using an Arduino Uno microcontroller board, a small fan, an off-the-shelf air freshener to deliver scents to a user of a serious game. A fuzzy logic system regulated the amount of scent delivered to the user based on their distance to the display. As a proof-of-concept, we developed a serious game intended to teach basic math (counting) skills to children. Learners (players) collect pineapples from the scene and then enter the amount of pineapples collected. As the pineapples are collected, a pineapple scent is emitted from the olfactory interface thus serving to supplement or complement the learner's senses and stimulate their affection and cognition. As part of our proof-of-concept, a 10 year old learner played the game and provided us with feedback regarding the olfactory interface and illustrated the potential of the system.

Keywords: Olfactory interface · Smell · Serious game · Microcontroller board · Fuzzy logic

1 Introduction

In the real world, our senses are constantly exposed to stimuli from multiple sensory modalities (visual, auditory, vestibular, olfactory, taste, touch, etc.), and although the process is not exactly understood, we can integrate/process this multisensory information in our acquisition of knowledge of objects in our environment [1]. Although a complete overview of the senses is beyond the scope of this paper, an excellent overview of the senses from a variety of perspectives is provided by [2]. The senses

© Springer Nature Switzerland AG 2021
C. Stephanidis et al. (Eds.): HCII 2021, LNCS 13095, pp. 3–16, 2021.
https://doi.org/10.1007/978-3-030-90963-5_1

interact with one another and alter each other's processing and ultimately our overall perception. Most scientific research suggests that the more modalities that are integrated into a virtual representation of our environment, the greater the sense of presence or immersion in that space (see e.g., [3, 4]). Additional modalities can reinforce existing information, or provide additional information that cannot be obtained by a single modality alone. For instance, although vision tends to dominate, auditory information can tell us what is behind a door, or behind or inside our bodies. With respect to learning, training and memory, most studies acknowledge that multiple sensory inputs result in improved processing and retention [5]. Moreover, when there is a deficit in one modality, another may be substituted: persons with hearing impairment sometimes perceive sound with touch, for example [6]. Tactile substitutions for vision are common (e.g. Braille), and "even a poor resolution sensory substitution system can provide the information necessary for the perception of complex images" [7, 8]. For a thorough overview of sensory substitution see [9].

Designers and developers of immersive 3D virtual environments including virtual simulations and serious games, typically aim to faithfully recreate real-world scenarios. In fact, it has been suggested that "achieving multisensory digital experiences is the holy grail of human-technology interaction" in general [10]. However, traditional emphasis is placed on recreating the visual, and (perhaps to a lesser extent), auditory scenes, while ignoring the other senses (including touch, smell, and taste) despite their importance in the real world [11]. Of course, simulating the sense of touch, smell, and taste is not trivial and presents many technological challenges and issues. Recently, there has been a large effort made on simulating the sense of touch (e.g., haptics) and this effort has been accelerated with the availability of consumer-level haptic devices.

Aside from some limited application in virtual environments, the sense of smell has been underused in human-computer interfaces, compared to the use of other senses [12] in multimodal HCI [13]. Studies regarding the role of sensory stimulation in virtual environments has highlighted olfactory stimulation as a potentially powerful yet underutilized therapeutic tool [14]. When incorporated into a virtual environment, the sense of smell (olfaction) may be useful in the treatment of post-traumatic stress disorder (PTSD), a mental health condition triggered by a terrifying event, either experiencing or witnessing it [14]. Furthermore, incorporating pleasant and congruent ambient scents into a virtual environment can lead to enhanced sensory stimulation, which in turn, can directly (and indirectly through ease of imagination) influence affective and behavioral reactions [10]. Finally, incorporating olfactory technologies into virtual environments has shown to be safe and effective for targeting several aspects of psychological and physical health such as anxiety, stress, and pain [15]. In addition, olfactory stimuli at the user interface (UI) may be beneficial in learning, including users' mood enhancement and stress reduction [12], shifting the learner's attention to focus on a particular event happening at the UI [13].

There are different techniques used for generating smells in olfactory human-computer interfaces. One of them works by spraying odors into the air [16], used by commercial off-the shelf air fresheners used in households and in other environments, as well as in computer-controlled olfactory interfaces, for example [17–19]. These and other projects cited elsewhere use microcontroller boards for controlling and activating sprays. A microcontroller board contains a microcontroller (a small computer on a chip) and extra electronic components that facilitate prototyping of physical computing applications using sensors [20]. Microcontroller boards are effective for controlling actuators such as motors and fans. [21] successfully tested a portable device that generated an odor to enhance user experiences in museums, containing a microcontroller board and two small fans.

However, very few reported olfactory display applications implement an efficient and carefully controlled way to diffuse scents in the air. For instance, [22] used fuzzy logic (it models human logic with intermediate possibilities between digital values YES and NO [23]), a motion sensor and a microphone connected to a microcontroller board for controlling an air freshener, activating it only when it was needed, as an olfactory stimulus to enhance user experiences in large venues. The fuzzy logic analyzed the noise levels and the number of people present in a venue to diffuse a pleasant odor accordingly.

2   Objective

Given the importance of olfaction within the human-computer interface and immersive environments such as virtual simulations and serious games, we have recently begun investigating the use of olfactory stimulation in virtual learning environments. Our ultimate goal is to develop effective virtual learning environments that maximize learning (knowledge acquisition and retention), and we believe this includes an environment where multiple senses (beyond audio and visual) are stimulated. In this paper, we describe the development of a simple, cost effective, and efficient olfactory interface that uses "off the shelf" equipment to provide olfactory stimulation within a typical serious gaming scenario (e.g., a learner seated in front of a computer display playing a math serious game). Inspired by the work of [24], the olfactory interface incorporates fuzzy logic running on an Arduino Uno (a very easy to use microcontroller board, useful in physical computing prototyping [25]), adjusting the amount of scent that it emits based on the distance between the learner (player) and the display (measured by an ultrasonic sensor), and controls a fan placed behind the scent dispenser (an off-the-shelf air freshener) to diffuse an odor. With the limited work focusing on olfactory displays and the growing interest in their use, the work presented here illustrates how an olfactory display can be developed and incorporated into a virtual learning environment in a simple and cost effective manner.

We decided to use fuzzy logic to control our olfactory interface's fan speed and to activate an air freshener, because when we tested the interface's ultrasonic sensor we found that when we directly mapped the distance between the player and the olfactory interface the fan speed was done in very small and linear increments, and participants who perceived the smell diffused by the fan did not notice any significant difference. After observing the same effect in a previous study about simulating physical wind in a racing game [26], we noticed in that study that direct mapping of a virtual car velocity to fan speed was done in very small and smooth increments, and participants who tested the fan system in that study did not notice small changes in wind speed. By applying fuzzy logic to control the fan speed in our olfactory interface, the fuzzy logic renders an effective fan speed control (and hence diffusing the smell to the user more effectively) with no perceived delay in the smell diffusion. This in turn could support a satisfactory player's olfactory experience. The next section provides a brief introduction to fuzzy logic and our fuzzy logic system.

3   What is Fuzzy Logic?

Fuzzy logic is an extension of classic Boolean logic (defining and using true/false values), uses the interval of real numbers between 0 (false) and 1 (true) to describe intelligent reasoning (e.g. 0.89 could mean it is "almost true"), taking into account uncertainties or inaccuracies dealing with imprecise logic values [23]. This has a gradual transition from falsehood to truth. Fuzzy logic is a technique applied in artificial intelligence (AI) to model human logical reasoning with imprecise statements in computer systems such as "it feels really windy outside" where we don't have a precise and discrete wind value that represents "very windy". It is based on human reasoning and decision making using a range of possibilities between YES and NO, such as:

- CERTAINLY YES
- POSSIBLY YES
- CANNOT SAY
- POSSIBLY NO
- CERTAINLY NO

Those possibilities from a fuzzy logic system are expressed verbally so people can better understand them, and used to represent a more "human-like" output from a system, and not a linear response to the user.

Fuzzy logic can be used to control devices such as motors and consumer products, such as washing machines. This technique may not give accurate reasoning, but acceptable reasoning, e.g. how a washing machine should properly wash dirty but heavy loads of clothes, so it will determine the right amount of water and temperature needed to wash those clothes. Fuzzy logic deals with uncertainty. For example, the speed of a fan can be controlled according to uncertain input values (e.g. distance, or temperature, or humidity changes) from the environment. Thus, it is often necessary to use sensors for measuring values from the environment and use those as input values in fuzzy logic.

In a fuzzy logic system, it is necessary to define fuzzy sets and rules to deal with fuzzy values. Fuzzy rules are conditionals coded in the form of *if-then* decisions and language functions, such as minimum or maximum value calculations that define behaviours and degrees of membership in a fuzzy system. For example, a fuzzy rule can be: "If it's forecasted 40% to 50% chance of rain this morning and the barometer is measuring a lower pressure, I will bring an umbrella to work".

A fuzzy set is an extension of classical crisp sets and are based on the fuzzy set theory. A fuzzy set can be defined as "any set that allows its members to have different grades of membership (membership function) in the interval [0, 1]" [27]. Fuzzy rules define degrees of membership to fuzzy sets. In our previous example, we define two fuzzy sets, one can be composed of rain chance and the other one will be barometric pressure values. Both fuzzy sets can have subsets (membership functions) such as "not likely", "likely", and "very likely". The universe of discourse is the possible range of all values for an input to a fuzzy system (e.g. from 0.0 to 100.0, or [0.0, 100.0]). The crossover point of a fuzzy set is an element at which its membership function is 0.5 [30].

In order to implement fuzzy logic to a real-world application, it must follow three main steps [30] (see Fig. 1):

1. Fuzzification: convert input (crisp) data into fuzzy data and define membership functions and fuzzy sets.
2. Fuzzy inference process: compute fuzzy rules with fuzzy sets to derive the fuzzy output.
3. Defuzzification: convert a fuzzified output obtained from the inference computations into a crisp value with respect to fuzzy sets and their subsets and fuzzy rules.

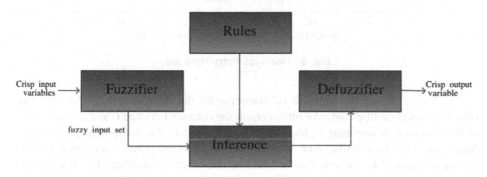

Fig. 1. The fuzzy logic process.

As Fig. 1 shows, the fuzzy logic system inputs crisp values coming from a sensor. The system outputs are crisp values, which will be used to activate an actuator such as a motor, a fan, etc.

3.1 Our Fuzzy Logic System

Since fuzzy logic deals with imprecise levels of truth simulating human reasoning, we defined using preliminary iterative testing with our olfactory interface three fuzzy sets: i) Close (20–40 cm), ii) Near (35–60 cm) and iii) Far (55–80 cm), for the measured distance using an ultrasonic sensor. Figure 2 shows the fuzzy sets. Those were crisp input variables used in our fuzzy logic system that ran on the Arduino Uno microcontroller board.

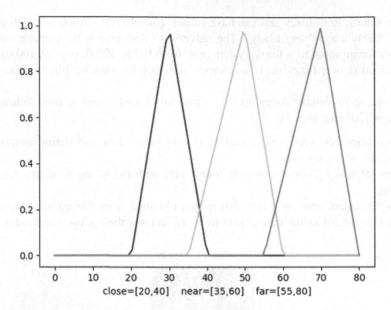

close=[20,40]   near=[35,60]   far=[55,80]

Fig. 2. Our three fuzzy input sets.

As Fig. 2 shows, the universe of discourse for the input values is [20, 80]. Our olfactory interface does not take into account the distance between 0 and 20 cms, since at that distance the user may be too close to the screen and the air freshener, receiving a huge amount of odor on the face, may negatively affect the player experience. Further testing is required to confirm this. In addition, the olfactory interface does not activate when the distance between the interface and the player exceeds 80 cms, meaning that the player is very far away from the computer, or not seated in front of the computer at all.

Our fuzzy logic rules are as follows:

- IF the player is 20 to 40 cms away from the computer screen THEN rotate the fan at low speed accordingly AND activate the air freshener.
- IF the player is 35 to 60 cms away from the computer screen THEN rotate the fan at medium speed accordingly AND activate the air freshener.
- IF the player is 55 to 80 cms away from the computer screen THEN rotate the fan at fast speed accordingly AND activate the air freshener.

Our fuzzy logic generated crisp output values (integer numbers) that fell between 0 (fan stops) and 255 (fan running at full speed). This is because the 8-bit pulse-width modulation (PWM) output function used by the Arduino microcontroller board works with discrete values from 0 to 255. PWM is a technique that can be used to control the spin of motors by setting up the width of pulses (square waves) in a signal generated by the Arduino microcontroller board [28]. The Arduino Uno board uses a programming function called *analogWrite(x)*, where *x*'s value can range from 0 to 255. The board automatically sets up the PWM pulses according to that function and sends that pulsing signal to one of the board's PWM-enabled output pins. We used a versatile and easy-to-use fuzzy logic library for the Arduino Uno board called FuzzyLibrary [29].

Figure 3 shows the resulting fuzzy sets with linguistic variables called "slow", "medium" and "fast", as applied by [24]. The variables helped to define an output value from 0 to 255 for controlling the fan using PWM technique. We conducted a software engineering testing method called "functional testing" [31] with our fuzzy logic program to see how it behaves under controlled inputs. In an initial functional test, we used the input value 60 cm for the distance between the computer and the user. As seen in Fig. 3, an example of a crisp output value was 195 (PWM value for the fan), represented with a vertical black line in Fig. 3. This value was sent to the microcontroller board to control the fan speed, which falls well within the "fast" subset with a membership degree of more than 0.5, and it somewhat belongs to the "medium" subset with a membership degree of less than 0.05.

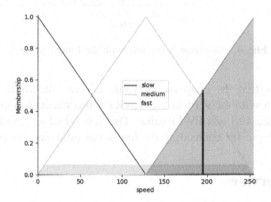

Fig. 3. An example of a crisp output value (195) computed in our fuzzy logic system with an input of 60 cms.

We ran another functional test with the input value of 50 cm. This was half of the universe of discourse of the input values defined in our fuzzy logic system ([20..80]). The result is shown in Fig. 4. As expected, the fuzzy logic system rightly defined the output crisp value as 128 (represented as a vertical black line), which fully belonged to the "medium" subset with a degree of membership of 1.0. Interestingly, the fuzzy logic system also determined that the output barely belonged to the "fast" subset, although this did not affect the output value. We believe this happened because of inaccuracies of floating point operations calculated by the fuzzy logic library, but we will need to confirm that in further analyses.

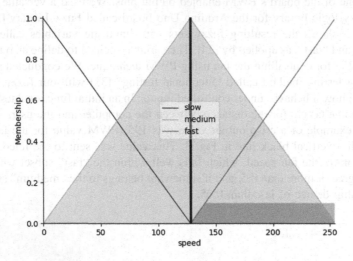

Fig. 4. Resulting fuzzy sets with the functional test.

Figure 4 shows that the crisp output value of 128 (shown at the center of the "medium" fuzzy set with the vertical bar) ran the fan connected to the Arduino Uno at medium speed, since 128 is a PWM value. This functional test confirmed the usefulness of the fuzzy logic for controlling the fan in our olfactory system.

4   System Overview

We developed a simple math serious game intended for young learners using the Panda3D game engine [32], to test it with our olfactory interface as a proof of concept. Panda3D has been used to develop serious games, such as in [33]. In our serious game, the player must count some pineapples and type in the resulting sum. If the number of pineapples is correct, the game sends a signal to the Arduino microcontroller board through the USB cable. The Arduino board activates the air freshener and changes the speed of the fan using a fuzzy logic analysis of the ultrasonic sensor data. If the player was seated "Close" to the computer, the olfactory interface spun the fan slower and thus sent a small amount of odor to the player. Conversely, if the player was seated "Far" from the computer, the olfactory interface increases the speed of the fan ensuring the odor reaches the player. The olfactory interface was placed very close to the computer screen. The serious game and the olfactory interface are shown in Fig. 5.

Fig. 5. A participant testing the serious game and the olfactory interface.

A closeup of the electronic interface is shown in Fig. 6.

Fig. 6. The olfactory interface.

The olfactory interface consists of the following components:

- An Arduino Uno microcontroller board and a USB cable connected to the computer that ran the serious game.
- A solderless breadboard for connecting the electronic components to it
- A 2N2222 transistor, used for controlling the fan rotation speed
- A 1 kΩ resistor for the 2N2222 transistor
- A second 2N2222 transistor, used for controlling the air freshener
- A 1 kΩ resistor for the 2N2222 transistor
- A 0.1 microfarad capacitor connected to the transistor, to reduce electrical noise.
- An HC-SR04 ultrasonic sensor, used for measuring the distance between the learner and the olfactory interface and the computer screen.
- A 12-V PC fan, used for diffusing the odor generated by the air freshener.
- A 12-V power source for the fan
- A a Glade Sense & Spray (TM) air freshener, containing a Hawaiian Breeze (TM) spray cartridge, with a smell of pineapple. We disabled the air freshener's motion sensor and its manual push-button and we connected it to the olfactory interface. The Arduino Uno activated the air freshener by grounding its push-button.

As seen in Fig. 6, we used a small box to raise the fan to diffuse the odor coming from the air freshener more efficiently.

5 Preliminary Test Case

One male player aged 10 years old initially tested our olfactory interface, shown in Fig. 5. We used the think-aloud protocol method [34] to obtain qualitative data on the usability of the olfactory system and player's verbal comments on the test of the serious game and the olfactory interface. The test showed that the pineapple smell generated by the air freshener worked as an efficient olfactory stimulation in the game, supporting a positive player experience. We found that the Arduino Uno microcontroller board can run the fuzzy logic without affecting its overall performance. The fuzzy logic program occupied approximately 25% of the Arduino's storage memory, allowing for the control of other sensors and fans that may be added in the future. The fuzzy logic system very rapidly activated the fan and the air freshener in the player's presence with no reported delays, changing the amount of smell by trying different distances between the player and the computer.

We found that a distance of 50 to 60 cm between the computer screen and the player (which is also recommended by ergonomists for a comfortable computer screen view [35]) was acceptable for perceiving enough odor from our olfactory interface. Further usability testing is needed with additional participants in an educational context of use such as a school computer lab to confirm our findings and our fuzzy sets.

6 Summary

The real world is multisensory and our experiences in this world are constructed by the stimulation of all our senses including visual, auditory, touch, and taste. Despite the importance of all the senses in providing us with and understanding of our world, virtual environments including virtual simulations and serious games, and the human-computer interface more generally, has predominantly focused on the visual and auditory sense solely. Simulating the other senses and the sense of touch and smell in particular can be beneficial (e.g., as previously described, olfaction within a virtual learning environment can increase learning). However, simulating these other senses within the human-computer interface including virtual environments is not trivial and although recently progress has been made with the simulation of touch with the availability of consumer-level haptic devices, less work and progress has been made with respect to simulating the sense of smell (olfaction). In this paper we presented a simple and cost-effective interface constructed using an Arduino Uno microcontroller board and a department store air freshener to deliver a scent to an user of a serious game. A fuzzy logic system was used to regulate the amount of scent delivered to the user based on their distance to the display. As a proof-of-concept, we developed a serious game intended to teach basic math (counting) skills to children. Learners (players) must collect pineapples from the scene and then enter the amount of pineapples collected. As the pineapples are collected, a pineapple scent is emitted from the interface thus serving to supplement or complement the learner's senses and stimulate their affection and cognition [38]. As part of our proof-of-concept, a 10 year old learner played the game and provided us with feedback regarding the interface and illustrated the potential of the system.

This work is ongoing and we are currently in the process of improving the interface and will then conduct more extensive user testing which will begin with one or more rounds of usability testing following an iterative development process. Feedback and suggestions for improvement from the usability testing will be integrated into the system after each round of testing. Upon completion of the usability testing phase, effectiveness testing will follow where we will examine the impact of the interface on learning (knowledge transfer and retention).

Future work will also build upon our own prior work on multimodal interactions that has examined the influence of sound on visual and haptic fidelity perception and task performance [36, 37]. Fidelity, that is, how realistic the virtual environment that the serious game is centered on must be in order to ensure effective learning, is influenced by multimodal interactions. We hypothesize that increased fidelity may help learning. To test our hypothesis we will evaluate our system in an experimental situation where we assess differences in learning with and without the system. This has potentially significant implications for designers and developers of virtual environments, given that with our current technology, we cannot faithfully recreate olfaction (we are actually far from being able to do so). However, just like sound can influence our perception of visual fidelity, future work will examine the influence of sound on olfaction perception with the goal of examining whether sound can be used to influence our perception of smell and more specifically, whether sound can increase our perception of olfaction perception. This may have large implications for developers of displays as it may allow low fidelity displays coupled with appropriate auditory cues, to be used in place of cost prohibitive and potentially complex displays.

References

1. Seitz, A.R., van Wassenhove, V., Shams, L.: Simultaneous and independent acquisition of multisensory and unisensory associations. Perception **36**, 1445–1453 (2007). https://doi.org/10.1068/p5843
2. Howes, D. (ed.): Senses and Perception: Critical and Primary Sources. Bloomsbury, London (2018)
3. Sheridan, T.B.: Musings on telepresence and virtual presence. Pres. Teleoper. Virtual Environ. **1**(1), 120–125 (1992). https://doi.org/10.1162/pres.1992.1.1.120
4. Witmer, B.G., Singer, M.J.: Measuring presence in virtual environments: a presence questionnaire. Pres. Teleoper. Virtual Environ. **7**(3), 225–240 (1998). https://doi.org/10.1162/105474698565686
5. Adelstein, B.D., Begault, D.R., Anderson, M.R., Wenzel, E.M.: Sensitivity to haptic-audio asynchrony. In: Proceedings of the 5th International Conference on Multimodal Interfaces, pp. 73–76. New York, NY (2003). https://doi.org/10.1145/958432.958448
6. Gault, R.H.: Touch as a substitute for hearing in the interpretation and control of speech. Arch. Otolaryngol. **3**, 121–213 (1926)
7. Bach-y-Rital, P., Kercel, S.W.: Sensory substitution and the human-machine interface. Trends Cogn. Sci. **7**(12), 541–546 (2003). https://doi.org/10.1016/j.tics.2003.10.013
8. Olsén, J.E.: Vicariates of the Eye: Blindness Sense Substitution, and Writing Devices in the Nineteenth Century. Mosaic Interdisc. Crit. J. **46**(3), 75–91 (2013)

9. Visell, Y.: Tactile sensory substitution: models for enaction in HCI. Interact. Comput. **21**(1–2), 38–53 (2009). https://doi.org/10.1016/j.intcom.2008.08.004
10. Flavian, C., Ibanez-Sanchez, S., Orus, C.: The influence of scent on virtual reality experiences: the role of aroma-content congruence. J. Bus. Res. **123**, 289–301 (2021)
11. Persky, S., Dolwick, A.P.: Olfactory perception and presence in a virtual reality food environment. Front. Virtual Real. **1**, 571812 (2020). https://doi.org/10.3389/frvir.2020.571812
12. Youngblut, C.: Educational use of virtual reality technology. Tech. Report. Inst. Defense Analyses, US (1998).
13. Richard, E., Tijou, A., Richard, P., Ferrier, J.L.: Multi-modal virtual environments for education with haptic and olfactory feedback. Virtual Reality **10**(3–4), 207–225 (2006)
14. Aiken, M.P., Berry, M.J.: Posttraumatic stress disorder: possibilities for olfaction and virtual reality exposure therapy. Virtual Reality **19**(2), 95–109 (2015). https://doi.org/10.1007/s10055-015-0260-x
15. Tomasi, D., Ferris, H., Booraem, P., Enman, L., Gates, S., Reyns, E.: Olfactory virtual reality (OVR) for wellbeing and reduction of stress. J. Med. Res. Health Sci. **4**(3), 1212–1221 (2021)
16. Kaye, J.J.: Making scents: aromatic output for HCI. Interactions **11**(1), 48–61 (2004)
17. The Smell of Success. Instructables. https://www.instructables.com/Smell-of-Success/. Accessed 18 May 2021
18. IoT Air Freshener (with NodeMCU, Arduino, IFTTT and Adafruit.io)., https://www.instructables.com/IoT-Air-Freshner-with-NodeMCU-Arduino-IFTTT-and-Ad/#step1. Accessed 19 May 2021
19. Herrera, N., McMahan, R.: Development of a simple and low-cost olfactory display for immersive media experiences. In: ImmersiveMe 2014, ACM (2014)
20. Garcia-Ruiz, M.A., Santana-Mancilla, P.C.: Creative DIY Microcontroller Projects with C: A Practical Guide to Building PIC and STM32 Microcontroller Board Applications with C Programming. Packt Publishing, Birmingham, UK (2021)
21. Sardo, J.D., Pereira, J.A., Veiga, R.J., Semião, J., Cardoso, P.J., Rodrigues, J.M.: Multisensorial portable device for augmented reality experiences in museums. Int. J. Educ. Learn. Syst. **3** (2018)
22. Vuppalapati, C., Vuppalapati, R., Kedari, S., Ilapakurti, A., Vuppalapati, J.S., Kedari, S.: Fuzzy logic infused intelligent scent dispenser for creating memorable customer experience of long-tail connected venues. In: IEEE International Conference on Machine Learning and Cybernetics (ICMLC), vol. 1, pp. 149–154 (2018)
23. Zadeh, L.A.: Is there a need for fuzzy logic? Inf. Sci. **178**(13), 2751–2779 (2008)
24. Kumar, L., Rawat, T. S., Pandey, M., Kumar, U.: Automatic control of fan speed using fuzzy logic. Int. J. Eng. Technol. Manag. Appl. Sci. **3**(4) (2015)
25. Garcia-Ruiz, M.A., Santana-Mancilla, P.C., Gaytan-Lugo, L.S.: Integrating microcontroller-based projects in a human-computer interaction course. Int. J. Comput. Inf. Eng. **12**(10), 946–950 (2018)
26. Garcia-Ruiz, M.A., Santana-Mancilla, P.C.: Development and usability testing of simulated wind in a racing video game. In: Proceedings of The 2015 IEEE Games, Entertainment, and Media (GEM) Conference, Toronto, Canada (2015)
27. Zadeh, L.A.: Fuzzy sets. Inf. Control **8**, 338–353 (1965)
28. PWM, https://www.arduino.cc/en/Tutorial/PWM. Accessed 18 May 2021
29. Fuzzy Library for Arduino, https://github.com/amimaro/FuzzyLibrary. Accessed 18 May 2021

30. Bai, Y., Wang, D.: Fundamentals of fuzzy logic control — fuzzy sets, fuzzy rules and defuzzifications. In: Bai, Y., Zhuang, H., Wang, D. (eds.) Advanced Fuzzy Logic Technologies in Industrial Applications. Advances in Industrial Control. Springer, London (2006). https://doi.org/10.1007/978-1-84628-469-4_2

31. Bertolino, A.: Software testing research: achievements, challenges, dreams. In: 2007 Future of Software Engineering, pp. 85–103. IEEE Computer Society (2007)

32. Panda3D. https://www.panda3d.org/. Accessed 18 May 2021

33. Henrich, V., Reuter, T.: CarDriver–Using Python and Panda3D to construct a Virtual Environment for Teaching Driving. Reykjavík University RUTR-CS08003 (2008)

34. Garcia-Ruiz, M.A., Santana-Mancilla, P.C.: Towards a usable serious game app to support children's language therapy. In: Proceedings of the IX Latin American Conference on Human Computer Interaction, pp. 1–4 (2019)

35. Canadian Centre for Occupational Health and Safety. https://www.ccohs.ca/oshanswers/ergonomics/office/monitor_positioning.html. Accessed 19 May 2021

36. Kapralos, B., Moussa, F., Collins, K., Dubrowski, A.: Fidelity and multimodal interactions. In: Wouters, P., van Oostendorp, H. (eds.) Instructional Techniques to Facilitate Learning and Motivation of Serious Games. Advances in Game-Based Learning. Springer, Cham (2017). https://doi.org/10.1007/978-3-319-39298-1_5.

37. Melaisi, M., Rojas, D., Kapralos, B., Uribe-Quevedo, A., Collins, K.: Multimodal interaction of contextual and non-contextual sound and haptics in virtual simulations. Informatics 5(4), 43 (2018)

38. Garcia-Ruiz, M.A., Edwards, A., Aquino-Santos, R., Alvarez-Cardenas, O., Mayoral Baldivia, G.M.: Integrating the sense of smell in virtual reality for second language learning. In: Proceedings of Elearn conference, Las Vegas, NV. Association for the Advancement of Computing in Education (AACE) (2008)

A Vibrothermal Haptic Display
for Socio-emotional Communication

Shubham Shriniwas Gharat[1], Yatiraj Shetty[2(✉)], and Troy McDaniel[2]

[1] School of Electrical, Computer and Energy Engineering,
Arizona State University, Tempe, AZ, USA
ssgharat@asu.edu
[2] The Polytechnic School, Arizona State University, Mesa, AZ, USA
{yshetty, troy.mcdaniel}@asu.edu

Abstract. Touch plays a vital role in maintaining human relationships through social and emotional communication. The proposed haptic display prototype generates stimuli in vibrotactile and thermal modalities toward simulating social touch cues between remote users. High-dimensional spatiotemporal vibrotactile-thermal (vibrothermal) patterns were evaluated with ten participants. The device can be wirelessly operated to enable remote communication. In the future, such patterns can be used to richly simulate social touch cues. A research study was conducted in two parts: first, the identification accuracy of vibrothermal patterns was explored; and second, the relatability of vibrothermal patterns to social touch experienced during social interactions was evaluated. Results revealed that while complex patterns were difficult to identify, simpler patterns, such as SINGLE TAP and HOLD, were highly identifiable and highly relatable to social touch cues. Directional patterns were less identifiable and less relatable to the social touch cues experienced during social interaction.

Keywords: Wearable tactile display · Thermal display · Spatiotemporal patterns · Social touch

1 Introduction

The sense of touch has an essential role in human interactions in social and emotional communication and is particularly significant in social interactions. A short touch by another person can elicit emotionally grounding and engaging experiences, from the comforting knowledge of being touched by one's spouse to the experience of anxiety when touched by a stranger [6]. The sense of touch can be stimulated in several ways: pressure, vibration, pain, temperature, movement, and position. Research into haptic displays has explored a variety of submodalities of touch such as vibrotactile [10], thermal [21], clenching [2], pressure [7], and dragging [8]. These haptic modalities were tested on various body parts using multiple form factors from head-mounted displays [3] to small thermo-electric wearables [17]. Haptic displays can render nuanced touch-based information, either tactile, kinesthetic, or both, to users in real, augmented, or virtual environments [3]. Touch can also enhance the meaning of other forms of verbal and non-verbal communication, e.g., touch intensifies emotions in addition to that displayed

© Springer Nature Switzerland AG 2021
C. Stephanidis et al. (Eds.): HCII 2021, LNCS 13095, pp. 17–30, 2021.
https://doi.org/10.1007/978-3-030-90963-5_2

by the face and voice [14]. Shaking, hugging, patting, squeezing, and stroking are examples of touch that convey emotions [4], such as love and anger.

Peltier units have been embedded into wearable devices to apply thermal stimulation. While there has been some exploration of thermal stimuli in spatiotemporal cues, high-dimensional patterns have not been investigated. Cang and Israr [1] explored the communication of socio-emotional sentiment using vibrotactile stimulation, but multimodal stimulation, such as thermal and vibrotactile, has potential to better simulate social touch and other multimodal non-verbal cues found in human interactions. This research aims to design, demonstrate, and test a multimodal haptic display using eccentric rotating mass (ERM) vibration motors and ceramic Peltier units on the forearm as a medium to transfer vibrotactile-thermal (vibrothermal) patterns toward simulating social touch cues.

2 Related Work

2.1 Haptic Feedback

Thermal Feedback. Wilson et al. [30] suggested that warm temperatures (>32 °C) could be used to convey the physical or social presence of other people. In contrast, cool temperatures (<30 °C) could convey people's absence. Additionally, users strongly agreed on the application of thermal feedback in social communication and rating-re-lated representations. Hot under the collar [31] made the first attempt to map a range of thermal stimuli to dimensional models of emotions and suggested that the distribution of points better fitted a vector model than the circumplex model, thereby making it difficult to convey the full range of emotions through thermal feedback alone, and could widen the range of emotions represented in the presence of other feedback modalities. While researchers have explored the utility of thermal bracelets [21] for spati-otemporal feedback, more complex patterns of higher dimensionality have not been investigated. A fascinating insight by Tewell et al. [26] is that increasing the stimulated skin area eases the perception of thermal signals. Thermal Feedback Identification in a Mobile Environment [29] tested two-dimensional thermal icons while sitting or walking, and concluded that the direction of change was a valuable thermal feedback parameter in mobile environments.

Lee and Lim [16] developed a structured approach about the quality of heat (thermal expression unit, thermal expression, and the two levels of thermal expression composition) and discovered the critical expression elements (temperature, duration, location, and temperature change rate). According to the results from K. Suhonen et al. [13], when touch was mapped to thermal stimuli, they found that cold messages conveyed negative feelings, whereas warmth communicated positive feelings. When thermal icons are designed based on the responses of the skin, they can be accurately determined with little training [24]. Researchers considered a lower limit of about 15 °C-17 °C and an upper limit of 45 °C-52 °C to avoid pain irritations associated with thermoreceptors [19]. A minimum of 15 s between different trials has been suggested to avoid the thermal adaptation effects. Wilson et al. [30] highlighted that the role of emotions could vary depending on the scenarios in which thermal stimulation is applied (e.g., happy memories, social closeness). Emotions are considered to be connected to sensed variations in temperature [23, 25], where warm temperatures were found to be comfortable, pleasant, and promoted social proximity, while colder temperatures were perceived as being uncomfortable to most. "Warm" temperatures have been associated with words like generosity, happiness, humor, and sociability [31].

Vibrotactile Feedback. A library of effects was created in Feel Effects [10], which altered the duration and intensity of tactile icons for testing on the backs of users. Turchet et al. [28] tested a walker's emotional states using a planar vibrotactile display embedded into footwear. Salminen et al. [22] studied emotional experiences and behavioral responses to haptic stimulations. Yoo et al. [37] identified parameters like perceived intensity, carrier frequency, duration, and envelope frequency to have a clear relationship to tactile stimuli's emotional responses, and develop design guidelines for tactile icons that have desired emotional properties. Vibro-glove [15] delivered seven facial expressions to the back of the hand through spatiotemporal vibrotactile feedback. Two-dimensional tactile moving strokes with varying frequency, intensity, velocity, and direction of motion were tested using Tactile Brush [9] on the backs of users. To study vibrotactile patterns and the value they contain in eliciting emotions, the Haptic Face Display (HFD) was designed and evaluated using a large set of spatiotemporal patterns to evoke affective responses [18]. Finally, the results from Haptic Empathy show that people can use vibratory feedback as a medium for expressing specific subjective feelings [12].

2.2 Multimodal Vibrotactile and Thermal Feedback

Thermal Icons [5] was the first study of intramodal and intermodal thermal and vibrotactile communication, where it was demonstrated that thermal and vibrotactile stimuli together do not appear to hinder interpretation across these submodalities, and hence, thermal changes may be a helpful addition to tactile icons. Wilson et al. [32] tried to expand the emotional expressivity of interfaces and provided examples of combining different modalities for affective states. Yang et al. [34] created a testbed using pin-array tactile and thermal feedback for psychophysical studies relating human touch sensation and perceived feelings of stimuli. Yang et al. [35] concluded through their study that multiple actuators are advantageous for simultaneously displaying combinations of amplitude and frequency. The perceived magnitude of vibrotactile stimuli was affected by temperature variation only for high frequency (>150) vibrotactile stimuli [33]. Yoo et al. [36] explored thermal cues' emotional responses through constant-temperature thermal stimuli and concluded that thermal and vibrotactile parameters have clear and somewhat independent effects on emotional responses.

3 Prototype Design

3.1 Hardware Design

The proposed vibrothermal haptic display was designed as a wearable device that fits the forearm and can produce high-dimensional spatiotemporal patterns—see Fig. 1.

Peltier units of size 20 mm × 20 mm × 5.1mm were used to generate thermal feed-back, and Eccentric Rotating Mass (ERM) motors of 8 mm diameter were used to generate vibrotactile feedback. Peltier units of this size were selected as they are smaller than the traditional ceramic Peltiers and can be easily arranged into a matrix, thereby providing scalability. This device was built using an Arduino UNO, where each of the actuating components was controlled through a MOSFET. Power to these components was provided through a 5V power supply or a battery bank for portable use. An HC-05 Bluetooth module connected the haptic display to custom software, through which pre-defined and user-defined unimodal and multimodal patterns can be created and sent to the haptic device for real-time display. Figure 2 depicts the arrangement of Peltier units and ERM vibration motors for the proposed design. The ceramic Peltiers and the ERM motors are arranged in a 3 × 3 staggered matrix pattern. The surface area of the skin covered by this device is 10 cm × 10 cm. Figure 3 depicts another view of the proposed display when not worn.

3.2 Software Design

An Android application was created to provide users with an interface for controlling the proposed haptic display. The Arduino UNO controls the temperature changes of the Peltier units and the vibrations of the ERM motors. According to the commands received from the android application, the output voltage of each pin of the Arduino UNO is precisely controlled through Arduino code. The Android application consists of different screens enabling control over the different modalities available for the device. The user can also select between pre-defined patterns or create new patterns using the keypad provided. The android application interacts with the hardware using a Bluetooth module connected to the Arduino UNO. Figure 4 displays different screens from the Android application.

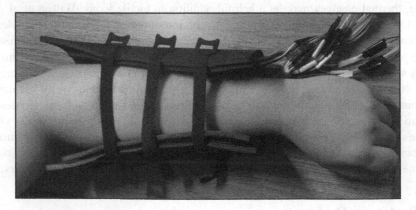

Fig. 1. Vibrothermal device on the forearm.

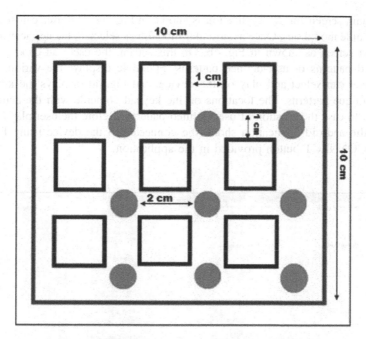

Fig. 2. Arrangement of peltiers and ERM motors

Fig. 3. Prototype of vibrothermal display.

The main screen for the application is shown in Fig. 4a. The user can select from three available modalities. Once a particular modality is selected, the application moves to the next screen as shown in Fig. 4b. On this screen, the user can choose between pre-defined patterns or user-defined patterns. Figure 4c displays the various patterns that the user can select and play on the device, and Fig. 4d displays the keypad for drawing unique patterns. The locations on the keypad coincide with the actuators on the device to ease the creation of user-defined patterns. Before the user plays different patterns, the android application should be connected to the device using Bluetooth from the CONNECT button provided in the application.

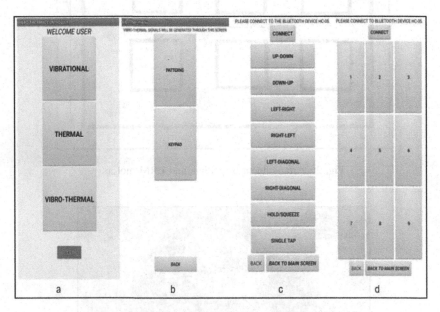

Fig. 4. Android application screens.

The proposed vibrothermal display can generate high-dimensional patterns in thermal and/or vibrotactile modalities. The main aim of testing vibrothermal patterns is to gather information about their relatability to social touch cues found in social interactions. Eight pre-defined vibrothermal patterns were designed. Figure 5 depicts the proposed pre-defined patterns for evaluation, namely UP-DOWN, DOWN-UP, LEFT-RIGHT, RIGHT-LEFT, LEFT-DIAGONAL, RIGHT-DIAGONAL, HOLD, and SINGLE TAP. Patterns like UP-DOWN, DOWN-UP, LEFT-RIGHT, and RIGHT-LEFT were commonly found in previous research [9, 15, 20]. The patterns on the diagonals, namely LEFT-DIAGONAL and RIGHT-DIAGONAL, were tested to research the change in spatiotemporal patterns across the forearm. Given their similarity to social touch cues commonly encountered during social interactions, patterns such as HOLD and SINGLE TAP were introduced to explore their reliability to social touch.

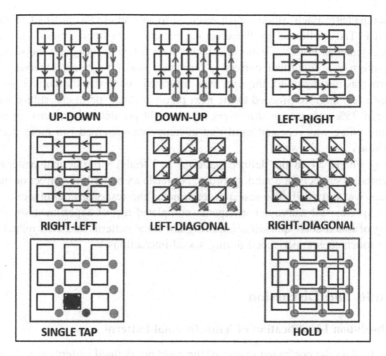

Fig. 5. Different patterns using vibrothermal modality.

4 Study Design

The aim of the proposed experiment was to determine the absolute identification accuracy of social touch patterns simulated in the vibrothermal modality, and their relatability to touch cues used during social interactions. The study was performed with ten participants (average age was 26 years old; 7 males and 3 females participated) recruited from Arizona State University (ASU). The study was approved by ASU's Institutional Review Board prior to recruitment. Two participants wore this device on their left hand while remaining subjects wore it on their right hand. The device was placed on the ventral part of the forearm, and a total of eight vibrothermal patterns were tested as shown in Fig. 5. A 15–20 s gap was provided between patterns to avoid thermal adaptation [11].

The study was conducted in the following steps:

- Informational Phase: All human subjects were informed about the research and its potential benefits.
- Familiarization Phase: All eight pre-defined patterns were presented and named for subjects for familiarization purposes before beginning training.

- Training Phase: Each pattern was presented to subjects in the order of HOLD and SINGLE TAP, followed by the diagonal patterns, and finally, the horizontal and vertical patterns. For each pattern, subjects were asked to recognize the stimulus. If the pattern was identified correctly, the guess was confirmed; otherwise, if the pattern was misidentified, the user was informed and given the correct answer to enhance learning. To proceed to the next phase of this experiment, subjects needed to attain 75% accuracy within a set of the eight pre-defined patterns, or else the training phase was repeated until that accuracy was attained (no more than three repetitions were allowed).
- Testing Phase: 24 (8 pre-defined patterns × 3 trials) vibrothermal patterns were presented to subjects in a random order. No feedback regarding correct or incorrect guesses was provided. The research team noted the responses of subjects.
- Post-Experimental Survey: Participants completed a post-experiment survey consisting of Likert-scale questions inquiring about the patterns and their relatability to social touch cues experienced during social interactions.

5 Results and Discussion

5.1 Absolution Identification of Vibrothermal Patterns

Figure 6 displays the confusion matrix of the eight pre-defined patterns tested using the proposed vibrothermal device. The pattern SINGLE TAP was highly accurate with an accuracy of 100%. The HOLD and RIGHT-DIAGONAL patterns have the same accuracy of 96.67%. The patterns RIGHT-LEFT, LEFT-DIAGONAL and LEFT-RIGHT were reasonably accurate with accuracies of 93.33%, 86.67%, and 80%, respectively. The patterns DOWN-UP and UP-DOWN were less accurate, with 66.67% and 63.33% accuracies, respectively. It can also be noted that the pattern UP-DOWN was more often confused with LEFT-RIGHT and DOWN-UP, whereas less often confused with the RIGHT-LEFT pattern. The DOWN-UP pattern was more frequently confused with RIGHT-LEFT, LEFT-RIGHT, and less frequently confused with the UP-DOWN pattern. The LEFT-RIGHT pattern was muddled with the DOWN-UP and RIGHT-LEFT patterns. The participants had a little confusion, of about 6.67%, with the RIGHT-LEFT pattern, which is relatively less than the previous patterns. In addition, the LEFT- DIAGONAL was confused with the LEFT-RIGHT and RIGHT-DIAGONAL patterns. The RIGHT-DIAGONAL and HOLD patterns had an identification accuracy of 96.67%, with around 3.34% being confused with the LEFT-DIAGONAL and SINGLE TAP patterns.

PATTERNS	UP-DOWN	DOWN-UP	LEFT-RIGHT	RIGHT-LEFT	LEFT-DIAGONAL	RIGHT-DIAGONAL	HOLD/SQUEEZE	SINGLE TAP
UP-DOWN	63.33%	13.33%	16.67%	6.67%	0%	0%	0%	0%
DOWN-UP	6.67%	66.67%	10%	16.67%	0%	0%	0%	0%
LEFT-RIGHT	3.33%	10%	80%	6.67%	0%	0%	0%	0%
RIGHT-LEFT	6.67%	0%	0%	93.33%	0%	0%	0%	0%
LEFT-DIAGONAL	0%	0%	6.67%	0%	86.67%	6.66%	0%	0%
RIGHT-DIAGONAL	0%	0%	0%	0%	3.34%	96.67%	0%	0%
HOLD	0%	0%	0%	0%	0%	0%	96.67%	3.34%
SINGLE TAP	0%	0%	0%	0%	0%	0%	0%	100%

Fig. 6. Pattern identification confusion matrix.

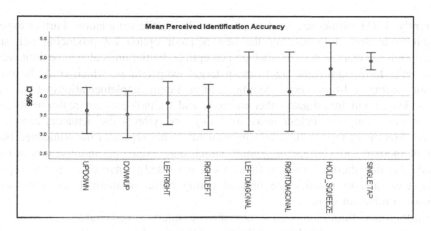

Fig. 7. Graphical interpretation of mean accuracies.

5.2 Relatability of Vibrothermal Patterns to Social Touch Cues

Responses on the relatability of the pre-defined patterns to social touch cues were noted on a 5-point Likert-scale and are depicted in Fig. 7. The patterns SINGLE TAP and HOLD were highly relatable, with mean values of 4.90 and 4.70, respectively. The patterns on the diagonals, i.e., the LEFT DIAGONAL and RIGHT DIAGONAL, had a mean value of 4.10 with a standard deviation of 1.5, which indicates some degree of interpersonal variation. The remaining four patterns, namely UP-DOWN, DOWN-UP, LEFT-RIGHT, and RIGHT-LEFT, had mean values between 3.50 and 3.80, which shows that these patterns were less relatable to social interactions. Patterns like SINGLE TAP and HOLD were intuitive in conveying social touch cues experienced during social interactions.

Summary. For most subjects, the pre-defined patterns were easily recognizable with little training. A few participants found that the SINGLE TAP and HOLD were easy to identify, whereas other patterns were more confusing and required more concentration for identification. One participant noted, "*It was easier to tell if the heat was on the Left or Right, but whether the heat was on the Top or Bottom was hard*". Most of the participants agreed that this device could be used to augment social interactions. Specifically, a user could use the technology to feel a social touch from a distance. A notable statement from one of the subjects mentioned that this device could be used in places where vocal communication is difficult, such as extreme environments; in particular, this participant mentioned interest in using the device while diving to communicate with diving partners. During the experiment's training phase, all participants obtained 75% accuracy—i.e., 6 out of 8 patterns were identified correctly in a single attempt across all subjects. This shows that with little training, it is possible to familiarize and identify spatiotemporal vibrothermal patterns on the forearm.

6 Limitations and Future Work

Currently, ERM motors are used to produce vibrotactile stimulation. Further experimentation is needed to identify the best actuator option for producing rich spatiotemporal vibrotactile patterns that are perceptible. Peltier units also have limitations; these units have significant lag to reach target temperatures, which could be problematic during real-time social communication. Future implementations of the proposed design will investigate other methods and technologies for real-time thermal stimulation. Moreover, Peltier units are bulky, and vibrotactile actuators cannot be placed directly on top of these heating elements. This separates the stimulated body sites of thermal and vibrotactile stimuli, which may reduce the intuitiveness of multimodal haptic patterns; however, future work is needed to investigate any perceptual differences, and to identify the optimal configuration of thermal and vibrotactile actuators on human skin.

Furthermore, future improvements to the user interface will enable users to directly draw patterns on a mobile device and interpret them on the proposed device, similar to [1]. Such a method may provide valuable insight when testing the device during a real-time phone call or video conversation.

Finally, a study to explore the emotional response to vibrothermal patterns using this device is needed to understand mappings that have potential for use in social scenarios. The main objective for such a study would be to explore a 3-dimensional graph of valence, arousal, and dominance/power (dominant vs. submissive) domains with a set of pre-defined patterns. A 3-dimensional projection [27] will provide researchers with more in-depth insight into the overall structure of emotional space than the previous 2-dimensional circumplex or vector model.

7 Conclusion

The proposed vibrothermal haptic display prototype can be deployed to provide rich vibrotactile and thermal stimulation for tactile interactions. This paper discussed a preliminary study to confirm the identification of such spatiotemporal patterns and their relatable to social touch cues. According to the results in Fig. 6, the confusion matrix for warm stimuli has more misclassifications for a particular pattern, which aligns with previous research performed [21]. Patterns like SINGLE TAP and HOLD were very relatable to social touch cues experienced during social interactions. Other patterns like UP-DOWN, DOWN-UP, LEFT-RIGHT, RIGHT-LEFT were less relatable to social interactions experienced by the users.

It was also noted that the spatial location of the vibrothermal patterns relative to the arm significantly affected their identification. Identifying patterns on the distal and proximal areas of the ventral side of the forearm was difficult for subjects. Detecting patterns on the periphery of the forearm was easier compared to the center of the forearm. Patterns drawn along the diagonals of the display were discernible, but their relatability to social interactions varied among subjects. Using these insights, future work will evaluate the detailed mapping of vibrothermal patterns to emotions within the specific context of social interaction. We believe that by utilizing the submodalities of touch, more tactile information could be conveyed in a compact form factor to elicit emotional responses from the users.

Acknowledgements. The authors would like to thank Arizona State University for their funding support through MORE (Mater's Opportunity for Research in Engineering) Scholarship and GPSA-GRSP (Graduate Research Support Program) for this research project. This work was also supported in part by the National Science Foundation (Grant No. 1828010).

References

1. Cang, X.L., Israr, A.: Communicating socio-emotional sentiment through haptic messages. In: IEEE Haptics Symposium HAPTICS (2020). https://research.fb.com/publications/communicating-socio-emotional-sentiment-through-haptic-messages/
2. Caswell, N.A., Yardley, R.T., Montandon, M.N., Provancher, W.R.: Design of a forearm-mounted directional skin stretch device. In: Proceedings of Haptics Symposium 2012, HAPTICS 2012, pp. 365–370 (2012). https://doi.org/10.1109/HAPTIC.2012.6183816
3. Chen, Z., Peng, W., Peiris, R., Minamizawa, K.: ThermoReality: Thermally enriched head-mounted displays for virtual reality. In: ACM SIGGRAPH 2017 Posters, SIGGRAPH 2017 **1**, 1–2 (2017). https://doi.org/10.1145/3102163.3102222
4. Gallace, A., Spence, C.: The science of interpersonal touch: an overview. Neurosci. Biobehav. Rev. **34**(2), 246–259 (2010)
5. Graham, W., Martin Halvey, S.A.B., Stephen, A.: Huges: thermal icons: evaluating structured thermal feedback for mobile interaction, p. 452 (2012)
6. Haans, A., IJsselsteijn, W.: Mediated social touch: a review of current research and future directions. Virtual Real. **9**(2–3), 149–159 (2006). https://doi.org/10.1007/s10055-005-0014-2

7. He, L., Xu, C., Xu, D., Brill, R.: Pneuhaptic: delivering haptic cues with a pneu- matic armband. In: ISWC 2015 - Proceedings 2015 ACM Internationa Symposium Wearable Computer, pp. 47–48 (2015). https://doi.org/10.1145/2802083.2802091

8. Ion, A., Wang, E., Baudisch, P.: Skin drag displays: dragging a physical tac- tor across the user's skin produces a stronger tactile stimulus than vibrotactile. In: Proceedings of Conference Human Factors Computing System, pp. 2501–2504 (2015). https://doi.org/10. 1145/2702123.2702459

9. Israr, A., Poupyrev, I.: Tactile brush: drawing on skin with a tactile grid display. In: Proceedings of Conference Human Factors Computing Systems, pp. 2019–2028 (2011). https://doi.org/10.1145/1978942.1979235

10. Israr, A., Zhao, S., Schwalje, K., Klatzky, R., Lehman, J.: Feel effects: enriching storytelling with haptic feedback. ACM Trans. Appl. Percept. **11**(3), 1–17 (2014). https://doi.org/10. 1145/2641570

11. Jones, L.A., Ho, H.N.: Warm or cool, large or small? the challenge of thermal displays. IEEE Trans. Haptics **1**(1), 53–70 (2008). https://doi.org/10.1109/TOH.2008.2

12. Ju, Y., Hynds, D., Chernyshov, G., Kunze, K., Zheng, D., Minamizawa, K.: Haptic empathy: conveying emotional meaning through vibrotactile feedback. In: Extended Abstracts of the 2021 CHI Conference on Human Factors in Computing Systems (2021)

13. Katja Suhonen, S.M., Rantala, J., Vaaanaanen-Vainio-Mattila, K., Raisamo, R., Lantz, V.: Haptically augmented remote speech communication: a study of user practices and experiences. In: Proceedings of the 7th Nordic Conference on Human-Computer Interaction: Making Sense Through Design, p. 834 (2012)

14. Knapp, M.L., Hall, J.A., Horgan, T.G.: Nonverbal Communication in Human Interaction. Cengage Learning (2013)

15. Krishna, S., Bala, S., McDaniel, T., McGuire, S., Panchanathan, S.: VibroGlove: an assistive technology aid for conveying facial expressions. In: Proceedings of Conference Human Factors Computing Systems, pp. 3637–3642 (2010). https://doi.org/10.1145/1753846. 1754031

16. Lee, W., Lim, Y.K.: Explorative research on the heat as an expression medium: Focused on interpersonal communication. Pers. Ubiquitous Comput. **16**(8), 1039–1049 (2012). https:// doi.org/10.1007/s00779-011-0424-y

17. Maeda, T., Kurahashi, T.: Thermodule: wearable and modular thermal feedback system based on a wireless platform. In: ACM International Conference Proceeding Series Association for Computing Machinery, March 2019. https://doi.org/10.1145/3311823. 3311826

18. McDaniel, T., Bala, S., Rosenthal, J., Tadayon, R., Tadayon, A., Panchanathan, S.: Affective haptics for enhancing access to social interactions for individuals who are blind. In: Stephanidis, C., Antona, M. (eds.) UAHCI 2014. LNCS, vol. 8513, pp. 419–429. Springer, Cham (2014). https://doi.org/10.1007/978-3-319-07437-5_40

19. Niijima, A., Takeda, T., Mukouchi, T., Satou, T.: ThermalBitDisplay: Haptic dis play providing thermal feedback perceived differently depending on body parts. In: Proceedings of Conference Human Factors Computing System Association for Computing Machinery, April 2020. https://doi.org/10.1145/3334480.3382849

20. Peiris, R.L., Peng, W., Chen, Z., Chan, L., Minamizawa, K.: ThermoVR: exploring integrated thermal haptic feedback with head-mounted displays, pp. 5452–5456 (2017). https://doi.org/10.1145/3025453.3025824

21. Peiris, R.L., Feng, Y.L., Chan, L., Minamizawa, K.: Thermalbracelet: Exploring thermal haptic feedback around the wrist. In: Proceedings of Conference Human Factors Computing System. Association for Computing Machinery, May 2019. https://doi.org/10.1145/ 3290605.3300400

22. Salminen, K., et al.: Emotional and behavioral responses to haptic stimulation. In: Proceddings of Conference Human Factors Computing System, pp. 1555–1562 (2008). https://doi.org/10.1145/1357054.1357298
23. Salminen, K., et al.: Emotional responses to thermal stimuli. ACM (2011)
24. Singhal, A., Jones, L.A.: Creating thermal icons - a model-based approach. ACM Trans. Appl. Percept. 15(2), 1–22 (2018). https://doi.org/10.1145/3182175
25. Song, S., Noh, G., Yoo, J., Oakley, I., Cho, J., Bianchi, A.: Hot & tight: exploring thermo and squeeze cues recognition on wrist wearables. In: ISWC 2015 - Proceedings 2015 ACM International Symposium Wearable Computing, pp. 39–42. Association for Computing Machinery, Inc. September 2015. https://doi.org/10.1145/2802083.2802092
26. Tewell, J., Bird, J., Buchanan, G.R.: The heat is on: a temperature display for conveying effective feedback. In: Proceedings of Conference Human Factors Computing System, pp. 1756–1767. Association for Computing Machinery, May 2017. https://doi.org/10.1145/3025453.3025844
27. Trnka, R., La'cevla'la'cev, A., Balcar, K., Ku'ska, M., Tavel, P.: Modeling semantic emotion space using a 3D hypercube-projection: an innovative analytical approach for the psychology of emotions. Front. Psychol 7, 522 (2016). https://doi.org/10.3389/fpsyg.2016.00522,www.frontiersin.org
28. Turchet, L., Zanotto, D., Minto, S., Roda, A., Agrawal, S.K.: Emotion rendering in plantar vibro-tactile simulations of imagined walking styles. IEEE Trans. Affect. Comput. 8(3), 340–354 (2017). https://doi.org/10.1109/TAFFC.2016.2552515
29. Wilson, G., Brewster, S., Halvey, M., Hughes, S.: Thermal feedback identification in a mobile environment. In: Oakley, I., Brewster, S. (eds.) HAID 2013. LNCS, vol. 7989, pp. 10–19. Springer, Heidelberg (2013). https://doi.org/10.1007/978-3-642-41068-0_2
30. Wilson, G., Davidson, G., Brewster, S.: In the heat of the moment: subjective interpretations of thermal feedback during interaction. In: Conference Human Factors Computing System, pp. 2063–2072. Association for Computing Machinery (2015). https://doi.org/10.1145/2702123.2702219
31. Wilson, G., Dobrev, D., Brewster, S.A.: Hot under the collar: mapping thermal feedback to dimensional models of emotion. In: Proceedings of Conference Human Factors Computing System, pp. 4838–4849. Association for Computing Machinery, May 2016. https://doi.org/10.1145/2858036.2858205
32. Wilson, G., Freeman, E., Brewster, S.A.: Multimodal effective feedback: Combining thermal, vibrotactile, audio and visual signals. In: ICMI 2016 – Proceedings of 18th ACM International Conference Multimodal Interaction, pp. 400–401. Association for Computing Machinery, Inc, October 2016. https://doi.org/10.1145/2993148.2998522
33. Yang, G.H., Kwon, D.S.: Effect of temperature in perceiving tactile stimulus using a thermo-tactile display. In: 2008 International Conference Control Automation System, ICCAS 2008, pp. 266–271 (2008). https://doi.org/10.1109/ICCAS.2008.4694562
34. Yang, G.H., Kyung, K.U., Srinivasan, M.A., Kwon, D.S.: Development of quantitative tactile display device to provide both pin-array-type tactile feedback and thermal feedback. In: Proceedings - Second Jt. EuroHaptics Conference Symposium Haptic Interfaces Virtual Environment Teleoperator System World Haptics 2007, pp. 578–579 (2007). https://doi.org/10.1109/WHC.2007.41
35. Yang, G.H., Yang, T.H., Kim, S.C., Kwon, D.S., Kang, S.C.: Compact tactile display for fingertips with multiple vibrotactile actuator and thermoelectric module. In: Proceeidngs of - IEEE International Conference Robotics Automation, pp. 491–496 (2007). https://doi.org/10.1109/ROBOT.2007.363834

36. Yoo, Y., Lee, H., Choi, H., Choi, S.: Emotional responses of vibrotactile-thermal stimuli: effects of constant-temperature thermal stimuli. In: 2017 7th International Conference Affective Computing Intelligent Interaction. ACII 2017, pp. 273–278 (2018). https://doi.org/10.1109/ACII.2017.8273612

37. Yoo, Y., Yoo, T., Kong, J., Choi, S.: Emotional responses of tactile icons: effects of amplitude, frequency, duration, and envelope. IEEE World Haptics Conf. WHC **2015**, 235–240 (2015). https://doi.org/10.1109/WHC.2015.7177719

Haptic Finger Glove for the VR Keyboard Input

Yuya Hoshi[1], Chenghong Lu[2], and Lei Jing[2,3](✉)

[1] The Graduate School of Computer Science, Tohuku University, Sendai, Japan
[2] The Graduate School of Computer Science, The University of Aizu,
Aizuwakamatsu, Japan
[3] Research Center for Advanced Information Science and Technology (CAIST),
The University of Aizu, Aizuwakamatsu, Japan
leijing@u-aizu.ac.jp

Abstract. With regards to use Virtual Reality headsets, people have many opportunities of key entry. However, current methods for key entry are suffering from low input speed and high error rate. In this paper, we suggest a new key entry system, Air keyboard with haptic finger glove. By applying haptic illusions such as phantom sensation and apparent movement, the finger glove could simulate the tactile feedback such as typing and unevenness sensation with low cost. Several controlled experiments were conducted to evaluate the efficiency and the accuracy of the air keyboard together with haptic finger glove. The result shows that the haptic finger glove could help user to better interact with the virtual keyboard. Moreover, a short-term training could increase the input efficiency and reduce the error rate, which is comparable or better than traditional pointing method with handheld controllers.

Keywords: VR keyboard · Haptic · Phantom sensation

1 Introduction

Virtual Reality (VR) headsets are getting customer levels. However, there are very few intuitive methods of key entry. One of the most general methods is pointing and selecting character by using handheld controller. This method has many downsides, such as the speed and accuracy of typing are relatively low and it is stressful to use. By the way, obviously, the most common method of key entry is Qwerty keyboard. Current VR headsets, Oculus Quest has feature of hand tracking. But there is no key entry system by using their own hand in current VR headsets. Can we implement keyboard in the VR environment? The goal of this study is to suggest new key entry method for VR environment which can enter text with high accurate, high speed, and less stressful. We can implement mid-air keyboard method, but inexistence of physical feedback makes it difficult to use keyboard as same as physical one. To achieve these goals, we focus on the haptic sensations which the user would feel as if they are using the

© Springer Nature Switzerland AG 2021
C. Stephanidis et al. (Eds.): HCII 2021, LNCS 13095, pp. 31–43, 2021.
https://doi.org/10.1007/978-3-030-90963-5_3

physical keyboard. The main issue of our research is how to simulate the haptic feedback from physical keyboard. The main feedback to simulate are typing the button and unevenness feedback when moving the finger across the buttons. We implement haptic finger glove by applying haptic illusions on finger to show those sensations. Haptic illusions enable user to show sensations by mistaking perceptions. Hence, we can give those sensations with more simple components with haptic illusion.

2 Related Works

T.M. Andualem, N. Atulya, R. David, and L.S. Emanuele searched about stiffness discrimination with visual only, tactile only, and both feedback [1]. They found visual feedback would compensate missed kinematic feedback in their experiment. We need to consider what feedback would be needed for our application use.

In terms of keyboard for VR environment, Facebook Reality lab searched about tactile feedback of mid-air keyboard [2]. In this study, they showed only touch and press sensations for fingers. They might be enough sensations to show for controlling keyboard, but we thought unevenness sensation across keys is also important information to show.

On the other hand, there are some key entry device researches which does not look Qwerty keyboard. C. Mehring, F. Kuester, K. Singh, and M. Chen have developed the glove type key entry system called Kitty [3]. User can input characters by pressing sensors on the glove with similar finger movements with Qwerty keyboard. However, it would need much training to improve input efficiency. In our system, we showed not only touch and type sensations, but also unevenness sensation across keys. Moreover, to reduce the learning cost, we used virtual Qwerty keyboard.

3 Method

3.1 Basic Theory

We used haptic illusions called phantom sensation and apparent movement. They enable user to show feedback points between actuators. Figure 1 shows the phenomena of phantom sensation. By changing amplitude of stimuli, the flexible sensation location can be achieved [4]. Figure 2 shows the phenomena of apparent haptic motion. Moving sensation is appeared when two stimulus amplitude were changed in time series. We applied these phenomenons on finger because it can reduce the number of actuators.

3.2 How to Show Unevenness Sensation

When user move their fingers on the keyboard as shown in Fig. 3, facing point on key is changed as they move their finger. We focus on this, and achieved

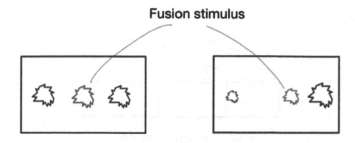

Fig. 1. Phantom sensation phenomena

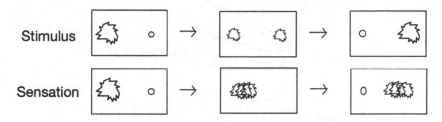

Fig. 2. Apparent haptic motion

this change by applying apparent haptic motion as shown in Fig. 3. User feels touching point as vibration. When they move their fingers on the keyboard, vibrating point is also moves based on their finger movement.

3.3 How to Show Type Sensation

When the user press a key, they get counter force from key in physical world, as shown in Fig. 4. We could not show the sensation of counter force with DC vibration motor, but we expressed this with vibration point and power change as shown in Fig. 4. We apply phantom sensation on finger to show stimuli on the point of finger where pressed the key.

4 System Design

4.1 Outline of System

Figure 5 shows the system outline. In our system, we use VR headset, Oculus Quest to show visual and audio feedback to user. Since Oculus Quest has a feature of hand tracking by image processing, we did not need any other additional tracking equipment. We use Oculus Link to connect PC and run software on Unity. For what at the PC side, we implement our virtual keyboard system. Based on the collision information on tracked finger in Unity, the virtual keyboard sends signals to finger glove controller via Bluetooth. Finger glove controller controls vibration motors to show real time haptic feedback.

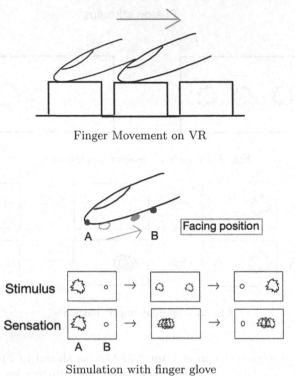

Fig. 3. Unevenness across keys

4.2   Implementation of Virtual Keyboard

We use an asset, Oculus integration, which is supported by Oculus to make use of Oculus Quest headset with hand tracking. Based on the information of finger position, we put spheres on the tip of fingers. In this system, user will use only thumb, index and middle fingers due to the accuracy of hand tracking. The user can type keyboard by colliding these spheres on the key. When finger touching on a key, user get haptic simulation of touch. If the user moves their finger with touching key, they get unevenness simulation. When user type key, they get type simulation. We made models of keyboard. Same as Qwerty keyboard, user can type capitalized character by holding shift key. When user type any keys, the keyboard output sound of type. In every several frames on Unity, this system sends signals to control haptic finger glove via Bluetooth.

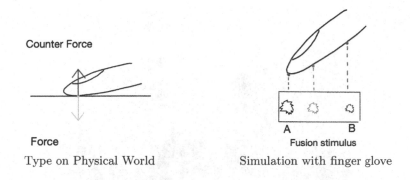

Type on Physical World   Simulation with finger glove

Fig. 4. Type a key

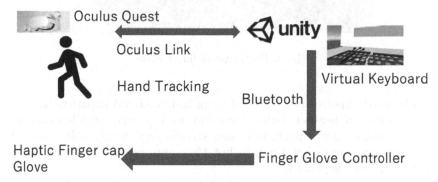

Fig. 5. System outline

4.3 Implementation of Haptic Finger Glove

Figure 6 is the prototype of finger glove. Haptic functions are showed by DC motors. Motors are controlled by ESP32 microcomputer. Figure 6 shows control circuit of DC motor. Each motor is controlled by NPN transistor (C1815), resistance (300Ω), diode (1N4007) and Pulse Width Modulation (PWM) signal. Due to the PWM pin number limits, we use the multiplexer to reduce the number of PWM pins (MUX, TC74HC153AP). MUX selects 4 PWM states by 2 bit digital signals. Figure 7 is our circuit image.

5 Experiment

5.1 Experiment Design

We conducted three experiments to evaluate the prototype system. First is about evaluating our new key entry method, Air keyboard with haptic finger glove perspectives from accuracy, speed, and mental workload of text entry. Second is about evaluating haptic functions of our Air Keyboard system. Third is about evaluating learnability of our system. Six subjects (age:20–24, 5M 1F) joined the

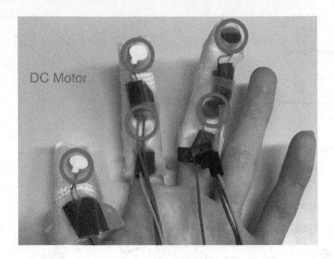

Fig. 6. Prototype of finger glove

first and second experiments. Three of them had much VR experiences, such as they have own VR headset. Other three did not have enough VR experiences. Third experiments participants were four student (age:20–26, 4M). All of their mother languages were not English, but they were familiar with English key entry with Qwerty keyboard.

5.2 Key Entry Experiment

Experiment Setting. We conducted controlled comparative experiments between handheld controller(HC) and Air keyboard without finger glove(AK) and Haptic Air keyboard with finger glove(HAK). One is most general key entry method in VR environment, pointing with handheld controller. We use Oculus Quest handheld tracer, shown in Fig. 8. User can enter character by pointing key and press trigger on the handheld controller. User gets only visual feedback. Second is our new method, air keyboard without haptic finger glove(AK), shown in Fig. 8. User gets sound and visual feedback from this system. Third is air keyboard with haptic finger glove(HAK), shown in Fig. 8. User gets sound, visual and haptic feedback in this system. In this experiment, participants were asked to complete displayed English phrases as quickly and accurately as possible. We used English phrase which MacKenzie, I. S. and Soukoreff, R. W. suggest to evaluate key entry method [5]. In each experiment, random English phrases from this English phrase set are appeared in the panel in front of the participant.

Each participant evaluated each method in terms of accuracy, speed, and mental workload quantitatively. We evaluate accuracy of key entry on a scale of Characters per Minutes (CPM), (1) and Error Rate (ER), (2).

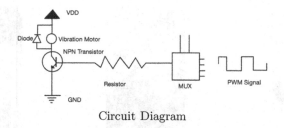

Circuit Diagram

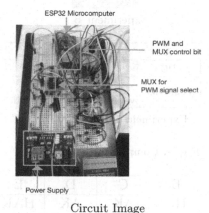

Circuit Image

Fig. 7. Haptic finger glove (circuit diagram and circuit image)

$$CPM = \frac{C}{M} \tag{1}$$

- where C is number of correct character, M is minutes.

$$ER = \frac{E}{C+E} * 100\% \tag{2}$$

- where E is the number of errors.

To measure mental workload, we used NASA Task Load Index (NASA-TLX) sheet [6]. NASA-TLX is the mental workload quantities assessment technique. NASA-TLX is consisted by 6 subjects, mental demand (MD), physical demand (PD), temporal demand (TD), own performance (OP), effort (EF), and frustration (FR). Participants answered these subjects by putting circles on line, and we scored in terms of the position of circle. Participants skipped weight phrase because we used Adaptive Weight Workload (AWWL) which Mitake and Kumashiro suggest [7]. Moreover, since all of participants were Japanese students, they were given Japanese translated sheet of NASA-TLX which Mitake and Kumashiro published [7].

Experiment A

Experiment B

Experiment C

Experiment	A	B	C
Abbr. Name	HC	AK	HAK
Method	controller	finger without haptic	finger with haptic

Experiment 1 Table

Fig. 8. Comparative experiments

	A	B	C	D	E	F
1	HC	HC	AK	AK	HAK	HAK
2	AK	HAK	HC	HAK	AK	HC
3	HAK	AK	HAK	HC	HC	AK

Fig. 9. Experiment order table

Participants sat on the chair and adjusted the position of keyboard according to their preference. Participants were asked to test typing 5 English phrases (ex. I am a student) before each experiment for practice. To prevent having influences in the experiment order, each participant did experiment in different order. Figure 9 shows the order of experiments. Participants were asked to complete displayed English phrase. Each experiment continued two minutes. In these experiments, only correct characters were inputted. Incorrect characters were just counted as mistakes. After the three experiments, participants were asked to complete NASA-TLX sheet.

Experiment Result. Figure 10 shows the CPM, and Fig. 11 shows the ER in each experiment. Figure 12 shows mental workloads who had no VR experiences, and Fig. 13 shows mental workloads who had much VR experiences.

Analysis. For speed of input, we confirmed that there are only small differences between three methods. On the other hand, for accuracy of input, our methods scored four times worse point. This result suggested that user cannot use the

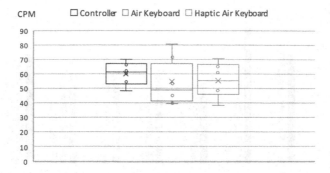

Fig. 10. Character per minutes

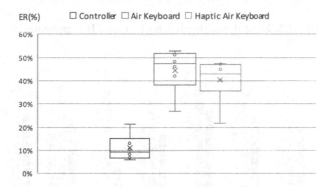

Fig. 11. Error rate

virtual keyboard system well without enough training. For mental workloads, we confirmed that there were big differences whether participants had much VR experience or not. Participants who did not have VR experiences got lower score in our system. On the other hand, participants who had much VR experiences answered higher score in our system. Particularly, participants who had much VR experiences answered the effort subject very low. It assumes that since they are already used to using handheld controller, they accept using it. However, participants who did not have much VR experiences prefer our system because our system is similar to usual Qwerty keyboard.

5.3   Haptic Function Evaluation

Experiment Setting. To evaluate our haptic function of finger glove, we asked participants about each sensations similarities compared to physical keyboard.

Experiment Sequence. Participants were asked to move their fingers. They were asked to type key, move finger from left to right, right to left, top to bottom, and bottom to top. After each movement, they were asked to score "How much

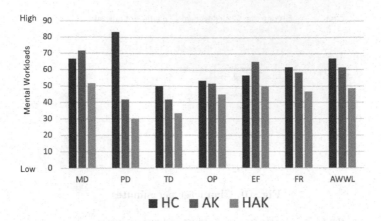

Fig. 12. Mental workloads who had no VR experiences

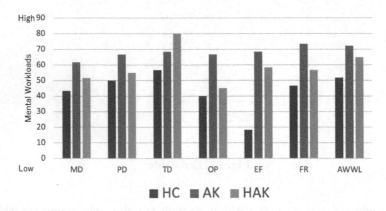

Fig. 13. Mental workloads who had much VR experiences

did you feel the sensation of them with comparing physical keyboard?" out of 7 points (1: completely different, 4: modestly same, 7: completely same).

Figure 14 shows the result of evaluations.

Experiment Result

Analysis. We confirmed that most of participants felt sensations that when they use keyboard. Five out of six participants felt the sensations of finger movement on keyboard. However, all of them did not notice before my asking. We assumed that those sensations could work unconsciously during using our system.

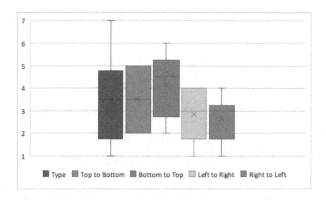

Fig. 14. Haptic function evaluation

5.4   Learnability Experiment

Experiment Setting. Judging by Experiment1, we thought that our system needs more pre-training to use well. Hence, we conducted 1 h experiment on four participants (age: 20–26, 4M) to measure the learning curve of our system.

Experiment Sequence. Participants did one minute experiment, same settings with experiment1. After 30 min training and 1 h training, participants did same experiment. In training session, We advised participants to practice the usage of Air keyboard. Participants choose to use their prefer fingers from one to three of each hand. Finger gloves were attached to only selected fingers, and user can type by only selected fingers.

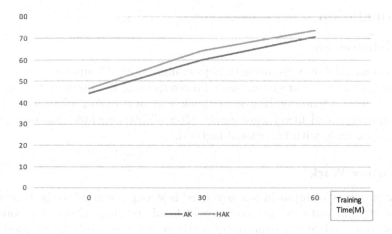

Fig. 15. CPM transition

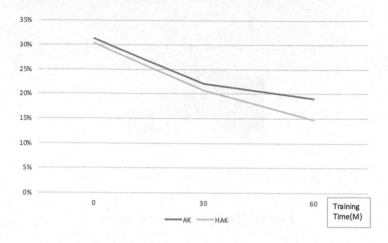

Fig. 16. ER transition

Figure 15 and Fig. 16 shows the transition of CPM and ER. One hour training resulted in improvement of typing speed and accuracy.

Analysis. We observed that one hour training increased input efficiency about 1.5 times, and reduce the error rate about one half. Compared to AK and HAK, HAK resulted better in CPM and ER after training session. Hence, our data suggested that the haptic finger glove could help user to better interact with the virtual keyboard. Compared to handheld controller in experiment1, our method resulted higher CPM after training. On the other hand, ER of our method was little bit higher than handheld controller.

6   Conclusion

6.1   Achievement

We implemented Air keyboard with haptic finger glove. Compared to general key entry method in VR, our system scored more speed of key input and comparable accuracy after 1 h training. Haptic feedback help users to control more accurately know their type and finger movement. After all, we conclude that our method can be replaceable with traditional method.

6.2   Future Work

The low accuracy of input in our keyboard is strongly related to the type recognition system in software and accuracy of hand tracking. There were some differences compared to our experiment settings, but this study [2] resulted lower than 3% error rate in mid-air keyboard. We estimate that improvement of typing software would improve the accuracy. Moreover, we will try to show haptic feedback with other methods.

References

1. David, R., Andualem, T.M., Atulya, N., Emanuele, L.S.: Wearable vibrotactile haptic device for stiffness discrimination during virtual interactions. Front. Robot. AI **4**, 42 (2017)
2. Kenrick, K., Kristensson, P.O., Aakar, G., Majed, S., Hrvoje, B.: Investigating remote tactile feedback for mid-air text-entry in virtual reality (2020)
3. Singh, K., Mehring, C., Kuester, F., Chen, M.: KITTY: keyboard independent touch typing in VR (2004)
4. Alles, D.S.: Information transmission by phantom sensations. IEEE Trans. Man-Mach. Syst. **1**, 85–91 (1970)
5. MacKenzie, I.S., Soukoreff, R.W.: Phrase sets for evaluating text entry techniques. In: Extended Abstracts of the ACM Conference on Human Factors in Computing Systems, pp. 754–755 (2003)
6. Hart, S., Staveland, L.: Development of NASA-TLX (task load index): results of empirical and theoretical research. Adv. Psychol. **52**, 139–183 (1988)
7. Shinji, M., Masaharu, K.: Subjective mental workload assessment technique. Jpn. J. Ergon. **29**(6), 399–408 (1993)
8. von Békésy, G.: Sensations on the skin similar to directional hearing, beats, and harmonics of the ear. J. Acoust. Soc. Am. **29**(4), 489–501 (1957)
9. Mingrui, Z., Sida, G., Ke, S., Xin, Y., Chun, Y., Yuanchun, S.: Atk: enabling ten-finger freehand typing in air based on 3D hand tracking data (2015)

Estimation of Empathy Skill Level and Personal Traits Using Gaze Behavior and Dialogue Act During Turn-Changing

Ryo Ishii[1]([✉]), Shiro Kumano[2], Ryuichiro Higashinaka[1], Shiro Ozawa[1],
and Testuya Kinebuchi[1]

[1] NTT Media Intelligence Laboratories, NTT Corporation, 1-1, Hikari-no-oka,
Yokosuka-shi, Kanagawa, Japan
ryo.ishii.ct@hco.ntt.co.jp
[2] NTT Communication Science Laboratories, NTT Corporation, 2-4, Hikaridai,
Seika-cho, Atsugi-shi, Kanagawa, Japan

Abstract. We explored the gaze behavior towards the end of utterances and dialogue acts (DAs), i.e., verbal-behavior information indicating the intension of an utterance, during turn-keeping/changing to estimate several social skills and personal traits in multi-party discussions. We first collected data on several personal indicators, i.e., Big Five, which measures personal traits, and Davis' Interpersonal Reactivity Index (IRI), which measures empathy skill level, utterances that include DA categories, and gaze behavior, from participants in four-person discussions. We constructed and evaluated models for estimating the scores of these indicators using gaze behavior and DA information. The evaluation results indicate that using both gaze behavior and DAs during turn-keeping/changing is effective for estimating all such scores with high accuracy. It is also possible to estimate these scores with higher accuracy by using the gaze distribution to the current speaker and listener and amount of speaking obtained during the entire discussion. We also found that the IRI scores can be estimated more accurately than those of Big Five.

Keywords: Personal traits · Empathy skill level · Gaze behavior · Dialogue act · Turn-taking

1 Introduction

Social communication skills are fundamental for successful communication in globalized and multi-cultural societies as they are central to education, work, and daily life. Although there is great interest in the notion of communication skills in scientific and real-life applications, the concept is difficult to generally define due to the complexity of communication, wide variety of related cognitive and social abilities, and huge situational variability [9]. Techniques that involve nonverbal behaviors to estimate communication skills have been receiving much attention.

C. Stephanidis et al. (Eds.): HCII 2021, LNCS 13095, pp. 44–57, 2021.
https://doi.org/10.1007/978-3-030-90963-5_4

For example, researchers have developed models for estimating public speaking skills [38, 43], persuasiveness [37], communication skills during job interviews [34] and group work [35], and leadership [42].

Most of these studies used the overall values of verbal/nonverbal behaviors during an entire discussion such as the amount of utterances and physical motion. However, Ishii et al. [20, 21] estimated communication skills with high accuracy from such behaviors in a short time during turn-changing. They developed an estimation model of scores of four indexes in Davis' Interpersonal Reactivity Index (IRI) [5] that uses the gaze behavior and dialogue acts (DAs) near the end of utterances during turn-keeping/changing as feature values. The model has a higher estimation accuracy than that using the overall values of verbal/nonverbal behaviors during an entire discussion used in many previous studies on skill estimation. This suggests that behavior during turn-keeping/turn-changing in a very short time is useful for estimating individual empathy skill level.

Ishii et al. [20, 21] focused on estimating only the score of one of the four indexes in IRI, which measures empathy skill level. It is necessary to demonstrate whether gaze behavior and DAs are useful for estimating various scores of indicators for measuring the characteristics and social skills of individuals other than IRI.

In this study, we explored whether gaze behavior and DAs during turn-keeping/changing are useful in estimating the scores of the other three IRI indexes, those of Big Five [4], for measuring personal traits, by constructing and evaluating estimation models for them. First, we collected data on the scores from each indicator plus utterances that include the DA categories such as provision, self-discourse, empathy, and turn-yielding, and gaze behavior from participants in four-person discussions. We constructed and evaluated models for estimating theses scores using gaze behavior and DAs. The evaluation results indicate that using both gaze behavior and DA information during turn-keeping/changing is effective for estimating all such scores with high accuracy. It is also possible to estimate these scores with higher accuracy by using the gaze distribution to the current speaker and listener and amount of speaking obtained during the entire discussion. We also found that the IRI scores can be estimated more accurately than those of Big Five.

2   Related Work

2.1   Personal Traits and Empathy Skill

We describe the importance of Big Five and IRI. Big Five is a taxonomy for five personality traits [4], i.e., "openness to experience (OP)", "conscientiousness (CO)", "extraversion (EX)", "agreeableness (AG)", and "neuroticism (NE)". OP reflects the degree of intellectual curiosity, creativity, and a preference for novelty and variety a person has. It is also describes the extent to which a person is imaginative or independent and depicts a personal preference for a variety of activities over a strict routine. CO reflects the tendency to be organized and dependable, show self-discipline, act dutifully, aim for achievement, and prefer planned rather than spontaneous behavior. EX reflects energetic, urgency, assertiveness, sociability, the tendency to seek stimulation in the company of others, and talkativeness. AG reflects the tendency to be compassionate and cooperative rather than suspicious and antagonistic towards others. It is also a measure of one's trusting and helpful nature and whether one is generally well-tempered. NE reflects the tendency to be prone to psychological stress, i.e., the tendency to experience unpleasant emotions easily such as anger, anxiety, depression, and vulnerability. It also refers to the degree of emotional stability and impulse control and is sometimes referred to by its low pole, "emotional stability".

As mentioned above, Davis' Interpersonal Reactivity Index (IRI) [5] includes four indexes of empathy: perspective-taking (PT), i.e., the tendency to adopt another's psychological perspective; fantasy (FS), i.e., the tendency to strongly identify with fictitious characters; empathetic concern (EC), i.e., the tendency to experience feelings of warmth, sympathy, and concern toward others; and personal distress (PD), i.e., the tendency to have feelings of discomfort and concern when witnessing others' negative experiences. IRI has been translated into many languages [6, 8] and used in a wide variety of fields such as neuroscience [1] and genetics [39]. In this context, some researchers in computer engineering developed models for estimating empathetic statements between people [31, 32]. Thus, measuring empathy skill level using IRI is considered invaluable in human communication.

The above three indicators are very important in measuring social skills and personality traits of individuals. Therefore, we focused on estimating the scores of a total of nine indexes of these two indicators. This study is the first attempt to demonstrate the relationships among such scores and gaze behavior and DAs during turn-changing/keeping during discussions.

2.2   Verbal and Gaze Behavior During Turn-Changing

Most research on elucidating the mechanism of turn-changing in conversation has been conducted in sociolinguistics. Sacks et al. [41] developed a turn-changing model in which turn-changing can only occur at transition-relevance points near the end of utterances. Several studies have reported that verbal behavior and nonverbal behavior, such as gaze, have an important association with the next speaker and the start of the next utterance [29].

Gaze behavior is especially important for smooth turn-taking. Kendon [29] reported that a speaker gazes at a listener in a two-person conversation as a "turn-yielding cue" at the end of an utterance. The listener glances at the speaker (mutual gazing) then looks away (mutual gaze ends) from the speaker and starts speaking, that is, takes the turn. These findings indicate that the transition of gaze behavior and mutual gaze are important for turn-changing. Some researchers [18, 25, 27] reported a similar tendency for the speaker to look at the next speaker when yielding the turn in multi-party discussions. On the basis of these findings, many studies have attempted to enable smooth turn-changing using verbal and gaze behavior in human-computer interaction [17, 40].

Fig. 1. Photograph of multi-party discussion

Several studies have explored the idea of automatically detecting whether turn-changing takes place in multi-party discussions by using gaze behavior near the end of an utterance and other behaviors [3,7,26,27]. In addition to estimating turn-changing, some studies have attempted to estimate who will become the next speaker during turn-changing and when the next utterance will start. Some previous studies have developed estimation models that feature three processing steps to estimate whether turn-changing or turn-keeping will occur, who the next speaker will be during turn-changing, and the start of the next speaker's utterance using the gaze-behavior features of gaze transition patterns (GTPs), which have an n-gram of gaze objects that includes mutual gaze information [12,18,24,25]. GTPs are the most useful patterns found thus far for estimating the next speaker and time of the next utterance.

Thus, people use verbal behavior and nonverbal behavior, such as gaze, near the end of utterances for smooth turn-changing. We assume that a high emotional and empathy skill level is needed to gaze depending on the DA information required for smooth turn-changing. In addition, there is a good possibility that such behavior may differ depending on personality traits. Our key idea is using DA information and gaze behavior during turn-keeping/changing to estimate emotion and empathy skill level and personal traits.

3   Corpus Data

In this section, we give details of the corpus of multi-party discussion. The corpus includes eight face-to-face four-person discussions held by four groups of four different people (16 participants in total). In each group, the four participants were Japanese women in their 20's and 30's who had never met before. They sat facing each other (Fig. 1). We labeled the participants, from left to right, P1, P2, P3, and P4. They argued and gave opinions in response to highly divisive questions, such as "Is marriage the same as love?", and needed to reach a conclusion within ten minutes. All four four-person groups took part in two discussions.

Table 1. Average values (Avg.) and standard deviations (SD) of 16 people for each indicator's indexes and Pearson's correlation coefficient r between indexes. The yellow and orange boxes are significantly correlated at significance level of $p < .05$ and $p < .01$ as result of uncorrelated test.

		Basic statistics		Correlation coefficient								
				Big five					IRI			
		Avg.	SD	OP	CO	EX	AG	NE	EC	PT	PD	FS
Big five	OP	4.36	0.52		0.081	0.515	0.110	−0.456	0.071	−0.107	0.072	−0.034
	CO	4.01	0.87	0.081		0.355	−0.051	0.338	0.205	0.161	0.034	0.022
	EX	4.85	0.77	0.515	0.355		0.114	0.115	0.020	0.388	−0.026	0.153
	AG	5.02	0.68	0.110	−0.051	0.114		−0.615	−0.006	−0.026	−0.206	0.105
	NE	4.34	1.06	−0.456	0.338	0.115	−0.615		0.074	−0.099	0.572	0.149
IRI	EC	2.59	0.80	0.071	0.205	0.020	−0.006	0.074		−0.114	0.383	0.622
	PT	3.10	0.45	−0.107	0.161	0.388	−0.026	−0.099	−0.114		−0.094	−0.101
	PD	2.52	0.54	0.072	0.034	−0.026	−0.206	0.572	0.383	−0.094		0.127
	FS	2.81	0.44	−0.034	0.022	0.153	0.105	0.149	0.622	−0.101	0.127	

The participants' voices were recorded with a pin microphone attached to their chests, and the entire discussions were videoed. Upper body shots of each participant (recorded 30 Hz) were also taken. From the collected data for all eight discussions (80 min in total) and from the recorded data, we constructed a multimodal corpus consisting of the following verbal/nonverbal behaviors and the participants' scores of the indexes of Big Five and IRI.

- Utterances and DAs: We built the utterance unit using the inter-pausal unit (IPU) [30]. The utterance interval was extracted manually from the speech wave. The portion of an utterance followed by 200 ms of silence was used as the unit of one utterance. From the created IPU, backchannels were excluded, and an utterance unit continued from the same person was considered as one utterance turn. IPU pairs adjoined in time, and IPU groups during turn-keeping/changing were created. The data for speech overlaps, i.e., when a listener interrupted during a speaker's utterance or two or more participants spoke simultaneously at turn-changing, were excluded from the IPU pairs for analysis. Eventually, there were 1227 IPUs during turn-keeping and 129 during turn-changing.
- Gaze objects: A skilled annotator manually annotated the gaze objects by using bust/head and overhead views in each video frame. The gaze objects were the four participants (labeled P1, P2, P3, and P4, as mentioned above) and non-persons, i.e., the walls or floor. Three annotators annotated the gaze behavior in our conversation dataset to verify the annotation quality. Conger's Kappa coefficient was 0.887. Based on the benchmarks of a previous study [10], the gaze annotations were of excellent quality.
- Personal traits: All participants were asked to complete a questionnaire that was based on IRI [5] and Big Five [4]. The scores of the five indexes of Big Five, i.e., OP, CO, EX, AG, and NE, and those of the four indexes of IRI, i.e., PT, FS, EC, and PD, for each participant were obtained from their responses. Table 1 shows the average values and standard deviations of 16 people for each

index and Pearson's correlation coefficients r among the 9 indexes of the two indicators. The following significant correlations between indexes were found.

- Correlation of indexes: there is a correlation [between OP and EX and between AG and NE of Big Five as well as between EC and FS of IRI.
- Correlation of indexes between the two indicators: there is a correlation between NE of Big Five and PD of IRI.

Thus, there is a correlation between several indexes.

All verbal and nonverbal behavior data were integrated 30 Hz for visual display using viewer software [36]. This software enables us to annotate multimodal data frame-by-frame and observe the data intuitively.

4 Feature Values

We used the gaze behavior and DAs during turn-changing/turn-keeping as feature values for developing estimation models of the scores of each indicator in reference to previous studies [15,20]. In this section, we give details of these feature values.

We first introduce gaze behavior. We focused on GTPs as features of gaze behavior, which are temporal transitions of participant's gaze behavior near the end of utterances according to previous studies [12,18,23,24]. A GTP is expressed as an n-gram, which is defined as a sequence of gaze-direction shifts. We demonstrated that the occurrence frequencies of GTPs differ significantly for a speaker and listener during turn-keeping and a listener who becomes the next speaker (hereafter, called "next-speaker") and listeners who do not become the next speaker (hereafter, called "listeners") during turn-changing. We also demonstrated that a GTP is effective for estimating the next speaker in multi-party discussions. Thus, we used GTPs as gaze-analysis parameters. To generate a GTP, we focused on the gazed object for 1200 ms: 1000 ms before and 200 ms after the utterance since the GTP during 1200 ms is important for turn-taking [12,18,23,24]. A GTP is composed of a person or object classified as "speaker", "listener", or "non-person" and labeled. We considered whether there was mutual gaze and classified gaze behavior using the following seven gaze labels.

- S: Person looks at a speaker without mutual gaze (speaker does not look at the listener.).
- SM: Person looks at the speaker with mutual gaze (speaker looks at a listener.).
- $L1$, $L2$, $L3$: Person looks at another listener without mutual gaze. Labels $L1$, $L2$, and $L3$ indicate different people. The sitting position does not matter. For example, if P1 who is speaking looks at P2 followed by P3 then P2 again, the gaze transition pattern of P1 is $L1$–$L2$–$L1$.
- $LM1$, $LM2$, $LM3$: Person looks at another listener with mutual gaze. Labels $LM1$, $LM2$, and $LM3$ indicate different people.
- N: Person looks at the next speaker without mutual gaze only during turn-changing.

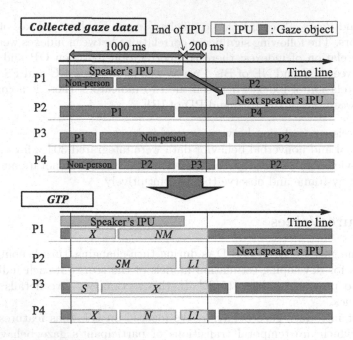

Fig. 2. Example of generating GTPs during turn-changing

- *NM*: Person looks at the next speaker with mutual gaze only during turn-changing.
- *X*: Person looks at non-persons, such as the floor or ceiling, i.e., gaze aversion.

Figure 2 shows how GTPs are constructed: P1 finishes speaking, then P2 starts to speak. Person P1 gazes at P2 after she gazes at a non-person during the analysis interval. When P1 looks at P2, P2 looks at P1; that is, there is mutual gaze. Therefore, P1's GTP is *X-NM*. Person P2 looks at P4 after making eye contact with P1; thus, P2's GTP is *SM-L1*. Person P3 looks at a non-person after looking at P1; thus, P3's GTP is *S-X*. Person P4 looks at P2 and P3 after looking at a non-person; thus, P4's GTP is *X-N-L1*.

A DA for each IPU was extracted using an estimation technique for Japanese [11,33] for DA analysis. This technique can estimate a DA of a sentence from among 33 DA categories using word n-grams, semantic categories (obtained from the Japanese thesaurus Goi-Taikei), and character n-grams. The technique outputs 33 DA categories. We grouped them into the following five major categories.

- Provision: Utterance for providing information
- Self-discourse: Utterance for disclosing oneself
- Empathy: Utterance intending empathy
- Turn-yielding: Utterance intending a listener to speak next (ex. utterance of question, suggestion, or confirmation)
- Others: Utterance not included in the above four categories

About 90% of utterances included the DA categories of Provision, Self-disclosure, Empathy, and Turn-yielding.

Ishii et al. [15,20] demonstrated that the occurrence frequencies of GTPs accompanying each DA category for the speaker and listeners during turn-keeping, and the speaker, next-speaker, and listeners during turn-changing in multi-party discussions, is effective for estimating a participant's EC score. We mainly used them as feature values of the estimation models of the scores of Big Five and IRI in this study.

5   Estimation Model

The goal of this study was to demonstrate that the gaze behavior and DAs during turn-keeping/changing are useful for estimating the individuals' scores of all nine indexes of Big Five and IRI. We constructed a model for estimating the index scores of each indicator using GTPs and DA information, one using utterance information such as duration of speaking and number of speaking-turns, and one using simple gaze information (which is the duration of looking at a speaker or listener in a discussion) to compare the usefulness of GTP and DA information. We also constructed two estimation models using GTPs and DA information and using GTPs, DA information, utterance information, and simple gaze information to evaluate the effectiveness of multimodal fusion.

We constructed the estimation models using a SMOreg [28], which implements a support vector machine (SVM) for regression in Weka [2], and evaluated the accuracy of the models and the effectiveness of each feature. The settings of the SVM, i.e., the polynomial kernel, cost parameter (C), and hyper parameter of the kernel (γ), were determined using a grid-search technique. The objective variable is the EC score of each person.

The details of the five estimation models are as follows.

- Chance-level model: This model outputs the mean value of all participants.
- Utterance model: This model uses the ratio of utterances and turns in the discussion.
- Simple-gaze model: This model uses the duration a person was looking at the speaker and listeners in the discussion.
- DA model: This model uses the frequency of occurrence of speech DA category.
- GTP model: This model uses the occurrence frequencies of GTPs. At this time, the occurrence frequencies of GTPs are not classified by DA category.
- GTP+DA model: This model uses the occurrence frequencies of GTPs for each DA category when the person is either the speaker or a listener during turn-keeping and the speaker, next-speaker, or a listener during turn-changing.
- All model: This model uses the ratio of utterances and turns, duration of looking, and occurrence frequencies of GTPs for each DA category. In other words, the features are integrated with an early-fusion method.

Table 2. Evaluation results of estimation models. Numbers indicate average absolute errors between estimated and actual scores. Those in parentheses indicate z-score of average absolute errors. Range of scores for each scale, average value obtained from participants, and distribution differ. We use z-score to compare magnitude of error between scales.

Model	Big five					IRI			
	OP	CO	EX	AG	NE	EC	PT	PD	FS
Chance level	0.422	0.725	0.639	0.516	0.828	0.627	0.306	0.406	0.295
	(0.809)	(0.834)	(0.828)	(0.760)	(0.784)	(0.783)	(0.678)	(0.746)	(0.676)
Simple gaze	0.693	0.724	0.423	0.383	0.738	0.609	0.232	0.458	0.315
	(1.329)	(0.833)	(0.549)	(0.565)	(0.699)	(0.761)	(0.517)	(0.841)	(0.724)
Utterance	0.497	0.883	0.666	0.669	0.970	0.698	0.340	0.472	0.328
	(0.953)	(1.016)	(0.863)	(0.986)	(0.919)	(0.871)	(0.754)	(0.866)	(0.754)
GTP	0.334	0.520	0.298	0.303	0.437	0.158	0.135	0.041	0.182
	(0.640)	(0.598)	(0.387)	(0.447)	(0.414)	(0.197)	(0.299)	(0.076)	(0.419)
DA	0.431	0.897	0.726	0.656	1.073	0.785	0.447	0.447	0.394
	(0.827)	(1.032)	(0.942)	(0.966)	(1.016)	(0.980)	(0.991)	(0.822)	(0.905)
GTP+DA	0.288	0.292	0.476	0.482	0.640	0.063	0.040	0.074	0.122
	(0.553)	(0.336)	(0.618)	(0.710)	(0.606)	(0.079)	(0.088)	(0.137)	(0.280)
All	0.272	0.458	0.232	0.287	0.222	0.147	0.051	0.061	0.209
	(0.521)	(0.527)	(0.342)	(0.423)	(0.210)	(0.183)	(0.114)	(0.112)	(0.481)

We used ten-fold cross validation with the data of the 16 participants. The mean absolute error of each estimation model is shown in Table 2.

The simple-gaze model estimated the EX, AG, and NE scores of Big Five and EC and PT of IRI more precisely than the chance-level model. The GTP model estimated all scores more precisely than the chance-level model. The DA model did not estimate any scores more precisely than the chance-level model. Among these models, the GTP model was the most accurate. The GTP+DA model was more accurate for OP, CO of Big Five and EC, PT, and FS of IRI. The accuracy was the highest for CO of Big Five and EC, PT, PD, and FS of IRI for all models.

The All model was the most accurate for OP, EX, AG, and NE of Big Five and PD of IRI. It was found that GTP alone is the most effective feature value in the models that use only one feature value and that the GTP+DA model or All model is most effective. The estimation errors were 0.063 for EC, 0.040 for PT, and 0.061 or less for PD of IRI. Also, among all the indexes, the error was 0.300 or less, and very accurate estimation was possible.

Next, to verify which indexes can be estimated higher and conversely lower, the difference in estimation accuracy among the indexes was analyzed. We compared the errors of the All model' with the highest precision among the other models. The estimation error in each index was divided using the standard deviation of the correct data to obtain a z-score. By comparing the z-scores of the errors in each index, the ease of estimation was examined among the indexes. One-way analysis of variance was conducted on the z-scores of 16 estimation errors of each index, which are the results of a 16 cross-validation, and significant differences were found among the indexes.

Table 3. Results of multiple comparison with Fisher's least significant difference method. * indicates that significance level is $p < .05$. ↑ indicates that estimation error is large compared with comparison target; conversely, ↓ indicates that estimation error is small compared with comparison target.

		Big five					IRI			
		OP	CO	EX	AG	NE	EC	PT	PD	FS
Big five	OP	■	n.s.	n.s.	n.s.	↑ *	↑ *	↑ *	↑ *	n.s.
	CO	n.s.	■	n.s.	n.s.	↑ *	↑ *	↑ *	↑ *	n.s.
	EX	n.s.	n.s.	■	n.s.	n.s.	n.s.	↑ *	n.s.	n.s.
	AG	n.s.	n.s.	n.s.	■	n.s.	↑ *	↑ *	↑ *	n.s.
	NE	↓ *	↓ *	n.s.	n.s.	■	n.s.	n.s.	n.s.	↓ *
IRI	EC	↓ *	↓ *	n.s.	↓ *	n.s.	■	n.s.	n.s.	↓ *
	PT	↓ *	↓ *	↓ *	↓ *	n.s.	n.s.	■	n.s.	↓ *
	PD	↓ *	↓ *	n.s.	↓ *	n.s.	n.s.	n.s.	■	↓ *
	FS	n.s.	n.s.	n.s.	n.s.	↑ *	↑ *	↑ *	↑ *	■

Next, we used multiple comparison and Fisher's least significant difference method to determine which index combination has a difference in estimation error. The results are listed in Table 3. The overall trend can be divided into two groups, i.e., large and small estimation errors, among the indexes. Specifically, errors tended to be smaller for NE of Big Five and EC, PT, and PD of IRI. On the contrary, the errors of OP, CO, EX, and AG of Big Five tended to be large.

6 Discussion

Our estimation models using GTP and DA information (i.e. DA+GTP model and All model) have been shown to accurately estimate the index scores of Big Five and IRI. Although gaze behavior and DAs, in the short term, during turn-keeping/changing are carried out unconsciously, they are effective in measuring social skills and personality traits. This is interesting with the findings that have been revealed for the first time. The results also suggest that it is possible to estimate such scores with higher accuracy by using both the gaze distribution to the current speaker and non-speaker obtained from the entire conversation and the amount of utterances in addition to GTPs and DAs.

We also compared the score-estimation accuracy among the nine indexes of the two indicators. NE of Big Five and EC, PT, and PD of IRI tended to have small errors. On the contrary, the errors of OP, CO, EX, and AG of Big Five, and FS of IRI tended to be large. When comparing how many indexes have relatively good accuracy within the indicators, one of the five indexes of Big Five and three of the four indexes of IRI were estimated with high accuracy (i.e. small accuracy error). Overall, Big Five's scores are considered to have large estimation errors and those of IRI have small estimation errors. From these results, the gaze behavior and DAs during turn-keeping/changing are less related to personality traits and more related to empathy skill level. During turn-changing, it is known that people care about the emotions of others and encourage them to speak using gaze behavior and speech. Therefore, such a result is considered very reasonable.

Finally, we describe the limitations of this research. First, we only used data from 16 people. Also, they were only Japanese women. Therefore, it is necessary to verify how common these results are. However, in spite of a small data set, high-accuracy estimation models could be constructed, so that the gaze behavior and DAs during turn-keeping/changing can be used to estimate the social skills and personality traits of various individuals.

7   Conclusion

We examined whether the gaze behavior, specifically GTPs, towards the end of utterance and DA information during turn-keeping/changing are useful for estimating the index scores of various social skills and personal characteristics indicators. It was shown that it is possible to estimate the scores of the nine indexes of Big Five and IRI with high accuracy by using the GTP and DA information during turn-keeping and changing. Although gaze behavior and DAs during turn-keeping/changing is done unconsciously, gaze behavior and DAs are very effective in measuring social skills and personality traits. The results also suggest that it is possible to estimate such scores with higher accuracy by using both the gaze distribution to the current speaker and non-speaker obtained from the entire conversation and the amount of utterances. Furthermore, the IRI scores can be estimated more accurately than those of Big Five. Therefore, the gaze and DAs during turn-keeping/changing may be more related to empathy skill level than personality traits.

For future work, we will explore how effective other behaviors [26], such as head movements [13,16], respiration [12,19,25], and mouth movement [14,22], are during turn-changing for estimating an individual's social skills and personal traits.

References

1. Banissy, M.J., Kanai, R., Walsh, V., Rees, G.: Inter-individual differences in empathy are reflected in human brain structure. NeuroImage **62**, 2034–2039 (2012)
2. Bouckaert, R.R., et al.: WEKA-experiences with a Java open-source project. J. Mach. Learn. Res. **11**, 2533–2541 (2010)
3. Chen, L., Harper, M.P.: Multimodal floor control shift detection. In: Proceedings of the International Conference on Multimodal Interaction, pp. 15–22 (2009)
4. Costa, P.T., McCrae, R.R.: The NEO personality inventory manual, FL Psychological Assessment Resources (1985)
5. Davis, M.H.: A multidimensional approach to individual differences in empathy **10** (1980)
6. De Corte, K., Buysse, A., Verhofstadt, L.L., Roeyers, H., Ponnet, K., Davis, M.H.: Measuring empathic tendencies: reliability and validity of the Dutch version of the interpersonal reactivity index. Psychologica Belgica **47**, 235–260 (2007)

7. De Kok, I., Heylen, D.: Multimodal end-of-turn prediction in multi-party meetings. In: Proceedings of the International Conference on Multimodal Interaction, pp. 91–98 (2009)
8. Fernandez, A., Dufey, M., Kramp, U.: Testing the psychometric properties of the interpersonal reactivity index (IRI) in Chile: empathy in a different cultural context. Eur. J. Assess. **27**, 179–185 (2011)
9. Greene, J.O., Burleson, B.R.: Handbook of Communication and Social Interaction Skills. Psychology Press, UK (2003)
10. Gwet, K.L.: Handbook of Inter-Rater Reliability: The Definitive Guide to Measuring the Extent of Agreement Among Raters. Advanced Analytics, LLC (2014)
11. Higashinaka, R., et al.: Towards an open-domain conversational system fully based on natural language processing. In: International Conference on Computational Linguistics, pp. 928–939 (2014)
12. Ishii, R., Kumano, S., Otsuka, K.: Multimodal fusion using respiration and gaze behavior for predicting next speaker in multi-party meetings. In: ICMI, pp. 99–106 (2015)
13. Ishii, R., Kumano, S., Otsuka, K.: Predicting next speaker using head movement in multi-party meetings. In: ICASSP, pp. 2319–2323 (2015)
14. Ishii, R., Kumano, S., Otsuka, K.: Analyzing mouth-opening transition pattern for predicting next speaker in multi-party meetings. In: Proceedings of the International Conference on Acoustics, Speech and Signal Processing, pp. 209–216 (2016)
15. Ishii, R., Kumano, S., Otsuka, K.: Analyzing gaze behavior during turn-taking for estimating empathy skill level. In: Proceedings of the 19th ACM International Conference on Multimodal Interaction, ICMI 2017, pp. 365–373. ACM, New York (2017)
16. Ishii, R., Kumano, S., Otsuka, K.: Prediction of next-utterance timing using head movement in multi-party meetings. In: Proceedings of the 5th International Conference on Human Agent Interaction, HAI 2017, pp. 181–187. ACM, New York (2017)
17. Ishii, R., Miyajima, T., Fujita, K., Nakano, Y.: Avatar's gaze control to facilitate conversational turn-taking in virtual-space multi-user voice chat system. In: Gratch, J., Young, M., Aylett, R., Ballin, D., Olivier, P. (eds.) IVA 2006. LNCS (LNAI), vol. 4133, p. 458. Springer, Heidelberg (2006). https://doi.org/10.1007/11821830_47
18. Ishii, R., Otsuka, K., Kumano, S., Yamamoto, J.: Predicting of who will be the next speaker and when using gaze behavior in multiparty meetings. ACM Trans. Interact. Intell. Syst. **6**(1), 4 (2016)
19. Ishii, R., Otsuka, K., Kumano, S., Yamamoto, J.: Using respiration to predict who will speak next and when in multiparty meetings. ACM Trans. Interact. Intell. Syst. **6**(2), 20 (2016)
20. Ishii, R., Otsuka, K., Kumano, S., Higashinaka, R., Tomita, J.: Analyzing gaze behavior and dialogue act during turn-taking for estimating empathy skill level. In: Proceedings of the 20th ACM International Conference on Multimodal Interaction, ICMI 2018, pp. 31–39. ACM, New York (2018)
21. Ishii, R., Otsuka, K., Kumano, S., Higashinaka, R., Tomita, J.: Estimating interpersonal reactivity scores using gaze behavior and dialogue act during turn-changing. In: Meiselwitz, G. (ed.) HCII 2019, Part II. LNCS, vol. 11579, pp. 45–53. Springer, Cham (2019). https://doi.org/10.1007/978-3-030-21905-5_4
22. Ishii, R., Otsuka, K., Kumano, S., Higashinaka, R., Tomita, J.: Prediction of who will be next speaker and when using mouth-opening pattern in multi-party conversation. Multimodal Technol. Interact. **3**(4), 70 (2019)

23. Ishii, R., Otsuka, K., Kumano, S., Matsuda, M., Yamato, J.: Predicting next speaker and timing from gaze transition patterns in multi-party meetings. In: Proceedings of the International Conference on Multimodal Interaction, pp. 79–86 (2013)

24. Ishii, R., Otsuka, K., Kumano, S., Yamato, J.: Analysis and modeling of next speaking start timing based on gaze behavior in multi-party meetings. In: Proceedings of the International Conference on Acoustics, Speech, and Signal Processing, pp. 694–698 (2014)

25. Ishii, R., Otsuka, K., Kumano, S., Yamato, J.: Analysis of respiration for prediction of who will be next speaker and when? In multi-party meetings. In: Proceedings of the International Conference on Multimodal Interaction, pp. 18–25 (2014)

26. Ishii, R., Ren, X., Muszynski, M., Morency, L.-P.: Can prediction of turn-management willingness improve turn-changing modeling?. In: Proceedings of the 20th ACM International Conference on Intelligent Virtual Agents (2020)

27. Jokinen, K., Furukawa, H., Nishida, M., Yamamoto, S.: Gaze and turn-taking behavior in casual conversational interactions. J. TiiS 3(2), 12 (2013)

28. Keerthi, S.S., Shevade, S.K., Bhattacharyya, C., Murthy, K.R.K.: Improvements to Platt's SMO algorithm for SVM classifier design. Neural Comput. 13(3), 637–649 (2001)

29. Kendon, A.: Some functions of gaze direction in social interaction. Acta Psychologica 26, 22–63 (1967)

30. Koiso, H., Horiuchi, Y., Tutiya, S., Ichikawa, A., Den, Y.: An analysis of turn-taking and backchannels based on prosodic and syntactic features in Japanese map task dialogs. Lang. Speech 41, 295–321 (1998)

31. Kumano, S., Otsuka, K., Matsuda, M., Yamato, J.: Analyzing perceived empathy based on reaction time in behavioral mimicry. IEICE Trans. Inf. Syst. E97-D(8), 2008–2020 (2014)

32. Kumano, S., Otsuka, K., Mikami, D., Matsuda, M., Yamato, J.: Analyzing interpersonal empathy via collective impressions. IEEE Trans. Affect. Comput. 6(4), 324–336 (2015)

33. Meguro, T., Higashinaka, R., Minami, Y., Dohsaka, K.: Controlling listening-oriented dialogue using partially observable Markov decision processes. In: International Conference on Computational Linguistics, pp. 761–769 (2010)

34. Nguyen, L., Frauendorfer, D., Mast, M., Gatica-Perez, D.: Hire me: computational inference of hirability in employment interviews based on nonverbal behavior. IEEE Trans. Multimed. 16(4), 1018–1031 (2014)

35. Okada, S., et al.: Estimating communication skills using dialogue acts and nonverbal features in multiple discussion datasets. In: Proceedings of the International Conference on Multimodal Interaction, pp. 169–176 (2016)

36. Otsuka, K., Araki, S., Mikami, D., Ishizuka, K., Fujimoto, M., Yamato, J.: Realtime meeting analysis and 3D meeting viewer based on omnidirectional multimodal sensors. In: ACM International Conference on Multimodal Interfaces and Workshop on Machine Learning for Multimodal Interaction, pp. 219–220 (2009)

37. Park, S., Shim, H.S., Chatterjee, M., Sagae, K., Morency, L.-P.: Computational analysis of persuasiveness in social multimedia: a novel dataset and multimodal prediction approach. In: Proceedings of the ACM ICMI, pp. 50–57 (2014)

38. Ramanarayanan, V., Leong, C.W., Feng, G., Chen, L., Suendermann-Oeft, D.: Evaluating speech, face, emotion and body movement time-series features for automated multimodal presentation scoring. In: Proceedings of the ACM ICMI, pp. 23–30 (2015)

39. Rodrigues, S.M., Saslow, L.R., Garcia, N., John, O.P., Keltner, D.: Oxytocin receptor genetic variation relates to empathy and stress reactivity in humans. Proc. Natl. Acad. Sci. U. S. A. **106**, 21437–21441 (2009)
40. Ruhland, K., et al.: A review of eye gaze in virtual agents, social robotics and HCI: behaviour generation, user interaction and perception. Comput. Graph. Forum **34**(6), 299–326 (2015)
41. Sacks, H., Schegloff, E.A., Jefferson, G.: A simplest systematics for the organisation of turn taking for conversation. Language **50**, 696–735 (1974)
42. Sanchez-Cortes, D., Aran, O., Mast, M.S., Gatica-Perez, D.: A nonverbal behavior approach to identify emergent leaders in small groups. IEEE Trans. Multimed. **14**(3), 816–832 (2012)
43. Wortwein, T., Chollet, M., Schauerte, B., Morency, L.-P., Stiefelhagen, R., Scherer, S.: Multimodal public speaking performance assessment. In: Proceedings of the ACM ICMI, pp. 43–50 (2015)

3D Hand Pointing Recognition over a Wide Area using Two Fisheye Cameras

Azusa Kuramochi and Takashi Komuro[✉]

Saitama University, Saitama, Japan
komuro@mail.saitama-u.ac.jp

Abstract. In this paper, we propose a user interface for large displays that allows pointing operations from a wide area. Two fisheye cameras installed on both sides of the display are used to capture images of a wide area in front of the display, and the system recognizes the user's skeleton and allows the user to perform pointing operation. Due to the wide viewing angle of the fisheye cameras, the baseline length between the cameras can be long. The experimental result showed that the pointing accuracy was higher with the fisheye cameras than with the standard cameras when operating at the same distance.

Keywords: Gesture recognition · Panoramic images · Pose estimation

1 Introduction

In recent years, large touch panel displays are becoming widespread, making it possible to provide interactive information in public places. However, there is a problem that a touch panel can only be used if when the user is near the display. Moreover, in the case of large displays, there are problems such as inaccessible places and the need to move large distances for operation.

On the other hand, systems that allows remotely selecting objects on a display by hand pointing have been proposed. However, some of them use markers [1–3] or devices [4, 5] for hand posture recognition, and a user need to wear them on his/her hand. Some other systems recognize hand pointing using cameras installed in the environment, such as on a wall or a ceiling [6, 7]. This makes it difficult to move the system, and also camera calibration is required after installation. There are some systems that use only a camera/cameras [8, 9] or a Kinect sensor [10] installed around the display, but the recognizable range is limited to the camera's field of view, and users have to perform operation within the range.

In this paper, we propose a user interface for large displays that allows pointing operations from a wide area. Two fisheye cameras installed on both sides of the display are used to capture images of a wide area in front of the display, and the system recognizes the user's skeleton and allows the user to perform pointing operation based on the information.

C. Stephanidis et al. (Eds.): HCII 2021, LNCS 13095, pp. 58–67, 2021.
https://doi.org/10.1007/978-3-030-90963-5_5

2   3D Pointing Recognition from Fisheye Camera Images

2.1   System

Figure 1 shows the configuration of the system and a user operating the system. The system utilizes two fisheye cameras to recognize a user's 3D hand pointing over a wide area. A cursor is displayed at the point where the user extended her arm toward the display.

Since the user's pointing operation is recognized using fisheye cameras, the user can operate the system from a wider range than using normal cameras. Figure 2 shows the field of view using standard cameras and that using fisheye cameras. Due to the wide viewing angle of the fisheye cameras, the baseline length between the cameras can be long, which would increase the positional accuracy in the depth direction. In this system, the two fisheye cameras were put on both sides of the display.

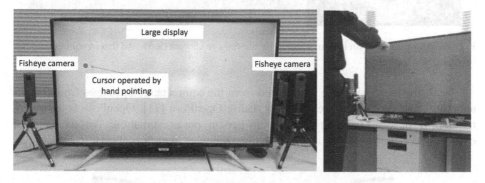

Fig. 1. Configuration of the system (left) and a user operating the system (right).

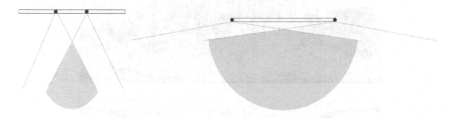

Fig. 2. Field of view using standard cameras (left) and that using fisheye cameras (right).

2.2   Hand Pointing Recognition

The system recognizes the user in front of the display from the omnidirectional image captured by the fisheye camera. First, the images acquired by the fisheye cameras are converted to those in the equirectangular format, which are represented by (θ, ϕ) coordinates. In this study, we used RICOH THETA V for the fisheye cameras, which has two fisheye cameras, one on the front and one on the back, and can output

360-degree panoramic images in the equirectangular format. However, we used only 180-degree part of the panoramic images that is captured by the front fisheye camera.

Figure 3 shows an example of an image captured by the fisheye camera, and the image converted to that in equirectangular format. The images captured by the fisheye cameras cover a large indoor area and can recognize a user's operations from a wide range.

Fig. 3. An example of an image captured by the fisheye camera (left), and that in equirectangular format (right).

Next, the user's skeleton is extracted from the equirectangular images from the left and right fisheye cameras, respectively, using OpenPose [11]. OpenPose is an implementation of deep-learning-based multi-person pose estimation. An example of extracted skeleton from left and right equirectangular images is shown in Fig. 4.

Fig. 4. An example of extracted skeleton from left and right equirectangular images.

The three-dimensional positions of the elbow and wrist of the user's right arm are used to calculate the pointing position. First, the coordinates (θ, ϕ) of each joint point in an equirectangular image is converted into plane coordinates (x, y) using the following equations. f is the focal length of the virtual camera and can be set to any value.

$$x = f \frac{\sin \theta \cos \phi}{\cos \theta}, \quad y = f \frac{\sin \theta \sin \phi}{\cos \theta}$$

Next, the 3D coordinates (X, Y, Z) of each joint are calculated from the planar coordinates of the corresponding joint points (x_l, y_l) and (x_r, y_r) in the left and right camera images using the following equations of parallel stereo. b is the baseline length between the left and right cameras.

$$X = \frac{b(x_l + x_r)}{2(x_l - x_r)}, \quad Y = \frac{b(y_l + y_r)}{2(x_l - x_r)}, \quad Z = \frac{bf}{x_l - x_r}$$

As shown in Fig. 5, a cursor is displayed at the point where the straight line passing through the 3D coordinates of the elbow (X_1, Y_1, Z_1) and wrist (X_2, Y_2, Z_2) intersects the display. By doing so, the cursor is displayed at the point where the user extends his/her arm.

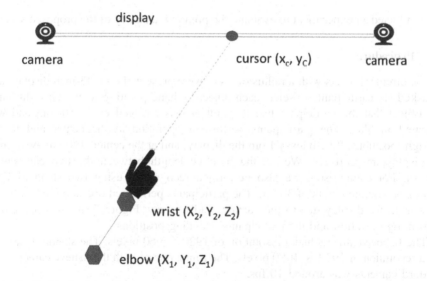

Fig. 5. Field of view using standard cameras (left) and that using fisheye cameras (right).

The coordinates of the cursor (x_c, y_c) are calculated by the following equations.

$$x_c = X_1 + k(X_2 - X_1), \quad y_c = Y_1 + k(Y_2 - Y_1), \quad k = -\frac{Z_1}{Z_2 - Z_1}$$

Since the cursor coordinates are calculated in a coordinate system in real space, they are converted to that in the display coordinate system. Figure 6 shows the 3D positions of the wrist and elbow, and the 2D cursor position calculated from the left and right equirectangular images in Fig. 6.

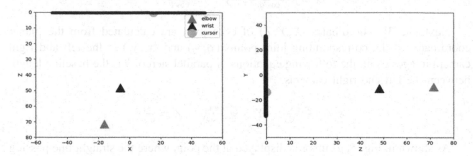

Fig. 6. 3D positions of the wrist and elbow, and the 2D cursor position.

3 Performance Evaluation

We conducted an experiment to evaluate the pointing accuracy of the proposed system.

3.1 Procedure

Fifteen circular objects with a radius of 5 cm were presented on a 43-inch display, and we asked six participants to select each object by hand pointing with their right hand. The object that the participant had to point at was changed every 10 min and was indicated in blue. The participants performed operation at the center and 60 cm left/right positions, 80 cm away from the display, and at the center, 140 cm away from the display, respectively. We set the baseline length between the two cameras to 120 cm. For comparison, we also performed recognition using two standard USB cameras a baseline length of 30 cm. The participants performed operation only 140 cm away from the display due to the narrow field of view. Figure 7 shows a participant performing operation and the participants' standing positions.

The fisheye cameras had a resolution of 1920 × 960 pixels. The standard cameras had a resolution of 1920 × 1080 pixels. The frame rate of both the fisheye cameras and standard cameras was around 10 fps.

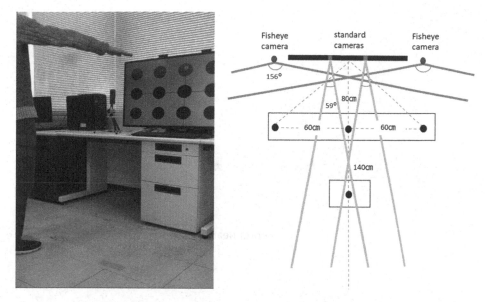

Fig. 7. A participant performing operation (left) and the participants' standing positions (right).

The following exponential smoothing filter was applied to the cursor positions to reduce jittering.

$$y_k = \alpha y_{k-1} + (1 - \alpha)x_k$$

We set the filter parameter α to 0.95. If the skeleton extraction by OpenPose fails, the value of the previous output y_{k-1} was used as the output y_k.

3.2 Results

Figure 8 shows the scatter plot of pointer coordinates when the participants were at the center, 80 cm away from the display. The last 50 pairs of coordinates in the 10 s of selecting one object were taken. The total of 300 pairs of pointer coordinates of six participants were taken for one object. The pointers that were inside the target object were plotted in orange, and those outside the target object were plotted in light blue. The pointers whose distances from the center of the target were more than 10 cm were not plotted.

Figure 9 shows the success rate for each operating position and object position, and Fig. 10 shows the number of failures in skeleton extraction. The success rate was over 90% for objects close to the operating position, but tended to drop as the object for objects farther away from the operating position. Also, operations near the display had a higher success rate than those away from the display.

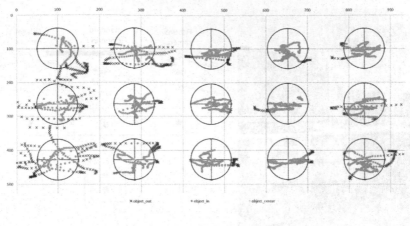

center near

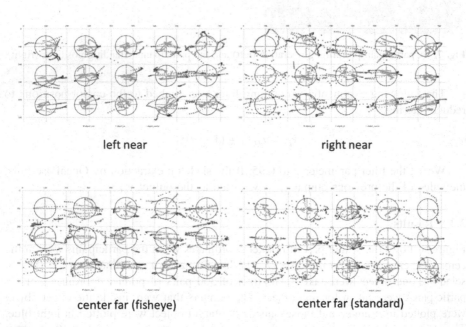

left near

right near

center far (fisheye)

center far (standard)

Fig. 8. Scatter plot of pointer coordinates for each operating position and object position.

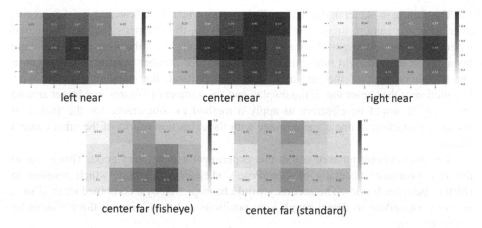

Fig. 9. Success rate for each operating position and object position.

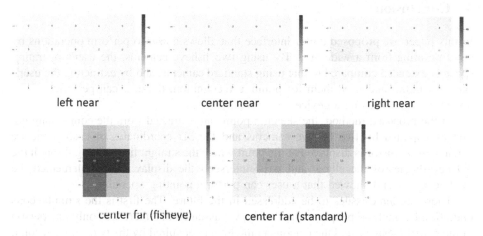

Fig. 10. Number of failures in skeleton extraction for each operating position and object position.

3.3 Discussion

The experimental results showed that the pointing accuracy of operations away from the display was lower than that of operations near the display. This is because the size of the user in the camera image becomes smaller as the user moves away from the camera, and the accuracy of skeleton extraction by OpenPose decreases.

However, even when operating at the same distance, the results were slightly more accurate with the fisheye cameras than with the standard cameras. This may be because the fisheye cameras have a longer baseline length, which results in a higher depth accuracy. Fisheye cameras have a wider field of view than standard cameras and the baseline length can be set longer, which is one of the advantages of using fisheye cameras.

The failure in skeleton extraction often occurs when the elbow and wrist appear to overlap in the camera image. As shown in Fig. 10, the number of failures increased when users are pointing at the target near the camera. Since the fisheye camera were installed on left and right sides outside the display, the number of failures was larger in the peripheral area of the display. On the other hand, the standard cameras were installed near the center top of the display and the number of failures was larger around that area. It would be effective to apply a method to compensate for the failure of skeleton extraction in one camera image with the extraction results of the other camera image.

The overall pointing accuracy in this experiment was not very good. This is due to the low positional accuracy of OpenPose's skeleton extraction, which resulted in shifting between frames. The accuracy would be improved by a combined method such as using OpenPose to detect rough joint positions and then aligning the positions by object tracking.

4 Conclusion

In this paper, we proposed a user interface that allows a user to perform operations by hand pointing from a wide area. By using two fisheye cameras, the user's operating space is extended compared to that using standard cameras, and by extracting the user's skeleton points and used them for pointing recognition, the user can perform remote operation without using a device.

In the proposed method, the skeleton points are extracted from the equirectangular images captured by two fisheye cameras and the 3D coordinates of each point are calculated. A cursor is displayed at the point where the straight line passing through the 3D coordinates of the elbow and wrist intersects the display. We implemented the method above and showed that a user can perform pointing operation.

There are three issues to be addressed in the future. The first is the simultaneous operation by multiple people. In this study, we assumed that there was only one person in the camera images, and the persons in the images acquired by the two cameras could be regarded as the same person. However, when there are multiple people in the images at the same time, it is necessary to recognize the same person in the left and right camera images.

The second is to improve the pointing accuracy. Possible solutions include compensating for false detection in one camera image with the other camera image, or a combination of skeleton extraction and object tracking.

The last is the variety of operations. In our method, the cursor is displayed and the user can only move the cursor to the object. Since OpenPose can recognize not only skeleton points of the body but also those of fingers, it would also be possible to make the system recognize operations using hand gestures.

References

1. Jota, R., Nacenta, M., Jorge, J., Carpendale, S., Greenberg, S.: A comparision of ray pointing techniques for very large displays. In: Proceedings of Graphics Interface, pp. 269–276 (2010)
2. Rateau, H., Rekik, Y., Grisoni, L., Jorge, J.: Talaria: Continuous drag & drop on a wall display. In: Proceedings of the ACM International Conference on Interactive Surfaces and Spaces, pp. 199–204 (2016)
3. Matulic, F., Vogel, D.: Multiray: multi-finger raycasting for large displays. In: Proceedings of the CHI Conference on Human Factors in Computing Systems, Article No. 245 (2018)
4. Pietroszek, K., Tahai, L., Wallace, J., Lank, E.: Watchcasting: freehand 3D interaction with off-the-shelf smartwatch. In: Proceedings of IEEE Symposium on 3D User Interface, pp. 172–175 (2017)
5. Haque, F., Nancel, M., Vogel, D.: Myopoint: pointing and clicking using forearm mounted electromyography and inertial motion sensors. In: Proceedings of the Annual ACM Conference on Human Factors in Computing Systems, pp. 3653–3656 (2015)
6. Schick, A., van de Camp, F., Ijsselmuiden, J., Stiefelhagen, R.: Extending touch: towards interaction with large-scale surfaces. In: Proceedings of ACM International Conference on Interactive Tabletops and Surfaces, pp. 117–124 (2009)
7. Hu, K., Canavan, S., Yin, L.: Hand pointing estimation for human computer interaction based on two orthogonal-views, In: Proceedings of International Conference on Pattern Recognition, pp. 3760–3763 (2010)
8. Matsuda, Y., Komuro, T.: Dynamic layout optimization for multi-user interaction with a large display. In: Proceedings of the International Conference on Intelligent User Interfaces, pp. 401–409 (2020)
9. Endo, Y., Fujita, D., Komuro, T.: Distant pointing user interfaces based on 3D hand pointing recognition. In: Proceedings of ACM International Conference on Interactive Surfaces and Spaces, pp. 413–416 (2017)
10. Makela, V., James, J., Keskinen, T., Hakulinen, J., Turunen, M.: It's natural to grab and pull: retrieving content from large displays using mid-air gestures. IEEE Pervasive Comput. **16** (3), 70–77 (2017)
11. Cao, Z., Hidalgo, G., Simon, T., Wei, S., Sheikh, Y.: OpenPose: realtime multi-person 2D pose estimation using part affinity fields. IEEE Trans. Pattern Anal. Mach. Intell. **43**(1), 172–186 (2021)

Design of an Interactive Device Based on e-Textile Material

Xuanzhu Meng and Qiong Wu[✉]

Tsinghua University, Beijing, People's Republic of China
mengxz18@mails.tsinghua.edu.cn,
qiong-wu@tsinghua.edu.cn

Abstract. Electronic textile (or e-Textile) is the material integrating digital information transmission ability and traditional fabric characteristics, which leads to great tactile interaction. However, the current research of the interaction of e-Textile are still influenced by the interaction mode adopted from electronic devices, such as the capacitive touch of the interactive elements. In this paper, we want to focus on how to interact with e-Textile in more textile characteristic ways, and pay more attention to the tactile semantics of materials in the process of interaction design. In order to apply the unique interactive way and interactive ability of e-Textile, this paper designs a group of interactive lighting devices. The lights combined with e-Textile can be used as output information to give feedback to the interactive behavior. The research for different interaction of e-Textile will expand the extension of fabric interaction mode, and tap the great potential of textile material properties in human-computer interaction.

Keywords: e-Textile · e-Textile Interaction · Material Affordance

1 Introduction

1.1 Background

Fabric is the object that has been in contact with people for the longest time in the world. It is the second layer of human skin and the next possible information presentation carrier. As an indispensable material in people's life, the significance of textiles is self-evident.

As a research field, e-Textile emerged with the development of conductive yarn. And its background is the prominent research fields such as wearable computing and entity interaction design [1]. E-Textile is the fabric that can embed digital components such as LED lights, minicomputers and sensors. As people are more and more interested in man-machine interface, the information input ability of e-Textiles can bring the possibility of digitalization to traditional fabrics, such as project Jacquard of Google [2]. and large-area display fabrics of Fudan University [3]. The texture of textile materials also provides a unique tactile experience for the interaction of e-Textile. But at present, the interaction of e-Textile is still using the traditional way adopted from electronic products.

© Springer Nature Switzerland AG 2021
C. Stephanidis et al. (Eds.): HCII 2021, LNCS 13095, pp. 68–81, 2021.
https://doi.org/10.1007/978-3-030-90963-5_6

In this paper, the electronic components are embedded and integrated into the traditional fabric, and we also design a tactile interaction device combining with the e-Textile interaction mode as the application.

1.2   Contribution

Although there are many researches on e-Textile today [4–6], the main point we focused on is the interactive way which is of great fabric characteristics.

We present two main contributions of this paper. On the one hand, combined with the existing research on tactile interactive material semantics, as well as the ability of information input and behavior monitoring of e-Textile, it provides the possibility of digital development for traditional fabrics.

On the other hand, instead of using the existing point-to-point interaction based on capacitive sensing to input information, this paper focuses on the physical properties and material properties of the fabric itself, and studies the functional significance of the structure and state of the fabric in electronic applications. It provides a research direction for the interaction of e-Textile to highlight the characteristics of material specialization and emotion.

2   Research on e-Textile

2.1   Development Status

In 1997, Rehmi Post and Maggie Orth introduced the interface with wire embroidery into the field of wearable computing [7]. However, e-Textile and wearable computing are two different concepts, because the key technology of e-Textile lies in the seamless integration of textiles and electronic components, such as microcontrollers, sensors and actuators.

Pailes Friedman [8] believes that the revolutionary significance of e-Textiles lies in that this integration method greatly expands the capability boundary of traditional fabrics, making them have the functions of energy exchange, storage and compilation for the first time.

E-Textile can provide multi-layer functions in a variety of new materials, including sensing, tactile, lighting and so on. As Dakova [9] pointed out, textiles reveal new ways of interaction and may support future innovative applications in the field of pervasive computing. At present, the interaction modes of e-Textile are click, slide, press, stretch and so on, and the capacitive touch is mainly used. The design of interactive elements refers to the buttons, sliders and so on in the entity interaction interface. In the e-Textile interface, it is the main form to imitate interactive elements through textile, embroidery and other ways.

In recent years, the research of e-Textile is more focused on embroidering conductive yarn on the fabric. Through user experiments, the recognition ability of individuals for interactive elements is studied, and the design principles in GUI field (such as Gestalt theory) are still applicable in the interface of e-Textile. Holleis [10] studied the structure of fabric interface. The author introduced the results of user research and summarized it as a guide for designing wearable accessories and clothing.

The Disadvantage of e-Textile Interaction. E-Textile interaction belongs to the category of entity interaction, but its interaction mode and feedback ability are different from entity interaction. Comparing capacitive touch input with entity interaction, due to the limitation of interface and the fact that the interactive elements of e-Textile have no entity button, there is no button feedback when clicking or touching. B. P. Challis & A. D. n. Edwards of the University of York in the UK [11] found that double-click is an inappropriate form of interaction in static display. If there is no tactile feedback, double-click will become very inefficient.

This violates the timeliness and effectiveness of the operation feedback design principle. E-Textiles should be developed to pay more attention to the properties of the fabric itself, and more in line with the nature of the fabric interaction, rather than limited by the interaction form of electronic products.

The Advantages of e-Textile Interaction. On the one hand, its deformation ability and softness enable the fabric to adapt to different shapes. The foldable and retractable features also make it portable and adaptable. On the other hand, the embedded integration of electronic components makes the form of information collection no longer limited to hard sensors.

Swatchbook [12] is an experimental project to study the interaction mode of e-Textile. Ramyah Gowrishankar and others mentioned that most e-Textiles still follow the interactive habit of electronic products [13]. In short, the advantage of e-Textile is the advantage of fabric itself. In order to give full play to the advantages of e-Textile interaction, we should explore and develop the material properties of the fabric itself.

2.2   Study on the Properties of Fabric Materials

In people's life, based on each individual's life experience, habits, and individual memories, people will build a cognitive knowledge base related to fabrics, in which different materials, products, shapes, touch, environment, vision, etc. related to fabrics have complex mapping and correlation with each other, and the cognition related to fabrics is complex and diverse. This chapter attempts to construct the cognitive knowledge base related to fabric by exhausting the physical state of fabric and the interaction ways related to fabric, and expand the extension of fabric interaction ways from the perspective of materials, so as to fully tap the great potential of textile material attributes in digital interaction.

Physical Properties of Fabric. The study of fabric cognition can start from exploring the physical properties of fabric itself. This paper attempts to focus on the overall fabric material categories, summarize the characteristics of fabric materials, and pay attention to the fabric materials and corresponding forms in daily life. Based on the summary of the physical properties mentioned by Ramyah Gowrishankar, this paper further summarizes the physical state of the fabric, so as to facilitate the follow-up research on the interaction mode related to the fabric, and make better use of the affordance of the fabric in the design practice, as shown in Fig. 1.

Among these attributes, the degree of association with fabric attributes is also different. The degree of association here refers to whether a certain physical property can only be possessed by fabric and cannot be replaced by other materials. For example, folding, tearing, turning over, storage and other physical states can be replaced by paper or other thinner flexible plastic materials. The physical functions such as draping, tying, weaving and stretching are relatively difficult to be replaced by other kinds of materials, that is, these physical functions are more closely related to the fabric.

Folding	Pleating	Braiding
Draping	Transparence	Knotting
Wrapping	Storage	Throwing open
Spreading	Attachment	Piercing
Crumpling	Portable	Twisting
Hanging	Drying	Turning inside out
Tearing	Tying	Wiping
Stretching		

Fig. 1. Study on the affordance of fabrics based on daily life experience and cognition.

In the design practice of this paper, we will try to choose the form from the summarized physical state of textiles, combined with the relevant interaction methods, to show the new form of fabric interaction with the material advantages.

Interaction Mode of Fabric. Due to the material characteristics of the fabric itself, the interaction of the fabric is relatively more unique. This paper summarizes the unique interaction modes of different forms and materials of fabrics. For fabrics in different states, people can interact with them in a variety of different ways (see Fig. 2).

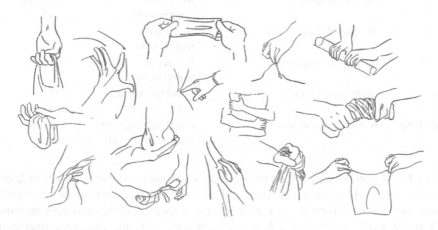

Fig. 2. A variety of different ways, including but not limited to stretching, lifting, tying, pressing, poking, hugging, touching, touching, grasping, twisting, pulling, curling, unfolding, lifting, etc.

Based on it, different kinds of interaction methods have requirements for the fabric's own state or material. This paper sorts out the fabric state requirements corresponding to the relevant interaction modes, as well as the fabric properties required in the corresponding state and the corresponding textile products and intentions, as shown in Table 1.

Table 1. Corresponding table of fabric state and interaction mode

Interaction /fabric	Fabric condition	Fabric properties	Product or intention
Carry	Loaded with heavy objects, and the structure has a portable part	No special requirements	Bag
Stretch	At least one end is not fixed	With tensile and resilience	Elastic band
Stamp	Tight or fluffy contents	With tensile and resilience	Plush toy, sofa
Hold up	Suspended with weight	No special requirements	Bag
Press	Tight or with fluffy contents	No special requirements	Cushion, sofa
Fasten	Slender in shape	Could be stretched to a certain extent	Shoelaces, belts, bandages
Stroke	No special requirements	Could be better with soft and plush material	Plush toy
Touch	No special requirements	No special requirements	No specific products
Brush	Overhanging state	No special requirements	Curtain
Hold on	No special requirements	No special requirements	No specific products
Press	Flat and supported	No special requirements	E-Textile products
Twist	No special requirements	No special requirements	Drain the water
Scroll	No special requirements	No special requirements	Scroll
Pull	Overhanging state	Could be stretched to a certain extent	No specific products
Hold tight	With fluffy contents	Could be better with soft and plush material	Cushion, sofa

Combined with the research on the emotional attributes and physical form of fabric, it is very able to show the interaction of fabric characteristics, such as "poke", "hold", "touch" and other interaction ways, which can be mapped with the emotional attributes such as "warmth" and "plush". It is also consistent with the emotional interaction design direction that this paper wants to try.

The above arrangement of fabric related interaction provides basic research support for the research on the interaction mode of e-Textile with material characteristics.

3 Interactive Device Design

3.1 Design Target

By studying the physical properties and material affordance of traditional fabrics, combined with the information input ability of e-Textiles, we finally completed a series of device designs that interact in the unique way of fabrics.

Because some fabrics give people warm, natural, close feeling and encourage people to touch. In physical characteristics, it is warm, soft, plush, thick and translucent. After consideration, we decided to present in the form of lamps combined with fabric. From the perspective of metaphor, there are some overlapping parts between the semantics of light and fabric, which involve warmth, trust and closeness. The light through the fabric can present a unique visual texture, giving people a soft feeling. From the perspective of signal transmission, the device integrates and processes the user"s behavior data, and finally converts it into the control of lighting parameters, such as switch, brightness, color temperature, flicker frequency, etc. The device is called ClothLight.

In the design process, this paper will consider the device form, fabric material affordance, device interaction mode, device light feedback form and device space display form.

3.2 Device Form Design

In the process of device design and scheme selection, this paper considers the following design elements as the principle to select the design scheme.

- The form of the fabric is integrated with the light.
- The state and form of the fabric seem to be interactive and could encourage interaction.
- The form of fabric is diversified.
- The matching of different fabric thickness and light transmittance with the brightness range of light source is considered.

To sum up, in the scheme design and selection, in order to promote the organic combination of light and fabrics, consider the interactivity of fabric form and highlight the sensing ability of fabric, this paper is more inclined to choose the fabric state with less rigid support structure in the scheme selection, as shown in Fig. 3, that is, the fabric is in a more natural state (such as hanging, hanging, hanging, etc.), in the form of unfolding.

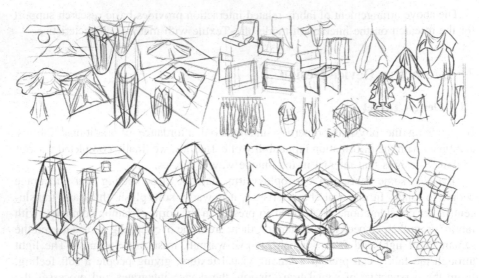

Fig. 3. Design of combination of fabric and light.

Referring to the implication of fabric demonstration and its form on interaction mode, we finally decided to combine five different fabric forms with light, and carry out device interaction in different interaction modes (see Fig. 4).

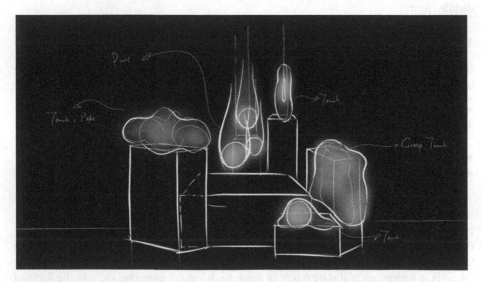

Fig. 4. The sketch of device. Among them, the five different states of fabric interaction are stretching, touching, touching, poking and lifting.

In order to better guide the users natural interaction, we also consider the encouraging effect of fabric texture on interaction behavior. For example, soft fabrics wrapped in cotton can cause people to want to hug, press or poke. We comprehensively consider the visual expression and tactile feeling, on the basis of comprehensively showing the uniqueness of traditional fabrics and the interactive ability of e-Textiles, we try to show the fabric performance and material characteristics (see Fig. 5).

Fig. 5. Device rendering effect

4 Device Implementation

From the perspective of information input and output, the implementation method of the device can be summarized as follows: the e-Textile detects the users interactive behavior and converts it into digital signal input control system, which converts the digital signal into light control signal and outputs it in the form of light change. After the formal design scheme is determined, we mainly need to make conductive fabrics and lamps.

4.1 Blending Experiment

The color and material of the ready-made conductive fabric are relatively single, and can't reflect the material and tactile characteristics of the fabric itself, while the conductive adhesive tape and conductive ink are attached to the fabric, both the function and interaction form are relatively limited.

Considering from the design goal, the combination of traditional fabric and conductive yarn can not only retain the texture of the fabric, but also give full play to the tactile characteristics and emotional cognitive attributes of the fabric. Combined with the experimental results of some conductive materials and the fabric requirements of the device design, after comparison and sample test, we finally decided to use two kinds of yarn blended weaving method for the production of e-Textile.

Conductive Yarn Selection. A series of experiments were carried out to screen conductive yarns. The selection goal is to retain the original traditional fabric properties as much as possible. On the basis of considering the processing difficulty, the two kinds of yarns should be organically integrated as far as possible. In this paper, we choose manual loom, electric loom, circular simple loom and simple shuttle loom to carry out small sample experiment. The experimental process is shown in Figs.6, 7, 8, 9, 10 and 11. The con-clusion is that silver fiber conductive yarn is more suitable for blending than stainless steel yarn.

Fig. 6. Experiment A: mixed knitting experiment of cotton yarn and stainless-steel yarn. Because the stainless-steel yarn is made of strong strands, when the non-conductive yarn and stainless-steel yarn are mixed and woven, there will be obvious wrinkles, twisting and not sticking.

Fig. 7. Experiment B: mixed knitting experiment of silk yarn and stainless-steel yarn. The wrinkles are not relieved.

Fig. 8. Experiment C: mixed knitting experiment of wool and stainless-steel yarn. When knitting on a simple circular loom, the thread is often jammed and the machine often needs to be adjusted. In the textile process, it is very easy to twine and be off-line, which greatly increases the difficulty of mixed textile.

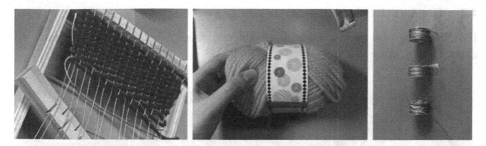

Fig. 9. Experiment D: mixed weaving experiment of wool and stainless-steel yarn. The woven method has higher requirements on the machine, and the conductive yarn with strong rigidity and low tensile property has poor tensile property.

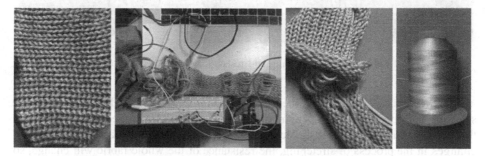

Fig. 10. Experiment E: mixed knitting experiment of wool and silver fiber conductive yarn. Silver fiber yarn is light and soft. The blended fabric of silver fiber yarn and non-conductive yarn basically retains the fabric characteristics of the original non-conductive yarn. This kind of conductive yarn has little interference to the traditional fabric and has good conductivity.

Non-conductive Yarn Selection. Combined with the form design and texture requirements of the five devices, we choose different yarn and stitch methods, which are: rib stitch method which can produce fabric with good tensile property combined with silk thread with strong draping feeling, mohair with soft plush combined with knitting method, coarse cotton thread combined with knitting method, etc.

Fig. 11. Comparison of fabrics before and after mixed weaving of conductive yarn and non-conductive yarn.

4.2   Conductivity Test

In this paper, the conductivity of conductive fabric, resistance change test and capacitance sensing test are carried out (Fig. 12).

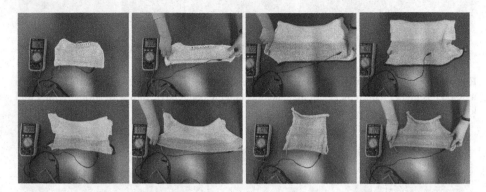

Fig. 12. Stretch sensing and resistance change sensing test.

The resistance change experiment shows that: due to the mixed textile of knitting structure and conductive yarn, a number of small coils will be formed in the fabric, and these coils will produce self-induction effect [14]. When the diameter of the coil changes in the process of stretching, the resistance of the whole fabric will change, so the stretching degree of knitted fabric can be detected by the change of fabric resistance. This device uses the mpr121 capacitance sensor, which has 12 interfaces, can judge the capacitance change of each interface and the conductive object connected with it, and can effectively and quickly accurately input the capacitance time point and duration. The results show that the change of fabric resistance caused by stretching is obvious.

The capacitive sensing experiment shows that the conductive yarn is embedded all over the whole fabric, and the signal input will be generated when touching the fabric in the capacitive sensing test.

4.3   Effect of Device

After the device design and practice, this paper finally completed a total of five groups of eight pieces of fabric lighting device (Figs. 13 and 14).

Fig. 13. Display effect of five kinds of e-Textile light device.

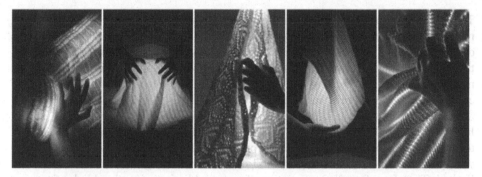

Fig.14. In the device interaction design, the interaction actions related to fabric materials are stretching, touching, repeatedly touching and stamping. The sensing methods are resistance change sensing and capacitance sensing. The feedback form is the increase of light intensity and the change of color temperature.

4.4   User Test

In order to verify the device interaction could reflect the fabric material affordance, and the accuracy of the device interaction can be implied by the material physical state and material characteristics, we use the observation method and interview method to carry out the user feedback experiment.

The sample size of the tested users is 54, including 48 teachers and students from various departments of Tsinghua University, 2 exhibition hall staff, and 4 visitors from outside the University. The experiment takes the form of camera shooting in the early stage and interview in the later stage. Without the interference of the researchers, the behavior of visitors is observed through the camera.

93% of the visitors interact with the device spontaneously without interactive guidance. This proves that the material properties of e-Textile can encourage people to interact with it. Among the five kinds of fabrics, the fabric with the highest probability of being touched is the fabric of plush material placed on the lamp ball, whose interaction probability is 98%. The fabric filled with cotton ranked second with 90%

interaction rate. For each form of fabric, the interaction behavior of visitors is different. For example, for the hanging fabric, 24 visitors touch the fabric, 11 visitors push it to shake it, only 7 visitors hold it up, and 2 visitors stretch it down.

After the observation, we interviewed the selected observers about their subjective evaluation. 94% of the respondents said that they could feel the warmth and softness brought by the fabric and light. It can also feel the behavior detection ability of the fabric through the lighting after touching. And 86% of the people said that the five groups of devices are very typical of the physical state of the fabric, and their form can well indicate the interaction mode of the device. Most people expressed full curiosity and expectation for future work.

5   Conclusion

This paper summarizes the physical properties, emotional cognitive properties and material semantics of fabric, discusses how to apply the traditional fabric affordance demonstration in the field of e-Textile interaction, and embeds the conductive yarn into the fabric. Combined with the material properties of traditional fabrics and the information collection and sensing ability of e-Textiles, the interaction mode with fabric characteristics is explored and tried.

However, in this paper, the research on the sensing ability of e-Textiles is only limited to capacitance sensing and resistance stretching sensing. The latter has some technical limitations in the application process. For example, for conductive fabrics with poor resilience, the sensing method of resistance change for the e-Textile is life limited. Therefore, from the perspective of technical limitations, other kinds of sensing methods will be tried in the future, or on this basis, the stability of the technology will be enhanced.

In addition, the research on the interaction mode of e-Textile is still in the exploratory stage. In the follow-up research, we will explore the practical application significance of e-Textile from a more valuable perspective.

Acknowledgement. . This research was supported by 2019 National Social Science Foundation Art Project "Interaction Design Method Research based on AI", the number is 19BG127.

1. References

1. Post, E R., Orth, M., Russo, P R.: E-broidery: Design and fabrication of textile-based computing. IBM Systems journal 39(3.4), 840–860(2000).
2. Poupyrev, I., Gong, N W., Fukuhara, S.: Project Jacquard: interactive digital textiles at scale. In: Proceedings of the 2016 CHI Conference on Human Factors in Computing Systems, pp. 4216–4227. (2016)
3. Large-area display textiles integrated with functional systems: Shi X, F., Zuo Y, S., Zhai P, T. Nature **591**, 240–245 (2021)
4. Loss, C., Gonçalves, R., Lopes, C.: Smart coat with a fully-embedded textile antenna for IoT applications. Sensors **16**(6), 938 (2016)

5. Klamka, K., Dachselt, R., Steimle, J.: Rapid Iron-On User Interfaces: Hands-on Fabrication of Interactive Textile Prototypes. In: Proceedings of the 2020 CHI Conference on Human Factors in Computing Systems, pp. 1–14. (2020).
6. Mečņika, V., Hoerr, M., Krieviņš, I.: Smart textiles for healthcare: applications and technologies. Rural Environment. Education. Personality **7**, 150–161 (2014)
7. Gilliland, S., Komor, N., Starner, T.: The Textile Interface Swatchbook: Creating graphical user interface-like widgets with conductive embroidery. In: International Symposium on Wearable Computers (ISWC), pp. 1–8. (2010).
8. Gaddis, R.: What is the future of fabric? these smart textiles will blow your mind. what-is-the-future-of-fabric-these-smart-textiles-will-blow-your-mind, (2014).
9. Mlakar, S., Haller, M.: Design Investigation of Embroidered Interactive Elements on Non-Wearable Textile Interfaces. In: CHI '20: CHI Conference on Human Factors in Computing Systems, pp. 1–10. (2020).
10. Holleis, P., Schmidt, A., Paasovaara, S.: Evaluating capacitive touch input on clothes. In: Proceedings of the 10th international conference on Human computer interaction with mobile devices and services, pp. 81–90. (2008).
11. Challis, B.P., Edwards, A.D.N.: Design principles for tactile interaction. In: Brewster, S., Murray-Smith, R. (eds.) Haptic HCI 2000. LNCS, vol. 2058, pp. 17–24. Springer, Heidelberg (2001). https://doi.org/10.1007/3-540-44589-7_2
12. Swatchbook Exchanges. The E-Textile Summercamps Electronic Textile Swatch Exchange, http://etextile-summercamp.org/swatch-exchange/videos/.
13. Gowrishankar, R., Bredies, K., Ylirisku, S.: A Strategy for Material-Specific e-Textile Interaction Design. In: Schneegass, S., Amft, O. (eds.) Smart Textiles. HIS, pp. 233–257. Springer, Cham (2017). https://doi.org/10.1007/978-3-319-50124-6_11
14. Fobelets, K.: Knitted Coil for Inductive Plethysmography. In: Multidisciplinary Digital Publishing Institute Proceedings, vol. 32, p. 2 (2019)

The Tap Strap 2: Evaluating Performance of One-Handed Wearable Keyboard and Mouse

Kristian Mrazek, Brian Holton, Tanner Klein, Izan Khan, Thomas Ayele, and Tauheed Khan Mohd[✉]

Augustana College, Rock Island, IL 61201, USA
tauheedkhanmohd@augustana.edu

Abstract. This paper presents an evaluation of Tap Strap 2, a one-handed wearable keyboard that uses tap combinations to type characters. The purpose of the Tap Strap 2 is to give the user a portable keyboard that is easier to use for mobile devices than the on-screen QWERTY keyboards included on those devices. The user taps different combinations of fingers on a surface to enter different characters and perform a variety of commands. By using the embedded sensors in each ring, the Tap Strap 2 can recognize which fingers are tapping at any given time. Tap Strap 2 also has a mouse mode that can be switched to from keyboard mode, allowing the user to browse websites on a mobile device as they would on a computer. The third mode that Tap Strap has is a gesture mode that can be used for mobile devices as well as in virtual reality settings. This article details what Tap Strap 2 is capable of and describes the hardware. It also provides an evaluation of the device's usability and tests an auto-correct algorithm meant to reduce the probability of spelling errors when using the Tap Strap 2.

Keywords: Keyboard · Wearable · Tap · Mobile · Touch

1 Introduction

As computer systems evolve, so do methods of human-computer interaction (HCI), particularly interfaces and the means through which input, such as text that the user wishes to type, is provided to the computer. The traditional QWERTY keyboard, in both its physical and onscreen forms, remains the dominant means of inputting text at the time of this paper. Unfortunately, the onscreen QWERTY keyboards on mobile devices can prove problematic to use due to the compact layout of the keys, which encourages spelling errors. These keyboards are also very difficult to use for the visually impaired, since the keys are small and flat. Currently, the solution to these issues is the implementation of a text-to-speech function on phones and smartwatches. However, even this has significant issues, as if the user does not speak clearly or there is too much noise in the surrounding environment, the device will incorrectly interpret the words and fail to produce the desired output.

© Springer Nature Switzerland AG 2021
C. Stephanidis et al. (Eds.): HCII 2021, LNCS 13095, pp. 82–95, 2021.
https://doi.org/10.1007/978-3-030-90963-5_7

As a potential solution to these problems, Tap Systems, Inc. introduced a wearable keyboard called the Tap Strap 2. Tap Strap 2 is a five-ringed device that can slip onto a hand and connect to a device using Bluetooth. The user slides each ring onto each finger, with the largest ring going on the thumb. Attached to the thumb ring are the power button and the mouse portion of the device, as shown in Fig. 1.

The Tap Strap 2 has three modes: the default keyboard mode, mouse mode, and air gesture mode. While in keyboard mode, the user can type by tapping different combinations of fingers at the same time on a solid surface. Taps are detected through the use of built-in accelerometers in each ring. This information is then sent to and processed by a microcontroller unit (MCU) in the thumb ring, determining the input. As is shown in Fig. 2, each combination corresponds to either a command key, such as tab or backspace, or a character key. For example, each vowel is created by tapping a single finger, beginning with "a" at the thumb and ending with "u" at the small fifth finger. Consonants are typed using two or more different fingers, and special characters, such as punctuation marks, are typed by tapping the same combination two or three times in rapid succession. Certain letters, such as "j" and "q", have difficult combinations that require the user to hold up their ring finger while tapping the two adjacent digits. To remedy this, shortcuts are implemented for these letters that require the player to simply tap one or two fingers twice in quick succession, similarly to special characters. The learning curve of the device is quite steep, as the user needs to memorize a brand new keyboard layout with many seemingly random combinations, though some of them, such as the vowels, are fairly straightforward to memorize. Some of the tapping combinations themselves can also be physically demanding to execute for individuals who suffer from low hand dexterity.

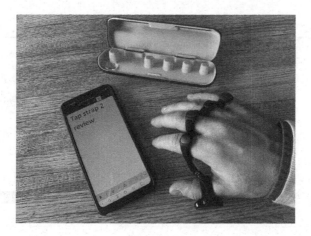

Fig. 1. The Tap Strap 2 and its case.

The Tap Strap 2's mouse mode works through the use of an optical chip embedded in the thumb ring. The user can activate mouse mode by resting their thumb on a surface. The cursor can then by guided by dragging the thumb across the surface in the direction the user wishes to move it. There are also several mouse commands, such as clicking and scrolling, that can be done by tapping fingers when in mouse mode. Mouse mode is disabled by simply lifting the thumb off the surface.

The third and final mode that this technology has is the air gesture mode. This is done through the use of a 6-axis inertial measurement unit, or IMU, which is built into the thumb ring. This unit is used in tandem with the accelerometers to determine the position of the hand in the air. Air gesture mode is triggered when the user holds their hand out in what the Tap Strap 2's official site refers to as a "handshake" position. By default, the air gesture mode turns the Tap Strap 2 into a mouse, where the user can direct the cursor with their hand and perform mouse commands (clicks, scrolling, etc.) by extending fingers and flicking them quickly in different directions. In addition to computers and mobile devices, the air gesture mode can also be used with Bluetooth television sets and media players.

In addition to the included manual and glossary, there is also an app called TapGenius, which is created to help the user learn the Tap Strap 2's inputs. TapGenius was designed with the help of Learning Neuroscience specialists at Stanford University. TapGenius teaches the user how to learn the Tap Strap 2's keyboard "layout," beginning with simple inputs such as vowels and later progressing to the more complicated consonants and punctuation marks. The training app breaks the alphabet into eight groups, ranked in order of difficulty. The app also teaches the user how to type words that employ characters that the user has already learned. The TapGenius app also gives the user a vibration in the thumb ring whenever an incorrect character is entered.

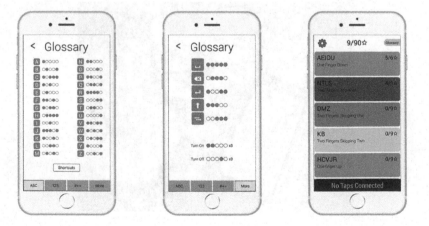

Fig. 2. The Tap Strap 2's glossary, accessed through the TapGenius app. Green circles indicate the fingers that are tapped to type a given character. (Color figure online)

2   Related Work

The past decade has seen the rise of wearable devices as a major force in technology and HCI. These "wearables" are a form of ubiquitous computing in which computing is embedded in seemingly mundane objects, with the most prominent of these being wristbands and smartwatches [1]. Many consumers across the globe have shown a strong interest in wearables. As a result, researchers and industry leaders seek new and innovative ways of interacting with daily devices, including smartphones, smart TVs and personal computers, besides the standard QWERTY keyboard. Moreover, the rise of augmented reality (AR) and virtual reality (VR) technologies in the computing and gaming world demands the existence of an input system that is based entirely on touch and gestures rather than eyesight [2].

2.1   An Overview of Wearables

Almost a decade ago, the North American PC gaming market saw a new addition in the form of the Peregrine Glove [3]. The glove comes with 18 touch zones that enable the user to communicate with any application where a keyboard is needed. With just a touch of the user's fingers, the user could perform any command they wanted to.

In 2013, Jing et al. [4] proposed the Magic Ring, a hands-free input device designed to recognize finger gestures. This device uses inertial sensors and can be used as a remote controller for electrical appliances such as televisions and radios. It does this by using an accelerometer to recognize gestures, much like the Tap Strap 2, then outputting an infrared signal that interacts with the object of interest. The Magic Ring also has the ability to accurately recognize when the user is performing a variety of day-to-day activities such as running, cooking, and writing. In tests performed with the Magic Ring, the rate of successful recognition was 97.2% [4].

In 2014, a system named Airwriting was developed at Germany's Karlsruhe Institute of Technology [5]. This used data from an IMU, accelerometer, and gyroscope, all of which were attached to the back of the user's hand, to detect gestures that correspond to the characteristic signal pattern for every alphabet letter. The gestures are then translated into editable text for phones, tablets, and other mobile devices. Tests run using this system yielded an average spelling error rate of 11%.

In 2012, Southern et al. [6] introduced a system called BrailleTouch. This is used to help blind people type on mobile devices, which is a challenge since most of these devices do not have physical keyboards attached to them. The device is set up in a way so that the blind user holds a phone facing away from them, with three fingers on each hand resting above dots on either side of the touchscreen. It is remarkably similar to the Tap Strap 2 in a sense, since the user types characters by tapping their fingers on the touchscreen using the same patterns as the Braille system. BrailleTouch was a much more affordable alternative to the comparable Braille Sense Plus system, which costs $6000.

TypeInBraille, another system that had emerged the previous year with the efforts of Mascetti et al. [7], similarly employed tap combinations. However, it generates all three rows of each Braille character separately. There are commands to raise both the left and right dots in each row as well as to move on to the next character. This proved to be both more accurate and efficient than the onscreen QWERTY keyboard, with 55% higher accuracy than the QWERTY in a noisy "tramcar" setting. Both BrailleTouch and TypeInBraille prove to be significant to this research, since while the Tap Strap 2 can prove useful for the blind due to relying on touch rather than sight, it suffers from a notable hindrance in that it requires them to learn a new alphabet rather than simply using the existing Braille system.

In 2015, Nirjon et al. [8] introduced the TypingRing, a wearable system in the form of a "ring" that can be slid onto the user's middle finger, enabling them to type as if an invisible standard QWERTY keyboard is lying on a surface underneath their hand. A user study states that Typing Ring yields a reasonable typing speed (e.g., 33–50 characters per minute), which improves over time as the users become more acquainted with the device.

In 2016, Gordon et al. [9] proposed the WatchWriter, a keyboard specifically designed for smart watches. Users can either use one tap per character or one gesture per word. This device helps since smartwatches are the next device in portable devices, and it can be difficult to accurately type out a message on one because of its size. The makers of WatchWriter decided to try to either optimize or change the current keyboard to help with the small size of the watch, while also making it easier for people to use the WatchWriter.

Wearable computing clearly improves the experience the user gets from technological devices, especially for those with sensory impairments. These devices will keep improving as more companies invest in research and innovation in the field. The wearables of the future will not only continue to make computing more ubiquitous, but they will be more user-friendly as well.

2.2 Comparing the Tap Strap 2 to Previous Technologies

Most consumers frequently employ information services from cellular towers and terminals to conduct various activities (e.g., checking e-mails, finding a route, texting, dialing a number). However, in order to use these services, the consumer has to pull the smartphone out of their pocket, which can be inconvenient. The advent of smartwatches did little to help. The available options in the market can provide data-driven notifications and timely updates; however, the smartwatch's small screen size means there is not enough space for solid gesture commands [9]. Therefore, the primary input method for a smartwatch is usually voice control. However, there are some technological limitations to this method. Due to the nature of speech recognition, background noises can hinder the device's capability to recognize the command. Moreover, voice control does little to preserve the user's privacy. In the meanwhile, glove-based input systems like the Peregrine Glove and Airwriting cover up the user's hand, which can impede the user in the execution of certain manual tasks. While the Magic Ring may cause little obstruction, it is poorly suited to typing. Most of these devices can replace a traditional keyboard, but using them involves complex gestures that require time and effort to master. Furthermore, if a user performs gestures without any support for the arm, the postures can be very uncomfortable.

The Tap Strap 2 seems better suited to its role than its counterparts. It has a series of embedded sensors that monitor the fingers and return mechanical information, such as acceleration, rotation, and orientation. The sensors then process data, and the finger-tap combinations are transformed into characters for output. The device is placed at the top of the fingers (close to the knuckles) and engages all five digits at the same time. Despite its user-friendly design and working mechanism, using "the Tap Strap" significantly constrains the user's interaction with the surroundings, though not to the extent of a glove. In comparison to this, the TypingRing can fulfill the user's typing requirements with minimal obstruction, but it requires the user to employ an extensive hard surface to type on (such as a wall or a table).

When compared with the original Tap Strap, the Tap Strap 2 comes with a new thumb ring glider and a more sensitive mouse functionality than its predecessor. When the first iteration of the Tap Strap was released, Tap stated that any surface could be used for typing. It was supposed be able to type virtually anywhere, as some individuals using it are traveling, leaving them with no solid surface to type on. However, following the release of the Tap Strap 2, Tap made it clear that any surface that is too soft or irregular may not work as intended.

3   Experimental Setup

Before the Tap Strap 2 was tested, information regarding the advantages and disadvantages of the device were collected from customer reviews on the Tap Strap 2 website, Amazon, and other review sites. This was done to see if this is truly groundbreaking HCI technology or merely a work in progress with some potential.

It was possible to locate some common complaints regarding the Tap Strap 2. Most of these were related to the hypersensitivity of the Strap's sensors. The device did not register characters as accurately as many users expected it to. In order to use the Strap, the user has to tap certain fingers and keep the rest stationary. Many encountered difficulty doing this and frequently produced errors. Users complained of typing the correct letter, but having the Strap produce the wrong output. For example, when one user was trying to type an "o", the Strap typed an "s", since the inputs for "o" and "s" are similar. When the consumer tried to fix the error, the Strap toggled the number pad and began to produce unwanted numbers instead.

3.1   Accuracy of the Tap Strap

Hard Surfaces. To test the overall accuracy of the Tap Strap 2, the device was used on hard, soft, and irregular surfaces. The first test was on a hardwood table. The test consisted of typing each letter one hundred times, only deviating from that when a shortcut is available. When a shortcut of the letter were available, fifty regular taps were tested alongside fifty shortcut taps.

Soft Surfaces. The same test was then performed on a bed. Lying in bed while using electronic devices is an activity that many people enjoy doing. The test of soft surfaces was performed to see if typing on a bed with the Strap is a plausible option, as well as to see how much accuracy is lost compared to hard surfaces. The test was conducted in the exact same format as the hard surfaces test.

Irregular Surfaces. This experiment is focused on the usability of the Tap while traveling. While away from home, there is not always a table available to type on. Often, the only way to use this device in these situations is on one's own leg. Even though Tap Systems, Inc. said that irregular surfaces may result in less accuracy with typing, a test on irregular surfaces was performed to see how much accuracy is lost. This test was performed in the same manner as the tests for hard and soft surfaces.

3.2   Recognizable Bluetooth

A major interruption noticed while using the Tap, if the device connected to the Tap would go into sleep mode or would turn off, Tap would not reconnect to the device. The test conducted for Bluetooth was to see if it would only disconnect on specific devices, or if each device would need to be manually reconnected. Before experimenting, the inner workings of Bluetooth and how it functions were researched. From the article by Bisdikian [10], Bluetooth uses asynchronous data that flows between the connected devices. This connection, allows the connection between the devices to be reestablished. Different devices used were cell phones, laptops, and computers.

3.3   Virtual Reality Capability

Virtual reality (VR) capability was another supposed feature of the Tap Strap 2. This feature was considered to be one of the main selling points of the device, since one can use the air gesture mode to interact with the VR setting. To test this feature, the device was hooked up to an Oculus Quest 2 headset. The goal of this was to test the functionality of the Tap Strap 2 in a VR setting.

3.4   Mouse Functions

Another important feature of the Tap Strap 2 was the built-in mouse. The usability of the mouse on the Tap Strap 2 was a major concern, so a series of tests were set up to test it. The specifications were researched for the mouse function in the Tap Strap 2 and they were compared to those of a regular computer mouse using the patent by Bieber [11]. The mouse in the patent is an optical mouse with laser illumination. The Tap Strap 2 also has an optical mouse with a laser sensor to detect movements. Both the efficiency and accuracy of the mouse will be quantified to determine its overall usability.

Efficiency. To test the efficiency of the mouse, it was determined how fast the mouse could scroll down a fifteen-page research paper. The test conducted used three different methods to get to the bottom of the page: the scroll bar on the right-hand side, the built-in scroll down function (mouse wheel), and the scroll lock. Each mouse was tested ten times with each scroll method.

The efficiency of the mouse's 'drag and drop' function was also compared to that of a normal mouse. For this test, a particular word or sentence was highlighted. Since the mouse could not tell when to stop highlighting, two different methods were tried. Method one let the mouse 'drag and drop' time out, the second method was clicking to get rid of the drag and drop.

Accuracy. At first use, it was apparent that the Tap mouse was quite sensitive, so it was also important to test the accuracy. To test the accuracy of the mouse on the Tap Strap 2, a test was performed where the user had to click on as many targets as possible in a minute. This was done first using a normal mouse, then with the Tap Strap 2's built-in mouse mode. The test was performed ten times for each mouse.

3.5 Accuracy of the Tap Strap with an Auto-correct Feature

A common critique of the Tap Strap 2 is that there is no built-in spell checker or auto-correct feature. This makes sense, as characters are typed by tapping different finger combinations, so the user will find themselves experiencing more input errors with the Tap Strap 2 than a normal QWERTY keyboard. While the auto-correct features on mobile devices will generally catch these errors, this is not the case with normal computers. It is especially problematic when one is using a text editor like Notepad, which has no built-in spell checker, since errors can easily go unnoticed. Spelling errors tend to also be a nuisance to fix, since the backspace command can add more unwanted characters if typed incorrectly.

In order to determine how much a built-in auto-correct feature improves the overall experience of the Tap Strap 2, a simple Notepad-like program was designed in Python, which incorporated three different spell checker modules. This was done in order to ensure that the auto-correct feature had the largest dictionary possible, preventing real words from getting corrected into other words. For the test, a set of 50 sentences was entered using the Tap Strap 2 into the normal Notepad (without any use of an auto-correct feature). These sentences, borrowed from the list of Harvard sentences, are useful because they provide a reasonable approximation of the frequency of every letter in the English language. Gordon et al. [9] employed a similar set to test the auto-correct feature for the watchWriter. The sentences were then entered into the Python text editor, which makes it easier to determine how effective the auto-correct feature was.

3.6   Obtaining Raw Data from the Device

There is a software development kit (SDK) available for the Tap Strap 2 on the TapWithUs GitHub. This contains code that allows the user to collect various forms of information from the device, such as inputs and raw sensor data, provided the Tap Strap 2 is connected to the computer and in developer mode. The raw accelerometer and IMU data is of particular interest here because if trends can be found in the data with respect to the character inputs themselves, it may be possible to propose a machine learning algorithm that will improve the accuracy of the device's readings. Therefore, for this experiment, the program was allowed to collect data in "raw sensors" mode while the alphabet was typed in order four times.

4   Experimental Results

Tables 1, 2 and 3 summarize the experiments done on Bluetooth connectivity, mouse functionality, and accuracy of Tap Strap 2's keyboard, respectively. When looking at the Bluetooth connectivity results, it can be seen that it failed to connect to both a desktop PC and a laptop in sleep mode. However, it successfully connected 100% of the time to a phone while the phone was in sleep mode and when the phone was restarted. Taking a look at the comparison between a regular mouse and the Tap Strap 2 mouse, it can be seen that the a regular mouse outperforms the Tap Strap 2 mouse in navigation speed, scroll wheel speed, and scroll lock speed. The Tap Strap 2 mouse was also tested for its drag and drop speed and clicking ability. For that experiment, the Tap Strap 2 was able to perform 2 out of 10 drag drops and 5 out of 10 clicks accurately. Moreover, it can also be seen that a regular mouse is approximately twice as accurate as the Tap Strap 2, hitting an average of 41.3 targets out of 60 while the Tap Strap 2 mouse hit an average of only 19.5 targets out of 60.

Figures 3, 4 and 5 summarize Tap Strap 2's accuracy on three types of surfaces: hard, soft, and irregular. The accuracy of the typing depended on the combination of finger taps required to produce a character. From the experiment performed, it was concluded that simple combinations using one finger or consecutive fingers tend to be more accurate than keys such as 'q' and 'w', which require the user to perform the difficult task of lifting the ring finger. In addition to that, it was also found that the letter 'a' had the highest accuracy, while the letter 'w' had the lowest accuracy. Lastly, the experiment helped identify that the Tap Strap 2 performs better on harder surfaces, with an average accuracy of 84.7%, while it has a 76.07% average accuracy on soft surfaces and a 80.23% average accuracy on irregular surfaces.

For the VR test, the Oculus Quest 2 headset connected to the Tap Strap 2 for a few seconds and disconnected. When reconnection was attempted, the Oculus failed to recognize the Strap entirely.

When looking the accuracy of the Tap Strap 2 with an Auto correct feature experiment. It was found that after typing a set of a 100 sentences, the Tap Strap

2 had an error rate of 16.39% without the use of auto-correct. In terms of the types of errors, this experiment yielded 90 character insertions, 71 substitutions, and 3 deletions. This shows that the overwhelming majority of errors happen due to the Tap Strap 2 detecting either the wrong input or a second input immediately after the intended one. Deletions, where the Tap fails to register a character at all, are comparatively rare. When auto-correct was used on this text, the error rate decreased to 4.39%. This shows that even a relatively simple auto-correct feature makes a considerable improvement to the accuracy of the device.

Lastly, the graph in Fig. 6 represents the raw data that was obtained from the Tap Strap 2 using the Tap SDK. In this case, the letter "a" was typed repeatedly by simply tapping the thumb on a table. The taps appear as spikes on the plot, and it is apparent that the accelerometer attached to the thumb ring shows a much higher acceleration than the other rings, as expected. It would be useful to obtain the actual input readings alongside the raw data; that is, determining whether an "a" was actually typed as opposed to some other character. This would assist in training a model to improve the accuracy of the input readings from accelerometer data, which would likely be done through the use of convolutional neural networks (CNNs) [12]. Unfortunately, however, the Tap SDK unfortunately only allows the user to extract either the raw data or the input information at once.

Table 1. Bluetooth connectivity

	Number of successful trials	Number of trials
Phone (Sleep)	10	10
Phone (Restart)	10	10
Computer (Sleep)	0	10
Laptop (Sleep)	0	10

Table 2. Regular mouse vs. Tap Strap 2 mouse efficiency

	Navigation speed (sec)	Scroll wheel (sec)	Scroll lock (sec)
Regular	1.94	5.47	1.97
Tap	7.33	29.17	7.01

Table 3. Regular mouse vs. Tap Strap 2 mouse accuracy

	Number of successful trials	Of attempts	Number of trials
Regular	41.3	60	10
Tap	18.5	60	10

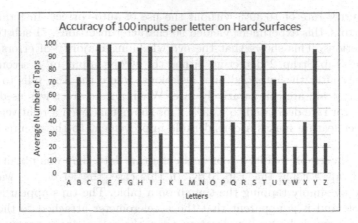

Fig. 3. Accuracy of the Tap Strap 2 keyboard on a hard surface

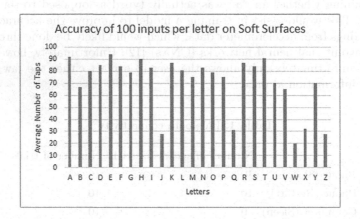

Fig. 4. Accuracy of the Tap Strap 2 keyboard on a soft surface

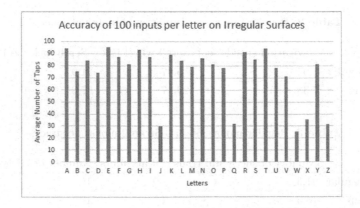

Fig. 5. Accuracy of the Tap Strap 2 keyboard on an irregular surface

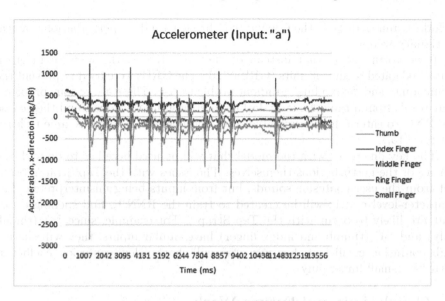

Fig. 6. Raw accelerometer data obtained while repeatedly typing the character "a."

It is evident that while using the Tap Strap 2 with an auto-correct mechanic significantly improves the accuracy of words, there are still certain situations in which the auto-correct feature fails. The most obvious example of this is when an input error results in a real English word; for example, typing in "bike" when attempting to enter "bake". Additionally, the program fails to fix even some errors that do not result in a word, such as accidentally typing "veut" instead of "vest," even though "vest" is in the dictionary and "veut" is not a real word in English. Since the implemented auto-correct feature simply looks for the most common similar words whenever it detects a spelling error, it cannot determine context within a sentence, causing it to miss these kinds of mistakes. The solution to this problem will be to implement a spell checker that uses a recurrent neural network, or RNN.

This RNN will be comparable to a nested RNN system developed by Li et al. [13]. This system consists of a character-level RNN, which examines the series of characters within a word and finds real words with similar spellings, nested within a word-level RNN, which uses the structure of a sentence to determine which word should be present. The result is a neural network system that focuses on both the spelling of a word and the surrounding context. It is remarkable due to its ability to reliably detect both real and non-real word errors, especially when compared to previous RNN-based and non-RNN-based spell checkers. Furthermore, this research has an interesting way of generating pseudo training data, using a confusion matrix that maps characters (or groups of characters) to other characters that represent phonetic sounds. High confusion coefficients correspond to characters or groups of characters that are often confused in spelling. The pseudo training data is then generated through random perturbations of real dictionary words.

It is worth noting that instead of "normal" RNNs, the work of Li et al. employed gated recurrent units (GRUs) [13]. The GRUs were used to prevent the "vanishing" and "exploding" gradient problems [14]. These are serious problems that result from a rapid spike or decline in error gradient values, and they cause the RNN to enter a highly unstable state and possibly cease to be able to learn entirely [15].

The key difference with the model that will be used here has to do with the nature of the perturbations themselves. The issues with the Tap Strap 2 occur not from the user confusing sounds, but from inputs being misinterpreted. The character-level matrix will be created to train the RNN to find spelling errors that are likely to occur with the Tap Strap 2. For example, since "a" (thumb only) and "n" (thumb and index finger) have similar inputs, they will share a high confusion coefficient; however, "a" will share a low confusion coefficient with "e" (small finger only).

5   Conclusions and Future Work

In this research, the overall usability of the Tap Strap 2 was investigated and evaluated with a particular focus on accuracy and efficiency. The device was able to consistently connect to a phone in sleep and restart mode, but failed to do so with laptop and desktop PCs. The device's mouse functionality was surpassed by a normal mouse in its ability to scroll quickly and accurately click targets. The Tap Strap 2 keyboard's accuracy was first found to be 84.7% when used on a desk, 76.07% when used on a bed, and 80.23% when used on a leg. Therefore, it can be stated with a reasonable level of confidence that the Tap Strap 2 functions nearly as well on soft or irregular surfaces as on flat, hard surfaces. However, the device was found to be unable to stay connected to a VR headset for more than a handful of seconds, which is a critical error since the device was marketed as being useful in VR settings. A simple Python-based spell checker was found to drop the word error rate of the Tap Strap 2 from 16.39% to 4.39%. Finally, an RNN-based machine learning model was presented with the goal of improving the spell checker's accuracy.

Hence, the Tap Strap is still surpassed by the traditional QWERTY keyboard and physical mouse setup in terms of overall usability. Compared to the QWERTY system, the Tap Strap 2 falls short in the key areas of learnability, efficiency, and accuracy. The two main niches this device would seem to satisfy would be VR users or the visually impaired. However, the device's VR capabilities did not work properly in this experiment, exposing them as error-prone at best, while it is surpassed by systems such as BrailleTouch for blind users in terms of learnability, since it does not require the user to learn a new alphabet. This is not necessarily claiming that the Tap Strap 2 does not have the potential to become a force in HCI in the future, as it does have the advantage of portability, especially when used with mobile devices. However, the device currently has little practical use and needs improvement in learnability, accuracy, and efficiency to compete with the QWERTY system. The next step in this research will be to implement the RNN-based spell checker into the Tap Strap 2 and determine how much this model improves the accuracy of the Tap Strap 2's output.

References

1. Seneviratne, S., et al.: A survey of wearable devices and challenges. IEEE Commun. Surv. Tutor. **19**(4), 2573–2620 (2017)
2. Meli, L., Barcelli, D., Baldi, T.L., Prattichizzo, D.: Hand in air tapping: a wearable input technology to type wireless. In: 2017 26th IEEE International Symposium on Robot and Human Interactive Communication (RO-MAN), pp. 936–941 (2017)
3. Taylor, J., Curran, K.: Glove-based technology in hand rehabilitation. In: Gamification: Concepts, Methodologies, Tools, and Applications, pp. 983–1002. IGI Global (2015)
4. Jing, L., Cheng, Z., Zhou, Y., Wang, J., Huang, T.: Magic ring: a self-contained gesture input device on finger. In: Proceedings of the 12th International Conference on Mobile and Ubiquitous Multimedia, pp. 1–4 (2013)
5. Amma, C., Georgi, M., Schultz, T.: Airwriting: hands-free mobile text input by spotting and continuous recognition of 3D-space handwriting with inertial sensors. In: 2012 16th International Symposium on Wearable Computers, pp. 52–59. IEEE (2012)
6. Southern, C., Clawson, J., Frey, B., Abowd, G., Romero, M.: An evaluation of BrailleTouch: mobile touchscreen text entry for the visually impaired. In: Proceedings of the 14th International Conference on Human-Computer Interaction with Mobile Devices and Services, pp. 317–326 (2012)
7. Mascetti, S., Bernareggi, C., Belotti, M.: TypeInBraille: quick eyes-free typing on smartphones. In: Miesenberger, K., Karshmer, A., Penaz, P., Zagler, W. (eds.) ICCHP 2012, Part II. LNCS, vol. 7383, pp. 615–622. Springer, Heidelberg (2012). https://doi.org/10.1007/978-3-642-31534-3_90
8. Nirjon, S., Gummeson, J., Gelb, D., Kim, K.-H.: TypingRing: a wearable ring platform for text input. In: Proceedings of the 13th Annual International Conference on Mobile Systems, Applications, and Services, pp. 227–239 (2015)
9. Gordon, M., Ouyang, T., Zhai, S.: WatchWriter: tap and gesture typing on a smartwatch miniature keyboard with statistical decoding. In: Proceedings of the 2016 CHI Conference on Human Factors in Computing Systems, pp. 3817–3821 (2016)
10. Bisdikian, C.: An overview of the Bluetooth wireless technology. IEEE Commun. Mag. **39**(12), 86–94 (2001)
11. Bieber, L., Willemin, M.: Motion detection mechanism for laser illuminated optical mouse sensor. US Patent 7,876,307 (25 January 2011)
12. Ignatov, A.: Real-time human activity recognition from accelerometer data using convolutional neural networks. Appl. Soft Comput. **62**, 915–922 (2018)
13. Li, H., Wang, Y., Liu, X., Sheng, Z., Wei, S.: Spelling error correction using a nested RNN model and pseudo training data. CoRR abs/1811.00238 (2018)
14. Chung, J., Gülçehre, Ç., Cho, K., Bengio, Y.: Empirical evaluation of gated recurrent neural networks on sequence modeling. CoRR abs/1412.3555 (2014)
15. Pascanu, R., Mikolov, T., Bengio, Y.: On the difficulty of training recurrent neural networks. In: International Conference on Machine Learning, pp. 1310–1318. PMLR (2013)

Development of a Pen-Type Device for SPIDAR-Tablet that Presents Force and Thermal Sensations

Kaede Nohara[1]([⊠]), Seiya Sekiwa[1], Makoto Sato[2],
Takehiko Yamaguchi[3], and Tetsuya Harada[1]

[1] Tokyo University of Science, 6-3-1 Niijuku, Katsushika-ku, Tokyo, Japan
[2] Tokyo Institute of Technology, 4259 Nagatsuta-cho, Midori-ku, Yokohama, Kanagawa, Japan
[3] Suwa University of Science, Toyohira, Chino-City, Nagano 5000-1, Japan

Abstract. The quality of education can be improved by combining information and communication technology (ICT) education using personal computers (PCs) and tablets, which have gained considerable popularity over the last few years with virtual reality (VR) technology. Many students have difficulty in comprehending various physical and mathematical phenomena intuitively even if they can be expressed in mathematical formulae. Sensitization (visualization, auralization, and tactileization) could help enhance the understanding of these phenomena. In this study, to increase the understanding of thermodynamic phenomena via force and thermal sensations, we used a tablet-type thermodynamics learning support system. In a previous study, a piston was displayed in a VR space on a tablet, and the pressure changes were presented as force sensation using a force feedback device and a SPIDAR-tablet. Using a pen-type thermal feedback device, the temperature changes were presented as thermal sensation; however, the current SPIDAR-tablet presents two issues: i) the force control unit and thermal control unit are separated during the development stage, and ii) the presented force is weak because the motor power is small; therefore, it is difficult to feel force changes. In this study, to solve these limitations, we first integrated the force and temperature control circuit, and then enhanced the presented force by changing the motor and fabricating a new frame. Then, we assessed and confirmed the improvement of the force that was presented.

Keywords: VR learning system · Force feedback · Thermal feedback

1 Introduction

Online connection and use of information and communication technology (ICT) devices such as personal computers (PCs) and tablets are currently used in education to enhance its quality [1]. Building an environment where people can learn independently, effectively, and without losing interest would promote the use of ICT in education [2].

The use of learning support systems based on VR technology is expected to help in devising effective learning programs. Such systems should allow learners to proactively participate [3].

C. Stephanidis et al. (Eds.): HCII 2021, LNCS 13095, pp. 96–105, 2021.
https://doi.org/10.1007/978-3-030-90963-5_8

In this study, we focus on haptic presentation in learning with tablet devices. Using tablets, which are extensively used in education, and extending the VR function with haptic presentation devices, we expect to reduce the cost of introducing a VR learning environment. In our previous study, we developed a device that can present force sensation for use in tablet operations [4]. Furthermore, the pen-type thermal sensation presentation device was added to the SPIDAR-tablet, and the force and thermal sensations were simultaneously presented to the tablet [5]. The issues that require to be addressed are the weakness of the presented force and circuit integration [5]. In this study, we fabricated the circuit board and frame for a new SPIDAR-tablet to improve the force sensation and integrate the force and thermal sensation circuits. Then, we conducted a quantitative evaluation of the force.

2   Previous Research

2.1   SPIDAR-Tablet

SPIDAR-tablet is a device that presents a force sense to the touch panel of a tablet. The string tension is controlled by motors attached to four corners of the frame, and a ring connected to the string can be attached to the finger to present the force sensation. Figure 1 shows the SPIDAR-tablet for iPad Pro [5].

This SPIDAR-tablet has a small circuit board and uses small motors; therefore, the frame is extremely compact and portable. However, the output is small and cannot present sufficient force sensation.

Fig. 1. SPIDAR-tablet for iPad [5]

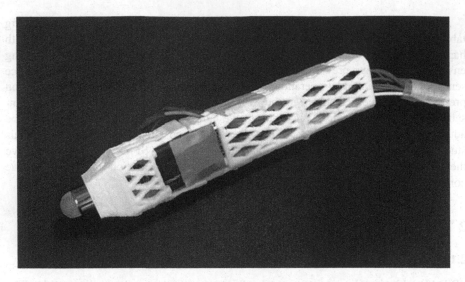

Fig. 2. Pen-type thermal sensation presentation device [5]

2.2 Pen-type Thermal Sensation Presentation Device

The pen-type thermal sensation presentation device shown in Fig. 2 adds thermal sensation to the user's fingertip. This device has a heat sink and fan in a frame produced using a 3D printer, a Peltier device, and a Cu plate to enable thermal sensation to the fingertip [5].

As shown in Fig. 3, by attaching SPIDAR-tablet strings to the pen tip, it can be used to present force and thermal sensations simultaneously. However, the limitation is that both force and thermal sensation control circuits are separated, and the wiring is complicated.

2.3 Thermodynamic Learning Support Application

We developed an application to assist students in learning thermodynamics using this device [5]. The virtual space was developed using Unity [6]. Figure 4 shows an example of the developed virtual space.

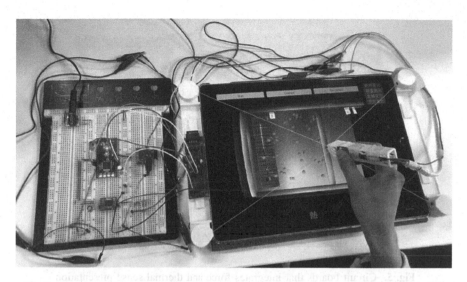

Fig.3. Combined use of pen-type thermal presentation device and SPIDAR-tablet [5]

For this application, the device shows the gas pressure and temperature in the cylinder as force and thermal sensation, respectively, and visually shows the movement and temperature change of the particles. After selecting one of the four thermodynamic state changes in the tablet menu, i.e. adiabatic, constant pressure, constant volume, and isothermal changes, when the learner moves the piston via tablet, the particle velocity and the indicated thermometer value changes.

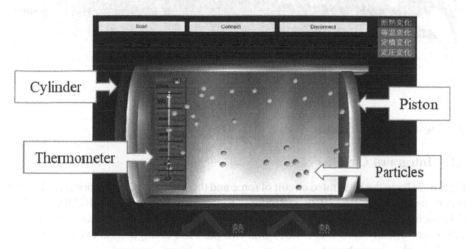

Fig. 4. Virtual space

Fig. 5. Circuit boards that integrates force and thermal sense presentation

Fig. 6. Combined the integrate circuit

3   Device Fabrication

3.1   Integrated Circuit

Figure 3 shows the integrated circuit of force and thermal control was fabricated. The PIC board used was a REWBPIC (Running Electronics LLC.) with PIC24FJ64GB004 (Microchip Technology Inc.). Figure 5 shows the integrated circuit board. As shown in Fig. 6, the circuit board was divided into two parts and configured in two stages. While installing the circuit board on the one side of the frame, we made it compact using a two-stage configuration just as we did with the conventional frame shown in Fig. 1. The connection between the circuit board and the pen is shown in Fig. 7. The pen is connected with a connector so that it can be removed when not in use.

3.2   System Configuration

Figure 8 shows the configuration of the force and thermal presentation system. First, the force and temperature values are calculated from the tablet via simulations. Then, these values are sent to the central processing unit (CPU) using Bluetooth Low Energy communication. In terms of the force sense, the CPU generates pulse-width modulation (PWM) signals, with the duty cycle corresponding to the received values and feed them to the motor drivers to control the torques of the motors. This allows to control string tension and demonstrates a force sense to the user. As for thermal senses, the CPU compares the target temperature with the temperature of the Peltier device and determines the PWM duty cycle using PID control. Consequently, the heat transfer of the Peltier element can be controlled and the user can get a thermal sensation.

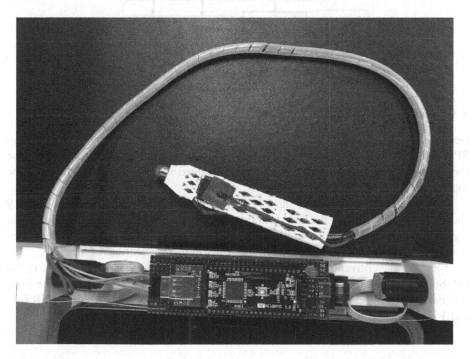

Fig. 7. The integrate circuit with the pen-type thermal presentation device

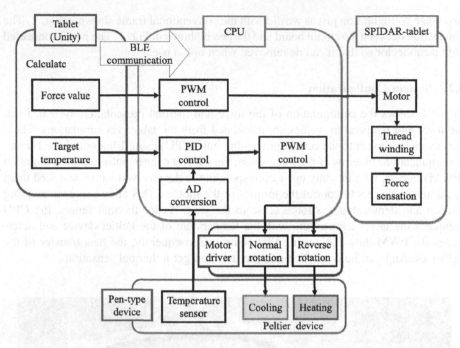

Fig. 8. The system configuration diagram

3.3   New Frame of SPIDAR-Tablet

Because of the motor performance, the magnitude of the force of conventional SPIDAR-tablet was weak, making it slightly difficult for the user to clearly perceive the force sensation changes. Therefore, we circumvented this limitation by changing the motor with a higher performance one.

In this study, the frame of the SPIDAR-tablet fabricated is described. Figure 9 shows the overall view of the newly fabricated force-enhanced frame. We designed the frame by adjusting its height, width, and the outlet height of the string from the pulley cover because the motor is larger than that used in the conventional frame.

First, for the conventional SPIDAR-tablet frame, the DC motor RF-300FA-12350 (Mabuchi Motor Co., Ltd.) was used; however, as mentioned above, because the force that can be presented is less, we used the DC motor 1724T006SR (FAULHABER Co., Ltd.). Table 1 lists a comparison of DC motor specifications.

Table 1. DC motor specifications

	RF-300FA-12350	1724T006SR
Rated voltage [V]	3	6
Rated torque [mNm]	0.48	4.2
Stop torque [mNm]	2.51	11.5
Weight [g]	22	27

Next, we described the change of the motor mounting method. For the conventional frame, the motor is vertically mounted to the tablet. For the new frame, the motor was horizontally mounted to the tablet, as shown in Fig. 10. The reason is that the outlet position of the string is considered. Because of the large axial length of the motor, if it is vertically installed as in the past, the outlet position of the string will be high. Therefore, by laying motor and pulley sideways, the height of the outlet is adjusted.

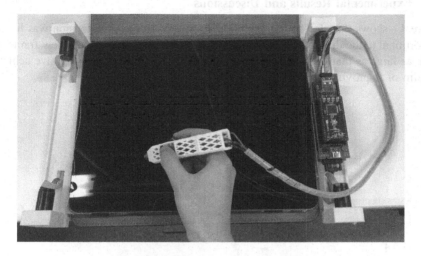

Fig. 9. The overall view of the force-enhanced frame

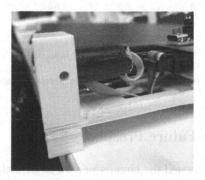

Fig. 10. A part of frame with motor installed

4 Evaluation Experiment

In this experiment, we evaluated the improvement of the magnitude of the presented force sensation, which has been a previously problem, by comparing the change in the string tension against the duty cycle of PWM control between conventional and new frame.

4.1   Experimental Method

In this experiment, we compared the string tension in the conventional frame and the new frame of the SPIDAR-tablet. The duty cycle of the PWM control was varied between 0% and 100%, and the string tension was measured at each point. The horizontal force was then measured against the string outlet of one motor.

4.2   Experimental Results and Discussions

Figure 11 shows that, for both conventional and new frames, the tension was linearly proportional to the duty cycle. Furthermore, the maximum force of the new frame was twice as large as that of the conventional frame. This indicates that we have achieved our aim of improving the force perception.

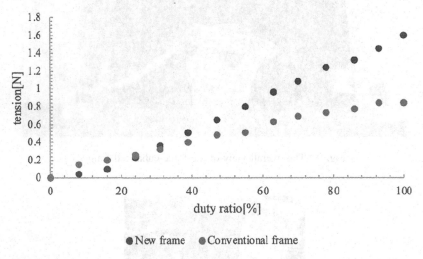

● New frame   ● Conventional frame

Fig. 11. The results of the string tension in the conventional and new frames of the SPIDAR-tablet

5   Conclusions and Future Prospect

In this study, we first integrated the circuits in a SIPDAR tablet and pen-type thermal presentation device. Consequently, we reduced the complexity of the connection between the SPIDAR-tablet and pen-type thermal presentation device and made the structure compact. Next, we replaced the motor of the SPIDAR-tablet and we designed a new frame to enhance the presentation force. By quantitatively evaluating the string tension in both old and new devices, we improved the presenting force.

As a future prospect, it is necessary to conduct the same experiment using the new device and evaluate performance as the previous study demonstrated that it was difficult to feel the force when the force and temperature were simultaneously presented [5]. Moreover, we will try to improve the thermal sensation presentation by enhancing the device structure and temperature control system. In addition, we aim to apply the system to the contents in wide areas using visual, force, and thermal sensation presentation as well as thermodynamics.

References

1. Ronald, M.: Hernandez: impact of ICT on education: challenges and perspectives. J. Educ. Psychol. Propósitos y Representaciones, **5**(1), 337–347 (2017)
2. Ratheeswari, K.: Information communication technology in education. J. Appl. Adv. Res. **3**(1), S45–S47 (2018)
3. Lee, E.-L., Wong, K.W.: A review of using virtual reality for learning. In: Pan, Z., Cheok, A. D., Müller, W., El Rhalibi, A. (eds.) Transactions on Edutainment I. LNCS, vol. 5080, pp. 231–241. Springer, Heidelberg (2008). https://doi.org/10.1007/978-3-540-69744-2_18
4. Tasaka, Y., et al.: Development of frame for SPIDAR tablet on windows and evaluation of system-presented geographical information. In: Yamamoto, S., Mori, H., (eds.) Human Interface and the Management of Information. Interaction, Visualization, and Analytics. HIMI 2018. LNCS, vol. 10904, pp. 358–368. Springer, Cham (2018) . https://doi.org/10.1007/978-3-319-92043-6_30
5. Nohara, K., Kubo, Y., Sato, M., Yamaguchi, T., Harada, T.: Development and evaluation of a pen type thermal sensation presentation device for SPIDAR-tablet. In: Stephanidis, C., Kurosu, M., Degen, H., Reinerman-Jones, L. (eds.) HCII 2020. LNCS, vol. 12424, pp. 231–240. Springer, Cham (2020). https://doi.org/10.1007/978-3-030-60117-1_17
6. Unity Technologies. https://unity.com

An HMD-Integrated Haptic Device for Force, Friction, and Thermal Sensations of Fingertip

Takahiro Ooshima[1]($\boxtimes$), Ryuichi Osaki[1], Shimpei Matsukiyo[1],
Makoto Sato[2], Takehiko Yamaguchi[3], and Tetsuya Harada[1]

[1] Tokyo University of Science, 6-3-1 Niijuku, Katsushika-ku, Tokyo, Japan
8120511@ed.tus.ac.jpm
[2] Tokyo Institute of Technology, 4259 Nagatsuta-cho, Midori-ku,
Yokohama, Kanagawa, Japan
[3] Suwa University of Science, 5000-1 Toyohira, Chino, Nagano, Japan

Abstract. We developed an HMD-integrated haptic device "SPIDAR-Fr," which can present contact and friction sensations to stiff objects. The device consists of two DC motors with a rotary encoder and a brake module attached to the HMD. A ring-shaped device which is the end-effector is attached to a string wound around the shafts. The user attaches the end-effector to the fingertip to obtain haptic experiences for virtual objects. When the user's fingertip comes into contact with a stiff object, the brake module stops the string from being pulled out, causing the string to collide with the fingertip and the reaction force to be perceived. Furthermore, if the finger is moved horizontally in that state, friction will occur between the skin of the fingertip and the fixed string, and the sensation of tracing can be perceived.

In this study, we used a spring-damper model and PWM control of the motors instead of the brake mechanism to enable SPIDAR-Fr to touch stiff and elasto-plastic objects and present its reaction force. In addition, we added a thermal sensation presentation mechanism using a Peltier element to present the warm or cold sensation of the touched object. We named this device "SPIDAR-H&F".

Keywords: Haptics · Force sensation · Friction sensation · Thermal sensation

1 Introduction

1.1 Background and Objectives

In recent years, HMDs have become increasingly high in specifications and low-priced due to their wide utilities by individuals and companies. The application of HMDs to virtual reality systems is limited to the presentation of audio and visual. Even though the controller attached to the HMD has the function of presenting skin sensation feedback by giving vibration [1], it is not possible to reproduce and present the sensation of force or friction. The haptic sensation is attracting attention as a sensory presentation following the advances in the visual and auditory senses. The development of a haptic sensation presentation device for operating directly the haptic sense and feeling the haptic sense using one's fingers are currently active [2–4]. In addition, wearable devices such as HMDs have the advantage of not hindering the user's

© Springer Nature Switzerland AG 2021
C. Stephanidis et al. (Eds.): HCII 2021, LNCS 13095, pp. 106–114, 2021.
https://doi.org/10.1007/978-3-030-90963-5_9

movements, since it is expected that wearable haptic presentation devices will be put into use and commercialized at an early stage.

2   Related Research

2.1   SPIDAR-Fr

SPIDAR-Fr is an HMD-integrated encounter type haptic device that presents force and friction sensation by a braking mechanism using solenoid [5]. We show SPIDAR-Fr in Figs. 1 and 2. SPIDAR-Fr detects the position of the finger using Leap Motion [6], and when the finger touches a virtual object in the virtual space, the brake is activated, stopping the rotation of the motors and the movement of the finger inserted into the end-effector connected with a string. When the finger is slid horizontally while in contact with the object, the finger slides on the string, and the user feels the friction of tracing the object.

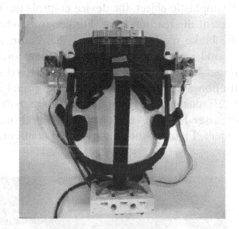

Fig. 1. SPIDAR-Fr

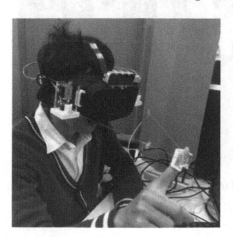

Fig. 2. SPIDAR-Fr in use

3 Proposed Device

3.1 Overview of SPIDAR-H&F

SPIDAR-H&F is an HMD-integrated parallel-wire haptic device that can present a feeling of contact and friction with both stiff and elastoplastic objects by controlling the torque of the motor of SPIDAR-Fr. As shown in Fig. 3, this device consists of five elements: the two brake modules attached to the left and right of the Oculus Rift S [7], the end-effector attached to the string extending from the brake modules, the Leap Motion attached to the front of the HMD, and the controller board attached to the rear. When the user wears the HMD and moves the hand with the end-effector attached to the finger, Leap Motion detects the 3D position of the finger and the hand avatar in the virtual space moves like a real hand. When the user comes into contact with an object, the device presents a different sense of reaction depending on whether the contacted object is a stiff object or an elastoplastic object. When it comes into contact with an elastoplastic object, the device controls the torque of the motor using PWM control to present the reaction force. Furthermore, when it comes into contact with a stiff object, the brake mechanism operates the motor, and the pulley around which the string is wound is fixed to present the reaction force. At this time, when the user moves the finger horizontally, it slides over the fixed string, this mechanism presents a sense of friction as if the user is tracing the virtual object. With these mechanisms, SPIDAR-H&F reacts to the feeling of contact regardless of whether the virtual object in front of the user is a stiff or elastoplastic object and reacts to the feeling of friction in a stiff object. Figure 4 shows the system configuration.

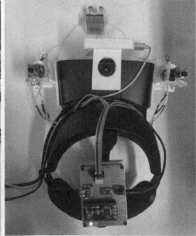

Fig. 3. SPIDAR-H&F

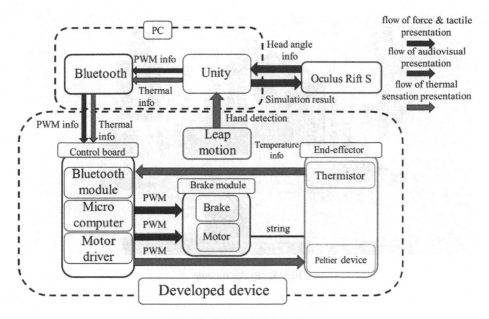

Fig. 4. System configuration

3.2 Components of SPIDAR-H&F

Brake Module. Figure 5 shows the brake module used for force and friction sense presentation. The upper part is a solenoid (Fig. 6, CBS08300120, TAKAHA KIKO Co., Ltd.) [8], and the lower part is a resin motor fixing frame created by a 3D printer. The motor (Fig. 7, RF-300FA-12350, MABUCHI MOTOR Co., Ltd.) [9] is in the frame on the lower side, and the rotating shaft is sticking out the top. A pulley is attached there, and the string is winded up. When the finger pushes an elastoplastic virtual object, the torque of the motor reacts to the spring-damper model and PWM control, and the reaction force is presented. When the finger pushes a stiff virtual object, the iron core of the solenoid presses down on the pulley, stopping the pulley from rotating, and as a result, the user feels a the contact with a stiff object.

End-Effector. We illustrate the end-effector in Fig. 8. The string extending from the motor penetrates the hole on the front of the end-effector and connects to the motor on the opposite side. The user is presented with a sense of force and friction sensation by attaching an end-effector to the fingertip. When the user is not in contact with the virtual object, the string does not come into contact with the belly of the finger due to the tension of the rubber attached to the left and right on the upper side of end-effector (Fig. 8(b)). When the user touches the virtual object, the string touches the finger and

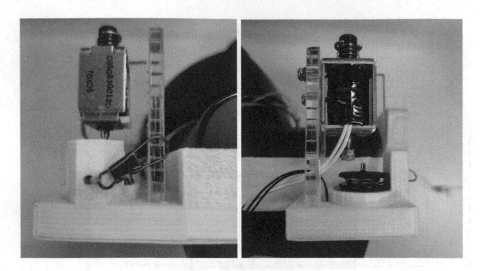

Fig. 5. Brake module

Fig. 6. Solenoid (CBS08300120) [8]

Fig. 7. DC motor (RF-300FA-12350) [9]

presents a feeling of contact. In this state, the user can trace over the fixed string by moving his finger along the string in lateral direction and with a feeling of friction. In addition, a copper plate for thermal sensation presentation is placed so that it touches the skin at the base of the nail, and a small Peltier element (Fig. 9, TES1-1102LT125, Laser Create Corporation) [10] with a heat sink and a thermistor (Fig. 10, 103JT-025, SEMITEC Corporation). [11] for temperature measurement are fixed to the copper plate. When a finger touches a virtual object, the thermal sensations react to the fingertip according to the temperature set for the virtual object.

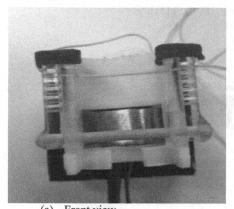   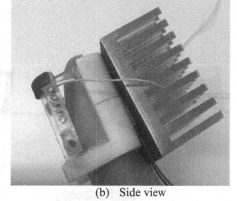

(a)   Front view   (b)   Side view

Fig. 8. End-effector

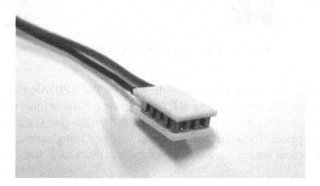

Fig. 9. Peltier element (TES1-1102LT125) [10]

Fig. 10. Thermistor (03JT-025) [11].

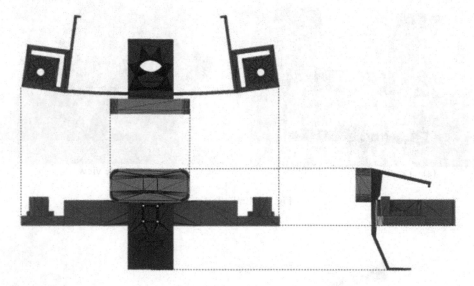

Fig. 11. Three views drawing of the frame

Frame. Figure 11 shows the three-view drawing of the SPIDAR-H&F frame. The frames are all made of resin printed by a 3D printer and consist of three pieces. Red part is a horizontal frame, blue part is a vertical frame, and yellow part is a frame to hold the Leap Motion in place. These frames are fixed together using screws and nuts. The horizontal and vertical frames have claws molded into them such that it can be fixed to the HMD.

Control Circuit Board. The control circuit board shown in Fig. 12 is used for Bluetooth communication with the PC and for controlling the force and thermal sensation presentation. The circuit uses a microcomputer board REWBPIC (Fig. 13, Running Electronics) [12] with PIC24FJ64GB004 [13] to control the motors and the solenoids of the brake modules, the Peltier element of the end-effector, and to read the thermistor thermometer of the end-effector.

Fig. 12. Control circuit board

Fig. 13. Microcomputer board REWBPIC [12]

3.3 Specifications of SPIDAR-H&F

The specifications of SPIDAR-H&F is shown in Table 1. The updated frequency of the sensory presentation is around 250 Hz and the weight of the device excluding the HMD is 561 g.

Table 1. Specifications of SPIDAR-H&F

Maximum force (breaking)	11.88N
Maximum force (motor)	0.90N
Usable zone	Depth < 60 cm, 140 × 120°
Update frequency	250 Hz
Weight (excluding the HMD)	561 g
Dimension (break module) $W \times L \times H$	78 mm × 56 mm × 42 mm
Dimension (end-effector) $W \times L \times H$	34 mm × 41 mm × 34 mm

4 Conclusion and Future Work

4.1 Conclusion

In this study, we improved the encounter-type HMD-integrated SPIDAR-Fr developed in the previous study, and developed SPIDAR-H&F, a device that can present force, tactile, and thermal sensations to both stiff and elastoplastic objects. The proposed device consists of an Oculus Rift S, Leap Motion, brake module, end-effector, and control board. Also, we designed and fabricated a control board that control the brake module and the thermal sensation presentation mechanism of the end-effector, and a frame that fix the Leap Motion and brake module to the Oculus Rift S. Finally, we verified and confirmed the final specifications.

4.2 Future Work

We are planning to conduct an evaluation experiment by constructing a virtual workspace with virtual objects that have various stiffness and temperature to check what kind of haptic experiences this device can provide to users.

References

1. Xu, P., Wu, Z., Wang, X., Fu, Y., He, Y.: An electromyogram-based tapping gesture model with differentiated vibration feedback by low-fidelity actuators. Virtual Real. **25** (2020)
2. Maereg, A.T., Nagar, A., Reid, D., Secco, E.L.: Wearable vibrotactile haptic device for stiffness discrimination during virtual interactions. Front. Robot AI **4**, 42 (2017)
3. Ayyildiz, M., Scaraggi, M., Sirin, O., Basdogan, C., Persson, B.N.J.: Contact mechanics between the human finger and a touchscreen. Proc. Natl. Acad. Sci. U. S. A. **115**(50), 12668–12673 (2018)
4. Berreiros, J., et al.: Fluidic elastomer actuators for haptic interactions in virtual reality. IEEE Robotics Autom. Lett. **4**(2), 277–284 (2019)
5. Yamaguchi, T., et al.: A newly designed string-based encountered-type head-mounted haptic display with having a brake mechanism enabling the sense of friction. In: IEEE World Haptics Conference 2019, July 2019
6. https://www.ultraleap.com/product/leap-motion-controller/. Accessed 14 May 2021
7. https://www.oculus.com/rift-s/. Accessed 14 May 2021
8. https://www.takaha-japan.com/product/cbs0830/. Accessed 14 May 2021
9. https://datasheetspdf.com/pdf-file/787897/MABUCHIMOTOR/RF-300FA-12350/1. Accessed 14 May 2021
10. https://www.lasercreate.com/products/tec/pdf/microTEC_131125.pdf. (in Japanese). Accessed 14 May 2021
11. http://www.semitec.co.jp/english/products/thermo/thermistor/jt/. Accessed 14 May 2021
12. http://www.runele.com/ca4/14/. (in Japanese). Accessed 14 May 2021
13. https://ww1.microchip.com/downloads/en/DeviceDoc/39940d.pdf. Accessed 14 May 2021

"Point at It with Your Smartphone": Assessing the Applicability of Orientation Sensing of Smartphones to Operate IoT Devices

Heinrich Ruser[1]([✉]) [iD] and Ilan Kirsh[2] [iD]

[1] Bundeswehr University Munich, Neubiberg, Germany
heinrich.ruser@unibw.de
[2] The Academic College of Tel Aviv-Yafo, Tel Aviv, Israel
kirsh@mta.ac.il

Abstract. The built-in orientation and motion sensors of smartphones along with their wireless communication abilities are utilized to control connected IoT devices from any place in a room, by pointing at them with the smartphone in the hand. The information of which device is targeted will be derived from the user's actual location, the spatial orientation of the smartphone and pre-knowledge regarding the positions of devices. Chosen devices are remotely operated with simple mid-air gestures performed with the smartphone. The feasibility of this cost-effective approach is assessed by user experiments. The continuous readings of the smartphone's inclination, rotation and magnetic field sensors are recorded with a dedicated freeware app. An algorithm combines the sensor readings to deliver the actual spatial orientation. Our preliminary experiments with different smartphone models and several users show that pointing at defined positions and performing gestures with a smartphone in the user's hand can be accurately sensed without latency and with small deviations of the orientation measurements in the range of up to 5 degrees, indicating the feasibility of this novel approach.

Keywords: Human-centered computing · Human computer interaction · Pointing devices · Universal remote control · Smartphone sensors · User experience

1 Introduction

A way to control technical devices in the living environment in a simple, consistent and intuitive manner would be highly desirable. One of the most intuitive and natural ways to address a visible object in front of the user but beyond the range of touch is to point in its direction with a finger, hand or arm [1]. In order to 'control' the targeted device the user would move a finger, hand or arm 'in the air' to perform basic gestures [2].

As experience shows, we are surprisingly good at pointing with a finger, hand or arm at visible targets in specific spatial directions. User studies (e.g. [3–6]) revealed that despite the parallax between eye and hand, the spatial accuracy of pointing at a target with a finger or arm of the dominant hand is usually below 10° both in horizontal and vertical dimensions.

C. Stephanidis et al. (Eds.): HCII 2021, LNCS 13095, pp. 115–131, 2021.
https://doi.org/10.1007/978-3-030-90963-5_10

The question is how to use this ability of precise direction pointing to control remote devices, i.e. how to address the devices and communicate with them in a flexible, natural and seamless way. We propose to use commodity smartphones for both, selecting a device from a distance and remotely controlling its basic functions.

The state-of-the-art of using smartphones as remote controls in a smart home environment with different appliances (TV sets, music boxes, lights, blinds, fans, etc.) accessible via Bluetooth or WLAN (so called IoT devices) is to launch the device-specific app and select and operate the device via the touchscreen. However, in many situations these display-based smartphone apps are perceived as not very user-friendly: It can be annoying to find the right app on the smartphone followed by maneuvering through menus and touching designated small and slippery 'software buttons' on the touchscreen. With dry, wet, cold or trembling hands, without glasses, being in a dark room or in a hurry or for users with visual impairments or hand movement disorders, this all may be challenging. In addition, the effort is often perceived as disproportionate to the simplicity of the task at hand, like dimming a light or switching off the TV.[1]

Smartphones are truly ubiquitous – most people carry their smartphone at almost all times wherever they are. Besides being a versatile and trusted always-on communication device, a smartphone is also a powerful measuring device, capable of sensing its environment with a variety of built-in-sensors. The ability to sense its spatial orientation can be used for our purpose.

We propose a new type of remote controls: phone-pointing remote apps [7]. Unlike touch-based apps, phone-pointing remote apps can be used with the phone's screen turned off. The interaction scheme is simple and intuitive: With a smartphone in the hand, the user points towards a visible but remote IoT device in a room to select it. Subsequently, holding the smartphone in the hand and performing some specific hand or arm motions 'in the air' the user remotely operates the chosen device, triggering several basic functions, like dimming a ceiling light, lifting window blinds or increasing the volume of a TV set or radio. The control information is sent to the chosen device via wireless communication between the smartphone and the wirelessly accessible IoT device.

Whereas phone-pointing to remotely operate IoT devices appears simple and straightforward, its underlying concept requires the determination of the smartphone's orientation and its localization in a room while using it as a pointing device. From the localization of the smartphone (and the user) and the spatial orientation, the 'pointing projection' will be calculated as a straight line in absolute 3D coordinates. Finally, positions along this projection will be matched with a list of known positions of devices to be remotely operated in that room in order to appoint the selected device.

To the best of our knowledge, there are no such implementations yet. In [7], the system architecture needed to turn ordinary smartphones into highly available, cost effective gesture-based remote controls is laid out. In the present paper, the applicability of the new approach of targeting different IoT objects from various user's

---

[1] Voice user interfaces, while easier to use, can show annoying performance drops due to disturbances from ambient noise or unclear pronunciation. Moreover, they meet reservations from the hesitation to speak to a technical device altogether and raise concerns regarding data privacy issues.

positions based on the information about the direction of pointing the smartphone in the user's hand is addressed.

The remaining of the text is organized as follows. In Sect. 2, related work regarding the usage of smartphones as pointing devices, for orientation sensing and for indoor localization is presented and discussed. In Sect. 3, the operating principles for phone-pointing remote controls are shortly described. In Sect. 4, we present results from experiments to verify the applicability (in terms of accuracy, repeatability and latency) of standard smartphone sensors for effective direction and motion sensing. The results and consequences are discussed in Sect. 5. A conclusion and an outline of future work are given in Sect. 6.

2 Related Work

As the information about the orientation and the localization of the smartphone in the user's hand are prerequisites for the novel approach, related work in these fields is briefly revisited.

2.1 Smartphones Used as Pointing Devices

A variety of approaches have been applied to allow for user interaction by pointing using smartphones, whether relying on direct pointing with attached flashlights or laser pointers, indirect pointing based on camera images or inertial sensing, using accelerometer and gyroscope sensor measurements.

Pointing with wearables has been widely investigated in the context of in-air remote interaction with large displays and screens [8, 9]. Examples are commodity devices like the *AirMouse* or special-purpose controllers like *XWand* [10] or *MagicWand* [11] based on orientation data provided by built-in inertial sensors. Usually, the goal has been to design a precise pointer that is usable simultaneously as an input device ('point-and-select', 'zoom-and-pan', 'drag-and-swipe' selected objects on the screen, etc. [12]) and also an output device (get information from the selected objects and other 'feedback'). A *PointerPhone* [13] was realized by attaching a laser pointer to a mobile phone and using a static camera to track the bright laser dot on the remote screen. Software buttons and fingertip gestures on the phone's touchscreen were proposed to address and manipulate the object pointed at on the remote screen. Re-calibration of the screen's position and orientation is required each time the positions of the camera or the screen change.

Phone-pointing techniques like *SmartCasting* [14] or *TiltCasting* [15] based on the smartphone's built-in inertial sensors have been proposed to be used in Augmented Reality (AR) applications to project the current smartphone display image via ray-casting into the surrounding 3D space. In AR/VR applications wearing a Head-Mounted Display (HDM), smartphones can be useful as virtual joysticks: a good motor control and dexterity are often expected from the users, as well as short selection times [16].

An interesting observation regarding the pointing accuracy of users in front of large screens has been repeatedly made (e.g. [17]): On average, pointing errors were larger when the user was in closer distance to the object displayed on the screen than if the screen was in a larger distance, presumably due to the larger parallax between the eye-to-target line and the arm-to-target line. However, since in closer distance the same object appears larger, the pointing accuracy is less demanding in this case and the larger errors are tolerable.

2.2 Smartphone Sensors for Orientation Sensing

Modern smartphones are equipped with a large number of miniaturized sensors which can be grouped into two categories:

- Position and motion sensors (magnetometer, accelerometer, gyroscope) measuring the strength of the surrounding magnetic field as a 3-component vector and the linear acceleration and rotational velocity of the smartphone along three axes;
- Environmental sensors (front and back cameras, thermometer, barometer, hygrometer, photometer) taking images and measuring the temperature, air pressure, air humidity and illumination.

The measured accelerations along all three axes (azimuth, roll, pitch, see Fig. 1) can be used, for example, to determine the smartphone's absolute 3D orientation (i.e., by what angle the phone is tilted) and to identify time-dependent movements such as rotation, swing or shake.

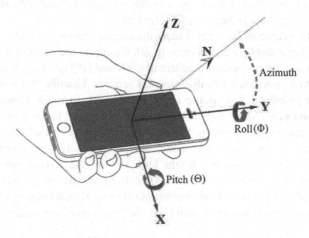

Fig. 1. Three fundamental axes and rotation vectors relative to a smartphone, with azimuth – the rotation angle about axis z (the gravity vector), pitch – the rotation angle about axis x and roll – the rotation angle about axis y. [18]

The angular velocities resulting from the gyroscope measurements describe the change in the rotation angle (pitch, roll and yaw) of the smartphone over time and therefore its relative, time variant orientation in 3D. If the initial orientation is known, the absolute orientation can be determined from it [19]. In most smartphones, the accelerometer and the gyroscope are combined in a miniaturized inertial measurement unit (IMU) [20–22].

In the absence of strong magnetic fields in the phone's proximity, the magnetometer's 3D measurement of the strength of surrounding magnetic fields is dominated by the Earth's magnetic field. From the combination of all 3 components, the absolute global orientation of the smartphone with respect to Magnetic North is derived (compass function) [23]. In Fig. 2, the azimuth angles calculated from measurements of the magnetic field sensor are shown when rotating the smartphone in the horizontal plane (used for calibration) demonstrating the high accuracy and repeatability.

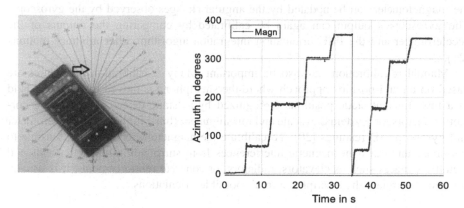

Fig. 2. Exemplary results from different orientation angle measurements using the smartphone's internal 3D magnetic field sensor.

With their constraints in size, weight, and power consumption, the miniaturized smartphone sensors have – compared to laboratory equipment – a restricted sensitivity and measurement range and are affected by noise and external disturbances to a larger extent (e.g. influences from electronic subsystems adjacent to the sensors, the Wi-Fi transceiver, battery, the package material, etc.) as well as can show long-term drifts in their measurements.

To reduce these influences and to suppress outliers and erroneous measurements, state estimation filters such as a Kalman filter and many more advanced algorithms have been applied [24]. Furthermore, the readings from different sensors can be combined and relied on each other and compared to known reference values. Such "software sensors" provide improved, smoothed estimates of the actual acceleration and orientation [25]. The typical update rate is approx. 200 measurements per second for the IMU and 100 measurements per second for the magnetometer, giving a sufficiently dense data stream for post-processing algorithms for many practical applications.

The accuracy of such "software sensors" after refining the raw sensor data was investigated in various studies. [26] confirms the presence of heterogeneities when gathering orientation output data from different smartphone devices pointing in exactly the same direction. For different smartphone models containing different sensor units, the measured orientation showed deviations from references of up to 2.1° and 6.6° for the pitch and roll angles, respectively. The accuracy achievable with smartphone acceleration sensors was shown to be sufficient for a successful recognition of unistroke symbols or letters written 'in the air' [27, 28].

A common way to improve the estimate of the absolute orientation is to combine (fuse) the readings from the IMU and the magnetometer, under the condition that the perpendicular axes of both sensors are aligned [29]. To ensure this, an occasional *re-calibration* has to be performed to correct for observed misalignments between the axes. Such automatic re-calibration could be performed e.g. at time intervals when the acceleration is measured only in the direction of gravity and the accelerations along the other axes are (almost) zero [30, 31]. Similarly, the (absolute) orientation angle from the magnetometer can be updated by the angular changes observed by the gyroscope. The gyroscope's output can again be calibrated by comparing the outputs of the accelerometer and the IMU orientation integration algorithm, after arbitrary motions [21].

Manual re-calibration can also be important. Many re-calibration procedures are based on a multi-position approach where the smartphone is moved by hand and held in a few different static positions (recognized by a 'static detector'), providing correction factors for (systematic) scale and misalignment (bias) for both the accelerometer and gyroscope 3D readings [29]. To calibrate the magnetometer, which is sensible to stationary and transient magnetic interferences from surrounding magnetic fields and metallic surfaces such as elevators, radiators, or concrete reinforcements, it is usually suggested to rotate the smartphone in all possible orientations.

2.3   Indoor Location Techniques with Smartphones

Using smartphones for indoor positioning is attractive for many applications where the ability to independently track people is important, e.g. in large offices or hospitals, factories and warehouses. A large variety of location techniques have been proposed and the obtained localization accuracies along with the effort and cost to achieve them have been extensively studied (see [25, 32, 33] for large in-depth surveys). During the Microsoft Indoor Localization Competition, organized in several rounds over the years 2014–2017, more than 100 teams from academia and industry deployed their indoor location solutions in quasi-realistic environments, allowing to directly compare the achieved accuracies and deployment costs [34].

However, no standard method has been brought up to date that would guarantee a similar accuracy, repeatability and seamless availability in indoor environments that global navigation satellite systems (GNSS) offer outdoors. Often, the average accuracy remains inadequate for many applications. Challenges for accurate indoor localization stem from the lack of a dense grid of absolute references for the built-in smartphones sensors for (occasional) re-calibration, the often complex indoor interior design enhancing multipath propagation or shadowing and the building materials themselves which distort or block radio and satellite signals. A major challenge for many localization-based systems, however, is the requirement for these systems to reliably track pedestrians in a highly dynamic environment, e.g., while they are walking with the smartphone in their pocket. As will be explained in Sect. 3, our application is different in this respect.

Generally, for indoor localization sensing with smartphones infrastructure-based and infrastructure-free approaches can be distinguished. Infrastructure-based approaches rely on the purposeful, optimized deployment of Bluetooth (BLE) beacons, or customized radio-frequency (RF), visible or infrared light sources or ultrasound transmitters. The signals transmitted by those beacons are picked up by appropriate smartphone sensors and translated into positions from the proximity to the closest beacon (BLE) or from the travel time of modulated signals, e.g. Ultra-Wide-Band (UWB), from the source. Often, the deployment costs remain high: Special-purpose hardware needs to be carefully deployed and hardwired or battery-powered in every area where indoor location services are needed. Whereas BLE proximity estimation allows only for a low average accuracy of about 3 to 10 m, most infrastructure-based techniques are reported to achieve localization accuracies of about 2 to 3 m in standard indoor scenarios [33].

Most infrastructure-free approaches focus on exploiting existing Wi-Fi signals from WLAN access points [35, 36], others on ambient FM radio or TV signals, geomagnetic or sound signals. As the source for indoor localization, a received signal strength (RSS) indicator is used, both for (manually) building an RSS distribution map of the ubiquitous signals in the specific indoor environment (a laborious work called 'fingerprinting') and later for finding the actual localization by matching the measured RSS to this map. Generally, the map will not be dense enough or the RSS will be unstable and distorted and hence the achievable accuracy is generally not better than 3 to 5 m [36]. A fine-timing protocol called *Wi-Fi location* includes the time it takes for the Wi-Fi signal to travel, enabling position estimation with improved accuracy of up to about 2 m [37].

Surveys revealed that due to its constant availability and high sensitivity, the best positioning accuracy could be achieved at no extra cost relying on the built-in IMU (e.g. [33, 34]). Based on double-integrating the continuously measures accelerations, the current position of the device is determined by accumulating the path vector from a known starting position (a class of techniques called 'dead reckoning'). However, small acceleration errors can rapidly accumulate to large positional errors of several meters [38]. If frequent re-calibration at reference points could be applied, e.g. at zero-points of the acceleration, the localization accuracy could be greatly improved [30].

Many realizations have been described which combine different technologies (hybrid systems) to improve the accuracy and availability of position estimates [25, 39]. For example, using IMU and WiFi RSS indicator readings and combining dead reckoning and a fingerprinting technique, localization accuracies in the range of 1 m could be achieved [32, 40]. In Table 1, average localization accuracies for selected smartphone sensors and sensor combinations are summarized.

Table.1 Average localization accuracies achieved with selected smartphone sensors and sensor combinations (adapted from [32, 33, 40]).

	Sensor	Sensor information (technique)	Approx. sampling rate per sec.	Average localization accuracy
Infra-structure-free	Magnetometer	Orientation (compass)	100	2...10° (static) (= 0.2...0.7 m in 4 m dist.)
	Accelerometer + gyroscope (IMU)	Orientation (azimuth, pitch) (dead reckoning)	200	1...3° (static) (= 0.1...0.2 m in 4 m dist.) 1...2 m
	IMU + Magnetometer	Orientation (compass + PDR)	100	0.3...1 m (static) 1.5...2.5 m (dynamic)
	Camera	Image series (optical flow)	20	2...3 m
	Barometer	Relative height (air pressure)	10	0.3...1 m
Infra-structure-based	GNSS	Global position	1	5...50 m
	WiFi	RSSI (Fingerprinting)	0.5	2...10 m
	Bluetooth	RSSI (Time difference of arrival)	1	3...10 m
	Photosensor	Position of light sources (illumination)	10	0.3...2 m
	Acoustic, Ultrasound	Distance to walls (Time of flight)	20	0.2...0.5 m

3   Operation Principles

We propose a universal, gesture-based remote control for operating electronic devices in the living environment, which would be very easy, almost intuitively to use. The built-in orientation and motion sensors of smartphones (magnetometer, accelerometer, gyroscope) along with their wireless communication abilities are utilized to control connected IoT devices in a room by pointing at them with the smartphone in the hand. The information of which device is targeted will be derived from the user's actual location, the spatial orientation of the smartphone and pre-knowledge regarding the positions of devices to be remotely operated.

A device would be marked as selected when three states are registered by the app: 1) The smartphone is pointed at a certain point in space for a longer while (i.e. the 3D coordinates of the smartphone's orientation are almost stable during a period of 1...2 s), 2) the projection of this orientation (roughly) matches with a 3D position from a stored list of devices' positions, and 3) the inclination (pitch angle) data show a short tilting or 'ticking' moment, which would stem from a natural and intuitive hand gesture by the user to confirm this selection. This 3-stage confirmation is to avoid any device to be accidentally operated by motions of the smartphone while using it for other purposes than as a remote control.

Selecting the right devices requires the app to find out the smartphone's (and hence the user's) approximate location in an indoor environment. Compared to many dynamic position-tracking applications where even approximate indoor position location finding with smartphones might be difficult (see Table 1), this problem would be facilitated here since during the process of device selection many parameters (e.g. the user's position, the smartphone's orientation) change very slowly and the number of potential positions a certain device might be selected from would be limited (by the size of the room, furniture, etc.) and/or known from previously recorded observations and teachings. Hence, the promising results from other studies for the localization accuracy obtained for IMU or magnetometer readings for static situations give positive indications regarding the feasibility of our approach.

After selecting a device by pointing at it with the smartphone, the user can specify an operation using movement gestures with the arm or hand while still holding the smartphone. A gesture is carried out with the hand-held smartphone describing 'a trajectory in the air'. For example, an upward forearm movement or a quick tilting of the smartphone (as to make a 'tick') can signal turn-on, whereas a downward movement can signal turn-off. Similarly, a clockwise rotation can signal volume-up, whereas a rotation in the opposite direction, counterclockwise, can signal volume-down. Only the relevant, intended part of the trajectory is evaluated for recognition; the delivery and final movements are discarded. By assigning the trajectory features to one of the predefined gesture classes, the gesture is automatically recognized. Knowing the basic gestures to remotely operate the main functions of the selected device, the recognized gestures can be automatically decoded by the app into device-specific commands (see Table 2).

Table.2 Example of a simple gesture lexicon and possible associated functions.

Gesture:				Could be associated with:	
No.	Acronym	Action	Trajectory	Device	Function
1	ON	Point at it, tilt	—	Lamp	Switch on
2	OF	Point at it, tilt	—		Switch off
3	UP	Move hand or arm straight bottom-up	Line bottom-up	Blind	Lift/open
4	DN	Move hand or arm straight top-down	Line top-down		Lower/close
5	LR	Move hand or arm straight left-to-right	Line left-to-right	Radio	Volume higher
6	RL	Move hand or arm straight right-to-left	Line right-to-left		Volume lower
7	CR	Turn/rotate hand or arm to the right	Circle or ellipse clockwise	Heater	Warmer
8	CL	Turn/rotate hand or arm to the left	Circle or ellipse counterclockwise		Colder

The exact gestures can vary from one implementation to another and could be customized by the user [41, 42]. The device-specific 'meaning' of the gestures performed with the smartphone in the user's hand will be sent wirelessly to the selected IoT device. The use of device-specific and also personalized gestures can be 'learned' by the app in a similar way: Users would demonstrate selections of devices by pointing at them from relevant locations and demonstrate gestures to remotely operate different functions of these IoT devices by arm and hand movements.

4 Experimental Results

The accuracy and consistency of orientation measurement were evaluated via offline calculation of experimental data, collected using a dedicated freeware app[2]. An algorithm combined and filtered the sensor readings to deliver the actual 3D orientation angles.

To make users consecutively point at specific positions in a room, a test room was prepared for the experiments with different numbered post-its ('markers') attached to different positions on a wall, in various spacings from 15 cm to 60 cm, horizontally and vertically, in heights from 0.5 m up to 2 m above the floor.

The user experiments were conducted as follows: Every user takes a position marked on the floor in a certain distance to the wall and starts recording the measurements of the built-in sensors via the dedicated app by touching the start/stop button on the smartphone's touchscreen. The user then points at a visible marker holding the smartphone with the upper edge (i.e. along the y axis, see Fig. 1) towards the marker for a short time, and possibly shortly ticks the smartphone to indicate the selection of an (imaginary) device at the marker's position. No "dry run" was performed for familiarizing the user with either the smartphone interface or the task. The user may then choose to point at additional markers consecutively in time. The position and orientation sensor readings are continuously recorded with a rate of approx. 100 measurements per second.

The data recording is continued until the user presses the smart/stop button on the touchscreen again. All recorded data are stored in a data sheet which after stopping the recording is ready to be sent from the smartphone to the computer to be further processed and visualized.

At this early stage of our investigations, the post-processing is limited to baseline reduction, phase-wrapping and motion detection, as to highlight the quasi-static orientation measurements (pointing) and differ them from the dynamic states (= motion between pointing instants; gestures). So far, no further automatic re-calibration has been carried out.

Figure 3 shows results from continued azimuth and pitch angle measurement with a smartphone held in the user's hand. Here, the user turns from West (270°) to South (180°) and back 4 times. In Fig. 3 the effect of tilting the smartphone while pointing (as to switch an imaginary device on or off) is also shown.

---

[2] Physics Toolbox Sensor Suite, https://www.vieyrasoftware.net/.

Figure 4 shows the potentially high pointing precision and accuracy. The test person consecutively swapped between pointing at two markers in a small distance to each other (15 cm horizontally). The absolute displacements of the smartphone's pointing positions were calculated from the known distance from the person's position to the markers (approx. 2.5 m here).

Figures 5 shows results from continued azimuth and pitch angle measurements when pointing the smartphone consecutively at different markers (their positions indicated as crosses in the 2D area plot). Below, the histograms of the azimuth and pitch measurements are given, showing a high precision (mean and maximum width of the histogram) and accuracy (deviation from the marker's azimuth positions).

Accuracies in the range of $\pm 5°$ can be achieved in detecting the direction of pointing with a smartphone. This accuracy range indicates the consistency of the user

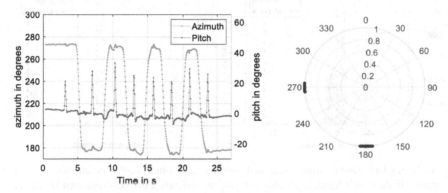

Fig. 3. (Left) Results from continued azimuth and pitch angle measurement with a smartphone held in the user's hand. Here, the user turns from West (270°) to South (180°) and back 4 times. Every time when pointing at these directions, the user slightly tilts the smartphone to indicate the wish to operate a device. (Right) Polar view of the azimuth angles when the smartphone is not moved and rests in the hand.

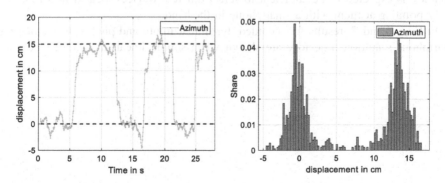

Fig. 4. Exemplary results from continued azimuth angle measurements with a smartphone in the user's hand, as a function of time (left) and histogram (right), when repeatedly pointing at two reference markers separated horizontally by 15 cm, from a distance of 2.5 m.

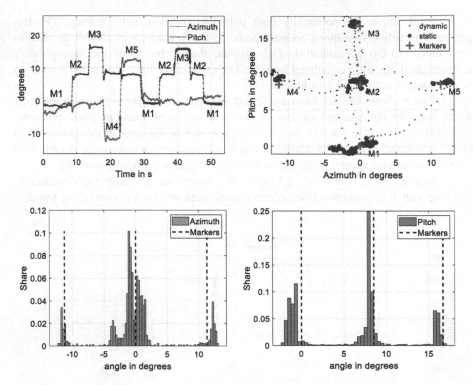

Fig. 5. Exemplary results from continued azimuth and pitch angle measurements with a smartphone in the user's hand, repeatedly pointing at 5 reference markers separated horizontally and vertically by 30 cm, from a distance of 2.5 m: Azimuth and pitch as a function of time and 2D plot of the orientation measurements (upper row), histograms of static azimuth and pitch measurements compared to the positions of markers (lower row).

operations rather than merely of the sensor measurements. For most applications, this accuracy is expected to be sufficient to select different devices located in a room by freely pointing at them with a smartphone in the hand.

In Figs. 6 and 7, results for recorded dynamic azimuth and pitch values along the smartphone's motion trajectory are shown when simple linear and circular gestures

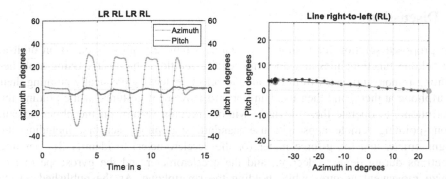

Fig. 6. (Left) Results from continued azimuth and pitch angle measurements with a smartphone in the user's hand, performing several left-right movements (Right) Trajectory in a chosen time interval and recognized gesture (in green). (Color figure online)

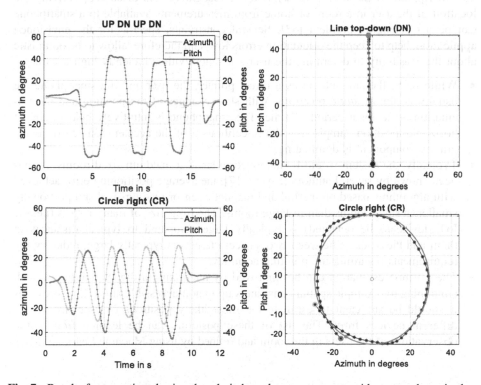

Fig. 7. Results from continued azimuth and pitch angle measurements with a smartphone in the user's hand, performing several straight up-down movements (top row) and clockwise circles (bottom row). In the right column, the performed trajectory of a chosen time interval along with the recognized gesture (in green) are shown. (Color figure online)

from the gestures lexicon are performed. To contribute those trajectories to several gesture classes, approximation fits of straight lines or ellipses are calculated.

5 Discussion

The proposed solution for a simplified seamless remote control is based on built-in smartphone functionalities and does not require additional hardware. Using a phone-pointing remote app, users would be able to select devices by physically pointing their smartphone at them, and then use hand or arm movement gestures, while holding the smartphone, to operate these devices, without needing to turn on the phone screen. Phone-pointing remote apps will use standard smartphone sensors, including the magnetometer and the g-force meter (or the accelerometer) to identify 3D pointing directions during device selection, and the accelerometer and the gyroscope to recognize movement gestures while holding the smartphone. As the published results revealed and our experiments confirm (see Sect. 4), the smartphone's spatial orientation is sensed by the built-in position sensors with high accuracy.

In order to use the smartphone as a direct pointing device, the current location of the smartphone in the users' hand has to be recognized. As discussed, deriving the location of the user in a room or home from measurements available to a smartphone can be a challenging problem [33]. Several constraints, specific for the envisioned application, help to keep the orientation errors low, and therefore, allow to be optimistic about the feasibility to determine the user's location with sufficiently high accuracy:

- While using the smartphone as a direct pointer, the user and the smartphone are usually at almost *static* positions, with slow changes of the position and the orientation angle for a period of time. The smartphone is intuitively held in almost horizontal position, simplifying the re-calibration of the acceleration sensor as the gravity component is dominating.
- Typically, the system would be deployed in small to medium sized rooms. As has been shown by several authors (e.g. [6, 17], the average positioning error achieved with algorithms based on inertial and magnetic sensor readings is disproportionally smaller in small rooms than in large rooms. The front size of many targets (i.e. the IoT device to be operated) is typically large compared to typical distances to them and the distance between two adjacent targets is typically large, reducing the requirements regarding the pointing accuracy.
- The position estimation can be improved by integrating a digital building model, containing for example spatial constraints up to non-accessible areas. In many cases it should be sufficient to estimate the most likely positions of users to operate different devices from. The list of these positions can be learned from initial observations of the users in the room and refined by using Machine Learning (ML).

6 Conclusion and Future Work

Commodity smartphones can be turned into ubiquitous, easy-to-use, intuitive gesture-based remote controls by making use of their built-in orientation sensors and wireless communication. Accordingly, they may be used as general-purpose, user-friendly alternatives to existing touch, voice or camera-based smart home interfaces, without the requirement of any extra hardware. We envisage that the proposed approach could be adapted to other contexts of mid-air interactions with multiple devices, beyond the smart home environment, like for example larger-range gestural interactions in workshops or factory halls, technology-enhanced public spaces, etc. with the aim to improve its usability, intuitiveness and experience.

We presented a novel approach to remote controlling, which combines smartphones with hand movement gestures. Unlike conventional remote control apps that use the smartphone touchscreen for input, with this approach, the phone's screen can remain turned off. Users select devices by pointing at them with their smartphone, and then use hand movements, while still holding the smartphone, to operate those devices. Although mobile phone-based interactions with remote screens have been investigated in the past, they have not been considered for applications in everyday tasks.

The promising results of preliminary experiments carried out with several users and with different smartphone models show that the novel remote control allows to accurately point at specific spatial markers without guidance or feedback (like visible dots from laser pointers). This is achievable with sufficient accuracy and repeatability, unaffected by the distances to the targeted device, obstructions along the imaginary line to that target or the ambient light conditions. Based on a high-quality orientation and motion reconstruction, with an improved separation between gesture classes the list of preferred quasi-intuitive gestures can be largely extended (including 'numbers' and other multi-stroke gestures), hence more devices and functions could be added.

As next steps, extensive validation tests to be deployed in the living environments of a larger number of test persons will be conducted and issues towards a real-time implementation of a phone-pointing app will be addressed.

References

1. Clark, H.H.: Pointing and placing. In: Kita, S. (ed.) Pointing: Where Language, Culture, and Cognition Meet, pp. 243–268. Taylor & Francis (2003)
2. Cartmill, E.A., Beilock, S., Goldin-Meadow, S.: A word in the hand: action, gesture and mental representation in humans and non-human primates. Philos. Trans. R. Soc Part B **367**(1585), 129–143 (2012)
3. Wong, N., Gutwin, C.: Where are you pointing? The accuracy of deictic pointing in CVEs. In: Proceedings of the CHI, pp. 1029–1038 (2010)
4. Cockburn, A., Quinn, P., Gutwin, C., Ramos, G., Looser, J.: Air pointing: design and evaluation of spatial target acquisition with and without visual feedback. Int. J. Hum. Comput. Stud., 401–414 (2011)
5. Akkil, D., Isokoski, P.: Accuracy of interpreting pointing gestures in egocentric view. In: Ubicomp 2016, Heidelberg (2016)
6. Flanagin, V.L., Fisher, P., Olcay, B., Kohlbecher, S., Brandt, T.: A bedside application-based assessment of spatial orientation and memory: approaches and lessons learned. J. Neurol. **266**(1), 126–138 (2019). https://doi.org/10.1007/s00415-019-09409-7
7. Kirsh, I., Ruser, H.: Phone-pointing remote app: using smartphones as pointers in gesture-based IoT remote controls. In: Stephanidis, C., Antona, M., Ntoa, S. (eds.) HCII 2021. CCIS, vol. 1420, pp. 14–21. Springer, Cham (2021). https://doi.org/10.1007/978-3-030-78642-7_3

8. Jota, R., Nacenta, M. Jorge, J., Carpendale, Sh., Greenberg, S: A comparison of ray pointing techniques for very large displays. In: ACM 36th Graphics Interface Conference, Ottawa (2010)

9. Nancel, M., Chapuis, O., Pietriga, E., Yang, X., Irani, P., Beaudouin-Lafon, M.: High-precision pointing on large wall displays using small handheld devices. In: Proceedings of the Conference on Human Factors in Computing Systems (CHI 2013), pp. 831–840 (2013)

10. Wilson, A., Shafer St.: XWand: UI for intelligent spaces. In: Proceedings of the Conference on Human Factors in Computing Systems (CHI 2003), pp. 545–552 (2003)

11. Ouchi, K., Esaka, N., Tamura, Y., Hirahara, M., Doi, M.: MagicWand: an intuitive gesture remote control for home appliances. In: IEEE International Conference on Active Media Technology (2005)

12. Spindler, M., Schuessler, M., Martsch, M., Dachselt R: Move your phone: spatial input-based document zoom & pan on mobile displays revisited. In: CHI 2014 Extended Abstracts on Human Factors in Computing Systems (CHI EA 2014), pp. 515–518 (2014)

13. Seifert, J., Bayer, A., Rukzio, E.: PointerPhone: using mobile phones for direct pointing interactions with remote displays. In: Kotzé, P., Marsden, G., Lindgaard, G., Wesson, J., Winckler, M. (eds.) INTERACT 2013. LNCS, vol. 8119, pp. 18–35. Springer, Heidelberg (2013). https://doi.org/10.1007/978-3-642-40477-1_2

14. Pietroszek, K., Kuzminykh, A., Wallace, J.R., Lank E.: Smartcasting: a discount 3D interaction technique for public displays. In: 26th Australian Computer-Human Interaction Conference on Designing Futures (OzCHI 2014), pp. 119–128 (2014)

15. Pietroszek, K., Wallace, J., Lank, E.: Tiltcasting: 3D interaction on large displays using a mobile device. In: Proceedings of the 28th ACM Symposium on User Interface Software & Technology (UIST 2015), pp. 57–62 (2015)

16. Hartmann, J., Vogel, D.: An evaluation of mobile phone pointing in spatial augmented reality. In CHI 2018 Extended Abstracts on Human Factors in Computing Systems (CHI EA 2018) (2018)

17. Plaumann, K., Weing, M., Winkler, C., Müller, M., Rukzio, E.: Towards accurate cursorless pointing: the effects of ocular dominance and handedness. Pers. Ubiquit. Comput. 22(4), 633–646 (2017). https://doi.org/10.1007/s00779-017-1100-7

18. Hosseinianfar, H., Chizari, A., Salehi, J.A.: GOPA: geometrical optics positioning algorithm using spatial color coded LEDs. arXiv:1807.06931v1 (2018)

19. Sato, K., Matsushita, M.: Object manipulation by absolute pointing with a smartphone gyro sensor. In: ACM Symposium on Spatial User Interaction (SUI 2019), New Orleans (2019)

20. Alce, G., Espinoza, A., Hartzell, T., Olsson, St., Samuelsson, D., Wallergård, M.: UbiCompass: an IoT interaction concept. Adv. Hum. Comput. Interact. 2018, Article ID 5781363 (2018)

21. Solin, A., Cortes, S., Rahtu, E., Kannala, J. Inertial odometry on handheld smartphones. In: 21st IEEE International Conference on Information Fusion (FUSION), pp. 1–5 (2018)

22. Gromov, B., Abbate, G., Gambardella, L., Giusti A.: Proximity human-robot interaction using pointing gestures and a wrist-mounted IMU. In: International Conference on Robotics and Automation (ICRA) (2019)

23. Odenwald, S.: Smartphone sensors for citizen science applications: radioactivity and magnetism. Citiz. Sci. Theory Pract. 4(1), 18, pp. 1–15 (2019)

24. Umek, A., Kos, A.: Validation of smartphone gyroscopes for mobile biofeedback applications. Pers. Ubiquitous Comput. 20, 657–666 (2016). https://doi.org/10.1007/s00779-016-0946-4

25. Correa, A., Barcelo, M., Morell, A., Vicario, J.L.: A review of pedestrian indoor positioning systems for mass market applications. Sensors 17(8), ID 1927 (2017)

26. Kuhlmann, T., Garaizar, P., Reips, U.-D.: Smartphone sensor accuracy varies from device to device in mobile research: the case of spatial orientation. Behav. Res. Methods **53**(1), 22–33 (2020). https://doi.org/10.3758/s13428-020-01404-5

27. Kela, J., Korpipää, P., Mäntyjärvi, J., Kallio, S., Savino, G.: Accelerometer-based gesture control for a design environment. ACM Pers. Ubiquitous Comput. **10**(5), 285–299 (2006)

28. Agrawal, S., Constandache, I., Gaonkar, Sh., Choudhury, R.R.: Using mobile phones to write in air. In: International Conference on Mobile Systems, Applications, and Services (MobiSys 2011), pp. 15–28. ACM (2011)

29. Kok, M., Schön, T.: Magnetometer calibration using inertial sensors. IEEE Sens. J. **16**(14), 5679–5689 (2016)

30. Li, X., Li, Z.: A new calibration method for tri-axial field sensors in strap-down navigation systems. Meas. Sci. Technol. **23**(10), 105105 (2012)

31. Salehi, S., Mostofi, N., Bleser, G.: A practical in-field magnetometer calibration method for IMUs. In: Proceedings of the IROS Workshop on Cognitive Assistive Systems: Closing the Action-Perception Loop, pp. 39–44 (2012)

32. Langlois, Ch., Tiku, S, Pasricha, S.: Indoor localization with smartphones. IEEE Consum. Electron. Mag. **10**(17), 70–80 (2017)

33. Nguyen, K.A., Luo, Zh., Li, G., Watkins, Ch.: A review of smartphones based indoor positioning: challenges and applications. IET Cybersyst. Robotics **3**(1), 1–30 (2021)

34. Lymberopoulos, D., Liu, J.: The microsoft indoor localization competition: experiences and lessons learned. IEEE Signal Process. Mag. **09**(17), 125–140 (2017)

35. Ashraf, I., Hur, S., Park, Y.: Indoor positioning on disparate commercial smartphones using wi-fi access points coverage area. Sensors **19**(19), 4351 (2019)

36. Retscher, G.: Fundamental concepts and evolution of wi-fi user localization: an overview based on different case studies. Sensors **20**(18), 5121 (2020)

37. Khalajmehrabadi, A., Gatsis, N., Akopian, D.: Modern WLAN fingerprinting indoor positioning methods and deployment challenges. IEEE Commun. Surv. Tutor. **19**(3), 1974–2002 (2017)

38. Real Ehrlich, C., Blankenbach J.: Indoor localization for pedestrians with real-time capability using multi-sensor smartphones. Geo-spat. Inf. Sci. (2019). https://doi.org/10.1080/10095020.2019.1613778

39. Pascacio, P., Casteleyn, S., Torres Sospedra, J.: Collaborative indoor positioning systems: a systematic review. Sensors **21**(3), 1002 (2021)

40. Landau, Y., Ben-Moshe, B.: STEPS: an indoor navigation framework for mobile devices. Sensors **20**(14), 3929 (2020)

41. Mezari, A., Maglogiannis, I.; An easily customized gesture recognizer for assisted living using commodity mobile devices. J. Healthc. Eng. **2018**, Article ID 3180652 (2018)

42. Madapana, N., Gonzalez, G., Zhang, L., Rodgers, R., Wachs, J.: Agreement study using gesture description analysis. IEEE Trans. Hum. Mach. Syst. **50**(5), 434–443 (2020)

Real-Time Estimation of Eye Movement Condition Using a Deep Learning Model

Akihiro Sugiura[1(✉)], Yoshiki Itazu[2], Kunihiko Tanaka[1], and Hiroki Takada[2]

[1] Gifu University of Medical Science, Seki, Gifu 454-0822, Japan
asugiura@u-gifu-ms.ac.jp
[2] Fukui University, Fukui 910-8507, Japan

Abstract. In this study, we conducted a basic investigation involving the discrimination of eye movement condition (peripheral and central vision) using deep learning techniques. The subjects were 6 males aged 21–23 years. They watched two three-minute videos for central vision and peripheral vision in a random order for a total of eight sessions (four sessions each). The subjects wore an eye movement measurement device, and their eye movements (viewing angles) during the viewing of each video were continuously. From the time series data for eye movement, with four different lengths (0.5 s, 1 s, 2 s, 3 s) and shift length of 0.5 s, short time series data for each 3 min was obtained in sets of 350, and the data were utilized for deep learning and its evaluation. For the deep learning model, input nodes according to data length were placed in the input layer. For the middle layer, seven to eight units were put in place that brought together the one-dimensional convolution layer, the batch-normalization layer, normalized linear function, and the max-pooling layer. The output layer consisted of the fully-connected layer, sigmoid function, and multi-class cross-entropy. As a result, the accuracy of the discrimination was improved as the data length increased, and it was possible to determine the condition with an accuracy of over 90% if the eye movement data was at least one second.

Keywords: Deep learning · Eye movement · Classification · Peripheral vision · Central vision · Convolutional Neural Network

1 Introduction

Dementia is a syndrome in which the capacity for memory, thought, behavior, and daily life activities is lowered. There are 50 million people with dementia worldwide, and 10 million new cases each year [1]. The symptoms of dementia can be broadly classified into "core symptoms" and peripheral symptoms called "behavioral and psychological symptoms of dementia" (BPSD) [2, 3]. Core symptoms include complete or partial loss of short-term or episodic memory, impaired orientation, executive dysfunction, and impairment of understanding and judgment in general. In BPSD, on the other hand, behavioral and psychological symptoms (peripheral symptoms) occur that are a complex combination of changes in mental status caused by core symptoms (strong anxiety and confusion, low self-esteem, etc.) and factors such as the surrounding environment, the

C. Stephanidis et al. (Eds.): HCII 2021, LNCS 13095, pp. 132–143, 2021.
https://doi.org/10.1007/978-3-030-90963-5_11

responses of others, and one's own experiences and personality. These symptoms include agitation, violence and verbal abuse, refusal of care, depression, anxiety, apathy, wandering, delusions, and hallucinations. These diverse symptoms develop and become severe as the condition progresses. Although dementia occurs primarily in the elderly, the symptoms show that it is not a normal phenomenon of aging. Dementia is a major cause of disability and dependency on care, and comprehensive measures are required, because it has physical, psychological, and socioeconomic effects for the person concerned, as well as the caregiver, the individual's family, and society. Because there is currently no cure for dementia, initiatives on the preventive side are particularly important.

Mild cognitive impairment (MCI) has received much attention in recent years [4, 5]. MCI is a condition that involves problems with some cognitive functions but does not interfere with daily life. There is thus concern over delayed detection and treatment. The percentage of people who progress to dementia from MCI is 10% per year [6], and it is estimated that about 40% of people will transition to dementia over 5 years. However, it has been suggested that early detection and treatment can potentially suppress the progression of MCI, with the possibility of recovery. Initiatives addressing lifestyle habits, such as diet and exercise, and social participation activities that are effective in maintaining and promoting cognitive function are expected to help [7, 8].

Decreased visual function is associated with symptoms of MCI. In an epidemiological study conducted in the United States on 635 older adults with cognitive impairment such as Alzheimer's disease, the patients were followed for more than 8 years in relation to visual function, and it was found that those in the favorable visual acuity group had a 63% lower risk of developing dementia [9]. In particular, visuospatial cognitive impairment is a common symptom observed in Alzheimer's dementia, and this shows that there is potentially a strong association between cognitive impairment and visual decline. It is therefore assumed that the promotion of strategic eye movement for visual function improvement is effective, because controlling decreases in visual function can potentially contribute to the prevention of dementia. Meanwhile, there remains the problem of whether the eye movement required by researchers for video observation is being carried out reliably. Visual confirmation of objects is broadly classified into the process carried out by the central visual field (hereafter, central vision) and the process carried out by the peripheral visual field (hereafter, peripheral vision), and eye movement also depends on the features of the visual confirmation method. Because the condition of eye movements changes easily depending on which visual confirmation method is used, it becomes important to monitor the state of eye movements in real time during observation. Therefore, in this study, we conducted a basic investigation involving discrimination of eye movement condition (peripheral and central vision) using deep learning technology.

2 Materials and Methods

2.1 Visual Stimulation and Eye Movements

Two videos were prepared for the experiment to efficiently elicit specific eye movements. Figure 1(a) shows a still image of the video for the central vision, and Fig. 1(b) shows a still image of the video for the peripheral vision. These videos were produced using computer graphics (CG) software. Multiple dots were arranged at random positions in the video, and movement of the entire image was realized by moving the CG camera in the space in a sinusoidal movement in a horizontal direction and a vertical direction at 0.25 Hz. As for the difference between the two videos, it was only the presence or absence of a gaze point. The yellow dot in (a) is the gaze point, which moved in the same way as the blue dot in the periphery. By continuing to follow this yellow dot, the gaze point was always captured in the central visual field. In contrast, in the video for peripheral vision, the subjects' gaze was not fixed, and the entire image would always be captured mainly in the peripheral visual field since subjects consciously tried to see the entire screen.

When visual confirmation of the entire screen of uniformly moving images is carried out with visual pursuit and central vision, unique eye movements can be observed. If the gaze point is continuously captured by the central vision, the line of sight is always fixed to the gaze point, and eyeball movement is dependent on the movement of the gaze point. In video (a), it is assumed that smooth pursuit eye movement of sinusoidal movement of 0.25 Hz is performed, because the gaze point is moving sinusoidally left/right and up/down at 0.25 Hz. In contrast, in video (b), given that visual stimulation has been input with the entire screen moving as one, it is assumed that there is slow eye movement (slow phase) and eye movement called optokinetic nystagmus (OKN), in which rapid eye movements (rapid phase) are repeated in reverse to the slow phase for resetting. Given that different eye movements are performed in central and peripheral vision, they can be distinguished by their characteristics. Meanwhile, in order to carry out discrimination of eye movements in real-time during video observation, which was the subject of our investigation, it is necessary to carry out discrimination from very short duration measurement results, and it can be said that evaluation using statistical attributes and analysis of frequency can be difficult. Consequently, in this study, we attempted a discrimination method that differed from conventional methods, using machine learning (deep learning technology).

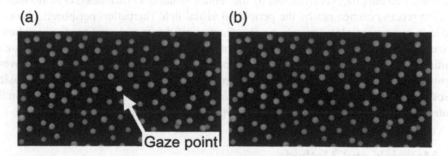

Fig. 1. Experiment video images: (a) Video image for central vision, (b) video image for peripheral vision2

2.2 Deep Learning

Deep learning is a machine learning technique that has attracted attention in recent years. Machine learning using an artificial neural network with multiple layers in the middle layer (Fig. 2) is called deep learning. In deep learning, there are learning methods that include supervised learning, unsupervised learning, and reinforcement learning, but in this study, we will only explain supervised learning, as only supervised learning was used in our study.

In supervised learning, a machine learns based on pre-specified correct answer labels, thereby optimizing the neural network model, and a model is constructed in which predictions are carried out as response values for a dataset. Conventional single-layer neural network models involve entries being made, manual extraction of attributes from certain data, and the use of attributes and data sets with correct answer labels. In contrast, in deep learning, the extraction of attributes is also carried out in the neural network, so manual extraction of attributes becomes unnecessary. In this study, eye movement angle data and viewing methods (central vision, peripheral vision) as correct answer labels were used as datasets.

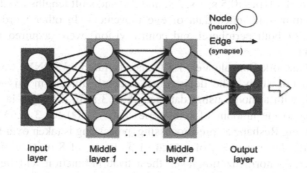

Fig. 2. Schematic representation of a deep neural network

2.3 Procedure and Design

Six healthy 21-to-23-year-old males (with vision correction used if necessary) were included in the study. Figure 3 shows a subject viewing the video. Subjects viewed peripheral and central vision movies on a 42-in. monitor with their chin on a chin rest 1 m away from the monitor, under an environment of approximately 10lx of ambient illuminance. After prior practice using central vision and peripheral vision with the experiment videos, a total of eight three-minute central vision videos and peripheral vision videos (four each) were observed in random order with small breaks in between. To record eye movements during video viewing, an eye movement measurement device based on the scleral reflection method (Manufactured by Takei Scientific Instruments Co., Ltd.) was attached in front of the subject's right eye. Eye movements (viewing angles) during each video viewing were continuously recorded at 500 Hz for the horizontal/vertical and left/right directions.

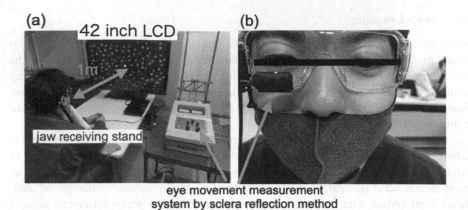

Fig. 3. Experiment set-up and eye movement measurement4

To verify the classification accuracy depending on different data lengths, we acquired short-duration series data in sets of 350 from the 3-min time series data, with data lengths fixed at 4 types (0.5 s, 1 s, 2 s, and 3 s) and shift lengths fixed at 0.5 s from the measured 3-min time series data of eye movement. In other words, 1,400 data (equal numbers for both peripheral and central vision) were acquired for each data length per person.

The Neural Network Console Ver. 1.57 (manufactured by SONY) was used for the deep learning in this study. The deep neural network utilized in this experiment is shown in Fig. 4, with a model using data length of 3 s. In the input layer, nodes are placed according to the amount of time series data (1,500 for 3 s). After sequence transformation using Reshape as pre-processing, processing is taken over by the middle layers. The middle layer consists of a total of 32 layers of 8 units, consisting of the convolution layer, the normalization layer, the activation function, and the max-pooling layer. Details of each layer are described below.

- Convolution layer: The convolution layer performs convolutional operations on the input time series data and extracts attributes. In our study, 64 processing results were obtained, because the size of the convolution kernel was set as 9, and a filter with 64 different parameters was applied to the input.
- Batch normalization layer: Batch normalization is a method used to make artificial neural networks faster and more stable through normalization of the input layer. Specifically, it is implemented to prevent vanishing gradient problems (where the gradient of the error function becomes 0) and exploding gradient problems (where the gradient diffuses).
- ReLU (Rectified Linear Unit [activation function]): The activation function transforms the summation of input signals into output signals and has data available to facilitate attribute learning. It is responsible for determining how the summation of input signals is output (fired) and for neuronal firing. ReLU is expressed in Eq. (1), where x is the input and y is the output.

$$y = \begin{cases} x(x \geq 0) \\ 0(x < 0) \end{cases} \tag{1}$$

- MaxPooling (Pooling Layer): This is often applied after the convolution layer and performs information compression using down sampling to deform the data into an easily-handled shape. In addition, down-sampling also helps to reduce the location dependence of attributes. MaxPooling outputs the largest data in the kernel-size area. In this study, the kernel size was set to 2, and each time pooling was carried out, the data were halved.

These four layers make up one unit with seven to eight units as middle layers. The output layer is composed of a fully-connected layer, a sigmoid function as an activation function, and a multi-class cross-entropy. In the learning process, learning was performed with a batch size of 64 and an epoch number of 100.

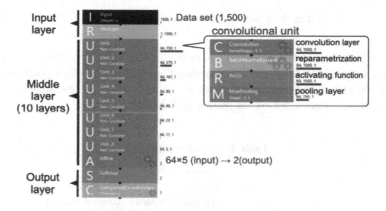

Fig. 4. Details of the deep neural network model used in this study

For learning and evaluation, the Neural Network Console was installed on a desktop PC (Windows 10 Professional, CPU: CORE i7-7700 3.6 GHz, Main memory: 16 GB, GPU: GeForce RTX 2070 SUPER 8 GB [NVIDIA]) and the subject-specific leave one out method was applied (Fig. 5). The leave one out method uses the datasets for all subjects for both learning and assessment. Five of the six subjects were utilized for learning, and the remaining one was utilized for evaluation. This was carried out sequentially on a subject-by-subject basis to obtain assessment results for six people. After that, final evaluation results were obtained by combining these results, to take into account the effect of individual differences.

2.4   Evaluation

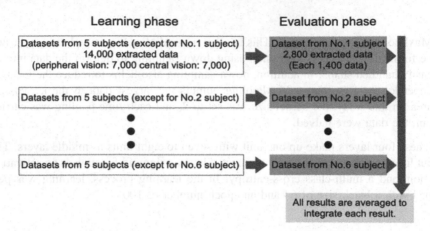

Fig. 5. Summary of the leave one out method

Several methods have been proposed for evaluating the accuracy of classification. In this study, a typical classification was calculated and evaluated. When positive was set as peripheral vision and negative was set as central vision, the evaluation could be expressed in a confusion matrix, as shown in Table 1.

Table 1. Confusion matrix 7

		Prediction of DL	
		Positive (peripheral vision)	Negative (central vision)
Actual classification	Positive (peripheral vision)	TP (True Positive)	FN (False Negative)
	Negative (central vision)	FP (False Positive)	TN (True Negative)

- Accuracy

$$Accuracy = \frac{TP + TN}{TP + FP + FN + TN} \qquad (2)$$

Accuracy shows the percentage of correctly predicted data. Unlike sensitivity and specificity, it is not restricted to positive and negative data but is the correct response rate calculated for all data and is the most fundamental measure.

- Precision

$$Percision = \frac{TP}{TP+FP} \qquad (3)$$

Precision is an index to be tested in respect of positives. Because formula (3) does not include FN, none of the missed values are considered, and if all positives are True (i.e., FP is 0), Precision is 100%. In this study, peripheral vision was set as positive and central vision as negative, and Precision represented the correct answer rate for the classification of peripheral vision.

- Recall

$$Recall = \frac{TP}{TP+FN} \qquad (4)$$

Recall is an index to be tested in respect of negatives. Since formula (4) does not include FP, none of the misdetected values are considered, and Recall is 100% if FN is 0. Recall represents the correct answer rate for classification of central vision.

- F-measure

$$F - measure = \frac{2Recall \cdot Precision}{Recall + Precision} \qquad (5)$$

This is the harmonic mean of Precision and Recall. It is often used as an overall evaluation because it is an indicator that balances the characteristics of both contrasting aspects.

3 Results

Firstly, the results of the measurements of eye movements obtained from the experiment are shown in Fig. 6. Figure 6(a) shows the results of central vision (pursuit), showing both the periodic eye movements that occur from the pursuit of the periodic movements of the gaze points and the spiking changes that result from blinking. In contrast, Fig. 6(b) shows the results of peripheral vision, which, unlike Fig. 6(a), shows that minute eye movements caused by OKN are always occurring during video observation. When the results of both measurements are compared, it is possible to discriminate between them easily, because the attributes of the waveforms differ greatly. However, when one part of a measurement result is observed limited to a short time (Fig. 7), the difference in the shape of the waveform can be obvious (Fig. 7(a), (b)), or the forms can be similar and it becomes difficult to discriminate only by visual features (Fig. 7(c)). Therefore, discrimination carried out with deep learning including attribute searches of the data is assumed to contribute to the improvement of the accuracy of the discrimination.

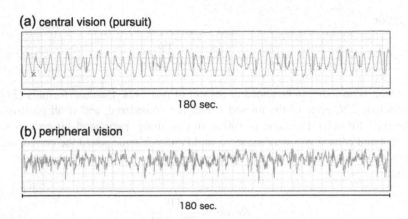

Fig. 6. An example of eye movement measurement results: (a) Central vision, (b) peripheral vision8

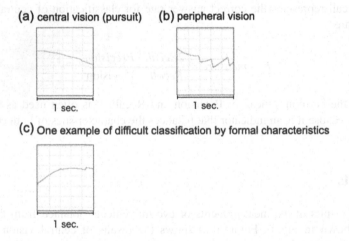

Fig. 7. Short-duration waveform of eye movement measurement: (a) Central vision, (b) peripheral vision, and (c) one example of difficult discrimination from waveform characteristics

Next, Fig. 8 shows the evaluation results of the accuracy of discrimination. Accuracy, Precision, Recall, and F-measure are shown in Figs. 8 (a)–(d), respectively, and all results showed improved accuracy with increasing data length. In particular, accuracy of at least 90% was able to be maintained when the data length was at least one second.

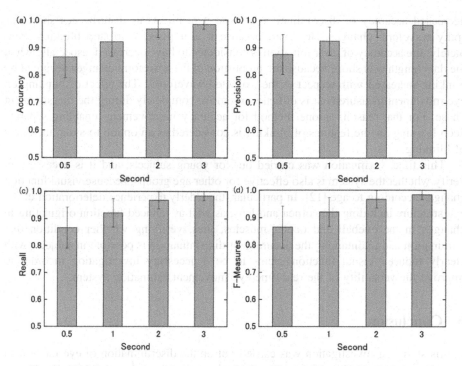

Fig. 8. Evaluation results: (a) Accuracy, (b) Precision, (c) Recall, (d) F-Measure9

4 Discussion

The results on accurate discrimination of eye movement condition showed a discrimination accuracy of 90% or higher if there was a data length of about one second (Fig. 8). This suggests that discrimination of condition can be made in real time with 90% accuracy, if a delay of about one second is accepted. The deep learning model used in this study is a Deep Convolutional Neural Network (DCNN) that has been commonly utilized in classification tasks in recent years. This network model is often applied to images and, in addition, it has been demonstrated that it exerts high accuracy for discrimination [10, 11]. If the convolutional layer of this model is reduced to one dimension, it is possible to apply the same model to one-dimensional time series data such as eye movement and heart rate variability, and as a result, high accuracy of discrimination is expected. Moreover, given that DCNN is a versatile model, it is expected to be applied in many fields, and this study will also potentially provide an example.

Both the quality and quantity of data prepared for deep learning are important and are strongly connected to good and poor evaluation accuracy. With regard to the quality of the data in this study, it is worth touching on the blinking that occurred during video observation. The subjects were instructed in advance to refrain from blinking as much as possible during the video observation. The reason for this is that in eye movement measurement, blinking in both central and peripheral vision can be the cause of decreased accuracy of discrimination because it manifests as disturbances shown as spiky waveform changes. However, because it is impossible to stop blinking completely, the accuracy of discrimination is considered to have decreased, especially when the data length was short, because the proportion of the waveform changes occupied by blinking increased with respect to the extracted waveforms. The effect of blinking on eye movement measurement is difficult to remove completely during the measurement phase. For that reason, as one method for accuracy improvement, enabling separate deep learning for the features of blinking is considered as an option to avoid the effect of blinking.

This time, verification was carried out for young subjects, and it is necessary to verify whether the system is also effective for other age groups, because visual function changes according to age [12]. In particular, the elderly experience deterioration of the eye structure including the cornea and lens, as well as reduced function originating in changes in the eyeball and ocular muscles; thus, verifying whether condition discrimination and maintaining the accuracy of discrimination is possible in subjects with clearly reduced visual function seems to be a necessary investigation in order to improve the versatility of the real-time eye movement estimation system.

5 Conclusion

In this study, an investigation was carried out on the discrimination of eye movement from measurement results of short duration using a deep learning model for the purpose of discriminating eye movement condition in real time during video observation. As a result, it was possible to carry out discrimination with accuracy of at least 90% if measurement data of at least one second were measured.

References

1. World Health Organization (WHO): Dementia Homepage. http://www.who.int/news-room/fact-sheets/detail/dementia. Accessed 1 June 2021
2. Cerejeira, J., Lagarto, L., Mukaetova-Ladinska, E.B.: Behavioral and psychological symptoms of dementia. Front. Neurol. 3, 73 (2012)
3. Seitz, D., Purandare, N., Conn, D.: Prevalence of psychiatric disorders among older adults in long-term care homes: a systematic review. Int. Psychogeriatr. 22, 1025–1039 (2010)
4. Petersen, R.C., Smith, G.E., Waring, S.C., Ivnik, R.J., Tangalos, E.G., Kokmen, E.: Mild cognitive impairment: clinical characterization and outcome. Arch. Neurol. 56, 303–308 (1999)
5. Petersen, R.C., et al.: Current concepts in mild cognitive impairment. Arch. Neurol. 58, 1985–1992 (2001)
6. Bruscoli, M., Lovestone, S.: Is MCI really just early dementia? A systematic review of conversion studies. Int. Psychogeriatr. 16, 129–140 (2004)
7. Kim, K.Y., Yun, J.-M.: Association between diets and mild cognitive impairment in adults aged 50 years or older. Nutr. Res. Pract. 12, 415–425 (2018)

8. Chandler, M.J., et al.: Comparative effectiveness of behavioral interventions on quality of life for older adults with mild cognitive impairment: a randomized clinical trial. JAMA Netw. Open. **2**, e193016 (2019)
9. Rogers, M.A.M., Langa, K.M.: Untreated poor vision: a contributing factor to late-life dementia. Am. J. Epidemiol. **171**, 728–735 (2010). https://doi.org/10.1093/aje/kwp453
10. Onishi, Y., et al.: Automated pulmonary nodule classification in computed tomography images using a deep convolutional neural network trained by generative adversarial networks. Biomed Res. Int. **2019**, 6051939 (2019)
11. Krizhevsky, A., Sutskever, I., Hinton, G.E.: ImageNet classification with deep convolutional neural networks. In: Pereira, F., Burges, C.J.C., Bottou, L., Weinberger, K.Q. (eds.) Advances in Neural Information Processing Systems 25, pp. 1097–1105. Curran Associates, Inc. (2012)
12. Meng, Q., et al.: Age-related changes in local and global visual perception. J. Vis. **19**, 10 (2019)

Development of SPIDAR-HMD
for a Standalone HMD

Yoshiki Takahashi[1]($\boxtimes$), Ryosuke Futatsumori[1], Makoto Sato[2],
Takehiko Yamaguchi[3], and Tetsuya Harada[1]

[1] Tokyo University of Science, 6-3-1 Niijuku, Katsushika-ku, Tokyo, Japan
[2] Tokyo Institute of Technology, 4259 Nagatsuta-cho, Midori-ku, Yokohama,
Kanagawa, Japan
[3] Suwa University of Science, 5000-1 Toyohira, Chino, Nagano, Japan

Abstract. The head-mounted display (HMD)-integrated force sense presentation device, SPIDAR-HMD, which we had developed, allows users to experience not only visual but also force sense in virtual reality (VR) space by
attaching the force feedback device on the HMD. In addition, because it is an
HMD-integrated type, there is no need to wear another device with the HMD,
which reduces the load on the user. However, the conventional SPIDAR-HMD
has the following problems: the target HMD is the Oculus Rift S, which requires
wiring to a high-performance PC to function, it can only operate under a
Windows environment, and the update frequency of force feedback is as low as
300 Hz. In this study, we focused on Oculus Quest, which is a standalone HMD
and uses Android as its operating system. Thus, we changed the microcomputer
used for the conventional SPIDAR-HMD controller from PIC24F to ESP32 and
added Wi-Fi UDP communication implemented in Unity standard C# and
Bluetooth serial port profile (SPP) communication function implemented in Java
for Android. In addition, a function for multiple players was implemented,
making it possible for multiple users to share the VR space with haptics. In the
evaluation experiment, the magnitude of the force and the update frequency
were measured. Regarding the presentation force, we could obtain two times the
magnitude of the conventional SPIDAR-HMD. Regarding the update frequency,
stable presentation of 800 Hz was possible in the Wi-Fi AP mode and Bluetooth SPP, but the performance was low in the Wi-Fi STA mode. These results
showed that higher performance could be obtained using Bluetooth SPP.

Keywords: Haptics · Force sensation · Standalone HMD · Wearable device

1 Introduction

Recently, various head-mounted displays (HMDs) for consumers, such as Oculus
Rift S and Oculus Quest 2 [1], have been developed and sold. As the latest devices,
standalone HMDs, such as Oculus Quest 2, have attracted enormous attention and
gained popularity because they are inexpensive, perform highly, and do not require a
connection to a PC, allowing virtual reality (VR) experience with them alone.

However, in the current VR technology, the development of devices that present
sensations other than visual and audio sensations has not progressed. In particular, it is

© Springer Nature Switzerland AG 2021
C. Stephanidis et al. (Eds.): HCII 2021, LNCS 13095, pp. 144–156, 2021.
https://doi.org/10.1007/978-3-030-90963-5_12

paramount to present haptic feedback as the next step; this will lead to the widespread use of VR technology in education, entertainment, and medical fields, such as rehabilitation.

Based on the above, we had developed a wearable HMD-integrated force feedback device called SPIDAR-HMD in our previous work [2]. SPIDAR-HMD was developed exclusively for the Oculus Rift CV1 and had a problem that it could not be easily attached to other HMDs with different shapes and operating systems. In addition, the update frequency of force feedback was as low as 300 Hz, and there was a problem that it was less than 1 kHz, which was necessary for the stable force feedback [3]. We describe the details of this device in the next section.

In this study, we selected Oculus Quest, a standalone HMD that allows users to move freely, as the target device; in addition, we aimed to improve its force feedback update frequency. Therefore, we designed and manufactured a mounting frame for Oculus Quest, changed the microcomputer used for the controller to a higher performance one, and tried a communication method of Bluetooth and Wi-Fi. Further, we constructed a system that allows two users to share a VR space simultaneously and experience haptic sensation using the hand tracking function built into Oculus Quest. Then, we measured the magnitude of the force presented by the device and evaluated the force feedback update frequency and screen frame rate with different communication methods.

2 SPIDAR-HMD

SPIDAR-HMD was developed for Oculus Rift CV1—a VR device for consumers developed by Oculus (currently Facebook Technologies LLC) [4]. Figure 1 shows the device in use. The device consists of two plastic frames made by a three-dimensional (3D) printer attached to the front and rear of the HMD. Three direct-current (DC) motors with rotary encoders are attached to the front frame, and a control unit is attached to the rear frame. The ends of the strings from the pulleys of each DC motor are connected at a point to which a ring (end effector) is attached. When the user moves a finger with the end effector on the finger, the length of the strings from each pulley changes, and the 3D position of the finger is measured by the rotary encoder. When the finger collides with a virtual object, the tensions of the strings are controlled by changing the duty ratio of the pulse-width modulation (PWM) signals to the DC motors, and the appropriate reaction force is felt at the fingertip. A mobile battery is used as the power source for the device, and serial communication using Bluetooth serial port profile (SPP) is used for communication with a PC. Table 1 shows the specifications of SPIDAR-HMD. The fingertip position measurement has three translational degrees of freedom (DOFs), and the force presentation has almost one DOF.

3   The Proposed Device

3.1   Outline of the Proposed Device

As shown in Figs. 2 and 3, the same as SPIDAR-HMD, the proposed device has three
DC motors equipped with rotary encoders fixed to the upper left and right and the lower
center of the front of the HMD, respectively, as well as a control unit attached to the
rear end of the head strap.

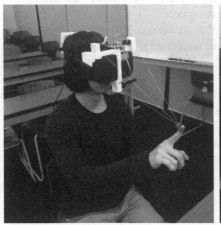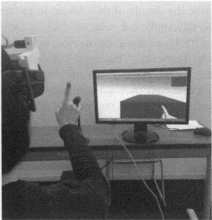

Fig. 1. SPIDAR-HMD in use

Table 1. Haptic specifications of SPIDAR-HMD

Maximum force	0.8 N
Position measurement	Translational 3 degrees of freedom
Update frequency	300 Hz
Weight (excluding battery and HMD)	344 g

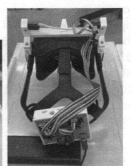

Overview   View from the front   View from the upper rear

Fig. 2. Configuration of the proposed device

 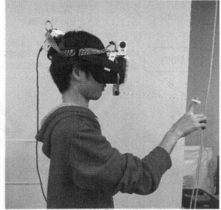

View from the front   View from the side

Fig. 3. State of wearing

3.2 System Configuration

As shown in Fig. 4, the system configuration consists of an HMD, which is the audiovisual presentation part, and the force feedback device. Unity—a game engine—was used as the software development environment for this device, and the force control values and the rotary encoder pulse count values were sent and received by Unity scripts. This communication was performed in Wi-Fi UDP STA mode via a wireless router, Wi-Fi UDP AP mode, or Bluetooth SPP. On the force feedback device, the HMD sends the force control value simulated by Unity to the device via Wi-Fi or Bluetooth as three force control values (each 10-bit unsigned integer). The force feedback device determines the duty ratios of the PWM signals based on the received values and sends these signals to the motor driver circuit to present the force sensation to the fingertip. This device also counts the pulses output from the three rotary encoders and sends the values (each 16-bit signed integer) to the HMD. The HMD uses these values to determine the 3D position of the finger on a Unity script. On the visual presentation part, Unity updates the VR space using the position of the finger and draws the image according to the position and angle of the HMD. In addition, using the original hand tracking function of the HMD, an avatar of the user's hand can be displayed.

3.3 Control Unit

As shown in Fig. 5, we used a development board—ESP32-DevKitC-32D (ESPRESSIF SYSTEMS CO., LTD.) [5]—equipped with a microcomputer—ESP-WROOM-32D—as the control unit. The DC motor used was 1724T006SR with rotary encoder IEH2-512 (FAULHABER MINIMOTOR SA) [6]. Figure 6 shows the flow-chart of the program installed.

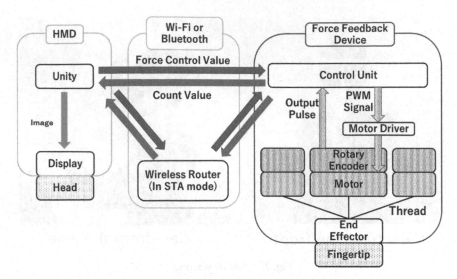

Fig. 4. System configuration

Fig. 5. Control unit

3.4   Simulation System

As shown in Fig. 7, we created a test content that allows the user to touch a flat wall with a fingertip and check the reaction force. In this content, a spherical object representing the proxy of the fingertip for reaction force calculation is displayed to check the operation of the program. The hand avatar is displayed by the hand tracking function, which is an original feature of Oculus Quest. Unity calculates the reaction force generated when the fingertip collides with an object in front of the user. During the collision, the finger penetrates the object, but the proxy does not penetrate the object, instead, it moves along its surface, following the movement of the finger. The reaction force (force sense information) is calculated via a spring-damper model using the difference between the fingertip and proxy positions. Figure 8 shows the flowchart of the force calculation and finger coordinate calculation of the simulation system. After establishing a connection with the motor controller, the simulation system sends the initial force control values. Next, the system receives the count values and calculates the coordinates of the finger position. Afterward, the system performs the collision check with the virtual object, and if there is a collision, it calculates the reaction force and sends the force control values to the control unit; otherwise, it sends the initial values.

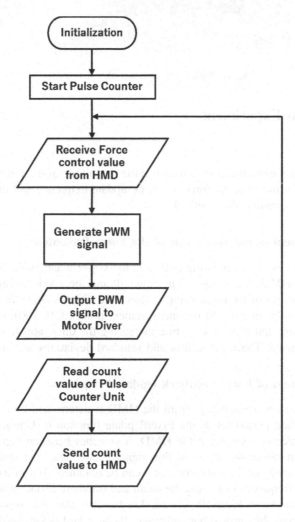

Fig. 6. Flowchart of the microcomputer control program

Fig. 7. Visual presentation of test content

4 Evaluation Experiment

4.1 Purpose

The purpose of this experiment is to measure the magnitude of the force presented and evaluate the performance in the force feedback update frequency and the screen frame rate due to the communication method.

4.2 Measurement of the Magnitude of the Force Presented

The plane formed by the three string outlets is the x–y–z plane, with the x-axis facing right toward the HMD, the y-axis facing upward, and the z-axis facing forward. The positional coordinates of the three string outlets were (98, 82, 0), (−98, 82, 0), and (0, −82, 0), respectively, in mm. At the measurement point (0, 0, 100), the presentation force was measured ten times each while increasing the duty ratio from 0% to 100% using 5% increments. The mean values and standard deviations are shown in Fig. 9.

4.3 Measurement of Force Feedback Update Frequency

The data transmission frequency f_s from the HMD is determined by a fixed timestep, which is the update period set in the FixedUpdate function of Unity. Each time the microcomputer receives data from the HMD, it switches between high and low on a certain output pin. Since one cycle of this signal is two times the update period, the reception frequency f_r of the microcomputer can be obtained. Ten measurements were made at each set frequency of f_s, and the mean and standard deviation were calculated. The results are shown in Figs. 10, 11, 12, 13, 14. The blue dots represent the mean value of f_r, whereas the vertical bars represent the standard deviation (left-hand axis).

The solid straight line represents $f_r = f_s$, and the gray straight lines above and below represent by the equation $f_r = f_s \pm 10$ [%], respectively (left-hand axis). The red dots represent the average screen frame rate (right-hand axis).

4.4   Results and Considerations

Evaluation Experiment of the Magnitude of the Force Presented. The approximate line shown in Fig. 9 is a linear approximation using the least-squares method. When the duty ratio is x [%] and the presenting force is F [N], the approximate equation is given by

$$F = 0.017x - 0.1136.$$

This approximation shows linearity from the coefficient of determination $R^2 = 0.9931 \approx 1$. Therefore, the above equation can be used to present a force of approximately $0-1.6$ N by changing the duty ratio of the PWM control. The maximum force of this device (1.6 N) was two times that of the conventional SPIDAR-HMD shown in 2.1 as 0.8 N, which was due to the change in the diameter of the pulley attached to the motor from 20 to 10 mm.

Evaluation Experiment of Force Update Frequency
Bluetooth SPP
In Figs. 10 and 11, the screen frame rate was kept at 72 Hz in all cases. The reception frequency f_r was within -10% of the transmission frequency f_s, except for the case with multiple players with hand tracking. Even for multiple players with hand tracking, it was within -10% in $f_s \leq 800$ Hz.

Wi-Fi UDP STA
In Figs. 12 and 13, the screen frame rate was kept at 72 Hz in all cases. The upper limit of the reception frequency f_r was in the range of 200–350 Hz when it was within -10% of the transmission frequency f_s, which was significantly inferior to other communication methods. This was probably because the system was connected to a LAN connected to the Internet and was therefore affected by other communication traffic.

Wi-Fi UDP AP
This was only the case without multiple players since hand tracking communication with another device over a normal Wi-Fi connection was impossible in this case. As shown in Fig. 14, the screen frame rate slightly decreased after 900 Hz but remained above 70 Hz, so there was no problem. The reception frequency f_r was within -10% in $f_s \leq 800$ Hz.

4.5   Consideration of Update Frequency

From *4.4.2.1* to *4.4.2.3*, it is considered appropriate to use Bluetooth SPP, which can ensure at least a communication speed close to 1 kHz, for all conditions in this environment.

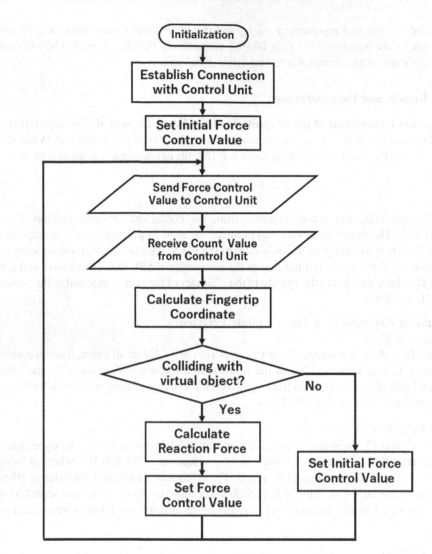

Fig. 8. Flowchart of force and coordinate calculation

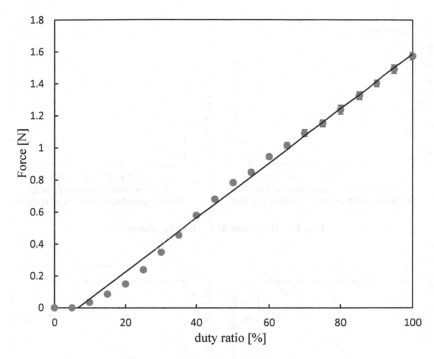

Fig. 9. Relationship between duty ratio and the magnitude of the force presented

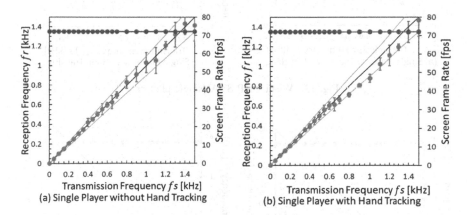

Fig. 10. Bluetooth SPP (single player).

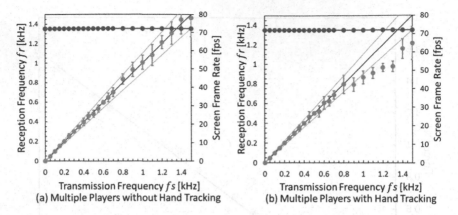

Fig. 11. Bluetooth SPP (multiple players).

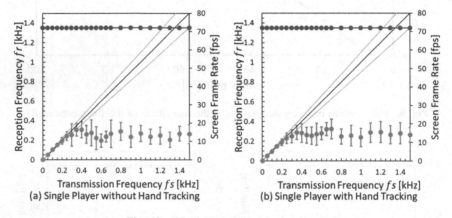

Fig. 12. Wi-Fi UDP STA (single player).

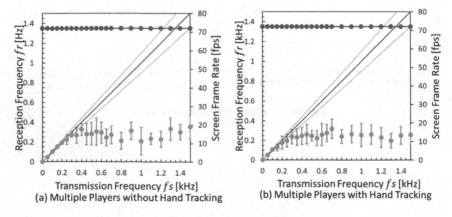

Fig. 13. Wi-Fi UDP STA (multiple players).

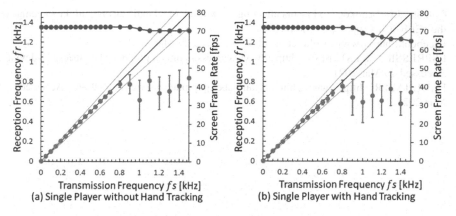

Fig. 14. Wi-Fi UDP AP (single player).

5 Conclusion and Prospects

In this study, we adapted SPIDAR-HMD, which was made for Oculus Rift CV1 in our previous study, to Oculus Quest, which stands alone and is easy to handle. The frame of the SPIDAR-HMD was redesigned, and the microcomputer of the controller was changed to ESP32 to build an environment that could function with various communication methods. Then, we evaluated the performance of the proposed device in terms of force feedback.

In the evaluation of the magnitude of the force presented, the proposed device could present a force of 1.6 N, which was two times that of the conventional SPIDAR-HMD. In addition, the relationship between the duty ratio and the presentation force was clarified.

For measuring force feedback update frequency, it was considered appropriate to use Bluetooth SPP, which could ensure at least a communication speed close to 1 kHz for all conditions in the environment. However, the increase in computational load of the HMD due to the complexity of VR space and increase in load due to the Internet connection for sharing VR space will affect the communication speed.

As a prospect, we would like to conduct haptic experiments of various shapes of virtual objects and explore the improvement possibilities of the proposed device. In addition, to achieving higher and more stable performance, we plan to make this device compatible with Oculus Quest 2, which is a successor to Oculus Quest with improved CPU performance.

References

1. Facebook: https://www.oculus.com/quest-2/. Accessed 1 Jan 2021
2. Sawata, M., Maruhashi, K., Tsukikawa, R., Yamaguchi, T., Sato, M., Harada, T.: Development of HMD Integrated Force Display Device "SPIDAR-HMD". The Institute of Electrical Engineers of Japan, pp.41–46 (2018). (in Japanese)

3. Colgate, J.E., Schnkel, G.: Factors affecting the z-width of a haptic display. In: Proceedings of the IEEE ICRA, pp. 3205–3201(1994)
4. Facebook: https://www.oculus.com/rift-s/. Accessed 29 Mar 2021
5. ESPRESSIF SYSTEMS: https://www.espressif.com/en/products/devkits/esp32-devkitc. Accessed 29 Mar 2021
6. FAULHABER: https://www.shinkoh-faulhaber.jp/products/series/ieh2-4096. Accessed 29 Mar 2021

Human Pose Estimation in UAV-Human Workspace

Ju Wang[1]([✉]), Wookjin Choi[1], Igor Shtau[2], Tyler Ferro[2],
Zhenhua Wu[1], and Curtrell Trott[1]

[1] Virginia State University, Petersburg, VA 23806, USA
{jwang, wchoi, zwu}@vsu.edu
[2] NSWC, Dahlgren, VA, USA
{igor, tyler.j.ferro}@navy.mil

Abstract. A 6D human pose estimation method is studied to assist autonomous UAV control in human environments. As autonomous robots/UAVs become increasingly prevalent in the future workspace, autonomous robots must detect/estimate human movement and predict their trajectory to plan a safe motion path. Our method utilize a deep Convolutional Neural Network to calculate a 3D torso bounding box to determine the location and orientation of human objects. The training uses a loss function that includes both 3D angle and translation errors. The trained model delivers <10-degree angular error and outperforms a reference method based on RSN.

Keywords: 6D pose estimation · Deep learning · UAV motion planning

1 Introduction

We investigate a deep learning method to estimate the 6D pose of humans for autonomous UAV motion control in both urban and indoor human environments. As autonomous robots/UAVs become integral parts of future workspace, they will interact and co-exist with humans in a close quarter. A fundamental requirement is that the autonomous robot must operate/navigate with safety assurance in unknown environments such as office buildings or factories. From the perspective of robot motion planning, autonomous UAVs must Simultaneously Localize and Map (SLAM), which in turn rely on the construction of a 3D occupancy map of the environment using onboard sensors [3, 4]. The 3D occupancy map allows the UAV to avoid collision into static obstacles. More importantly, the UAVs must detect dynamic human objects, estimate their 6D poses, and predict their trajectory to plan a safe path.

In both 2D/3D human pose estimation [1, 2, 9], keypoints such as the pelvis, arms, head, and calves are often used to construct a mapped skeleton data structure. With the emerging AI frameworks and GPU hardware, many Machine Learning (ML) approaches [2, 5, 9] have been studied with promising results. Compared to many existing methods, the main difference of our method is that we predict 6D human pose

The project is supported by NSF award 1818655, Raytheon Space and Intelligence, and NEEC award N001742110011.

C. Stephanidis et al. (Eds.): HCII 2021, LNCS 13095, pp. 157–167, 2021.
https://doi.org/10.1007/978-3-030-90963-5_13

instead of 2D skeleton keypoints. The skeleton keypoints in existing methods are all 2D, and they do not offer direct information of the body orientation and the distance information. Our network is trained to detect a 3D bounding box instead of the skeleton keypoints. The benefit of our method is that the 3D bounding box is relatively invariant even though the human body can be in vastly different poses. The network processing pipeline consists of (1) a deep CNN network that processes RGB video frames and generates pose proposals of human objects, (2) an extended Kalman filter to select pose candidates using the pose estimation from past frames. We mainly discuss human pose representation and the implication on the design of the training process. As the human body is not rigid, there are many alternative ways to define the bounding box and the human pose. Accordingly, the training process and the loss function will differ. Two pose representations are studied here: (1) our proposed Torso Box Pose (TBP) derived from a set of 3D keypoints, and (2) selected skeleton points used in the coco human dataset. We provide a close examination of the prediction accuracy for both.

The rest of the paper consists of the following sections: Sect. 2 describes UAV perception and motion planning Architecture. Section 3 details the network structure and the regression layer design. We will discuss the human pose representations and the loss function. Section 4 provides a performance evaluation of our system as well as demonstration cases in UAV motion planning.

1.1 Related Work

Robot motion planning requires some form of map and knowledge of its location. In the early systems, a prior knowledge (map) of the environment is often required for motion planning/execution. The navigation map can be a topological or grid-based occupancy map, with the latter containing more terrain detail for turn-by-turn motion commands. In contrast to fixed maps, a more flexible and robust approach is Simultaneous Localization and Mapping (SLAM), which requires the robot to map the environment with onboard sensors on the flight [3, 4]. A brief overview of recent advances in SLAM is presented in [11]. Recently graph-based approaches to solve SLAM problems are gaining popularity [10]. In graph SLAM, the robot's pose nodes are optimized by minimizing the distance to observation nodes and edges.

Human pose information is critical to many computer vision tasks, such as human behavior recognition and human-computer interaction. Deep learning-based human pose detection has attracted many researchers in the last decade [2, 5, 9, and 12]. To accurately recognize a human's posture, body keypoints in appropriate locations such as the pelvis, arms, head, and calves are typically detected. For location-sensitive vision problems such as human pose estimation, semantic segmentation, and object detection, high-resolution representations are required.

In High-Resolution Net (HRNet) [9], keypoints in an image and the location confidence of the keypoint are used to construct mapped skeletal data that represents the original human pose. Frameworks such as ResNet and VGGNet first encode input images with low-resolution representations using subnetworks created by sequentially connecting high-resolution convolutions, and then recover high-resolution representations from encoded low-resolution representations. The HRNet maintains a high-resolution representation through the whole process instead of recovering high resolution from low resolution and exchanges information across various resolutions. The advantage is that the resulting representation is richer in both semantic and spatial features. A closely related work is Residual Steps Network (RSN) [12]. RSN aggregates feature with the same spatial size (Intra-level features) efficiently to obtain delicate local representations, which retain rich low-level spatial information and result in precise keypoint localization. Most of the existing works have focused on detecting skeleton points while overlooking the body orientation, which is the main focus of our approach.

2   UAV Perception and Motion Planning Architecture

We briefly describe the overall architecture of the UAV navigation stack. To safely operate in complex environments, the UAV's motion is controlled by a collection of subsystems performing sensing, perception and motion planning. The overall system architecture is shown in Fig. 1. The real or simulated UAV provides sensor data include the RGB/depth camera data, lidar scan, the IMU data, the barometer data, and optionally the GPS data. Both the camera depth image and the Lidar scan are used to create a 3D map of the environment and estimate the visual odometry. To navigate a target location, the UAV's high-level controller searches the 3D map and calculates a feasible path based on the static map. The motion planning subsystem corrects the local map using the current sensor data and optimizes the local path at the motion control level. The local correction is essential to avoid collision with dynamic objects such as humans. A significant amount of vision processing is required to obtain the updated information of the 3D occupancy map, and a GPU-based object detection module assists this task.

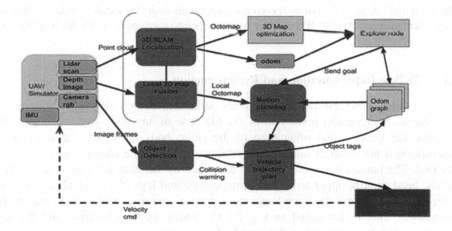

Fig. 1. UAV motion control software stack and information flow.

The perception and motion planning tasks are carried out by several computing nodes:

- 3D-SLAM-node: Construct a 3D occupancy map using the depth image input [7].
- Object-detection-node: This node is a deep Convolutional Neural Network (CNN) trained to recognize human objects and estimate human pose. The rest of the paper will focus on this node.
- Motion-planning-node: This node computes the feasible trajectory to reach a near-range waypoint based on a combined local 3D map.

3   Pose Detection Network Pipeline

We now describe how the 6D human pose can be represented and detected by a deep learning network. We will first discuss our proposed 3D Torso Box Pose (TBP). This is followed by an explanation of the deep CNN and training method. We then discuss the construction of the 6D pose from the coco human pose data serving as a comparison.

Fig. 2. (left)17 skeleton keypoints in coco pose, arm location and leg locations indicate different body orientation. (right) pose 3D bounding box (blue points) obtained in our model. (Color figure online)

3.1   6D Pose Representation and Reconstruction

In rigid body pose estimation, the body structure is well defined and remains unchanged. A successful prediction of the 6D pose of any body part is sufficient to describe the location and orientation of the entire body. However, the rigid body assumption is not valid in human pose estimation; hence the situation is more complicated. The human poses are typically described by skeleton keypoints such as the pelvis, head, mouth, upper arms, low arms, calves, and legs [8, 9, 12]. However, it is difficult to directly use the bone locations to form a consensus about the human body orientation. This is illustrated in Fig. 2(left), where the arm location and the leg locations indicate a completely different body orientation.

We define the human pose as the minimum 3D bounding box containing selected torso parts.

Assuming the camera coordinate system, we define $\vec{x_i} = (x_i, y_i, z_i)$, i = 1 ... N as a set of N keypoints. The corresponding 3D bounding box is defined by the convex cube:

$$\vec{B} = \{p = (x, y, z) | min\,\vec{x_i} < x, y, z < max\,(\vec{x_i})\}$$

An immediate question arises: *which keypoints should be included to construct the 3D bounding box?* Intuitive thought is to use all skeleton keypoints like the case of 2D bounding box for simple human detection. The problem, however, is that the resultant 3D bounding box might not align with the 3D torso bounding box. On the other hand, limiting to only a few torso keypoints will make the network training difficult since fewer human features are used. As a tradeoff, we include obvious joints such as the pelvis, upper arm, and calves. We further decide to have the head keypoint to allow enough features in the detection phase. Elbow and front arms are considered too 'free-moving and not used here.

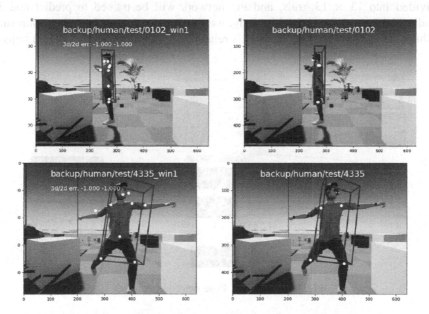

Fig. 3. 3D bounding boxes: ground truth vs. estimated from two different cases. (Color figure online)

With the 3D bounding box of the human body defined, the 6D pose can be estimated using the predicted 2D keypoints using a Perspective-n-Point (PnP) pose estimation method [17]. In our case, PnP uses only eight such control point correspondences and provides an estimate of the 3D rotation matrix R and 3D translation t of the object in the camera frame. Mathematically, the PnP find the optimum 3D transformation parameters $(R, t)^*$ that has the minimum 3D-2D projection errors over the 3D bounding box:

$$(R, t)^* = argmin_{R,t}(\sum_{i:keypoints}||p_{im,i} - A[R|t]P_{c,i}||)$$

Here $p_{im,i}$ represent the pixel location in the image plane, and $P_{c,i}$ is the keypoint in camera coordinate.

Figure 3 shows the estimated 6D pose (blue-box) and the ground truth (green-box) for two test cases. The distance of the human object to the camera is 8 m and 4 m, respectively. In both cases, the predicted 6D poses are very close to the ground truth.

3.2   Torso Box Pose Detection Network

Our approach is inspired by the success of the single-shot 6D pose estimator [5]. Our network architecture is shown in Fig. 4, which utilizes the convolutional layers of a YOLOv2 to predict the 2D projections of 9 keypoints for a human's 3D torso bounding box. We adopt the grid-cell concept of the YOLO2 network, where the original image is divided into 13 × 13 grids, and the network will be trained to predict one 3D bounding box per grid cell. In this study, we fixed to one anchor box dimension since the shape variation of the human body is relatively small compared to random objects.

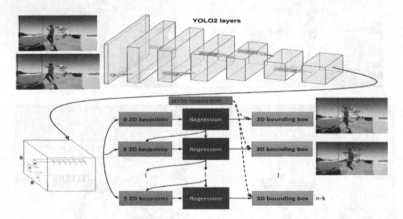

Fig. 4. Torso Box Pose detection network

For a 13 × 13 grid, the output of the last convolutional layer consists of about 169 3D bounding box proposals, each with the center inside the corresponding grid cell. Each box proposal predicted will contain nine pairs of normalized pixel coordinates plus the classification and confidence. After the convolutional layers, a final regression layer follows. We use a loss function that explicitly calculates the 3D bounding box errors to train the network. The loss function L consists of three parts:

1. l_{angle}: the error measured in quaternion distance between the projected rotation matrix R and the ground truth R*, We minimize the following loss function to train our complete network.

2. l_{trans}: the 3D distance error between the projected translation vector t and the ground truth t*.

3. $\sum_{i:keypoints} \|p_i - p_{i,gt}\|$: the sum of the pixel distance between the projected and the actual keypoints.

$$L = \lambda_1 l_{angle} + \lambda_2 l_{trans} + \lambda_3 \sum_{i:keypoints} \|p_i - p_{i,gt}\|$$

We also use the predicted results of the past k frames to exploit the temporal correlation in the video data. Since the predictions of the previous frames are strongly correlated to the current frame, they provide a tie-break for complex cases when human objects are partially observed or occluded. During network training, the old predictions contribute to the loss function and gradient calculation. At the testing/inferencing time, the old predictions refine the current prediction to improve the spatial accuracy.

3.3 RSN Comparison

To compare to some existing methods in human pose estimation, we also tested a state-of-the-art 2D pose estimation method using the MMPose toolbox, an open-source toolbox for pose estimation based on PyTorch and is a part of the OpenMMLab project [13]. The reference method we will compare to is the Residual Steps Network (RSN) [12], which won the 2019 COCO Keypoint Challenge.

The multi-stage network architecture of the RSN pose estimation is cascaded by multiple RSN. RSN uses effective intra-level feature fusion to learn delicate local representations. RSN differs from ResNet in the architecture of constituent units. RSN consists of Residual Steps Blocks (RSBs), while ResNet consists of "bottleneck" blocks. RSN is designed for learning delicate local representations through dense element-wise sum connections. Each human joint has a different scale. The scale of the eye, for example, is small, whereas the scale of the hip is large. As a result, architecture with a broader range of receptive fields is better suited to extracting characteristics related to various joints. Furthermore, a large receptive field aids in learning more discriminating semantic representations, which is beneficial to the keypoint classification task. The RSN creates extensive connections within RSB features with small-gap receptive fields. The deeply connected architecture aids in learning delicate local representations, which are critical for accurate human pose estimation. A Pose Refine Machine (PRM) is used in the last stage. Features are mixed after intra- and inter-level aggregation, containing low-level precise spatial information and high-level discriminant semantic information. Keypoint localization benefits from spatial information, whereas keypoint classification benefits from semantic information.

It is noteworthy that the keypoints location predicted by RSN, like many similar works, is in the 2D image domain. This makes it difficult to make a direct comparison between RSN and our model. To use the output of the RSN in 6D pose reconstruction, the 17-points coco keypoints are converted to the 8-points keypoints for the 3D bounding box by a simple process. We use the shoulder skeletons to derive the approximate location of the four (4) upper body torso keypoints. The offset of the nose to the center of the shoulder points determines the squadron. The conversion algorithm to obtain four shoulder points works as following:

1.   def SkeletonTo4ShoulderPoints((shoulder_l, shoulder_r, knee_l, knee_r, nose):
2.   nose_off=nose-(shoulder_l+shoulder_r)/2
3.   if nose_off[0]>0:
4.   faceleft=1
5.   else:
6.   faceleft=0
7.   m,c = get_line_equs(shoulder_r, shoulder_l)
8.   m1,c1,m2,c2= get_lines_tang (shoulder_r, m,c) # approx with tangent line
9.   p1,p5 =get_line_y(m1,c1, shoulder_r)   ## front/back keypoints near left shoulder
10.   p0,p4 =get_line_y(m2,c2, shoulder_l)   ##   keypoints near right shoulder

The keypoints near the knee are obtained similarly. After this, we apply the PNP method to estimate the coordinate transformation matrix representing the 6D pose. Figure 5 illustrates the keypoints outcome of the conversion process.

Fig. 5. Pseudo 3D box keypoints derived from RSN skeleton points

4   Experiment Results

4.1   Train Result

We use a game engine with 3D graphics and a physics engine to generate photo-realistic images and ground truth poses data to train and evaluate our network. Figure 6 shows the results of our model. Using a total 190 training images, the network parameters converge within 40 epochs of training. The mean error of the keypoints is 8.6 pixels, while the average angular error is less than 8°.

The detection speed of the network benefits from the efficient implementation of the Yolo2. Our experiment shows that the system can process 20 frames/sec on NVIDIA Jetson TX2.

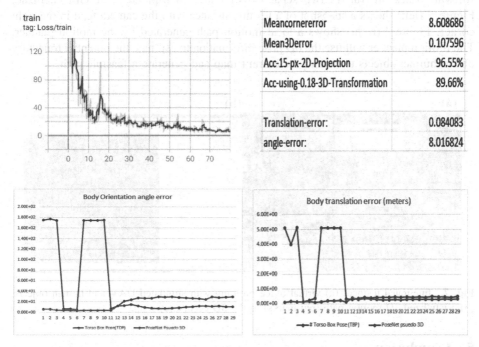

Meancornererror	8.608686
Mean3Derror	0.107596
Acc-15-px-2D-Projection	96.55%
Acc-using-0.18-3D-Transformation	89.66%
Translation-error:	0.084083
angle-error:	8.016824

Fig. 6. Model train result and error: (a) loss function of a training session, (b) overall 2D and 3D errors, (c) 3D angle errors comparison, (d) 3D translation error comparison. (Color figure online)

Figure 6 C and D show the 6D pose error comparison between the proposed Torso Box Pose and the modified RSN method. The angle error is computed between the projected 3D pose vector and the ground truth pose vector. The angle error for TBP is uniformly under 20° and half of which are within a single-digit error.

We also noticed seven fail cases for the modified RSN method where the angle errors reach almost 170–200°. The failure is due to the fact that the simple 2D-3D mapping algorithm could not calculate a pose solution when the left and right shoulder points are too close. Such behavior is expected since the 2D skeleton points have limited 3D expressing power. Among the good testing cases, the angle error for the modified RSN method is about 30% higher than that of TBP. For translational error, the two methods are very comparable, with TBP has a slight edge.

4.2   Integrated Motion Planning Test

To test the pose detection algorithm, we created a testbed consisting of a 3D game environment (Unreal Engine 4) and an external software stack described in Sect. 2. The autonomous UAV in the game engine communicates with the external software components through the Airsim plugin framework [14]. The game engine and the UAV software stack are run in two separate computers to separate their GPU demand. Figure 7 (left) shows a snapshot of a testing instance with the camera feed in the right corner. Figure 7 (right) shows a local motion path generated by the motion planner. The motion planner will use the 6D pose information to estimate the potential trajectory of the human objects to amend the current map and generate a feasible path.

(a)   **(b)**

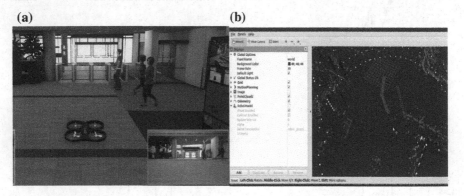

Fig. 7. Integrated testbed: (a) virtual office building with simulated UAV and human objects. (b) Visualized 3D motion path (red marks) in the 3D occupancy map.

5   Conclusion

We present a deep CNN-based pose estimation method to predict the true 6D pose information of human objects. This algorithm is an integral part of the motion planning stack for autonomous UAV control in human environments. We utilize a deep Convolutional Neural Network to estimate a 3D torso bounding box to determine the location and orientation of human objects. Our results show that the torso bounding box reflects the human pose well and is trainable through transfer learning.

References

1. Munea, T.L., Jembre, Y.Z., Weldegebriel, H.T., Chen, L., Huang, C., Yang, C.: The progress of human pose estimation: a survey and taxonomy of models applied in 2D human pose estimation. IEEE Access **8**, 133330–133348 (2020). https://doi.org/10.1109/ACCESS.2020.3010248
2. Pavllo, D., Feichtenhofer, C., Grangier, D., Auli, M.: 3D human pose estimation in video with temporal convolutions and semi-supervised training. In: CVPR (2019)

3. Laird, J.E., et al.: A standard model for the mind: toward a common computational framework across artificial intelligence, cognitive science, neuroscience, and robotics, AI Magazine **38**(4), 13–26 (2017)
4. 3D Mapping & Navigation. https://www.wilselby.com/research/ros-integration/3d-mapping-navigation/
5. Tekin, B., et al: Real-time seamless single shot 6D object pose prediction. In: CVPR (2018)
6. Li, S., Chan, A.B.: 3D human pose estimation from monocular images with deep convolutional neural network. In: Cremers, D., Reid, I., Saito, H., Yang, M.H. (eds.) ACCV 2014. LNCS, vol. 9004, pp. 332–347. Springer, Cham (2015). https://doi.org/10.1007/978-3-319-16808-1_23
7. Sünderhauf, N., Protzel, P.: Towards a robust back-end for pose graph SLAM. In: Proceedings of International Conference on Robotics and Automation, pp. 1254–1261 (2012)
8. Lin, T.Y., et al.: Microsoft COCO: common objects in context. In: Fleet, D., Pajdla, T., Schiele, B., Tuytelaars, T. (eds.) ECCV 2014. LNCS, vol. 8693, pp. 740–755. Springer, Cham (2014). https://doi.org/10.1007/978-3-319-10602-1_48
9. Wang, J., et al.: Deep high-resolution representation learning for visual recognition. IEEE Trans. Pattern Anal. Mach. Intell. (2020). https://doi.org/10.1109/TPAMI.2020.2983686
10. Thrun, S., Montemerlo, M.: The graph SLAM algorithm with applications to large-scale mapping of urban structures. Int. J. Robot. Res. **25**, 403–429 (2006)
11. Cadena, C., et al.: Past, present, and future of simultaneous localization and mapping: toward the robust-perception age. IEEE Trans. Robot. **32**, 1309–1332 (2016)
12. Cai, Y., et al.: Learning delicate local representations for multi-person pose estimation. In: Vedaldi, A., Bischof, H., Brox, T., Frahm, J.M. (eds.) ECCV 2020. LNCS, vol. 12348, pp. 455–472. Springer, Cham (2020). https://doi.org/10.1007/978-3-030-58580-8_27
13. MMPose Contributors: OpenMMLab Pose Estimation Toolbox and Benchmark (2020). https://github.com/open-mmlab/mmpose
14. Shah, S., Dey, D., Lovett, C., Kapoor, A.: AirSim: high-fidelity visual and physical simulation for autonomous vehicles. In: Hutter, M., Siegwart, R. (eds.) Field and Service Robotics. SPAR, vol. 5, pp. 621–635. Springer, Cham (2018). https://doi.org/10.1007/978-3-319-67361-5_40

Current Status of User Experience of the Keyboard on Smartphones: An Overall Questionnaire Analysis

Yincheng Wang[1], Tong Lin[2], Jingxin Yu[2], Lu Wang[2], Jibo He[1], and Luoma Ke[1(✉)]

[1] Tsinghua University, Beijing 100084, People's Republic of China
wang-yc18@tsinghua.org.cn,
hejibo666@mail.tsinghua.edu.cn
[2] Beijing Forestry University, Beijing 100083, People's Republic of China
umi077@bjfu.edu.cn

Abstract. The present status of the user experience of the keyboard on smartphones (UXKS) remains ambiguous because of the fast-changing developments of smartphones. This study adopted an online questionnaire ($N = 866$) to explore users' current experience, habits, and preferences towards specific objects, including large smartphones and the dual-task input when interacting with their smartphones and the keyboards. The results concluded the user profile of UXKS, and found that users were suffering from long-time use of large smartphones. Additionally, the dual-task operation has become common, with increasing numbers using type or swipe keyboards while driving and walking in particular. The study could provide research objects and basis for organizations and corporations to enlighten future studies on the optimization of the smartphone keyboard design under various scenarios.

Keywords: Smartphone keyboard · User experience · Human-computer interaction

1 Introduction

As a consequent method of human-smartphone interaction, keyboard input is becoming an increasingly ubiquitous and integral part of modern lives. Moreover, with the vast user base of smartphones expanding, it has got millions of users [1–4]. For instance, China Internet Network Information Center's latest statistics [5] have shown the scale of China's smartphone users reached 986 million, and the Sogou Mobile Keyboard had 473 million daily average users in 2020 [6]. Therefore, the optimization of keyboard input design has become a popular topic of psychological and ergonomic research and a key mercantile point for corporations and companies.

User experience of the keyboard on smartphones (abbreviated as UXKS) could be defined as the effectiveness, efficiency, and subjective experience of the input method used by a specific user in a specific environment for a specific purpose under a single input task, as well as the mutual influence of the input task and other tasks [7–9].

C. Stephanidis et al. (Eds.): HCII 2021, LNCS 13095, pp. 168–182, 2021.
https://doi.org/10.1007/978-3-030-90963-5_14

Nevertheless, the current status of UXKS in the 2020s remains unknown, for the fast-changing development of smartphones and keyboards.

The larger-sized phones may be an important point affecting UXKS. With the boom of screen technology, 5.5-in. and above smartphones taking up nearly 80% of 2021's first season's sales in the smartphone market, indicating a growing manufacturing trend toward larger screens [10]. Although the enlarged screen aimed to improve users' viewing experience, it has changed the gravity, size, and weight of smartphones, which may not correspond with the physiological structure of the hand and lead to poor input effectiveness, efficiency, and subjective feelings like discomfort in hand, including muscle pain, tenosynovitis, arthritis, etc. [11–14].

Another important perspective of UXKS involves the interaction between the use of keyboard input and other tasks (the dual-task operation), including the impact of input tasks on other tasks. With the amount of instant messaging app users soaring, keyboard input tasks may collide with various scenarios like having a meeting or class, walking, or even driving. In particular, although China prohibits the use of mobile phones while driving, this behavior has been repeatedly banned, which brings a lot of risks to driving safety [15, 16]. As of the end of 2020, the number of motor vehicles in China was 372 million, and the number of motor vehicle drivers reached 456 million [17]. According to statistics, using smartphones while driving has been one of the main reasons for traffic accidents, and more than 1/5 of the accidents are caused by texting messages on smartphones while driving [18–20]. Therefore, typing under a dual-task scenario is also an inseparable aspect of the research on the UXKS.

Despite abundant existing research on smartphone keyboard use, few have deeply explored UXKS from users' perspectives. Users' experience, habits, and preferences towards specific objects such as big-sized phones, traditional Qwerty layout, and dual-task input scenarios in daily smartphone use are still unknown and needed to be further investigated. The purpose of this study is to mainly concentrate on the current status of UXKS in China by an overall questionnaire analysis, and also to test whether the applications of input methods under the single task and those under the dual-task context are both important research objects for the human-smartphone interaction research.

2   Method

2.1   Procedure and Participants

This study launched an online questionnaire on Credamo (Creator of Data and Model, a professional research and modeling integrated data platform). A sample of 926 Chinese participants was recruited, and all of them had registered as users with real names. Sixty participants were excluded from the analysis for providing inconsistent or irrelevant responses. Therefore, 866 participants (321 females; aged from 16 to 58, $M = 26.47$, $SD = 5.72$) were included in the current study (mean answering time = 218.83 s, $SD = 177.65$).

This study was approved by the Ethics Committee of the Department of Psychology at Tsinghua University.

2.2   Design of the Questionnaire

The questionnaire consisted of 22 items in 4 parts: demographic statistics, users' experience and habits when interacting with their smartphones, users' experience and habits when using smartphone keyboards, and users' experience of the dual-task operation on smartphones. The main items include users' smartphone size, average daily usage time, hand discomfort and diseases caused by smartphone usage and its reasons, keyboard input preference (gestures, methods, and layouts), and scenarios and frequency of keyboard input under the dual-task condition. The whole list of items is shown in Appendix.

2.3   Data Analysis

We used SPSS 23.0 to analyze the data. First, we sorted the data from all aspects with visualizations. Second, a hierarchical multiple regression analysis on the keyboard satisfaction score was carried out.

3   Results

3.1   Demographic Statistics

Among the 866 the copies of effective questionnaire, 112 are left-handed (13.05%), 591 are right-handed (68.24%), and the rest are ambidexters (18.82%). 163 of them are in Guangdong Province (18.82%), 68 in Shandong Province (7.85%), 63 in Jiangxi Province (7.27%), 63 in Henan Province (7.27%), etc.

3.2   User Experience of Smartphones

Figure 1 shows a comprehensive view of the user experience of smartphones.

The distribution of users' smartphone operating systems is shown in Fig. 1(a). Android system users (675, 77.94%) account for the majority of all the users.

As shown in Fig. 1(b) and 2(c), the size of users' smartphones are large ($M = 6.31$ in., $SD = 0.55$), and their usage time reaches 6.95 h per day ($SD = 2.58$) on average. 82.79% of users are using smartphones larger than 6.0-in., and 65.59% of users are using smartphones for more than 6.0 h per day.

After using the smartphone, 849 participants (98.04%) feel discomfort in hand (frequency $M = 0.39$, $SD = 0.22$), as shown in Fig. 1(d). Among those, there are 509 participants (59.95%) who have pains in the thumb and thenar eminence, 295 participants (34.75%) who have discomfort between the thumb and the index finger, 376 participants (44.29%) who suffer from wrist discomfort, and 5 participants (0.59%) have other discomforts, like little finger discomfort.

265 participants (30.60%) suffer from hand diseases, as shown in Fig. 1(e). Among those, 223 participants (84.15%) suffer from thumb tenosynovitis, 133 participants (50.19%) have carpal tunnel syndrome, and 4 participants (1.51%) have other diseases like hand muscle strain and fatigue.

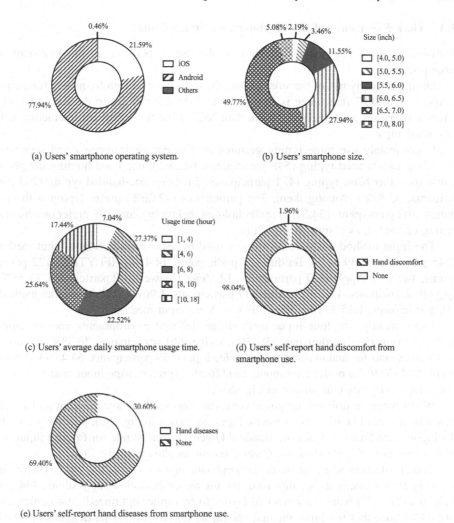

(a) Users' smartphone operating system.

(b) Users' smartphone size.

(c) Users' average daily smartphone usage time.

(d) Users' self-report hand discomfort from smartphone use.

(e) Users' self-report hand diseases from smartphone use.

Fig. 1. The comprehensive view of the user experience of smartphones.

The reasons for hand discomfort and diseases that participants report are as follows: the large size of smartphone screen (37.41%), the heavyweight of smartphones (43.30%), using the smartphone for too long (77.37%), more requirements on sophisticated hand and finger movements while playing games on smartphones (42.73%), and lacks ergonomic design of mobile App interface (such as keyboard, game interface, etc.) (23.21%).

3.3   User Experience of the Keyboard on Smartphones

Figure 2 shows a comprehensive view of the user experience of the keyboard on smartphones.

During the daily use of the smartphone, the users have a mean frequency (i.e., input frequency) of 0.57 (the range is from 0.00 to 1.00, $SD = 0.22$) to do text input, i.e., when a user uses a smartphone, more than half of the time they are interacting with keyboard input.

Users mainly use three typing gestures in different environments and scenarios, including two-handed typing (548 participants, 63.28%), one hand holding the phone while the other hand typing (471 participants, 54.39%), one-handed typing (293 participants, 33.83%). Among them, 366 participants (42.26%) prefer typing with both hands, 302 participants (34.87%) prefer holding and typing, and 198 prefer one-handed typing (22.86%), as shown in Fig. 2(a).

The input method software commonly used by users include Sogou input method (345 participants, 39.84%), Baidu (125 participants, 14.43%), iFLYTEK (122 participants, 14.09%), Apple (107 participants, 12.36%), Huawei (100 participants, 11.55%), QQ (40 participants, 4.62%), Google (17 participants, 1.96%), and other input methods (10 participants, 1.15%) like Mi, OPPO, or Vivo input methods.

Users mainly use four input methods in different environments and scenarios, including type (603 participants, 69.63%), swipe (661 participants, 76.33%; including 454 participants for handwriting input), voice input (558 participants, 64.43%). Among them, 502 (57.97%) prefer type input, 230 (26.56%) prefer swipe input, and 132 prefer voice input (15.24%), as shown in Fig. 2(b).

When typing in different language contexts, users tend to have different preferences towards keyboard layouts. For Chinese input, as shown in Fig. 2(c), 42.49% prefer the T9 layout, and 56.81% prefer the standard Qwerty layout. While for English input, 81.41% of users prefer the standard Qwerty layout, as shown in Fig. 2(d).

The satisfaction score of users for keyboard input ($M = 72.95$, $SD = 19.23$; full score is 100) remains to be improved. As for the optimization suggestions, 434 participants (50.12%) want the keyboard layout to be further optimized; 364 participants (42.03%) hope that the input method should be improved; 658 participants (75.98%) hope that the algorithms including automatic correction, fuzzy recognition, etc. can be optimized.

709 participants (81.87%) report that they once have been performing a certain main task while using the smartphone for keyboard input, i.e. type under the dual-task context, as shown in Fig. 2(e). The average frequency (i.e., dual-task input frequency) is 0.52 (the range is from 0.00 to 1.00, $SD = 0.21$).

Among all the participants, 223 participants (25.75%) use keyboard input while in a meeting; 326 participants (37.64%) use it while in class; 78 participants (9.01%) use it while driving; 95 participants (10.97%) use it while riding a bike; 501 participants (57.85%) use it while walking; 508 participants (58.66%) use it while chatting offline.

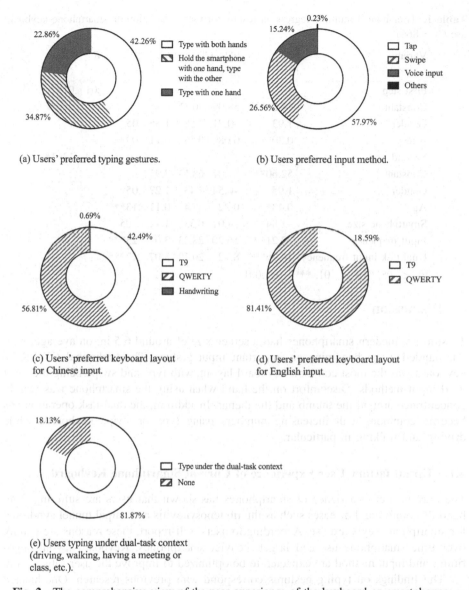

(a) Users' preferred typing gestures.

(b) Users preferred input method.

(c) Users' preferred keyboard layout for Chinese input.

(d) Users' preferred keyboard layout for English input.

(e) Users typing under dual-task context (driving, walking, having a meeting or class, etc.).

Fig. 2. The comprehensive view of the user experience of the keyboard on smartphones.

3.4 Regression Analysis

Hierarchical multiple regression was applied to find potential factors that influenced user satisfaction on smartphone keyboard use.

The results in Table 1 show that both input frequency and dual-task input frequency have a significant positive correlation with user satisfaction on keyboard use.

Table 1. Hierarchical multiple regression results for user satisfaction on smartphone keyboard use ($N = 866$).

Variable	B	95% CI		SE	β	R^2	ΔR^2
		LL	UL				
First step						.01	.01*
Constant	64.20***	58.09	70.31	3.11			
Gender	1.93	−0.71	4.58	1.35	.05		
Age	0.30**	0.08	0.53	0.11	.09**		
Second step						.14	.13***
Constant	52.60***	37.07	68.13	7.91			
Gender	1.95	−0.54	4.43	1.27	.05		
Age	0.43***	0.22	0.64	0.11	.13***		
Smartphone size	−1.84	−4.01	0.33	1.11	−.05		
Input frequency	22.21***	16.20	28.23	3.07	.25***		
Dual-task input frequency	14.76***	8.72	20.79	3.07	.17***		

$*p < .05, **p < .01, ***p < .001$

4   Discussion

To sum up, modern smartphones had a screen size of around 6.5 in. on average, with one-handed usage becoming an important input gesture. The traditional QWERTY keyboard was the most common keyboard layout, with type and swipe being the most used input methods. Discomfort on the hand when using the smartphone was mainly concentrated around the thumb and the thenar. In addition, the dual-task operation has become common, with increasing numbers using type or swipe keyboards while driving and walking in particular.

4.1   Unsatisfactory User Experience of Current Smartphone Keyboard

The current user experience of smartphones has shown that users are suffering from hand discomfort and diseases such as thumb tenosynovitis and carpal tunnel syndrome for smartphone keyboard use. According to users' self-report, these reasons are mainly over time smartphone use and larger, heavier smartphones. Keyboard layout, algorithm, and input method are expected to be optimized to improve the user satisfaction.

The findings on typing gestures correspond with previous research. One-handed input is a commonly adopted input gesture for smartphones. The thumb is limited in typing flexion and extension when securing the device with only one palm and four fingers [21]. Compared with those using smartphones by both hands, one-handed smartphone users suffer from more serious input discomfort, large smartphone users in particular [22–24]. Moreover, our results have shown that 22.86% of users prefer one-handed operation because it frees the other hand to perform other tasks, thereby improving overall work efficiency [25, 26]. Therefore, the optimized interaction design for one-handed usage is in urgent need.

Therefore, these results had achieved a basic exploration of user experience of the keyboard on smartphones, indicating a vast improving space for keyboard input design.

4.2 Status of Input Under the Dual-Task Context

The findings on the single and dual-task input scenarios indicated that the impact of input behavior on the dual-task context is one of the main focuses of human-smartphone interaction research. The use of input methods under multitasking operations has become a common behavior in human life. Our results have shown that more than 80% of people had been using smartphones for text input when performing a certain task, including driving, indicating a high safety risk.

Also, according to the regression model, there is a significant positive correlation between the input frequency, the dual-task input frequency, and the score of smartphone input method satisfaction. This accorded with the previous research that user stickiness and satisfaction were tightly correlated, and satisfaction was a dominant factor of continuous use intention [27, 28].

4.3 Inspirations for Future Study

This study also has some limitations which could be optimized in future studies. Firstly, we could enlarge the sample size and recruit more participants from other regions with more details on user profiles, e.g., the education level and the occupation. Secondly, we could investigate more on the applications of input under the single or the dual-task context, e.g., input behaviors while walking and driving.

Based on the findings, in the future, researchers could conduct more in-depth research in the following directions.

First, the design of the smartphone keyboard needs further optimization from aspects of layouts, algorithms, and other input methods. Numerous keyboard designs and concepts have been proposed, including scaling up or down the keyboard button size and curved design keyboards, e.g., Microsoft WordFlow Keyboard [29], and changing the keyboard button positions, e.g., IJQwerty [30], Quasi-Qwerty [31], etc. In addition to changing the keyboard layout, designers could try to optimize the input algorithm, which may contribute to a better user experience. Functions like fuzzy recognition or correcting erroneous input automatically based on natural language processing (NLP) could be beneficial [32–34]. Also, various input methods, including type, swipe, hand-gesture, eye-tracking, and brain-computer interface, may be conducive to optimizing the human-smartphone interaction process [35–37].

Second, more emphasis should be put on the safety issue in the dual- or multitask context. Our results have shown the dual- or multitask input scenarios have become increasingly common, which may bring a high safety risk, driving [19], walking, and riding a bike in particular. The government and researchers should consider these and take appropriate measures, e.g., ban the text input function when Map apps usage is detected in real-time.

Third, further optimization for input under diverse dual- or multitask scenarios should be investigated. Scenarios such as input in a meeting or class often require as little distraction as possible for the main task and are often accompanied by one-handed use. The applications for such specific input scenarios are in crucial need of an optimized input method.

To summarize, the overall results could provide research objects and basis for organizations and corporations to enlighten future studies on the optimization of the smartphone keyboard under various scenarios.

Appendix

The whole list of the questionnaire items.

Part	Item
	1. What's your gender?
	○ Male
	○ Female
	2. What's your age?
Demographic statistics	_____
	3. Which one is your dominant hand?
	○ Right hand
	○ Left hand
	○ Both
	4. What's the operating system of your smartphone?
	○ iOS
	○ Android
	○ Others
Users' experience and habits when interacting with their smartphones	5. What's the size of your smartphone?
	_____
	6. What's the average daily usage time on your smartphone?
	_____
	7. How often do you feel uncomfortable with your hands when (after) using your smartphone? (0%–100%)
	_____

8. Where are your hand discomforts mainly concentrated in your hand?

☐ The thumb and thenar eminence

☐ Between the thumb and the index finger

☐ Wrist

☐ Others

☐ None

9. What hand diseases have you ever suffered from smartphone use?

☐ Thumb tenosynovitis

☐ Carpal tunnel syndrome

☐ Others

☐ None

10. What do you think are the reasons for "hand discomfort caused by smartphone usage"?

☐ The large size of smartphone screen

☐ The heavyweight of smartphones

☐ Using the smartphone for too long

☐ Playing games on smartphones requires more sophisticated hand and finger movements

☐ Mobile App interface design is not ergonomic enough (such as keyboard, game interface, etc.)

☐ Others

11. how often do you use the smartphone keyboard for text input? (0.00–1.00)

0.00   1.00

12. What typing gestures have you used (i.e., in a certain environment, you may use this method)?

☐ Type with both hands

☐ Hold the smartphone with one hand, type with the other

☐ Type with one hand

Users' experience and habits when using smartphone keyboard

13. What's your first choice of typing gesture?

○ Type with both hand

○ Hold the smartphone with one hand, type with the other

○ Type with one hand

14. What's your most frequently used text input method software?

○ Huawei input method

○ Baidu input method

○ Sogou input method

○ QQ input method

○ Apple input method

○ iFLYTEK input method

○ Google input method

○ Others

15. Which input methods have you used when using your smartphone (i.e., in a certain environment, you may use this method)?

☐ Tap

☐ Swipe

☐ Voice input

☐ Handwriting

☐ Others

16. What's your first choice of input method?

○ Tap

○ Swipe

○ Voice input

○ Handwriting

○ Others

17. What's your preferred keyboard layout for Chinese input?

○ T9

○ Qwerty

○ Others

18. What's your preferred keyboard layout for English input?

○ T9

○ Qwerty

○ Others

19. What's the satisfaction score of your current input method? (0–100)

0   100

20. Have you ever used your smartphone for keyboard input while performing a main task (such as messaging while having a meeting), and what following scenarios are included?

☐ Using the smartphone while driving

☐ Using the smartphone while in a meeting

☐ Using the smartphone while in class

☐ Using the smartphone while riding a bike

Users' experience of the dual-task operation on smartphones

☐ Using the smartphone while walking

☐ Using the smartphone while chatting face to face

☐ Others

☐ Never

21. When use a smartphone for keyboard input, how often do you perform another or multiple main tasks at the same time? (0.00–1.00)

0.00   1.00

22. What aspects of the smartphone keyboard input method you use now need to be improved?

☐ The keyboard layout

☐ The input method

☐ The algorithms including automatic correction, fuzzy recognition, etc.

☐ Others

o: single-choice questions. ☐: multiple-choice questions.

References

1. Baidu Inc.: Big Data Annual Report of 2017 on Baidu Input Method. https://mp.weixin.qq.com/s/9TJRiv0c6qP-kpE3dl2aFQ. Accessed 18 May 2021
2. Lee, S., Zhai, S.: The performance of touch screen soft buttons. In: SIGCHI Conference on Human Factors in Computing Systems on Proceedings, pp. 309–318. ACM, Boston (2009)
3. Smith, A.L., Chaparro, B.S.: Smartphone text input method performance, usability, and preference with younger and older adults. Hum. Factors **57**(6), 1015–1028 (2015)
4. Smith, B.A., Bi, X., Zhai, S.: Optimizing touchscreen keyboards for gesture typing. In: 33rd Annual ACM Conference on Human Factors in Computing Systems on Proceedings, pp. 3365–3374. ACM, New York (2015)
5. China Internet Network Information Center, CINIC, The 47th China Statistical Report on Internet Development. http://cnnic.cn/hlwfzyj/hlwxzbg/hlwtjbg/202102/P020210203334633480104.pdf. Accessed 19 May 2021
6. Sogou Inc.: Sogou 2020 Annual Report. Annual Reports. http://ir.sogou.com/index.php?s=120. Accessed 18 May 2021
7. ISO, ISO 9241-210: Ergonomics of human-system interaction – Part 210: human-centred design for interactive systems. https://www.iso.org/obp/ui/#iso:std:52075:en. Accessed 18 May 2021
8. ISO, ISO 9241-11: Ergonomics of human-system interaction – Part 11: usability: definitions and concepts. https://www.iso.org/obp/ui/#iso:std:iso:9241:-11:ed-2:v1:en. Accessed 18 May 2021
9. ISO, ISO 9241-210: Ergonomics of human-system interaction – Part 210: human-centred design for interactive systems. https://www.iso.org/obp/ui/#iso:std:iso:9241:-210:ed-2:v1:en. Accessed 18 May 2021
10. China Academy of Information and Communications Technology, CAICT, Monitoring Report on the Characteristics of Interactive Carriers of Domestic Mobile Phone Products (4th edition in 2020). http://www.caict.ac.cn/kxyj/qwfb/qwsj/202101/P020210125327586418628.pdf. Accessed 18 May 2021
11. Chachris, E.A., Sirinya, V., Lucy, R.: Musculoskeletal disorder and pain associated with smartphone use: a systematic review of biomechanical evidence. Hong Kong Physiother. J. **38**(2), 77–90 (2018)
12. Chang, J., Choi, B., Tjolleng, A., Jung, K.: Effects of button position on a soft keyboard: muscle activity, touch time, and discomfort in two-thumb text entry. Appl. Ergon. **60**, 282–292 (2017)
13. Eitivipart, A.C., Viriyarojanakul, S., Redhead, L.: Musculoskeletal disorder and pain associated with smartphone use: a systematic review of biomechanical evidence. Hong Kong Physiother. J. **38**(2), 77–90 (2018)
14. Gehrmann, S.V., Jie, T., Zong, M.L., Goitz, R.J., Windolf, J., Kaufmann, R.A.: Motion deficit of the thumb in CMC joint arthritis. J. Hand Surg. **35**(9), 1449–1453 (2010)
15. Caird, J.K., Johnston, K.A., Willness, C.R., Asbridge, M., Steel, P.: A meta-analysis of the effects of texting on driving. Accid. Anal. Prev. **71**(10), 311–318 (2014)
16. White, K.M., Hyde, M.K., Walsh, S.P., Watson, B.: Mobile phone use while driving: an investigation of the beliefs influencing drivers' hands-free and hand-held mobile phone use. Transp. Res. F: Traffic Psychol. Behav. **13**(1), 9–20 (2010)
17. Ministry of Public Security of the People's Republic of China. https://app.mps.gov.cn/gdnps/pc/content.jsp?id=7647257. Accessed 18 May 2021 (in Chinese)
18. Goodchild, S.: Kwik Fit: 18% of 18–34s involved in driving incident while using phone. https://www.tyrepress.com/2019/08/kwik-fit-18-of-18-34s-involved-in-driving-incident-while-using-phone/. Accessed 7 June 2021
19. He, J., Chaparro, A., Nguyen, B., Burge, R.J., Crandall, J., Chaparro, B., et al.: Texting while driving: is speech-based text entry less risky than handheld text entry? Accid. Anal. Prev. **72**, 287–295 (2014)

20. National Highway Traffic Safety Administration: Visual-manual NHTSA driver distraction guidelines for portable and aftermarket devices. U.S. Department of Transportation, National Highway Traffic Safety Administration (2016)
21. Lai, J., Zhang, D.: ExtendedThumb: a target acquisition approach for one-handed interaction with touch-screen mobile phones. IEEE Trans. Hum. Mach. Syst. **45**(3), 362–370 (2014)
22. Girouard, A., Lo, J., Riyadh, M., Daliri, F., Eady, A.K., Pasquero, J.: Onehanded bend interactions with deformable smartphones. In: 2015 CHI Conference on Human Factors in Computing System, pp. 1509–1518. ACM, Seoul (2015)
23. Lee, M., Hong, Y., Lee, S., Won, J., Yang, J., Park, S.: The effects of smartphone use on upper extremity muscle activity and pain threshold. J. Phys. Ther. Sci. **27**(6), 1743–1745 (2015)
24. Trudeau, M.B., Asakawa, D.S., Jindrich, D.L., Dennerlein, J.T.: Two-handed grip on a mobile phone affords greater thumb motor performance, decreased variability, and a more extended thumb posture than a one-handed grip. Appl. Ergon. **52**, 24–28 (2016)
25. Azenkot, S., Zhai, S.: Touch behavior with different postures on soft smartphone keyboards. In: 14th International Conference on Human-Computer Interaction with Mobile Devices and Services, pp.251–260. ACM, San Francisco (2012)
26. Holman, D., Hollatz, A., Banerjee, A., Vertegaal, R.: Unifone: designing for auxiliary finger input in one-handed mobile interactions. In: 7th International Conference on Tangible, Embedded and Embodied Interaction, pp. 177–184. ACM, Barcelona (2013)
27. Fang, I.C., Fang, S.C.: Factors affecting consumer stickiness to continue using mobile applications. Int. J. Mob. Commun. **14**(5), 431–453 (2016)
28. Kang, S.: Factors influencing intention of mobile application use. Int. J. Mob. Commun. **12**(4), 360 (2014)
29. Microsoft Garage, Word Flow Keyboard. https://www.microsoft.com/en-us/garage/profiles/word-flow-keyboard. Accessed 7 May 2021
30. Bi, X., Zhai, S.: IJQwerty: what difference does one key change make? Gesture typing keyboard optimization bounded by one key position change from Qwerty. In: 2016 CHI Conference on Human Factors in Computing Systems on Proceedings, pp. 49–58. ACM, San Jose (2016)
31. Bi, X., Smith, B.A., Zhai, S.: Quasi-qwerty soft keyboard optimization. In: Proceedings of the SIGCHI Conference on Human Factors in Computing Systems, pp. 283–286. ACM, Atlanta (2010)
32. Ahmed, F., Luca, E.W.D., Nürnberger, A.: Revised n-gram based automatic spelling correction tool to improve retrieval effectiveness. Polibits **40**, 39–48 (2009)
33. De Amorim, R.C., Zampieri, M.: Effective spell checking methods using clustering algorithms. In: Proceedings of the International Conference Recent Advances in Natural Language Processing RANLP 2013, pp. 172–178. INCOMA, Hissar (2013)
34. Kukich, K.: Techniques for automatically correcting words in text. ACM Comput. Surv. **24**(4), 377–439 (1992). https://doi.org/10.1145/170791.171147
35. Cutrell, E., Tan, D.: BCI for passive input in HCI. In: Proceedings of CHI, vol. 8, pp. 1–3. ACM, New York (2008)
36. Panwar, M., Mehra, P.S.: Hand gesture recognition for human computer interaction. In: 2011 International Conference on Image Information Processing, pp. 1–7. IEEE, Waknaghat (2011)
37. Feit, A.M., Williams, S., Toledo, A., Paradiso, A., Kulkarni, H., Kane, S., et al.: Toward everyday gaze input: accuracy and precision of eye tracking and implications for design. In: Proceedings of the 2017 Chi Conference on Human Factors in Computing Systems, pp. 1118–1130. ACM, New York (2017)

HCI in eXtended Reality

Extended Reality (XR) Applications in Architectural Practice: Towards a Development Framework

Maryam Abhari$^{(\boxtimes)}$, Kaveh Abhari⬤, Madison Drinkwine,
and Jordan Sloan

San Diego State University, San Diego, CA, USA
mabhari@sdsu.edu

Abstract. Extended Reality (XR) applications allow designers to experiment with design concepts and examine design solutions in mixed-reality environments. XR technologies, from virtual reality to augmented reality, have proven potentials to enhance the design process and improve design outcomes. However, XR applications in architecture, engineering, and construction are limited mainly due to primitive XR technology—both software and hardware. Further research on how to develop these applications thus deems necessary. This study focused on XR use cases in architectural practice, identified six key XR affordances through a case study and then discussed their relationships with three components of the creative design process in architecture (concept, knowledge, and environment). The results are presented as a framework that can serve a reference for developing the next generation of XR applications for architectural practice.

Keywords: Extended Reality · Augmented reality · Design process · Concept-knowledge design theory · Architectural practice · Architects · Affordances

1 Introduction

Digital Media such as Extended Reality (XR) offers experiential design opportunities in mixed reality environments [1]. XR combines real and virtual design environments and supports a new form of contextual and multi-dimensional human-machine interaction [2]. This can foster creativity, enhance requirement analysis, boost design productivity, and facilitate feasibility studies in architecture, engineering, and construction [3–6]. While XR has proven potentials to enhance the design process and improve design outcomes, XR applications in these domains are limited mainly due to primitive XR software and hardware [7, 8]. Hence, research on the XR development is the necessary first step to address the challenges associated with the industry-wide adoption and effective use [2, 8]. To this end, this research focuses on XR use cases in architectural practice with the hope of offering a novel approach to XR software development in general.

This study proposes a framework recognizing the key requirements for XR-supported design in architecture. Within this framework, we examine the features,

© Springer Nature Switzerland AG 2021
C. Stephanidis et al. (Eds.): HCII 2021, LNCS 13095, pp. 185–196, 2021.
https://doi.org/10.1007/978-3-030-90963-5_15

benefits, and limitations of current XR tools on the market, align the analysis of those tools with the best practices of the field, and identify when and why they can meet design process requirements. As a result, we identify six key affordances related to developing the design concepts, examining design concepts, enriching design environment, simulating design scenarios, validating design solutions, and improving design logic. Further, we explain how design process requirements are fulfilled by these affordances with reference to the *concept-knowledge-environment framework*—an extended version of the *concept-knowledge design (process) theory* [9]. The final framework proposed by this study can inform the design of future XR applications, allow professionals to select the right tools that best suit their needs, and help researchers understand the adoption and implications of XR technology in architectural design.

2 Background

XR technologies offer unprecedented opportunities to revolutionize architectural practice by enhancing design productivity while reducing errors and saving the trifecta (time, money, and resources) [4, 8, 10]. In this study, we refer to XR as a broad category of many types of real-and-virtual environments generated by digital technologies including Augmented Reality (AR), Mixed Reality (MR), Augmented Virtuality (AV), and Virtual Reality (VR)—see Table 1 for the definitions [8, 11]. For example, XR includes both AR and MR affordances as users can virtually interact with the environment in real-time with or without occlusion between virtual content and the real-world. Similarly, XR benefits from AV and VR technologies that can recreate a virtual version of reality within a digitally regenerated world. However, beyond AV and VR, XR combines elements of the virtual world and allows them to interact within the real world. XR application goes beyond traditional virtual rendering methods used in VR applications that have both been proven inadequate in support of creative design and in particular, architectural design [12–15].

Table 1. The definition of XR components

Augmented reality	The real world still exists with all its objects and features; however, virtual objects or information are purposefully added to allow real-time interactions
Mixed reality	The real and virtual worlds combine to form one completely new hybrid and interactive reality rather than the mere addition of elements to reality
Augmented virtuality	Th display of real objects or information onto a virtual world. The user would be within the virtual reality while manipulating real objects
Virtual reality	The digitalized version of a real environment or virtual representation of a reality in which objects and information are only limited to that regenerated reality

XR has shown the potential to revolutionize the architectural design process [4, 8]. The appeal of XR tools in architecture lies in the idea that they can more efficiently support the design solutions and construction efforts (e.g. programming, material selection, lighting, and circulation). XR applications allow the project stakeholders to interact with the environment, experiment with design scenarios, and examine different options before actual construction [5, 6].

Recently introduced VR applications fall short in satisfying these needs [14, 16, 17]. Firstly, VR is not a viable choice when the design or the design environment is complex, constantly changing, or hard to verify. This is a commonly cited problem with the available VR applications that renders 3D models for the walkthrough. Secondly, VR environments are also isolated from both real-world and project stakeholders. While in certain cases such as training simulators, this can be considered a benefit of the program, it is not an asset when it comes to the architectural design process. Architecture is fundamentally a socio-cultural endeavor; meaning that user, designer, builder, and other stakeholders must be in constant communication and deliberation. Therefore, reducing all design elements into a purely virtual environment may isolate the stakeholders from reality and limit their interactions. Thirdly, the accuracy and fidelity of the regenerated reality in a VR environment is an issue when it comes to architectural design, engineering, and construction. This is due to the inherent separation of realities and the complexity of digitalization of all the details in VR environments. Lastly, enhancing productivity is challenging in using current VR tools. For example, time could be spent on correcting mistakes in a virtual environment, rather than taking the object in actual reality and merely adding virtual elements onto it for a more efficient assessment.

Advance augmentation can address the aforementioned issues to a great extent. For example, AR applications in construction have proven to have intuitive visualization capabilities serving functions such as review of different layers of information, quality control, illustrating the location of concealed works, and facilities operations and maintenance. Similar benefits have been realized in engineering and architectural applications as well. The question is, however, how these applications can systematically and formally support the design process. To answer this question, we use the concept-knowledge design theory as a guide to operationalize the architectural design process and then to discuss how this process can be supported by the next generation of XR applications.

3   Concept-Knowledge (C-K) Design Theory

C-K Design (Process) Theory looks at the reasoning applied throughout the design process and strives for continuous and incremental improvement [18]. First introduced by Armand Hatchuel and his colleagues, the theory has proven to be a practical way to model the requirements of a robust and well-reasoned design process [19]. This theory defines design-reasoning as a logic of design development, refinement and organization processes—when a new object (concept or knowledge) is generated. The C-K theory is traditionally structured around three pillars: knowledge, concepts, and operators. *Knowledge* within this theory (K) is defined as a set of propositions with a logical status according to the current knowledge of the designers. The K space within design describes all objects and known facts from the point of view of the designer and that can be organized and documented for current or future reference. *Concepts* (C) refer to a set of design propositions or possible solutions within concept space. *Operators* build upon the premises of knowledge, concepts, and their interactions. The four central operators, K to C (disjunction), C to K (conjunction), C to C (C expansion), and K to K (K expansion), collectively denote the design process that is illustrated in Fig. 1 [18, 20].

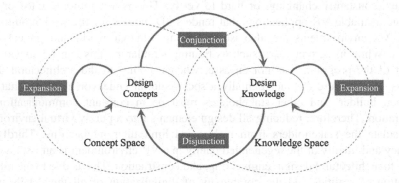

Fig. 1. C-K Design Theory based on the Hatchuel and Weil's *Design Square*

Overall, the C-K theory not only offers a comprehensive formalization of design processes, irrespective of the design domain, but also allows explaining the design discovery process when assisted with computer technology. We argue that modern architectural practice can be modeled after the C-K design theory. In architecture professional practice, the initial design is decided upon using propositions from existing design concepts and knowledge. At the start of the project, previous knowledge informs new design concepts (disjunction). For example, preliminary design takes place after the first meeting with a client to capture their needs and preferences. Schematic designs are developed next in line with what the client requests, available resources, zoning, topological and geographical restrictions among many other factors. These designs are then, explored, expanded, given added details, and elaborated upon by different project stakeholders (C expansion). This refers to design development that requires further meetings and communications with the client. This is where most of the work takes place as plans and schematics are further refined and readied for possible use in the third stage, which is the construction document. After several rounds of iterations, the final design becomes new knowledge informing construction (conjunction). Lastly, this process contributes to the expansion of K that guides future designs. Conjunction and knowledge expansion contribute to both project's knowledgebase and the firm's knowledgebase (e.g., construction specifications). Figure 1 serves as a visual representation of the four processes.

While the C-K theory can be applied and explained how modern architectural practice operates, it falls short in explaining the role of 'environment' and its impact on concept and knowledge expansion [9]. The environment is the key element that defines both design opportunities and constraints. While in the real world, we are not able to expand the environment (in the sense we develop design concepts and knowledge), virtualization and augmentation technology allow us to experiment with the design concepts and verify our knowledge in an extended reality environment. Therefore, to model the architectural design process, we adopt the extended version of the C-K Design Theory: Concept-Knowledge-Environment or CKE framework [9, 18, 20]. This framework suggests that creative design practice can be modeled as the interplay between three interdependent spaces with different structures and logics: the space of concepts (C), the space of knowledge (K), and the design environment (E)—an extended or mixed environment in our case. Accordingly, we can use the CKE framework to model architectural design practice as three external operations (inter-actions between C, E, and K) and three internal operations (concepts, knowledge, and environment expansions). These operations—conceptualized below and illustrated in Fig. 2—refer to the key 'design process requirements' in this study.

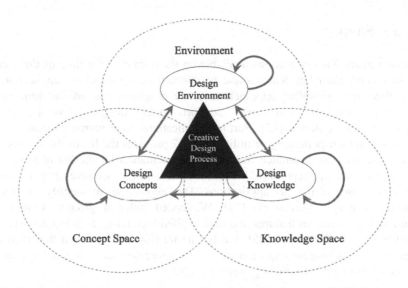

Fig. 2. Creative design process: Concept-Knowledge-Environment (CKE) framework

- **The interplay between C and E**: Architects should be able to modify the design environment according to their design concepts and define new concepts based on the target environment.
- **The interplay between E and K**: Architects should be able to model the environment to formulate new knowledge or interpret knowledge to understand the environment.
- **The interplay between K and C**: Architects should be able to develop innovative design concepts (e.g., design alternatives) based on existing knowledge or validate new concepts (e.g., design prototypes) as new knowledge.
- **Concept expansion**: Architects should be able to develop design concepts cre-atively, independently, or in collaboration with project stakeholders including their clients.

- **Knowledge expansion**: Architects should be able to expand their knowledge critically and contribute to both project and the firm's knowledgebases.
- **Environment expansion**: The design environment could be expanded with the new layer of internal or external information or objects related to the site variables (e.g. climate) or conditions (e.g. geography).

With knowledge of how the CKE framework is applied and how modern architectural practice operates, we can examine the features of XR applications and determine their affordances. This would help ensure that the requirements of the architectural design process identified earlier can be met by the next generation of XR applications. Further, this approach would pave the way for co-design in architectural practice [21].

4   Case Study

We reviewed six XR applications available on the market at the time of this study in order to identify their key features and functionalities. To select the applications, we used a theoretical sampling approach to select programs that are recommended in architectural   journals   and   that   support   both   design   development   and documentation/presentation [22]. Further, applications were narrowed down to three cases based on their popularity or utility. Table 2 provides the list of these tools. After the case selection, we examined the tools' documentation for the list of features and coded data for each application [23]. Then, the relevant features were categorized based on their use cases across the applications. This allowed us to identify the intended functions (designed affordances) [24]. We coded different groups of affordances enabled by each group of features and then applied hierarchies to select and verify the key categories of affordances [25]. Lastly, the relationships between the listed affordances and design process requirements were enumerated and examined according to the Needs-Affordances-Features perspective [26].

Table 2. The list of applications reviewed as part of case study

AR Tool name	Tool description
ARki (iOS application)	ARki allows instant augmented reality experiences with features such as real-time lighting and layering of various 3D models
Morpholio (iOS application)	Morpholio trace supports augmented reality sketch-walkthrough with features such as 3D model augmentation, dynamic and live walkthrough, and real-time tracing and design alteration
Unity reflect (Desktop application)	Create real-time 3D experiences, including in AR and VR, from Autodesk Revit, BIM 360, Navisworks, SketchUp, and Rhino

Features were grouped based on the design process requirements informed by the CKE framework (Table 3). As expected, features supported more than one requirement, such as virtual tours, interaction with XR objects, import and export files, and create simulations. The key features were centered around empowering the design team, including architects, to create XR models, join workspaces, and utilize XR visualizations for both design development and presentation. However, the analysis revealed that there was a significant difference in the utility of these applications in terms of interactivity and collaboration. However, all tools offered features supporting XR tours at the actual construction site. These features provided greater synergy between clients and architects during the design development phase.

We examined the features in the relationship with three components of the CKE framework—concept, knowledge, and environment—to identify the required affordances enabled by different groups of features. Design concept development, independently or interdependently to knowledge space or environment, could be supported by a group of features allowing on-site visualization and rendering different design options. These features enabled designers and other project stakeholders to design in a dynamic environment supported by augmented reality or virtuality. The case review also showed that the programs with more virtualizing features such as tracing, real-time lighting, and interactive layering fulfilled more experiential design needs than traditional AR or VR tools that focus on presentation. These features mainly corresponded with the expansion of the environment and how it supports both concept and knowledge development. The evaluation of design in both virtual and augmented environments was an example facilitated by features such as dynamic scaling to lighting. We assumed that clients/users could be part of the environment and therefore, they should contribute to the concept development. Supporting this assumption, the XR technologies studied here could connect the design team to the client and engage the client with features such as presentation, co-design, and critique. One of the noted benefits was the design team's capability to define different design scenarios and allow the client to experiment with them.

Table 3. The summary of XR feature categories and their relationships with design process requirements

Feature Categories	C⇔C	K⇔K	E⇔E	C⇔K	C⇔E	K⇔E
Build virtual models	X			X	X	
Create dynamic XR environments	X			X	X	
Interact with XR environment	X		X		X	X
Augment objects/information			X		X	X
Virtual and dynamic tours	X		X	X	X	X
Simulation (e.g., lighting)	X	X	X	X		X
Experimentation (e.g., materials)	X	X	X	X	X	X
Knowledge management		X		X		X
Workspace management				X		X
Collaboration features	X			X	X	X
Documentation features	X	X	X	X	X	X
Integration (with design tools)	X			X	X	
Integration (with XR tools)			X		X	X
Integration (with knowledge-base)		X		X		X

The findings suggested that knowledge-related features play an important role in design evolution and selection. The first group of features was related to integration (e.g. import and export 3D models), project documentation (e.g. journaling), and knowledge-management (e.g. building information modeling) that could help with both design and construction. Other examples included features such as sharing, commenting, and redlining. In the relationship between concept and environment, the design team however retained editing and similar admin level rights. These possibilities not only allowed expanding the existing knowledge but also contributed to firms' knowledgebase when the design is finalized.

The results of mapping the identified features on the architectural design process revealed that concept-related features can differentiate design products within the environment, attract attention, and enhance the design approval by the clients. Design concepts are further enhanced when the XR application enables the development and examination of a design concept in collaboration with the client. In the same way, the examination of the design concepts is also facilitated by XR technologies more realistically and practically. For example, these technologies allow clients to monitor design concepts as they evolve while encouraging them to provide more timely and thoughtful feedback. In the same way, participatory design processes require interactional experiences that afford real-time experimentations with 3D models in an augmented environment. XR applications enable project stakeholders to explore potential design options, share knowledge, examine their findings, collaborate, and seek feedback from other members in an environment enriched with augmented information. This minimizes the misunderstandings between the parties and ultimately enhances the quality of the design outcome.

XR applications facilitate the simulation of potential design solutions that can create a more reliable and detailed understanding of possible designs. Making well-reasoned design decisions can also motivate the use of XR applications that afford design validation. Furthermore, architects have a vested interest in tracking and analyzing the use of their time and resources. Hence, dynamic integration between design and other knowledgebases (enabled by XR applications) can optimize the use of resources in validating a design solution. Also, the design process can be enhanced when architects and design teams can have more control over the utility of time and, therefore, make more reasonable decisions during the design process. For example, by using simulation and validation functionalizes, architects and clients can co-regulate the design decisions for the benefit of time. Additionally, architects need to be able to share knowledge with external collaborators including the clients which are paramount to an effective design process.

The environment is the source of inspiration for architects especially if it is enriched with information that is not readily available in a dynamic manner such as data related to lighting, temperature, and traffic. XR applications, with the power of simulation, can enhance the design team's creativity in understanding the environment and how different design elements including materials interact with the design environment. This can foster the evaluation of complex design concepts and forward the design development. Besides, this may lead to a higher level of engagement with the client and project team and thereby nurturing the culture of co-design. XR applications allow clients to experience the proposed design concepts in a more natural setting. This invites more constructive feedback and therefore, optimizes the number of iterations in the design and later minimizes changes in the construction document or plan. Lastly, augmented reality and virtuality both give the client a 'sense of control'. For example, a client can freely experiment with a 3D model before approving a design. This sense of control also enhances the client's trust in architects.

5 Discussion

The relationships between the features of XR applications and the requirements of the architectural design process helped us to identify six functional affordances. These affordances could potentially guide the development of future XR applications for architecture and engineering design in general. The implementation of these functional affordances would ensure that XR lives up to its promise of solving a plethora of design challenges. Our identified affordances include:

- develop design concepts
- examine design concepts
- enrich design environment
- simulate design scenarios
- validate design solutions
- improve design logic

Develop design concept enables designers including architects to develop their creative conceptual ideas and generate innovative design concepts in a shared augmented environment that enables project stakeholders to view, interact and manipulate the ideas. *Examine design concepts* refers to supplying an augmented environment that accepts mixed inputs—from human and non-human sources—and generates experiential design elements during the design concept development. *Enrich design environment* supports the design process by modeling and representing the possibilities, constraints, and expectations in an extended environment. *Simulative design scenarios* refer to XR technologies affordances that can assist architects by examining various design scenarios as part of the approval process. *Validate design solutions* are XR affordances that help test design concepts based on a mix of inputs such as environmental survey data, site constraints, and building codes and compliances. *Lastly, improve design logic* enhances design solutions by offering real-time access to project information, project knowledgebase, and existing design solutions in an augmented environment.

We claim our identified XR design affordances can satisfy the design requirements suggested by the CKE framework in the following manner [9, 18, 20]. Design ideas can be expanded by design concept development in XR environments. XR applications that afford examine design concepts help test the design options in an augmented environment. XR applications can enrich the design environment by augmenting the environment with an added information, knowledge, or concepts. Design scenario simulations allow experimenting with various design solutions in an augmented design environment. XR applications can facilitate the design solution validation by supporting a critical and systematic review of new design concepts based on existing knowledge or new knowledge activated by new concepts. XR applications can support knowledge expansion—related to both design process and design outcome—when it affords to improve design logic. We summarize these relationships in Fig. 3.

The alignment between the identified XR affordances and creative design requirements, if actualized, could support architects at different levels (a) design solution development (e.g. balance between creativity, possibilities, client's expectations, and other project's constraints by providing an immersive design experience), (b) collaborative examination of complex design solutions, (c) design verification and experimentation (e.g. minimize misinterpretation and accelerate approval process), and (d) design process and outcome performance for all project stakeholders (e.g. as a result of design efficiency, improved accuracy and access to up-to-date information). The proposed framework can be used not only as a guide to review the existing XR applications used in architecture but also as a blueprint to design and develop new XR applications.

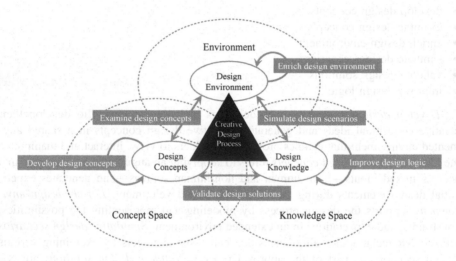

Fig. 3. The proposed framework for designing XR affordances based on the CKE framework

6   Conclusion

This study provides the opportunity for adaptive and effective XR application analysis on the part of developers, users, and researchers. Our proposed framework offers XR developers a guide for understanding architectural design and its requirements to hone the next generation of XR applications to address those requirements. In designing future XR applications, developers could use our framework to systematically analyze the key requirements of architectural practice. For example, developers could identify which affordances satisfy given requirements and which features should be implemented to enable those functional affordances. This has the potential to improve the chance of XR application success in terms of usability and adoption. Moreover, this framework can inform the evaluation of existing XR solutions for practical applications. For example, architects can use our framework to choose the application that suits their specific needs in six identified domains, development, examination, augmentation, simulation, validation, and improvement. The framework may also be used in the reverse method. For example, architectural firms can identify what design requirements are being addressed by certain features of the XR application in use and then use that knowledge to address any gaps present in their practice.

Examining the effects of each group of affordances on design outcomes is a rich avenue for future inquiry. For instance, future research could empirically examine how XR affordances may be designed, orchestrated, and presented to achieve the most meaningful and engaging experiences for architects, and clients alike. Researchers in technology fields can also adopt, test, and expand our framework to further investigate the role of XR applications in enhancing the design process in engineering and construction. Further, study into XR applications can propose more effective collaboration and communication mechanisms between different project stakeholders.

References

1. Veas, E., Grasset, R., Kruijff, E., Schmalstieg, D.: Extended overview techniques for outdoor augmented reality. IEEE Trans. Vis. Comput. Graph. **18**, 565–572 (2012)
2. Chuah, S.H.-W.: Why and who will adopt extended reality technology? Literature review, synthesis, and future research agenda. SSRN Electron. J. (2019). https://doi.org/10.2139/ssrn.3300469
3. Kose, A., Tepljakov, A., Petlenkov, E.: Real time data communication for intelligent extended reality applications. In: CIVEMSA 2020 - IEEE International Conference on Computational Intelligence and Virtual Environments for Measurement Systems and Applications, Proceedings. Institute of Electrical and Electronics Engineers Inc. (2020)
4. Alizadehsalehi, S., Hadavi, A., Huang, J.C.: From BIM to extended reality in AEC industry. Autom. Constr. **116**, 103254 (2020)
5. Stals, A., Caldas, L.: State of XR research in architecture with focus on professional practice–a systematic literature review. Archit. Sci. Rev. 1–9 (2020). https://doi.org/10.1080/00038628.2020.1838258
6. Ahn, K., Ko, D.S., Gim, S.H.: A study on the architecture of mixed reality application for architectural design collaboration. In: Lee, R. (ed.) Applied Computing and Information Technology, vol. 788, pp. 48–61. Springer, Cham (2019). https://doi.org/10.1007/978-3-319-98370-7_5
7. Sagnier, C., Loup-Escande, E., Lourdeaux, D., Thouvenin, I., Valléry, G.: User acceptance of virtual reality: an extended technology acceptance model. Int. J. Hum. Comput. Interact. **36**, 993–1007 (2020)
8. Wu, S., Hou, L., Zhang, G.: Integrated application of BIM and eXtended reality technology: a review, classification and outlook. In: Toledo Santos, E., Scheer, S. (eds.) Proceedings of the 18th International Conference on Computing in Civil and Building Engineering. LNCE, vol. 98, pp. 1227–1236. Springer, Cham (2021). https://doi.org/10.1007/978-3-030-51295-8_86
9. Kazakçi, A.O., Tsoukias, A.: Extending the C-K design theory: a theoretical background for personal design assistants. J. Eng. Des. **16**, 399–411 (2005)

10. Banfi, F., Brumana, R., Stanga, C.: Extended reality and informative models for the architectural heritage: from scan-to-bim process to virtual and augmented reality. Virtual Archaeol. Rev. **10**, 14–30 (2019)
11. Çöltekin, A., et al.: Extended reality in spatial sciences: a review of research challenges and future directions. ISPRS Int. J. Geo-Inf. **9**, 439 (2020)
12. Park, M.K., Lim, K.J., Seo, M.K., Jung, S.J., Lee, K.H.: Spatial augmented reality for product appearance design evaluation. J. Comput. Des. Eng. **2**, 38–46 (2015)
13. Sun, C., Hu, W., Xu, D.: Navigation modes, operation methods, observation scales and background options in UI design for high learning performance in VR-based architectural applications. J. Comput. Des. Eng. **6**, 189–196 (2019)
14. Su, P., Wang, S.: Virtual reality practice in architecture design. In: Proceedings - 2012 IEEE Symposium on Electrical and Electronics Engineering, EEESYM 2012, pp. 98–101 (2012)
15. Hill, D., George, B.H., Johnson, T.: How virtual reality impacts the landscape architecture design process during the phases of analysis and concept development at the master planning scale. J. Digit. Landscape Archit. **2019**, 266–274 (2019)
16. Phan, V.T., Choo, S.Y.: Interior design in augmented reality environment. Int. J. Comput. Appl. **5**, 16–21 (2019)
17. Kulkarni, M.: Impact of software and technology on architectural design practice. Int. J. Eng. Res. **7**, 165–167 (2018)
18. Hatchuel, A., Weil, B.: C-K design theory: an advanced formulation. Res. Eng. Des. **19**, 181–192 (2009). https://doi.org/10.1007/s00163-008-0043-4
19. Hatchuel, A., Weil, B., Le Masson, P.: Towards an ontology of design: lessons from C-K design theory and forcing. Res. Eng. Des. **24**, 147–163 (2013)
20. Hatchuel, A., Weil, B.: A new approach of innovative design: an introduction to CK theory. In: DS 31: Proceedings of ICED 03, 14th International Conference on Engineering Design, pp. 1–15 (2003)
21. Abhari, K., Davidson, E.J.: Creative co-production: the adaption of an open innovation model in creative industries. In: Lugmayr, A., Stojmenova, E., Stanoevska, K., Wellington, R. (eds.) Information Systems and Management in Media and Entertainment Industries. ISCEMT, pp. 119–130. Springer, Cham (2016). https://doi.org/10.1007/978-3-319-49407-4_6
22. Yin, R.K.: Case Study Research: Design and Methods. Sage Publications, Thousand Oaks (2009)
23. Adžgauskaitė, M., Abhari, K., Pesavento, M.: How virtual reality is changing the future of learning in K-12 and beyond. In: Stephanidis, C., et al. (eds.) HCI International 2020 – Late Breaking Papers: Cognition, Learning and Games. LNCS, vol. 12425, pp. 279–298. Springer, Cham (2020). https://doi.org/10.1007/978-3-030-60128-7_22
24. Hartson, R.: Cognitive, physical, sensory, and functional affordances in interaction design. Behav. Inf. Technol. **22**, 315–338 (2003)
25. Kaptelinin, V., Nardi, B.A.B., Hall, B., Irvine, U.C.: Affordances in HCI: toward a mediated action perspective. In: Proceedings of the 2012 ACM Annual Conference on Human Factors in Computing Systems, pp. 967–976. ACM Press, New York (2012)
26. Karahanna, E., Xu, X.S., Xu, Y., Zhang, N.: The needs–affordances–features perspective for the use of social media. MIS Q. **42**, 737–756 (2018)

A Cost-Effective Immersive Telexistence Platform for Generic Telemanipulation Tasks

Reem Al-Remaihi[1], Aisha Al-Raeesi[1], Reem Al-Kubaisi[1],
Mohammed Al-Sada[1,2(✉)], Tatsuo Nakajima[2], and Osama Halabi[1]

[1] Department of Computer Science and Engineering,
Qatar University, Doha, Qatar
alsada@dcl.cs.waseda.ac.jp, ohalabi@qu.edu.qa
[2] Department of Computer Science and Communications Engineering,
Waseda University, Tokyo, Japan
tatsuo@dcl.cs.waseda.ac.jp

Abstract. Robots are expected to become an essential part in tackling the global corona virus pandemic. However, acquiring robotic technology in economically-challenged nations is very difficult for a variety of factors. This work aims at developing a low-cost Telexistence systems that can be used for remote manipulation. We propose a system comprising components on the local site, which comprise a commonly available VR headset, a tracking system and a 3D-printed haptic exoskeleton. The remote site comprises a small robot arm. We discuss the implementation specifics of our approach. We evaluated our system by comparing usability and performance in two tasks while using the VR headset and a monitor. Users were able to complete the two tasks successfully with our system. Moreover, results show superiority of the VR headset, however, the screen also show promising results, and thereby offer a cheaper deployment option.

Keywords: Telexistence · Teleoperation · VR · Haptics · HRI

1 Introduction and Motivation

Robots are expected to become powerful instruments in tackling global issues such as the challenges caused by the global Corona virus epidemic that severely overwhelmed the world and transformed our lives. The resulting lockdowns have tremendous impact on our work and daily lives. A critical challenge is the difficulty of people's presence in work environments due to emergency constraints, which has impact tasks and activities that require physical interaction like operation of industrial machinery, taking care of patients at hospitals or hands-on training contexts.

Previous works in telexistence and telepresence technologies [1–5] have long been investigated as approaches that utilize robots to accomplish physical tasks with high sense of presence. However, the complexity and cost of such systems have constrained their deployment within various industries, especially within developing countries that face challenges to access, develop and deploy such technology.

© Springer Nature Switzerland AG 2021
C. Stephanidis et al. (Eds.): HCII 2021, LNCS 13095, pp. 197–208, 2021.
https://doi.org/10.1007/978-3-030-90963-5_16

This work attempt to bridge the gap into developing a cost-effective teleoperation robotic system that is able to accomplish a variety of physical manipulation capabilities, while being easy to use and providing high sense of presence and agency in the remote locations. Accordingly, we explain the specifics of our implementation and follow with an evaluation of the system usability and the effect of the level of immersion, using an HMD and a desktop screen, on task accuracy in two physical manipulation tasks. The overall results are encouraging to pursue deeper evaluations. Lastly, we provide our conclusion and future research direction.

Our contribution is summarized as follows: 1) we design and implement a telepresence robotic system based on off-the-shelf components to ensure ease of accessibility and deployment in developing countries. 2) Evaluate the effect different levels of immersion on the accuracy achieving different tasks.

2 Related Works

Telexistence and telepresence has long been investigated in previous literatures. Telexistence is a term that refers to a group of technologies and approaches that focus on high sense of presence within remote environments [1, 2, 3, 4, 5]. Various previous works proposed robotic platforms that enabled locomotion and multimodal interactions within remote environments. Generally, these works focused on enabling high sense of presence, therefore, engaging multiple senses such as vision, olfactory and haptic to deliver high sense of agency and presence with the relayed remote environment. Haptics is indispensable for such systems as it increase the sense of presence and accuracy of doing tasks [6, 7]. It also enhances the memory retention that lead to better performance [8]. A telepresence presents a group of technologies to enable a person to feel as if they are in other locations [9, 10]. Research has thoroughly investigated a variety of methods for telepresence, with varied levels of immersion, interaction modalities and sense of presence with the remote environments. Telepresence robotics focuses on enabling users to remotely access and interact with a remote environment [10].

Despite the robustness of previous efforts, we believe that most existing robotic telepresence systems and telexistence are inaccessible to economically-challenged nations, whether in terms of cost, attainability of equipment or availability within such nations. In comparison to previous works, our approach focuses on bridging the gap in deployability and cost for telexistence systems. Therefore, we use off-the-shelf components that are commonly available, without much reliance on industrial or custom-made components. Second, we use cost-effective components to reduce the cost as much as possible. These two aspects ensures that our implementation can be duplicated based on easily available components, or similar alternative components. Likewise, our software infrastructure uses commonly available technologies, such as Unity3D [11], SteamVR [12], and network connectivity based on websockets, which are all commonly available and attainable for free (with varied licensing for commercial use).

3   System Design and Implementation

The system is divided into two sub systems, local site (controller site) and remote site (robot site), as shown in Fig. 1. Next sections will explain every sub system:

3.1   Local Environment

The local site is designed to enable high sense of presence, similar to telexistence systems. The local site comprises a 3D-printed haptic exoskeleton that can both sense user's finger locations and deliver haptic feedback (based on [13]), as shown in Fig. 2. The exoskeleton is controlled through a Pololu Mini Maestro controller [14]. The user can see the remote site by wearing virtual reality (VR) head mounted display (HMD) with trackers placed on the user's hands to track their hand movements (HTC Vive system).

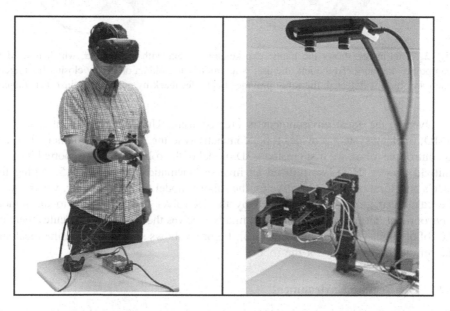

Fig. 1. Left) The exoskeleton haptic glove with attached tracker and HMD in Local environment. Right) The stereoscopic camera and the robot.

Before holding an object	After holding an object

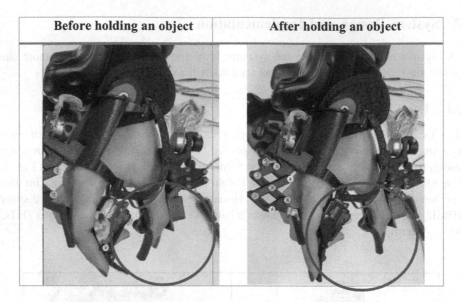

Fig. 2. This image shows the haptic exoskeleton system with the tracker, which is used to manipulate the robot. To the left, the user is attempting to hold an object by closing his fingers, when an object is detected, the robot provides haptic feedback by pressing against their fingers.

Overall, the local environment is created using Unity3D, which integrates the HMD, tracking system provides robot connectivity to the remote environment. In order to control the robot, we first created a 3D model of the robot arm and imported it to our unity3d project. Next, we utilized an inverse kinematic (IK) solver [15] setting the user's arm location as an objective for the robot's model to reach. Finally, we extracted the calculated joint angles produced by the IK solver and sent them to the remote environment. The remote environment finally receives the angles and executes them on the robot similar to previous works [16]. Figure 3 shows snapshots from the local and the remote environment for the robot.

3.2   The Remote Environment

The remote site comprises a stereoscopic camera that is positioned above the robot arm to provide live streaming to the local site, and a robot arm based on Robotis Manipulator X with a gripper end-effector equipped with force-sensitive sensors (FSR) to detect touch forces, see Fig. 4. The client-server architecture was used to enable controlling the robot in remote locations. Overall, the control system of the remote environment is deployed on a PC, while the FSR's data is captured through a Pololu Mini Maestro controller, which is also connected to the PC to forward the data to the local environment. Lastly, we used a ZED Mini Stereoscopic Camera to transmit the stereoscopic feed through WebRTC [17].

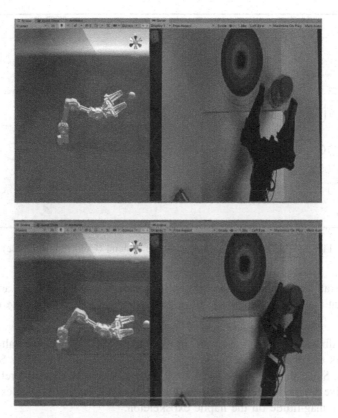

Fig. 3. Screenshots from the local and the remote environment. The left side of each picture shows the Unity3D scene with the imported robot model and IK solver. The right side of the image shows the camera feed from the remote environment with the robot attempting to follow the user's movement in the local environment.

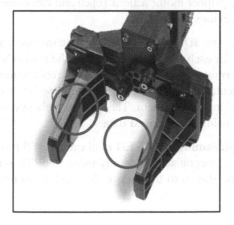

Fig. 4. An FSR is attached on each side of the end-effector to provide the ability to sense the applied pressure on the manipulated objects. The captured pressure data is sent to the local environment where they are conveyed as haptic feedback to the user.

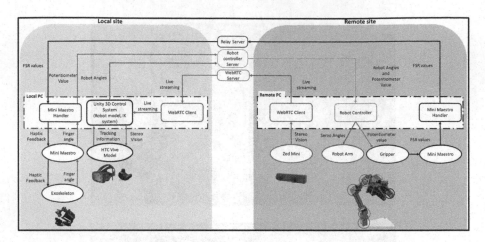

Fig. 5. The overall architecture of the system. (Color figure online)

The overall architecture of the system is explained in Fig. 5. There are four main modules that comprise data flow within the system (color coded in the diagram for clarity):

Haptic Feedback: The Mini Maestro in the remote PC will read the values from the FSR sensors that are attached on the gripper and send it to the Relay Server using websockets. Since the PC at the local environment is connected to the relay server, it would receive the FSR data, and map such readings into servomotor angles that control the feedback magnitude on the haptic exoskeleton.

Robotic Gripper Control: The Mini Maestro connected to the PC at the local environment will read the values from the potentiometer sensors that are attached on the exoskeleton and send them to the Robot Controller Server using websockets. Accordingly, the remote site's system will map the potentiometer readings into one angle that controls the gripper motor actions (open and close) using the robotic control system used in our previous work [16].

Robot Arm Control: The 3D model Unity3d is implemented and the IK solver to find out the robot's angles for each posture is used. Also, the tracker's location on the user's hand is used to determine the target location the robot's model should move to. Accordingly, the calculated robot angles are these angles are transferred through websockets to the remote site's system. The remote site's system will read the angles and control the robot using the received data.

Stereoscopic Video Streaming: The ZED mini camera will provide the system a live stereoscopic streaming, integrated within unity using webRTC server. The stereoscopic image is processed and shown to the user in the local environment.

The system is generally comprised of both off-the shelf components or 3D printed ones. The local environment utilizes consumer-level and 3D-printed components that can easily be obtained and are cost-effective. The chosen robot arm is also capable of lifting up to 500 g, with an effective workspace of 450 mm, and its end-effector exchangeable to meet other application domains (e.g., 5-finger hand). Therefore, we believe our design and implementation is easy to follow and customizable to match different applications. Moreover, with the falling costs of HMDs and actuators in the market, we believe a system based on the proposed architecture would be very cost-effective yet efficient for a variety of tasks, serving both industrial, hobbyist or research applications.

4 Evaluation

4.1 Objectives and Design

The main objective is to investigate the overall usability of the system as well as explore the effect of using different immersive displays on the task accuracy. In the experimental setup, HMD used as very high immersive display and a desktop display as a lower immersive level as can be seen in Fig. 6. Two types of manipulation tasks were considered in the study: 1) Lift and place an object (a plastic bottle of water) from one location and placing it to different locations on the table (T1), which is a common task within object manipulation contexts [16], 2) holding an instrument and pointing it towards a specific target (T2), which resembles taking a Corona virus swab. Both tasks are shown in Fig. 7 and Fig. 8.

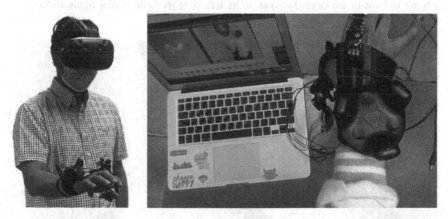

Fig. 6. The conditions of the experiment. We compared the user's accuracy and usability of our system on the HMD (Left) and a monitor (Right).

The accuracy was measured in terms of percentage of ±5 mm range in both tasks. As shown in Fig 7, if the user places the bottle in the middle of the target (yellow circle), they get 100, and with each measured 5 mm from the center, the user loses 5 points.

We used the same calculation method for both T1 and T2. Moreover, we set some more rules to calculate the percentages, for example, if the bottle/poking device falls from the robot during operation, the accuracy will be counted as 0%. Also, users were not allowed to modify the position of the bottle or poke the target after their initial touch or poke. In addition to measuring the task accuracies, we also measured the time to complete each trial.

In addition to demographic data, we created a questionnaire to measure user's impressions regarding the two tasks under the HMD and monitor conditions. We also evaluated our system's usability using the SUS questionnaire [18, 19].

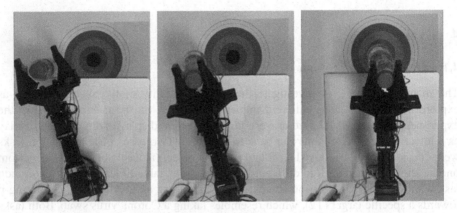

Fig. 7. Task 1 (T1): users had to pick up a bottle and place it at the middle of the target. This task was executed based on three conditions depending on the starting location of the bottle, which are in-front of the target location, to its left, or to its right. (Color figure online)

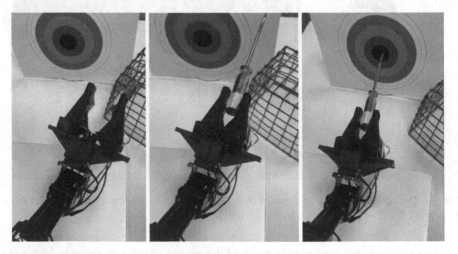

Fig. 8. Task 2 (T2) resembles a swab test. Participants had to pick up the screw-driver and poke the target in the middle. T2 was also executed in two basic conditions that alternated the locations of the screw-driver, placing it to the left or right of the target mark.

4.2   Participants and Procedure

Participants: We recruited 10 participants (all females, age m = 23.1, std = 2.96), who were students from various disciplines. Six participants indicated that they were familiar with VR, while the rest were not.

Flow: After a brief familiarization session, each participants took a demographic questionnaire, followed by the user study conditions. Participants did task 1, then task 2, using the HMD and followed by the monitor conditions, where each trial was repeated 3 times similar to previous works [20]. Overall, each participants undergone 10 trials (6 for T1, 4 trials for T2), where the experiment took approximately 60 min per participant. Upon finishing the trials, participants took a questionnaire that gauged their overall impression of the system and tasks, in addition to the SUS questionnaire.

4.3   Results and Analysis

Task Accuracy: The accuracy of manipulating the two tasks was higher when using HMD display than standard monitor as shown in Fig. 9. This demonstrates the superiority of immersive stereoscopic view in telexistence systems.

As shown in Table 1, the overall accuracy and time needed to accomplish both T1 and T2 was better in the HMD than the monitor. In T1, the average accuracy was slightly higher in the HMD than the monitor. However, in T2, the accuracy was remarkably higher in the HMD. We believe such results are in-line with previous telexistence results that showed the superiority of stereoscopic vision during physical manipulation tasks as users are able to perceive the depth of objects and thereby control the robot arms efficiently.

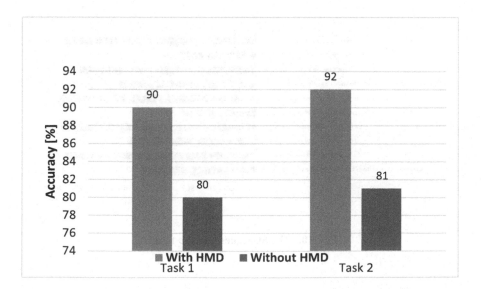

Fig. 9. The accuracy of achieving tasks for different levels of immersion.

Table 1. Average time on task and accuracies for each condition, with standard deviation values between brackets.

Tasks	Average time on task seconds (SD)	Average accuracy % (SD)
T1 (Monitor)	161 (44.8)	87.66 (8.89)
T1 (HMD)	145 (28.4)	88.83 (7.62)
Task2 (Monitor)	236 (18.2)	80.5 (8.87)
Task2 (HMD)	202 (35.3)	91 (8.52)

User Impressions: The participants were asked whether they preferred the HMD or the screen to accomplish the tasks. Seven participants preferred the HMD, mentioning that the sense of depth, better dimensions and realism of the remote objects seen through HMD and stereoscopic feed made them accomplish the tasks better. Participants who preferred the monitor mentioned aspects of dizziness and clarity of vision since these participants could not use their glasses with the HMD. When tasked to rate the difficulty of both tasks (5 means very difficult), participants rated T1 and T2 in terms of difficulty with 1.20 (std = 0.42) and 2.80 (std = 0.91), respectively. These results indicate that the participants generally though that the tasks were generally easy to accomplish.

SUS Questionnaire Results: Participants liked the system and found it very useful and usable. High scores in the questions related likeness, well integrated, easy to use, and confidence to use the system with scores over 80%. However, the lowest scores were in the questions related to complexity, inconsistency with scores less than 40% (Fig. 10). Nevertheless, final SUS score was 73.5, which is considered good as the average score for SUS to be considered usable is 68.

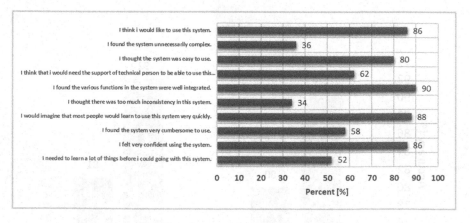

Fig. 10. The SUS questionnaire results.

Overall, we believe the results are encouraging to pursue further work. Users were able to accomplish two fundamental physical manipulation tasks remotely, therefore, we believe the control system was generally successful. Although the HMD proved to be superior to the monitor, we believe that using the monitor is a viable option and users had generally good results. Therefore, we believe that the results show the flexibility of deploying similar systems without the use of HMDs, which can contribute to reducing the overall cost.

5 Conclusion

This paper presents the design, implementation, and evaluation of a low-cost telexistence robotic system. We believe the presented architecture is cost-effective yet highly capable in terms of task accuracy and usability. The evaluation results also revealed the superiority of the HMD and stereoscopic vision for the evaluated physical manipulation tasks. However, replacing the HMD with a screen is also a viable option, and it produced acceptable results. Therefore, we believe that both deployment options can accomplish a variety of tasks, and future work should further evaluate the advantages of using a monitor for telemanipulation tasks.

A critical direction to research is to explore potential applications of telepresence robotics within daily usage contexts [16]. Moreover, as the context of use in economically challenged nations could be different than developed nations, we believe that focus groups and brainstorming workshops should be held within target countries. These workshops would enable us to capture design requirements or application domains that we have not initially thought about [21]. Accordingly, such data can be used as bases to advance our architecture to fit specific deployment domains.

We hope that this work will inspire further research that contributes to advancing of cost-effective technologies and exploring potential deployment domains that addresses the daily life constraints imposed by the corona pandemic.

Acknowledgement. This paper was jointly supported by Qatar University M-QJRC-2020-7. The findings achieved herein are solely the responsibility of the authors.

References

1. Tachi, S.: Telexistence: enabling humans to be virtually ubiquitous. IEEE Comput. Graph. Appl. **36**, 8–14 (2016). https://doi.org/10.1109/MCG.2016.6
2. Tachi, S.: Telexistence. J. Robot. Soc. Japan (2015). https://doi.org/10.7210/jrsj.33.215
3. Alhalabi, M.O.O., Horiguchi, S.: Haptic cooperative virtual workspace: architecture and evaluation. Virtual Reality **5**, 160–168 (2000). https://doi.org/10.1007/BF01409421
4. Inoue, Y., Kato, F., Tachi, S.: Master-slave robot hand control method based on congruence of vectors for telexistence hand manipulation. In: 2019 22nd 2019 IEEE International Symposium on Measurement and Control in Robotics: Robotics for the Benefit of Humanity (ISMCR), ISMCR 2019, pp. 1–4 (2019). https://doi.org/10.1109/ISMCR47492.2019. 8955688

5. Fernando, C.L., Furukawa, M., Minamizawa, K., Tachi, S.: Experiencing ones own hand in telexistence manipulation with a 15 DOF anthropomorphic robot hand and a flexible master glove. In: 2013 23rd International Conference on Artificial Reality and Telexistence, pp. 20–27 (2014). https://doi.org/10.1109/icat.2013.6728901

6. Halabi, O., Halwani, Y.: Design and implementation of haptic virtual fixtures for preoperative surgical planning. Displays **54**, 9–19 (2018). https://doi.org/10.1016/j.displa.2018.07.004

7. Halabi, O., Bahameish, M.A., Al-Naimi, L.T., Al-Kaabi, A.K.: Response times for auditory and vibrotactile directional cues in different immersive displays. Int. J. Hum.-Comput. Interact. **35**, 1578–1585 (2019). https://doi.org/10.1080/10447318.2018.1555743

8. Halabi, O., Al-Mesaifri, F., Al-Ansari, M., Al-Shaabi, R., Miyata, K.: Incorporating olfactory into a multi-modal surgical simulation. IEICE Trans. Inf. Syst. E97.D, 2048–2052 (2014).https://doi.org/10.1587/transinf.E97.D.2048

9. Björnfot, P., Kaptelinin, V.: Probing the design space of a telepresence robot gesture arm with low fidelity prototypes. In: ACM/IEEE International Conference on Human-Robot Interaction, Part F1271, pp. 352–360 (2017). https://doi.org/10.1145/2909824.3020223

10. Yamen Saraiji, M., Sugimoto, S., Lasantha Fernando, C., Minamizawa, K., Tachi, S.: Layered telepresence: simultaneous multi presence experience using eye gaze based perceptual awareness blending. In: Proceedings of ACM SIGGRAPH 2016 Emerging Technologies (2016)

11. Unity3D: Unity Game Engine. https://unity.com

12. Steam: Stream VR. https://store.steampowered.com/app/250820/SteamVR/

13. youbionic: youbionic. https://www.youbionic.com/handexohand

14. Pololu Corporation: Pololu. https://www.pololu.com/product/1354

15. Starke, S., Hendrich, N., Zhang, J.: Memetic evolution for generic full-body inverse kinematics in robotics and animation. IEEE Trans. Evol. Comput. 23 (2019). https://doi.org/10.1109/TEVC.2018.2867601

16. Al-Sada, M., Höglund, T., Khamis, M., Urbani, J., Nakajima, T.: Orochi: investigating requirements and expectations for multipurpose daily used supernumerary robotic limbs. In: Proceedings of the 10th Augmented Human International Conference 2019 on - AH2019, pp. 1–9. ACM Press, New York (2019)

17. StereoLabs: ZED mini. https://www.stereolabs.com/zed-mini/

18. Brooke, J.: SUS: a "quick and dirty" usability scale. In: Usability Evaluation in Industry, pp. 207–212. CRC Press (1996)

19. Brooke, J.: SUS : a retrospective. J. Usability Stud. **8**, 29–40 (2020)

20. Al-Sada, M., Jiang, K., Ranade, S., Kalkattawi, M., Nakajima, T.: HapticSnakes: multi-haptic feedback wearable robots for immersive virtual reality. Virtual Reality **24**(2), 191–209 (2019). https://doi.org/10.1007/s10055-019-00404-x

21. Al Sada, M., Khamis, M., Kato, A., Sugano, S., Nakajima, T., Alt, F.: Challenges and opportunities of supernumerary robotic limbs. In: CHI 2017 Workshop on Amplification and Augmentation of Human Perception (Amplify 2017), Denver, CO, USA (2017)

Motion Primitive Segmentation Based on Cognitive Model in VR-IADL

Taisei Ando[1(✉)], Takehiko Yamaguchi[1], Norito Kohama[2],
Maiko Sakamoto[3], Tania Giovannetti[4], and Tetsuya Harada[5]

[1] Suwa University of Science, Toyohira, Chino, Nagano 5000-1, Japan
GH20502@ed.sus.ac.jp, tk-ymgch@rs.sus.ac.jp
[2] Tokyo University of Science, Yamazaki, Noda, Chiba 2641, Japan
[3] Saga University, 5-1-1 Nabeshima, Saga, Saga, Japan
[4] Temple University, Philadelphia, PA 19122, USA
[5] Tokyo University of Science, 6-3-1 Niijuku, Katsushika, Tokyo, Japan

Abstract. Recently, many studies have been conducted using virtual reality (VR) technology in the medical field. Our research group has been developing a virtual kitchen challenge (VKC), which is a system to evaluate instrumental activities of daily living (IADL) using VR technology. In the previous study, we focused on motion primitives, which are the smallest unit of motion in VKC. In this study, we focused on the motion of the VKC task when there is no contact with the screen and developed a model that can be segmented by motion primitives. Furthermore, using a two-step process based on time-series data of the subject's fingertip velocity during the VKC task, we developed a model that can be segmented in terms of motion primitives. Therefore, the segmentation accuracy was 83.4%, and the percentage of false positives was as high as 28%.In the future, we plan to revise the feature set.

Keywords: Virtual reality · Motion primitive segmentation method

1 Background

1.1 Aging and Dementia Problem

Currently, the elderly population in Japan is increasing due to the declining birthrate and aging population, also in 2019, the elderly population aged 65 years and older was 35.88 million, accounting for 28.4% of the total population of Japan [1]. As the population ages, the number of dementia patients continues to increase. As of 2012, 4.62 million people were living with dementia, with the number estimated to increase to approximately 7 million by 2025 [2]. The increasing number of dementia patients is a major social problem not only in Japan but around the world. According to the International Alzheimer's Association, the number of dementia patients worldwide is estimated to be 50 million in 2018 and is expected to increase to 82 million by 2030 and 152 million by 2050 [3]. Dementia can be classified into Alzheimer's disease and cerebrovascular dementia according to its cause. Alzheimer's disease is responsible for 40%-60% of all cases. The causes of Alzheimer's disease are still unknown, and no definitive treatment has been established.

© Springer Nature Switzerland AG 2021
C. Stephanidis et al. (Eds.): HCII 2021, LNCS 13095, pp. 209–218, 2021.
https://doi.org/10.1007/978-3-030-90963-5_17

1.2   MCI

Mild cognitive impairment (MCI) is a condition that occurs between aging and dementia people. MCI is classified into four subtypes according to the presence and pattern of impairment in memory and other cognitive functions. MCI is classified into four subtypes according to the presence or absence and pattern of memory and other cognitive impairments: 1) Amnestic MCI Single Domain, 2) Amnestic MCI multiple domains, 3) Non-amnestic MCI Single Domain, and 4) Non-amnestic MCI multiple domains. It has been reported that each subtype of MCI can lead to dementia, but it has also been reported that MCI patients can return to a normal state with appropriate rehabilitation [5]. Therefore, early detection of MCI is critical in terms of dementia prevention. It is a problem that cognitive function tests, such as MMSE, have low discrimination accuracy, with a rate of approximately 30% in the MCI stage. Therefore, it is necessary to consider screening methods for MCI by evaluating functions other than cognitive function.

1.3   Instrumental Activities of Daily Living

Instrumental Activities of Daily Living refers to a group of activities that includes meal preparation, public transportation, and money management. IADL requires more thought than ADL (Activities of Daily Living), which includes activities such as bathing, eating, and toileting. Recently, according to the results of objective and subjective assessments, MCI patients show a functional decline in these activities compared to healthy elderly people. Based on an objective evaluation study, Giovannetti et al. conducted the Naturalistic Action Test (NAT) task on healthy elderly people, MCI patients, and patients with Alzheimer's disease, and the number of human errors during the NAT task was counted and compared. The number of human errors during the NAT task was counted and compared among the three groups. Therefore, it was reported that the number of human errors in MCI patients was significantly higher than in healthy elderly people [6]. Based on a subjective evaluation study, Cintra et al. conducted a questionnaire about IADL for family members and caregivers of healthy elderly, MCI patients, and Alzheimer's patients and analyzed the questionnaire scores. The results showed that MCI patients were significantly lower than those of healthy elderly people [7].

1.4   Virtual Kitchen Challenge System

Our research group has been developing a VKC system, which is an assessment tool to evaluate the meal preparation among IADLs [8]. Two tasks are implemented in VKC. The first is the Toast & Coffee task, which simulates the breakfast preparation. The second is the Lunchbox task, which simulates lunch preparation. In both of these two tasks, some kitchen items are necessary to perform the task, while some are not. The data output by the VKC includes the time from the start to the end of the task, the name of the item touched, and the touch flag. The VKC consists of three layers; the main task, the subtasks required to execute the main task, and the behavior primitives required to execute the subtasks. The smallest unit of motion in the VKC is the behavior primitive.

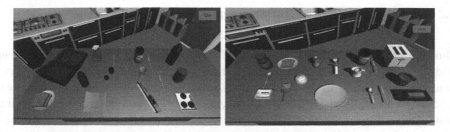

Fig. 1. Screenshot of VKC (left: Lunchbox task, Right: Toast & Coffee task).

2   Previous Study

2.1   Frequency Analysis of Behavioral Primitives in VKC Tasks

In a previous study, we focused on the frequency of occurrence of motion primitives such as touch and drag [9]. The frequency of occurrence of motion primitives in the VKC task of university students, healthy elderly people, and MCI patients was determined, and frequency data was generated (see Fig. 2). Clustering was performed on the frequency data using a topic model (LDA: Latent Dirichlet Allocation). Therefore, college students and MCI patients were divided into independent topics. Additionally, the topics of the healthy elderly were not identified, while the topics of the university students and MCI patients were divided into both. This suggests that healthy elderly people have characteristics similar to college students and MCI patients. The results of this study propose that MCI can also be screened using frequency analysis of movement primitives in the VKC task [9].

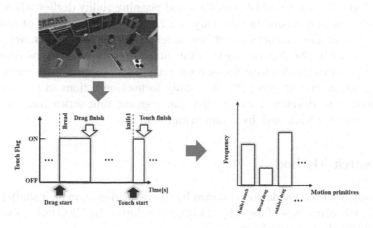

Fig. 2. Flow of motion frequency analysis.

2.2   Relationship Between Human Cognitive Models and Motion Planning

Humans pay attention to the necessary information received through sensory organs and interpret, judge, and execute such information based on previous memories. Atance et al. defined planning as the ability to think about what actions to select and execute in a series of action flows [10]. In this study, we defined action planning as the preliminary action of task execution in the cognitive model based on Atance et al.'s definition of planning.

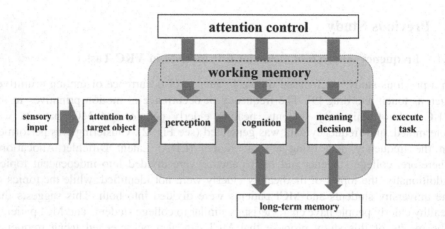

Fig. 3. Model of human cognition (modified from a figure in Yamaguchi (2019) [11]).

It has been shown that IADL functions and planning ability decline when working memory dysfunction occurs. In this study, we focused on the behavior of participants when they were not in contact with the screen because the characteristics of the behavior caused by the decline in IADL functions appear during motion planning.

While previous studies have focused on actions that occur during screen contact, such as touching and dragging [9]; this study focuses on actions that occur without screen contact to develop a model that can segment time-series data of fingertip velocities during a VKC task by action primitives.

3   Research Method

In this study, we used the dataset obtained by Giovannetti et al. in their study [12]. The 3D positional coordinates of the subject's fingertips during the VKC task, as well as the experimental videos, were obtained.

3.1   Participant

In this study, we used the dataset obtained from the study by Giovannetti et al. [12]. There were 22 subjects; fourteen healthy university students, five healthy elderly, and three MCI patients, with a mean age of 40.2 years (SD = 27.23), which are 7 males and 15 females.

3.2   Lunchbox Task in VKC

The Lunchbox task used in this study consists of three main tasks (sandwich, water bottle, and cookie task) and several subtasks necessary to accomplish them. The details of the main and subtasks are shown below.

(1) Sandwich task
     This task consists of eight subtasks: (1) Place a piece of bread on a piece of aluminum foil. (2) Open the lid of the peanut jam. (3) Scoop out the peanut jam with a knife and spread it on the bread. (4) Open the lid of the blueberry jam. (5) Scoop out the blueberry jam with a knife and spread it on the bread. (6) Sandwich it with another piece of bread. (7) Wrap the bread in aluminum foil. (8) Put the wrapped bread into the Lunchbox.
(2) Water bottle task
     This task consists of five subtasks: (1) Open the lid of the juice. (2) Pour the juice into the water bottle. (3) Close the inner lid of the water bottle. (4) Close the outer lid of the water bottle. (5) Place the water bottle in the Lunchbox.
(3) Cookie task
     This task consists of three subtasks (1) Place three cookies on a piece of aluminum foil. (2) Wrap the three cookies with aluminum foil. (3) Put the wrapped cookies into the Lunchbox.

After completing the three main tasks, close the lid of the Lunchbox and press the Quit button on the upper right corner of the screen to exit.

3.3   Segmentation Method

In this study, we performed segmentation in two steps, following the method proposed by Iwashita et al. [13]. In the first stage, we segment the time-series of fingertip velocities obtained during the VKC task at the zero intersections of the acceleration. Furthermore, some segment boundaries are incorrectly set. In the first segmentation step, some segment boundaries are incorrectly set in the first stage, thus, we corrected the incorrect segment boundaries in the second step. The second stage involves applying machine learning to the primary correct data obtained in the first stage, as well as the segment interval features, to correct the primary correct data, i.e. the incorrect segment points.

3.4   Differences Between Wandering and Pointing in Terms of Angle Statistics

Wandering is included in the movement in motion planning defined earlier. Wandering is a movement in which a person is lost while moving his or her fingers minutely. Wandering was more common in healthy elderly people and MCI patients than in university students. This is because the cognitive functions of elderly people and MCI patients are lower than that of university students, resulting in slower decision-making speed. In extracting features, we focused on wandering and pointing. Wandering was mistakenly perceived as a series of pointing, resulting in incorrect segmentation. Therefore, we focused on the direction vector of the motion per unit time.

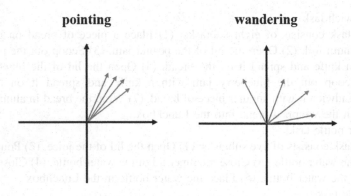

Fig. 4. Polar coordinate display of motion direction vector per unit time.

When pointing, the variation of the direction vector per unit time is small, but large when wandering. As shown in Fig. 4, when the direction vectors per unit time are displayed in polar coordinates, wandering and pointing are different in terms of angle statistics. Therefore, we decided to model these two motions using angle statistics.

Figure 5 shows the velocity waveform during pointing and the adjustment time. In the case of pointing, a segment interval is defined from the start to the end of the motion. However, when the adjustment time occurs, the segment boundary is incorrectly set at 34.33 s as shown in Fig. 5, and the segment is divided into two segments.

The adjustment time is the amount of time taken for the visual feedback loop to move the hand precisely to the target stimulus while adjusting the hand speed [14].

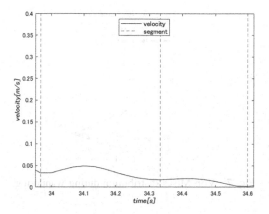

Fig. 5. Velocity waveform during pointing including adjustment time with incorrectly set segment boundaries.

3.5 Von Mises Distribution

To model wandering and pointing from the viewpoint of angle statistics, we focused on the von Mises distribution. The von Mises distribution has two parameters, the mean μ, and degree of concentration κ ($\kappa \geq 0$). The random variable is the angle θ ($0 \leq \theta$ 2π or $-\pi \leq \theta \leq \pi$). The probability density function is defined by the Eq. (1).

$$f(\theta) = \frac{1}{2\pi I_0(\kappa)} exp\{\kappa cos(\theta - \mu)\} \tag{1}$$

Where $I_0(\kappa)$ is the first type of transformed Bassel function of rank 0. Concentration becomes a sharp distribution.

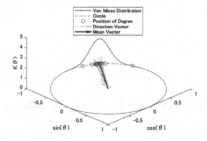

Fig. 6. Von Mises distribution during pointing.

As shown in Fig. 6, based on the characteristics of the von Mises distribution, the degree of concentration increases during pointing.

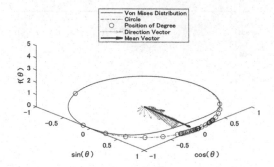

Fig. 7. Von Mises distribution during wandering.

However, the concentration decreases during wandering because of the characteristics of the von Mises distribution, as shown in Fig. 7.

To solve the problem of incorrectly setting segment boundaries, as well as including adjustment time in the velocity waveform during pointing, we focused on the correlation between the average direction vectors of the previous and following segment segments. Furthermore, we focused on the correlation between the average direction vectors of the segments before and after the pointing time, which is the inner product of the average direction vectors of the segments before and after the pointing time.

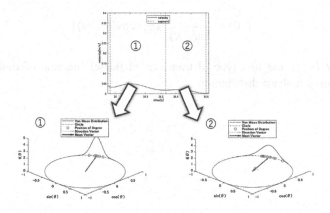

Fig. 8. Average direction vector during pointing including adjustment time.

3.6   Data Set

In this study, we created a data set by extracting the data from the motion in the screen and the motion when not in contact with the screen. 6-dimensional features were created. Specifically, (1) the time of the segment, (2) the maximum value of the velocity of the segment, (3) the ratio of the velocity during the segment to the maximum value of the velocity of the segment, (4) the presence or absence of screen contact in the next segment, (5) the temporal variance of κ in the von Mises distribution, and (6) the inner product of the mean direction vectors of the previous and next segments. The total number of data sets is 1738.

4   Result

The results of modeling the dataset using decision trees are shown in Fig. 9. The overall detection accuracy was 83.4%, true positives were 89%, true negatives were 72%, false positives were 28%, and false negatives were 11%.

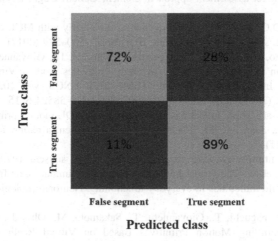

Fig. 9. Evaluation of segmentation by a confusion matrix.

The segment categorized as a false positive had an arc-like pointing pattern. Although pointing should be recognized as a single segment, it is possible that the pointing was divided into two segments because the correlation between the mean direction vectors of the segment before and after the pointing was low.

5   Conclusion

In this study, we developed a model that can segment time-series data of fingertip velocities in the VKC task by motion primitives using the dataset obtained by Giovannetti et al. The segmentation's overall accuracy was 83.4%, but 28% of the data were categorized as false positives. In the future, we plan to revise the feature set to correctly categorize segments that were categorized as false positives.

Acknowledgments. This work was supported by Grant-in-Aid for Scientific Research (C) 18K 12118 and National Institute on Aging (NIA) R01AG062503.

References

1. Statistics Bureau of Japan. https://www.stat.go.jp/index.html
2. Comprehensive Promotion of Measures for Dementia-Ministry of Health, Labour and Welfare (2019). https://www.mhlw.go.jp/content/12300000/000519620.pdf
3. World Alzheimer Resort 2018: The Global Impact of Dementia, p. 34 (2018)
4. Petersen, R.C., Morris, J.C.: Mild Cognitive Impairment as a clinical entity and treatment target. Arch. Neurol. 1160–1163 (2005)
5. Melk-Ahmadi, M.: Reversion from mild cognitive impairment to normal cognition: a meta-analysis. Alzheimer Dis. Assoc. Disord. **30**(4), 324–330 (2016)
6. Giovannetti, T., et al.: Characterization of everyday functioning in mild cognitive impairment: a direct assessment approach. Dement Geriatr. Cogn. Disord. **25**(4), 359–365 (2008)
7. Cintra, F.C.M.D.C., et al.: Functional decline in the elderly with MCI: cultural adaption of the ADCS-ADL scale. Rev. Assoc. Med. Bras. **63**(7), 590–599 (2017)
8. Prasasti Martono, N., Abe, K., Yamaguchi, T., Ohwada, H., Giovannetti, T.: Generating Rules of Action Transition in Errors in Daily Activities from a Virtual Reality-Based Training Data. In: Yamamoto, S. (ed.) HIMI 2017. LNCS, vol. 10274, pp. 166–175. Springer, Cham (2017). https://doi.org/10.1007/978-3-319-58524-6_15
9. Shirotori, A., et al.: Topic model-based clustering for IADL motion primitives (2019)
10. McCormack, T., Atance, C.M.: Planning in young children: a review and synthesis. Dev. Rev. 1–31 (2011)
11. Yamaguchi, H. https//www.dcnet.gr.jp/pdf/journal/t_2019_sousetu_19708.pdf
12. Giovannetti, T., et al.: The virtual kitchen challenge: preliminary data from a novel virtual reality test of mild difficulties in everyday functioning. Neuropsychological **26**(6), 823–841 (2019)
13. Iwashita, Y., Yamaguchi, T., Giovannetti, T., Sakamoto, M., Ohwada, H.: Discriminative Model for Identifying Motion Primitives Based on Virtual Reality-Based IADL. In: Stephanidis, C., Antona, M., Gao, Q., Zhou, J. (eds.) HCII 2020. LNCS, vol. 12426, pp. 574–585. Springer, Cham (2020). https://doi.org/10.1007/978-3-030-60149-2_44
14. Takashima, K.: Osaka University Knowledge Archive. http://hdl.handle.net/11094/1520

Virtual Reality for Simulation and Evaluation: Technology Acceptance Models for Automotive Consumer Electronics

Vassilis Charissis[1]([⊠])(iD), Kweku F. Bram-Larbi[1], Ramesh Lagoo[2],
Shu Wang[3], Soheeb Khan[1], Samar Altarteer[4], David K. Harrison[1],
and Dimitris Drikakis[5](iD)

[1] School of Computing, Engineering and Built Environment,
Glasgow Caledonian University, Glasgow, UK
[2] Core Lab + Ltd., Research and Development, Glasgow, UK
[3] Volkswagen, Research and Development, Beijing, China
[4] Dar Al-Hekma University, School of Design and Architecture,
Jeddah, Saudi Arabia
[5] University of Nicosia, Defence and Security Research Institute,
Nicosia, Cyprus

Abstract. The design, development and evaluation of consumer electronics pose many challenges in the transition from initial concept to final product market release. In the automotive sector, in particular, due to the nature of these devices and to alleviate users' safety concerns, the evaluation of such devices could be primarily performed in simulated and virtual environments. Device functionality can be evaluated objectively by measurement of user performance indicators. User acceptance of these technologies and attitude towards future use is, however, more difficult to formally access, but is considered as important a determinant of the success or failure of a product. The paper presents the virtual simulation requirements of two prototype AR HUD systems and two variations of Technology Acceptance Models (TAM) designed exclusively for their evaluation. The reasoning behind virtual simulations and utilisation of TAM variants in accessing and predicting user experience outcomes and intentions is discussed. In conclusion, a future plan for examining further the virtual simulation environments and additional TAM structures is proposed.

Keywords: Augmented Reality · Virtual Reality · Technology Acceptance Model · Collision avoidance · Head-Up Display · Smart Cities · Simulation

1 Introduction

En masse production of consumer electronics has to deliver on their functionality promise and ought to comply with several quality standards. Additionally, they have to fulfil users' expectations and support future consumer electronics ecosystems. As such, the development of a successful product is usually not a one-step process but adheres to a certain sequential methodology, which relies on the development of the product through a series of experimentations and adjustments as required. One of the most

C. Stephanidis et al. (Eds.): HCII 2021, LNCS 13095, pp. 219–234, 2021.
https://doi.org/10.1007/978-3-030-90963-5_18

important parts of this sequence is the User Experience (UX) evaluation of the product during the different stages of design, research and development period. Failure to satisfy and produce a conducive user experience typically results in an overall commercial failure. Physical prototypes could facilitate an initial appraisal, yet the production of different physical prototype models might prove costly and potential changes to the product could not be directly accommodated to the same testing model. Health and safety risks might also hinder the development and testing process of consumer electronics, particularly in the automotive or building sector.

Virtual and Augmented Reality (VR/AR) has already been employed by various industries to test and improve products before physical prototyping and manufacturing [1]. To this end, the development of VR immersive simulators could offer the luxury of infinite repetitions of an experiment and easy customisation of a product. Furthermore, the evaluation of any product's efficiency can be processed in a safe virtual environment enabling the developers and the users to identify potential issues in manufacturing and usage issues that could not be performed in real-life [2].

For this reason, we developed a Virtual Reality Driving Simulator (VRDS Lab) designed to evaluate various in-vehicle infotainment systems [3, 4]. The paper will present the design and evaluation process of two prototype AR HUD interfaces, aiming to increase safety by reducing driver distraction typically caused by in-vehicle information or/and passengers respectively.

The first AR HUD system employs gesture recognition for the direct manipulation of selected AR icons which could present infotainment data in a timely and safe manner to the driver [3]. The second interface provides an assortment of infotainment activities (i.e. educational information, games, navigation data, and local news) that could be superimposed in the real-surroundings, and occupy the rear passengers during commuting or long-distance travelling, improving the driver's attention to the road.

This paper will present the use of customised Technology Acceptance Models (TAM) applied to measure the users' experience, satisfaction, and acceptance of the emergency technologies tested in the virtual environment [5, 6]. The TAM results of the two aforementioned cases of AR HUD interfaces will be discussed in contrast to the simulation performance achieved by the users. Finally, the paper will discuss the potential of the VR evaluation of various product designs, aiming to perfect and appraise them before the final level of production and will offer a development framework for the customisation of TAM constructs for VR evaluations in Consumer Electronics.

2   Consumer Electronics

2.1   Current Consumer Electronics' Trends

Technological advancements have enabled the development of current consumer electronics that follow an exponential progression in the miniaturisation of the devices with increased computational processing speed and capabilities. Yet, this fast pace provision of systems and devices can present major challenges with regards to users' expectations, satisfaction and acceptability [7]. Once these consumer electronics (i.e.

mobile phones, smart-tablets, smart-watches and televisions amongst other devices) are already developed in a functional prototype version, numerous user-experience (UX) methods could be employed to assess the level of user satisfaction [8].

To this end, user experience and intention for purchasing and using new electronic products could be focused on the user's expectations and related to products' performance, the effort required to operate it, the social influence that could enhance users' image, and the facilitating conditions, which are stemming from the unified theory of acceptance and use of technology (UTAUT) [9]. Yet, particular devices and systems that could affect user's safety (i.e. car consumer electronics) are typically tested in simulated and/or controlled physical environments that could mask any potential user hazards [2, 4]. In previous work, during the design and development process, it was observed that the evaluation performed through immersive simulation (VR Simulation) could offer a better understanding of users' expectations and intentions to use the prototype product [4, 5, 10].

2.2 Vehicular Prototype Devices – AR HUD Case Studies

To define a framework for the development of a Technology Acceptance Model (TAM) that could facilitate the evaluation for similar consumer electronics designed for the automotive sector, this work will present and discuss two case studies related to AR HUD systems and the TAMs designed for the evaluation of each system.

The aforementioned Head-Up Display devices currently offer an alternative to traditional dashboard infotainment systems (Head-Down Displays) with the immediate benefit of maintaining the driver's gaze on the road [11–13]. The HUD design mantra largely involves the presentation of useful information directly in the driver's field of view by superimposing them to the windscreen producing significant advantages in contrast to HDD [13, 14]. To superimpose the selected information, HUD devices employ a projection system (i.e., image projector or laser projector) and a glass combiner that enhances the projected image. The majority of the current commercial versions of HUDs are falling within the small to medium estate and as such do not augment information directly to the real-environment. Our previous studies focused on the large-scale estate HUDs which utilised Augmented Reality to superimpose information directly onto the real-objects in close proximity to the vehicle enabling the driver to identify potential hazards and reduce the probability of collisions [13, 15].

Previous studies in the provision of crucial information to the driver via AR HUD system were evaluated primarily to define the actual driver performance benefits in relation to braking response times (RTs), manoeuvring choices and ultimately user's ability to avoid imminent collisions with the use of the prototype HUD systems in contrast to existing dashboard bound HDD systems. Although the HCI designs were meticulously tested in different driving simulators and driving scenarios revealing the significant performance gains achieved with the use of AR HUDs, it had not yet fully assessed the drivers' intention to use and subsequently purchase these devices in the future [15–17].

The necessity to define and quantify the users' behavioural intentions was deemed essential in the latest two projects which are related to the provision of in-vehicle infotainment. These two projects are presented in this paper as case studies, whilst aiming to minimise the risk of driver distraction and consequently reduce collision occurrences. These two AR HUD prototypes are presented succinctly below.

(a) Driver's AR HUD system: This system presents three types of information namely navigation, mobile phone text messages and phone calls as shown in Fig. 1. The latter could be withheld during manoeuvring or high-speed travelling. In this case, a text message provided the caller's contact details that the driver could call when a safe driving pattern is resumed. In contrast to current HUD systems that only present some information mirroring the HDD functions, the proposed AR HUD is fully interactive as the driver can operate the AR icons through a simple gesture recognition interface. This approach offers a direct manipulation capability to the user interface that imitates real-life interactions and enables the driver to access infotainment data safely [3, 4, 13].

Fig. 1. Case 1:Driver's AR HUD and gesture recognition for controlling infotainment sources.

(b) Passenger's AR HUD system: This second system is designed explicitly for the passengers to present infotainment activities that enrich daily commuting or long-distance travelling whilst reducing the interaction with the driver. This approach aims to reduce driver distraction by proxy of increasing the distraction of the passengers. The in-vehicle passenger distractions are responsible for a significant number of collisions, particularly when the rear passengers are children [18]. The provision of the AR HUD infotainment could also use the external scenery to superimpose educational information and games. The interaction with the aforementioned activities is performed with the use of console controllers as illustrated in Fig. 2.

Fig. 2. Case2: Passengers' AR HUD system for controlling infotainment sources.

Both systems were evaluated in a custom-built VR driving simulator described in detail in the following section. The same driving scenario was applied following on from previous AR HUD systems and collision avoidance interfaces' evaluations [4, 5, 13]. The driving scenarios entailed several potential collisions based on real-scenarios provided by the local traffic police department. Maintaining uniformity in the evaluation systems, environment and scenarios was deemed essential for future comparison and evaluation purposes. In the following sections, the paper will further elaborate on the differences and similarities of the evaluation TAM tool that have been designed for each system.

3   Simulation

The vast majority of electronic and engineering products are typically tested at a physical or virtual prototype level to identify the benefits and drawbacks of each system. This process is primarily concerned with the functionality of the systems, yet, the identification of User Experience (UX) and acceptability of the provided technologies, products and services is also an essential requirement. In particular, products such as software applications and small devices could be evaluated through functional prototypes.

However, this is not the case for systems and/or devices which need to be incorporated in larger products such as vehicles [2, 15]. The evaluation limitations could further extend in safety and ethical considerations. In the case of new in-vehicle systems such as car infotainment devices that could affect a driver's response time (RT) to potential collision situations the user evaluation, at least at the first stages, should comply with strict regulations before performing physical prototype testing.

The provision of a simulation that could replicate closely the majority of the affecting attributes and conditions offers an ideal testing environment. To this end, the employment of VR technology for driving simulation enabled us to simulate a large range of configuration options without the need to build a physical mock-up. Based on the accurate representation of an existing motorway environment in Scotland, we simulated the effects of different icon types, positioning, and global calibration parameters [15]. Using spatially immersive, stereoscopic projections we achieved a simulation at 1:1 scale including effects of depth perception and weather conditions as Fig. 3 shows.

Fig. 3. Top view schematic of the Virtual Reality Driving Simulator laboratory (VRDS Lab) during the user evaluations of the two AR HUDS (a) Driver's and gesture recognition version (b) Passengers' version

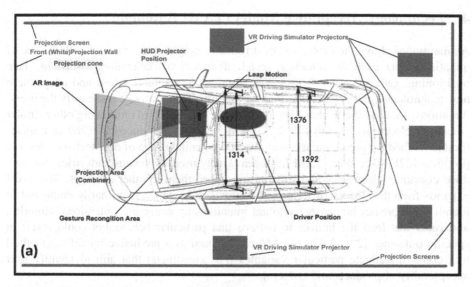

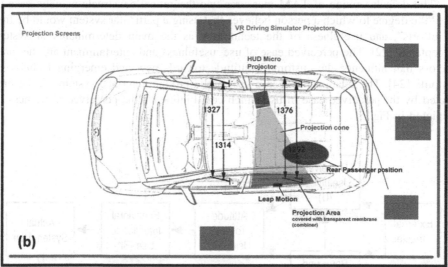

Fig. 4. Top view schematic of the Virtual Reality Driving Simulator laboratory (VRDS Lab) during the user evaluations of the two AR HUDS (a) Driver's and gesture recognition version (b) Passengers' side windows' version.

The simulator entails a real-life vehicle (Mercedes A-Class 2003 model) that is enclosed within a CAVE (Cave Automatic Virtual Environment) projection system and enriched with 5.1 surround audio and vibrotactile devices to imitate tarmac inconsistencies. The VRDS laboratory space and equipment offer a flexible and customisable environment for prototyping and evaluating various consumer electronics related to vehicles and road infrastructure as can be seen in Fig. 4 a&b.

4 Technology Acceptance Model (TAM) Rationale

As mentioned above the evaluation of driver's responses was achieved with the use of quantitive data such as vehicle's speed, deceleration/acceleration, collisions, lane positioning, gathered every 0.03 s. Yet, the driver's intention to use and adopt these new technologies and devices was unclear [15, 16]. To investigate and clarify the users' intentions, we used the Technology Acceptance Model (TAM) following other similar consumer electronics studies [18–21]. TAM has been introduced in 1989 as a quantifiable method for predicting the usability and potential usage of new technologies and products [22]. Since then, TAM has been widely used by several industries that produce consumer electronics and software or embed them to other products. The TAM expands from the Theory of Reasoned Action (TRA) which is primarily employed to identify and predict human behavioural intentions by analysing, intentions, attitudes, and rules that lead the human to believe that particular behaviours could result in specific outcomes [23]. As such TAM can be used as a predictive modelling method that could investigate particular variables (i.e., constructs) that aim to identify user acceptability of products and outcomes.

The default version of TAM measures two theoretical constructs namely: ease of use "the degree to which a person believes that using a particular system would be free of efforts", and usefulness of the technology as the main determinants of system acceptance [22]. The perceived ease of use, usefulness and entertainment are the main factors that influence the customer's attitude towards new and emerging technology outputs [24]. The relation between a user and a product/interface system can be predicted by the perceived ease of use which could influence the perceived usefulness as depicted in Fig. 5.

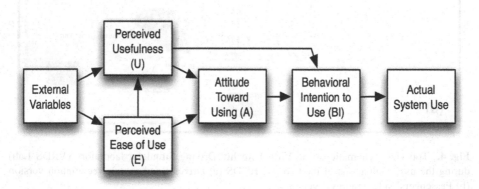

Fig. 5. First modified version of Technology Acceptance Model TAM [22].

Although the aforementioned variables are the essential constructs that could explain the acceptability of technologies and products, additional variables could contribute towards the formation of attitudes and views towards technological advancements [21]. This ability to incorporate bespoke constructs in a modular manner provides much-needed flexibility to the TAM for accommodating different variables depending on the technology products, and the relevant users' population.

In addition, previous studies demonstrated that several other common construct variables can be used to gauge technology adoption and acceptance, such as Behavioural Intention (BI), Attitude Towards Technology (ATT), and Anxiety (ANX) [9, 25, 26].

As such research studies that investigate different technologies and outcomes such as electronics, engineering, medical, and e-commerce applications could enhance the main TAM structure by adding new constructs, designed to reveal users' behavioural intentions (BI) for specific technological products and services. Yet, it could be argued that the users' BI to use a product doesn't necessarily reflect the real-life, actual usage outcome. To this end, previous studies revealed that the BI is likely to be correlated with actual usage. In contrast, the main TAM constructs (i.e., PEU and PU) are less likely to be correlated with actual usage and as such caution is advisable when these constructs are utilised outwith the original context that the TAM was intended to be used [27]. In the automotive consumer electronics domain, a variety of TAM structures have been modified and employed to identify the user's intentions to use and ultimately purchase specific electronic devices or the car itself [28–30].

To accommodate the individual factors/variables that affect users' BI, different studies can develop additional constructs that are integrated into the default TAM model constructs. The establishment of new constructs is based on the system characteristic and tasks' nature. For the particular case studies presented in this paper, two variations of the main TAM structure were used as described below:

(a) The AR HUD for the Driver used a modified TAM to include further constructs that were deemed essential in determining the usability aspects and the perceived risk of the proposed system. This TAM adhered to the previous TAM 2 structure and evaluations where the Attitude Towards Using (A) was excluded from the default structure [30–32]. Although the value of (A) is debated in previous studies, in this particular case it was considered unnecessary as the system under investigation, was in the initial development phase and any minor differences in the results wouldn't have a major impact. The additional construct Perceived Risk of Use (PRISK) is incorporated and measured in the original TAM structure consisting of the Perceived Usefulness (PU) and Perceived Ease of Use (PEOU) in relation to the user's Behavioural Intention (BI). The different hypotheses (H) that affect the relationship between the constructs are described in detail as follows:

- *H1: A driver's perceived usefulness of a HUD utilising contactless gestures while driving has a positive effect on his/her behavioural intention to use the system.*
- *H2: A driver's perceived ease-of-use of HUD with contactless gestures has a positive effect on his/her behavioural intention to use the car infotainment system.*
- *H3: A driver's perceived ease-of-use of HUD with contactless gestures has a positive effect on his/her perceived usefulness of the car infotainment system.*
- *H4: The increased perceived risk of an HDD with touch gestures in comparison to HUD with contactless gestures has a negative effect on his/her behavioural intention to use the car infotainment system.*

- *H5: The increased perceived risk of an HDD with touch gestures in comparison to HUD with contactless gestures has a negative effect on the usefulness of the system.*
- *H6: The increased perceived risk of an HDD with touch gestures in comparison to HUD with contactless gestures has a negative effect on perceived ease of use of the system.*

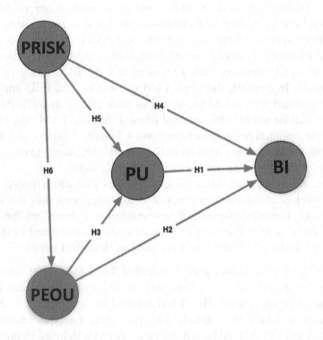

Fig. 6. Case A: TAM for Driver's AR HUD with Contactless Gestures for infotainment system.

Based on TAM 2 and the custom TAM constructs used in this research were assessed by items of the questionnaire with PU having 9 items, PEOU with 7 items, Perceived risk with 5 items and BI with 4 items. After the trial, the user was asked to evaluate the system by going through the 25 questions using a 5-point Likert scale (5: Strongly agree, 5: Agree, 4: Neutral, 3: Disagree, 1: Strongly disagree).

(b) In contrast to the first case study, the Passengers' AR HUD used a modified model of TAM to include additional constructs. In this case, the Perceived Risk of Use (PRISK) has been replaced by the Perceived Entertainment value (PE) but the Attitude Towards Use (A) was maintained following closely the original TAM structure. Supplementary values were also investigated but not presented on this version, such as perceived presentation attractiveness (PPA), and perceived playfulness (PP) [29]. This factor (PE) has been incorporated into the model following previous TAM models that investigated the playfulness and enjoyment factors of specific technologies as is illustrated in Fig. 7 [28–32].

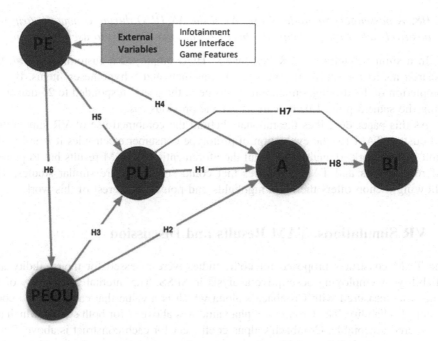

Fig. 7. Case B: TAM for Passengers' AR HUD for infotainment system.

The different hypotheses (H) that affect the relationship between the constructs are described in detail as follows:

- *H1: A passenger's perceived usefulness (PU) of the AR HUD system positively affects his/her behavioural intention (BI) to use the system.*
- *H2: A passenger's perceived ease-of-use (PEOU) of the AR HUD system positively affects his/her behavioural intention (BI) to use the system.*
- *H3: A passenger's perceived ease-of-use (PEOU) of the AR HUD interface design will positively affect the participants' perceived usefulness (PU)of the system.*
- *H4: The perceived entertainment (PE) and educational value of the AR HUD in comparison to traditional means (i.e., smartphones/tablets, talking to the driver/passengers) will positively affect the participants' attitude of use (A) the proposed system.*
- *H5: The perceived entertainment (PE) and educational value of the AR HUD in comparison to traditional means (i.e., smartphones/tablets, talking to the driver/passengers) will positively affect the participants' perceived use (PU).*
- *H6: The perceived entertainment (PE) and interface design of the AR HUD in comparison to traditional means (i.e., smartphones/tablets, talking to the driver/passengers) will positively affect the participants' perceived use (PU).*
- *H7: A passengers' perceived usefulness (PU) of the AR HUD utilizing during commuting/trip will positively affect the participants' behavioural intention (BI) to use the system.*

- *H8: A passengers' attitude of use (A) of the AR HUD during commuting/trip will positively affect the participants' behavioural intention (BI) to use the system.*

In a similar mantra the AR Passengers' HUD employed a customised TAM, the research model for study (a), examines 5 constructs and 8 hypotheses' items. By the completion of the driving simulation experiment, the users' responded to 25 questions using the same 5-point Likert scale as per the previous case.

As this paper describes the rationale behind the combined use of VR simulations and custom TAM for the evaluation of prototype consumer electronics it is not in the remit of this work to analyse in detail the aforementioned TAM results but to present different options and TAM structures that could support future similar studies. The following section offers the main highlights and points of interest of this work.

5   VR Simulations, TAM Results and Discussion

The TAM constructs proposed for both studies were assessed for their validity and reliability by employing descriptive analysis in SPSS. The internal consistency of all items was measured with Cronbach's alpha which is a value that calculates the coefficient of reliability. The Cronbach alpha value was above .7 for both studies which are considered acceptable. Cronbach's alpha coefficient for each construct is above .7 and ranges between 0.720 to 0.826. The mean value of each item depicts the overall consistency and has been calculated for each item. The mean value of each TAM construct and its items is above 3.5 which is acceptable and proves that the accumulated data is consistent. The individual hypotheses (H) for both cases were examined using regression analysis. The hypotheses testing values presented p values and correlation coefficient in the significant range (p < 0.01 and a correlation coefficiency above 0.5) as required to support the hypotheses.

Irrelevantly to the TAM structure of choice (with or without the Attitude of Use) both studies presented valuable, measurable feedback which informed the immediate changes on the prototype applications. The subjective suggestions and the experimenters' observations verified further the users' responses whilst the quantitative data related to collision occurrences and driver's RTs also reinforced the TAM results. On some limited occasions, it was identified, a disparity between the users' BI and the actual performance achieved (for collision avoidance) with the prototype devices. Although these were negligible in the particular samples of users, 50 for each system evaluation, it would be of interest to explore further the reason and outputs that affected the users' BI.

As described in the previous section in a simulated synthetic environment it is feasible to reconstruct almost an infinite number of variables with no safety infringes. Furthermore, the system development could be achieved and re-evaluated on the spot and users' feedback could be applied significantly faster than in real-life working prototypes. A physical prototype would be eventually developed for the final product testing, yet, all the intermediate major or minor alterations could be applied in a considerably cost-effective manner through simulation [33–36].

In particular, human factors engineering attributes could be applied promptly throughout every stage of the development. Digital human modelling and accurate environment visualisation can provide the product engineers with crucial information concerning the benefits or problems that might appear in the real product. Identifying and resolving the potential issues well in advance offer a significant advantage to the typical testing environments and processes.

Additionally, VR can be employed also in cases that need to imitate the depth of field or various physical conditions, weather conditions and AI collision scenarios [2, 13, 14, 35].

Another significant attribute of VR simulation is the ability to incorporate any object (3D model) into the testing environment with no physical constraints as weight and overall size limitations. The drawback of VR simulations is that the initial 3D modelling and programming of interactions and physics could be an elaborate process, however, any future required changes could be applied rapidly and at a lesser cost than a physical prototype. On rare occasions, users could also demonstrate motion sickness if the evaluation of the prototype product requires the user to move in the virtual environment.

6 Conclusions

The paper presented a pipeline for the evaluation of vehicular consumer electronics with the use of VR driving simulators and customized Technology Acceptance Models. The paper discussed the flexibility of the VR simulators and the diversity between the products, actions and environments that could be replicated in a synthetic setting as well as the acceptance of such technologies by the prospective users.

In addition, this paper presented the virtual simulation requirements of two prototype multimodal AR HUD systems that both aim to reduce driver distraction either by the contemporary infotainment devices or by the interaction with the passengers. The evaluation of both systems was performed by 50 users and resulted in improving the driver's response time and situational awareness as the collision occurrences were reduced significantly in both cases.

The evaluation of both prototype systems has been accommodated in a high-fidelity full-scale VR driving simulator developed to replicate realistically driving scenarios of high probability collisions. In future work, we intend to exchange the TAM structures for the two studies and re-evaluate the proposed AR HUD systems aiming to identify potential differences in the user's behavioural intentions with and without the attitude towards use (A) construct.

References

1. Falcão, C.S., Soares, M.M.: Application of virtual reality technologies in consumer product usability. In: Marcus, A. (ed.) DUXU 2013. LNCS, vol. 8015, pp. 342–351. Springer, Heidelberg (2013). https://doi.org/10.1007/978-3-642-39253-5_37

2. Charissis, V., Ramsay, J., Sharples, B., Naef, M., Jones, B.S.: 3D stereoscopic design of submersive rescue vehicle and rescue mission simulation. In: International Conference of Warship 2008: Naval Submarines, The Royal Institution of Naval Architects, pp. 13–19, Glasgow, UK (2008)

3. Karapanos, E.: User experience over time. In: Modeling Users' Experiences with Interactive Systems. Studies in Computational Intelligence, vol. 436. Springer, Berlin, Heidelberg (2013). https://doi.org/10.1007/978-3-642-31000-3_4

4. Lagoo, R., Charissis, V., Harrison, D.K.: Mitigating driver's distraction: automotive head-up display and gesture recognition system. IEEE Consumer Electron. Mag. 8(5), 79–85 (2019). https://doi.org/10.1109/MCE.2019.2923896

5. Wang, S., Charissis, V., Lagoo, R., Campbell, J., Harrison, D.K.: Reducing driver distraction by utilising augmented reality head-up display system for rear passengers. In: IEEE International Conference on Consumer Electronics (ICCE), Las Vegas, USA (2019). https://doi.org/10.1109/ICCE.2019.8661927

6. Altarteer, S., Charissis, V.: Technology acceptance model for 3D virtual reality system in luxury brands online stores. IEEE Access J. 7, 64053–64062 (2019). https://doi.org/10.1109/ACCESS.2019.2916353

7. Andrae, A.S.G., Andersen, O.: Life cycle assessments of consumer electronics are they consistent? Int. J. Life Cycle Assess 15, 827–836 (2010). https://doi.org/10.1007/s11367-010-0206-1

8. Lin Kuo-Yi, Y., Pei-I, A., Pei-Chun, C., Chen-Fu, C.: User experience-based design of experiments for new product development of consumer electronics and an empirical study. J. Ind. Prod. Eng. 34(7), 504–519 (2017). https://doi.org/10.1080/21681015.2017.1363089

9. Venkatesh, V., Morris, M.G., Gordon, B.D., et al.: User acceptance of information technology: toward a unified view. MIS Q. 27(3), 425–478 (2003)

10. Wang, S., Charissis, V., Harrison, D.K.: Augmented reality prototype HUD for passenger infotainment in a vehicular environment. Adv. Sci. Technol. Eng. Syst. J. 2(3), 634–641 (2017)

11. Okumura, H., Hotta, A., Sasaki, T., Horiuchi, K., Okada, N.: Wide field of view optical combiner for augmented reality head-up displays. In: 2018 IEEE International Conference on Consumer Electronics (IEEE ICCE) (2018)

12. Wang, J., Wang, W., Hansen, P., Li, Y., You, F.: The situation awareness and usability research of different HUD HMI design in driving while using adaptive cruise control. In: Stephanidis, C., Duffy, V.G., Streitz, N., Konomi, S., Krömker, H. (eds.) HCII 2020. LNCS, vol. 12429, pp. 236–248. Springer, Cham (2020). https://doi.org/10.1007/978-3-030-59987-4_17

13. Charissis, V., et al.: Employing emerging technologies to develop and evaluate in-vehicle intelligent systems for driver support: infotainment AR HUD case study. Appl. Sci. 11(4), 1397 (2021). https://doi.org/10.3390/app11041397

14. Wu, W., Blaicher, F., Yang, J., Seder, T., Cui, D.: A prototype of landmark-based car navigation using a full-windshield head-up display system. In: AMC 2009: Proceedings of the 2009 workshop on Ambient media computing, October 2009, pp. 21–28 (2009). https://doi.org/10.1145/1631005.1631012

15. Charissis, V., Papanastasiou, S.: Human-machine collaboration through vehicle head-up display interface, international journal of cognition, technology and work. In: Cacciabue, P. C., Hollangel, E. (eds.) Springer London Ltd Volume 12, Number 1, pp. 41–50 (2010). https://doi.org/10.1007/s10111-008-0117

16. Charissis, V., Papanastasiou, S., Chan, W., Peytchev, E.: Evolution of a full-windshield HUD designed for current VANET communication standards. In: IEEE Intelligent Transportation Systems International Conference (IEEE ITS), The Hague, Netherlands, pp. 1637–1643 (2013). https://doi.org/10.1109/ITSC.2013.6728464

17. Charissis, V., Papanastasiou, S., Mackenzie, L., Arafat, S.: Evaluation of collision avoidance prototype head-up display interface for older drivers. In: Jacko, J.A. (ed.) HCI 2011. LNCS, vol. 6763, pp. 367–375. Springer, Heidelberg (2011). https://doi.org/10.1007/978-3-642-21616-9_41

18. Barker, J.: Driven to distraction: children's experiences of car travel. Brunel University, UK, (2009). https://doi.org/10.1080/17450100802657962

19. Planing, P., Britzelmaier, B.: Understanding consumer acceptance of advanced driver assistance systems – a qualitative study on the German market. Int. J. Sales Retail. Market. (2012)

20. Kuo-Yi, L., Pei-I, Y., Pei-Chun, C., Chen-Fu, C.: User experience-based design of experiments for new product development of consumer electronics and an empirical study. J. Ind. Prod. Eng. **34**(7), 504–519 (2017). https://doi.org/10.1080/21681015.2017.1363089

21. Altarteer, S., Charissis, V., Harrison, D., Chan, W.: Product customisation: virtual reality and new opportunities for luxury brands online trading. In: Proceedings of the 21st International Conference on Web3D Technology (Web3D 2016). Association for Computing Machinery, New York, NY, USA, pp. 173–174 (2016). https://doi.org/10.1145/2945292.2945317

22. Davis, F.D., Bagozzi, R.P., Warshaw, P.R.: User acceptance of computer technology: a comparison of two theoretical models. Manage. Sci. **35**(8), 982–1003 (1989)

23. Madden, T.J., Ellen, P.S., Ajzen, I.: A comparison of the theory of planned behavior and the theory of reasoned action. Pers. Soc. Psychol. Bull. **18**(1), 3–9 (1992). https://doi.org/10.1177/0146167292181001

24. Kim, J., Forsythe, S.: Sensory enabling technology acceptance model (SE-TAM): a multiple-group structural model comparison. Psychol. Market. **25**(9), 901–922 (2008)

25. Fetscherin, M., Lattemann, C.: User acceptance of virtual worlds. J. Electron. Commer. Res. **9**(3), 231–242 (2008)

26. Shumaker, R. (ed.): VAMR 2013. LNCS, vol. 8022. Springer, Heidelberg (2013). https://doi.org/10.1007/978-3-642-39420-1

27. Turner, M., Kitchenham, B., Brereton, P., Charters, S., Budgen, D.: Does the technology acceptance model predict actual use? Syst. Lit. Rev. Inf. Softw. Technol. **52**(5), 463–479 (2010). https://doi.org/10.1016/j.infsof.2009.11.005

28. Planing, P., Britzelmaier, B.: Understanding consumer acceptance of advanced driver assistance systems – a qualitative study on the german market. Int. J. Sales, Retail. Market. 32–40 (2012)

29. Planing, P.: Innovation acceptance: the case of advanced driver-assistance systems, Springer Gabler (2014)

30. Legris, P., Ingham, J., Collerette, P.: Why do people use information technology? a critical review of the technology acceptance model. Inf. Manage. **40**, 191–204 (2003)

31. Surendran, P.: Technology acceptance model: a survey of literature. Int. J. Bus. Soc. Res. (IJBSR) **2**(4), 175–178 (2012)

32. Marangunić, N., Granić, A.: Technology acceptance model: a literature review from 1986 to 2013. Univ. Access Inf. Soc. **14**(1), 81–95 (2014). https://doi.org/10.1007/s10209-014-0348-1

33. Choi, S., Jung, K., Noh, S.D.: Virtual reality applications in manufacturing industries: past research, present findings, and future directions. Concurrent Eng. **23**(1), 40–63 (2015). https://doi.org/10.1177/1063293X14568814

34. Berg, L.P., Vance, J.M.: Industry use of virtual reality in product design and manufacturing: a survey. Virtual Reality **21**(1), 1–17 (2016). https://doi.org/10.1007/s10055-016-0293-9

35. Frank, M., Drikakis, D., Charissis, V.: Machine-learning methods for computational science and engineering. Computation **8**, 15 (2020)

36. Choudhry, A., Premchand, A.: Digital transformation using immersive technologies in manufacturing and utilities. In: Favorskaya, M.N., Mekhilef, S., Pandey, R.K., Singh, N. (eds.) Innovations in Electrical and Electronic Engineering. LNEE, vol. 661, pp. 433–443. Springer, Singapore (2021). https://doi.org/10.1007/978-981-15-4692-1_33

Modeling Viewpoint of Forklift Operators Using Context-Based Clustering of Gaze Fixations

Jouh Yeong Chew[✉], Takashi Okuma, Eiichi Yoshida,
and Yukikazu Koide

National Institute of Advanced Industrial Science and Technology, AIST
Tsukuba Central 1, 1-1-1 Umezono, TsukubaIbaraki 305-8560, Japan
{jy.chew,takashi-okuma,e.yoshida,
yukikazu.koide}@aist.go.jp

Abstract. This study proposes a method to find optimal viewpoints for Human Machine Interface (HMI) of teleoperation system using human visual pattern. Forklift operation is used as a case study due to its operation complexity consisting of multiple work contexts such as driving and cargo handling. It is challenging to model human viewpoint because there is usually no prior knowledge of the behavior, complicated steps to process behavioral data, and difficulty to represent dynamic behavior throughout the operation. Therefore, a method is proposed to model human viewpoint using setups in a virtual environment that is reconstructed from a real laboratory environment mimicking the warehouse. Gaze points are measured during experiments in virtual environment, and the clustering methods are used to find natural spherical clusters resembling human foveal vision at different work contexts. Viewpoints of several category of forklift operators are derived from the proposed method, and their common viewpoints at each work context is represented using a piecewise function defining distribution of cluster centroids from the origin of local coordinate system. Spatial analysis of gaze pattern suggests distribution of gaze centroids are generally spatially independent between work contexts. More importantly, the common viewpoint is spatially correlated with the viewpoints of different category of operators. This suggests the proposed model is representative of the general viewpoint of forklift operation.

Keywords: Work context · K-means clustering · Hierarchical clustering · Gaze fixations · Human viewpoint · Teleoperation · Spatial analysis · Clark-Evans criterion

1 Introduction

Teleoperation systems are getting more common due to the need to reduce contact and mobility. However, implementation of a good and easy-to-use teleoperation system is not easy. This section describes the significance of a suitable viewpoint to facilitate teleoperation and the related studies. The objective and hypotheses of this study are also discussed. The proposed method is also benchmarked with related studies and the contributions are elaborated.

© Springer Nature Switzerland AG 2021
C. Stephanidis et al. (Eds.): HCII 2021, LNCS 13095, pp. 235–249, 2021.
https://doi.org/10.1007/978-3-030-90963-5_19

1.1   Viewpoint for Teleoperation

Transition from manned to remote operation is challenging because it is usually not clear what visual stimuli should be presented on the Human Machine Interface (HMI). Presenting the optimal visual stimuli on HMI is important to achieve telepresence so that operators can acquire any viewpoints needed for remote operation like they are physically present at the distant working environment. Several methods were discussed in the previous studies. [1, 2] proposed to acquire viewpoints of monitoring robots to facilitate remote operation. This solution works well but requires one or more autonomous robots to trail the teleoperated robot. Other suggestions include real time control of position and orientation of a remote camera [3], and presenting the 3D reconstructed working environment [4]. These solutions are helpful to present the optimal and augmented visual stimuli, but they are not easy to use. For example, real time control of camera is not easy because camera motion can be restricted. Computing power also limits real time 3D reconstruction of working environment.

This study proposes a novel method to find the optimal viewpoints for remote operation HMI. This approach uses cognition of visual search pattern during manned operation. Forklift operation is used as a case study due to its operation complexity consisting of multiple work contexts such as driving and cargo handling [5, 6]. Experiments were carried out to measure gaze attention of forklift operators from different skills categories, and the data were modeled as viewpoint relative to the local coordinate system of the fork. The contribution of this paper is the method to model and evaluate the common human viewpoint. This viewpoint model is advantageous because it can be expanded to develop a cognitive HMI for remote operation without supporting systems such as monitoring robots [1, 2]. For example, cameras can be mounted on the remotely operated forklift, and optimal visual stimuli acquired from these cameras can be presented on HMI at any work contexts using the proposed viewpoint model.

1.2   Objectives

Results of the preceding studies [5, 6] suggest operators tend to behave differently at each work context. Therefore, this study proposes a human viewpoint model for forklift operation and answers two research questions. The first question evaluates how well the proposed human viewpoint model generalizes to different skills level or category of operators. The second question evaluates how human viewpoint varies from one work context to another. Spatial analysis of the distribution of gaze points are carried out to test the following null and alternative hypotheses. For the first and second questions, comparisons are made between point distributions of different work contexts and between different category of operators, respectively.

H_0: Two point distributions are spatially independent. Each distribution follows an identical homogeneous Poisson distribution independently

H_1: Two point distributions are spatially correlated. They are spatially attractive (repulsive) with each other

2   Methodology

The methodology of this study is discussed in this section. First, the experiment conditions to acquire human behavioral data are elaborated. This is followed by the clustering approach to derive human viewpoint from these data. Evaluation of the proposed human viewpoint model is explained at the end of this section.

2.1   Experiment Conditions

An experiment was carried out using the forklift simulator developed in the preceding study [5] to acquire behavioral data of manned forklift operation. Experiments in the virtual environment are preferred to minimize safety issues and to facilitate data analysis. More importantly, results of [5] suggest the simulator elicited behavior like operation in the real environment, as evaluated using Face Validity [7] which compares temporal behavior in the real and virtual environments using dynamic time warping algorithm [5].

This experiment was carried out according to the rules and regulations of the National Institute of Advanced Industrial Science and Technology (AIST) of Japan. Informed consents were obtained from all human subjects and the experiment protocol was reviewed and approved by the Human Factor experiment committee of AIST. There are 57 experiment subjects from four skill categories and all of them possess forklift driving license in Japan. The categorial descriptions of subjects are given in Table 1. The recruitment plan is 15 subjects for each category. Although the number of recruited participants differs from the plan due to recruitment difficulty, behavioral analysis for 3 subject categories is not affected.

Table 1. Gaze metrics of crane operators for the experiment task.

Category	n	Work experience
Expert	17	≥ 10 years
Novice	16	<2 years
Intermediate	23	≥ 2 years, <10 years
Instructor	1	Instructor of forklift training

During the experiment, subjects wore the HTC Vive Pro Eye Head Mounted Display (HMD) with eye tracking capability and performed the same task consisting of a series of basic work contexts commonly done at workplaces such as warehouses and factories. These work contexts include but not limited to driving forward and reverse, with and without the pallet, approaching the shelf, and loading/unloading the pallets (see Fig. 1). Each subject performed the task three times, excluding once during the training session.

Work Context	Load	
	No	Yes
Stop	①	⑧
Forward	②	⑨
Approach	③	⑩
Adjust heading	④	⑪
Load/Unload	⑤	⑫
Retreat	⑬	⑥
Reverse	⑭	⑦

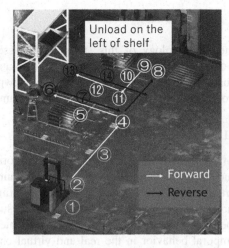

Fig. 1. Task performed during the experiment consists of 14 work contexts commonly done at workplaces such as warehouses and factories. These work contexts form a complete cycle which is typically repeated for each pallet/cargo.

2.2 Modeling of Human Viewpoint

The common viewpoint of forklift operators is represented using $\mathbf{G(s)}$ in Eq. (1) consisting of s sets of 3D gaze centroids $\mathbf{g}$ for each work context, and N_s represents the total number of centroids (i.e. cluster number of gaze fixations) for the sth work context. All gaze points take reference from the origin of the fork as in Fig. 2. The fork is used as the reference because it is the moving part of the forklift which attracts attention. This definition is useful especially for cargo handling operations when attention tends to be focused near the fork. The steps to process gaze data using clustering methods are adapted from [8, 9] and summarized in Fig. 3.

$$
\mathbf{G(s)} = \begin{cases} \{\mathbf{g}_1, \mathbf{g}_2, \ldots, \mathbf{g}_{N_1}\}, s = 1 \\ \{\mathbf{g}_1, \mathbf{g}_2, \ldots, \mathbf{g}_{N_2}\}, s = 2 \\ \qquad \vdots \\ \{\mathbf{g}_1, \mathbf{g}_2, \ldots, \mathbf{g}_{N_{14}}\}, s = 14 \end{cases} \tag{1}
$$

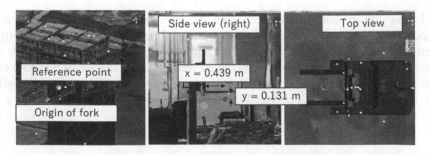

Fig. 2. All gaze points including centroids of point clusters take reference from fork's origin.

The first step discriminates 3D gaze data for each category of operators into saccades and fixations because human attention is better represented by gaze fixations [10, 11, 14, 15]. The second step clusters gaze fixations based on their positions in the work environment, after being translated to the local coordinate system of the fork as in Fig. 2. The K-means clustering is used for this purpose and the optimal K is determined using the silhouette plot and elbow method since there is no prior knowledge of the salient points of forklift work contexts. Therefore, viewpoints for each category of operators at each work state can be obtained. The final step uses hierarchical clustering to cluster the viewpoints of all categories of operators at each work state to obtain Eq. (1). Details of each step are given in the following sections.

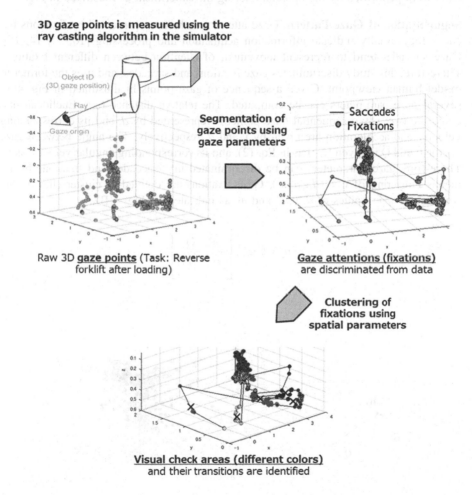

Fig. 3. Experiment subjects wore HMD with eye tracking functions, and gaze points were measured using the ray casting algorithm in the forklift simulator. For each work context and each category of operator, gaze points are discriminated into saccades and fixations prior to clustering the fixations to find the viewpoint (visual check areas).

Definition of Work Contexts. Behavior of biological systems can be represented by sequential work contexts discriminated using different methods like GMM [16] and other machine learning methods. In the preceding study [6], six basic work contexts are defined and represented using state flow method. However, the model is not representative of all basic work contexts commonly carried out at workplaces. For example, forward and reverse operations are not discriminated by the model. In a typical scenario, operators tend to look at the direction of motion, i.e. looking at the front when going forward and back when reversing. Therefore, this study expands the work contexts into 14, taking into consideration the limitations of the previous model and the typical working conditions at workplaces such as factories and warehouses. These work contexts were performed by the operators during the experiment as illustrated in Fig. 1.

Segmentation of Gaze Pattern. Gaze attention is better represented by fixations because they usually indicate information acquisition and processing [10, 11, 14, 15]. Gaze saccades tend to represent movement of attention between different fixations. There-fore, this study discriminates gaze fixations and saccades, and uses the former to model human viewpoint. Given a sequence of gaze points hi illustrated in Fig. 4(a), several gaze parameters can be computed. The relative distance (e.g. Euclidean distance) be-tween two sequential gaze points is represented by d, and its corresponding velocity and acceleration are given by v and a, respectively. The angle between gaze vector $\vec{P}$ and $\vec{Q}$ is given by θ as in Eq. (2), and its corresponding angular velocity as ω. There-fore, gaze parameters can be discriminated into saccades and fixations by K-means clustering of $u = (d,v,a,\omega)$. Gaze fixations are defined as clusters having the smallest average values of d, v, a, and ω, as indicated by Fig. 4(B).

$$\theta = \cos^{-1}\left[\frac{\vec{P} \cdot \vec{Q}}{|\vec{P}| \cdot |\vec{Q}|}\right] \tag{2}$$

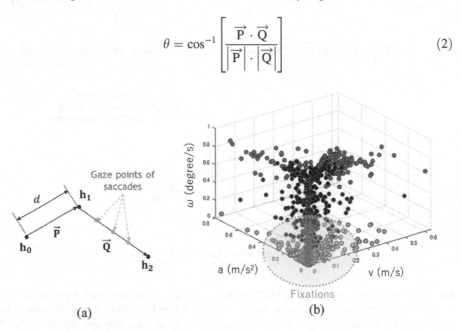

(a)   (b)

Fig. 4. (a) A sequence of gaze points to compute gaze parameters and (b) visualization of the clustering results of gaze parameters to find fixations.

Clustering of Gaze Fixations. Gaze fixation points are used for K-means clustering to identify the spherical natural clusters. To the best knowledge of the authors, there are no prior studies on the attention of forklift operators. Therefore, the optimal K for clustering is selected using the silhouette plot [12] and elbow method [13]. Figure 5 illustrates the selection of K based on these two methods. The elbow method is used to estimate the optimal K by selecting the K explaining at least 90% of the variance. The silhouette plot cross checks by giving a graphical representation of silhouette value for every point within K clusters. This measures the distance of each point to members of its own cluster compared to distance to members of neighboring clusters. A high silhouette value indicates the point is well-matched to its cluster and vice versa. Therefore, gaze fixations of different types of operators at each work context can be defined by K number of clusters represented by their centroids as explained in Sect. 3.1.

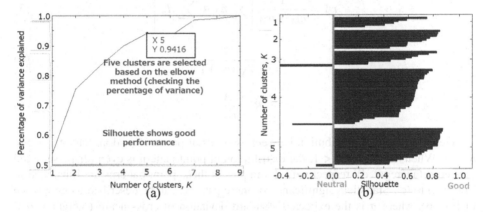

Fig. 5. The quality of K-means clustering is determined using (a) elbow, (b) silhouette method.

Common Viewpoint. Instead of viewpoint for each category of operator discussed in the preceding section, this section explains the method to find the common viewpoint to represent attention of forklift operation in general. This is motivated by the fact that any systems developed from such operator viewpoint should be applicable to different types of users. The results in Sect. 3.1 also indicate similarity of viewpoint for different category of operators, especially for major clusters. The hierarchical clustering method is used to find the common viewpoint using the gaze centroids of all categories of operators at each work context. The threshold of hierarchical clustering is the mean of Euclidean distances between two gaze centroids. Therefore, a set of gaze centroids for each work context as defined in Eq. (1) can be obtained to represent common viewpoint of forklift operation.

2.3   Spatial Analysis of Human Viewpoint

Evaluation of viewpoints derived from Sect. 2.2 is carried out using spatial analysis which is commonly used for evaluation of point patterns [17–19] in different scenarios.

The primary objective is to evaluate how the proposed common viewpoint model in Eq. (1) describes the viewpoints of each category of operators. The secondary objective is to compare viewpoint model for each work context. Given two sets of points P_A and P_B, the mean of cross nearest neighbor distances rA can be computed using Eq. (3) so that spatial influence on each other can be evaluated. The distance from the ith P_A to its nearest P_B point is defined by d_{Ai}, and the distance from the ith P_B to its nearest P_A point is defined by d_{Bi}. The number of points for P_A and P_B are represented by m_A and m_B, respectively. The Clark-Evans criterion [20, 21] is used to describe the point pattern. The expected mean of cross nearest neighbor distances rE can be computed as a function of number of points $m = m_A + m_B$, and the volume V containing these points in Eq. (4), where V is defined as the cuboid containing all the gaze centroids. The Clark-Evans criterion R is given in Eq. (5).

$$rA = \frac{1}{m_A + m_B} \left[\sum_{i=1}^{m_A} d_{Ai} + \sum_{i=1}^{m_B} d_{Bi} \right] \tag{3}$$

$$rE = \frac{1}{2\sqrt{(m/V)}} \tag{4}$$

$$R = \frac{rA}{rE} \tag{5}$$

Generally, spatial distribution between two sets of points is random (chaotic) when $R = 1$. When $R > 1$ and $R < 1$, the distribution of point pattern is even (dispersed) and clustered (aggregated), respectively. Examples of these point patterns are illustrated in Fig. 6(a) to (c). Statistical significance of these patterns can be described using z-score in Eq. (6), where σ is the expected standard deviation of cross nearest neighbor distances in Eq. (7). To reject the null hypothesis that two sets of points are spatially independent, z-score > 1.96 or z-score < -1.96 at the two tails of Fig. 6(d). And $R < 1.0$ for a clustered (attracted to each other) point pattern, and $R > 1.0$ for even (dispersed from each other) point pattern.

$$z = \frac{rA - rE}{\sigma} \tag{6}$$

$$\sigma = \frac{0.2612}{\sqrt{m^2/V}} \tag{7}$$

3   Results

The clustering results for each category of operators at each work context is visualized and discussed in this section. Pairwise comparisons of viewpoints as described in Sect. 2.3 are also summarized. Specifically, generalization of the common viewpoint model in the first research question, and the difference of viewpoints for work contexts in the second research question are answered here.

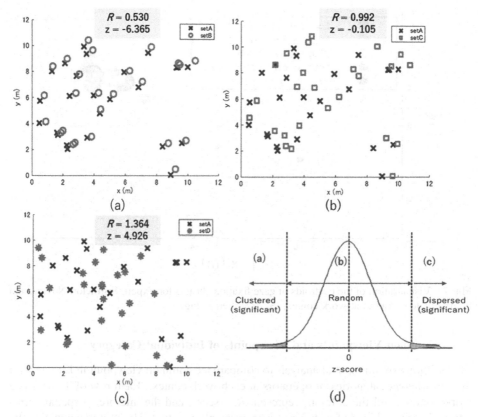

Fig. 6. Point pattern analysis using cross nearest neighbor distance and Clark-Evans criterion *R*. (a) clustered when two sets of points are attracted to each other, (b) random when there is no clear spatial relationship, (c) even when the points are dispersed, and (d) significance of point pattern based on z-score.

3.1 Viewpoints of Different Categories of Operators

The viewpoints of each category of operators for each work context can be represented by Fig. 7 which shows the view from top down of the forklift with the reference point to the fork's origin (in black). Each plot is the centroid of gaze fixation clusters, and the size defines the weight (cluster size) of that viewpoint. Visual comparison of viewpoint between different categories of operators indicates similarity of major viewpoints. Therefore, the hierarchical clustering method is used to find the common viewpoints between all categories of operators for each work context, as represented by Eq. (1). This is motivated by the fact that it is usually necessary for a model to generalize for different category of users.

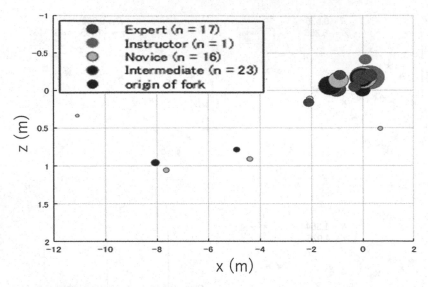

Fig. 7. Visualization of the centroids of gaze fixation clusters for Expert, Instructor, Novice, and Intermediate operators at work context ⑨ described in Fig. 1.

3.2   Common Viewpoints and Viewpoints of Individual Category

This section explains spatial analysis to compare the common viewpoint in Eq. (1) with that of different categories of operators at each work context. Each row of Table 2 is a work context, and the columns represent R, z-score, and the interpreted spatial correlations based on Fig. 6, for different categories of operators. The footnote explains the three types of spatial correlations and the significance of pattern based on Fig. 6(d). Generally, the spatial correlations between the common viewpoint and that of different categories of operators are significantly clustered as represented by notation cl*, i.e. the point pattern in Fig. 6(a) when $R < 1.0$ and $z < -1.96$. Although some cases of Expert, Novice and Intermediate are random with insignificant pattern as represented by notation rd, it is noteworthy that $R < 1.0$ for almost all cases, indicating a relatively weak clustered pattern like Fig. 6(b).

This suggests the common viewpoint derived from Sect. 2 is representative of the viewpoints of different types of operators, except for Instructor. However, the differences between common viewpoint and that of Instructor is expected since there is only one operator in this category. In other words, the common viewpoints for most work contexts are spatially correlated (attracted) to viewpoints of Expert, Novice, and Intermediate. Therefore, the null hypothesis of spatial independence can be rejected in cases with cl*, and the common viewpoint model can be regarded as a general model of forklift operation.

Table 2. Clark-Evans criterion R for comparison of spatial correlations between common viewpoint and viewpoints of individual category of operators at each work context.

Common viewpoint at work context	Expert			Novice			Intermediate			Instructor		
	R	z	Pattern	R	z	Pattern	R	z	Pattern	R	z	Pattern
①	0.304	-5.491	cl*	0.332	-5.272	cl*	0.189	-6.766	cl*	1.966	6.408	dv*
②	0.417	-4.598	cl*	0.246	-6.287	cl*	0.293	-5.739	cl*	0.710	-2.288	cl*
③	0.464	-4.475	cl*	0.465	-4.464	cl*	0.918	-0.650	rd	0.596	-3.628	cl*
④	0.275	-6.358	cl*	0.436	-4.945	cl*	0.465	-4.579	cl*	0.542	-4.113	cl*
⑤	0.398	-5.021	cl*	0.748	-1.985	cl*	0.872	-0.980	rd	0.354	-5.528	cl*
⑥	0.570	-3.489	cl*	0.550	-3.852	cl*	0.595	-3.467	cl*	0.903	-0.832	rd
⑦	0.986	-0.125	rd	0.466	-4.906	cl*	0.356	-6.039	cl*	1.192	1.686	rd
⑧	0.479	-4.232	cl*	1.112	0.883	rd	0.718	-2.351	cl*	2.244	8.248	dv*
⑨	1.295	2.460	dv*	0.286	-6.111	cl*	0.371	-5.111	cl*	1.787	5.834	dv*
⑩	0.832	-1.512	rd	0.429	-5.128	cl*	0.383	-5.664	cl*	1.443	3.493	dv*
⑪	0.494	-4.109	cl*	0.493	-4.447	cl*	1.463	3.653	dv*	1.273	2.091	dv*
⑫	0.698	-2.952	cl*	0.572	-4.179	cl*	0.735	-2.430	cl*	0.286	-7.102	cl*
⑬	0.862	-1.290	rd	0.899	-0.869	rd	0.581	-3.927	cl*	0.346	-5.736	cl*
⑭	0.783	-1.948	rd	0.610	-3.256	cl*	0.778	-1.855	rd	0.436	-4.453	cl*

cl: clustered (aggregated) pattern
rd: random (chaos) pattern
dv: even (dispersed pattern)
*: significance ($p < 0.05$) of spatial correlation pattern

3.3   Common Viewpoints Between Different Work Contexts

This section explains spatial analysis between viewpoints of different work contexts. Table 3 uses the same notation as Table 2 to represent the different spatial correlations explained in Fig. 6 and their significance. The columns and rows of Table 3 represent work contexts, and each table element indicates spatial correlations between these work contexts using R, z-score, and the spatial pattern. The results suggest most of the spatial correlations are statistically insignificant or random with insignificant pattern as represented by notation rd. It is noteworthy that $R > 1.0$ or $R \approx 1.0$ in most cases which indicate a pattern like Fig. 6(c), i.e. even or dispersed pattern. Therefore, the null hypothesis of spatial independence cannot be rejected for most cases, except for work contexts⑦ and from ⑨ to ⑭. Viewpoints in these work contexts are significantly clustered as indicated by cl*. These are the work contexts after picking up the cargo on pallets. It is likely that view occlusions by cargo resulted in similarity of viewpoints for these work contexts.

Table 3. Clark-Evans criterion R for comparison of spatial correlations between common viewpoints of different work contexts.

Work context		②	③	④	⑤	⑥	⑦	⑧	⑨	⑩	⑪	⑫	⑬	⑭
①	R	1.346	1.264	1.238	0.847	0.973	0.877	1.132	0.843	1.036	0.922	0.977	1.022	1.007
	z	3.177	2.471	2.279	-1.401	-0.257	-1.199	1.188	-1.437	0.348	-0.717	-0.229	0.216	0.070
	Pattern	dv*	dv*	dv*	rd	rd	rd	rd	rd	rd	rd	rd	rd	rd
②	R		0.608	0.544	1.479	1.197	1.139	1.117	1.071	1.107	1.098	0.986	0.909	0.931
	z		-3.756	-4.448	4.491	1.882	1.383	1.071	0.664	1.045	0.917	-0.149	-0.904	-0.663
	Pattern		cl*	cl*	dv*	rd	rd	rd	rd	rd	rd	rd	rd	rd
③	R			0.425	1.435	1.316	1.205	1.152	1.208	1.212	1.076	0.933	1.005	0.910
	z			-5.720	4.159	3.083	2.079	1.428	1.992	2.112	0.731	-0.701	0.055	-0.880
	Pattern			cl*	dv*	dv*	dv*	rd	dv*	dv*	rd	rd	rd	rd
④	R				1.260	0.964	0.940	0.866	0.903	0.932	0.908	0.906	0.834	0.788
	z				2.534	-0.360	-0.623	-1.285	-0.948	-0.688	-0.897	-0.998	-1.708	-2.113
	Pattern				dv*	rd	rd	rd	rd	rd	rd	rd	rd	cl*
⑤	R					0.797	0.517	1.061	0.560	0.984	0.855	0.885	1.006	0.992
	z					-1.938	-4.805	0.559	-4.125	-0.154	-1.356	-1.187	0.057	-0.076
	Pattern					rd	cl*	rd	cl*	rd	rd	rd	rd	rd
⑥	R						0.738	1.012	0.857	0.689	1.061	0.665	0.959	0.856
	z						-2.655	0.117	-1.368	-3.093	0.580	-3.514	-0.416	-1.403
	Pattern						cl*	rd	rd	cl*	rd	cl*	rd	rd
⑦	R							1.093	0.411	0.719	0.601	0.548	0.763	0.717
	z							0.911	-5.860	-2.898	-3.969	-4.896	-2.480	-2.867
	Pattern							rd	cl*	cl*	cl*	cl*	cl*	cl*
⑧	R								0.877	0.625	0.854	0.838	0.866	0.849
	z								-1.125	-3.593	-1.343	-1.640	-1.305	-1.415
	Pattern								rd	c *	rd	rd	rd	rd
⑨	R									0.601	0.560	0.596	0.722	0.673
	z									-3.892	-4.123	-4.161	-2.767	-3.127
	Pattern									cl*	cl*	cl*	cl*	cl*
⑩	R										0.690	0.708	0.770	0.658
	z										-3.024	-3.111	-2.367	-3.399
	Pattern										cl*	cl*	cl*	cl*
⑪	R											0.609	0.699	0.684
	z											-4.025	-2.989	-3.026
	Pattern											cl*	cl*	cl*
⑫	R												0.594	0.531
	z												-4.398	-4.914
	Pattern												cl*	cl*
⑬	R													0.480
	z													-5.268
	Pattern													cl*

cl: clustered (aggregated) pattern
rd: random (chaos) pattern
dv: even (dispersed pattern)
*: significance ($p < 0.05$) of spatial correlation pattern

4   Discussions

This section discusses the results from two aspects. First, the importance of gaze segmentation into fixations and saccades by clustering the gaze parameters. Then, we discuss the impact of the proposed model for developing work support technology.

4.1   Segmentation of Gaze Pattern

As discussed in Sect. 2.2, the model is developed based on gaze fixations of operators. Therefore, this section discusses the importance of gaze parameters for segmenting gaze pattern into fixations and saccades. Although there are other methods for discriminating gaze pattern [7–11], it is noteworthy that the methods are mostly for 2D scan paths. The approach of this study can also be used for 3D scan paths. Figure 8 illustrates two cases of clustering with and without the angular velocity of scan path ω. The results indicate that clustering gaze parameters d, v, a, and ω is helpful to discriminate gaze points that belong to saccade pattern. This is important so that the resulting clusters will not bias towards gaze points forming straight lines that is more representative of gaze transition (saccade) behavior.

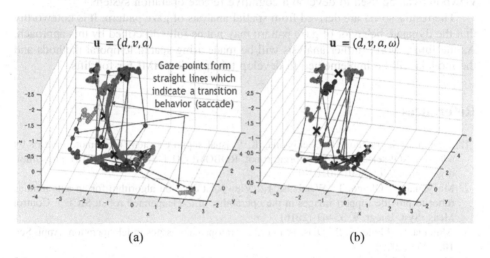

(a)   (b)

Fig. 8. Segmentation of gaze pattern into fixations and saccades is more effective using ω with other gaze parameters. (a) gaze points forming straight lines are discriminated as fixations and used for clustering, resulting in strange formation of clusters as represented by different marker colors, (b) gaze points forming straight lines are discriminated as saccades and not used for clustering, resulting in better formation of clusters.

4.2   Impact of Human Viewpoint Model

The proposed spatial model describes the important viewpoints during forklift operation using the local coordinate system as reference. This definition is useful in multiple scenarios. For autonomous operations like vision-based navigation, the proposed model can be used for foveal analysis of acquired images, where only the salient region is processed with high resolution, and the non-salient region is processed with low resolution. Since image acquisition using wide-angle cameras like omnidirectional [22] or fisheye cameras [23] is a norm, such approach is helpful to reduce computing load and increase response speed of autonomous systems. And for teleoperations, the model is useful to provide the optimal visual stimuli so that operators can work like they are present in the remote working environment.

5 Conclusions and Future Works

A method to model human viewpoint for forklift operation is proposed in this study. Comparisons between the common viewpoint with viewpoints of individual operator category suggests the model is representative of general forklift viewpoint. Comparisons of common viewpoints between different work contexts also suggest most work contexts prior to loading the cargo are spatially independent, i.e. operators exhibit different viewpoint at these work contexts. Compared to [1–4], the proposed human viewpoint can be used to develop a cognitive remote operation system.

The results so far are derived from spatial analysis of gaze pattern. It is noteworthy that the dynamic behavior of gaze pattern may not be fully described by this approach. As the future work, further analysis will be made using spatial-temporal methods and the models will be implemented to develop teleoperation HMI for forklifts.

References

1. Samejima, S., Fozilov, K., Sekiyama, K.: Visual support system for remote control by adaptive ROI selection of monitoring robot. ROBOMECH J. **5**(1), 1–21 (2018). https://doi.org/10.1186/s40648-018-0103-0
2. Maeyama, S., Okuno, T., Watababe, K.: Viewpoint decision algorithm for an autonomous robot to provide support images in the operability of a teleoperated robot. SICE J. Control Meas. Syst. Integr. **9**, 33–41 (2016)
3. Almeida, L., Menezes, P., Dias, J.: Interface transparency issues in teleoperation. Appl. Sci. **10**, 6232 (2020)
4. Thomason, J., et al.: Adaptive view management for drone teleoperation in complex 3D structures. In: Intl Conf Intelligent User Interfaces, Limassol, Cyprus (2017)
5. Chew, J.Y., Okayama, K., Okuma, T., Kawamoto, M., Onda, H., Kato, N.: Development of a virtual environment to realize human-machine interaction of forklift operation. In: Intl Conf Robot Intelligence Tech Applications (RiTA), Daejeon, South Korea (2019)
6. Kawamoto, M., Okayama, K., Okuma, T., Kato, N., Kurata, T.: Work analysis using human operating data based on a state transition model. In: Int Symp Circuits and Systems (ISCAS), Florence, Italy (2018)
7. Schreuder, H.W., Persson, J.E., Wolswijk, R.G., Ihse, I., Schijven, M.P., Verheijin, R.H.: Validation of a novel virtual reality simulator for robotic surgery. Sci. World J. (2014). https://doi.org/10.1155/2014/507076
8. Konig, S.D., Buffalo, E.A.: A nonparametric method for detecting fixations and saccades using cluster analysis: removing the need for arbitrary thresholds. J. Neurosci. Methods **227**, 121–131 (2014)
9. Chew, J.Y., Ohtomi, K., Suzuki, H.: Glance behavior as design indices of in-vehicle visual support system: a study using crane simulators. Appl. Ergon. **73**, 183–193 (2018)
10. DiStasi, L.L., et al.: Gaze-entropy as a task load index for safety-critical operators: military pilots and surgeons. J. Vis. **16**, 1341 (2016)

11. Allsop, J., Gray, R.: Flying under pressure: effects of anxiety on attention and gaze behavior in aviation. J. Appl. Res. Memory Cognit. **3**, 63–71 (2014)
12. Rousseeuw, P.J.: Silhouettes: a graphical aid to the interpretation and validation of cluster analysis. Comput. Appl. Math. **20**, 53–65 (1987)
13. Syakur, M.A., Khotimah, B.K., Rochman, E.M.S., Satoto, B.D.: Integration K-means clustering method and elbow method for identification of the best customer profile cluster. IOP Conf. Ser. Mater. Sci. Eng. **336**, 012017 (2018)
14. Chew, J.Y., Ohtomi, K., Suzuki, H.: Skill metrics for mobile crane operators based on gaze fixation pattern. Adv. Human Aspects Transp. Adv. Intell. Syst. Comput. **484**, 1139–1149 (2016)
15. Chew, J.Y., Ohtomi, K., Suzuki, H.: Gaze behavior and emotion of crane operators for different visual support system. In: HCII Posters 2017 (Part I), Communications Computer and Information Science, vol. **713**, pp. 287–292 (2017)
16. Chew, J.Y., Kurabayashi, D.: Quantitative analysis of the silk moth's chemical plume tracing locomotion using a hierarchical classification method. J. Bionic Eng. **11**, 268–281 (2014)
17. Eglen, S.J., Lofgreen, D.D., Raven, M.A., Reese, B.E.: Analysis of spatial relationships in three dimensions: tools for the study of nerve cell patterning. BMC Neurosci. **9**(68) (2008)
18. Pandit, K., Bevilacqua, E., Mountrakis, G., Malmsheimer, R.W.: Spatial analysis of forest crimes in Mark Twain National Forest, Missouri. J. Geospatial Appl. Nat. Resour. **1**(3) (2016)
19. Ward, S., Cohen, E.A.K., and Adams, N.: Testing for complete spatial randomness on three dimensional bounded convex shapes. Spatial Stat. **41**, 100489 (20121)
20. Clark, P.J., Evans, F.C.: Distance to nearest neighbor as a measure of spatial relationships in populations. Ecology **35**, 445–453 (1954)
21. Ripley, B.D.: Tests of randomness for spatial point patterns. J. R Statist. Soc. B **41**, 368–374 (1979)
22. Taha, Z., Chew, J.Y., Yap, H.J.: Omnidirectional vision for mobile robot navigation. J. Adv. Comput. Intell. Intell. Inform. **14**, 55–62 (2010)
23. Silva, V.D., Roche, J., Kondoz, A.: Robust fusion of lidar and wide-angle camera data for autonomous mobile robots. Sensors **18**, 2730 (2018)

Study on Virtual Reality Performance from the User's Individual Characteristics

Daiji Kobayashi$^{(\boxtimes)}$ ⓘ and Seiji Kikuchi$^{(\boxtimes)}$

Chitose Institute of Science and Technology, Bibi Chitose Hokkaido,
Chitose 758-65, Japan
{d-kobaya, d-kobaya}@photon.chitose.ac.jp

Abstract. In this study, we aimed at revealing the difference and diversity of users working in a virtual environment and the relation between individual characteristics, performance, and sense of embodiment (SoE). Therefore, we conducted two experiments including multiple design factors in the virtual environment and carefully observed the participants' task performances. The participants were 20 students in the first experiment and 8 students in the second experiment. The task was to quickly hit the button on the desk in a virtual environment with a hand avatar. Thus, the participants hit the button setting on the real desk; therefore, they had to recognise the sense of depth and size in the virtual environment while performing the task. Task performance was measured by time, performance level, and SoE score proposed in our previous study. As a result, the relationship between the user's physical or psychological characteristics and the task performance and the SoE are revealed. Although the number of participants and the relation among the design factors, user characteristics, and SoE is not sufficient, some clues for designing tasks and virtual environments are obtained.

Keywords: Virtual environment · Individual characteristics · Sense of embodiment

1 Introduction

In recent years, head-mounted displays connected to a personal computer wirelessly has been commonplace and the users' sphere of action has expanded such that they can move around the virtual environment as if they behave in the physical world. This technical progress permits the users to perform more complicated tasks such as office work in the virtual environment; therefore, the quality of the virtual environment, including the condition of the user's body attached to a head-mounted display in the physical world, should be more comfortable for the user. In this regard, the quality of the virtual environment should be adequately designed, although the virtual environment we developed could have some artefacts such as unnatural visual and/or haptic presentation due to system imperfections. Therefore, from the user's experience, an evaluation of the virtual environment quality is required to improve the system.

Our recent study evaluated two virtual environments implemented using the same head-mounted display and different types of haptic interfaces. The virtual environment

C. Stephanidis et al. (Eds.): HCII 2021, LNCS 13095, pp. 250–261, 2021.
https://doi.org/10.1007/978-3-030-90963-5_20

was compared to a real environment using the same task based on the participants' performance and SoE [1–3]. The performance was measured using electromyography, and the SoE was assessed using our SoE questionnaire. As a result of observing the respective performance for the experimental task, we could specify the averaged SoE of the two virtual environments that implemented different haptic interfaces as a quality measure of the virtual environment; however, we considered that the SoE could be changed depending on the user's skills or capabilities of adapting to the virtual environment. In this regard, this concerns the validity of SoE as a quality measure of the virtual environment, and clarifying the relation between the SoE and the user's performance in a virtual environment is necessary.

On the contrary, some people experience motion sickness and are allergic to virtual reality, whereas some users can adapt to tasks in a virtual environment. Thus, the quality of the virtual environment affects the user's performance and can depend on various factors related to individual factors, including the user's perceptual characteristics. Moreover, the user is required to be accustomed to the virtual environment as soon as possible to perform the task well; therefore, we considered that the comfortable virtual environment not only increased the SoE but also increased the user's environmental perception in the virtual environment. This indicates that the environmental perception that can be built by performing tasks should be evaluated to estimate the virtual environment comfort.

Therefore, we investigated the performance of the respective users executing tasks in unfamiliar virtual environments from the viewpoint of environmental perception.

2 Methods

2.1 Experimental Overview

To observe the user's performance in an unfamiliar virtual environment, we designed a virtual environment for performing simple tasks, such as hitting a button in front of the user in the virtual environment. Further, the virtual environment was composed of fewer components such as a table, a button on the desk, an indicator over the desk, and a right-hand avatar with less texture in contrast with them in reality. In other words, we created a simple virtual environment, had fewer visual cues affecting a sense of distance, depth, or size of the object, and presented fewer cues to perform correctly; therefore, the virtual environment can be an unfamiliar environment for the user performing tasks.

We conducted two experiments using the virtual environment to observe the participants' performance and environmental perception. The participants' task in both experiments was hitting a button (target button) immediately after hearing a buzzer rung. The virtual environment presented via a head-mounted display, including a right-hand avatar; however, presenting the right-hand avatar was a trial condition herein. In this regard, the relation between the hand avatar and sense of agency (SoA) was considered [4]; therefore, we expect the effect of the hand avatar as a design factor in the virtual environment to facilitate the task.

Virtual components such as the target button on the desk and right-hand avatar were of their actual size, and the target button was located on a desk at the corresponding position in the virtual environment. Therefore, the participant looked at the target button in the virtual environment and hit the target button in the physical environment. In this regard, the target button tactually presented the gap between the right palmar and the centre and top of the target button owing to its domical shape, and the participants could evaluate the accuracy or relative position of the target button and palmar in every trial. Therefore, during the task, the participant could grasp the sense of distance, depth, or scale by the correspondence relation between visual and haptic perception. This indicates that the trials or task could progress the participants' environmental perception in an unfamiliar virtual environment (Fig. 1).

Fig. 1. Scene that a participant with the head-mounted display executed a task seeing the virtual environment and hit the target button by his right palmar in the real world.

The first experiment was conducted to test whether the virtual environment could be perceived correctly by the participants. They were instructed to hit the target button as quickly as possible after lighting their visual field in the head-mounted display and the buzzer was rung. After hitting the target button, they had to push another button (left button) set near the left-hand side without delay by the left palmar after an indicator over the desk in the virtual environment, and then their visual field darkened at once. This sequence was a procedure for the participant trial, which was repeated 60 times per participant. However, we moved the position of the target button on the real desk further from its width from the correct location every five times, although the position presented in the virtual environment was not changed and the participants did not know that. Thus, in the first experiment, a right-hand avatar presenting the posture of the right palmar was indicated in the virtual environment.

After all trials, to investigate whether the respective participants could perceive the virtual environment, we interviewed the participants regarding their perception of the virtual environment. Concretely, we asked the participants whether they could hit the target button well every trial, why they could not hit the target button well every time, and their opinion about the task, in other words, the attribution of the case wherein the participant did not hit the target button well.

The participants were seventeen right-handed and three left-handed students ranging in age from 21 to 22 years, and it included three females; however, we checked that they could perform the task well and we took all participants' informed consent in advance.

The second experiment, which was conducted three months after the first experiment, was conducted to investigate the relation between the skill of the task and the SoE. Eight students participated in the first experiment. The task was the same as in the first experiment; however, the target button was randomly located anywhere in nine positions comprising three squares (vertical) by three squares (horizontal) during every trial, as shown in Fig. 2. We silently moved the target button to the positions in accordance with the directions registered on the personal computer in each trial. In the first step, the participants attempted the task 25 times without the right-hand avatar in the virtual environment. Subsequently, they tried 15 times with the avatar in the second step. After these steps, the participants were interviewed about the SoE questionnaire described later and their opinions about the tasks. The scenes of these sessions were recorded using a video camera.

Fig. 2. Real-world task environment in the second experiment. The height of the desk was 40 cm from the respective participants' eye level.

2.2 Apparatus

The domical target button and the left button both had a diameter of 10 cm and were attached to an aluminium case having dimensions $15 \times 10 \times 3$ cm^3; these were used for the first and second experiments. The signal from the target button and the left button was sent to a personal computer (LENOVO LEGION T730) through a USB I/O terminal (Contec AIO-160802AY-USB). Furthermore, the participant's hand motion was captured using a motion capture device (Leap Motion) attached to a head-mounted display (HTC VIVE PRO EYE). Thus, the virtual environment, including the right-hand avatar, was presented via the head-mounted display and the motion sensor. Further, eye-tracking during the participant executed the task was recorded by a personal computer using the head-mounted display. Moreover, the buzzer was presented using a head-mounted display.

The virtual environment was built using UNITY with Microsoft Visual Studio 2019 Enterprise Edition on Windows 10 Pro installed on a personal computer. The sizes of every part in the virtual environment were at the real-world scale, in accordance with the real experimental environment. In this regard, the environmental perception of the participants in the first experiment could affect task performance in the second experiment. Therefore, the height of the desk in front of the participants was 25 cm from their eye level in the first experiment and 40 cm in the second experiment in both the real and virtual environments. Figure 3 shows the two visual fields for the two experiments.

Fig. 3. Two visual fields for the first and second experiments.

To evaluate the task performance of the participants, we extracted the duration from their performances according to the aim of the task in every experiment; therefore, the virtual scene while the participant performed the task was the participant's sight indicated by the head-mounted display, and this was recorded by the personal computer as well as their performance in real time was recorded by the video camera.

2.3   SoE Questionnaire

Our previous study proposed a questionnaire for assessing the SoE for tasks in virtual environments based on Gonzalez-Franco and Peck's embodiment questionnaire [5]. The foci of the embodiment questionnaire were covered via six characteristics: body ownership, agency and motor control, tactile sensations, location of the avatar's body, avatar's external appearance, and response to external stimuli. In other words, the questionnaire was for the task, i.e., the avatar was used to control some objects, and the user could receive haptic feedback from the objects in the virtual environment. Therefore, we arranged the questionnaire to the task of this study in a virtual environment by selecting nine statements from the embodiment questionnaire. Therefore, the task in the virtual environment, including the right-hand avatar, could be assessed using the arranged questionnaire. In this regard, the questionnaire was not applicable to the task without an avatar in the second experiment.

The concept of the embodiment questionnaire was that the SoE was composed of a sense of body ownership, SoA, and sense of self-location. Furthermore, we assume that SoBO, SoA, and SoSL have equal impact on the SoE in a previous study. The nine questionnaire statements we chose, therefore, were composed of three categories, as shown in Table 1. From the results of a previous study, we observed that the questionnaire statements were useful for assessing the quality of the virtual environment in accordance with the participants' experience in the task and their performances. Therefore, we applied the questionnaire statement herein.

The questionnaire was provided to the participants at the end of the second experiment after they tried the second task with the hand avatar. In this regard, the questions were related to the participants' experience during the experiment; therefore, we instructed the participants to answer the questionnaire while recalling the situations described in each item using a seven-point Likert scale. The Likert scale ranged from strongly disagree (−3) to disagree (−2), somewhat disagree (1), neither agree nor disagree (0), somewhat agree (+1), agree (+2), and strongly agree (+3).

In this study, the SoE score for the RTT was composed of the SoBO, SoA, and SoSL scores, which were estimated as follows:

SoBO score = (− Q1 − Q2 − Q3)/3.
SoA score = (Q4 + Q5 − Q6 − Q7)/4.
SoSL score = (Q8 − Q9)/2.
SoE score = (− Q1 − Q2 − Q3)/3 + (Q4 + Q5 − Q6 − Q7)/4 + (Q8 − Q9)/2.

Table 1. Nine questionnaire statements for investigating the SoE in this study [3].

Category	Questionnaire statement
SoBO	1. It felt as if the hand avatar I saw was moved by someone else
	2. It seemed as if I might have more than one right hand
	3. I felt a sensation that I did not move my hand when I saw the right-hand avatar moving, or I felt a sensation that I moved my hand when I saw the right-hand avatar stopped
SoA	4. It felt like I could control the right-hand avatar as if it was my hand
	5. The movements of the right-hand avatar was caused by my behaviour
	6. I felt as if the movements of the right-hand avatar was influencing my behaviour
	7. I felt as if the right-hand avatar was moving by itself
SoSL	8. I felt as if my hand was located where I saw the right-hand avatar
	9. I felt as if the right-hand avatar is my real hand drifting toward my hand I see or as if the right-hand avatar I see was drifting toward the right-hand avatar in my real hand

2.4 Performance Measure for the Task

To contrast the SoE score with the performance of the respective participants, we extracted performance measures from the scene recorded by a personal computer and video camera. In the first experiment, the target button was moved from the correct location every five times; therefore, we applied the time to the performance measure from the point when the participant hit the target button right to the point when he/she pushed the left button by the left hand after making sure that the above indicator went on 300 ms after hitting the target button. Thus, we called the time taken to push the left button after hitting the target button "Post-hitting." Meanwhile, we used time as the performance measure from the point when the buzzer rung to when the participant hit the target button was extracted from the video in the second experiment, that is, "Pre-hitting."

The postures of their right palmar for hitting the target button were different; therefore, we identified the normal posture for respective participants based on their performance by using video and judged the participant's performance for classifying into three levels and quantified as missed (0), abnormal (1), and normal (2) according to the way of hitting depending on the respective participants. Further, we considered the performance where the participants hit a location off the target button and then hit the target button subsequently as Missed (0).

3 Results

3.1 Post-hitting Time in the First Experiment

According to the results of our interview with all participants in the two experiments and after checking the experimental results, we observed that the results were due to all participants' efforts. However, 13 participants were aware that the location of the target button was sometimes incorrect in contrast with 7 participants who were not aware of the button's incorrect location regardless of their dominant hand and gender. Figure 4 shows that the post-hitting time of these two groups and the left bar of each group indicates the post-hitting time in the case of hitting the target button located in the correct position, and the right bar indicates the time when the target button was in an incorrect position. Thus, the case of the correct location was 48 out of 60 trials per participant, and the case of the incorrect location was the remaining 12 trials. Therefore, the seven participants unaware of the incorrect location of the target button required significantly more post-hitting time when they hit the target button located in an incorrect position, in contrast to the 13 participants who were aware of the incorrect button's location (see Fig. 4).

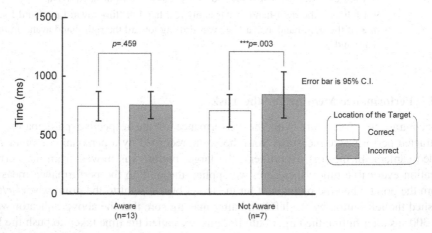

Fig. 4. Post-hitting time in case of hitting the target button at the correct/incorrect location by two groups.

In the interview, we asked the participants about attribution of the case where they did not hit the target button well, and we classified their answers into two types— environment and internal. The environment means that they attributed their bad hitting to the incorrect button's location. The internal type was the case wherein the participants thought the reason their skill of the task was poor [6]. The number of participants for each attribution type is shown in Table 2.

Table 2. Number of participants for each attribution type.

Group	Attribution type	
	Environmental	Internal
Aware	11	0
Not aware	1	8

Table 2 suggests that the participants who were not aware that the location of the target button was sometimes incorrect tended to attribute their abnormal hitting to their inner factors such as skill and effort. Concretely, they want to perform well, although they cannot grasp the sense of depth, distance, or scale in the virtual environment.

3.2   SoE Score

The SoE scores of the participants in the second experiment are listed in Table 3. These scores were obtained after the participants finished all experiments; therefore, the score suggests the evaluation result of the virtual environment for testing by the respective participants.

Table 3. Respective participants' SoE score in the second experiment.

Participant	SoA	SoBO	SoSL	SoE
P1	2.75	1.33	2.5	6.58
P2	1	1.67	2	4.67
P3	2.25	2	0	4.25
P4	0.5	2	1.5	4
P5	1.5	2.67	−0.5	3.67
P6	2	0.33	0.5	2.83
P7	−0.75	0	−0.5	−1.25
P8	−1.25	−0.33	−2.5	−4.08
Mean	1.00	1.21	0.36	2.58
SD	1.43	1.08	1.62	3.49

Table 3 shows that the SoE score of the participants P7 and P8 are less than the other participant's score. Thus, we analysed the respective participants' performance focusing on P7 and P8.

3.3   Performance in the Second Experiment

As a result, we obtained the performance data based on two performance measures: pre-hitting time and performance level. Figure 5 shows the trends of the averaged pre-hitting time of every five trials from the 1st to 25th for each participant. The left-hand line graph shows the averaged times in the case of the trials without the right-hand avatar, in contrast with the right-hand line graph showing the case of the trials with the right-hand avatar. The dotted line shows the change in the average pre-hitting time for participants P7 and P8.

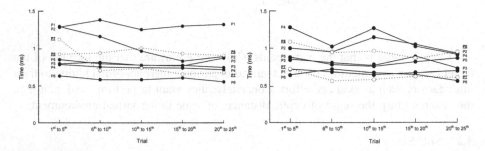

Fig. 5. Averaged pre-hitting time for every five trials in the second experiment. The left-hand side shows the change of averaged pre-hitting time for every five trials without the right-hand avatar and the line graph of the right-hand side shows as well, although the line graph indicates pre-hitting times for the trials with the right-hand avatar.

Tables 4 and 5 show that the respective participants' performance level (0 to 3) we had judged were based on their posture of the right hand hitting the target button, although the performance levels are averaged for every five trials, as shown in Fig. 5 as well.

Table 4. Averaged performance level for every five trials without the right-hand avatar.

Participant	Trial				
	1st to 5th	6th to 10th	10th to 15th	15th to 20th	20th to 25th
P1	0.8	0.6	0.8	0.8	1.6
P2	0.4	0.6	1.6	1.8	1.4
P3	1.2	1.6	1.6	1.8	1.5
P4	1.4	1.8	1.6	2.0	2.0
P5	1.2	1.4	1.4	1.2	1.6
P6	0.8	1.4	1.6	1.6	1.6
P7	1.2	1.4	1.4	1.4	1.4
P8	0.8	1	0.8	1	1.2
Mean	0.98	1.23	1.35	1.45	1.47
SD	0.33	0.45	0.35	0.42	0.15

Table 5. Averaged performance level for every five trials with the right-hand avatar.

Participant	Trial				
	1st to 5th	6th to 10th	10th to 15th	15th to 20th	20th to 25th
P1	1.8	1.6	1.6	2	1.8
P2	1.6	2	1.6	1.4	1.8
P3	1.6	1.4	1.8	2	1.6
P4	1.8	2	1.8	1.6	1.8
P5	1.4	2	1.2	1.6	1.8
P6	1	1.6	1.6	1.6	1.8
P7	1.2	1	1.4	1.8	1.4
P8	0.8	1.4	1.2	1.2	1.2
Mean	1.40	1.63	1.53	1.65	1.65
SD	0.37	0.36	0.24	0.28	0.23

4 Discussion

4.1 Attribution in the Virtual Environment

The performance data in the first experiment demonstrated that the participants who were not aware of the incorrect location of the target button tended to perform slowly after hitting the button. Further, the participants tended to think about why they could not hit the target button as they could not have a sense of depth, distance, or scale in the virtual environment. This indicates that it was difficult for them to grasp the sense in the virtual environment, and they attributed their poor performance to their skill or effort. Therefore, users who tend to apply internal attribution cannot grasp the cue to develop or improve their skills in the virtual environment. Looking at another aspect, they made an effort to think about the gap between visual and haptic perception when they hit the target button setting the incorrect location in the real world. In this regard, Synofzik et al. proposed a two-step account of agency, which is a model explaining the concept of SoA [7]. Based on this model, we experimentally confirmed that a user confused by an unexplainable situation in the virtual environment has a reduced SoA until the user obtains the best explanation [1]. Therefore, as shown in Fig. 4, the post-hitting time after hitting the target button at an incorrect location could be significantly longer.

The results of the first experiment suggest that users are not skillful at perceiving the virtual environment and tend to explain their poor performance by inner attribution. Thus, for working or living comfortably in a virtual environment, it is necessary to build a virtual environment, including appropriate cues to perceive the virtual space based on the concept of visual perception, such as Gibson's ecological approach [8].

4.2 Attribution in the Virtual Environment

The aim of the second experiment was to reveal the user's individual differences while performing tasks in a virtual environment. As a result, the user's performance in training the task varied among different participants. For instance, in the case of P1, the average pre-hitting times without the right-hand avatar did not change during the task, in contrast with the average pre-hitting times of the other participants. In the interview, Participant P1 said that it was a difficult task for him, and he hit the target button without rushing through the task. Therefore, his performance level progressed at the end of the trial (see Table 4), and the SoE score could be higher than that of the others, as shown in Table 3.

Focusing on P7 and P8, whose SoE scores were lower than the others', the change in averaged pre-hitting time was flatter than that of the other participants, and the performance level at the end of the trials were also lower. P1, P7, and P8 used to get carsick, and P8 had experienced cybersickness. Although these three participants used to get motion sickness, P1 knew that performing slowly and carefully was the best way for him, in contrast with P7 and P8, who made an effort to do it as quickly as possible. In this sense, for a user who has negative symptoms in a virtual environment, training in the virtual environment should be made slowly and carefully. Regarding cybersickness, there are many recent studies, such as [9].

5   Conclusion

In this study, we aimed at revealing the difference and diversity of users who work in a virtual environment and the relation between individual characteristics, performance, and SoE. Therefore, we conducted two experiments, including multiple design factors in the virtual environment, and observed the task performance when adopting the virtual environment. As a result, the relation between the user's physical or psychological characteristics and the task performance and the SoE was observed. Although the number of participants and the relation among the design factors, user characteristics, and SoE is insufficient, some clues for designing tasks and virtual environments are obtained.

References

1. Kobayashi, D., Shinya, Y.: Study of Virtual Reality Performance Based on Sense of Agency. In: Yamamoto, S., Mori, H. (eds.) HIMI 2018. LNCS, vol. 10904, pp. 381–394. Springer, Cham (2018). https://doi.org/10.1007/978-3-319-92043-6_32
2. Kobayashi, D., et al.: Effect of Artificial Haptic Characteristics on Virtual Reality Performance. In: Yamamoto, S., Mori, H. (eds.) HCII 2019. LNCS, vol. 11570, pp. 24–35. Springer, Cham (2019). https://doi.org/10.1007/978-3-030-22649-7_3
3. Kobayashi, D., Ito, Y., Nikaido, R., Suzuki, H., Harada, T.: Virtual Environment Assessment for Tasks. In: Stephanidis, C. (ed.) HCII 2020, LNCS, vol. 12428, pp. 1–15. Springer, Heidelberg (2020)
4. Kong, G., He, K., Wei, K.: Sensorimotor experience in virtual reality enhances sense of agency associated with an avatar. Conscious. Cogn. **52**, 115–124 (2017)
5. Gonzalez-Franco, M., Peck, T.C.: Avatar embodiment. towards a standardized questionnaire. Frontiers in Robotics and AI. https://doi.org/10.3389/frobt.2018.00074. Accessed 20 May 2020

6. Weiner, B., Frieze, L.H., Kukla, A., Reed, L., Rest, S., Rosenbaum, R.M.: Perceiving the cause of success and failure. In: Jones, E.E. et al. (Eds.) Attribution: Perceiving the Cause of Behavior, General Learning Press, New Jersey (1971)

7. Synofzik, M., Vosgerau, G., Newen, A.: Beyond the comparator model: a multi-factorial two-step account of agency. Conscious. Cogn. **17**(1), 219–239 (2008)

8. Gibson, J.J.: The ecological approach to visual perception: Lawrence Erlbaum Associates, New Jersey (1986)

9. Wang, G., Suh, A.: User adaptation to cybersickness in virtual reality: a qualitative study. In: Twenty-Seventh European Conference on Information Systems (ECIS2019) Proceedings, Stockholm-Uppsala, Sweden (2019)

Training Tool on Structured Knowledge for Risk Management with VR Technology

Noriyuki Kushiro[1(✉)], Koshiro Nishinaga[1], and Toshihiro Mega[1,2]

[1] Kyushu Institute of Technology, Kawazu Iizuka, Fukuoka 820-8502, Japan
kusiro@mx1.ttcn.ne.jp
[2] Mitsubishi Electric Building Techno-Service Co., Ltd.,
Arakawa, Tokyo 116-0002, Japan

Abstract. In this paper, fundamental issues in legacy risk trainings were discussed on data obtained through experiments by a tool with eye tracking and motion sensors for totally 22 field overseers. Then, risk training tool on experts' structured risk knowledge with VR technologies was proposed on the discussion. Capability of the proposed tool was evaluated through risk trainings for 3 field overseers in detail. As a result, we confirmed that the tool succeeded in obtaining structured knowledge for risk perception and management, and the tool also contributed to build meta-knowledge (procedural knowledge) besides domain knowledge both for novices and experts.

Keywords: Risk recognition training · Structured knowledge for risk perception and management · VR technologies

1 Introduction

In 2020, 125,611 workers were injured or killed by industrial accidents in Japan. Most companies provide "work procedure manuals" to prevent the accidents, and all the workers are obliged to take "risk training" regularly, e.g. KYT(Japan), JSA(USA), STARRT(Europa). Nevertheless, the number of industrial accidents is increasing [1]. Prior to the study, we conducted questionnaire survey in major maintenance company in Japan. As a result, 80% of workers met situations involving exposure to risk and 60% workers felt issues for legacy risk trainings composed of "work procedure manuals" and "risk training". For examples, some workers indicated as the followings:

- Difficulties to improve skills for risk perception and management due to lack of experiences
- Requirements to establish practical risk training tool, which can provide virtual experiences exposed in risk

C. Stephanidis et al. (Eds.): HCII 2021, LNCS 13095, pp. 262–281, 2021.
https://doi.org/10.1007/978-3-030-90963-5_21

In this paper, issues in legacy "work procedure manual" and "risk training" were discussed on the results of experiments with eye tracking and motion sensors for totally 22 field overseers. "risk training tool" on experts' structured risk knowledge with VR technologies was proposed on the discussion, and capability of the tool was evaluated through minute investigation for 3 field overseers.

The rest of paper is composed of the followings 4 sections: The next section reviews literatures about risk perception, management and training tools. The third section describes overview of experiments to clarify issues in legacy "work procedure manual" and "risk training" and results of these experiments. The forth section mentions about the proposed risk training tool on experts' structured knowledge and the results of feasibility study for 3 actual field overseers. Then, the study is concluded in the last section.

2   Literature Review

There are numerous studies in the field of risk perception, management and training tools. In reflecting serious conditions around the OHS, general literature review for occupational safety and health (OHS) were conducted very frequently. For examples, [2–4] surveyed significant topics, e.g. risk perception, risk management and training tools for the OHS. As for the topic of risk training tools, [5] confirmed that knowledge of risk affected heavily to attitude for risk perception and management, and training for obtaining practical risk knowledge was effective to prevent occupational risks. [6] investigated relations between human errors (cause) and occupational risks (effect) and described these relations as association rules on the historical data of work related accidents. [7] introduced a motion sensor to analyze causes of risks objectively on data obtained from the sensor. [8] developed a training tool with VR technologies and confirmed the tool with VR technologies had advantages in increasing concentration and attention to the training in comparison with the legacy risk training. [9] also confirmed that the tool with VR technologies was superior to the legacy training in daily or repetitive risk trainings.

Based on results of the literature review, a tool, which was composed of an eye tracking sensor and a motion sensor, was realized both for discussing fundamental issues in legacy risk trainings on data, and for obtaining practical risk knowledge used in actual field. Furthermore, a training tool with VR technologies was proposed to educate structured risk knowledge including procedural knowledge for risk perception and management.

3   Research Questions and Research Methods

At the first step of the study, we set the following research questions:

Research Question 1. What are fundamental issues in legacy training tools?
Research Question 2. Which kinds of tools are effective to solve these issues?

The following two experiments were conducted for answering the questions:

Experiment 1. A tool for promoting verbalization of latent risk perception and management knowledge in actual field overseers with eye tracking and motion sensors was developed. An algorithm for visualized logical structures of knowledge both in utterances extracted from field overseers and sentences in work procedure manual was also realized. The tool and the algorithm were applied to risk training for 22 field overseers in total, and the algorithm was also applied to analyzing work procedure manual for answering the research question 1.

Experiment 2. A risk training tool was designed for solving the fundamental issues discussed in the experiment 1. The training tool was applied to 3 field overseers and capability of the training tool was evaluated.

4 Experiment 1: Clarifying Fundamental Issues in Legacy Risk Trainings

In the experiment 1, two kinds of experiments were conducted for clarifying fundamental issues in legacy risk training and work procedure manual. To achieve the goal of the experiment, a tool for extracting latent knowledge used in field overseers and an algorithm for visualizing logical structures in utterances of field overseers and sentences in work procedure manual were developed.

4.1 Tool for Extracting Latent Knowledge Used in Field Overseers

Overview for the tool for extracting latent knowledge from field overseers, and their basic capabilities are described in the section. Risk knowledge itself has difficulty to be verbalized, because it involves a kind of the tacit dimension of knowledge [10]. Therefore, workers often face to the difficulties for verbalizing their knowledge and process for risk perceiving in the risk training. The tool for promoting verbalization of latent risk knowledge in field overseers, and the algorithm for structuring knowledge as propositional network were developed in the study.

Composition and Function. The tool consists of a PC, monitors and/or head mount display, an eye tracking sensor and a motion sensor (Fig. 1).

Fig. 1. Configuration of tool for extracting latent knowledge used in field overseers

As backend of the tool, a cluster of eight PCs assists in visualizing eyes movements and structure of utterances. The eye tracking sensor identifies positions of intention look at every frame in the video and the motion sensor records the trainee's utterances and behaviors during the training. The PC shows videos to trainees on a monitor or a head mount display. All the utterances and trails of intention look during the training are reserved in the PC. Eye tracking sensor was not necessary, when the trainee wears head mount display besides monitor. Because the trainee tends to watch objects closely in the center of their sight [11]. The center of panoramic moving picture of 360° view is regarded as the trainee's intention points.

The tool provides the following four functions for extracting knowledge used in field overseers (Table 1).

Table 1. Function lists of tool for Exp.1

Categories	Outline
Eyes	1. Visualize present positions of eyes on videos
	2. Visualize trails of eyes around present position as heat map
	3. Analyzing transitions of gazed object
Utterances	4. Converting utterances to semiformal descriptions and structuring logical relations as propositional network

Capability. Accuracy of the eye tracking sensor was evaluated by 6 subjects prior to the study [12]. The subjects gazed 21 points deployed on the monitor, and the differences between the truth and the identified positions by the sensor were estimated. As a result, average errors were 18 pixels for x axis and 12 pixels for y axis (resolution of the screen: 1980 × 1080). The maximum error was 45 pixels for x axis and 62 axis for y axis for the subjects worn thick glasses for supporting heavy astigmatism. We confirmed that the errors were allowable to the experiment 1.

4.2 Algorithm for Visualizing Logical Structure of Knowledge

The algorithm for visualizing logical structure of knowledge is described in the section. Utterances and sentences in the work procedure manual are converted as atomic propositions and logical relations among atomic propositions are visualized as propositional network on the algorithm.

Process. The processes for converting trainees' utterances to propositional network are shown in Fig. 2. At the first step, the trainees' utterances are converted into texts with the voice-to-text function in Google Document. Then, the texts are converted into semiformal description [14] by the algorithm called "semiformalizer". The "semiformalizer" converts every utterance into simple sentences by using parsers, e.g. Stanza [16] for English, and KNP [17] for Japanese. Then, the "semiformalizer" formalizes simple sentences with semiformal description [14] to reduce ambiguity based on "cases" and "case frame" [18] as grammatical informations. The "semiformalizer" also identifies logical relations among atomic propositions, e.g. ∧, ∨, and →, etc. [15]. At the last step, the algorithm called "proponet" draws semiformal descriptions as propositional networks for visualizing the logical structure of the utterances.

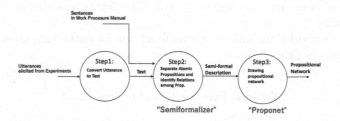

Fig. 2. Process for visualizing logical structure of knowledge

Algorithm. Utterances and sentences in natural language contain a lot of complex and compound sentences. To simplify formalization, all the utterances and sentences are converted into simple sentences. For example, "When the stick was originally a very handsome one and the stick has been so knocked, a town practitioner carried the stick." [19] are converted as the following three simple sentences: "the stick was originally a very handsome one", "the stick has been so knocked", and "a town practitioner carried the stick" on dependencies analyzed by the parser.

Then, every sentence is formalized to semiformal description. The algorithm shapes simple sentences to semiformal descriptions for reducing ambiguity in natural language, e.g. inconsistent wordings, etc., and to clarify dependencies relations among words or phrases in every sentence. Words in a sentence are assigned as elements in an atomic proposition according to lexical categories and "cases" on the algorithm. The simple sentences are formalized as the following steps:

1. The algorithm searches verbs (inflections) in a sentence, and the verbs in the sentence are placed at the head of atomic proposition.
2. The other words in the sentence are regarded as phrases, and the words are combines as phrases on dependency structure analyzed by the parser. For examples, the words: "very", "handsome" and "one", are combines as a phrase "very_handsome_one" at the second step.
3. Then, the phrases are deployed in atomic proposition on the dependency structure. As a result, the subject and the object phrases are allocated at adjacent to the verbs in the atomic proposition. The simple sentence assigned in the atomic proposition is called as atomic primitive in the paper.

Atomic primitives are joined each other with logical relations based on the features for morphemes and phrases, which are identified by the parser [20]. The logical relations among the atomic primitives are described with the fundamental logical symbols: "Not(!)", "And(&)", "Or(—)" and "Implication(→)". Furthermore, the following four symbols: "One", "Exclusive", "Inclusive" and "Require", are supplemented to express complex conditions among the atomic primitives. These relations among the atomic primitives are expressed by using "p_constraint" on the notation syntax shown. The order of precedence among logical symbols is based on general mathematical order. The logical relations among atomic primitives are defined on the rules for each logical relation, which are established through authors' surveying features of sentences.

Semiformal descriptions themselves illustrate logical relations explicitly, however, it remain still difficulty to grasp complex logical relations because of their textual notation. The "proponet" visualizes logical relations among semiformal descriptions as a propositional network (Fig. 3). In the propositional network, each atomic primitive is illustrated as an element of the network (the part encircled with broken line in Fig. 3), and logical relation among the atomic primitives are depicted with structural expression defined in Fig. 3.

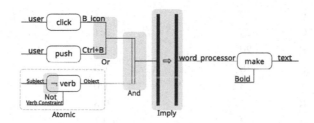

Fig. 3. Visualization of logical structure as propositional network

Capability. Basic capability of the algorithm was estimated by the experiments. Prior to the study, 5 documents were evaluated to confirm basic capability of the algorithm. The precision and recall for converting sentences to atomic primitives and identifying their relations were validated by comparing the results converted manually by 4 engineers for the same documents. As a result, the average precision and recalls were 0.76 and 0.89 [13]. We confirmed that the tools satisfied practical capability for applying the experiment.

4.3   Experiment 1−1

The tool, which promotes verbalization of latent knowledge with eye tracking and motion sensors, and the algorithm for visualized logical structures of knowledge, were applied to risk training for 22 field overseers in the experiment 1−1. Domain and meta-knowledge for risk perception and management were extracted through the experiment.

Process and Subjects' Profile in Experiment 1−1. The experiment 1−1 was conducted on the following two steps:

Step1: each subject watched three movies, while taking memos of risks his/her noticed

Step2: each subject supplemented annotations about the reasons why he/she looked the portions on the screen, referring to the trails of eyes and their memos

12 subjects are categorized 3 groups from the view points of the experiences for outdoor overseers (Table 2).

Table 2. Subjects for Experiment 1−1

Categories	Subjects	Total years of experience	Experience in Outdoor:Indoor
Experts	A	21	17:2
Experts	B	24	20:3
Experts	C	35	20:12
Experts	D	27	19:5
Middles	E	13	8:3
Middles	F	19	3:13
Middles	G	25	6:15
Middles	H	20	1:16
Novices	I	8	1:3
Novices	J	3	1:0
Novices	K	7	0:3
Novices	L	3	0:1

Targeted Scene for Risk Training in Experiment 1−1. Three videos including typical work scenes for constructions of a parabolic antenna were applied to the experiment. The outlines of each video are described in Fig. 4.

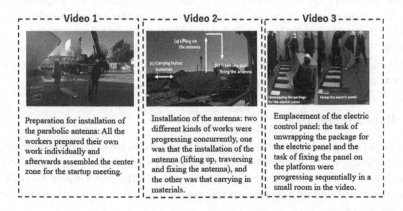

Fig. 4. Targeted video for training in Experiment 1

4.4   Experiment 1−2

We tried to clarify differences of knowledge between used in actual field and described in a manual. The differences were explained by comparing propositional networks obtained from utterances of actual field overseers and from the manual.

Process and Subjects' Profile in Experiment 1−2. At the first step of the experiment 1−2, the risk recognition knowledge in the work procedures manual (Table 4) was structured as the following steps:

Step 1−1: Make a noise word dictionary, which contains nouns appearing frequently in the manual, e.g., demonstrative pronoun. "lifting" is set as initial keyword

Step 1−2: Extract all nouns, which appear in the same sentence with the key word

Step 1−3: Remove words included in the noise word dictionary from the extracted nouns in Step 2 and store them as candidates of co-occurred nouns

Step 1−4: Select a word from the candidates of co-occurred nouns and set the word as the new key words

Step 1−5: Repeat from Step 1−2 to Step 1−4 during new nouns being discovered or until predetermined number of repeat times

Step 1−6: Extract sentences which include the candidates of co-occurred nouns from the manual

Step 1−7: Analyze all the sentences extracted in Step 1-6, with the proposed algorithm

At the second step, the utterances were elicited through the same process described in the Sect. 4.3 from the trainees.

10 field overseers in a construction company (Table 3) attended the experiment 1−2.

Table 3. Subjects for Experiment 1−2

Categories	Subjects	Total years of experience
Experts	A	34
Experts	B	23
Experts	C	20
Middles	D	10
Middles	E	13
Middles	F	15
Middles	G	15
Novices	H	1
Novices	I	1
Novices	J	1

Targeted Manuals and Risk Scene for Training in Experiment 1−2.

Panoramic moving picture of 360° view for "lifting" (Fig. 5) was used as a scene for risk training in the experiment 1−2. Details for work procedure manuals for the experiment 1−2 was shown in Table 4.

Table 4. Targeted work procedure manual for Experiment 2

Items	Contents
Targeted task	Lifting (lifting heavy load to roof)
Targeted manual	Work procedure manual of a construction company for building facilities
Number of pages	81 pages (3 sections), 8466 morphemes

Lifting up and down heavy materials on roof of buildings by crane from ground.
Two workers were supporting for unloading the Heavy materials.

Fig. 5. Panoramic View of 360° for Experiment 1−2

4.5   Results of Experiment 1

Differences of eyes and knowledge between novices and experts, and differences among knowledge used by actual field overseers and that described in work procedure manual are discussed on the results.

Differences of Eyes and Knowledge Between Novices and Experts.
Big differences in movement of eyes and knowledge existed between experts and novices. Experts observed larger areas in each scene, and frequently repeated the extensive observation and the gaze to small area more than novices did (Fig. 6). On the other hand, novices tended to pursue the moving objects attentively.

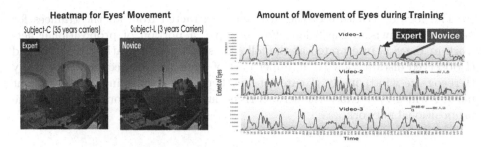

Fig. 6. Differences in eyes' movement between experts and novices

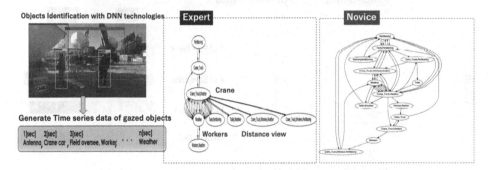

Fig. 7. Transition of gazed objects for experts and novices

For analyzing transitions of subjects' intent objects, objects in the videos were identified with the DNN technologies and time-series data of gazed objects at every second were generated (Fig. 7). The expert frequently focused both crane and distance view to check potential hazard caused by weather and operation of crane, and also paid attentions to workers and their allocations to grasp general conditions of construction site concurrently. The experts managed his intentions based on their procedural knowledge, because all the objects, to which the experts paid attentions, were appeared in their utterances. On the other hand, the novice observed each scene exploratory on declarative knowledge obtained from the work procedure manual. Many objects were not appeared in the novice's utterances. As a result, the followings were confirmed for the eyes:

- The experts surveyed the screen widely to grasp the risk scenarios and perceived more than one risk scenarios and payed their attention to every risk scenarios concurrently
- The experts did not only check their immediate risks, but also the feature risks predicted on the risk scenario and checked latent risks, e.g. hazard of weather, intrusion of persons, workers' motivation perceived from the surroundings in each scene on their knowledge for field overseers
- The experts controlled attentions on their procedural knowledge, however, the experts should break their fixed way for observing objects in order to perceive unexpected events

The logical structure of the utterances extracted from all the trainees for video 1 is drawn in Fig. 8 left. For example, a portion of propositional network in Fig. 8 is interpreted as the followings: (I observe weather_forecast) and (I observed distant view (tree, upper part of crane, cloud, electric wire)) imply (I recognize wind) imply (I care for weather). The former incidents or latent hazard which may cause the serious risks, are located the former parts of the propositional network.

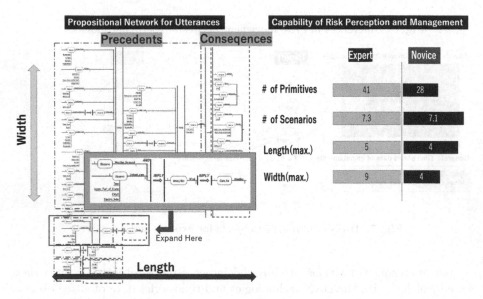

Fig. 8. Propositional network for utterances of experts and novices during training

The width of the network indicates capability for predicting the obvious risks widely from the several former incidents. The length of the network expresses capability for predicting the obvious risks earlier. Thus, as the network is wider and longer, the capability of the field overseers will be higher. The performances of Experts and Novices were scored with the length and width of propositional network (Fig. 8 right). The experts were superior to the novices at the points of number of primitives and width of knowledge.

The utterances for each trainee were also analyzed with the algorithm. Figure 9 shows an example of experts' utterances during training. The utterances of experts were organized from 5 kinds of risk knowledge: the utterances in red area were knowledge for immediate "risks", which were perceived directly from the scene, the utterances in blue area were "counter measures" for the risks and the utterances in green area showed "precedents" both for "risks" and "impeding factors". On the other hand, the utterances of novices neglected precedents both for risks and impeding factors. The structured knowledge were perceived and managed as the following processes in the experts:

1. Perceive two parallel tasks (installation of antenna and carrying in materials) by observing working site widely
2. Recall risk knowledge for each tasks (sideswipe accidents between antenna and workers, intrusion of workers into prohibited area) described in the work procedure manuals
3. Suppose precedents 1 (antenna's vibration by wind, defect of partition for work area) to increase probabilities of risk occurrence
4. Recall measures to avoid risks (rope to lead antenna, standby area for workers)
5. Suppose precedent 2 to invalidate the risk avoidances (shortage of rope's length, absence of supervisor)

Since the order of the propositional network was regarded as causeeffect relations, the precedents were appeared at the former positions, and risks and counter measures for avoiding risks were located at the later positions in the propositional network (Fig. 8).

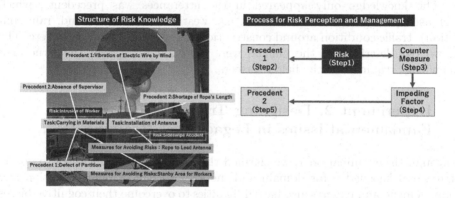

Fig. 9. Experts' risk recognition process

Differences Among Knowledge Used in Actual Field and that Involved in Manual. We tried to clarify differences of knowledge between used in actual field overseers and knowledge described in a manual. The differences were explained by comparing propositional networks obtained from utterances of actual field overseers and from the manual (Fig. 10).

794 atomic proposition were obtained as risk recognition knowledges for "Lifting heavy load to roof" from the manual, and 228 atomic propositions were obtained from the utterances. The risk recognition knowledge both extracted from the work procedures manual and the utterances of field overseers were merged on the algorithm, after correcting orthographical variants. As a result, total of 984 atomic propositions were obtained through the examination. Greater part of the risk recognition knowledge (**76.8%**) was obtained from the manual, slight few knowledge (**3.9%**) were shared with the knowledge obtained from the utterances and from field overseers. The proportions of the shared knowledge

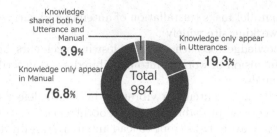

Fig. 10. Risk recognition Knowledge from manual and utterances

between the manual and the field overseers were quite small, even it takes consideration that the targeted video might not contain risk scenes described in the manual. **19.3**% of the risk recognition knowledge was only appeared in the utterances of the field overseers.

The knowledge only appeared in the utterances was precedents, which increased probability of serious risks, e.g. weather conditions (wind, rain condition), traffic condition around construction site, workers' assignment, etc. The knowledge described in the manual were not enough to cover the structured knowledge required for the field overseers.

5   Experiment 2: Designing Training Tool to Solve Fundamental Issues in Legacy Risk Training

Through the examination 1, we clarified that novices have difficulties to obtain structured knowledge for domain and meta-knowledge of risk perception and management, and experts also have difficulties to overcome their cognitive biases (fixed way for observing objects) from their long experience as field overseers. The risk training tool was designed to solve the above issues, and was applied to risk trainings for 3 field overseers.

5.1   Design of Risk Training Tool with VR Technology

The followings concepts were set for a risk training tool on the results of experiment 1:

1. To learn structured risk knowledge, which are composed of risk, counter measures for avoiding risk, precedent to risk, impeding factor for the counter measure, and precedent to impeding factor
2. To learn both domain knowledge and meta-knowledge (procedural knowledge) for risk perception and management
3. To learn the above domain and meta-knowledge heuristically based on Andragogy [21], in order to use the knowledge obtained through the training in practical

Based on the above concept, we designed a risk training tool with VR technologies (Fig. 11). The tool is composed of head mount display and its controllers, monitor for organizing risk knowledge and PC. PC is connected to Google Cloud Speech via internet, to transcribe utterances as texts, which were gathered by the head mount display. The tool has the following three functions:

1. Collecting elements of structured risk knowledge from trainees. The tool provides panoramic moving picture of 360° view to the trainee. The trainee perceives risk and precedents from the movie and annotates them sticking on the moving picture directly (Fig. 11 left).
2. Structuring element of knowledge on framework for risk perception and management knowledge. The elements collected during risk training, are arranged on the knowledge scheme in accordance with navigation of the tool.
3. Providing risk knowledge preserved in Data Base: When the elements of risk knowledge are insufficient to fill out the scheme. Candidates of risk knowledge, which are accumulated on DB, are provided to compensate knowledge of the trainee (Fig. 11 right).

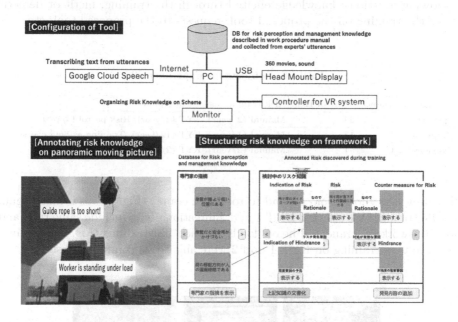

Fig. 11. Risk training tool with VR technologies

5.2 Setups for Experiment 2

3 trainees were attend to the experiment 2 (Table 5). The experiment 2 was conducted on the following processes (Fig. 12):

Step1: Surveying trainees' profiles: name and experiences as field overseers were inquired for each trainee

Step2: Training on legacy risk training (KYT1): each trainee was trained by legacy risk training on the illustration shown in Fig. 13 left.

Step3: Training on the proposed risk training tool: each trainee conducted risk training with proposed tool with VR technologies as the following steps:

  Step3−1: Lecturing operation for the proposed tool: the trainer explained the trainee processes of the examination and lectured operation of the tool for few minutes

  Step3−2: Searching risks on the tool: the trainee searched risks and perceptions on the tool and annotated utterances on panoramic moving picture directly as texts with Google Cloud Speech

  Step3−3: Structuring elements of risks and perceptions on the scheme: the trainee structured each risk elements (risks and perceptions) annotated at Step 3−2, and compensated risk knowledge from the DB provided by the tool

Step4: Training on legacy risk training again (KYT2) : each trainee was re-trained on legacy risk training with illustration shown in Fig. 13 right.

Step5: Inquiring impression on the tool: the trainer asked trainees as the following questions: knowledge elicited through the training, merit or demerit of the training on the proposed tool, requests to the proposed tool, etc.

Table 5. Subjects for Experiment 2

Categories	Trainee	Years of Exp.	Risk training usually disciplined
Experts	A	24	Manual (2/year), KYT (2/year), Risk patrol (4/year)
Experts	B	13	Manual (1/year), KYT (12/year), Training as field overseer
Novices	C	1	Manual (2/year), KYT (2/year), Risk patrol (4/year)

"Loading heavy load from ground to roof with crane" (Fig. 5) was utilized again for the training. We selected KYT 1 and 2 intentionally to include same risks and objects (workers, crane and heavy loads) in their illustrations (Fig. 13), because the results of training on KYT 1 and 2 were able to be compared easily.

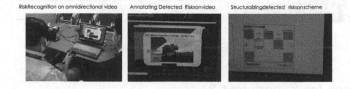

Fig. 12. Process for Examination 2

5.3   Results of Experiment 2

KYT 1 and 2 were selected to include same risks and objects in their illustrations, we can compare the results of training on KYT 1 and 2 easily. Capability of risk perception and management for each trainee in KYT 1 and 2 were scored with the same indexes used in Fig. 8 (Fig. 13). Number of atomic primitives obtained through the trainings was increased, and the length of propositional network was prolonged for all trainees. On these results, we confirmed that the tool contributed to obtain structured knowledge for risk perception and management both for experts and a novice. Especially, for the novice, the length of scenario was prolonged drastically. We can also confirm that the tool was succeeded in providing meta-knowledge (procedural knowledge for risk perception and management) besides domain knowledge for the novice. The experts, who had over 10 years experiences as field overseers, perceived more risk scenarios after the trainings on the tool. The results suggested that the experts broke their cognitive biases and expanded their viewpoints through the training on the proposed tool.

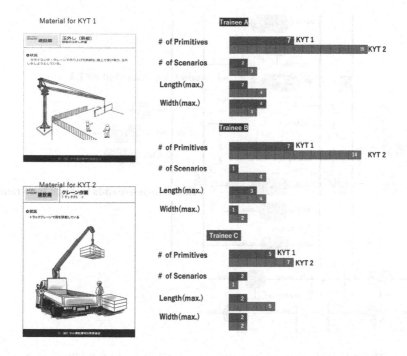

Fig. 13. Capability of risk perception and management for each subject

Figure 14 and Fig. 15 were propositional networks for risk knowledge elicited through KYT 1 and KYT 2. The colored atomic primitives in Fig. 14 and Fig. 15 were appended knowledge in the KYT 2. For example, the trainee A perceived the following two risk scenarios in KYT 1:

– move (operator, crane, miss operation) ∧ is (load, unstable) → hit (load, workers)
– is (load, heavy) → fall down (crane,)

The trainee A just intended the risks included in the illustration, and did not care for precedents and counter measures for the risks.

In KYT 2, the trainee A perceived the following three risk scenarios:

– work (crane, wide) ∧ work (workers, narrow workspace) ∨ !observe (operator, workspace) → is (guide rope, no) ∨ !have (worker, refuge area, at load fall) ∨ !care for (operator, workers,) → work (workers, under load) ∧ fall down (load,) → hit (load, workers).
– !observe (operator, workspace) ∧ work (operator, crane, miss operation) → fall down (crane,).
– work (operator, crane, on public space) → set (field overseer, work area, on public space) → avoid (field overseer, intrusion, outsider).

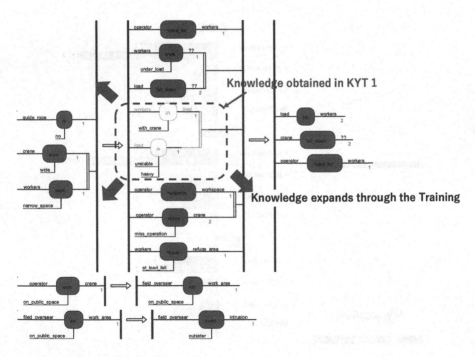

Fig. 14. Differences between results of KYT 1 and 2 for Trainee A

We can confirmed that the utterances in KYT 2 included precedents and counter measures for the risks clearly. The same were observed in the results of trainee B and C.

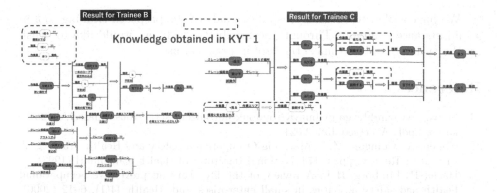

Fig. 15. Differences between Results of KYT 1 and 2 for Trainee B and C

6 Conclusions

In this paper, issues in legacy "work procedure manual" and "risk training" were discussed on the results of experiments with eye tracking and motion sensors for totally 22 actual field overseers. Through the examination, we clarified that novices had difficulties to obtain structured knowledge of risk perception and management, and experts also had difficulties to overcome their cognitive biases on their long experience as field overseers. The risk training tool was designed for solving the above fundamental issues. The training tool was applied to 3 field overseers and efficiency of the training tool was evaluated. As a result, we confirmed that the training tool was succeeded in teaching both structured knowledge and procedural knowledge for novices and experts. We would like to answer the following research questions set in the Sect. 3:

Question 1. What are fundamental issues in legacy training tools?
- Risk knowledge had a structure, which was composed of risks, counter measures for avoiding risk, precedents to risk, impeding factors, and precedents to impeding factor
- Legacy "work procedural manual" just described risks and counter measures, and did not referred to precedents to the risks and precedents to the impeding factor
- Legacy "risk training", e.g. KYT, also failed to express precedents in illustrations used in the training and failed to train procedural knowledge

Question 2. Which kinds of tools are effective to solve the issues?
- The tool, which can handle structured knowledge and procedural knowledge, is indispensable
- Panoramic moving picture of 360° view and VR technologies are hopeful solutions to teach structured knowledge and procedural knowledge, because these kinds of knowledge deploy in spatial and chronological around risk scenes

We have a plan to enhance feasibility study of the proposed training tool in a maintenance company. Through the feasibility study, we would like to brush up the training tool and make the tool in practical use.

References

1. https://www.mhlw.go.jp/bunya/roudoukijun/anzeneisei11/rousai-hassei/dl/20-kakutei.pdf. Accessed June 2021
2. Cohen, A., Colligan, M.J.: Assessing Occupational Safety and Health Training, A Literature Review, pp. 1–174. National Institutes of Health, Cincinnati (1998)
3. Hasle, P., Limborg, H.J.: A review of the literature on preventive occupational health and safety activities in small enterprises. Ind. Health 44(1), 6–12 (2006). https://doi.org/10.2486/indhealth.44.6
4. Andersen, J.H., et al.: Systematic literature review on the effects of occupational safety and health (OSH) interventions at the workplace. Scand. J. Work Environ. Health **45**(2), 103–113 (2019)
5. Arezes, P.M., Sergio Miguel, A.: Does risk recognition affect workers' hearing protection utilization rate? Int. J. Ind. Ergon. **36**, 1037–1043 (2006)
6. Bevilacqua, M., Ciarapica, F.E.: Human factor risk management in the process industry: a case study. Reliab. Eng. Syst. Saf. **169**, 149–159 (2018). https://doi.org/10.1016/j.ress.2017.08.013
7. Manghisi, V.M., Uva, A.E., Fiorentino, M., Gattullo, M., Boccaccio, A., Evangelista, A.: Automatic ergonomic postural risk monitoring on the factory shopfloor. Procedia Manuf. **42**, 97–103 (2020)
8. Sacks, R., Perlman, A., Barak, R.: Construction safety training using immersive virtual reality. Constr. Manag. Econ. **31**(9), 1005–1017 (2013). https://doi.org/10.1080/01446193.2013.828844
9. Pedram, S., Perez, P., Palmisano, S., Farrelly, M.: Systematic approach to evaluate the role of virtual reality as a safety training tool in the context of the mining industry. In: Proceedings of the 16th Coal Operators' Conference, Mining Engineering, University of Wollongong, pp. 433–442 (2016)
10. Polanyi, M.: Tacit Dimension, Reissue edition. University of Chicago Press (2009)
11. Kushiro, N., Nishinaga, K., Aoyama, Y., Mega, T.: Difference of risk knowledge described in work procedure manual and that used in real field by field overseers. Procedia Comput. Sci. **159**, 1928–1937 (2019). https://doi.org/10.1016/j.procs.2019.09.365
12. Kushiro, N., Fujita, Y., Aoyama, Y.: Extracting field oversees' features in risk recognition from data of eyes and utterances. In: IEEE International Conference on Data Mining Workshop (ICDMW) (2017)
13. Aoyama, Y., Kuroiwa, T., Kushiro, N.: Executable test case generation from specifications written in natural language and test execution environment. In: 2021 IEEE 18th Annual Consumer Communications & Networking Conference (CCNC), pp. 1–6 (2021)
14. Rolland, C., Achour, C.B.: Guiding the construction of textual use case specifications. Data Knowl. Eng. **25**(12), 125–160 (1998)
15. Myers, G.J., Sandler, C., Badgett, T.: The Art of Software Testing, 2nd edn., pp. 65–84. Wiley (2004)
16. Manning, C.D., Surdeanu, M., Bauer, J., Finkel, J., Bethard, S.J., McClosky, D.: The Stanford CoreNLP natural language processing toolkit. In: Association for Computational Linguistics (ACL) System Demonstrations, pp. 55–60 (2014)

17. Kawahara, D., Kurohashi, S.: A fully-lexicalized probabilistic model for Japanese syntactic and case structure analysis. In: Human Language Technology Conference of the North American Chapter of the Association of Computational Linguistics, pp. 176–183. Association for Computational Linguistics (2006)

18. Fillmore, C.J.: The case for case. In: Bach, E., Harms, R. (eds.) Universals in Linguistic Theory. Holt, Rinehart, and Winston (1968)

19. Doyle, A.C.: The Original Illustrated Sherlock Holmes. In: CASTLE, pp. 343–344 (1902)

20. Bird, S., Klein, E., Loper, E.: Natural Language Processing with Python. O'Reilly (2010)

21. Knowles, M.: Andragogy in Action. JosseyBass, San Francisco (1984). ISBN 0-608-21794-8

An Industry-Adapted AR Training Method for Manual Assembly Operations

Traian Lavric[1,2(✉)], Emmanuel Bricard[2], Marius Preda[1],
and Titus Zaharia[1]

[1] IP Paris, Telecom SudParis, Evry, France
{traian.lavric,marius.preda,
titus.zaharia}@telecom-sudparis.eu
[2] Elm Leblanc SAS, Drancy, France

Abstract. The adoption of Augmented Reality (AR) in the industry is in early stages, mainly due to technological and organizational limitations. This research work, carried out in a manufacturing factory, aims at providing an effective AR training method for manual assembly, adapted for industrial context. We define the *2W1H (What, Where, How) principle* to formalize the description of any manual assembly operation in AR, independently on its type or complexity. Further, we propose a head-mounted display (HMD)-based method for conveying the manual assembly information, which relies on low-cost visual assets - i.e. text, image, video and predefined auxiliary content. We evaluate the effectiveness and usability of our proposal by conducting a field experiment with 30 participants. Additionally, we comparatively evaluate two sets of AR instructions, low-cost vs. CAD-based, to identify benefits of conveying assembly information by using CAD models. Our objective evaluation indicates that (i) manual assembly expertise can be effectively delivered by using spatially registered low-cost visual assets and that (ii) CAD-based instructions lead to faster assembly times, but persuade lower user attentiveness, eventually leading to higher error rates. Finally, by considering the diminishing utility of the AR instructions over three assembly cycles, we question the worthiness of authoring CAD-based AR instructions for similar industrial scenarios.

Keywords: AR · Industry · Manual assembly · Training · Visual asset · CAD · Case study · Field experiment

1 Introduction

AR is an emerging technology with a great potential in numerous fields of application, from gaming and entertainment to manufacturing and medical [1–4]. AR as a training tool is not a new idea. Previous studies show that AR leads to lower error rates, improved training times and decreased mental workload when compared to classical training procedures [5–8]. However, the adoption of AR in industrial sectors is lagging due to organizational, technological and human limitations [9, 10]. Most AR solutions are designed and tested in laboratory settings [1, 11, 12] and focused on specific segments [2], therefore risking to not answering industrial needs and requirements [9]. Consequently, the utility and effectiveness of these applications in real world use cases are not proven.

© Springer Nature Switzerland AG 2021
C. Stephanidis et al. (Eds.): HCII 2021, LNCS 13095, pp. 282–304, 2021.
https://doi.org/10.1007/978-3-030-90963-5_22

We aim to address this concern by elaborating an AR training solution for a concrete use case, a boiler-manufacturing factory. Our proposal is guided by industrial requirements identified during a long-term case study, specifically conducted to this purpose. We use a Human-centered design (HCD) approach to provide an intuitive, hands-free AR training method adapted to the considered use case and potentially to a wide range of other manual assembly scenarios. This paper has an industrial focus, however it explores relevant AR-related research topics identified by Kim et al. [13], including interaction techniques, user interfaces (UI), AR applications, evaluation, AR authoring, visualization and multimodal AR. Additionally, it addresses AR assembly concerns identified by Wang et al. [14], which include time-consuming authoring procedures and appropriate guidance for complex, multi-step assembly tasks. Finally, it tries to answer a research question inquiring optimal ways for conveying instructions in Industrial Augmented Reality (IAR) [15].

The rest of the paper is organized as follows. The related work is discussed in Sect. 2. Section 3 presents the case study and the research context. Section 4 describes the proposed AR training method. Section 5 presents the field experiment and the interpretation of the results. We discuss the evaluation results in Sect. 6. Finally, Sect. 7 concludes the paper and opens perspectives for future work.

2 Related Work

One of the first AR industrial exploration studies was conducted in 1992 in the context of aircraft manufacturing [16]. Since then, the potential benefits of AR have been exemplified in numerous research works. Tang et al. [17] demonstrated that AR could improve significantly the performance and relieve mental workload on assembly tasks, in comparison to printed manuals or images displayed on LCD or HMD. Quite a few other studies evaluate as well the effectiveness of conveying instructions by using AR (see-through or projected), compared to classical ways of training or guidance like paper instructions, LCD or tablet displays [8, 18–21]. Some, however, identify that classical training methods still perform better than AR in some aspects (i.e. completion time) [22, 23]. Other techniques for conveying assembly instructions in AR are proposed in the literature: 3D in-situ, 2D in-situ, 3D wire and side-by-side [24]. The evaluation environments used in these studies (e.g. Duplo Blocks) however, makes it hard to anticipate the adaptability and effectiveness of these systems in industrial context. Gattullo et al. [15] claimed that more studies are needed to identify optimal ways for conveying AR instructions in industrial sectors. Similarly, Wang et al. [14] concluded that future work should examine the appropriateness of AR guidance for more complex assembly tasks and provide a robust hands-free interaction.

Funk et al. [25] proposed a hands-free AR information conveyance alternative based on SAR (Spatial Augmented Reality), eliminating the need of visual assets. However, SAR and other AR-projection techniques do not seem to be adapted to manual production environment because of the initial effort required to install and calibrate such systems, their lack of mobility and adaptability, reveal our and other industrial studies [26, 27]. An alternative was proposed by Fiorentino et al. [28] with a Screen-Based Video see-through Display (SBVD) technique. Likewise, the hardware setup is complex and rigid while the potential benefits of SBVD systems are questioned by the features proposed in the state-of-the-art HMD devices. Finally, we identified a more pragmatic approach [29], demonstrating a HMD First-Person View (FPV) video technique for conveying task instructions. We note the authoring advantages and the usability of such technique, potentially addressing some of the industrial requirements discussed in Sect. 3.

We observe that numerous AR training methods and techniques are proposed in the literature, however, their adoption in the industrial sectors is questioned by organizational and technical limitations [9, 10]. Palmarini et al. [30] claimed that AR technology is not sufficiently mature for complying with industrial requirements of robustness and reliability. Recent surveys reveal that most AR studies are conducted in controlled environments and laboratory settings. Dey et al. [1] found in an AR usability study that only 54 out of 369 are field studies. Merino et al. [11] noted as well that a majority of user studies reported on MR/AR are conducted in laboratory settings. Egger and Masood [12] identified that only 30 out of 291 papers with a focus on AR in manufacturing have an industrial context and call future research to focus on AR in practice. Furthermore, it seems that requirements identified in the academic world differ from the ones identified in the industrial context [9]. Sousa et al. [2] identified that a considerable number of developed applications (48%) are not focused on specific industry, but rather developed for a general segment and that 97% of the studied AR applications are tested to ensure their viability and compare AR pros and cons against traditional methods, while only 5% are implemented in production.

It seems that most AR solutions are designed outside the context of their expected usage, without the direct involvement of the end users. Consequently, these systems fail to answer effectiveness and usability requirements imposed by concrete use cases, potentially explaining the low adoption rate of AR solutions in industrial sectors.

3   Case Study and Research Context

To elaborate a training methodology adapted to the manual assembly industry, we carried out a 2.5 year-long study in a boiler-manufacturing factory. Our objective was to identify industrial requirements and design an AR training methodology with the direct involvement of the end users, as suggested in the literature. Our analysis was focused on informal meetings, open discussions, contextual inquiries and demonstrations with more than 30 experts (e.g. managers, team leaders, shop floor workers, etc.) from multiple departments (e.g. production, planning, IT, etc.) of the factory. The key success factors identified during the study are effectiveness and viability. A summary of the most relevant challenges that an AR training system should address, in order to be considered for adoption in such context, are further listed. We note that both the authoring (the creation of the AR instructions) and the training (the assembly information conveyance) are concerned by these aspects.

- The system should not be dependent on existing digital assets or external services.
- The system should be mobile, flexible and easy to use and maintain.

- The system should be effective in other manual assembly scenarios than the one analyzed in the considered case study.
- The system should not require expert knowledge or AR experience.

Further, we analyzed the assembly process and the existing digital resources of the factory, to identify how these aspects could affect the design of our proposal. The most significant findings of our subjective analysis are that:

- The assembly workstations are complex environments, consisting of a very diverse set of components and operations, potentially explaining the lack of standardized methods for capturing manual assembly expertise by using AR.
- The existing digital assets of the factory are either not reliable (e.g. assembly instructions) or AR-friendly (e.g. CAD models). Preliminary tests indicate that the existing CAD models require a mesh simplification and a file format conversion.

Requirements for IAR applications identified in the literature [9, 31–34] support these findings. Costs, data privacy and ergonomics have also been identified as potential concerns, but not considered a priority until the proposed method validates the points aforementioned in a field experiment.

4 Proposed Method

We justify the most relevant choices on which the proposed method relies in Sect. 4.1. We discuss the main design principles of our approach in Sect. 4.2. Finally, we detail the training methodology in Sect. 4.3.

4.1 AR Device, Visual Assets and Spatial Registration

Hardware Device. From a hardware perspective, cable-less HMD AR devices seem to answer best the challenges presented in Sect. 3. Handheld devices (i.e. Smartphones) do not answer the hands-free requirement while SAR systems are not viable for the considered industrial context, shows our analysis. We choose to rely the implementation of the proposed AR training method on microsoft® HoloLens 2 [35].

Visual Assets. Digital assets used to convey information in AR include text, audio, static 2D/3D and dynamic 2D/3D [16]. The visual ones are classified as text, sign/symbol, image/picture, video, drawing, 3D model and animations [15, 36]. However, as identified in a recent study [15], there is no agreement in the literature regarding optimal ways of conveying instructions via AR. Tainaka et al. [37] however empirically observed that low-cost assets provide satisfactory results in conveying most assembly operations. Similarly, Lee et al. [29] demonstrated the potential of FPV videos for conveying task instructions. The advantage of low-cost assets is that, unlike CAD models, they can be captured by current AR devices, in-situ, as part of the AR authoring procedure itself. The authoring of the AR instructions is therefore not limited by existing content, preparation or post-processing steps, as proposed by commercial AR tools like Vuforia Expert Capture [38] and Microsoft Dynamics 365 Guides [39].

The most relevant concerns related to the usage of CAD models in AR, identified during our informal experiments are: availability [34] and preparation, positioning during the authoring, spatial registration accuracy particularly for objects in motion and occlusion. Finally, not depending on spatially registered CAD models removes the risk of rendering poor AR experiences or even introducing potential safety issues in the considered manual assembly use case, due to imprecise spatial registrations. We rely therefore our AR training methodology on low-cost visual assets, including text, images, video and predefined auxiliary content.

Content Registration Methods and Techniques. Content registration is a core function of many AR systems, including ours, still an open issue of research. The three main types of information registration methods for HMD-based AR are object, head and environment-based [37]. Marker-based represents the most utilized (57%) registration technique among industrial applications [2]. Other techniques - i.e. 2D/3D recognition, sensor-based, location-based and marker less - do not comply with industrial requirements and are generally limited to test environments [2]. To address robustness and precision requirements, we rely our training proposal on head (head-gaze technique) and environment (marker-based technique) registration methods.

4.2   Design Principles

User acceptance is identified as one of the most important success factors in the literature [9, 33] and during our case study. Our informal experiments performed with shop floor workers suggest that a simplistic UX is potentially the most adapted, considering the profile of the end users and the organization of the production environment. To ensure the usability of the proposed training method, we follow a HCD approach. We analyze and adopt information-presentation methods (i.e. registration, media types, semi-transparent effect and rotation) proposed as guidelines for AR assembly task support [37] and explore information access and peripheral awareness methods discussed in a study related to information access methods for HMD AR [40]. We finally design a hybrid method, by combining and adjusting these guidelines [37] and techniques [29], to provide a contextualized information conveyance method adapted to the considered use case. We use implicit interaction techniques, including eye tracking and head position, along with common interaction techniques [41] like speech and touch, an information outlined in Table 1. A summary of the main design principles around which our proposal is designed, is listed below:

- *Familiarity*: use familiar UI patterns (buttons, arrows) and assets (text, images and video) to increase the user confidence and trust during the usage of the application.
- *Guidance*: use visual cues and implicit interaction techniques to guide the user during the training procedure, in the least intrusive manner.
- *Simplicity*: use a standard information delivery method regardless the variety of the assembly operations. Require deliberate input from the user only when necessary.
- *Comfort and safety*: do not clutter the UI and render graphical elements spatially registered to key locations in the real word environment.

4.3   Methodology

The 2W1H Principle (What, Where, How). In the absence of a standardized method for digitally capturing and conveying manual assembly operations in AR, we propose a technique that aims to address this concern. We note that each assembly operation, independently of its type and complexity, can be described by three variables: *What*, *Where* and *How*. By using this technique, we try to replicate the oral human-to-human explanation of a manual operation as noted during our assembly training and observations. *What* describes briefly the assembly operation, *Where* indicates the physical location of the operation and *How* describes how the assembly is performed. This approach is based on the principle proposed by the Greek philosopher Aristotle, known as the *Five Ws* (*Who, What, When, Where* and *Why*) and *How*, which represent the six basic questions in problem solving. In the considered use case, *Who* – the trainee, *When* – now and *Why* – training/authoring procedure, are known, therefore not considered as variables. Our hypothesis is that by following the *2W1H principle*, the authors of the AR instructions will be able to describe any manual operation effectively and in a formalized manner, independently on the assembly environment and process. We aim to ensure a simple and consistent assembly information conveyance, potentially easy to follow by shop floor workers, people without AR experience.

Assembly Instructions Chunking. For the *2W1H principle* to be applicable, each AR instruction must describe a single assembly operation. As an example, the assembly instruction *"grab an upright and place it on the structure"* as defined in the existing paper instructions, becomes two separate *"2W1H-friendly"* instructions: (1) *"grab an upright"* and (2) *"place the upright on the structure"*. By using this technique, we expect the following benefits: (i) the authoring and the training are consistent for any assembly process; (ii) asking the trainee to perform a single task at a time potentially decreases the complexity, the mental workload and the error rate; and (iii) limit the number of virtual elements to avoid the UI clutter. Advantages of a similar chunking technique were recently demonstrated in the literature [37].

Visual Representation of an Assembly Task. We apply the *2W1H principle* for describing assembly operations by using the aforementioned low-cost visual assets. Each assembly operation is therefore visually composed of three elements:

- (*What*) A **text** instruction, briefly describing the assembly operation.
- (*Where*) An **arrow** pointing to the physical location of the operation.
- (*How*) A FPV **image** or **video** illustrating complex assembly operations (optional).

User Interface and Assembly Information Conveyance. Let us detail how the assembly information is conveyed and how the user interacts with the visual elements, during the training procedure. An example is presented in Fig. 1. Note that Fig. 1d) illustrates the usage of a cad model, replacing the location arrow (see Sect. 5.2).

Fig. 1. Example of how the assembly information is conveyed via AR. Instruction 1: "*Grab 2 uprights*". a) Text & indication arrow; b) Location arrow & FPV photo; Instruction 2: "*Place the first upright*". c) Text & indication arrow; d) FPV video & CAD model.

What: Each task starts by displaying a text instruction panel (Fig. 1. a)) in front of the user, between 0.6 to 0.7 m away. The instruction panel follows user's head for 1s (head registration) then it stops (environment registration). We ensure that the text instruction is not overlooked by the user and at the same time that the panel does not visually interfere for more than necessary. The "*sticking time*" of 1s is adjusted for our use case, based on the required movements of the user during the assembly procedure. The user hides the panel by clicking a "*hide*" button or by using the voice command "*hide*". Complementing the "*hide*" button with a voice command was necessary for cases when the panel is rendered behind the physical environment, unreachable to hand touch. Our use case validates the requirement of multimodal interfaces discussed in [42].

Where: The next step consists in identifying the assembly location, pointed at by a spatially registered arrow (Fig. 1. b)). If the location is not in the Field Of View (FoV) of the user, a fixed-screen registered arrow (Fig. 1. a) and c)) will guide the user toward it. Other techniques for localizing out-of-view objects in AR, like EyeSee360 and audio-tactile stimuli [43] and the "*virtual tunnel*" [44] are proposed in the literature. However, we rely on the arrow guidance-based technique for several reasons: (i) arrows are familiar visual cues, potentially easy to follow in unfamiliar environments like AR; (ii) visually, arrows are less intrusive and easier to integrate with other graphical elements; (iii) the implementation of such technique does not represent a challenge. A similar spatial cue technique was recently proposed in [29].

How: Optionally, a FPV image or video (Fig. 1 d)) describing the assembly operation is displayed in the proximity of the assembly location. Its position is spatially registered so that the visual asset and the assembly location are in the FoV of the user, minimizing therefore user's head movement while switching the attention between the two. The eye gaze controls the video playback, meaning that the video plays as long as the user looks at it. The implicit video playback interaction technique allows the user to follow video instructions without requiring deliberate input. We address thus the hands-free requirement while avoiding the UI clutter with the classical visual playback controls. We respect the design principles discussed in Sect. 4.2, by allowing the trainee to focus on the assembly process, not on the application usage.

The user visualizes the next/previous instruction by clicking the *"next"/"previous"* button or by using the corresponding voice command. The *"help me"* voice command brings the instruction panel in front of the user. We note that unlike [29], our proposal makes use of text and images, in addition to video and indication arrows. We use predefined arrows as AR visual cues, spatially registered during the authoring by using instinctual interaction [45]. In our approach, the FPV instructional video is presented during the training experience exactly as captured in the authoring procedure.

Table 1 presents a summary of the AR interaction techniques while Table 2 summarizes the UI and the information conveyance techniques adopted by our approach. We use the Frame of Reference (FoR) notation for referring to the registration methods: Screen-Fixed (SF) and World-Fixed (WF) [46].

Table 1. Interaction techniques

Interaction technique	User input	Output
Speech	*next, previous*	Goes to the next / previous instruction
	help me, hide	Shows / hides the text instruction (panel)
Touch	Touch virtual elements (buttons)	Hides the text instruction by touching the *"hide"* button with the fingertip; goes to the next / previous by touching the corresponding button
Head gaze	Implicit interaction	Controls the position & orientation of the panel and the orientation of the images & videos
Eye gaze	Implicit interaction	Controls the video playback

Table 2. UI and information conveyance

	Media type	FoR	Information	User action
What	Text instruction	SF / WF	Briefly describes the assembly operation	Reads text, then hides or ignores the panel
Where	Indication arrow	SF	Guides the user toward the assembly location	Turns the head towards the indicated direction
	Location arrow	WF	Indicates the assembly location	Identifies the location
How	Image / video	WF	Illustrates the assembly action	Performs the assembly

5 Field Experiment

We evaluate the proposed training method in a field experiment. The condition of the assembly workstation on which we perform the experiment is not adjusted in any way for the purpose of the evaluation.

5.1 Objectives

The main objectives of our evaluation are the following:

- (**O1**) Determine if low-cost visual assets are sufficient for effectively conveying manual assembly expertise via AR.
- (**O2**) Identify potential benefits of exploiting CAD models by comparing two sets of AR instructions: low-cost vs. CAD-complemented.
- (**O3**) Answer a research question [15] suggesting that studies are needed to identify optimal ways to convey instructions in industrial sectors via AR.
- (**O4**) Validate the HCD principles discussed in Sect. 4.2, by measuring the perceived usability of the system and the mental workload of the participants.

5.2 Experiment Set-Up and Instruction Sets

The experiment requires performing the assembly of a boiler frame. The procedure consists of 38 assembly tasks performed on the mobile structure of the first workstation of a manual assembly line. Figure 2 presents the most relevant assembly steps, referred to later in this paper. We group the Assembly Tasks (**ATx**) into four types:

- 14 x **AT1** – picking (assembly components and tools)
- 8 x **AT2** – installing / placement (assembly components)
- 12 x **AT3** – screwing & riveting (screws and rivets)
- 4 x **AT4** – manipulating (assembly structure and tools)

We used our HMD-based AR authoring tool designed during the case study and addressing the requirements discussed in Sect. 3, to author two sets of AR instructions. The first set relies solely on low-cost visual assets. The second is identical with the first, except that CAD models replace the location arrows in assembly instructions of type AT2. Every instruction of type AT2 has a FPV video associated to it in the first instruction set and complemented with a CAD model in the second instruction set. There is no potential benefit in complementing with CAD models the other assembly types (AT1, AT3 and AT4). The first instruction set addresses objective O1 while the second one addresses objective O2. A comparison between the two instruction subsets of type AT2 addresses objective O3. Finally, an overall subjective evaluation of the two instruction sets addresses objective O4.

The training application is developed for Microsoft® HoloLens 2 [35], by using Unity 3D (v. 2019.4) [47] and MRTK (v. 2.4.0) [48]. The application requires an internet connection and a unique QR code for spatial registration purposes.

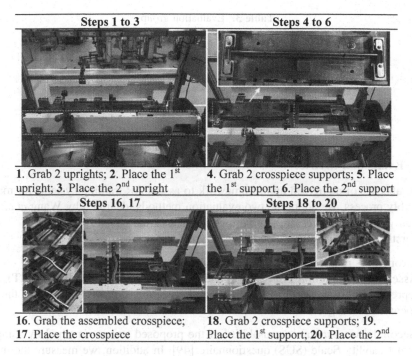

Steps 1 to 3	Steps 4 to 6
1. Grab 2 uprights; 2. Place the 1st upright; 3. Place the 2nd upright	4. Grab 2 crosspiece supports; 5. Place the 1st support; 6. Place the 2nd support
Steps 16, 17	Steps 18 to 20
16. Grab the assembled crosspiece; 17. Place the crosspiece	18. Grab 2 crosspiece supports; 19. Place the 1st support; 20. Place the 2nd

Fig. 2. Field experiment: relevant assembly steps

5.3 Participants

We acquired 30 participants from the factory, 22 males and 8 females, with a wide range of age, education level and professional positions, from shop floor workers to engineers and managers. We create two groups, **G-LA** and **G-CAD**, each composed of 15 participants, for evaluating the two instruction sets: **LA = Low-cost Assistive** based instruction set and **CAD = CAD**-based instruction set. Five participants have assembly experience in each group. We create two subgroups for each group: **G-LA-N = N**ovice participants from G-LA and **G-LA-E = E**xperienced participants from G-LA. Similarly for G-CAD: **G-CAD-N** and **G-CAD-E**. We group the participants as such, to identify if assembly or AR experience has a notable influence on the training performance. The smaller number of participants with assembly experience is an organizational limitation, presumably sufficient to identify potential significant performance differences between the subgroups. Table 3 outlines this information.

Table 3. Evaluation groups

Group	G-LA		G-CAD	
Subgroup	G-LA-N	G-LA-E	G-CAD-N	G-CAD-E
Number of participants	10	5	10	5
Assembly experience	No	Yes	No	Yes
Instruction set number	1		2	

5.4 Evaluation Metrics

In the absence of an agreed upon framework to assess AR training systems for manual assembly process, we adopt the two evaluation methods identified by Wang *et al.* [14] in their AR assembly research survey: effectiveness and usability.

Firstly, we evaluate the effectiveness by measuring the:

1. Error rate – measured (counted) by the evaluator,
2. Assembly Completion Time (**ACT**) and the Instruction Reading Time (**IRT**). ACT represents the time spent for completing an assembly task; IRT represents the time spent on reading the low-cost visual assets (text, image and video).

Secondly, we evaluate the usability of the proposed training method by using the System Usability Scale (SUS) questionnaire [49]. In addition, we measure the mental workload by asking participants to complete the NASA-TLX questionnaire [50]. Finally, we designed a specific questionnaire, for identifying the user profile, mainly the assembly and the AR experience, and gather subjective feedback.

5.5 Experimental Evaluation Procedure

The experiment takes 60 to 100 min per participant and it is conducted as follows:

1. 5 to 10-min discussion to present the goal of the experiment and perform the eye calibration in Hololens
2. The participant learns to interact with virtual buttons.
3. 30 min at the workstation, time in which the participant performs up to four assembly cycles, depending on his skills.
4. 5 to 10-min discussion right after the experiment, to debrief the training experience and collect first impression remarks.
5. Hand the three questionnaires (SUS, NASA-TLX, ours).
6. Open discussion to analyze the experience in detail.

During the experiment, the evaluator is in the proximity of the participant to ensure his safety and observe the procedure. When an error is committed, the participant is interrupted and the evaluator performs and explains the assembly operation. The participant resumes the experiment with the next assembly operation.

5.6   Experimental Results and Interpretation

Table 4 presents the number of participants, per group, performing the nth assembly cycle (78 in total). For each assembly cycle, we present the percentage of participants committing errors, the average error rate per instruction set, the total ACT and IRT (% of the ACT), and finally the average ACT of tasks of type AT2. We measure the IRT to identify differences and to estimate the utility of low-cost visual assets over multiple assembly cycles, in both instruction sets. A comparison between the two subsets of type AT2 is performed separately. Table 4 however, presents the reported statistics collected on all instructions, in order to identify the impact of the CAD-based instructions over the whole instruction set, a practical evaluation approach for the considered use case.

Table 4. Evaluation measurements

Group	G-LA			G-CAD		
Cycle no	1	2	3	1	2	3
Participants no	15	12	8	15	15	9
Participant error rate (%)	66%	25%	0%	66%	20%	0%
Total number of errors	13	3	0	18	3	0
Error rate per set (%)	2.2%	0.6%	0%	3.1%	0.5%	0%
Avg. ACT (s)	884s	538s	367s	838s	475s	336s
ACT progress (n^{th}-1)		39%	31%		43%	29%
Avg. IRT (%)	37%	29%	25%	31%	27%	19%
Avg. ACT of AT2 (s)	290s	165s	98s	268s	130s	74s

Error Rate. The error rate is calculated per total number of assembly tasks, given by the number of participants per cycle × 38 tasks/cycle. We observe that all assembly errors are committed on operations of type AT2, during the first two cycles. These are illustrated in Fig. 2 (assembly steps: 2, 3, 5, 6, 17, 19 and 20) and represent seven out of the eight tasks of type AT2. Except one, all errors consist in a wrong installing of the assembly component. Few riveting and screwing mistakes have been committed because of the lack of assembly experience. These were detected and fixed without the intervention of the evaluator and therefore not accounted as errors.

Figure 3 illustrates an assembly error example: the crosspiece is placed upside-down.

Fig. 3. Assembly error example: wrong orientation

The two green marks underline the arrow on the 3D model and in the video, indicating the orientation of the component. However, some participants fail to notice this detail. It seems that subtle assembly details are prone to be overlooked, especially by participants without assembly experience, which commit more errors as shown in Table 5. We observe during the first assembly cycle, further referred to as the **W**orkstation **E**xploration **C**ycle (**WEC**), that some participants are guessing the orientation of the component, as the assembly structure allows the placement of the component with an incorrect orientation. An informal evaluation of all assembly tasks of the line shows that subtle assembly operations are frequent; therefore, a better visual modality is needed to highlight key assembly details, particularly during the WEC. A simple potential fix, as suggested by the participants, consists in detailing the text instruction, a solution in agreement with the authoring constraints and with our design guidelines. We note that audio-complemented instructions could represent a better alternative for other use cases than the one considered in this work.

Table 5 presents the average error rate committed per participant in each subgroup during the WEC. The error rates of the following cycles are not significant, therefore not discussed.

Table 5. Error rates per subgroup during the WEC

Group	G-LA		G-CAD	
Subgroup	G-LA-N	G-LA-E	G-CAD-N	G-CAD-E
Avg. errors per participant	1.1	0.4	1.4	0.8
Novice vs. experienced	−63%		−42%	
G-LA vs G-CAD	+ 38%			

We note that participants with assembly experience commit fewer errors in both groups (−63% and −42%) and that G-CAD commits more errors than G-LA (38%). The IRT measurement discussed in the next section reveals that G-CAD participants watch the videos less (during AT2 instructions), potentially explaining their higher error rate during the WEC.

By considering the error rate of the WEC, we make two hypotheses: 1) CAD-based instructions (including low-cost visual assets) are not reliable for conveying assembly information of type AT2 and 2) low-cost assistive visual assets are sufficient for effectively conveying assembly information of type AT1, AT3 and AT4.

The convergence of the error rate to zero after three assembly cycles in both groups (LA and CAD) does not support the hypothesis that any of the two instructions sets is not reliable for conveying assembly information of type AT2. A realistic usage of the solution in the industrial context however might require human supervision during the WEC. Our assumption, considering the evaluation results, is that a slightly better technique for highlighting subtle assembly details will lead to an error rate converging to zero, for both instruction sets, even during the WEC. The subjective post-evaluation shows that all participants from both groups agree that spatially registered low-cost visual assets are sufficient to effectively conveying assembly information. Few suggest that CAD-based instructions are easier to follow but the spatial registration needs to be improved for moving parts, as well as the rendering modality, which visually interfere with the assembly location and perturb the assembly operation.

Assembly Completion (ACT) and Instruction Reading (IRT) Times. We discuss the ACT and the IRT of the WEC and of all cycles separately. For the WEC, we compare the ACT and the IRT of the two AT2 subsets, as the other instructions are the same in both instruction sets.

First Cycle (WEC). Table 6 presents the reported ACT and IRT of the WEC, per group. We observe that G-CAD performs slightly faster than G-LA. G-CAD participants use 18% less time for reading the low-cost visual assets; however, the overall ACT is decreased by only 5% compared to G-LA participants.

Table 6. ACT and IRT of the WEC

Dimension (no. of tasks)	Group		Difference
	G-LA	G-CAD	
ACT for ATx (38)	884s	838s	−5%
IRT for ATx	328s	268s	−18%
ACT for AT2 (8)	295s	281s	−7%
IRT for AT2	152s	107s	−29%

A visual representation of the ACT and IRT of assembly tasks of type AT2 is depicted in Fig. 4. We observe a constant lower value of IRT-CAD in comparison to IRT-LA, potentially indicating that participants prefer CAD-based guidance to FPV videos. G-CAD participants use 29% less time for watching videos, leading to a 7% decrease in the ACT. However, as observed in Table 5, CAD-complemented instructions lead to an increase in the error rate by 38%.

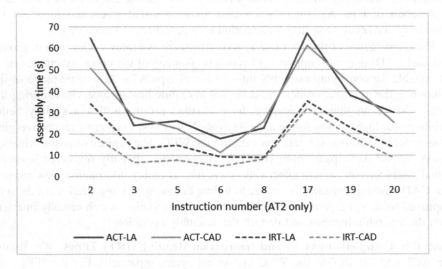

Fig. 4. ACT and IRT of AT2 instructions during the WEC

All Cycles (3) for All Participants. Table 4 shows that the overall ACT decreases, on average for both groups by 41% in the second assembly cycle and by 30% in the third one. The mean (M) and the standard deviation (SD) between the ACT over the three cycles presented in Table 7, support the WEC paradigm and indicate that the participants start familiarizing with the assembly operations at a rapid pace.

Table 7. Mean and standard deviation of the ACT and IRT over three assembly cycles

Cycle number	1		2		3	
Global ACT/IRT	ACT	IRT	ACT	IRT	ACT	IRT
M	22.67	7.85	13.34	3.80	9.26	2.07
SD	13.04	6.89	6.73	3.07	4.04	1.32

Figure 5 illustrates the average ACT of all participants, per cycle. The ACT "flattening" over the three assembly cycles supports the previous claim and demonstrates the learning progress. The overall value of the IRT decreased by 47.5%, respectively by 35.7% in the second and third cycles indicate that participants become less dependent on the AR instructions at a fast pace (see Table 7). Note that Table 5 and Fig. 5 do not consider the first assembly instruction of any cycle, as the participants receive in-app explanations during the first instruction of the WEC.

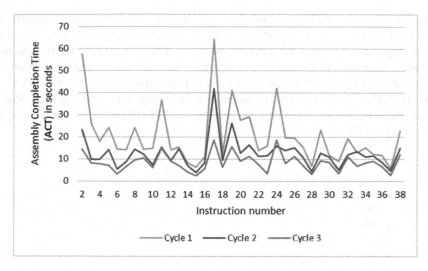

Fig. 5. ACT per instruction over 3 assembly cycles

By considering only the AT2 subset, we observe that CAD-complemented instructions lead to a faster assembly progress. G-CAD participants require less time to perform AT2 compared to G-LA participants: -7% in the first cycle, -18% in the second and -24% in the third (see Table 4). We deduce that CAD-complemented instructions improve the ACT of assembly operations of type AT2, particularly after the WEC.

Subjective Measurements. We present subjective measurements organized by subgroups: G-La, G-CAD, experienced (**G-experienced**) and novice (**G-novice**) participants.

NASA-TLX Score (Raw). Figure 6 presents the raw NASA-TLX scores reported for G-LA $(S = 24.42,\ SD = 4.75)$, G-CAD $(S = 24.22,\ SD = 5.00)$, G-Experienced $(S = 25.25,\ SD = 6.13)$ and G-Novice $(S = 23.85,\ SD = 5.49)$. A one-way analysis of variance (ANOVA) finds no statistical significant differences $(P > .05)$ between all groups and on all dimensions. However, our post-experiment evaluation reveals that participants with assembly experience have higher expectations from a temporal perspective, affecting their perceived performance level. Figure 7 support these claims, where the most notable differences can be observed between G-Experienced and G-Novice for PD $[F(1,28) = 1.96,\ P = 0.17)]$, T $[F(1,28) = 1.52,\ P = 0.22)]$ and P $[F(1,28) = 2.23,\ P = 0.14)]$.

SUS Score. We used the SUS questionnaire to evaluate the overall usability of the proposed training method, by using a five-item likert scale ranging from *strongly agree* to *strongly disagree* (Fig. 7). A one-way analysis of variance reveals no significant differences between G-LA and G-CAD $[F(1,28) = 0.01,\ P = 0.89)]$ or between G-Experienced and G-Novice $[F(1,28) = 0.71,\ P = 0.40)]$. The overall reported perceived usability for all the participants is 4.53 $(SD = 0.25)$, indicating that the proposed method validates the HCD principles presented in Sect. 4.2. However, we observe that the lowest overall score is reported on Q4 (S = 3.80): some participants claim that human supervision is required particularly during the WEC. The effectiveness measurements presented in the previous sections, especially the error rate, support this hypothesis. At the same time, Q4 reports a significant difference between G-LA vs. G-CAD [F(1,28) = 5.34, P = 0.02)] potentially indicating that CAD models lead to higher user confidence, evidence supported by the IRT difference of assembly operations of type AT2.

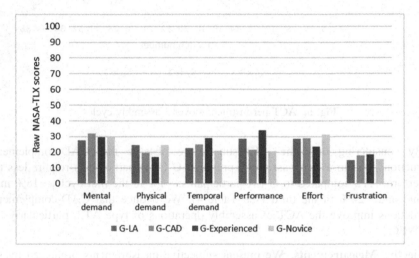

Fig. 6. Raw NASA-TLX scores per dimension and per group

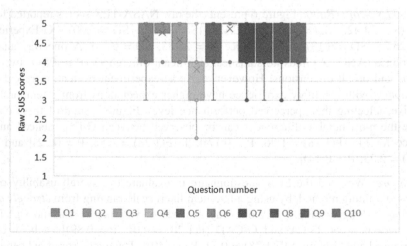

Fig. 7. Overall raw SUS score

6 Discussion

6.1 Relevant Findings

The number of participants committing errors during the WEC invalidates the hypothesis that novice workers can perform the training unsupervised. CAD-complemented instructions lead to faster ACT but to a higher error rate during the WEC, for components with a high degree of symmetry as observed in Fig. 2, assembly steps 4 to 6 and 18 to 20. Videos seem to be more reliable for error-prone assembly operations; however, the experiment results indicate that participants prefer CAD-based guidance. We acknowledge however that the quality of the visual assets plays a crucial role in the comprehension of the assembly and we speculate that user attention and cognitive abilities have a significant impact on the error rate and assembly speed. A single error of type non-AT2 was reported, indicating that low-cost assistive visual assets can effectively convey assembly information of type AT1, AT3 and AT4. Additionally, all participants agree that spatially registered low-cost visual assets are sufficient for conveying assembly instructions in AR. Our picking method differs from the one proposed in [44], however, the effectiveness of pick-by-AR technique is supported by the results of our experiment.

Assembly experience leads to a better training performance. Experienced participants perform significantly faster in AT3 tasks (screwing and riveting) and they commit fewer errors during the WEC. They do not commit errors during the following cycles and their ACT progresses faster. AR experience however does not affect the performance. We do not observe a lower mental workload nor usability advantages for participants with AR experience, validating the usability of the method.

G-CAD participants appreciate CAD-based instructions because the position and orientation of the assembly components can be easily identified. However, some negative remarks were noted: (i) a correct spatial registration requires the mobile assembly structure to keep its initial position; (ii) spatially registered CAD-models interfere visually with the assembly location, making it difficult to perform assembly operations in non-obvious locations (see Fig. 2, assembly steps 2, 3 and 17). The latter issue is observed in video-based instructions as well, where some of the participants spend more time than expected to identify the corresponding real world assembly location indicated in the instructional FPV video.

Finally, it seems that successive and repetitive assembly operations like screwing and riveting can be grouped as a single assembly instruction. Participants performing at least three assembly cycles either suggest or agree on this affirmation, indicating that the instruction chunking technique is not adapted for certain repetitive operations, particularity after the WEC.

6.2 Objectives' Conclusions

(O1) Both the subjective and objective evaluation results support the hypothesis that low-cost visual assets are sufficient for effectively conveying manual assembly instructions via AR, particularly after the WEC. However, a decisive claim cannot be made for AT2 operations, independently on the visual assets (low-cost or CAD models) used to convey the assembly information.

(O2) CAD-complemented instructions lead to faster ACT especially after the WEC. On the other hand, CAD models persuade lower user attentiveness, eventually leading to an increased error rate for subtle assembly operations.

(O3) We identify potential optimal visual assets for conveying assembly instructions via AR as follows: spatially registered (i) visual cues (i.e. arrows) for indicating physical locations, (ii) text and/or image for describing easy assembly operations like picking, (iii) a combination of text and FPV videos for complex assembly tasks. CAD models can complement and potentially replace other visual assets as long as a reliable spatial registration is ensured. We firmly believe that certain assembly operations require video explanations, animations or a combination of multiple assets. Our study does not assess the effectiveness of other visual assets [15] and audio.

(O4) All participants were able to complete the assembly experiment, independently on their AR or assembly experience. AR experience does not significantly affect the perceived usability of the system and the mental workload or the assembly performance, potentially validating the HCD principles discussed in Sect. 4.2.

6.3   Observations and Lessons Learnt

- Quite a few participants do not follow the instructions as told. User attentiveness and cognitive skills seem to have an impact on the assembly performance, independently on the information conveyance method.
- In-app explanations are understood and assimilated by the participants significantly faster than the ones performed outside AR.
- Rarely, during the experiment, some participants triggered without intention voice commands and virtual buttons. Similarly, the Hololens menu was occasionally triggered, as the device was not set in "kiosk mode".
- Few system-related errors occurred during the evaluations, without apparent reason, requiring the restart of the headset. No negative remarks regarding the comfort of the headset were made by the participants.

7   Conclusion and Perspectives

In this paper, we have elaborated and proposed an AR training method for manual assembly, adapted to industrial context. This research work reveals that spatially registered low-cost assistive visual assets conveyed via a HMD AR device might represent the best compromise for addressing organizational and technical challenges and requirements identified in the considered industrial use case. We assessed the effectiveness and usability of our proposal by conducting a field experiment. The evaluation results suggest that the proposed method can be effectively used for training novice workers, with a remark that human assistance might be required during the WEC.

Secondly, we comparatively evaluated a CAD-complemented instruction set with the initial one, to identify potential benefits of conveying assembly information by using CAD models. We found that CAD models persuade lower user attentiveness, eventually leading to higher error rates for components with a high degree of symmetry, but to faster overall assembly completion times, after the WEC. By considering the progress of the time spent by the participants in reading the AR instructions over three assembly cycles, we question the worthiness of authoring CAD-based instructions in similar industrial use cases.

From all the participants performing the third assembly cycle, none committed errors while the ACT decreased on average by 59% and IRT by 73% compared to the WEC. The overall reported effectiveness and usability scores are favorable, indicating that our proposed training method can potentially be used in concrete real world industrial use cases, with a remark that a better technique for underlining subtle assembly details is required for ensuring error-free, completely unsupervised AR trainings. We expect that our approach can be generalized and adopted in other manual production use cases where the *2W1H principle* can be applied.

The main limitation of our work is that the proposed training method was evaluated on a single assembly workstation. To obtain unquestioning statistical data regarding its effectiveness and usability, full training procedures on novice assembly workers and on multiple workstations might be required. We anticipate that future evaluations considering detailed user profiles (e.g. education background, cognitive skills) will reveal important findings regarding optimal ways of conveying profile-adapted assembly instructions in AR.

Finally, we believe that the industry does not need to wait for better registration techniques, 3D content authoring processes or interfaces. We demonstrated that easy to author, low-cost visual assets together with specific interaction and visualization techniques available in state-of-the-art AR devices could provide effective AR training experiences in complex industrial environments. At the same time, we proved that organizational and technical AR challenges could be overcome, as long as the conception of the solution is performed in the correct context and with the direct involvement of the end users.

In future work, we will determine the validity of our expectations by evaluating the training method in other manual assembly use cases and by extending the current evaluation to multiple workstations and ideally performing complete training procedures on multiple novice workers.

References

1. Dey, A., Billinghurst, M., Lindeman, R.W., Swan, J.E.: A systematic review of 10 Years of augmented reality usability studies: 2005 to 2014, Front. Robot. AI, **5** (2018). https://doi.org/10.3389/frobt.2018.00037
2. de Souza Cardoso, L.F., Mariano, F.C.M.Q., Zorzal, E.R.: A survey of industrial augmented reality, Comput. Ind. Eng. **139**, 106159 (2020). https://doi.org/10.1016/j.cie.2019.106159
3. Röltgen, D., Dumitrescu, P.R., Stief, P., Dantan, J., Etienne, A., Siadat, A.: Sciencedirect functional and physical architecture of existing products for an assembly product family identification classification of industrial augmented reality use cases classification of industrial augmented reality use cases. Proc. CIRP **91**, 93–100 (2020). https://doi.org/10.1016/j.procir.2020.01.137

4. Bellalouna, P.F.: Industrial use cases for augmented reality application, pp. 10–18 (2020). https://doi.org/10.1109/CogInfoCom50765.2020.9237882
5. Bosch, T., Könemann, R., de Cock, H., van Rhijn, G.: The effects of projected versus display instructions on productivity, quality and workload in a simulated assembly task. In: Proceedings of the 10th International Conference on PErvasive Technologies Related to Assistive Environments (PETRA '17). Association for Computing Machinery, pp. 412–415. New York, NY, USA (2017). https://doi.org/10.1145/3056540.3076189
6. Sanna, A., Manuri, F., Lamberti, F., Paravati, G., Pezzolla, P.: Using handheld devices to support augmented reality-based maintenance and assembly tasks. In: 2015 IEEE International Conference on Consumer Electronics (ICCE), pp. 178–179. Las Vegas, NV (2015). https://doi.org/10.1109/ICCE.2015.7066370
7. Hahn, J., Ludwig, B., Wolff, C.: Augmented reality-based training of the PCB assembly process. In: Proceedings of the 14th International Conference on Mobile and Ubiquitous Multimedia (MUM '15). Association for Computing Machinery, pp. 395–399. New York, NY, USA (2015). https://doi.org/10.1145/2836041.2841215
8. Funk, M., Kosch, T., Schmidt, A.: Interactive worker assistance: comparing the effects of in-situ projection, head-mounted displays, tablet, and paper instructions. In: UbiComp 2016 – Proceedings 2016 ACM International Jt. Conference Pervasive Ubiquitous Computing, pp. 934–939 (2016) https://doi.org/10.1145/2971648.2971706
9. Masood, T., Egger, J.: Augmented reality in support of industry 4.0—implementation challenges and success factors, Robot. Comput. Integr. Manuf. 58, 181–195 (2019). https://doi.org/10.1016/j.rcim.2019.02.003
10. Martinetti, A., Marques, H., Singh, S., Dongen, L.: Reflections on the limited pervasiveness of augmented reality in industrial sectors. Appl. Sci. 9, 3382 (2019). https://doi.org/10.3390/app9163382
11. Merino, L., Schwarzl, M., Kraus, M., Sedlmair, M., Schmalstieg, D., Weiskopf, D.: Evaluating mixed and augmented reality: a systematic literature review (2009–2019) (2020) https://doi.org/10.1109/ISMAR50242.2020.00069
12. Egger, J., Masood, T.: Augmented reality in support of intelligent manufacturing – a systematic literature review, Comput. Ind. Eng. 140, 106195 (2020). https://doi.org/10.1016/j.cie.2019.106195
13. Kim, K., Billinghurst, M., Bruder, G., Duh, H.B.L., Welch, G.F.: Revisiting trends in augmented reality research: a review of the 2nd Decade of ISMAR (2008–2017). IEEE Trans. Vis. Comput. Graph. 24(11), 2947–2962 (2018). https://doi.org/10.1109/TVCG.2018.2868591
14. Wang, X., Ong, S.K., Nee, A.Y.C.: A comprehensive survey of augmented reality assembly research. Adv. Manuf. 4(1), 1–22 (2016). https://doi.org/10.1007/s40436-015-0131-4
15. Gattullo, M., Evangelista, A., Uva, A.E., Fiorentino, M., Gabbard, J.: What, How, and Why are visual assets used in industrial augmented reality? a systematic review and classification in maintenance, assembly, and training (from 1997 to 2019), IEEE Trans. Vis. Comput. Graph. 2626, 1 (2020). https://doi.org/10.1109/tvcg.2020.3014614
16. Caudell, T.P., Mizell, D.W.: Augmented reality: an application of heads-up display technology to manual manufacturing processes, 2, 659–669 (2003). https://doi.org/10.1109/hicss.1992.183317
17. Tang, A., Owen, C., Biocca, F.: Comparative effectiveness of augmented reality in object assembly (2003) https://doi.org/10.1145/642611.642626
18. Loch, F., Quint, F., Brishtel, I.: Comparing video and augmented reality assistance in manual assembly. In: 2016 12th International Conference on Intelligent Environments (IE), pp. 147–150 (2016). https://doi.org/10.1109/IE.2016.31

19. Henderson, S., Feiner, S.: Exploring the benefits of augmented reality documentation for maintenance and repair. IEEE Trans. Vis. Comput. Graph. **17**(10), 1355–1368 (2011). https://doi.org/10.1109/TVCG.2010.245
20. Ceruti, A., Marzocca, P., Liverani, A., Bil, C.: Maintenance in aeronautics in an industry 4.0 context: the role of augmented reality and additive manufacturing, J. Comput. Des. Eng. **6** (4), 516–526 (2019) https://doi.org/10.1016/j.jcde.2019.02.001
21. Lai, Z.H., Tao, W., Leu, M.C., Yin, Z.: Smart augmented reality instructional system for mechanical assembly towards worker-centered intelligent manufacturing, J. Manuf. Syst. **55**, 69–81, (2020) https://doi.org/10.1016/j.jmsy.2020.02.010
22. Werrlich, S., Daniel, A., Ginger, A., Nguyen, P.A., Notni, G.: Comparing HMD-based and paper-based training. In: Proceedings 2018 IEEE Internatioanl Symposium Mixed Augmental Reality, ISMAR 2018, pp. 134–142 (2019) https://doi.org/10.1109/ISMAR. 2018.00046
23. Gavish, N., et al.: Evaluating virtual reality and augmented reality training for industrial maintenance and assembly tasks. Interact. Learn. Environ. **23**(6), 778–798 (2015). https://doi.org/10.1080/10494820.2013.815221
24. Blattgerste, J., Renner, P., Strenge, B., Pfeiffer, T.: In-Situ instructions exceed side-by-side instructions in augmented reality assisted assembly. In: Proceedings of the 11th PErvasive Technologies Related to Assistive Environments Conference, pp. 133–140 (2018) https://doi.org/10.1145/3197768.3197778
25. Funk, M., Mayer, S., Schmidt, A.: Using in-situ projection to support cognitively impaired workers at the workplace. In: ASSETS 2015 - Proceedings 17th Interanational ACM SIGACCESS Conference Computing Access, pp. 185–192 (2015). https://doi.org/10.1145/2700648.2809853.Des
26. Mengoni, M., Ceccacci, S., Generosi, A., Leopardi, A.: Spatial augmented reality: an application for human work in smart manufacturing environment. Procedia Manuf. **17**, 476–483 (2018). https://doi.org/10.1016/j.promfg.2018.10.072
27. Uva, A.E., Gattullo, M., Manghisi, V.M., Spagnulo, D., Cascella, G.L., Fiorentino, M.: Evaluating the effectiveness of spatial augmented reality in smart manufacturing: a solution for manual working stations. Int. J. Adv. Manuf. Technol. **94**(1–4), 509–521 (2017). https://doi.org/10.1007/s00170-017-0846-4
28. Fiorentino, M., Uva, A.E., Gattullo, M., Debernardis, S., Monno, G.: Augmented reality on large screen for interactive maintenance instructions. Comput. Ind. **65**(2), 270–278 (2014). https://doi.org/10.1016/j.compind.2013.11.004
29. Lee, G.A., Hoff, W.: Enhancing first-person view task instruction videos with augmented reality cues, pp. 666–676, (2020). https://doi.org/10.1109/ISMAR50242.2020.00078
30. Palmarini, R., Erkoyuncu, J.A., Roy, R., Torabmostaedi, H.: A systematic review of augmented reality applications in maintenance. In: Robotics and Computer-Integrated Manufacturing, vol. 49, pp. 215–228, ISSN 0736–5845 (2018). https://doi.org/10.1016/j.rcim.2017.06.002
31. Quandt, M., Knoke, B., Gorldt, C., Freitag, M., Thoben, K.D.: General requirements for industrial augmented reality applications. Proc. CIRP **72**, 1130–1135 (2018). https://doi.org/10.1016/j.procir.2018.03.061
32. Nicolai, T., Sindt, T., Kenn, H., Witt, H.: Case study of wearable computing for aircraft maintenance. In: 3rd International Forum Applicable Wearable Computing, pp. 1–12 (2006)
33. Masood, T., Egger, J.: Adopting augmented reality in the age of industrial digitalisation, Comput. Ind., **115**, 103112 (2020) https://doi.org/10.1016/j.compind.2019.07.002
34. van Lopik, K., Sinclair, M., Sharpe, R., Conway, P., West, A.: Developing augmented reality capabilities for industry 4.0 small enterprises: lessons learnt from a content authoring case study, Comput. Ind., **117**, 103208 (2020). https://doi.org/10.1016/j.compind.2020.103208

35. HoloLens 2. https://www.microsoft.com/en-us/hololens/hardware. Accessed 6 Jul 2021
36. Li, W., Wang, J., Jiao, S., Wang, M., Li, S.: Research on the visual elements of augmented reality assembly processes. Virtual Real. Intell. Hardw. **1**(6), 622–634 (2019). https://doi.org/10.1016/j.vrih.2019.09.006
37. Tainaka, K.: Guideline and tool for designing an assembly task support system using augmented reality, pp. 654–665 (2020) https://doi.org/10.1109/ISMAR50242.2020.00077
38. PTC. Vuforia Expert Capture (2021). https://www.ptc.com/en/products/augmented-reality/vuforia-expert-capture. Accessed 27 April 2021
39. Microsoft. Mixed Reality Dynamics 365 Guides (2021). https://dynamics.microsoft.com/en-us/mixed-reality/guides/. Accessed 27 Apr 2021
40. Lu, F., Davari, S., Lisle, L., Li, Y., Bowman, D.A.: Glanceable AR: evaluating information access methods for head-worn augmented reality. In: 2020 IEEE Conference on Virtual Reality and 3D User Interfaces (VR), pp. 930–939 (2020) https://doi.org/10.1109/VR46266.2020.00113
41. Muhammad Nizam, S., Zainal Abidin, R., Che Hashim, N., Lam, M.C., Arshad, H., Abd Majid, N.A.: A review of multimodal interaction technique in augmented reality environment. Int. J. Adv. Sci. Eng. Inf. Technol., **8**(4–2), 1460 (2018) https://doi.org/10.18517/ijaseit.8.4-2.6824
42. Irawati, S., Green, S., Billinghurst, M., Duenser, A., Ko, H.: An Evaluation of an Augmented Reality Multimodal Interface Using Speech and Paddle Gestures. In: Pan, Z., Cheok, A., Haller, M., Lau, R.W.H., Saito, H., Liang, R. (eds.) ICAT 2006. LNCS, vol. 4282, pp. 272–283. Springer, Heidelberg (2006). https://doi.org/10.1007/11941354_28
43. Marquardt, A., Trepkowski, C., Eibich, T.D., Maiero, J., Kruijff, E., Schoning, J.: Comparing Non-Visual and Visual Guidance Methods for Narrow Field of View Augmented Reality Displays, IEEE Trans. Vis. Comput. Graph., 1 (2020). https://doi.org/10.1109/tvcg.2020.3023605
44. Hanson, R., Falkenström, W., Miettinen, M.: Augmented reality as a means of conveying picking information in kit preparation for mixed-model assembly. Comput. Ind. Eng. **113**, 570–575 (2017). https://doi.org/10.1016/j.cie.2017.09.048
45. Introducing instinctual interactions. https://docs.microsoft.com/en-us/windows/mixed-reality/design/interaction-fundamentals. Accessed 06 Jul 2021
46. Gabbard, J.L., Fitch, G.M., Kim, H.: Behind the glass: driver challenges and opportunities for AR automotive applications. Proc. IEEE **102**(2), 124–136 (2014). https://doi.org/10.1109/JPROC.2013.2294642
47. Unity 3D, v2019.4. https://unity3d.com/get-unity/download/archive
48. Microsoft Mixed Reality Toolkit v2.4.0. https://github.com/microsoft/MixedRealityToolkit-Unity/releases/tag/v2.4.0. Accessed 06 Jul 2021
49. https://www.usability.gov/how-to-and-tools/methods/system-usability-scale.html
50. Hart, S.G.: Nasa-Task Load Index (NASA-TLX); 20 Years Later. In: Proceedings of the Human Factors and Ergonomics Society Annual Meeting, pp. 904–908. https://doi.org/10.1177/154193120605000909

Interacting with FEM Simulated Tubes in AR

Manuel Olbrich[1,2(✉)], Andreas Franek[1,2], and Daniel Weber[1,2]

[1] Fraunhofer IGD, Darmstadt, Germany
{manuel.olbrich,andreas.franek,daniel.weber}@igd.fraunhofer.de
[2] TU Darmstadt, Darmstadt, Germany

Abstract. This paper presents the results of a study the authors conducted to identify the opportunities and challenges of interfacing complex engineering simulations run on dedicated systems with mobile devices visualizing the simulation results and providing inputs in real-time. We build upon an existing finite element method (FEM) simulation, which we tuned to deliver snapshots to an Augmented Reality (AR) application for real-time visualization. On this basis we develop interaction designs for tablets and Optical See-Through Head-Mounted Displays (OST-HMD) utilizing the interaction methods available on such mobile devices to manipulate FEM simulated tubes in AR, as well as an evaluation of these interaction designs.

Our design goal is an intuitive workflow concept that allows usage of an AR application without training overhead. To this end we introduce movable proxies on the virtual tube that provide the simulation with input data. Since the described client devices belong to very different device classes, we show intuitive interaction designs for all of them.

Our client application is supposed to be run at the tube installation site, so we can not rely on stable high bandwidth connections to the simulation server in every case. Therefore, we implemented an asynchronous communication, enabling the use with reduced update rates.

Our system enables the user to quickly reconfigure tube configurations and compare different approaches. At the same time the interaction is intuitive so training the user is unnecessary.

Keywords: Conceptual design and planning · HCI in Industry and Business · Mixed reality and environments · Natural user interface · UX (User Experience) · Simulation · FEM · Network

1 Motivation

Flexible tubes are a staple of industrial construction. Due to their flexible nature, accurately planning their position in CAD (Computer Aided Design) processes proofed to be challenging. Finite element simulations (FEM) allow to simulate the elastic behavior and thereby allow engineers to accurately plan how they will behave in the real world.

© Springer Nature Switzerland AG 2021
C. Stephanidis et al. (Eds.): HCII 2021, LNCS 13095, pp. 305–317, 2021.
https://doi.org/10.1007/978-3-030-90963-5_23

Tube planning is also relevant when connecting objects in existing installations. In this case, model-based simulation would require modelling all involved parts before the simulation can be run.

AR has proven itself in planning scenarios, where new elements are added into an existing environment, allowing the user to perceive the planned assembly in a realistic way, and even make changes on the go.

A key factor for AR in these scenarios is the user's ability to quickly get an understanding of how a planned (virtual) object interacts with existing geometry. This allows recognizing problems early in the design process instead of noticing issues during installation. Especially when working in existing environments, only the data of structures believed to be essential is gathered. Thus obstacles might go unrecognized and need to be dealt with at time of installation.

Even in completely new installations, it might be beneficial for the user to be able to quickly visualize different alternatives. This might also be beneficial in engineering education, since the system can be used to experience the tubes behavior in different situations without any setup time, and the student can gather hands-on experience on how little changes impact the tubes behavior and show the generated stresses.

The rest of the paper is organized as follows. In Sect. 2 we discuss studies related to FEM simulation in AR and the contribution of this paper. Section 3 shows our approach to the different components of our experimental setup including the simulation, uses of AR and interaction technologies as well as interaction design. The implementation of this setup is described in detail in Sect. 4. Section 5 concludes the paper with a summary and perspective.

2   Related Work

Huang et al. [1] use AR to enhance the visualization and interaction with finite element analysis (FEA) of structures. They describe interactions that enable the user to directly influence the FEA in AR by applying weights or even modifying the structure. Fiorentino et al. [2] have a similar approach where they visualize the FEM simulation of a body tracked via fiducial markers and overlay the internal stress onto the body. In contrast to these our focus is on intuitive and realistic interactions with FEM simulated tubes in a workplace environment.

Olbrich et al. [3] aims to solve a problem like the one described in this paper, but in a different setting and with different materials. Here, steel pipe models taken from CAD are loaded into the application, and the user corrects the bends on his tablet device (shown in Fig. 1) before sending the pipe to construction. This intermediary step is necessary, because big ships are individual products, and the scale of the overall project can result in discrepancies to the planning model that prevent pipes from fitting correctly if produced as planned. While no simulation or networked connection are necessary in order to solve the given problem, the requirement to have users modify key points of a pipe run are similar to our need to have the user modify points on a flexible tube. While Olbrich et al. [3] opts to modify the coordinates of bends in 3D space via UI

Fig. 1. The image shows the virtual pipe planning application from [3], running on a tablet-PC. A user can interactively modify virtual pipe segments by touch interaction.

elements, we choose to allow our users to directly modify the positions in 6D via device interaction.

The main contributions of this paper are:

- An approach to manipulating FEM-simulated tubes via pre-defined proxies that constitutes the basis for the interaction designs presented here.
- A design for interacting with FEM-simulated tubes via proxies on OST-HMDs using hand tracking.
- A design for interacting with FEM-simulated tubes via proxies on tablets using touch interaction as well as the 3D position of the tablet in relation to the simulated tube.
- An evaluation of the described interaction designs.

3   Approach

Our aim is to combine the advantages of AR with the benefits of FEM tube simulation, allowing a user to interactively experiment with different tube positioning, while observing the simulated behavior in real-time.

To reach this goal, we build upon the advanced tracking capabilities of the Microsoft HoloLens 2 (as shown in Fig. 2) and the Apple iPad Pro. Both devices provide excellent tracking in indoor environments. To allow our application to use known geometries as a spatial reference for the planned tube, we integrate the computer vision library visionLib[1], which enables us to locate the 6D position of known models in the device's camera images in the applications coordinate system. After this step, we can rely on the device's tracking system to keep track of the relative positions of recognized objects.

To utilize the computationally intensive FEM simulation in a real-time environment, we outsource it to a graphics workstation, where it can run on powerful GPUs (Graphics Processing Units). While solving the computational disadvantages of the mobile platforms, this introduced challenges linked to distributed systems. By building up our communication upon WebSockets, we ensure that

---

[1] https://visionlib.com/.

Fig. 2. A user working with the HoloLens application.

the client can communicate with the server even in more restricted environments. Especially in corporate environments, network connections are sometimes limited, but since WebSockets are elevated http connections, they are most of the time even usable in restricted networks. This is especially relevant in the HoloLens case, because it depends on Wi-Fi for all of its communication, while on iPads cellular modems are available.

3.1 FEM Simulation

For simulating the motion of elastic objects, we rely on the partial differential equations for linear elasticity, which we spatially discretize with linear tetrahedral finite elements. For the AR-application, we adapted the approach from our previous work [4,5], which we briefly describe in the following.

In order to solve the equations of motion, we require a volumetric discretization, *i.e.* a tetrahedral mesh. As input, we require a triangle mesh of the to-be-simulated geometry, which we feed into CGAL[2] for generating the volumetric mesh. Linear elasticity exhibits volumetric artefacts, *i.e.* unrealistic volume growth, especially when the object is subject to rotational motion. Therefore, we adopt the approach of corotational elasticity introduced by Mueller *et al.* [6]. There, the rotational component is determined per tetrahedral element by means of a polar decomposition of the deformation gradient. The resulting rotation matrix is used to correct the strain measure and eventually avoids the volumetric artefacts. More details can be found in [4], or [6].

The high computational speed of the finite element simulation is achieved by executing all necessary building blocks on a GPU using NVIDIA CUDA[3] as the programming interface. Therefore, expensive transfers between CPU and

---

[2] https://www.cgal.org/.
[3] https://developer.nvidia.com/cuda-zone.

GPU memory are avoided. In addition, all algorithms are designed to expose fine-grained parallelism. This enables a massively parallel execution on GPUs and therefore high speed. We build on our previous work (see [7]), where the following building blocks are described in more detail: computing initial element stiffness matrices in a pre-processing step, and in every time step extracting the rotation matrix per tetrahedron, generating the global stiffness matrix, discretizing the time-dependent equation by employing implicit time integration (Baraff and Witkin [8]), setting up and solving the linear system with the conjugate gradient method and finally updating vertex positions. In addition, we rely on techniques introduced by Mueller-Roemer *et al.* [9], namely the specialized Bin-BCSRStar data structure for sparse matrices, which enables GPU-friendly access for sparse matrix-vector multiplications, and on efficient routines for determining the memory layout and assembling the global stiffness matrix. For solving the linear system we use the method of conjugate gradients, as the matrix is symmetric and positive definite. We fix the number of conjugate gradient iterations to 200, which is helpful to limit the run time for computing one time step. In contrast to other computer graphics approaches for deformation simulation (*e.g.* [ABC], [7]), we use a comparably high number of fixed iterations to increase the accuracy for this engineering simulation. Please note that our implementation does not yet support the simulation of collisions. Hence, it was not possible to consider contact with the environment and to base the interaction on collisions. Instead, we predefined interaction points on the flexible geometry, which can be moved freely.

3.2   User Interface

Owed to the different forms of user input available on different classes of AR device, we implemented specific ways to interact with objects in the 3D scene. Keil *et al.* [10] explains the significance of clear and coherent interaction, so while interaction is partly platform dependent, we keep a common pattern to provide a unified experience. The main difference is the interaction used to manipulate the interaction points into their desired position.

When the user moves these points, their position is transmitted to the FEM Service, which applies them to the simulation and sends tube updates back to the client. The client displays the received tube along the given points. The FEM simulation does not only provide movement of the tube, but also the stresses (the internal elastic forces) generated by its bending and stretching, which are displayed as the tubes surface color.

3.3   Mental Model

The shape of a tube is determined by several factors, some of which a user can influence. Ideally the only inputs would be the position and orientation of the tube's end points, and those are the first factors the user can control. Both ends can be positioned in 3D space, and rotated on all axes. While having two axes of rotation would be sufficient to orient the tube ends, the third can apply a pretension to the tube, significantly influencing its form.

Ideally, the tube's shape would be further restricted by the geometries conflicting with its natural position. Since our solver is not yet capable of handling collisions with geometry, we cannot simply simulate the collision of the tube with an articulated hand model. Instead, another type of input from the user is needed. By adding pass-through points along the tube, the user can define locations where the tube must pass through, *e.g.*, openings in solid sheet of metal.

These two 6D transformations and optional 3D points are the only inputs that the user needs to manipulate the simulation. In the rest of this paper, these added points, where the user can interact with the simulated tube are called proxies. While these proxies define a common way to interact in the application, the form in which this interaction is implemented depends on the used devices.

3.4   Communication

The communication between the visualization device and the simulation service is designed to make the two operate independently from each other as far as possible. To this end it is built completely on asynchronous messages. The general communication design is shown in Fig. 3.

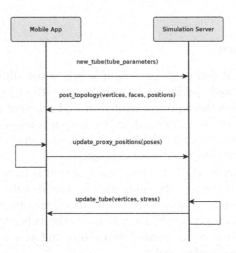

Fig. 3. Schematic depiction of the communication between mobile application and simulation server. The shown calls are in pseudocode.

After a connection is established the mobile application requests a new tube defined by parameters like length and radius. The simulation service then sends initial mesh attributes. To minimize the load on the renderer we define the attributes only once when a new tube is requested. During the interaction, only the vertex position and vertex colors of the mesh are updated continuously. The vertex colors are based on the simulated stress for the respective vertex. When the user manipulates the proxies their new positions are constantly transmitted to the simulation service. These position updates are used as an input to the FEM simulation. On the server, the simulation is executed in pre-defined intervals, independent of the position update message frequency. The simulation results are then sent back to the mobile application. We choose the interval at which we send simulation results based on the connection quality and the load on the interaction application. The simulation service keeps sending these updates until the simulation stabilizes. Further updates are only necessary, if there is new input from the user.

3.5   Environment Tracking

To allow a user to engineer something that has to interact with its surroundings in AR, the interaction device needs to keep track of its own position in the interaction space, so that the worked on virtual object can be displayed at a fixed position. Earlier AR applications like [3] often used simultaneous localization and mapping [11] (SLAM) based approaches with a simple camera, which required the user to work with a steady hand to hopefully not lose track.

Modern AR devices like OST-HMDs or smartphones/tablets provide this camera tracking as a service. While in most cases also being based on SLAM, these services are highly optimized for the specific device, and also use data from other sensors, like IMUs or even depth cameras to keep track of the environment. In case of the HoloLens 2, multiple cameras are used to visually track the devices movement.

The API for these services is specific to the OS, *e.g.* Windows Mixed Reality on the HoloLens, ARKit on iOS devices and ARCore on Android. While each of them are also providing specialized features (some of them will be mentioned later when describing the way user inputs on different devices are implemented), they all provide the needed tracking of the device in space. With AR Foundation[4] Unity3d provides a middleware for this functionality. This allows us to rely on the devices tracking without having to focus on which platform is currently used.

3.6   Environment Reconstruction

Even if the user can position the tube accurately, it might look off since a real-word object that should occlude the tube is unknown to the application and therefore it seems the tube can be seen through walls. When using a tracked model, this can be used to prevent this effect very accurately, but this is only possible for objects with existing models.

Another approach is to reconstruct the environment during runtime. While this is far less accurate then most models, it can provide enough detail to "hide" the tube behind other objects and therefore allow the user to get a better understanding of its position in the real world.

---

[4] https://unity.com/unity/features/arfoundation.

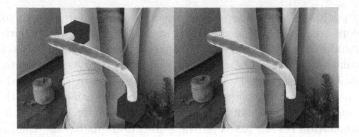

Fig. 4. A simulated Tube with and without an occlusion mesh.

AR Foundation supports Meshing on some platforms, which can be used to generate a low poly mesh of the environment during runtime. Figure 4 shows the improvement of having the environment occlude virtual objects.

3.7 HMD Interaction

OST-HMDs are a great way to present an AR scenario. The real world is still visible in full detail. If the calibration is done right, the user experiences the depth of displayed objects as realistic. This enables the user to understand the location of virtual objects in the real world.

A long-time struggle with these devices has been user input. Earlier models like the Epsons Moverio BT-300 relied on external controllers as input devices. In many cases, this forced the developers to leave it up to the 3D environment to implement some pointer like interaction. This is sufficient for selection tasks, but not for manipulating objects in 3D space. The original HoloLens was one of the first devices of this class that allowed to use the user's hands in a reliable way. If the users hand is held correctly, the device can distinguish between open and closed hand, and also returns the hand position reliably. Since both hands can be tracked, gestures can be used to manipulate objects in other ways then just dragging.

On the HoloLens 2, accurate hand tracking is available, which we use to manipulate our proxies singlehandedly without too much effort. Figure 5 shows the perspective of a user manipulating one of the tube proxies through the HoloLens 2 display.

3.8 Tablet Interaction

While current tablets like the iPad Pro provide sufficient computational power for our application, we were not able to create a user interaction as intuitive as with the HoloLens 2. Even simple interactions like dragging one of the proxies through touch interaction does not relate to behavior that all users expect.

One possible translation from touch interaction to tube manipulation is to restrict the resulting movement to the XY-, ZY- or XZ-plane. Which of these planes to use can be chosen at runtime by calculating the angle between the

Fig. 5. The application as seen by the user wearing the HoloLens 2. The vertical rainbow artefact are caused by taking a picture through the hololens optics.

plane's normal and the camera forward direction The plane with the smallest angle is then selected. While this allows for great precision in movements, it has two significant disadvantages. The behavior is not very intuitive for people not used to work with 3D applications, and the working environment can make it impossible to reach the right position to select the axis you need.

Our solution was to reduce the touch interaction to a secondary form of interaction, since it also does not offer an obvious way to rotate the proxies. Touch interaction is still used, but the dragged proxy is moved on a plane parallel to the screen.

Our main way to manipulate proxies with the tablet is to grab one proxy simply by touching it, and then move the device through space. The object is thereby statically coupled to the device and can be moved and rotated by a similar movement of the device. Due to the coupling, the proxy will always stay on screen and thereby visible to the user.

4 Implementation

With the FEM solver existing as a working project, there are three main implementation tasks:

- Defining a protocol to satisfy our communication needs between client and server
- Extending the solver runtime with a network interface, speaking our newly defined protocol
- Implementing the clients

While the first two steps come with predefined complexity, the clients went through some iterations in which we worked through problems in our interaction design.

The communication protocol is implemented based on Protocol Buffers[5], Google's language-agnostic library for serializing structured data. This allows for implementing without focusing too much on the different languages used in client and server. It also makes the components easily exchangeable. The combination of Unity3D, HoloLens 2 and Protocol Buffers only works with a particular version of Protocol Buffers. This is caused by some C# system functions not being available in the runtime that is cross-compiled for the HoloLens using IL2CPP in Unity3D. To be able to create and connect to WebSockets the simulation service uses Simple-WebSocket-Server[6] while the Unity3D application used NativeWebSockets[7].

HoloLens 2 rendering capabilities are not sufficient for the task at hand. To ensure quasi real-time interaction on the HoloLens 2 we had to limit the simulation updates 3 Hz. The bottleneck is the writing of new vertex coordinates into the mesh.

Fig. 6. Our application as seen by an iPad user.

4.1   Client Applications

The clients are implemented with the Unity3D engine, which enables us to easily deploy our application to both the HoloLens and the iPad. This also allows us to deploy a desktop version of the client to more easily verify our network communication. For handling user input, we diverge between the platforms. The iPad app, shown in Fig. 6, is built on Unity's interaction framework, only using

---

[5] https://developers.google.com/protocol-buffers.

[6] https://github.com/eidheim/Simple-WebSocket-Server.

[7] https://github.com/endel/NativeWebSocket.

the camera position provided by AR-Foundation as a non-standard input. To be able to use the hand tracking features available on the HoloLens we integrate Microsofts MRTK[8]. This provides us with virtual hand representations, which are used to manipulate specially tagged objects simply by grabbing and moving them.

5   Evaluation

Due to the restrictions brought on by the current pandemic, we were forced to choose an easily available environment and restrict the number of people who got first-hand experiences with our setup. Especially the HoloLens 2 is problematic, since the user has direct face contact with the device. The iPad is easy to disinfect, so most users got to try the tablet-based interaction.

To show the technology in an industrial context and a sufficiently complex environment, we test it on a rack-sized fuel cell, intended for server room emergency power supply. When opened, the unit provides different compartments between which we position tubes and visualize the resulting stresses.

5.1   Task

The participants were given a moment to familiarize themselves with the interaction patterns, before they were directed to the fuel cell to connect different elements with tubes, with only the location of points provided by an instructor. After the first connection, the color coding was explained, and the users were tasked to modify the tube to reduce stresses. After that, participants were asked to make two additional connections while optimizing for stresses.

5.2   Evaluation Results

The interaction with the HoloLens is easy to learn for users. With the benefit of depth perception, they are easily able to position the proxies in the desired places. Some users got into positions, where they blocked the hand tracking with their arms, which they easily learned to avoid.

On the iPad, users quickly understand how to manipulate proxies, which works great in free space. One problem of our interaction approach is that proxies can only be rotated if the user is able to rotate the tablet around the proxy. However, this movement might be restricted by the environment.

Because of the missing depth perception, users often need to look from different perspectives to ensure that the proxy is in the desired position. This problem was lessened when we introduced the environment reconstruction in Sect. 3.6, since the user is now able to see occlusions with the environment. This enables the user to position the proxy with more confidence. Nevertheless the interaction is still more intuitive with the depth perception of a HMD.

---

[8] https://github.com/microsoft/MixedRealityToolkit-Unity.

6   Conclusion

Combining FEM simulation with an AR environment enables the user to gauge how a flexible tube will behave in a certain setting. Extending this with intuitive interaction adds the possibility to optimize the fit of the tube and minimize the stress acting on it.

During Evaluation, a significant shortcoming in the tablet interaction became visible: The user needs to be close to the proxy to easily rotate it based on the tablet movements. This is very restrictive if the proxies location is too far (>1 m) from the user, or it is located in an environment, which prevents the user from moving the tablet freely (like the inside of a machine). In these cases, it would be beneficial to have alternative means to rotate the proxy, without moving the tablet excessively.

On the Hololens, the current implementation of the tube updates proved to be a bottleneck which causes significant drops in the framerate during updates. Only updating the vertices while keeping the mesh structure improved the situation, but further improvements are necessary to free users from this irritation.

While we greatly improved the reliability of our network connection, further work into automatically adjusting the frequency with which simulation updates are sent based on the current connection would improve network overhead and user experience.

Currently the FEM simulation does not consider collisions of the flexible tube with the environment. A real-time collision simulation would enable the user to fit the tube more realistically into a given assembly. Devices like the iPad or the HoloLens 2 provide a rough 3-dimensional map of the environment in real time. This could be used in combination with real-time collision simulation to allow for realistic interaction with an unknown environment.

Modern rendering engines enable extending our interaction approach for different use cases. One possible example is using tags of modeled 3D objects, which is a common feature to identify them as possible connection endpoints in a scene. The tube proxies can then be scripted to snap to these endpoints in a desired way. Another possibility would be a menu that lets the user switch between tube models while the proxies are fixed in space. This way tubes with different characteristic features could be evaluated for a certain use case.

There is a physical tool introduced in [3], which is mounted in wall pass throughs and visually tracked. This is used to align pipe segments in the editor to these pass throughs. A similar tool could be used for our application to physically set the position of tube fittings or similar items.

References

1. Huang, J., Ong, S.K., Nee, A.Y.: Visualization and interaction of finite element analysis in augmented reality. Comput. Aided Des. **84**, 1–14 (2017)
2. Fiorentino, M., Monno, G., Uva, A.: Interactive "touch and see" fem simulation using augmented reality. Int. J. Eng. Educ. **25**(6), 1124–1128 (2009)

3. Olbrich, M., Wuest, H., Riess, P., Bockholt, U.: Augmented reality pipe layout planning in the shipbuilding industry. In: 2011 10th IEEE International Symposium on Mixed and Augmented Reality, pp. 269–270 (2011)
4. Weber, D., Kalbe, T., Stork, A., Fellner, D., Goesele, M.: Interactive deformable models with quadratic bases in Bernstein-Bézier-form. Vis. Comput. **27**, 473–483 (2011)
5. Weber, D., Mueller-Roemer, J., Altenhofen, C., Stork, A., Fellner, D.: Deformation simulation using cubic finite elements and efficient p-multigrid methods. Comput. Graph. **53**(PB), 185–195 (2015)
6. Müller, M., Gross, M.: Interactive virtual materials. In: Proceedings of Graphics Interface 2004, GI 2004, School of Computer Science, University of Waterloo, Waterloo, Ontario, Canada, Canadian Human-Computer Communications Society, pp. 239–246 (2004)
7. Weber, D., Bender, J., Schnoes, M., Stork, A., Fellner, D.: Efficient GPU data structures and methods to solve sparse linear systems in dynamics applications. Comput. Graph. Forum **32**(1), 16–26 (2013)
8. Baraff, D., Witkin, A.: Large steps in cloth simulation. Comput. Graph. **32**, 43–54 (1998)
9. Mueller-Roemer, J.S., Stork, A.: GPU-based polynomial finite element matrix assembly for simplex meshes. Comput. Graph.Forum **37**(7), 443–454 (2018)
10. Keil, J., Schmitt, F., Engelke, T., Graf, H., Olbrich, M.: Augmented reality views: discussing the utility of visual elements by mediation means in industrial AR from a design perspective. In: HCI (2018)
11. Leonard, J., Durrant-Whyte, H.: Simultaneous map building and localization for an autonomous mobile robot. In: Proceedings IROS 1991: IEEE/RSJ International Workshop on Intelligent Robots and Systems, vol. 3, pp. 1442–1447 (1991)

Improving Learnability Capabilities in Desktop VR Medical Applications

Laurie-Jade Rochon[1]([⊠]), Alexander J. Karran[1], Frédérique Bouvier[1],
Constantinos K. Coursaris[1], Sylvain Sénécal[1], Jean-François Delisle[2],
and Pierre-Majorique Léger[1]

[1] HEC Montréal, Montréal, QC H3T27, Canada
{laurie-jade.rochon,pierre-majorique.leger}@hec.ca
[2] CAE Inc., Saint-Laurent, QC H4T1G6, Canada

Abstract. The main objective of this study was to evaluate the implicit and explicit learning experiences of two distinct training segments, a tutorial and a Free Play Mode (FPM), of a desktop-based virtual reality (VR) medical operations simulator to assess aspects of learnability for a first-time user. Our goal was to evaluate the tutorial simulator and User Interface (UI) design by interpreting results through the lens of Mayer's principles of multimedia learning. The experiment was conducted remotely and the study sample comprised of ten upper-year medical students. The video recording from the participant's desktop camera was retrieved to determine their affective responses by analyzing facial micro-expressions and infer valence pain points (VPPs). Participants performed the simulation's tutorial followed by the FPM tasks, partitioned into two types: twelve retention tasks designed to verify how well users learned UI elements through the tutorial, and an exploration task to observe how the user explored the interface when few instructions were given. Results showed that the explicit user experience did not differ between the tutorial and the retention tasks. In contrast, users reported significantly higher cognitive load and lower system usability during the exploration task than during the tutorial. A negative correlation was found between perceived self-efficacy and perceived cognitive load. Results pertaining to VPPs indicated that FPM tasks were associated with more negative affective responses when compared to the tutorial. The manuscript concludes with methodological guidelines to assess the learnability of complex, ecologically valid simulations while reinforcing the need to use complementary methods to assess the users' experience.

Keywords: Multimedia learning · Learnability · Virtual reality · VR · User experience · Valence pain points · Automated facial expression analysis

1 Introduction

Virtual environments (VE) are becoming an essential learning tool for various industrial domains such as aerospace, medicine and engineering [1–3]. Learning in a Virtual Reality (VR) settings has been shown to have beneficial effects on knowledge acquisition, retention, motivation and enjoyment [4–6], providing users with a robust

© Springer Nature Switzerland AG 2021
C. Stephanidis et al. (Eds.): HCII 2021, LNCS 13095, pp. 318–336, 2021.
https://doi.org/10.1007/978-3-030-90963-5_24

environment to facilitate the comprehension of complex conceptual knowledge and procedures through observation, imitation and participation [7].

It has been widely accepted that applying the principles of multimedia learning for the design of multimedia environments generates deeper, better learning experiences [8]. However, to our knowledge, no work has investigated the use of these principles to generate heuristic recommendations for the improvement of virtual environments (VE) in a learning context. Therefore, it becomes necessary to develop a method of evaluating user training that accounts for the complexity of such ecologically valid simulations.

The main objective of the present study is to evaluate the implicit and explicit learning experience of two distinct segments – a guided tutorial and an FPM – of a desktop VR medical operations simulator to assess elements of learnability for a first-time user. Specifically, our goal is to evaluate the simulator's User Interface (UI) design by interpreting results through the lens of Mayer's design principles of multimedia learning [8]. To form the basis of our study, we posed the following research question: To what extent can the evaluation of the user training experience through implicit and explicit measures inform the design of learning experiences within desktop VR simulations?

2   Literature Review

2.1   VR for Medical Training

VR technology and VE's have been defined by Schroeder [9] as "a computer-generated display that allows or compels the user (or users) to have a sense of being present in an environment other than the one they are actually in, and to interact with that environment". Immersion, interactivity, and presence are particular features of VR that distinguish it from other representational technology [10]. VE's may be displayed on a computer screen, a head-mounted display, or projection screen, whereas in desktop VR, interaction usually occurs through a computer monitor using a keyboard, a touch screen, mouse, or joystick [11]. VR offers several advantages, such as real-world familiarity, allowing learners to rehearse sequences of procedures with high physical and psychological fidelity, enabling immediate feedback in a controlled environment [12–15].

A recent meta-analysis of eight studies of inpatient deaths put the number of preventable deaths at just over 22,000 a year in the United States [16]. Therefore, refining medical training procedures is pivotal in saving thousands of lives. However, a lack of training personnel and equipment scarcity constrain medical practitioner's training [17]. VR training provides a realistic environment and is an attractive hands-on training method to address this need as it provides practical know-how while simultaneously minimizing the risks to patients. Moreover, VR-based simulators can offer a large number of diverse use cases, allowing the training of rare but dangerous complications which a trainee might not otherwise experience during a residency program [18]. Finally, VR is relatively inexpensive and widely available, reducing costs associated with booking operating rooms and accelerating the training of medical personnel [18]. To train effectively using VR, one must determine the skills to be learned, distinguishing between basic manipulative skills and procedural skills [18]. The present study focuses on procedural skills aligned with cognitive processes such as problem identification and selecting an appropriate response by the trainee [18].

2.2   Principles for Multimedia Learning

The effectiveness of training depends on multiple factors, namely the training method and the learning processes involved. Learning is viewed as "a process of model transformation, a progression through increasingly sophisticated mental models where each reflects an adequate understanding of the target software" [19]. A novice user can form a system mental model in three different ways independently or simultaneously: through using it (mapping via usage), by drawing analogies from similar systems that are familiar to them (mapping via analogy), and through training (mapping via training) which is the focus of this study [19]. Learning outcomes can be measured through retention tests that emphasize remembering and transfer tests that emphasize understanding [20], and this study focuses on retention as a learnability outcome during user training.

The Cognitive Theory of Multimedia Learning has shed light on the notable effects of learning support on learning outcomes [21]. The theory proposes three main assumptions. Firstly, there are two separate channels for processing information, the auditory and visual channels. Secondly, each channel has a finite capacity. Thirdly, learning is an active process that requires filtering, selecting, organizing, and integrating information based upon prior knowledge to generate meaningful learning [21]. By a series of research that was tested through more than 200 experimental tests, Mayer articulated 15 principles of multimedia learning which are separated into three categories (See Table 1): principles meant to reduce extraneous processing – cognitive processing that does not serve the instructional goal; principles for managing essential processing – cognitive processing needed to acquire the essential information; and principles to foster generative processing – cognitive processing aimed at making sense of the material [8]. These principles were translated into design recommendations, making it easy for designers to build high-quality multimedia material [8].

Table 1. Principles of multimedia learning and their goal [8]

Representative instructional principle	Goal
1. Multimedia	Basis for the theory
2. Coherence	Reduce extraneous processing
3. Signalling	Reduce extraneous processing
4. Redundancy	Reduce extraneous processing
5. Spatial contiguity	Reduce extraneous processing
6. Temporal contiguity	Reduce extraneous processing
7. Segmenting	Manage essential processing
8. Pre-training	Manage essential processing
9 Modality	Manage essential processing
10. Personalization	Foster generative processing
11. Voice	Foster generative processing
12. Image	Foster generative processing
13. Embodiment	Foster generative processing
14. Immersion	Foster generative processing
15. Generative activity principle	Foster generative processing

2.3   Implicit and Explicit Measurement in a Learning Context

User experience (UX) is defined by the ISO 9241-210 standard as a "person's perceptions and responses resulting from the use and anticipated use of a product, system or service" [22], including emotions, beliefs, preferences, and physiological responses among others. Most UX research utilizes self-reported qualitative (e.g., interviews, observations, open-ended questionnaire questions) and quantitative (e.g., closed questionnaire questions) measures to capture these responses. Self-reported questionnaires allow the measurement of different aspects of UX, for instance, perceptions of usability [23], cognitive load [24], and perceived efficacy [25], among others. However, it is difficult for users to report on their own experience. The evaluation of perceptual emotional reactions at the end of an interaction is associated with a significant loss of moment-to-moment user reactions throughout a task, potentially resulting in important differences between what a user felt during an experience and how it was recalled afterwards [26]. This type of evaluation corresponds to a global perspective that has shown to be impacted by multiple biases such as the peak effect and the peak-end rule [27].

Collecting quantitative psychophysiological data to measure UX in real-time has shown to provide a deeper understanding of UX while reducing methodological biases associated with the sole use of perceptual measures [28]. Combining complementary methods through the measurement of implicit antecedents in parallel with explicit measurements via self-report renders a more complete and reliable portrait of UX [28]. The recognition of facial expressions is a psychophysiological measure used to calculate emotional valence, i.e., the emotional spectrum ranging from unpleasant (negative valence) to pleasant (positive valence) [29]. The method of identifying psychophysiological pain points (PPPs) developed by Giroux-Huppé, et al. [30] generates a better representation of a user journey as it includes automatic, often unconscious, negative physiological manifestations of the user. Shown in Table 2 is a summary of the constructs investigated in the present study along with their definitions.

Table 2. Constructs of interest.

Construct	Definition
Valence Pain Points *Implicit*	Frequency of moments of negative emotions during the execution of training task, defined by low valence (lowest 10%)
Cognitive workload *Explicit*	Participant's perceptions of workload during the training task and VR application used
Perceived usability *Explicit*	Participant's perceptions of the VR application used
Self-perceived Efficacy *Explicit*	Participant's perceptions of self-efficacy during the training task

3   Hypothesis Development

Our objective was to evaluate the implicit and explicit learning experience of two distinct segments of a desktop VR medical operations simulator to assess elements of learnability for a first-time user. The broader aim of this research is for the results to inform the design of learning experiences within desktop VR simulations.

We hypothesized that an effective tutorial should allow a user to complete retention tasks successfully without frustration. Conversely, an ineffective tutorial will evoke frustration, as indicated by an increased number of VPPs and difficulty completing the task. This expected outcome is due to much of the tutorial affording participants the opportunity to passively process information, whereas users are actively engaged in interaction during free play mode (FPM) tasks. Accordingly, we expect users to experience more moments of frustration when struggling to complete a task than when passively following a tutorial. Therefore, to test the implicit training experience of users, we propose the hypothesis that (H1) a user will experience a significantly higher number of VPPs per minute during an FPM task - for both the retention tasks (H1a) and the exploration task (H1b) - than during a tutorial, translating to a more negative affective experience.

Instructional design aims to control the cognitive load while also stimulating learners to use their available cognitive capacity for better learning [31]. When completing FPM tasks, users must constantly interact with the VE and various interface elements, which has been shown to have beneficial effects on engagement and motivation [5]. When motivated, learners are more likely to exert more cognitive effort to schema construction and automation to improve their cognitive task performance [31]. Previous studies also showed task procedural complexity to be positively associated with intrinsic cognitive load [32, 33]. Essential processing is analogous to intrinsic cognitive load in cognitive load theory [34]. An FPM task complexity is higher than that of a tutorial in that a user must remember the exact steps of a procedure and replicate them to complete it. Hence, we hypothesize that a user's perceived cognitive load will be significantly higher during an FPM task when compared with a tutorial, for both the retention tasks (H2a) and the exploration task (H2b), as a user interacts with the interface. During their interaction with the interface, the chance of encountering new pain points increases, which can impact the perceived usability of a system.

The work of de Guinea et al. [28] has shown that when frustration is high, neurophysiological memory load has a negative impact on perceived system usability, while conversely, a low level of frustration positively influences a user's perceived system usability. Hence, we posit that effects of frustration and cognitive load experienced when interacting with the medical desktop VR simulator will lead to a lower perceived system usability for both the retention tasks (H3a) and the exploration task (H3b) relative to the tutorial.

Previous studies have also identified a negative correlation between the levels of self-perceived efficacy and cognitive load, where high self-perceived efficacy led to lower cognitive load than low self-efficacy [35, 36]. In that sense, a participant's low perceived efficacy for clinical skills will result in more difficulty completing a task and increased cognitive load. We thus hypothesize that (H4) the level of self-perceived efficacy will be negatively related to a user's perceived cognitive load.

4   Method

Due to COVID-19 restrictions, the experiment was conducted remotely in the presence of a moderator as part of the deployment of a new desktop VR medical platform designed to reproduce clinical environments and train anaesthetists to treat patients. A user had to complete a continuously guided tutorial that showed the basic functionality of the system. After completion of the tutorial, a built-in FPM allowed a user to freely explore the simulation environment. This FPM simulator mode allowed participants to reproduce various tasks learned through the tutorial and perform an exploration task. Hence, a one-factor within-subject experimental design was used, where the tutorial task and the FPM tasks measures were compared for each participant.

4.1   Participants

Ten medical students were recruited by word-of-mouth to participate in this study. Selected participants were required to have completed a minimum of two years in a university medicine program and speak at an advanced English level. Four participants were 3rd-year students, three participants were 4th-year students, two students were 5th-year students, and one student was a postgraduate student completing a residency training in anaesthesia. Participants included five men and five women, ranging from 22 to 25 years old, with a mean of 23.4 years (SD = 1.07). Nine participants spoke French as a first language and reported being bilingual, and the remaining participant spoke English. Before the experiment, participants had to read and sign a consent form;

they received compensation in the form of a $30 gift card at the end of the experiment. Our institution's ethics committee approved this project (2021-4305).

4.2 Procedure

The experimental procedure is shown in Fig. 1. The training course (stimulus) for this study consisted of two segments, a guided tutorial and an FPM. First, participants had to follow the interactive guided tutorial of a desktop-based VR medical operations simulator designed to teach them the basic functionalities of the interface. The tutorial included segments of information presented in text boxes. Users were asked to turn the simulation's sound on to hear the information read by a narrative voiceover. At multiple times, the participant was required to step into the tutorial to try various interface features. A participant would complete the tutorial steps at their own pace, but without the possibility of performing backtracking, nor exploring features other than those presented in real-time during the tutorial. When the tutorial was complete and before the FPM task started, the user switched to a questionnaire tab on their computer to complete an online questionnaire.

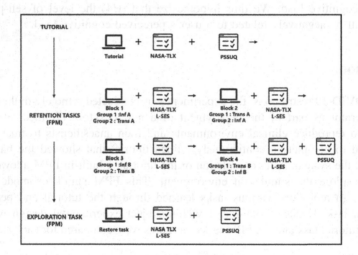

Fig. 1. Experimental procedure.

Next, a user had to complete twelve retention tasks and one exploration task in a linear sequence using the simulator's FPM. The individual task descriptions were presented in the questionnaire window; a user would hence navigate back and forth between the questionnaire and simulator windows.

The retention tasks aimed to verify how first-time users learned UI elements through the tutorial, defined as "executing the exact steps in a training task that were previously shown" [20]. Six tasks were "informational" where the intent was to acquire information (e.g., Identify the patient's heart rate), and six tasks were "transactional" where the intent was to perform an activity (e.g., Perform five manual ventilations)

[37]. Empty fields in the questionnaire tab allowed participants to write down their answers to informational questions. Retention tasks were separated into four blocks; after each block, the participant filled out questionnaires. The order of presentation of tasks within a block was randomized, and the presentation order of the blocks was counterbalanced in two equal groups of participants who were randomly assigned to a group.

The exploration task aimed to investigate how users explored the interface when few instructions were provided. We call this task "restore", which consisted of restoring the patient's condition to the best of the participant's ability. The participant would collect information about the patient in the simulated operating room and perform various procedures whose effects could be observed in real-time. Participants were allocated five minutes to complete the task but could tell the experiment moderator they were done before so, which immediately ended the task. This was followed by the completion of a series of questionnaires by switching to the computer's questionnaire tab.

Participant (explicit) cognitive load was assessed using the NASA Task Load Index (NASA-TLX), a widely used subjective multidimensional scale designed to obtain workload estimates that can be used during task completion or immediately afterwards [24]. The scale's six items are Mental, Physical, and Temporal demand, Frustration, Effort, and Performance, each rated on a 100-point range with 5-point intervals, which are then averaged (as no weights were applied to each item) to give the task load index [24]. The user's experience with the simulator was assessed using the Post-Study System Usability Questionnaire (PSSUQ), a 16-item instrument that allows participants to provide an overall evaluation of the system they used [23]. The items are 7-point Likert Scales ranging from "Strongly disagree" (1) to "Strongly agree" (7) and a "Not applicable" (N/A) point outside the scal. The scale's psychometric evaluation revealed three factors, i.e., System Usefulness, Information Quality and Interface Quality [23], which were also assessed in this study. The perceived self-efficacy for the clinical skills of medical students was assessed using the cognitive domain of the Learning Self-Efficacy Scale (L-SES) [25], which includes 4 items rated on 5-point Likert Scales ranging from "Disagree" (1) to "Agree" (5). The L-SES was used to distinguish any difficulties encountered in tasks by users because of a lack of prior knowledge of clinical skills.

To capture emotional valence from participant video recordings, we utilized Facereader v6.0 (Noldus, Wageningen, NL) and CUBE HX was used to synchronize the data [38, 39]. This software uses the Facial Action Coding System (FACS) developed by Ekman and Friensen [29] to provide inference for six basic emotions, happiness, sadness, anger, disgust, fear, and surprise, with the addition of the neutral emotion [40]. Video acquisition and analysis was acquired following guidelines for collecting automatic facial expression detection data synchronized with a dynamic stimulus in remote moderated user tests from Giroux et al. [41]. These inferences are provided as a value between 0 and 1, from negative to positive [40]. VPPs were derived based on the participant's peak intensity of negative emotions, which crossed the tenth percentile of emotional valence threshold [30, 42].

Performance was assessed for the retention tasks using task completion time, success rate and partial success rate as proxies. A task was marked as failed if a participant required help from a moderator or if they did not complete a task and moved on to the next. A partial success was counted if a participant navigated to the correct interface element but indicated an incorrect final response (informational task) or incorrectly adjusted a parameter (transactional task) [43].

4.3   Analysis

Using SAS 9.4 (SAS, Cary, USA), the NASA-TLX, PSSUQ and L-SES results were tested with a linear regression with random intercept model (Holm-Bonferroni corrected) at the task level as they were assessed directly after the tasks. To test the difference in the mean number of VPPs between the tasks, a 2-tailed Wilcoxon signed rank test was used.

5   Results

One informational task was excluded from all analyses because its formulation led to confusion in 6 participants who failed or skipped the task.

5.1   Descriptive Statistics

Prior to answering the research question, we investigated whether task characteristics influenced the results. The eleven retention tasks were divided into two groups of tasks, five informational tasks and six transactional tasks [37]. Table 3 shows the mean ratings (and standard deviation) of task completion time, success and partial success rates, perceived cognitive workload, and numbers of VPPs per minute for informational and transactional task types.

Table 3. Mean and standard deviation of six dependent measures for informational and transactional tasks.

Measure	Informational task	Transactional task	P-value
1. Performance			
Completion time	37.75 (32.8)	144.2 (97.9)	$p < .001$
Success rate	0.95 (0.122)	0.87 (0.199)	$p = .153$
Partial success rate	0.05 (0.122)	0.08 (0.183)	$p = .638$
2. Perceived cognitive load	24.72 (17.4)	31.4 (17.3)	$p = .011$
3. VPPs per minute	27.81 (15.5)	21.79 (12.9)	$p = .322$

The analysis performed indicate that transactional tasks took significantly more time to perform when compared to informational tasks (B = (−6.0063), SE = 1.4678 (df = 29, t = −4.09), p < 0.001). Overall, the tasks were successfully completed; no significant difference for success and partial success rates were found between informational and transactional tasks. Results indicate that there is an effect associated with the nature of tasks for perceived cognitive load, which was perceived significantly higher by participants when performing transactional tasks when compared to informational tasks (B = (–0.3065), SE = 0.1131 (df = 29, t = –2.71) p = 0.0112). The affective experience of users, however, did not differ significantly across both task types.

5.2 Hypothesis 1: A User Will Experience a Significantly Higher Number of VPPs Per Minute During an FPM Task -,for Both the Retention Tasks (H1a) and the Exploration Task (H1b) - Than During a Tutorial

The first prediction is that the mean number of VPPs will be higher during the FPM tasks as compared with the tutorial. To examine the results from the analysis of VPPs, we produced a "valence journey map" relating participant affective responses with tasks performed within the simulation. The results indicated that both the retention tasks (Z = 17.5, p = 0.0391, r = 0.78) and the exploration task (Z = 20.5, p = 0.0117, r = 0.91) were associated with more negative affective responses when compared to the tutorial task. These results support Hypothesis 1a and 1b that the FPM tasks induced a significantly higher number of VPPs per minute than the tutorial.

5.3 Hypothesis 2a and 2b: User's Perceived Cognitive Load Will Be Significantly Higher During an FPM Task - for Both the Retention Tasks (H2a) and the Exploration Task (H2b) - When Compared with a Tutorial

The mean ratings (and standard deviation) of perceived cognitive workload, perceived system usability, and numbers of VPPs per minute for the three tasks performed (i.e., the tutorial, the retention tasks and the exploration task) are shown in Table 4.

Table 4. Mean and standard deviation of four dependent measures for the tutorial, retention and exploration tasks.

Hypothesis measure	Task				
	Tutorial task	Retention task	P-value Tut-Ret	Exploration task	P-value Tut-Exp
Perceived cognitive load	22.82 (16.5)	28.06 (17.5)	p = .221	53.00 (23.1)	p < .001
Perceived system usability	6.15 (0.487)	5.993 (0.59)	p = .185	5.706 (0.80)	p = .017
VPPs per minute	11.15 (7.66)	23.95 (10.9)	p = .039	20.16 (7.45)	p = .012

The second hypothesis posited that participants will report higher levels of cognitive load during the FPM tasks compared with the tutorial. The results from this analysis indicate that there is an effect associated with perceived cognitive load, in this case between the exploration task and the tutorial (B = (0.8847), SE = 0.2065 (df =

47, t = 4.28), p = < 0.001), where the perceived cognitive workload was perceived higher during the exploration task. Our analysis for the NASA-TLX individual items revealed a significant difference for the levels of temporal demand between the tutorial and the exploration task (B = (4.44), SE = 1.7528 (df = 48, t = 2.82), p = 0.0208); Participants perceived the pace of the exploration task to be more rushed or hurried. Moreover, results indicate a significant difference in the levels of perceived effort between the tutorial and the exploration task (B = (3.6111), SE = 1.3829 (df = 48, t = 2.61), p = 0.036); Participants felt like they had to work harder to accomplish their level of performance during the exploration task. These results do not support Hypothesis 2a, i.e. that the perceived cognitive load induced by a retention task would be significantly higher than that of a tutorial. However, results support Hypothesis 2b, as the perceived cognitive load was reportedly higher during the exploration task than during the tutorial.

5.4   Hypothesis 3a and 3b: Users Will Perceive a Lower System Usability for Both the Retention Tasks (H3a) and the Exploration Task (H3b) Relative to the Tutorial

The third hypothesis posited that participants will report lower levels of system usability during the FPM tasks as compared with the tutorial. The perceived system usability was rated significantly higher by users during the tutorial than during the exploration task (B = (−0.4432), SE = 0.1526 (df = 47, t = −2.9), p = < 0.05). We observed the same tendency for reported results of perceived information quality (B = (−0.6646), SE = 0.1679 (df = 47, t = −3.96), p = < 0.001), indicating that the tutorial task provided a better-perceived level of information quality when compared to the exploration task; and system usefulness (B = (−0.5428), SE = 0.1936 (df = 47, t = −2.8), p = < 0.05), indicating in this case that participants perceived a higher level of system usefulness during the tutorial than during the exploration task. No significant differences were found when comparing the perceived interface quality of the tutorial with that of the retention tasks and the exploration task. These results do not offer support for Hypothesis 3a, i.e. that the users would report significantly lower system usability during retention tasks when compared to a tutorial as no significant difference was observed across tasks. However, results offer support for Hypothesis 3b, as system usability was perceived to be lower for the exploration task than for the tutorial.

5.5   Hypothesis 4: Self-efficacy Will Be Negatively Related to a user's Perceived Cognitive Load

The last hypothesis posited that the level of self-efficacy will negatively affect a user's perceived cognitive load. Our results confirmed a negative correlation between the levels of perceived cognitive load and those of perceived self-efficacy (B = (−1.6483), SE = (df = 38, t = −10.13), p < 0.0001) for all the FPM tasks combined. These results provide support for Hypothesis 4 and are consistent with the idea that self-efficacy can positively impact learning [44].

6 Discussion

The objective of this study was to evaluate the implicit and explicit learning experience of two distinct segments of a desktop VR medical operations simulator to assess elements of learnability for a first-time user. Overall, results suggest that users' training experience was more positive during the tutorial than during the retention and exploration tasks. The results of explicit and implicit measures contribute differently but jointly to explain the training experience of users.

We first discuss the implicit experience of users. The number of VPPs per minute during FPM tasks was significantly higher than during the tutorial. We interpret this result using four situations for illustration. Firstly, a tutorial presents interface functionality adequately, and because of this, the user manages to perform an associated FPM task easily, this inducing a non-significant amount of VPP's during both training segments. Secondly, the presentation of interface functionality during the tutorial is misunderstood by a user, which induces a VPP. While in FPM, a user has difficulty performing the task which induces a new VPP. The number of VPPs in this situation is equal between the two segments. Thirdly, the tutorial shows an interface function and immediately requires a user to test it. The user struggles, and a VPP occurs; however, when a user performs the same task in FPM, they understand the task and no VPP is recorded. The number of VPPs is, therefore, higher during the tutorial. Lastly, the tutorial explains a feature that the participant believes they understand. They perform it for the first time during an FPM task, and they struggle, which induces a VPP. The number of VPPs is now higher during FPM than during the tutorial. It is possible that the last situation presented manages to adequately explain why the number of VPPs was higher during the FPM tasks. This also suggests that designers would benefit from including more interactive segments during a tutorial, which supports the design principle of generative activity, which states that individuals learn better when guided in carrying out activities such as summarizing, mapping, or like in our case, self-testing, by fostering generative processing [8]. These results can additionally be explained by the fact that users are more passive during a tutorial than during FPM tasks. Indeed, a portion of the tutorial time is dedicated to listening and reading, whereas users continually interact with the interface when performing tasks such as in FPM; thus, the opportunities for a pain point to arise are thus more numerous in the latter case.

We now discuss the explicit experience of users. Results highlight that the explicit training experience of users was more positive during the tutorial than during the exploration task, as indicated by lower measures of perceived cognitive load, temporal demand, effort, and higher perceived system usability, information quality and system usefulness. However, the explicit experience did not differ when comparing the tutorial with retention tasks; thus, Hypothesis 1b and 1c were not supported. Indeed, we found no significant change in the levels of perceived cognitive load nor perceived system usability for these tasks. In addition, our results indicate that the levels of perceived cognitive workload are negatively correlated with measures of self-perceived efficacy.

We hypothesized that the perceived cognitive load would be higher during retention tasks when compared to the tutorial; this was justified through an appraisal of the cognitive processes involved during the execution of retention tasks. Previous work that studied the limitations of subjective cognitive load in simulation-based procedural training supported essential load as synonymous with the NASA-TLX mental demand item, while extraneous and generative cognitive loads were not reflected in the questionnaire [45]. The fact that instrinsic load is positively correlated with the complexity of the performed task, and negatively correlated with the learner's expertise [32, 33], suggests that retention task complexity was not high enough to impact a user's perceived cognitive load significantly. The failure rate for the retention tasks was 2.73% for all participants, indicating that tasks were completed successfully by participants and this suggests that participants were able to recall the steps shown during the tutorial without involving significantly greater cognitive resources, which together seem to indicate that the tutorial was effective in achieving its goal overall.

Users perceived a significantly higher cognitive load during the exploration (or restore) task when compared to the tutorial. The restore task required users to refer to external knowledge and to understand interface features regardless of their context of use, which characteristics correspond to those of a transfer test, i.e. by verifying if learners can apply what they have learned in various situations [20]. Engaging in generative processes proved to lead to better performance outcomes in transfer tests [8]. Since the cognitive load is negatively correlated with the learner's expertise [32, 33], results related to self-efficacy – which indicate a negative correlation between self-efficacy and perceived cognitive load – can inform our interpretation of the NASA-TLX results. In this case, the low level of self-efficacy during the exploration task caused an increase in users perceived cognitive load due to the lack of mastery of the external knowledge required to perform the medical procedures. We know from the retention task results that users remembered the various interface features. However, the restore task results do not allow us to infer whether they were understood.

Interestingly, during the tutorial, several VPPs occurred when principles that foster generative processes were not respected. Notably, the tutorial narration was performed by a robotic non-human voice using formal dialogue. This contradicts the personalization and voice principles, which are based on the premise that human to human communication fosters the creation of a conversational bond. Without this bond, a user must try harder to make sense of what the author is saying [8]. The increase in perceived effort can be explained by the users' need to recover prior knowledge activated from long-term memory to select the VE's important signals, then organize this information into a coherent structure mentally, and integrate it [21]. The increase in perceived temporal demand can be explained by two different factors. First, immersion is a defining characteristic of VE. When immersion is high, users tend to lose track of time [46]. When task difficulty increases at a fast rate, immersion decreases [47]. It is therefore possible that a lower level of immersion during the exploration task led to higher perceived temporal demand. Second, users had five minutes to complete the exploration task whereas they could take the time that they needed to complete the tutorial, which could have created pressure for participants during the exploration task.

In line with the work of [28, 42] which showed that when frustration is high, cognitive load negatively impacts perceived system usability, we hypothesized that as a result of an anticipated higher number of VPPs per minute and higher perceived cognitive load, the perceived system usability would be lower during retention tasks. In our case, negative affective responses were more frequent during retention tasks, but perceived cognitive load remained constant as did the perceived system usability. Usability problems are caused by the combination of user interface design factors and factors of usage context [48]. As all the participants had access to the same VE and functionalities to complete the tutorial and retention tasks and the context of use was the same, participants could have encountered the same usability problems.

Participants rated the usability of the system significantly lower during the exploration task. In this case, the VE was the same as during the tutorial, but the context of use was different, as users had not previously been shown the exact steps to complete the task. We observed a change in the participants' strategies to complete the task. It is therefore possible that the interface was less suitable for this type of inter-action. For example, participants would cease to make an intense use of the quick access buttons menu and they would instead directly look for clues within the simu-lation's VE by clicking on medical objects and tools. In this case, results support our hypothesis and the work of [28], i.e., the highest number of VPPs per minute occurred during the exploration task, when the perceived cognitive load was accordingly higher and this influenced negatively perceived system usability. Results also pointed towards lower perceived information quality and lower usefulness, whereas no significant difference in perceived interface quality was observed. This suggests that it was likely the information given to participants to perform the task rather than the interface itself that led to this perceived decline in usability. Once again, the self-efficacy reported by users is aligned with these results, as users felt they did not have the knowledge at their disposal to complete the task. It is interesting to note that some multimedia principles that were put forward during the tutorial were not applied during the FPM tasks. For example, while the tutorial interface elements being presented were highlighted in yellow (referring to the signaling principle [8]), this was not the case during FPM tasks. Emphasizing elements of simulation during FPM tasks could redirect novice users' attention and thus guide them to the right solution [49].

The combination of the explicit and implicit experience measures clearly informs us that the experience of users was suboptimal during the exploration task of the FPM when compared with the tutorial. However, the sole use of perceptual measures would have had no significant difference between the experience of participants when fol-lowing the tutorial and when completing a retention task. Additionally, the method of identification of VPPs allows to distinguish principles of multimedia learning that seem to impact the training experience of users the most. For example, in a situation where VPPs occurred 50% times more frequently when the robotic voiceover was playing, one could infer that the voice principle should be revisited in priority. Taken together, these results are in line with extant literature that suggests that the combination of explicit and implicit methods provides a deeper understanding of UX [28, 42].

This study has limitations that need to be considered for future studies. First, the sample size used for this study respected the minimum number of 9 participants required to find more than 80% of VPPs, as indicated by Lamontagne, et al. [50]. Nevertheless, follow-up studies should be conducted with a larger sample and with other VR training applications to ensure and reinforce the results' validity. Second, the sample used in this study included upper-level medical students ranging from their third undergraduate year to postgraduate training, nine students of which frequented the same university at the graduate level. The characteristics of these participants were therefore necessarily not identical to those of practicing physicians. Being at a lower level of training than the end-users could have negatively impacted the results. Moreover, the attendance of the same school by a vast majority of participants could also have reduced the generalizability of the results, as these students were exposed to the same learning and training methods in their academic environment. Third, this study prioritized ecological validity by using the orientation module of a real medical simulator. The use of such technology meant that it was not possible to control all the stimuli present in the simulation, as it would have been the case for a simulator specifically built for the purpose of the study. Moreoever, participants would complete a block of three short tasks followed by the completion of the self-efficacy question-naire. We did this because retention tasks had to be the same to those previously shown during the tutorial. Administering the questionnaire after each task would have taken too much time. In a controlled VE however, it would be beneficial to create longer tasks to administer the self-efficacy questionnaire once before each task. This would allow to have a better idea of which specific skill was less mastered by participants; this would ensure removing any peak-end effect; and above all it would ensure that the perceived performance of participants with the task did not influence questionnaire response regarding self-efficacy. Fourth, this study only used automated facial expression analysis to infer emotional valence and thus measure the psychophysio-logical state of participants using remote physiological recording [51]. Previous research has shown however that at least two physiological measures should be assessed at the same time to avoid extraneous noise and to give a richer comprehension of the affective and cognitive state of the user [52–54]. The psychophysiological pain points (PPPs) identification method used by Giroux-Huppé, et al. [30] which derives valence-arousal PPPs and valence-cognitive PPPs from measures of electrodermal activity, pupillometry and user facial expressions generates a deeper representation of a user's journey and should thus be used in follow-up studies [55, 56]. In lab data collection could also allow for a better understanding of the learner cognitive engagement via the use of electroencephalography [57].

7 Conclusion

This article contributes to the multimedia literature by evaluating the training experi-ence of two distinct segments of a desktop VR medical operations simulator to assess elements of learnability for a first-time user. This study presents a first effort in understanding how the combination of implicit and explicit measures can render a deep comprehension of a user's VR medical training experience to inform heuristic rec-ommendations based on the design principles of multimedia learning [8]. Our results show that whereas the number of negative affective responses was significantly higher during the retention and exploration tasks of the FPM as compared with the tutorial, only the exploration task explicit results (i.e., perceived cognitive load and perceived system usability) were different than those of the tutorial. The results also support previous work that showed a negative correlation between the levels of self-efficacy and those of perceived cognitive load [35, 36], and underline the importance of paying attention to task characteristics in VR training assessment. We finally propose a method to inform designer teams of usability problems' severity and UI elements optimization to improve learnability outcomes in complex medical desktop VE.

Acknowledgements. The authors would like to thank CAE Inc for its collaboration and funding as well as the NSERC-PROMPT Industrial Research Chair in UX.

References

1. Hays, R.T., Jacobs, J.W., Prince, C., Salas, E.: Flight simulator training effectiveness: a meta-analysis. Mil. Psychol. **4**(2), 63–74 (1992). https://doi.org/10.1207/s15327876mp0402_1
2. Izard, S.G., Juanes, J.A., García Peñalvo, F.J., Estella, J.M.G., Ledesma, M.J.S., Ruisoto, P.: Virtual reality as an educational and training tool for medicine. J. Med. Syst. **42**(3), 1–5 (2018). https://doi.org/10.1007/s10916-018-0900-2
3. Wang, P., Wu, P., Wang, J., Chi, H.L., Wang, X.: A critical review of the use of virtual reality in construction engineering education and training. Int. J. Environ. Res. Public Health **15**(6) (2018). https://doi.org/10.3390/ijerph15061204
4. Chittaro, L., Buttussi, F.: Assessing knowledge retention of an immersive serious game vs. a traditional education method in aviation safety. IEEE Trans. Visual Comput. Graph. **21**(4), 529–538 (2015)
5. Makransky, G., Borre-Gude, S., Mayer, R.E.: Motivational and cognitive benefits of training in immersive virtual reality based on multiple assessments. J. Comput. Assist. Learn. **35**(6), 691–707 (2019). https://doi.org/10.1111/jcal.12375
6. Mayer, R.E.: Incorporating motivation into multimedia learning. Learn. Instr. **29**, 171–173 (2014)
7. Goodyear, P., Retalis, S.: Learning, technology and design. In: Technology-Enhanced learning: Brill Sense, pp. 1–27 (2010)
8. Mayer, R.E.: Multimedia Learning, 3rd edn. Cambridge University Press, Cambridge (2020)
9. Schroeder, R.: Defining virtual worlds and virtual environments. J. Virtual Worlds Res. **1**(1) (2008)
10. Mandal, S.: Brief introduction of virtual reality & its challenges. Int. J. Sci. Eng. Res. **4**(4), 304–309 (2013)
11. Lee, E.A.-L., Wong, K.W.: Learning with desktop virtual reality: low spatial ability learners are more positively affected. Comput. Educ. **79**, 49–58 (2014)
12. Feng, Z., González, V.A., Amor, R., Lovreglio, R., Cabrera-Guerrero, G.: Immersive virtual reality serious games for evacuation training and research: a systematic literature review. Comput. Educ. **127**, 252–266 (2018)
13. McComas, J., MacKay, M., Pivik, J.: Effectiveness of virtual reality for teaching pedestrian safety. Cyberpsychol. Behav. **5**(3), 185–190 (2002)
14. Rose, F.D., Attree, E.A., Brooks, B.M., Parslow, D.M., Penn, P.R.: Training in virtual environments: transfer to real world tasks and equivalence to real task training. Ergonomics **43**(4), 494–511 (2000)
15. Smith, S., Ericson, E.: Using immersive game-based virtual reality to teach fire-safety skills to children. Virtual Real. **13**(2), 87–99 (2009)
16. Rodwin, B.A., et al.: Rate of preventable mortality in hospitalized patients: a systematic review and meta-analysis. J. Gen. Intern. Med. **35**(7), 2099–2106 (2020). https://doi.org/10.1007/s11606-019-05592-5

17. Makled, E., et al.: PathoGenius VR: VR medical training. In: Proceedings of the 8th ACM International Symposium on Pervasive Displays, 2019, pp. 1–2 (2019)
18. Riener, R., Harders, M.: VR for medical training. In: Virtual Reality in Medicine. Springer, London (2012). https://doi.org/10.1007/978-1-4471-4011-5_8
19. Bostrom, R.P., Olfman, L., Sein, M.K.: The importance of learning style in end-user training. MIS Q. **14**(1), 101–119 (1990). https://doi.org/10.2307/249313
20. Pellegrino, J.W., Chudowsky, N., Glaser, R.: Knowing what students know: The science and design of educational assessment. ERIC (2001)
21. Mayer, R.E.: Cognitive theory of multimedia learning. The Cambridge Handbook of Multimedia Learning, vol. 41, pp. 31–48 (2005)
22. B. ISO and B. STANDARD: Ergonomics of human-system interaction (2010)
23. Lewis, J.R.: IBM computer usability satisfaction questionnaires: psychometric evaluation and instructions for use. Int. J. Hum. Comput. Interact. **7**(1), 57–78 (1995). https://doi.org/10.1080/10447319509526110
24. Hart, S.G., Staveland, L.E.: Development of NASA-TLX (Task Load Index): results of empirical and theoretical research. In: Hancock, P.A., Meshkati, N. (eds.) Advances in Psychology, vol. 52, North-Holland, 1988, pp. 139–183 (1988)
25. Kang, Y.N., Chang, C.H., Kao, C.C., Chen, C.Y., Wu, C.C.: Development of a short and universal learning self-efficacy scale for clinical skills. PLoS ONE **14**(1), e0209155 (2019). https://doi.org/10.1371/journal.pone.0209155
26. Eich, E., Kihlstrom, J.F., Bower, G.H., Forgas, J.P., Niedenthal, P.M.: Cognition and Emotion. Oxford University Press on Demand, Oxford (2000)
27. Cockburn, A., Quinn, P., Gutwin, C.: Examining the Peak-End Effects of Subjective Experience, presented at the Proceedings of the 33rd Annual ACM Conference on Human Factors in Computing Systems, Seoul, Republic of Korea (2015). https://doi.org/10.1145/2702123.2702139
28. de Guinea, A.O., Titah, R., Léger, P.-M.: Explicit and implicit antecedents of users' behavioral beliefs in information systems: a neuropsychological investigation. J. Manag. Inf. Syst. **30**(4), 179–210 (2014)
29. Ekman, P., Friesen, W.V.: Manual for the Facial Action Coding System. Consulting Psychologists Press, Palo Alto (1978)
30. Giroux-Huppé, C., Sénécal, S., Fredette, M., Chen, S.L., Demolin, B., Léger, P.M.: Identifying psychophysiological pain points in the online user journey: the case of online grocery. In: Marcus, A., Wang, W. (eds.) Design, User Experience, and Usability. Practice and Case Studies. HCII 2019. Lecture Notes in Computer Science, vol. 11586, pp. 459–473. Springer, Cham (2019). https://doi.org/10.1007/978-3-030-23535-2_34
31. Paas, F., Tuovinen, J.E., Van Merrienboer, J.J., Darabi, A.A.: A motivational perspective on the relation between mental effort and performance: optimizing learner involvement in instruction. Educ. Tech. Res. Dev. **53**(3), 25–34 (2005)
32. Van Merriënboer, J.J.G., Sweller, J.: Cognitive load theory in health professional education: design principles and strategies. Med. Educ. **44**(1), 85–93 (2010). https://doi.org/10.1111/j.1365-2923.2009.03498.x
33. Sewell, J.L., Boscardin, C.K., Young, J.Q., Ten Cate, O., O'Sullivan, P.S.: Learner, patient, and supervisor features are associated with different types of cognitive load during procedural skills training: implications for teaching and instructional design. Acad. Med. **92**(11), 1622–1631 (2017). https://doi.org/10.1097/ACM.0000000000001690
34. Sweller, J.: Cognitive load theory. In: Psychology of Learning and Motivation, vol. 55, pp. 37–76. Elsevier (2011)

35. Redifer, J.L., Bae, C.L., Zhao, Q.: Self-efficacy and performance feedback: impacts on cognitive load during creative thinking. Learn. Instr. **71**, 101395 (2021). https://doi.org/10.1016/j.learninstruc.2020.101395

36. Vasile, C., Marhan, A.M., Singer, F.M., Stoicescu, D.: Academic self-efficacy and cognitive load in students. Procedia Soc. Behav. Sci. **12**, 478–482 (2011). https://doi.org/10.1016/j.sbspro.2011.02.059

37. Broder, A.: A taxonomy of web search. In: SIGIR Forum, vol. 36, no. 2 (2002)

38. Léger, P.M., Courtemanche, F., Fredette, M., Sénécal, S.: A cloud-based lab management and analytics software for triangulated human-centered research. In: Davis, F., Riedl, R., vom Brocke, J., Léger, P.M., Randolph, A. (eds.) Information Systems and Neuroscience. Lecture Notes in Information Systems and Organisation, vol. 29, pp. 93–99. Springer, Cham (2019). https://doi.org/10.1007/978-3-030-01087-4_11

39. Léger, P.M., et al.: Precision is in the eye of the beholder: application of eye fixation-related potentials to information systems research, 2014. Association for Information Systems (2014)

40. Loijens, L., Krips, O.: FaceReader methodology note, a white paper by Noldus Information Technology, Noldus. Zugriff am, vol. 16, p. 2018 (2018)

41. Giroux, F., et al.: Guidelines for collecting automatic facial expression detection data synchronized with a dynamic stimulus in remote moderated user tests. International Conference on Human-Computer Interaction, Forthcoming.

42. Lamontagne, C., Sénécal, S., Fredette, M., Labonté-LeMoyne, É., Léger, P.M.: The effect of the segmentation of video tutorials on user's training experience and performance. Comput. Hum. Behav. Rep. **3**, 100071 (2021). https://doi.org/10.1016/j.chbr.2021.100071

43. Dargent, T., Karran, A., Léger, P.M., Coursaris, C.K., Sénécal, S.: The Influence of Task Types on User Experience after a Web Interface Update.

44. Schunk, D.H., Dibenedetto, M.K.: Self-efficacy theory in education. Handbook of Motivation at School, vol. 2, pp. 34–54 (2016)

45. Naismith, L.M., Cheung, J.J., Ringsted, C., Cavalcanti, R.B.: Limitations of subjective cognitive load measures in simulation-based procedural training. Med. Educ. **49**(8), 805–814 (2015). https://doi.org/10.1111/medu.12732

46. Brown, E., Cairns, P.: A grounded investigation of game immersion. In: CHI 2004 extended abstracts on Human factors in computing systems, 2004, pp. 1297–1300 (2004)

47. Qin, H., Rau, P.-L.P., Salvendy, G.: Effects of different scenarios of game difficulty on player immersion. Interact. Comput. **22**(3), 230–239 (2010). https://doi.org/10.1016/j.intcom.2009.12.004

48. Manakhov, P., Ivanov, V.D.: Defining usability problems. In: Proceedings of the 2016 CHI Conference Extended Abstracts on Human Factors in Computing Systems, 2016, pp. 3144–3151 (2016)

49. Mayer, R.E., Fiorella, L.: Principles for reducing extraneous processing in multimedia learning: coherence, signaling, redundancy, spatial contiguity, and temporal contiguity principles. In: Mayer, R.E. (ed.) The Cambridge Handbook of Multimedia Learning, 2 ed. Cambridge Handbooks in Psychology. Cambridge University Press, Cambridge, pp. 279–315 (2014)

50. Lamontagne, C., et al.: User test: how many users are needed to find the psychophysiological pain points in a journey map? In: Ahram, T., Taiar, R., Colson, S., Choplin, A. (eds.) IHIET 2019. AISC, vol. 1018, pp. 136–142. Springer, Cham (2020). https://doi.org/10.1007/978-3-030-25629-6_22

51. Vasseur, A., et al.: Distributed remote psychophysiological data collection for UX evaluation: a pilot project. In: International Conference on Human-Computer Interaction Forthcoming

52. DIS, I.: 9241-210: 2010. Ergonomics of human system interaction-Part 210: Human-centred design for interactive systems (formerly known as 13407), International Standardization Organization (ISO). Switzerland (2010)
53. Charles, R.L., Nixon, J.: Measuring mental workload using physiological measures: a systematic review Appl. Ergon. **74**, 221–232 (2019). https://doi.org/10.1016/j.apergo.2018.08.028
54. Ganglbauer, E., Schrammel, J., Deutsch, S., Tscheligi, M.: Applying psychophysiological methods for measuring user experience: possibilities, challenges and feasibility. In: Workshop on User Experience Evaluation Methods in Product Development, 2009: Citeseer (2009)
55. Dawson, M.E., Schell, A.M., Filion, D.L.: The electrodermal system (2017)
56. Sweller, J., Ayres, P., Kalyuga, S.: Measuring cognitive load. In: Sweller, J., Ayres, P., Kalyuga, S. (eds.) Cognitive Load Theory. Explorations in the Learning Sciences, Instructional Systems and Performance Technologies, vol. 1, pp. 71–85. Springer, New York, NY (2011). https://doi.org/10.1007/978-1-4419-8126-4_6
57. Lackmann, S., Léger, P.-M., Charland, P., Aubé, C., Talbot, J.: The influence of video format on engagement and performance in online learning. Brain Sci. **11**(2), 128 (2021)

Towards Improving Situation Awareness of Maritime Field Operators Using Augmented Reality

Marcel Saager[✉], Marcus Behrendt, and Patrick Baber

OFFIS Institute for Information Technology,
Escherweg. 2, 26121 Oldenburg, Germany
{saager,behrendt,baber}@offis.de
https://www.offis.de/

Abstract. The work of ensuring safety at sea is characterised by the spatial separation between operators in control rooms (CRO) and operators in the field (FO), such as maritime patrols. In this process, the FOs are assigned by the CROs to check reports of vessels behaving anomalously at the scene of the incident. In order to carry out this type of assignment correctly and avoid misjudgements, FOs must be able to develop accurate situational awareness (SA). However, this often proves difficult. On the one hand, situations involving vessels with abnormal behaviour are challenging for an FO to oversee from his normal perspective. On the other hand, the spatial separation from the CRO who assigned the verification of the anomaly report complicates the flow of information. To mitigate these problems, our approach is to support the FO in his work by means of augmented reality (AR). In this way, we believe we can improve the SA of the FO, which will lead to fewer errors in the assessment of anomalies. We have developed an AR application specifically for maritime FOs, which we have tested in a pilot study on test subjects. For the pilot study, selected scenarios with anomalies at sea were transferred to a meadow. Our hypothesis is that with AR support, misclassification of anomaly reports can be reduced by at least 60%.

Keywords: Situation awareness · Augmented Reality · Maritime safety · Cognitive engineering · Human factors · Human machine interaction

1 Introduction

International and national waters are places where crimes such as drug smuggling and pollution as well as accidents such as cargo losses occur. Therefore, it is important to clarify or prevent such incidents with wide-area live monitoring in order to ensure or restore safety at sea [3]. For such monitoring, data and information from sea areas are pooled in control centres and presented to a

Supported by organization x.

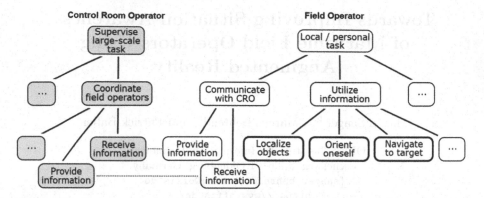

Fig. 1. Shared task model: To detect anomalies, the CRO and FO each handle their own specific tasks and communicate with each other to be more effective.

Control Room Operator (CRO) who evaluates them. Among this information, there are also reports on vessels that exhibit anomalies.

An example of an anomaly is a vessel entering a prohibited area, or a vessel's current reported position being strikingly different from its previous position. These anomalies may have been detected either by automatic classification procedures or by witnesses.

However, abnormal behaviours of vessels themselves do not yet constitute crimes or accidents that endanger safety at sea. They can, however, be an indication of such. The first step in an investigation chain is thus to check whether the reported anomaly has been correctly classified and thus truthfully describes the situation at sea. To do this, the CRO directs a *Field Operator* (FO) to check the reported anomaly. An FO is a maritime patrol that is able to travel to the location of the anomaly and assess the situation.

As shown in Fig. 1, the CRO and FO exchange information for the assessment of the anomaly: The CRO directs the FO to locate the anomaly and the FO provides feedback to the CRO on whether to confirm or reject anomaly.

In order to verify the correctness of a reported anomaly, accurate situation awareness (SA) [4] is a prerequisite for the FO. In order to achieve SA, the FO must first perceive all vessels in a scene (SA Level 1). The identified vessels must then be classified by the FO according to whether they belong to the reported anomaly or are uninvolved. Only then can the FO judge the correctness of the anomaly (SA Level 2).

However, there are two obstacles that make it difficult for the FO to develop an accurate SA for himself. The first obstacle is the normal perspective that the FO takes on a vessel floating on the surface of the water. It hinders his Level 1 SA of the vessels in a scenery. For example, vessels can be hidden behind other vessels. Furthermore, the normal perspective also impairs SA Level 2: It makes it difficult to estimate vessel positions and the relative arrangement between vessels. Often, however, this estimate must be very precise in order to be able to identify vessels involved in the anomaly and those not involved.

The second obstacle is the spatial separation between CRO and FO. It hinders an accurate and fast flow of information between the CRO and FO. The CRO will only provide the FO with a visual indication on a nautical chart and possibly a verbal description of the anomaly. The verbal description is often too imprecise to describe complex situations at sea. Furthermore, it is difficult for the FO to transfer the bird's eye view of the nautical chart into his normal perspective.

In our work, we want to improve the FO's SA by developing an application that makes it possible to present anomalies to the FO using augmented reality (AR). By means of AR, we expect that the FO will obtain better SA. On the one hand, AR helps him to have a better overview of the situation from his normal perspective. On the other hand, AR, in our opinion, improves the exchange of information between the CRO and FO, as the augmented anomalies are self-explanatory and require few queries.

The hypothesis that we want to put forward and test in this paper is therefore

Hypothesis 1 (H1). *The use of AR reduces errors of judgement on reported anomalies by 60%.*

To test our hypothesis, we conducted a within-subjects pilot study. In the pilot study, typical scenarios at sea were represented with cardboard vessels on a meadow. Subjects then had to judge, both with and without the AR application, whether the anomalies reported to them actually applied to situations in the meadow.

To provide a complete description of our work, this paper is organised as follows: Sect. 2 serves as a starting point, where we briefly review related work. Section 3 describes how our AR application works. The evaluation of our postulated hypothesis is given in Sect. 4 where we describe our study and the results obtained. Finally, Sect. 6 is a discussion of our work.

2   Related Work

There is already some work that deals with the topics of augmented reality (AR) in control centres. In this section we present an overview of papers that address AR, control centres and situation awareness (SA) in combination. An example of AR in the maritime sector is the work of Vasilijevic et al.[7]. They described AR in combination with handheld devices, such as smartphones, as a technology with great potential.

Using AR technologies to improve individual SA is not a new idea. The paper from Fromm et al. [5] also deals with SA in emergency control centres and wants to improve it with the help of AR. In the paper, an approach is taken to filter data from social media and visualise it in an AR environment. With this, a task analysis is then performed to identify SA requirements for emergency responders. The methodology, or strategy to filter data was determined together with experts in an interview study. The handling of large amounts of data was identified as a particular challenge. This shows there is already research on the topic of AR in control centres. However, the work of Fromm et al. has a different focus and a completely different data basis than this paper.

An example from another domain of how geolocation-based technology can be used is the approach developed by Sadhu et al. [6]. Here, drones are used to support a rescue centre in case of house fires, thus assisting humans in performing their tasks. This plan is adopted in the present work by developing geo-based AR technology to support personnel at sea. In addition, both variants are safety-critical and thus require a high degree of user safety.

Baber et al. [1] has already given a proposal to conduct a study to validate an AR app for visualising anomalies at sea. The authors also developed an application that uses geospatial data to visualise locations and anomalies. Baber et al. proposed a study design using a boat with test subjects at sea to search for objects in the water. These objects are equipped with GPS transmitters so that they can communicate their positions to the AR application. Baber et al. concluded that this topic needs further research. For this very reason, in our paper, building on the work of Baber et al., we developed a proposal to evaluate an AR application on a meadow first, as this promises to be much less time-consuming.

3 Concept and Implementation

This section describes the process of developing a prototype AR application to be used by Field Operators (FO) for improving their Situation Awareness (SA). There are many classes of anomalies such as a vessel not transmitting AIS data, or incoming AIS data from several vessels with same MMSI (Maritime Mobile Service Identity) and same IMO (International Maritime Organization number). In this work, we concentrated on two classes of anomalies, that are very typical. These are:

1. Inconsistent Position (IP)
2. Restricted Area (RA)

The first one (IP) is a vessel sending AIS position data that is inconsistent to prior position data sent. For example, a vessel sends a position where it is physically impossible for it to be, given the positions previously sent. The second anomaly (RA) is a vessel navigating through an area where it is not allowed to be. For example, such a restricted area could be a military zone.

To be able to run on as many mobile devices as possible, we developed our AR application with *Viro React*. The application can rely on several data sources to display anomalies, such as WebSocket connections for live data or static data in JSON format for testing purposes. To display anomalies, we transform geo-positions of respective vessels into the internal coordinate system of our AR application. For both classes of anomalies, our application draws a red semi-transparent kite as a marker on exactly that position where an anomaly has been reported. With this approach, we expect the FO to be able to assess the situation in front of his eyes very quickly: To decide whether the anomaly has

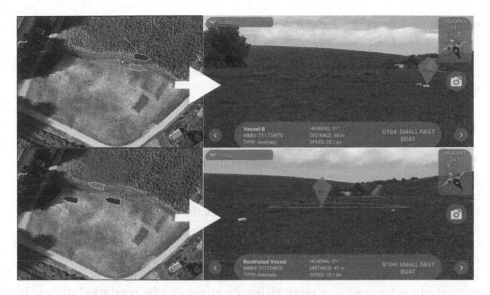

Fig. 2. The two classes of anomalies considered in this paper: This figure depicts the bird's eye view and the view through our AR application on an anomaly. The upper half shows an *Inconsistent Position (IP)* anomaly. The bottom half illustrates a *Restricted Area (RA)* anomaly. The semi-transparent markers point to the position of a reported anomaly. Both anomalies in the figure are correct because there is always a vessel at the respective marker position.

been correctly reported, the FO must pay attention to whether a vessel is really at the position of the marker. Otherwise, if at the position of the marker is no vessel, the FO can be quite sure that the anomaly has been reported by mistake. In addition to that, our application draws red lines for representing borders of restricted areas. We think that this even further helps the FO to understand the situation for RA anomalies.

Figure 2 illustrates how anomalies may look like in the bird's eye view and how they may look in our application. Besides the anomalies and restricted areas, our application is able to provide the FO with extra information about the situation. This is for example the distance to anomalies, data of the vessels, and the FO's cardinal direction. For the communication with the Control Room Operator (CRO) as shown earlier in Fig. 1, the application has the ability to send a screenshot.

After the application was roughly finished, we tested its suitability for outdoor use. The first question that concerned us was whether the display would remain readable during use in strong sunlight. Fortunately, this was the case when the display brightness was set to maximum. The battery life was also acceptable. After about two hours of intensive use, the battery was still a little more than half full. Next, we tested shaking the smartphone vigorously to see if the markers held their position. This test also passed, because we could not observe any changes in the marker positions after shaking. Even switching the smartphone on and off and switching to another app did not change the marker positions. Only starting the app with an insufficiently calibrated compass sometimes shifted the marker positions slightly, by a few degrees. In the end, however, this was not much of a problem, as the compass can be calibrated with little effort before starting the application.

4   Planning and Execution of the Study

This section explains the planning and implementation of a pilot study. The purpose of this pilot study is to investigate whether an AR application can be used to reduce misinterpretation of scenarios at sea. This could provide initial indications as to whether the shared task model presented in Fig. 1 is valid and whether technical solutions could be derived from it to improve the work of maritime safety forces. Since typical scenarios can also be simulated under certain conditions on a meadow, this pilot study was first launched before the issues are investigated in a real test environment at sea. This means that if the pilot study is successful, a more elaborate study can be conducted at sea. In order for the specific conditions mentioned to be fulfilled, the perspective of the FO on the meadow must be the same as at sea. These conditions were simulated on a meadow with dimensions of 50 m × 65 m. In addition, ships were developed as cardboard displays with dimensions of 50 cm × 30 cm.

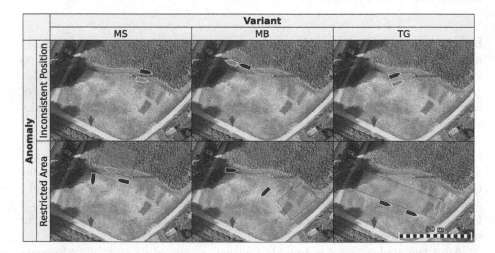

Fig. 3. The 6 scenarios used for the study: Two classes of anomalies, each in three variants and each in true and false, were investigated. The subject's location is illustrated as ▼. In each scenario, there was one vessel reported having an anomaly ⬄ If the reported anomaly was false the vessel would be at the position of ⬄. Uninvolved vessels in the scenario are depicted as ⬄. Restricted areas are shown as ▢.

Fig. 4. Point of view from a FO in direction to the meadow with

Figure 4 shows an example of the meadow from the FO's point of view. Also visible are the white cardboard stands that are supposed to simulate the ships. The cardboard displays are placed according to the different scenarios that we defined in advance. The anomalies identified in Fig. 3 were used for this purpose. We created a total of 6 scenarios. These are each the classes of the anomaly Inconsistent Position (IP) and Restricted Area (RA) in three different variants. In addition, these six variants have a ground truth expression.

Figure 3 shows an overview of the different scenarios and their variants.

For the execution, each subject received information about the task, the application and the scenarios. Then they had to evaluate the correctness of anomalies in six scenarios. Half of the test persons had to assess the first three scenarios with the AR app. The remaining three scenarios had to be assessed by the test persons without technical support. This procedure was reversed for the second half of the subjects. The ground truth gave the subject the opportunity to identify a true scenario as true or false. The same applies to identifying a false scenario as true or false.

The ground truth expression of the 6 scenarios per subject was randomised. The combination of anomaly class and variant occurred exactly once per subject and not twice. The order of the 6 scenarios was randomised so that in each of the two halves of the 6 scenarios an anomaly class occurred either once or twice per subject. Regardless of whether subjects were currently using the AR-App, for each run of a scenario they were given a situation map representing the situation in the meadow. What this situation map looks like and how it was developed can be seen in Fig. 5.

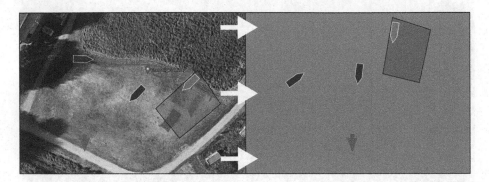

Fig. 5. Explanation from the visualisation meadow to the abstract map for the subjects

The scenarios were transferred step by step to the structure of the meadow. Scenario Restricted Areas with the variant MB serves as an example for this. Here, ships and a restricted area were inserted. In the real environment, the display was placed at the positions of the ships on the map. The restricted area, on the other hand, is only visible in the AR application. Since the test person receives a situation map with each run, the background was changed and replaced by a monochrome background, light blue. This was done in order to remove landmarks from the map, which looks more like the situation map at sea.

After the subject has gone through the scenarios, he had to complete a standardised questionnaire for the usability of the AR application. The System usability Scale questionnaire was chosen. The questionnaire has 10 questions, which can then be interpreted using an evaluation method. One experimental run per subject was about 1 h with introduction. This included the actual experiment and the completion of the questionnaire. A total of 11 subjects took part in the study, none of them had a professional background.

5   Evaluation

After the all the subjects finished the experiment on the meadow, we evaluated the data.

5.1 Evaluation of the Study

The first thing, we compared was the accuracy of the subjects in classifying the correctness of anomalies with the help of AR and without the help of AR. The accuracies are depicted in Fig. 6. When using AR, to our astonishment, there was no scenario at all that was misclassified. Thus, the maximum accuracy of 1 was achieved here. The reason for this could be that the AR application was simple, clearly structured and worked accurately. Thus, as will be mentioned in Sect. 5.2, it met with great user acceptance.

Conversely, without AR support, more errors were made in the classifications. Here the accuracy was only about 0.548. The first statement we can make based on our study is that AR support is strongly correlated with classification outcome, as Fisher's exact test showed a significance value of $p = 1.824e - 05$,

Since no misclassifications were made when AR was used, we will now focus on the runs without AR support. First, we were interested to see which reported anomaly caused more problems in classification when subjects did not receive AR support. The result is illustrated in Fig. 7. The subjects in the study had a slightly lower accuracy for the Restricted Area (RA) anomaly. It was 0.5, while the Inconsistent Position (IP) anomaly was 0.6. It should be noted, however, that Fisher's exact test with a value $p = 0.7224$ still showed no correlation. But our guess is that the boundaries of restricted areas are harder to detect without AR support than inconsistent vessel positions. But more data would have to be collected to clarify this question.

The next interesting thing to investigate would be whether the accuracy in classification differs between the variants. Each of the two experimenters created a variant for each anomaly. In addition, the TG variant was created by both experimenters in collaboration. Thus, there could well be differences in accuracy in the classifications between the variants. The result is illustrated in Fig. 8. Again, the test showed no significance with $p = 0.6597$. However, the collaboratively created TG variants in the experiments have a noticeably lower accuracy (0.4 vs. 0.6 and 0.636). Perhaps a larger data set would show that collaboratively created variants are more difficult to classify, since collusion produces variants that can be very ambiguous for the classifier.

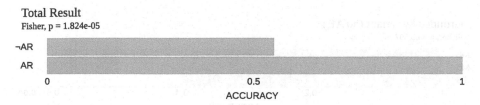

Fig. 6. Overall comparison of the subjects' accuracies in classifying reported anomalies without AR (0.548) and with AR (1.0).

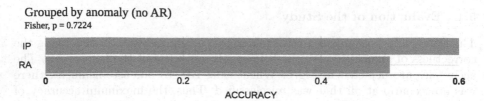

Fig. 7. Comparison by anomaly without the use of AR: Although no significance was found, subjects in the study performed slightly better in the IP anomaly (0.6) than in the RA anomaly (0.5) when no AR was used.

Finally, with regard to the non-use of AR, it is important to find out to what extent the ground truth of a situation influences the correctness of classifications. The Fig. 9 shows that subjects have more problems recognising a falsely reported anomaly than recognising a correctly reported anomaly. The accuracy for detecting incorrectly reported anomalies is 0.333, while it is 0.636 for detecting correctly reported anomalies. Although Fisher's exact test has a somewhat low significance level with $p = 0.2329$, no correlation can yet be established due to the insufficient data. It would be interesting to know whether subjects are more often under the assumption that reported anomalies must be correct. However, more data would have to be collected for this.

The main question we want answer in this paper is whether our postulated hypothesis 1 is correct. Therefore, the last thing we did was a binomial test. The statistical population used to determine the probability of error p in the classification of reported anomalies was all trials performed by the subjects without the support of AR. In this way, we calculated an error value of $p = 0.452$. We then used the classifications made by the subjects using AR for a left-tailed binomial test. The significance value of $p = 8.16e - 09$ resulting from the test shows, in addition to the previously performed Fisher test, that the use of AR is significantly different from the use without AR. The 95% confidence interval was $[0.0, 0.092]$. We calculated that the upper bound of the confidence interval represents a 79.6% reduction in misclassifications compared to the statistical population. With all this insight, we are able to reject the null hypothesis, that

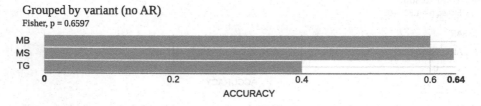

Fig. 8. Comparison by variant without the use of AR: In the study, there was a small difference between the MB (0.6) and MS (0.636) variants when AR was not used. The accuracy of the variant TG was the lowest (0.4). The differences were not shown to be significant.

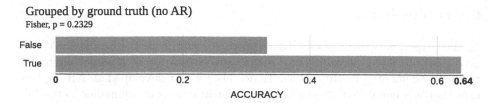

Grouped by ground truth (no AR)

Fisher, p = 0.2329

Fig. 9. Comparison by ground truth without the use of AR: There was a noticeable difference in the accuracies between classifying scenarios with different ground truths. Subjects were less accurate in classifying falsely reported anomalies (0.333) than in classifying correctly reported anomalies (0.636).

there is no significant difference in the use of AR. We also showed that the reduction of misclassifications is greater than 60%.

5.2 System Usabilty Scale

The System Usability Scale (SUS) questionnaire was developed by John Brooke [2] in the 1980s and is still one of the common quantitative evaluation methods in the field of user research. After the test person has used the AR app, he or she is to answer the SuS questionnaire. Figure 10 shows the conversion of the SUS score into quartiles, acceptability and adjectives. The red line represents the achieved SuS score of the AR application. In total, all 11 test subjects completed the SuS questionnaire. The evaluation resulted in a SuS score of 90.45. Thus, the app can be considered very good and accepted by the users. The test persons stated that they could handle the AR app well. Nevertheless, the only thing that came out was that the users imagined that they might need support in using it and therefore did not feel confident in using it. This could be due to the fact that, as described in Sect. 3, the application does not yet function properly.

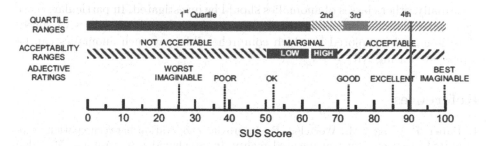

Fig. 10. SuS - Score Result of the Study from a usability perspective

6   Discussion

In this paper, we have presented an approach to improve the Situation Aware-ness (SA) of Field Operators (FO) during the verification of reported anomalies through Augmented Reality (RA). To do this, we first developed an AR applica-tion that was capable of displaying two different classes of anomalies to the FO. To initially test our approach with simple resources, we conducted a pilot study. For this pilot study, subjects had to assess anomalies, which were simulated on a meadow using cardboard vessels. The subjects were in the role of the FO and had to make this assessment both with and without AR support.

Our initial hypothesis 1, that the use of AR reduces errors in classifications of reported anomalies by 60%, can be accepted after evaluation of the study data. To our amazement, the support provided by the AR application was so good that not a single mistake was made in the classification during its use. A SuS test carried out indicates that the reason for the lack of errors could be the accuracy, ease of use and clear structuring of the application.

The pilot study is a strong indication for us that our AR approach could also work for the classification of real reported anomalies at sea. It therefore paves the way to conduct a larger-scale study similar to the one described in [1].

Such a follow-up study would investigate another possible positive effect of AR support. As also pointed out in [1], the processing time required by a subject to classify a reported anomaly could be measured. If an anomaly is confirmed more quickly, actions could thus be taken very early to limit the possible con-sequential damage of the anomaly. The hypothesis here is that the processing time with AR support is shortened compared to the processing time without AR support.

The pilot study identified variables that could have an effect on classification accuracy in the absence of AR support. Among these variables were the class and ground truth of an anomaly and the person who created the anomaly. More data would need to be collected in a follow-up study to better investigate these effects.

Finally, other classes of anomalies should be investigated. In particular, those that have dynamic properties, such as a vessel travelling at excessive speed. Here it must be explored in which comprehensible way such anomalies can be represented using AR.

References

1. Baber, P., Saager, M., Wortelen, B.: Improving cooperation between spatially sep-arated operators using augmented reality. In: Stephanidis, C., Antona, M. (eds.) HCII 2020. CCIS, vol. 1225, pp. 3–8. Springer, Cham (2020). https://doi.org/10.1007/978-3-030-50729-9_1
2. Bangor, A., Kortum, P.T., Miller, J.T.: An empirical evaluation of the system usabil-ity scale. Int. J. Hum. Comput. Interact. **24**(6), 574–594 (2008)
3. Diwell, L, e.a.: Masterplan leitstelle 2020 (2013). https://zoes-bund.de/wp-content/uploads/2015/10/Masterplan-Leitstelle-2020-ZOES.pdf

4. Endsley, M.R., Garland, D.J.: Situation Awareness Analysis and Measurement. CRC Press, Cambridge (2000)
5. Fromm, J., Eyilmez, K., Baßfeld, M., Majchrzak, T.A., Stieglitz, S.: Social media data in an augmented reality system for situation awareness support in emergency control rooms. Inf. Syst. Front. 1–24 (2021)
6. Sadhu, V., Salles-Loustau, G., Pompili, D., Zonouz, S., Sritapan, V.: Argus: Smartphone-enabled human cooperation via multi-agent reinforcement learning for disaster situational awareness. In: 2016 IEEE International Conference on Autonomic Computing (ICAC), pp. 251–256. IEEE (2016)
7. Vasilijevic, A., Borović, B., Vukić, Z.: Augmented reality in marine applications. Brodogradnja **62**, 136–142 (2011)

Semi-automatic Reply Avatar for VR Training System with Adapted Scenario to Trainee's Status

Tomohiro Tanikawa[✉], Keisuke Shiozaki[✉], Yuki Ban,
Kazuma Aoyama[✉], and Michitaka Hirose[✉]

The University of Tokyo, 7-3-1 Hongo Bunkyo-ku, Tokyo, Japan
{tani,jnakano,narumi,hirose}@cyber.t.u-tokyo.ac.jp

Abstract. For service industry, quality of customer service skills and customer satisfaction are very important topic. However, it is difficult to learn and master this kind of service skill without on-the-job-training (OJT). In this research, we propose a service VR simulator in which user can train man-to-man service by using VR technologies (Fig. 1). For service skill, it is important not only physical behavior and valval skills which can be learn by using manual, but also emotional control and sensing skills. Thus, to training the emotional skill on man-to-man service, we propose and construct preliminary service VR simulator to master emotional skills.

Our service VR simulator consist of mental/emotional sensing devices, estimating algorithm and intervention approaches. At first, to sensing mental/emotional state of trainer, we developed vital sensor attached HMD (Fig. 2). By sensing vital signal, such as heart beat and respiration, we can estimate mental/emotional state of trainer during VR training. Next, we also develop mental/emotional intervention which can induce emotion of users. For example, we can alleviate user's tension with altered auditory feedback. Finally, our proposed system can control difficulty of training according to trainer's mental state and skills. Combining these mental/emotional sensing and feedback technologies enables effective training of emotional control and expression skills.

In addition, by utilizing advantage of the characteristics of VR, our system can be expected to be more effective than training conducted on actual sites. For example, by switching to customer's viewpoint from trainer's own viewpoint, trainer can find and understand his/her problem easily. Also, by replaying and rewinding man-to-man service simulation, trainer can try-and-error and find solution during training.

Keywords: Augmented reality · Digital museum · Mobile device · Public exhibition

1 Introduction

For service industry, quality of customer service skills and customer satisfaction are very important topic. However, it is difficult to learn and master this kind of service skill without on-the-job-training (OJT). In this research, we propose a service VR simulator in which user can train man-to-man service by using VR technologies.

© Springer Nature Switzerland AG 2021
C. Stephanidis et al. (Eds.): HCII 2021, LNCS 13095, pp. 350–355, 2021.
https://doi.org/10.1007/978-3-030-90963-5_26

For service skill, it is important not only physical behavior and valval skills which can be learn by using manual, but also emotional control and sensing skills. Thus, to training the emotional skill on man-to-man service, we propose and construct preliminary service VR simulator to master emotional skills.

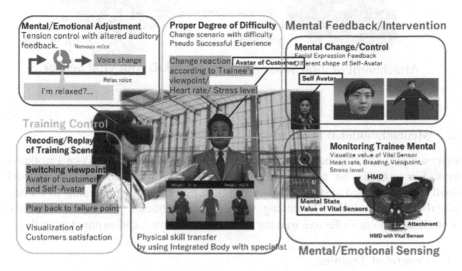

Fig. 1. Concept of service VR training system

2 System Concept

Conventional VR system consist of sensing and display devices. VR system sense user's physical behavior by using head/motion tracking, data grove, etc., and present generated visual/auditory/haptic sensation according to user's physical behavior.

For training services, emotional skills are very important. Thus, our service VR simulator consist of mental/emotional sensing devices, estimating algorithm and intervention approaches (Fig. 1).

2.1 Mental/Emotional Sensing

At first, to sensing mental/emotional state of trainer, we developed vital sensor attached HMD (Fig. 2). By sensing vital signal, such as heartbeat and respiration, we can estimate mental/emotional state of trainer during VR training.

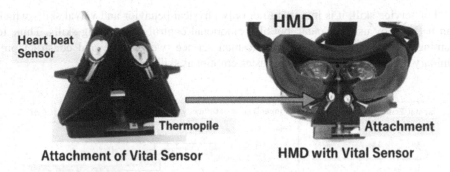

Fig. 2. HMD with vital sensor

2.2 Mental/Emotional Feedback

Next, we also develop mental/emotional intervention which can induce emotion of users. For example, we can alleviate user's tension with altered auditory feedback. Finally, our proposed system can control difficulty of training according to trainer's mental state and skills. Combining these mental/emotional sensing and feedback technologies enables effective training of emotional control and expression skills.

2.3 Control of Training

In addition, by utilizing advantage of the characteristics of VR, our system can be expected to be more effective than training conducted on actual sites. For example, by switching to customer's viewpoint from trainer's own viewpoint, trainer can find and understand his/her problem easily. Also, by replaying and rewinding man-to-man service simulation, trainer can try and error and find solution during training by his/herself.

3   Prototype System

Based on this concept, we developed preliminary prototype system to show effectiveness of service VR training system (Fig. 3).

Figure 4 shows trainee's view. Trainee interact with customer's avatar with his/her speech. Our system detects trainee's speech and behavior and change customer's reaction (Fig. 5). When trainee mistake in service scene, trainer play back before making mistake and trainee can go back and try again. By this trying and error, trainee understand well what is important in customer service.

And trainee can check self avatar's facial expression by looking upper-right sub-window. It is important that trainee recognize how customer are seeing his/her for customer service training.

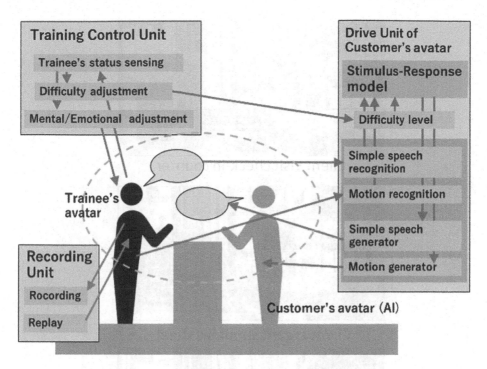

Fig. 3. System diagram of service VR training system

Fig. 4. Trainee's view of service VR training system

Client visit check-in counter

Client cream about his sheet

Trainee choose her dialogue

If her dialogue is wrong, client anger to her

Fig. 5. Test scene

4 Conclusions

Current prototype system provides limited choice in speech. In future, we will implement intelligent avatar by using AI technologies and customer services data. For this purpose, we are logging many kinds of training data, such as motion capture data, voice, facial expression, etc., which captured in real training scene. By accumulating huge amounts of data, we can realize natural interaction with virtual customer avatar.

Acknowledgement. This work was supported by Council for Science, Technology and Innovation, "Cross-ministerial Strategic Innovation Promotion Program (SIP), Big-data and AI-enabled Cyberspace Technologies" (funding agency: NEDO).

Reference

1. Naruse, K., Yoshida, S., Takamichi, S., Narumi, T., Tanikawa, T., Hirose, M.: Estimating confidence in voicesusing crowdsourcing for AlleviatingTension with altered AuditoryFeedback. In: Asian CHI Symposium: Emerging HCI Research Collection in ACM Conference on Human Factors in Computing Systems (CHI) 2019, 4–9 May (2019)

A Pilot Study on Progress of Driving Skills with Immersive VR Driving Simulator

Yuejun Xu[1](✉) and Makio Ishihara[2](✉)

[1] Graduate School of Fukuoka Institute of Technology, Fukuoka, Japan
mfm19201@bene.fit.ac.jp
[2] Fukuoka Institute of Technology, Fukuoka, Japan
m-ishihara@fit.ac.jp

Abstract. Some people have lack of opportunities for practice driving after obtained their driver license. If they had insufficient driving experience, they would be highly prone to traffic accidents. One of the prospective solutions to these concerns is VR driving training for beginners to practice before driving on a real road. In recent years, VR equipment has become affordable and research activities on impact of VR driving training on driving skills have been conducted so far. To see how VR driving training can improve the driving skills, the authors build a VR driving simulation system with three types of weather conditions (clear sky, rain and foggy) and three types of road conditions (urban road, mountain road and highway). This manuscript conducts a pilot experiment on progress of users driving skills. The results initially show validity of the authors' simulation system from the fact that it is more hard for users to manoeuver the car along the optimal driving line in foggy condition in comparison with clear sky ones. As for progress of theirs driving skills, users manoeuver the car more safely as they drive more time, and they also do safely even at the early time of driving in the fog condition in terms of optimal driving lines and safe driving speed.

Keywords: Driving skills · Driving simulator · Immersive virtual reality

1 Introduction

Learning to drive in a driving school is generally very expensive. Some people are lack of opportunities for practice driving after obtained the driver's license. If they have insufficient driving experience, they are prone to accidents. To deal with this problem, driving simulators have been recognized to be a reliable tool which incorporates with intuitive input, cognitive processing and behavioral output [1]. A virtual reality system is a promising training and learning tool to properly familiarize drivers with a car. Compared with non-immersive driving simulators, users show unsafe gaze patterns and a higher levels of anxiety when

© Springer Nature Switzerland AG 2021
C. Stephanidis et al. (Eds.): HCII 2021, LNCS 13095, pp. 356–365, 2021.
https://doi.org/10.1007/978-3-030-90963-5_27

operating the VR driving simulator [2]. It would help beginners eliminate the fear of driving. It can also save the time and cost of practice of driving and it could help them learning driving skills quickly. K. Likitweerawong et al. [3] built a VR serious game with realistic physics and natural feels. S.M. Taheri et al. [4] showed that controlling the car, speed, tendencies and fatigue are closely related to the performance of driving even if using a VR simulator. M. Koashi et al. [5] has been found that the information on the longitudinal distance and the lateral displacement between cars plays a central roles in determining avoidance behavior.

The purpose of this manuscript is to study how VR driving simulators can improve driving skills such as obedience to traffic rules and driving with safety speed on the best driving line without sudden brakes or acceleration. Section 2 explains our VR driving simulator and Sect. 3 conducts a pilot experiment on progress of driving skills. Section 4 gives the concluding remarks.

2   VR Driving Simulation System

The map is developed by Unity 3D game engine. Various types of road conditions are developed using a free unity plug-in of Road Architect which can create dynamic intersections, bridges and many other road objects. The total distance of a driving course used in the experiment is about 1.5 km and it takes 2 to 3 min for drivers to complete a single lap.

2.1   3D Virtual City

Figure 1 shows a virtual city used in the experiment. In order to adjust the challenge level faced by the subjects [6], the virtual city has set up different types of roads such as urban roads, mountain roads and expressways.

Fig. 1. Virtual city environment

2.2   Main Features of Car

This driving simulation system employs a gear transmission which is closer to the real automatic transmission of cars, and it is also equipped with GPS navigation system as shown in Fig. 2.

Fig. 2. Car simulation

2.3   Weather Simulation System

Weather conditions are created by the Enviro - Sky and Weather. Figure 3 shows the driver's view in a weather condition of clear (left), rainy (middle) and foggy (right). In the rainy weather, the friction between the wheels and the road surface will be reduced compared with the clear weather [7], and there will be simulated raindrops and they will appear on the windshield of the car.

Fig. 3. Driver's view under different weather conditions

2.4   Optimal Driving Line

The traffic rules of the VR driving simulation system stipulate that users should drive the car on the right lane of the road. The optimal driving line is defined as the center line on the right lane of the road, which is depicted as a yellow line in Fig. 4. The line can be set to be visible or invisible. When it is set to be visible, the user can clearly see it from the cab of the car. When the user is driving the car on the road, the system will obtain the shortest distance between the car and the optimal driving line in real time as the lateral deviation data of the car.

Fig. 4. Optimal racing line (Color figure online)

3 Experiment

3.1 Purpose

The purpose of this experiment is to confirm the feasibility of our VR driving simulator for improving driving skills and to see progress of the subject's driving skills in terms of optimal driving line.

3.2 Experiment Setups

A high-performance desktop computer with an intel Core i7-9700 CPU 3 GHz, a 16 GB RAM and a NVIDIA GeForce GTX 1660 Ti graphics card is employed to run our driving simulator. HTC VIVE is used to provide an immersive driving environment and Logicool G29 steering wheel is used as input system as well (Fig. 5).

Fig. 5. Experiment setup

3.3   Procedure

Subjects are instructed to drive in different road environments and weather conditions. They are also asked to fill in about their personal information and driving experience in Japan and their home countries. There are 8 subjects in this study, 7 of them have driver's license and 6 of them are male and 2 are female.

This experiment includes three kinds of weather conditions: clear sky, rainy and foggy. The subjects need to drive 3 laps in each weather condition, resulting in 9 laps in total.

$$8\,\text{subjects} \times 3\,\text{weather conditions} \times 3\,\text{laps} = 72\,\text{laps in all}$$

When the subjects are driving, there will be an assessor next to them to teach them about the map and how to improve their driving skills, and make them pay attention to drive along the center of the driving lane as safely and precisely as possible. The experimental procedure is as follows:

1. Eight people are selected as subjects
2. Before the experiment, each subject drives freely for a short period of time to adapt to our VR driving simulator. In this step, the green guide arrow is set to be visible.
3. Each subject is asked to perform a task of driving from the position of the blue arrow in the lower right of the map along the blue navigation route as shown in Fig. 6.
4. He/she will first goes through a section of downhill road and highway, then uphill road and city road, the total distance of the course is 1.5 km.
5. Car's current speed, subject's input, car position and lateral deviation from the optimal driving line will be recorded every 0.1 s.

3.4   Results

The results of Fig. 7, 8, 9, 10, 11 and Fig. 12 came from subject 8 as the representative data, and the data from the other 7 subjects are similar to his. Figure 7–9 is the driving path on the first narrow corner. The horizontal axis and the vertical axis is geographic coordinates in meter. After the practice, the subject can better drive along the optimal driving line. Figure 10–12 show comparisons of the recorded lateral deviation data of the first lap to the third lap in each weather condition. The horizontal axis is a percentage of a lap, and the vertical axis is the lateral distance in meter. For the third lap, the lateral deviation rate has a tendency to remain at a low level.

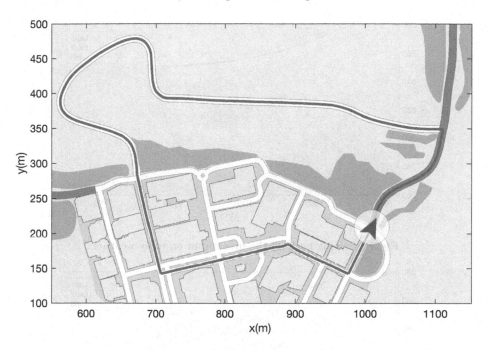

Fig. 6. Driving course

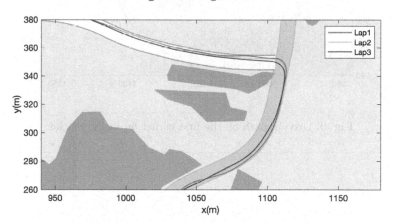

Fig. 7. Driving path on the first corner on clear weather

To confirm the tendency, Fig. 13 shows the average and standard deviation of the lateral deviation at each weather condition for each lap across all the subjects. The horizontal axis is the type of weather conditions and the vertical one is the lateral distance in meter. From the figure, there is a significant change

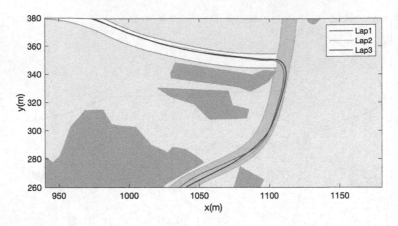

Fig. 8. Driving path on the first corner on rainy weather

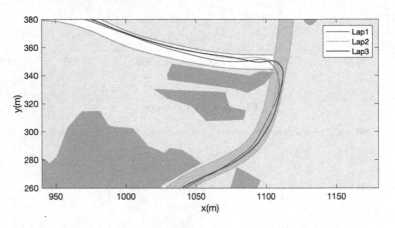

Fig. 9. Driving path on the first corner on foggy weather

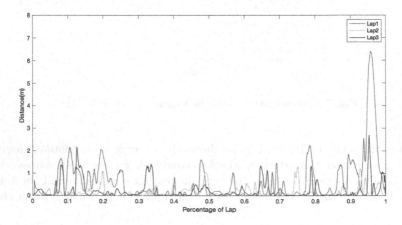

Fig. 10. Lateral deviation on clear weather

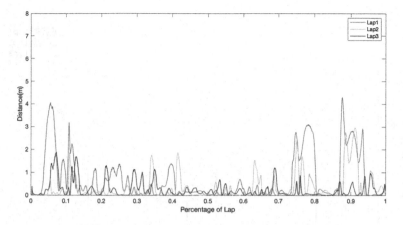

Fig. 11. Lateral deviation on rainy weather

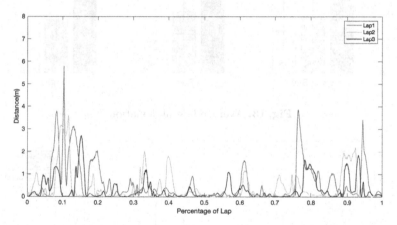

Fig. 12. Lateral deviation on foggy weather

in lateral deviation between Lap1 and Lap2 [$t(23) = 3.0295, p < .01$], Lap2 and Lap3 [$t(23) = 3.9201, p < .01$] across all the weather conditions. Figure 14 shows the average of the elapsed time to complete each lap at each weather condition. The horizontal axis is the type of weather conditions and the vertical one is the elapsed time in minute. From the figure, there is a significant change in elapsed time between clear sky and rainy [$t(23) = -4.0579, p < .01$], rainy and foggy [$t(23) = 4.5451, p < .01$] across all the laps.

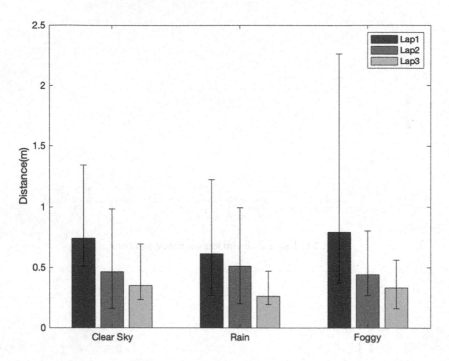

Fig. 13. Average lateral deviation

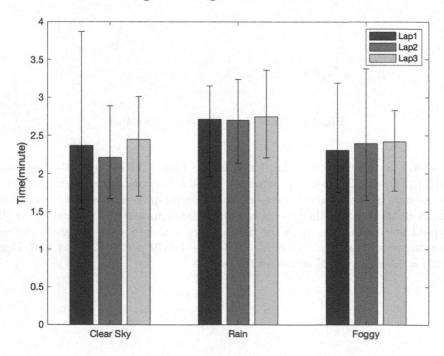

Fig. 14. Average times

4   Conclusion

According to the results, VR driving could improve the driving ability of the car. As the number of experimental driving laps increases, subjects can better driving along optimal driving line for later laps, and gradually adapt to different weather conditions. Especially, the improvement is considerably seen at former laps for clear sky and foggy.

As regards the elapsed time, it varies in weather conditions meaning that different levels of stress on attention are successfully given subjects.

In the future, we will increase the number of experiments and add night driving to test the help of VR driving training to adapt to low visibility driving. We will also make different routes and improve the experimental procedures to explore whether familiarity with the road will affect the results of the experiment.

References

1. Lew, H.L., et al.: Predictive validity of driving-simulator assessments following traumatic brain injury: a preliminary study. Brain Inj. **19**, 177–188 (2005)
2. Wade, J., et al.: A virtual reality driving environment for training safe gaze patterns: application in individuals with ASD. In: Antona, M., Stephanidis, C. (eds.) UAHCI 2015. LNCS, vol. 9177, pp. 689–697. Springer, Cham (2015). https://doi.org/10.1007/978-3-319-20684-4_66
3. Likitweerawong, K., et al.: The virtual reality serious game for learning driving skills before taking practical test. In: ICDAMT, pp. 158–161 (2018)
4. Taheri, S.M., et al.: Virtual reality driving simulation for measuring driver behavior and characteristics. Jour. Trans. Tech. **7**, 123–132 (2017)
5. Koashi, M., et al.: Measurement and modeling of collision avoidance behavior of drivers using three dimensional driving simulator. In: SICE 2003 Annual Conference (IEEE Cat. No.03TH8734), vol. 1, pp. 623–627 (2003)
6. Fan, J., et al.: EEG-based affect and workload recognition in a virtual driving environment for ASD intervention. IEEE Trans. Biomed. Eng. **65**(1), 43–51 (2018)
7. Khaleghian, S., et al.: A technical survey on tire-road friction estimation. Friction **5**, 123–146 (2017)

Artificial Intelligence and HCI

Ethical AI for Social Good

Ramya Akula(✉)🆔 and Ivan Garibay🆔

University of Central Florida, Orlando, USA
ramya.akula@knights.ucf.edu, igaribay@ucf.edu

Abstract. The concept of AI for Social Good(AI4SG) is gaining momentum in both information societies and the AI community. Through all the advancement of AI-based solutions, it can solve societal issues effectively. To date, however, there is only a rudimentary grasp of what constitutes AI socially beneficial in principle, what constitutes AI4SG in reality, and what are the policies and regulations needed to ensure it. This paper fills the vacuum by addressing the ethical aspects that are critical for future AI4SG efforts. Some of these characteristics are new to AI, while others have greater importance due to its usage.

Keywords: Ai for social good · Artificial intelligence · Ethics · Fairness · Equitable · Responsible AI · Human centered AI

1 Introduction

The concept of AI for Social Good(AI4SG) is gaining momentum within the AI community. The models that fall under AI4SG are very diverse and include models to forecast clinical manifestations, game-theoretic models to avoid phishing, online reinforcement learning to focus on HIV education, statistical methods to prevent harsh policing, and promote student retention name a few. Indeed, new AI4SG applications emerge regularly, providing socially beneficial results that were previously unattainable, impractical, or expensive. There have lately been many methodologies for the formulation, development, and operation of ethical AI in general. Nevertheless, a common accord for "AI for the Social Good" is an open topic. Encountering AI4SG Adhoc [3], as an annual summit for the AI industry and the government, has been done by analyzing specific application areas such as famine relief or disaster management. Since 2017, United Nations' Sustainable Development Goals[1], an interdisciplinary approach neither explains nor suggests how the development of AI4SG solutions leads to harnessing their full potential. Because designers of AI4SG confront at least two significant challenges: pointless losses and unexpected accomplishments, having a clear grasp of what makes AI socially beneficial in principle, what qualifies as AI4SG in reality, and how to replicate its first achievements in terms of the policy is an issue.

Human values influence AI software, which, if not properly chosen, may result in "good-AI-gone-wrong" situations. Consider the failure of IBM's oncology-support software, which detects malignant tumors using machine learning, but

---

[1] United Nations' Sustainable Development Goals. https://aiforgood.itu.int/about/.

© Springer Nature Switzerland AG 2021
C. Stephanidis et al. (Eds.): HCII 2021, LNCS 13095, pp. 369–380, 2021.
https://doi.org/10.1007/978-3-030-90963-5_28

the medical practitioners on the ground reject the algorithm. The system was trained on artificial data and was not yet sophisticated enough to understand confusing, nuanced, or otherwise messy patient health information. It also depended on US medical procedures that are not universally applicable. Misdiagnoses and incorrect treatment recommendations resulted from the software's hasty rollout and poor design, jeopardizing physicians' and hospitals' confidence. Context-specific design and deployment may assist in avoiding such value mismatch and provide more consistent AI4SG initiatives. Simultaneously, accurate socially beneficial AI results may emerge by coincidence, such as an unintentional deployment of an AI solution in a different environment. However, because of a lack of knowledge of AI4SG, this achievement was just coincidental; it is unlikely to be replicated in the future. AI4SG would benefit from examining the critical elements that underpin the design of effective AI4SG systems to prevent needless failures and successes. This paper aims that an AI4SG project concentrates on aspects that are especially important to AI as a technology intended and utilized to promote social good.

Four categories of limitations to AI use

Critical barriers for most domains	Critical barriers for select cases¹	Contextual challenges	Potential bottlenecks
● Data accessibility	● Data volume	● Data availability	● Access to software libraries and other tools
● Data quality	● Data labeling	● Data integration	
● High-level AI-expertise availability	● AI-practitioner talent availability	● Access to technology	● Organizations able to scale AI deployment
● High-level AI-expertise accessibility	● AI-practitioner talent accessibility	● Privacy concerns	
● Regulatory limitations	● Access to computing capacity	● Organizational receptiveness	
● Organizational-deployment efficiency			

Fig. 1. List of challenges mentioned by AI researchers and Social Sector experts. Source: McKinsey Global Institute Analysis

2 Definition of "AI for Social Good"

AI is one of the most rapidly expanding areas in the technology industry. The use of AI has extended to a wide range of industries, including healthcare, transportation, and security. As a result of this expansion, competent AI experts are in high demand across various sectors. An AI4SG project is adequate if it contributes to reducing, mitigating, eradicating a specific issue of moral importance by overcoming potential challenges shown in Fig. 1 by McKinsey Global Institute Analysis[2]. The following working definition serves as the foundation for our investigation into the critical elements for effective AI4SG: *The design, development, and deployment of AI systems in such a way that they prevent, mitigate, or resolve problems that negatively impact human life and the well-being of the natural world, and enable socially preferable and environmentally*

---

[2] https://www.mckinsey.com/featured-insights/artificial-intelligence/applying-artificial-intelligence-for-social-good.

sustainable developments. It means that AI should be beneficial to both humans and the natural environment, and AI4SG initiatives should not only adhere to but also reaffirm this concept. Although beneficence is a crucial requirement of AI4SG, it is not adequate in and of itself since the beneficial effect of an AI4SG project may be neutralize by the development or amplification of additional risks or harms. When it comes to AI4SG projects, ethical analysis that informs the design and deployment process is critical in minimizing the predictable risks of unintended effects and potential misuses of the technology.

3   Ethical AI for Social Good

Entrepreneurs and enterprises may enjoy the advantages of AI while simultaneously being aware of possible downsides and taking cautious measures to minimize their impact. In this section, we elaborate on characteristics of Ethical AI for Social Good as shown in Fig. 2.

Fig. 2. Characteristics of Ethical AI for social good

3.1   Explainability and Interpretability

AI4SG applications need transparency to make the operations and results of these systems understandable and their goals visible. Since the operations and results of AI systems reflect the broader goals of human designers, these two needs are naturally intertwined. An essential ethical concept in AI is the need for systems to be understandable. Moreover, considering the growing widespread deployment of AI systems, it has gotten greater attention lately. As discussed above, AI4SG initiatives should provide Explainability and Interpretability tailored to the specific needs of the recipient group they are addressing. In various methods, the designers of AI4SG programs have attempted to make decision-making systems more understandable to the public. For example, machine learning predicts academic difficulty in certain studies [6]. School administrators interpret the system utilized predictors based on things they recognized and valued, such as grade point averages and socio-economic classifications. According to the researchers, reinforcement-learning techniques can assist authorities at homeless shelters in educating homeless adolescents about HIV. By selecting which homeless adolescents to teach, based on the likelihood that homeless youths would pass on their knowledge, the system learns how to maximize the impact of HIV education [14]. One version of the technology revealed the identity of the selected youngster by exposing their social network graph. Although these explanations seemed counter-intuitive to the homeless shelter administrators, they believed that they might impact users' knowledge of how the system operated and, as a result, their confidence in the system as a whole. When describing an AI-based conclusion, these two examples demonstrate how critical it is to use the proper conceptualization. Because AI4SG initiatives range significantly in terms of their goals, subject matter, context, and stakeholders, the appropriate conceptualization is likely to change across them. Explainability and Interpretability must establish as the first step to communicate anything to someone.

3.2   Privacy Protection

Privacy is probably the most researched area with a substantial amount of material available. Because privacy is an essential prerequisite for safety, human dignity, and social cohesiveness, among other things, this should not come as a surprise. Moreover, previous generations of digital technologies had a significant effect on privacy. When a state obtains influence over people via privacy infringements, jeopardizing the safety of those persons. Respect for privacy is also a fundamental prerequisite of human dignity. We may consider personal information to be the building blocks of an individual, and depriving someone of their records without their permission is likely to be considered a breach of their dignity. Individual privacy is a fundamental right, and the idea of privacy as a fundamental right underpins court judgments. When individuals deviate from social standards without offending, and when societies retain their social structures, privacy undergirds the individual's social cohesion and cohesiveness. Tensions may develop between people who have various levels of consent. In life-or-death circumstances such as national catastrophes and pandemics, the stress is often at its highest level. Consider the epidemic of Ebola in West Africa in 2014, which presented a problematic ethical quandary [9]. In this particular instance, the quick release and analysis of call-data records from mobile phone users in the affected area may have enabled epidemiologists to monitor the spread of the fatal illness in the area in question. When promptness is not essential, it is feasible to seek a subject's permission for and before the use of their personal information. The amount or kind of permission requested may vary depending on the situation.

In healthcare, it is possible to establish an assumed consent threshold. Reporting a medical problem to a doctor is deemed to represent assumed permission on the patient's side. It will be more reasonable in other situations to set a threshold for informed consent. However, since informed consent requires researchers to acquire a patient's explicit permission before using their data for a non-consented purpose, practitioners may select a clear consent threshold for general data processing, including medical use. Another option is developing dynamic consent, which allows people to monitor and modify their privacy choices on a more detailed level as their circumstances change; otherwise, it disregards informed consent. Similarly, the recent development of machine learning algorithms to forecast the prognosis of ovarian cancer patients based on retrospective analysis of anonymized pictures was a case in point [7]. The use of patient health data in the development of AI solutions without the patients' permission has also piqued the interest of data protection authorities. However, it is still possible to balance protecting patient privacy and developing successful AI4SG technologies. However, even if adopting a computer vision-based solution to the issue has obvious technological benefits, privacy laws prohibit video recording. Even in situations where video recording is permitted, access to the recordings is often restricted. Instead, the researchers used depth pictures, which do not reveal the participants' identities, thus protecting their anonymity. In the process of complying with privacy regulations, the researchers' non-intrusive method managed to beat previous systems, even though they lost key visual appearance signals in the process. Finally, consent in the internet environment is fraught with difficulties; consumers often lack choice when using online services. The relative absence of protection or permission for the second-hand use of personal data that is openly accessible on the internet allows for the creation of ethically problematic AI technologies.

3.3 Data Infringement

AI to anticipate future trends or patterns is becoming more common in AI4SG settings, with applications ranging from using automated prediction to correct an academic failure to prevent unlawful policing and identify corporate fraud. The prediction capability of AI4SG is subject to two risks: manipulation of input data and over-reliance on noncausal indicators such as correlation coefficient. The manipulation of data is not a new issue, and it is not confined to AI systems alone. However, AI has the potential to aggravate it, and it is a significant danger for any AI4SG effort since it has the potential to degrade the predictive capacity of AI and lead to the avoidance of socially beneficial actions on an individual basis. Because of the scale at which AI is usually implemented, the advent of AI complicates problems. The information used to forecast an inevitable result may be known by an agent with such knowledge. The value of each predictive variable can be changed to prevent intervention. There is also a danger that excessive reliance on noncausal indicators - that is, data associated with phenomena but is not causal of it - may divert attention away from the context in which the AI4SG designer is attempting to intervene. Instead of focusing on noncausal predictors, any such human-centered intervention should aim to address the fundamental causes of a particular issue, such as poor corporate governance or detecting fraudulence [15]. To do otherwise is to run the danger of merely treating the symptoms of a problem rather than the underlying cause. These dangers indicate that the usage of safeguards as a design element for AI4SG projects should be considered. Strict guidelines for AI4SG initiatives may restrict the selection of indicators to be utilized in their design. These indicators should impact human-centered interventions and the level of openness that should be applied to how indicators influence decisions. As a result, the following best practice is established: AI4SG designers should include safeguards that guarantee that noncausal indicators do not unduly bias interventions and restrict, where appropriate, knowledge of how inputs influence outputs from AI4SG systems in order to avoid manipulation.

3.4   Human-Centered Intervention

Technology should intervene in the lives of users only in ways that are respectful of their independence. Note that this is not an issue emerging when AI intervenes, although AI brings additional concerns. In particular, developing human-centered interventions that balance present and future benefits is a significant issue for AI4SG initiatives. It comes down to a matter of temporal choice interdependency, which is well-known in the field of preference elicitation research. In the present, an human-centered intervention may elicit user preferences, which the program can then rationalize future interventions to the specific user in question. Thus, a user autonomy-preserving intervention approach may be unsuccessful in collecting the information needed for appropriately contextualized future interventions. On the other hand, an human-centered intervention that oversteps the bounds of a user's autonomy may impact the consumer to shun the technology, making future interventions in that situation challenging to perform. This balancing act is something that most AI4SG projects have to deal with. Take, for example, interactive activity detection software for individuals with cognitive impairments, becoming more popular. The program intends to cause the least amount of disruption to their overall objectives, to encourage patients to keep a routine activity. Each human-centered intervention contextualizes such that the program learns the frequency of future interventions based on the reactions to previous interventions, which is a powerful feature. Furthermore, only significant human-centered intervention offers, and yet all interventions are only partly voluntary since rejecting one prompt results in a subsequent prompt with similar information. In this case, there was a worry that patients might leave a device that was too invasive; thus, exploring the middle ground. In our second case, there is a lack of this balance. A game-theoretic application meddles in the patrols of wildlife security agents by suggesting other paths to follow [5]. However, if physical barriers obstruct a track, the program cannot offer alternate route recommendations in this case. Officers may choose to disregard the advice by pursuing an alternative path. However, they must do so without abandoning the application and easing restrictions for users to reject an intervention while accepting additional, more appropriate interventions in the form of advice later on. These case studies demonstrate the significance of considering users as equal partners in designing and implementing autonomous decision-making systems. Adopting this frame of thinking may have contributed to the sad loss of two Boeing 737 Max aircraft in October 2017 [11]. In part, it seems that the pilots of these aircraft failed to correct a software problem caused by defective sensors, which may exacerbate by the lack of optional safety measures that Boeing offered at an extra cost. In many cases, the danger of false positives is equally as severe as the risk of false negatives. Appropriate intervention in the context of the receiver accomplishes a reasonable degree of disruption while maintaining autonomy via options. This contextualization underpins knowledge about users' capabilities, preferences, and objectives and the conditions in which the human-centered intervention will be implemented and assessed.

3.5 Fairness and Discrimination

For the most part, AI developers depend on data that may skew in socially important ways. As a result, the algorithmic decision-making that underlies many AI systems may skew in unjust ways for the decision-making process. AI4SG efforts that depend on skewed data may end up perpetuating that skewed data via a vicious loop. In such a scenario, a limited dataset helps guide the initial phase of AI decision-making, resulting in discriminatory behaviors, which would then lead to the gathering and use of more biased data. For instance, there has been a long-standing prejudice against African-American women in the U.S. seeking care because of negative historical assumptions for preterm birth [10]. In this case, AI can make a significant dent in the glaring racial gap, but only provided the same historical prejudice is not reproduced in AI systems. Alternatively, consider the use of predictive policing tools. According to software developers, progressive policing software may pre-train on data from the police department that includes deeply entrenched biases. When prejudice has an impact on arrest rates, it gets ingrained in the data collected during prosecutions. Such biases may lead to discriminatory judgments, which in turn feedback in the more skewed datasets, resulting in a vicious cycle of discrimination. Designers must, without a doubt, clean up the datasets used to train AI. The danger of using too powerful a disinfectant will remove crucial contextual subtleties that might help enhance ethical decision-making down the road. As a result, designers must guarantee that AI decision-making remains sensitive to variables that are essential for inclusivity in the first place. A word processor, for example, should ensure that all human users, regardless of their gender and race, have a similar experience. However, we should also expect it to function in a non-equal and still fair manner by assisting individuals with visual impairments. Let us compare AI to a word processor. It allows for a much greater variety of decision-making and interaction modalities, many of which base on possibly biased input. Natural language in training datasets may include unjustified connections between genders and words, which in turn may have normative force due to their normative nature. In other settings and use cases, an equitable approach may need variations in communication depending on variables such as gender to be fair.

Consider the example of the virtual teaching assistant who, when informed that a user was expecting a child, failed to differentiate between men and women in its replies, praising the males while dismissing the women [4]. An investigation by the BBC News revealed an even more extreme example: a mental health chat bot[3] designed for children could not comprehend a kid reporting underage sexual assault to a mental health professional. The ability to recognize and respect situational fairness is critical for the effective deployment of AI4SG. A long-standing issue has been the impact of past biases on decision-making in the future. Erroneous reinforcement learning processes, on the other hand, can entrench these biases in, strengthen them, and repeat them over and over again.

AI4SG must enable people to curate and nurture their semantic capital, which is any material that may improve someone's ability to provide meaning and make sense of things for it to be effective. We may have the technological capability to automate the production of meaning and sense (connotations) using AI. Still, if we do it carelessly, we may create distrust or injustice. Two issues arise: The first issue is that AI software may define connotations differently from our personal preferences. A similar issue may emerge if AI software supports connotations based on previously used terms. It would be difficult for AI software to define all meanings and sensations in a social context, which is the second issue. For example, only legally authorized agents have the authority to determine the legal meaning of the term violation [1]. In the same way, the meaning and sense of emotional symbols, such as facial expressions, is dependent on the kind of agent who is displaying a particular indication. Effective AI may identify an emotion; for example, a fake agent may correctly say that a person looks sad, but it cannot alter the meaning of the feeling. It is necessary to differentiate between those responsibilities that may and should not outsource to a computerized system of some kind. AI should be used to enable human-friendly semantic annotation rather than to offer semantic annotation itself. For example, when it comes to individuals who have Alzheimer's disease. Research on caregiver-patient relationships identifies three aspects [2]. First and foremost, caregivers perform a significant, though time-consuming, role in reminding patients of their involved tasks, such as taking medicine. Second, caregivers are essential in ensuring that patients have meaningful interactions with one another. Third, when caregivers remind patients to take their medication, the patient-carer relationship may be weakened due to the patient being annoyed. The caregiver may lose part of their ability to offer empathy and meaningful support. As a result, researchers have created AI software that strikes a balance between reminding the patient and irritating the patient. By using reinforcement learning, it is possible to learn and optimize the equilibrium. The researchers created the method so that caregivers may spend the majority of their time giving empathetic support and maintaining a meaningful connection with the patient rather than administering medications. Using AI to automate formulaic activities while maintaining human-friendly connotations is feasible.

---

[3] Child Advice Chatbots Fail Sex Abuse Test https://www.bbc.com/news/technology-46507900.

3.6   Adaptability and User Friendliness

Despite considerable work over the last decade to create data-driven techniques for automated log analysis and troubleshooting, the research has concentrated only on algorithms and methods. There is still less focus on the performance of these algorithms and techniques. Toward the opposite end of the spectrum, new advancements in the MLOps and AIOps fields have placed more emphasis on managing data and models, in addition to the underlying infrastructure and platforms. While many components and subtleties are needed to integrate goods, applications, and working methods effectively, the overall picture is positive. These go much beyond simply algorithms and platforms, and they have a broader impact. The following characteristics are helpful for effective AI adaptability: (1) Large technology companies with multiple product offers want to maximize the usage of software re-use to enhance their bottom line as much as feasible. The following people re-use the work in [2]: Linnaeus package should be operated and controlled without any code modifications without the need to comprehend the underlying information technology architecture. They are putting a strong focus on a small memory footprint so that Linnaeus may use resource-constrained systems prevalent in telecommunications. Because it minimizes the attack surface, this approach indirectly addresses specific security issues. It only uses the necessary modules and nothing more-providing a very versatile REST interface that can accommodate almost all working styles across different Ericsson design groups. Implementing sufficient flexibility in feature representation and model selection ensures that Linnaeus classification performance is optimum regardless of the underlying log format and semantics is a high priority. Because Linnaeus uses character n-grams, it can work with both Syslog log formats and the JSON log format; as a result, no need for specific pre-processing if both log types are in the same log. (2) High-quality labeled data is essential for supervised learning. (3) Because telecommunications systems are considered essential infrastructure, considerable focus is put on the development of observability methods that assist in tracking and understanding system behavior. (4) Explainability modules may assist troubleshooters and data scientists better understand the rationale behind categorization findings.

3.7   Verification and Validation

Verification and validation are essential considerations. For technology in general and AI4SG applications, in particular, to be accepted and have a significant beneficial effect on human life and environmental welfare, trustworthiness are crucial. However, although there is no everyday experience or guideline that can assure or guarantee integrity, subjectivity is a critical aspect to consider when enhancing the trustworthiness of technology applications in general and AI4SG applications specifically. Falsifiability entails the specification of one or more urgent requirements and the possibility of empirical testing of those requirements. A critical need is a condition, resource, or means required for a capability to be fully operational and without which something could or should not function. Safety is an unquestionably vital necessity. As a result, for an AI4SG system to be reliable, its safety must be verifiably safe. Unless demonstration of falsifiability, it is impossible to verify the essential requirements [12]. Therefore the technology should not be considered trustworthy. As a result, falsifiability is a critical consideration for any AI4SG initiatives that are feasible. Unfortunately, we will not determine for certain whether or not a particular AI4SG application is safe until we have tested the program in every conceivable scenario. In an unpredictable and fuzzy environment with numerous unexpected circumstances, the potential of knowing when a certain essential need is not implemented or maybe failing to function correctly is within reach. As a result, if the essential criteria are falsifiable, we can determine whether the AI4SG application is not reliable, but we cannot determine if the application is trustworthy. With an iterative deployment cycle, it is important to validate the most critical requirements. Unintended harmful consequences may only become apparent after testing. Software should only be tested in the actual world if it is safe to do so, although this should not be the case all of the time. To accomplish this, developers must follow a deployment cycle that includes the following steps: (a) Verification, (b) conducting inferential statistics (c) Validation across increasingly wacky environments. When developing AI4SG applications, formal methods may use to attempt to test key requirements. They might, for example, incorporate formal verification to guarantee that autonomous cars and AI systems in other safety-critical settings would choose the morally preferable option when given the opportunity [13]. As far as falsifiability is concerned, such techniques provide safety checks that may show high accuracy. Simulations may provide assurances that are approximately comparable to those provided by experiments. A simulation allows one to determine whether or not key criteria fulfill under a set of formal assumptions by running the simulation. In contrast to a formal demonstration, a simulation may not always show that the necessary characteristics in all circumstances. However, a simulation often allows one to test a far larger range of situations that cannot deal with formally, for example, owing to the intricacy of the argument, than can be done in a formal setting. The use of formal properties or simulations alone to disprove an AI4SG application would be erroneous and counterproductive. The assumptions behind these models limit the application of any conclusions drawn in the actual world. Furthermore, assumptions may out to be wrong in practice. What one may show to be right via formal proof or what one may believe to be correct through simulation testing may be refuted later on when the system deploys in the real world. For example, authors of a game-theoretic model for wildlife protection assumed that the terrain was generally level and free of significant obstacles. The program that they initially created included an erroneous definition of an optimum patrol route, due to which the software was subsequently updated. The application's incremental testing allowed for refining the optimum patrol route by demonstrating that the presumption of a flat terrain was incorrect. After deployment, identifying and rectifying valid inferences is a strategy when faced with new problems in real-world settings that need altering previous assumptions established in the lab. An alternative is to use an on the fly or runtime system, which allows for continuous updating of a program's processing of the inputs it receives. However, there is a slew of issues with this method as well. For example, Microsoft's notorious Twitter bot, Tay [8], gained meanings in a very loose sense at run time when it learned how to react to messages from Twitter users, which accomplishes via machine learning. In the real-and often vicious-world of social media, the bot's capacity to modify its conceptual understanding continuously became an unpleasant flaw, as Tay learned and regurgitated foul language and unethical connections between ideas from other users after being deployed. When dealing with the falsifiability of requirements, a supervised learning method poses difficulties comparable to those encountered when using a predictive approach. It is significant since supervision is the main technique to learn from data. Germany's strategy to regulate autonomous cars is an excellent example of taking a gradual approach to regulation. Constrained autonomy may test in deregulated zones, and after raising the levels of trustworthiness, manufacturers can test cars with greater degrees of autonomy in more regulated zones. Indeed, establishing such unregulated zones was one of the recommendations for a more ethical AI strategy at the EU level.

4   Conclusion

According to the seven characteristics, achieving effective AI4SG involves striking two types of balances: intra- and inter-organizational credits. Each factor may require a system's intrinsic balance. For example, when deciding on human-centered interventions, there may be a need to balance the risks of over-and under-intervening; or when deciding on protection by obfuscation versus security by enumeration of salient differences between people's intended goals and circumstances. As the AI4SG community continues to grapple with the general issue of whether one is ethically obligated to design, create, and deploy a particular AI4SG project, the topic has become more complex and challenging to answer. This article provides a framework of essential elements that must be examined, understood, and assessed in the context of a particular AI4SG project. Design, development, and deployment happen at the same time. The development of AI4SG will probably offer additional chances to enhance such a framework of critical variables in the future. Individual and systemic balances are essential to maintaining in any system. AI itself may assist in managing its life cycle by giving, in a meta-reflective manner, tools to assess how to achieve the greatest possible individual and systemic balances. This article aims to set the groundwork for both good practices and policies and an additional study into the ethical concerns that should underpin AI4SG initiatives and the "AI4SG project" as a whole in the future.

Acknowledgments. This research is funded by University of Central Florida provost scholarship for joint research with National Academy members.

References

1. Al-Abdulkarim, L., Atkinson, K., Bench-Capon, T.: Factors, issues and values: revisiting reasoning with cases. In: Proceedings of the 15th International Conference on Artificial Intelligence and Law, pp. 3–12 (2015)
2. Burns, A., Rabins, P.: Carer burden in dementia. Int. J. Geriatr. Psychiatry 15(S1), S9–S13 (2000)
3. Butler, D.: Ai summit aims to help world's poorest. Nat. News 546(7657), 196 (2017)
4. Eicher, B., Polepeddi, L., Goel, A.: Jill Watson doesn't care if you're pregnant: grounding AI ethics in empirical studies. In: Proceedings of the 2018 AAAI/ACM Conference on AI, Ethics, and Society, pp. 88–94 (2018)
5. Fang, F., et al.: Deploying paws: field optimization of the protection assistant for wildlife security. In: Twenty-Eighth IAAI Conference (2016)
6. Lakkaraju, H., et al.: A machine learning framework to identify students at risk of adverse academic outcomes. In: Proceedings of the 21th ACM SIGKDD International Conference on Knowledge Discovery and Data Mining, pp. 1909–1918 (2015)
7. Lu, H., et al.: A mathematical-descriptor of tumor-mesoscopic-structure from computed-tomography images annotates prognostic-and molecular-phenotypes of epithelial ovarian cancer. Nat. Commun. 10(1), 1–11 (2019)
8. Mathur, V., Stavrakas, Y., Singh, S.: Intelligence analysis of Tay twitter bot. In: 2016 2nd International Conference on Contemporary Computing and Informatics (IC3I), pp. 231–236. IEEE (2016)
9. Oliver, N.: Big data for social good: opportunities and challenges. In: 12th World Telecommunication/ICT Indicators Symposium (WTIS 2014) [Date of reference 20 May 2015] (2014). http://www.itu.int/en/ITU-D/Statistics/Documents/events/wtis2014/003INF-E.pdf
10. Petersen, E.E., et al.: Vital signs: pregnancy-related deaths, united states, 2011–2015, and strategies for prevention, 13 states, 2013–2017. Morb. Mortal. Wkly Rep. 68(18), 423 (2019)
11. Tabuchi, H., Gelles, D.: Doomed boeing jets lacked 2 safety features that company sold only as extras. The New York Times, 21 March 2019
12. Taddeo, M., Floridi, L.: How AI can be a force for good. Science 361(6404), 751–752 (2018)
13. Taddeo, M., Floridi, L.: Regulate artificial intelligence to avert cyber arms race (2018)
14. Yadav, A., et al.: POMDPs for assisting homeless shelters – computational and deployment challenges. In: Osman, N., Sierra, C. (eds.) AAMAS 2016. LNCS (LNAI), vol. 10003, pp. 67–87. Springer, Cham (2016). https://doi.org/10.1007/978-3-319-46840-2_5
15. Zhou, W., Kapoor, G.: Detecting evolutionary financial statement fraud. Decis. Support Syst. 50(3), 570–575 (2011)

A Change in Perspective About Artificial Intelligence Interactive Systems Design: Human Centric, Yes, But Not Limited to

Pietro Battistoni⬡, Marco Romano(✉)⬡, Monica Sebillo⬡, and Giuliana Vitiello⬡

Università di Salerno, 84084 Fisciano, SA, Italy
{pbattistoni,marromano,msebillo,gvitiello}@unisa.it

Abstract. In this paper, we want to show how the evolution of Artificial Intelligence must lead to change the point of view of the design of interactive systems based on it. It is necessary to re-think the decision-making paradigm where a user makes a decision with the support of the electronic system or where an Artificial Intelligence makes a decision autonomously. The new paradigm must consider that both the user and the Artificial Intelligence are two entities capable of making decisions and for which the decision-making process may be even a mediation between the human and artificial intelligence, taking into account that one can progressively mutually learn from the other. For this reason, in this work, we explain through a *Decision Perception Model* how to adapt the *Human-Centred Design* process to meet the requirements and necessities of Artificial Intelligence giving it the same importance as the user within the design.

Keywords: Human-centred design · Artificial intelligence · Decision-making process

1 Introduction

In our previous research [5, 6], we investigated how Artificial Intelligence based on neural networks could play a relevant role in sign language learning. AI was employed to recognize user errors performing sign language gestures. We wanted users to learn from mistakes by adapting to Artificial Intelligence assessments. Based on the user experience studies we performed and our observations, we can state that the users willingly adapted their learning process to the Artificial Intelligence input. Indeed, those users established with the system a sort of disciple-mentor relationship. On the other hand, the system design had to consider that gestures and the same users' hands are never exactly the same, so Artificial Intelligence had to go through a process of inference to recognize the gesture variants, thus aligning itself with the unique characteristics of each user. In some way, both the human and the artificial intelligences

Partially supported by MIUR PRIN 2017 grant number 2017JMHK4F004 and MIUR 2019 grant number AIM1872991-2.

were collaborating by aligning to each other. However, this kind of positive human-artificial relationship is not always the case. In support of this, Stanton and Jensen [12] state: "*the actual trustworthiness of the AI system is influential insofar as it is perceived by the user. Trust is a function of user perceptions of technical trustworthiness characteristics*". Indeed, Sneiderman in [2] analyzing the literature on artificial intelligence and autonomous systems stated that in general all the analyzed works share a common point: humans do not trust the system and spend more energy monitoring and trying to control it rather than exploiting it.

Our sensitivity to the potential errors of artificial intelligence is evident. Talking about cases such as a fighter-bomber mistakenly shot down by AI-controlled friendly fire [3] is very sensationalistic, however friendly fire is unfortunately common in battle. It seems that human mistakes are intrinsically more accepted than the machine errors. Although disaster examples are of course very impacting on our collective imagination and explain the lack of trust in similar situations, such lack of trust is present at various levels of autonomous systems [2].

Users' Feelings. In our opinion, there is a need to redesign the relationship between Artificial Intelligence and humans to make people generate a feeling of trust towards the system.

In [11], in the context of the Internet of Things, the authors explain the importance of designing physical objects in a way that they can generate users' positive feelings. Indeed, in contrast to a software interface that when not needed is turned off, a physical object remains in the physical world and we must deal with it in space, take care of it and even just see it daily. Similarly, as in the case of the commercial voice assistants, even if we do not see Artificial Intelligence, it remains active by exploring and listening to the context and being ready to assist the user. It is a passive but continuous interaction between Artificial Intelligence and the user. Therefore, also in this case, the relationship between a user and AI should generate positive feelings.

Moreover, positive feelings can be obtained for example by providing an interaction perceived more natural to humans, as the conversational interfaces do [4]. Indeed, such systems pretend to be human by communicating through a natural spoken language. However, this may be not sufficient, because often the decision-making power is an exclusive responsibility of the human part, while in a natural human-human interaction both the parts are able to make a decision for which the final decision is made by mediation.

Decision-Making Approach. Recently, new approaches were proposed as the *cooperative approach* in [7]. The authors state that the machines must learn to find a common ground between AI and Humans. The authors list four elements of cooperative intelligence: *Understanding, Communication, Commitment* and *Norms,* remarking the similarity with human cooperation activities. We agree that a paradigm shift is required to establish a new form of deeper cooperation between humans and AI, which can bring huge benefits, exactly like it happens when people with different abilities cooperate to find or improve a solution. These changes can be basically summarized in two goals: redimension the fears about AI and enhance the communication to improve the understanding.

Who Fears AI. However, as we have seen before, fear is a not uncommon users' feeling. It is our opinion that the fear arises mostly from knowledge that AI-powered systems are based on probability and uncertainty. Then the question to answer can be: *is there any human that has not experienced that the whole life is governed by probability and uncertainty?* Just thinking about the quantum mechanical revolution or reading the book *"The quantum moment"* [8], is easy to find scientific evidence, but even by daily experiences it is possible to catch the signal. The following example is to argue that defining the AI decision as riskier than a human decision is not rational.

The *"Self-driving car dilemma"*, which is frequently used as an example of a scary decision that an AI cannot take, is about a self-driving car that at a certain point has to decide if it sacrifices the people in the car or the people distractedly crossing the road in front of it. The survey in [9] shows how such a decision is even harder for a human and depends on so many factors that it is even impossible to decide which decision is right and which is wrong.

Enhanced Interaction. While the fear about AI is mainly a social bias of humans versus the AI, the communication between Humans and AI is almost a matter of interfaces.

Relationships almost always involve a mixture of shared and conflicting interests in the real world. Finding a common vocabulary to communicate the intentions is an effective solution to reinforce the trust in the human relationship as well as in *Human - AI Cooperation* (H-AC). Furthermore, there is an advantage in the H-AC. It is that the AI is fully honest. While human cooperation can end whenever a conflict of interests arises in the cooperators or someone betrays the initial agreement, these cases must not be considered in H-AC. The user interest is undoubtedly the only interest.

User Experience. In Fig. 1, we show the factors that can influence the user experience in an Artificial Intelligence system. Some factors, such as usability, satisfaction in completing a task, interface ergonomics, or comfort, are typical factors of UX, while other factors are more closely related to AI. In particular, they are the type of decision-making process, the level of interaction, and the feelings that the system is capable of arousing in users.

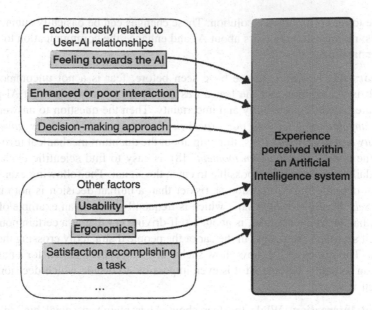

Fig. 1. A figure caption is always placed below the illustration. Short captions are centered, while long ones are justified. The macro button chooses the correct format automatically.

2   A Change in Perspective: The *Intelligence-Centred Design*

In this position paper, we argue that Artificial Intelligence, in the same way as the user, should be placed at the center of the system design. It should be considered as another user with different characteristics and with specific needs, capable of making decisions independently or in agreement with the user, but in a way that is perceived as natural. This would make Artificial Intelligence nearer to the user and able to generate trust and a better user experience. In this perspective, also the decision-making process should be evolved towards a cognitive process mediated by two intelligences. Such a process should be similar to the one adopted by two persons playing a *cooperative balancing game (Fig. 2)*. It is an intuitive game where two players do not compete but work together to solve a challenge. A ball placed on a wooden board has to go through a labyrinth. The corners of the board are supported by four nylon threads, the ends of the threads are held by the players. Every decision and movement of one of the two players irremediably affects the other. Initially, there are possible misunderstandings and mistakes but quickly the two players will learn to understand the decisions made by the other, to imitate them, to predict them and build a common strategy.

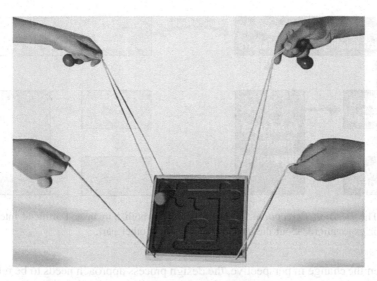

Fig. 2. A *cooperative balancing game*: players have to move together the nylon wires sustaining a wooden tablet to push a marble through a labyrinth.

To better explain this approach, we present the *Decisions Perception Model* depicted in Fig. 3. It is an actualization of the *Context Perception Model* presented by [1], which was used to explain the awareness mismatch between the user and a context aware system. Our model shows that the user's expectations of AI decisions depend on the current context and previous experience. Similarly, AI perceives the current context through data collected by environmental sensors and interpreted by its neural network which has been trained for specific cases and which can continue improving and adapting through the reinforcement learning process. Given the current context, AI will be able to make decisions but also to expect the decisions made by the user.

A decision made by AI may not be expected by the user due to the different perceptions of the context and previous experience. However, this is not necessarily bad. The user may appreciate AI's decision by recognizing that it is better than the expected one and thus aligning the one's perception for the future. On the other hand, if the decision of the AI were not appreciated, it would learn from the situation and align itself with the user's expectations. Practically, the decisions made by both the two intelligences are a continuous alignment of expectations that allow them to grow as users of the same interactive system.

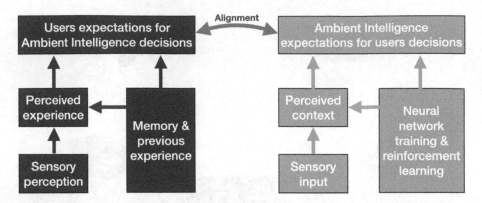

Fig. 3. The *Decision Perception Model* explains how both human and artificial intelligences build their expectations about the decision made by the other part.

Given the change in perspective, the design process approach needs to be rethought. When we design an interactive system, we are used to paying particular attention to the users' needs and goals. Now, given the involvement of Artificial Intelligence, we should consider it as an active and integral part of the design process. This approach may seem to tend towards *technology-driven design* however it does not want to eliminate the user-centricity, rather it wants to give equal importance to AI and user in the design.

On a par with the user, Artificial Intelligence has its own requirements to be satisfied to ensure a correct communication between the Artificial Intelligence and the humans. Some requirements, as for the humans but from an Artificial Intelligence perspective, are related to usability, the kind of interaction, and the cognitive approach to the decision-making. Meeting them means directly dealing with the experience of the user.

Table 1 presents a list of possible AI requirements.

Table 1. Possible AI requirements and their rationale.

AI requirements	Rationale
Easy to learn	User interaction must be adequate to facilitate the *reinforcement learning* process. This is to allow the network to improve by learning from mistakes, user requests, and the context
Easy to interpret	User interaction must be enough unequivocal to rarely require the *reinforcement learning* process
Interaction based on the context	Depending on the type of environmental and technological context, AI may require a specific type of interaction, such as voice, gesture or text. This includes the way in which users can give feedback to AI
Kind of decision-making approach	The decision-making process can be collaborative, that is, the intelligence and the user make a shared decision, fully automated, when the decision is made only by the Ambient Intelligence, user-dependent, when the decision is made by the user independently or, finally, a mix of the previous ones
Single or multiple users interaction	Ambient intelligence may have to interact with a single user or with multiple distinct users at the same time or at different times

At this point, given that both users and AI requirements must be considered and met to enhance the user experience, the classic *Human-Centred Design* process referring to ISO 9241-210:2019 needs to be extended. In Fig. 4, we show the *Intelligence-Centred Design* (ICD) process where the study and analysis of the context of use lead designers to define both the user and AI requirements. The solution will therefore be designed starting from both sets of requirements and its evaluation must be performed against both users and AI's requirements.

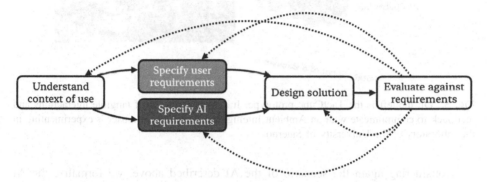

Fig. 4. *Intelligence-Centred Design*: the traditional *Human-Centred Design* process is extended to introduce the AI requirements at the same level of users' requirements.

3   A Scenario Based on Our Experience

While experimenting with the tangible interface of [10, 13], the following scenario came out. Figure 5 shows the prototype of a mobile controller that allows users to interact and receive feedback from various devices placed in a space controlled by an Ambient Intelligence. The controller allows users to exploit a large variety of gestures in various combinations of rotations.

A user entering a dark room, governed by an *Ambient Intelligence* (AmI), manipulates its interactive device to request more light. He expected that a lamp was powered to satisfy the requirement, but the AmI, instead, opened the curtains, making the light enter from the outside. AmI took the decision based on electricity consumption data (unknown to the user) and a constraint requiring them to save energy when possible. Although the AmI decision was not expected, it made sense and could be accepted by the user if (s)he could know the rationale behind it. On the other end, the AmI decision could not be accepted if the user prefers not to open the curtains for privacy reasons. In this case, the AmI needs to reinforce its learning to consider such a necessity next time.

The example shows the design weakness of the tangible interface. Indeed, although *Human-Centred Design* for interactive systems (ISO 9241-210:2019) principles were followed, the lack of attention to the needs of AmI to communicate, accordingly the same principles led to a rich set of input commands for the user but to poor haptic feedback, limiting the conversation from the AmI toward the user.

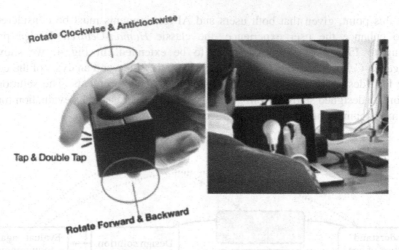

Fig. 5. On the left is the TactCube prototype. It allows a rich set of tangible interactions and feedback to communicate with an Ambient Intelligence. On the right a user is experimenting in the laboratory of the University of Salerno.

Considering again the scenario of the AI described above, we formalize the AI high-level requirements using Table 1:

Easy to Learn. Since user needs and expectations can vary from one user to another, AI needs to be able to easily evolve and adapt to the user and context. For example, asking for more light in an office could generate the expectation of natural light, as the user goes to that room to work several hours, and natural light can be more relaxing. On the other hand, when a user enters a bedroom one may want a more intimate environment, preferring to have blinds closed. The relationship between the time needed to learn and the amount of information correctly learned by AI must produce a rapid learning curve.

Easy to Interpret. In unambiguous cases, AI should not learn all the time, for example when the user asks to perform a specific task such as turning on the TV. In this case, the interaction must be immediately interpretable.

Interaction Based on the Context. The system environment is frequented by multiple users, then audio interactions can generate privacy problems or confusion. A multimodal interaction able to give enough expressiveness to the communication must be selected but respecting the limitations of the environment.

Kind of Decision-Making Approach. In our case, the type of decision-making process is primarily cooperative. For example, the user expresses the necessity to have more light and Artificial Intelligence offers the most appropriate solution according to the context it perceives and to its previous "experience" with the user. The user can agree or not, can ask to modify the decision or even be convinced.

Single or Multiple Users Interaction. The AI must relate to different users in the same space. Therefore, each user must be easily distinguishable by AI to allow it to correctly pursue its decision-making process.

If designers took into consideration only the AI requirements, they would probably design a communication based on low-level interfaces that are incomprehensible to the user. Therefore, designers must mediate the AI requirements with those of the users. For example, there will be cases in which a verbal interaction can be defined as usable by both AI and users and cases in which for technical or privacy limitations it can be discouraged.

4   Conclusions Final Remarks

In this work, we expressed our position about the approach to be adopted when designing an interactive system based on Artificial Intelligence. To improve the user experience, and increase the sense of trust, we have identified the need to rethink both the relationship between Artificial Intelligence and users, and the *Human-Centred Design* process that must put on the same level of importance the needs and requirements of Artificial Intelligence and humans.

It is worth clarifying that although the human and AI must equally be involved in the design, this does not mean that AI can have its own interests but the human ones.

The only AI requirements that must be considered are those finalized to achieve the human interests exclusively.

The study presented here is limited in its scope, since our position is expressed on the basis of our experience and scientific literature, but it must be evaluated to confirm its feasibility by involving designers and users.

References

1. Musumba, G.W., Nyongesa, H.O.: Context awareness in mobile computing: a review. Int. J. Mach. Learn. Appl. **2**(1), 5 (2013)
2. Shneiderman, B.: Human-centered artificial intelligence: reliable, safe & trustworthy. Int. J. Hum. Comput. Interact. **36**(6), 495–504 (2020). https://doi.org/10.1080/10447318.2020. 1741118
3. Blackhurst, J.L., Gresham, J.S., Stone, M.O.: The autonomy paradox. Armed Forces Journal, pp. 20–40 (2011). http://armedforcesjournal.com/the-autonomy-paradox/
4. Jentzsch, S.F., Höhn, S., Hochgeschwender, N.: Conversational interfaces for explainable AI: a human-centred approach. In: Calvaresi, D., Najjar, A., Schumacher, M., Främling, K. (eds.) EXTRAAMAS 2019. LNCS (LNAI), vol. 11763, pp. 77–92. Springer, Cham (2019). https://doi.org/10.1007/978-3-030-30391-4_5
5. Battistoni, P., Di Gregorio, M., Romano, M., Sebillo, M., Vitiello, G., Solimando, G.: Sign language interactive learning - measuring the user engagement. In: Zaphiris, P., Ioannou, A. (eds.) HCII 2020. LNCS, vol. 12206, pp. 3–12. Springer, Cham (2020). https://doi.org/10. 1007/978-3-030-50506-6_1

6. Battistoni, P., Di Gregorio, M., Romano, M., Sebillo, M., Vitiello, G.: AI at the edge for sign language learning support. In: The International Journal of Humanized Computing and Communication, vol. 1, no. 1, pp. 23–42. KS Press (2020)
7. Dafoe, A., Bachrach, Y., Hadfield, G., Horvitz, E., Larson, K., Graepel, T.: Cooperative AI: machines must learn to find common ground. Nature **593**(7857), 33–36 (2021). https://doi.org/10.1038/d41586-021-01170-0
8. Crease, R.P., Goldhaber, A.S.: The Quantum Moment: How Planck, Bohr, Einstein, and Heisenberg Taught Us to Love Uncertainty. W. W. Norton & Company, New York (2014)
9. Maxmen: Self-driving car dilemmas reveal that moral choices are not universal. Nature, 24 Oct 2018. https://www.nature.com/articles/d41586-018-07135-0
10. Battistoni, P., Sebillo, M.: A tactile user device to interact with smart environments. In: Artificial Intelligence in HCI, Virtual, vol. 39. https://doi.org/10.1007/978-3-030-77772-2_30
11. Rowland, C., Goodman, E., Charlier, M., Light, A., Lui, A.: Designing connected products: UX for the consumer Internet of Things. "O'Reilly Media, Inc." (2015)
12. Stanton, B., Jensen, T.: "Trust and artificial intelligence." Tech. Rep., NIST (2020)
13. Battistoni, P., Gregorio, M., Romano, M., Sebillo, M., Vitiello, G.: TactCube: designing mobile interactions with Ambient Intelligence. In: Ardito, C., et al. (eds.) INTERACT 2021. LNCS, vol. 12935, pp. 599–609. Springer, Cham (2021). https://doi.org/10.1007/978-3-030-85610-6_34

Virtual Control Panel API: An Artificial Intelligence Driven Directive to Allow Programmers and Users to Create Customizable, Modular, and Virtual Control Panels and Systems to Control IoT Devices via Augmented Reality

Shreya Chopra[✉]

University of Calgary, Calgary, AB T2N 1N4, Canada
shreya.chopra@ucalgary.ca

Abstract. An incremental tide in IoT devices prompts a centralized control system where physical controls such as buttons and knobs can become virtual and centralized via augmented reality: especially headset AR. I conduct a literature mapping to identify gaps and create a front-end based virtual control panel API tool to allow programmers and end-users to rapidly create headset augmented reality-based virtual control systems for physical devices. I probe on how an artificial intelligence back-end aids in such a system in terms of panel creation and automation as well as panel usage and control scenarios. I delve into use cases of the virtual control panel API including mass usage and specialized scenarios. Furthermore, I specify the guidelines for a requirements elicitation study for such a system along with potential points of derivation. Next, I probe into implications and limitations of such a system in terms of artificial intelligence, usage, and precision. My work has implications for programmers and users of a virtual control system backed by artificial intelligence for the purpose of controlling physical IoT devices in mass usage as well as in specialized scenarios.

Keywords: Virtual control panel · User centered design · Application programming interface · API · Artificial Intelligence · Machine learning · User experience design · Augmented reality · Virtual reality · Control panel · Control system · Block programming · Requirements elicitation · Customization · Internet of Things · Consumer and industrial application domains · Ethical and trustworthy AI · Generative UX/UI design · Human-centered AI

1 Introduction

1.1 Background

With the continual increase of ubiquitous computing in recent times, devices that were not conventionally embedded with computer-like abilities are now able to connect to the cloud, "talk" to one another, as well as be controlled via a user utilizing a control

© Springer Nature Switzerland AG 2021
C. Stephanidis et al. (Eds.): HCII 2021, LNCS 13095, pp. 391–400, 2021.
https://doi.org/10.1007/978-3-030-90963-5_30

point. While utilizing a remote control for a television has made sense for users in the past, the rate at which the amount of IoT devices are popping up as a part of one environment calls for multiple such remote controls. Alternatively, Augmented Reality (AR) provides the user with the ability to control multiple devices on a single platform.

1.2   Motivation

I am motivated by aiming to provide further functionality on physical objects and controls. One example of this being a physical music player being augmented with AR to program interactions [5] and the *Reality Editor* [4]. Everyday control panel use cases include a pilot's controls, a radio jockey's controls, an industrial technician's controls as well as an oven used for cooking. When considering any of these, the environment and corresponding environmental affordances also must be kept in mind. The respective environments are a cockpit, factory/industrial, a radio station, and a home. The interface spectrum going from physical controls, mixed controls, and virtual controls can be considered for potential designs. Physical controls are fixed in space, provide physical/haptic feedback to hands, can be used by multiple users in the room, and are a part of a physical environment. Virtual controls offer portability, remote operation, remote collaboration, replace hardware with software, training simulators, customized panels, high level of security, and virtually unlimited real estate. Mixed controls offer partial portability, software level protection, ease of manipulation, virtually unlimited real estate, physical as well as mixed feedback, as well as the Internet of Things Application. I look towards allowing users to create and customize their own virtual control panels to go along with their physical devices: backed via an artificially intelligent procedure. The artificial intelligence backend has two main objectives in mind: (1) to facilitate automation of panel creation based on situational as well as user preferences and (2) to predict and suggest or automatically trigger control sequences based on artificial intelligence learnings based on specific or generic users.

2   Related Works and Literature Review

2.1   Related Works

I look towards pre-existing device discovery standards in IoT to determine and build upon what kind of backend/application programming interface instructions could correspond to the design. The *Amazon Dash Button*, before it became recently discontinued, allowed the consumer to program it [1]. Applications of this wi-fi enabled mechanism included Netflix, coffee, hotel bookings, and more, and actions were triggered based on taps on the button. Particular device discovery standards include iBeacon Bluetooth Beacons [12], Physical Web [11], and Wifi Aware WiFi Alliance [13]. Universal Plug and Play is another device discovery standard which is compatible with many household devices and comes with developer tools [10]. IFTTT or If This Then That is a service that allows users to connect devices and apps to each other so that an event on one may trigger an action on the other. Applications include Google,

Youtube, and more with an example being turning on Phillips Hue porch lights when a Domino's delivery is on the way [6].

Applications of such IoT enabled virtual control panels range from personal to industrial usage. The Rolls Royce Remote Controlled Augmented Ship allows two people to control the entire ship (manned) where the windows of the bridge serve as augmented reality displays of the vessel's surroundings including hazards that are usually invisible to the human eye [9]. Research is going into remote controlling the ship which would also allow one person to contribute to controlling multiple ships. Industrial control rooms are also a use case for such virtual control: one such being oil and gas. The Audi Smart Factory is an initiative by Audi to create an IoT based factory [7]. In terms of personal uses, the Lykan Hypersport sports car has a holographic display to control the radio and sound system in the car [8]. Other personal use cases include home scenarios of controlling IoT devices via AR [2, 3].

2.2 Literature Review

I conduct a literature review of relevant works using the following formulae:

1. Abstract: (((Immersive OR Augmented OR Mixed OR Virtual) AND (Reality OR Environment)) AND (Tangible Interfaces) AND ((Ubiquitous Computing) OR (Internet of Things)))
2. Abstract: ((Immersive OR Augmented OR Mixed OR Virtual) AND (Reality OR Environment)) AND (Abstract:(tangible interfaces)) AND ((Ubiquitous Computing) OR (Internet of Things))
3. Abstract: (Immersive Control Room OR Augmented Control Room OR Mixed Control Room OR Virtual Control Room OR Immersive Control Panel OR Augmented Control Panel OR Mixed Control Panel OR Virtual Control Panel)
4. Abstract: ((Augmented Reality Knobs) OR (Virtual reality knobs) OR (Mixed Reality Knobs))

   The result is that there are 72 pieces of work that are relevant to my research, and I conduct a literature mapping to identify the gaps in research. In order to do so, I map the readings by six facets visually as seen in Figs. 1 and 2. The bulk of the additional mapping literature can be found here in my extended work [2]. The *Contribution facet* factors in research that either contributes a design method, technical tool, or metric. The *Variability Context facet* factors in what the variability of the contribution is such as a system requirement, implementation, or verification. The *Research facet* factors in the type and formatting of the research including validation, evaluation, solution proposal, philosophical, experience report, and opinion. The *Platform facet* makes note of what kind of interaction platform was used including AR with glasses, virtual reality, mixed reality, touchscreen, physical/combination, or multimodal. The *Purpose facet* makes note of the application of the work including operator training simulator, remote operation, remote collaboration, augmenting information over physical parts, non-remote immersive workspace, and survey of physical control panel. The *Controls Virtuality* facet maps what kind of virtuality spectrum the work lies on including entirely physical controls, entirely virtual controls, physical and virtual control components, entirely touchscreen controls, physical and touchscreen combo controls, and survey of multiple technologies. The literature mapping reveals that the sparse areas require further contributions. I follow this lead to build a tool that can be used to program customizable, modular, virtual control panels and systems.

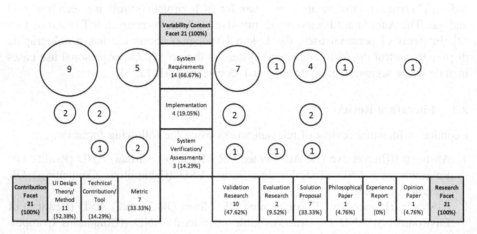

Fig. 1. Part one of the literature mapping. This part reveals that the existing literature resides mostly on system requirements that are either based on design methodology, metrics, validation research or solution proposals.

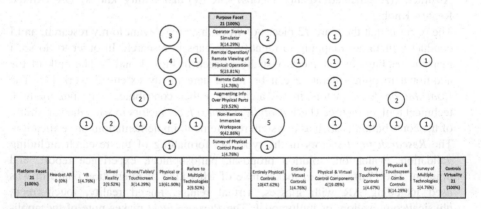

Fig. 2. Part two of the literature mapping. This part reveals that the existing literature resides mostly for the purpose of remote operation/remote viewing of physical operation or operator simulator training where the platform is physical or a combination of physical and virtual. Additionally, the work based on non-remote immersive workspace relies on a combination or physical platform as well or has entirely physical controls.

3 The Solution

3.1 Augmented Reality Front-End

By identifying the gaps in research, I propose a front-end based Application Programming Interface (API) design methodology that enables programmers to rapidly create virtual control panels for the purpose of controlling IoT devices. Furthermore, the front-end nature of this programming interface makes it akin to block programming and thus enables non-programmers or end-users to create these virtual control panels. The mechanism being that each front-end component holds programmed instructions of the API. The literature review reveals a need for customizable immersive control panels, and I build towards such a solution. I look to mainstream IDE's (Integrated Development Environment) such as Microsoft Visual Studio for inspiration to design the front-end based API design. Furthermore, I aim for the solution to encapsulate three major design aspects:

1. **Virtual tool:** Encapsulates the benefits of virtual control along with the feedback benefit of both the virtual control as well as the physical devices themselves. The augmented reality-based interaction such as via a Microsoft HoloLens headset is vital to the Internet of Things interaction that allows the user to be able to control multiple devices via one medium: augmented reality. The software nature of control panels allows them to also be modular and customizable.
2. **Modular:** The modularity aspect allows the user to rapidly and simply create minimal viable product panels and either keep adding to them or simply multiplying many of the same ones.
3. **Customizable:** The customizable aspect allows the user to program interactions as per their personal as well as device specific and environmental needs. The customization also plays into the solution's compatibility with an artificially intelligent back end. Customization can be based on personal preferences as well as those of users as a whole as learned by the AI.

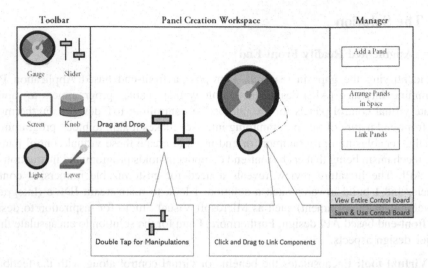

Fig. 3. Prototype of the virtual control panel creation tool. This tool can be implemented directly in headset augmented reality as well as on a computer where once virtual control panels are created, they can be utilized in headset AR as control points to control IoT devices. This API tool allows the user to program a customizable, modular, and virtual control panel or control system for physical devices.

The Virtual Control Panel Programming Interface has three components: the toolbar, the panel workspace, and the manager which are laid out like an IDE. The **Toolbar** holds visual components which are usually seen on control panels such as a gauge, slider, screen, knob, light, and lever, and more. These components are pre-programmed/hold generic instructions on behaviour in regard to how they will interact with each other and with physical devices the user may choose to control. In this way, this interface becomes a front-end based API for end users and programmers. The toolbar components can be dragged and dropped into the **Panel Creation Workspace**. This is where the visual look of the virtual control panel can be designed by the programmer/user. Once dragged into this space, the toolbar components can be *double tapped* for manipulation such as visual rotation of the tool. One tool can be clicked and dragged to another to create a linkage of functionality between two tools. For example, a slider can be linked to a light so that it lights ups when the slider hits a certain value. The **Manager** allows the user to manage panels once they have been created in the panel creation workspace. The user can *Add a Panel* so that there are multiple panels. Additionally, they can also *Arrange Panels in Physical Space* so that they may find a panel exactly where they need it in physical space the next time that they put on their augmented reality headset. For example, a user may place their television's virtual control panel at head-level in front of their couch so that it is always available. Moreover, the user can *Link Panels* to each other so that they are all used to control something together. One example would be a cockpit where multiple control panels may be required. The bottom of the manager holds two more options. The user may *View the Entire Control Board* once it is all created and arranged as well as *Save and*

Use the Control Board to exit the panel creation mode and enter control mode. After I created the prototype in Fig. 3 above, interns joined the lab, and I programmed a preliminary, augmented reality-based, exclusively front-end prototype of the toolbar section (where some tools can be dragged and dropped to another space but without any ability) with them as a means to teach them how to code line-by-line.

3.2   Artificial Intelligence Enabled Backend

My design-based approach to an API for a universal control panel as well as the emphasis on modularity and customizability enables the system to more readily rely on and benefit from artificial intelligence. One major aspect being automated design. Once the user/programmer makes use of the API a few times, the AI backend can start predicting the user's preferences on the design and begin automating control panel designs. Neural networks can be used to predict the design a specific user will create based on what the system has learned from their customizations including: what tools would be used in the panel, how many panels there would be, where the panels would be placed in space, what devices would be controlled, and more. This can be achieved via deep learning or non-deep learning. To go from artificial narrow intelligence towards a higher level of artificial intelligence, hidden neural network layers can be utilized. User-testing can be implemented to determine key factors of customization that users want the system to provide via neural networks. The system may perform personal or generic user customizations based on previous user data. One aspect that may be specific to certain users may be whether they choose to use the same controls for multiple devices or have separate ones for each. Artificial Intelligence and machine learning also aid in this design as means of performing the control itself. The AI backend may predict the time a user usually gets home based on when they use the controls to turn on the lights. In turn, the system may control/provide suggestions to facilitate actions on other IoT devices in sequence such as adjusting the thermostat or suggesting a dinner recipe at that time based on what is available in the fridge. Feedback and feedforward backed by AI are direct beneficiaries in such a system for the creation of panels as well as the controlling of devices. Thus, an AI backend provides: automated design of customizable control panels or control systems as well as prediction support of actions to be triggered or automated triggers when the panels are being used to control devices.

4   Discussion: Use Cases

The solution offers many use cases including mass usage for the general public as well as specialized uses. Mass usage includes smart cities and tourism applications, home based scenarios as well as workplace scenarios. Mass usage also includes personal usage in any setting, personal usage for individuals with cognitive and physical disabilities, and personal usage in conjunction with tracking personal data. Specialized usage includes industrial and factories including collaboration, single person usage, remote control of hazardous scenarios, non-remote control, as well as field work such as oil and gas and mining. Another specialized use case is for the purpose of teaching how to program such as is with block programming. Data-tracking may be used as a powerful tool in conjunction with mass usage as well as specialized use cases: especially in collaboration with artificial intelligence. This would result in extensive data that may be utilized back for process improvement and further innovation.

5   Future Work: Elicitation Study Design and Derivatives

The key to implementation of such a system is to elicit requirements from the user. Thus, as I establish the prototype in Fig. 3, I also establish an elicitation study structure that makes use of two groups of people. Group A would be put through a creative ideation stage where they make use of *drawing* and *ideating*. Next, they would refine given ideas. Possible techniques to use may be *paper prototype testing* where they are provided with a low-fidelity prototype and asked to use it and make suggestions and *wizard of oz* where they may be provided with a high-fidelity software prototype that they believe they are controlling and asked to make refinement suggestions from there. The target users of this study would be *domain experts* who regularly make use of industrial or home-based control panels (that may or may not be virtual), *software experts* who create or work with API's, IDE's, and front-end tools, and lastly, *non-technical users* who are not programmers but would be possible end-users to make use of such a virtual control panel. Such an elicitation study would have quantitative derivatives such as *completion time, number of clicks*, and *likert scale satisfaction values*. The qualitative derivatives the study would provide would be *body language and talk out loud, usability interview* via a semi-structured interview, and *field observations*. A key outcome of this would be to determine what kind of predictions the user and programmer want from the artificial intelligence of the system to make it easier to create a customized universal control system. The elicitation study will allow further user-centered implementation of the solution in augmented reality.

6   Considerable Implications

There may be some limitations and implications to consider in such a system. An entirely virtual control means that there is *no physical/haptic feedback* on the hands. Although there may be other physical indicators of successful control manipulation on the device such as something turning on/off, haptic feedback currently serves the user with the knowledge of having accomplished something as soon as it is done. Haptic feedback may also be an indicator of amount of control (such as how much one turns a steering wheel when driving). *Precision and accuracy* may also be a factor that is limited by the factors such as hardware and the lag that one may experience while using augmented reality. However, these would likely improve further over time. Although environmental affordances may aid the user when interacting with IoT, *environmental disturbances* could also be present. Examples being using augmented reality when surrounded by too many people or using it outside where unpredictable interferences may occur. Additionally, *artificial intelligence* itself presents a multitude of points that may be hard to predict when designing such a system and thus becomes black box decision making. Factors include how well and quick the agent may learn and implement suggestions and triggers including feedback and feedforward, customizations of panel design, and more. The bias factor in an AI equation such as in a neural network is also something to consider as that could change and refine further over time. Another factor to consider is how collaboration may or may not work when *screen/interface sharing* is not easy to implement.

7 Conclusion

I discussed the motivation of providing augmented reality interactions for controlling physical IoT devices. I delved into related work in terms of industrial applications and device discovery standards in addition to conducting a more extensive research centric visual literature mapping. I took the literature mapping results as a que to prototype a front-end based virtual control panel API tool to allow programmers and end users to create virtual control systems for their IoT devices. I also discussed the artificial intelligence application of the backend with two key points in mind: 1) automation of panel/control system creation as well as 2) prediction and suggestion/triggering of control actions based on specific or generic users and their environments. Next, I discussed the use cases of the virtual control system API including specialized as well as mass usage and emphasized that data science may be used in collaboration with artificial intelligence in turn for further product improvement. Then, I delved into future work with specific planned detail on my requirements elicitation study design and derivatives to re-iterate on front-end and back-end user-centric specifications for my product. Lastly, I considered the implications and limitations of such a system in terms of artificial intelligence, usage, and precision. My work has implications for programmers and users of virtual control systems backed by artificial intelligence for the purpose of controlling physical IoT devices via augmented reality.

Acknowledgements. I would like to thank Dr. Frank Maurer, head of the Agile Surface Engineering group at the Department of Computer Science at the University of Calgary under whose supervision I did this work as a commencement of my graduate studies.

References

1. Amazon Virtual Dash Button Service. Amazon Developer. https://developer.amazon.com/virtual-dash-button-service. Accessed 16 May 2021
2. Chopra, S.: Evaluating User Preferences for Augmented Reality Interactions for the Internet of Things. Master's thesis. University of Calgary, Calgary, Canada (2019)
3. Chopra, S., Maurer F.: Evaluating user preferences for augmented reality interactions with the Internet of Things. In: Proceedings of AVI 2020: International Conference on Advanced Visual Interfaces (2020)
4. Heun, V., Hobin, J., Maes, P.: Reality editor: programming smarter objects. In: Proceedings of the 2013 ACM Conference on Pervasive and Ubiquitous Computing Adjunct Publication (UbiComp 2013 Adjunct)

5. Heun, V., Kasahara, S., Maes, P.: Smarter objects: using AR technology to program physical objects and their interactions. In: Extended Abstracts on Human Factors in Computing Systems (CHI 2013) (2013)
6. IFTTT Homepage. https://ifttt.com. Accessed 16 June 2021
7. Interesting Engineering: Audi's Smart Factory is A Glimpse Into The Future. Transportation (2017). https://interestingengineering.com/audis-smart-factory-glimpse-future. Accessed 16 May 2021
8. Lykan Hypersport Holographic Display. https://www.youtube.com/watch?v=5zJi7JQ9sTE. Accessed 16 May 2021
9. Prigg, M.: Rolls Royce Reveals 'Roboship' with Augmented Reality Control Decks That Can Automatically Spot Hazards in the Water. DailyMail (2014). https://www.dailymail.co.uk/sciencetech/article-2875205/Rolls-Royce-reveals-roboships-augmented-reality-control-desks-automatically-spot-hazards.html. Accessed 16 May 2021
10. UPnP Developer Resources. https://openconnectivity.org/developer/specifications/upnp-resources/upnp-developer-resources/. Accessed 16 May 2021
11. Walk Up and Use Anything, Physical Web. http://google.github.io/physical-web/. Accessed 16 May 2021
12. What are iBeacons, iBeacon Insider. http://www.ibeacon.com/what-is-ibeacon-a-guide-to-beacons/. Accessed 16 May 2021
13. Wifi Aware. https://www.wi-fi.org/discover-wi-fi/wi-fi-aware. Accessed 16 May 2021

How to Explain It to Facility Managers? A Qualitative, Industrial User Research Study for Explainability

Helmut Degen[1(✉)], Christof J. Budnik[1], Kunal Chitre[2], and Andrew Lintereur[2]

[1] Siemens Technology, Princeton, NJ 08540, USA
{helmut.degen, christof.budnik}@siemens.com
[2] Siemens Smart Infrastructure, 9225 Bee Caves Road, Austin, TX 78733, USA
{kunal.chitre, andrew.lintereur}@siemens.com

Abstract. In this research, we focus on a building management system (BMS) and the facility managers as users. The application under research is a BMS which reports building related incidents to facility manager (e.g., an air conditioning system is not working properly), including causal factors and related measurements. The information should enable facility managers to select and initiate a responsive action. We wanted to know whether facility managers have the same or different expectations for a BMS application, using an machine-learning (ML) based technology (producing uncertain results), compared to the use of a rule-based technology (producing certain results). We interviewed four facility managers. The research found out that all four interviewed facility managers have different expectations for the use of ML-based technology, compared to a rule-based technology with the following differences: D.1) Show several options per incident. D.2) Annotate each option with a confidence level. D.3) Provide detailed information for each option (outside-in content), expressed in the building technology domain. Two observations are resulting from our case study. ML-generated content enables facility managers to select a proposed incident option and to validate a proposed incident option against their experience. Proposed options with a high confidence level that are validated by facility manager as correct build up even more trust in ML-based technology. Options with a high confidence level which is validated as incorrect can receive feedback by the facility manager, so that the ML-based technology can learn and improve. The limited research indicates that explainability content needs to be expressed as "outside-in content". The result also suggests that a user-centered approach is needed to identify which content is outside-in content which effectively enables option selection and option validation. Such an outside-in content can be used to specify requirements for the development of an ML-technology.

Keywords: HCI · Explainable AI · Trustworthiness · AI · Building technology · Qualitative user research · Root cause · Cognitive walkthrough with user

© Springer Nature Switzerland AG 2021
C. Stephanidis et al. (Eds.): HCII 2021, LNCS 13095, pp. 401–422, 2021.
https://doi.org/10.1007/978-3-030-90963-5_31

1 Introduction

With a constantly improving maturity of machine-learning-based technology, more and more consumer and industrial domains leverage these technologies to introduce new features and improve product quality. Machine-learning-based technologies, or ML-based technology in short, is the dominant branch of artificial intelligence where systems learn from data, identify patterns, and can make decisions with minimal human interaction.

ML-based technology is a subset of artificial intelligence-based (AI-based) technologies. A key characteristic of ML-based technology is the included uncertainty in produced results, i.e., the correctness of the outcome is less than 100% accurate. The reason is that training and test data are incomplete. Another subset of AI-based technology is a rule-based technology. Rule-based technology produces results with a certainty of 100%. Due to its given certainty, we infer that concerns regarding trust and explainability do not apply to rule-based technology. The research about explainability and trust, as scoped in this paper, applies to ML-based technology, not to rule-based technology.

Several known challenges and concerns have been identified when using ML-based technology: Trustworthiness, Ethics, and Human-centered AI [4, 5, 11, 17, 20, 22, 27, 33, 36, 44].

One promising approach to effectively address the topic of trustworthiness is AI Explainability [1, 3, 41]. Explainability is given by presenting the influencing factors of ML-based decisions to users. This eases the user's choice whether to consider ML-based decisions for their actions, or not.

To the best of our knowledge, two different groups of users have been identified as interested in explanations. One group of users are end-users. Their interest is to use the system of interest, defined by the intended use. The system of interest supports them to conduct defined user tasks in order to achieve defined user goals. We call this group of users "outside-in users". We call the content provided to the users to perform the user tasks "outside-in content".

The second group of users belong to the system development team. Their interest is the successful development of the system, so that outside-in users can perform the user tasks. We call this group of users "inside-out users". The content (e.g., performance attributes, safety attributes, reliability attributes, functions) needed by the inside-out users to develop it successfully is called "inside-out content". The majority of the outside-in content and the inside-out content is different.

This research focuses on explainability content for outside-in users. Similarly, the work of [7, 18] investigated how to translate explainability from the system (inside-out view) to the application domain (outside-in view).

One known distinction between using ML-based technology and traditional, rule-based technology is the level of certainty of the system generated results. Results derived from rule-based technology are deterministic and their rules are coded by humans. These results are considered as certain. Results from an ML-based technology are probabilistic which defines its own set of rules based on data output. Due to limited training and testing data, results of ML-based technology are not certain.

To not introduce potentially wrong assumptions about explainability early on, we will take a step back in this research project. A reasonable question to ask is: How does uncertainty influence the expectations of outside-in users knowing that an ML-based system introduces uncertainties, compared to a traditional rule-based system?

To answer that question, we reinforce the problem by two research questions (RQ):

- RQ.1 Do outside-in users have different expectations for the use of a system, using an ML-based technology, compared to a system, using a traditional, rule-based technology?
- RQ.2 If RQ.1 is answered with no: Why not? If RQ.1 is answered with yes: What are such differences?

We support our research by performing an industrial case study within the building technology domain. One group of outside-in users within that domain are facility managers. The system of interest is a smart building system which reports building incidents that need to be addressed by appropriate actions as early as possible. The selected research approach taken is qualitative research based on a case study [10].

The contribution of the research results report in this paper are: 1) A set of research methods to gain expectations about explainability with a user-centered approach. 2) The distinction between the outside-in perspective and the inside-out perspective for explainability. 3) The expectations and preferences for the industrial domain "building technologies".

The paper is structured in the following way. Section "Related work" mentions publications which are related to the research reported in this paper. Section "Application domain" introduces the application domain of building monitoring systems, the user role "Facility Manager" and the structure of a root cause analysis. The section "Research method" describes how the qualitative research was performed. The results and reported in the section "Results", followed by the Section "Conclusions and future work".

2 Related Work

Explainability has become a growing body of various research in recent years. Survey research provides a good selection of papers with insights into explainability as well as its relationship to trust [1, 3, 16, 41]. However, most research seems to be influenced by technical capabilities and its black box characteristics as machine-learnings-based enablers. There is still a gap between user needs and design exploration and design concepts, explored and validated by end users. Furthermore, it has not been identified which explainability differences exist between traditional, rule-based technology and an ML-based technology.

We focused our literature study at research which considered the use of ML-based technology with user involvement, i.e., where ML directly affects users' trust and decision-making efficiency, thus also affecting the adoption of ML-based solutions. To relate this research with the state-of-the-art, the following classification (C) criteria have been applied:

- C.1 Research method: Analysis vs. evaluation
- C.2 Application domain: Consumer domain vs. industrial domain
- C.3 System capabilities: ML-based technology only (ML-based) vs. comparison between rule-based technology and ML-based technology (comparison)

Van der Waar et al. [42] investigated rule-based and example-based contrastive explanations for a recommendation system for diabetes patients. The target users are patients with diabetes mellitus type 1. The application's intended use is to aid those patients in terms of insulin dosage. The research found out that both explanation types do not improve task performance, compared to no explanations. The research focusses on the evaluation (C1: evaluation) of an industrial medical application (C2: industrial) and comparing systems (C3: Comparison).

Chen, Yan and Wang [6] performed a user study to understand the impact of sentiment-based recommendations explanations for high-value consumer products (e.g., digital cameras). The research showed that sentiment-based explanations can significantly increase users' product knowledge. The research focused on an evaluation (C1: evaluation) of a consumer application (C2: consumer) for an ML-based system (C3: ML-based).

Rana & Bridge [35] created so called Recommendation-by-Explanation (r-by-e). It means that explanations are used as recommendations. Their research shows that such explanations as recommendations achieve a higher precision than a comparable recommender, while both produce recommendations with roughly equal levels of diversity and serendipity. The research focused on evaluation (C1: evaluation) of a consumer application (C2: consumer) for a ML-based system (C3: ML-based).

The research presented in this paper uses an analysis technique (C.1: Analysis) for industrial applications (C2: Industrial) and with comparing system capabilities (C.3: Comparison). We have not found published research which focuses on the analysis for ML-generated content (C1: Analysis) for an industrial application (C2: Industrial) and comparing rule-based and ML-based technology (C3: comparison).

3 Application Domain

3.1 Building Management System

Many commercial buildings, incl. campuses, and large residential buildings are nowadays equipped with several control systems including fire alarm systems, power systems, heating and cooling systems, ventilation systems as well as security systems. To observe and operate all those systems at the same time facility managers are supported by a building management system (BMS). Its purpose is to inform the facility manager about the building status and reporting issues to keep occupants safe and comfortable. Based on defined setpoints, the BMS constantly measures the building control properties to operate in a certain value range. Let the temperature of a room for example a building property. The temperature setpoint for that room can then be defined to 72 °F (Fahrenheit). A tolerance range can be set to plus/minus 4 °F. If the measure room temperature is below 68 °F or above 76 °F, the BMS will activate the heating or cooling system to bring the temperature back within the tolerance area of the temperature set point. The monitoring and controlling of the systems are done fully automated by the BMS, so the facility manager does not need to intervene.

BMS also have the capability to report incidents. Incidents in the context of BMS are deviations of building conditions and equipment which require the intervention of the facility manager and in many cases a repair which could turn into a replacement of equipment. For instance, a temperature set point might accidentally drop to a lower value. The changed setpoint reduces the volume of water pumped which then overheats the coils of the heating system. The incident of overheated coils is reported, and the facility manager intervenes by changing the setpoint to the correct value.

3.2 Facility Manager

Our target user role is the facility manager. A building is maintained by one or more facility managers. A facility manager represents an outside-in user of a building management system. A facility manager has two main goals (G):

- G.1) Keep the occupants safe and comfortable and
- G.2) Optimize building operation and maintenance costs.

To achieve G.1, the facility manager uses the BMS to define setpoints for comfort relevant building properties (e.g., temperature, humidity, light). If the actual building properties meet the setpoints within given ranges, the occupants should feel comfortable and safe. In case a building property is not correct (e.g., a room temperature is too cold), the facility manager needs to adjust certain setpoints. Another reason for adjusting a building's system can be an incident.

An incident is an event which requires a facility manager's intervention to initiate a corrective, and maybe preventive action. Such actions can be:

- Change a building parameter (e.g., a temperature setpoint)
- Replace or repair broken equipment
- Enhance system by adding new equipment

These days reported incidents contain information about measured values of equipment properties such as actual values read by a sensor or set by an actuator. The actual value can be of different types including binary (e.g., on/off), discrete (e.g., 5%, 10%, 15%, ...) or continuous (e.g., 3.57, 3.58, ...).

Reported incidents provide measured values for sensors and actuators. The facility manager derives causal factors from such reported values. A causal factor is understood as any contributor to an incident (a wrong value or undesirable condition), that if eliminated would have either prevented the occurrence of the incident or reduced its severity or frequency. However, the ability to find such causal factors requires many years of experience in the field. Since there can be thousands of measured values, the manual identification of causal factors for a reported incident is time-intense and error-prone. It is not uncommon for facility managers to take up to a week identifying causal factors for a single reported incident.

Thus, facility managers need help in reducing the time to resolve all incidents demanded as their daily duties. The time to resolve one incident starts from the time when an incident is reported to the time an effective action is initiated, performed and completed. One beneficial way to save time is by aggregating all relevant values of a reported incident to allow a faster identification of the causal factors.

The use of a rule-based application uses measurements to identify causal factors that resulted in a reported incident. The use of an application with ML-based technology can not only find casual factors but furthermore identify responsive actions to address those causal factors. The difference between a rule-based application and an ML-based technology application is the level of certainty. Rule-based applications are assumed to determine results with 100% certainty (based on the defined rules), while ML-based technology is assumed to determine results with less than 100% certainty, due to the use of limited training and testing data.

3.3   Root Cause Analysis

Another important entity used in our research is the root cause analysis. It is essential to understand the structure and elements of a root cause analysis. The process of a root cause analysis (RCA) consists of the following steps (based on [43]):

- RCA.1 Identify and describe the problem
- RCA.2 Establish a timeline from the normal situation up to the time the problem occurred
- RCA.3 Establish a causal graph between the root cause and the problem.

The result of a root cause analysis can be a causal graph showing dependencies between the occurred problem, intermediate causal effects, and the root cause. For practical reasons, it can also contain corrective and preventative actions (see Fig. 1).

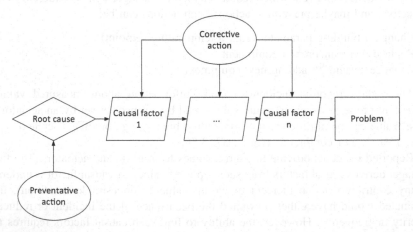

Fig. 1. Causal graph, connecting the problem with the root cause via causal factors, including corrective and preventative actions. One root cause can be multiple paths of causal factors.

A corrective action is applied to one or more causal factors. However, the corrective action does typically not address the root cause. A preventative action addresses the root cause.

To illustrate this, we use the example of an air conditioning (AC) system. Assuming the AC system takes too much energy to cool (problem). A causal factor can be a dusty air filter (causal factor). Not replacing the air filter on time is another factor (causal factor). The root cause could be that the replacement of the air filter is not part of the maintenance manual. By adding an air filter check to the maintenance manual (preventative action), the problem could be avoided in the future. To fix the current situation, the air filter needs to be replaced (corrective action). The corrective action without the preventative action would not avoid the same problem in the future.

A facility manager would benefit if a BMS can identify the causal factors and the root cause for a reported incident. A ML-based technology can do that, a rule-based technology not.

4   Research Preparation

4.1   Target Users, User Goals, User Tasks

To conduct the research with facility managers, we prepared two concepts for a smart building application. Both concepts are represented as lo-fi mockups, visualized as wire frames. Concept 1 represents a concept based on rule-based technology. It reports an incident, causal factors, and related measurements. Concept 2 is based on ML-based technology. It reports an incident, causal factors, related measurements, and actions. They are described in more detail below. Both concepts were created with the help of building management domain experts from the Siemens Smart Infrastructure (SII) business unit. Please note that the facility managers were not involved in any kind at any time in the creation of these concepts.

For both concepts, our target user group are facility managers (outside-in user). The addressed user's goal is to recognize an incident and initiate a response.

The two concepts enable a different set of user tasks (UT):

- UT.1 Recognize the existence of an incident.
- UT.2 Understand causal factors and system measurements.
  Both user tasks should enable facility managers to derive actions, based on the user's experience and knowledge with buildings and their equipment. Concept 1 does not propose responsive actions. Concept 2 extend the supported user tasks of concept 1. In addition to the two mentioned user tasks, it enables another user task:
- UT.3 Select possible actions which are intended to address the causal factors.
  The two concepts are described in more detail in the subsequent subsections.

4.2   Target Users, User Goals, User Tasks

The first set of stimulus material shows an interaction concept for a rule-based system (see Figs. 2 and 3). They were presented to the facility managers as concept 1.

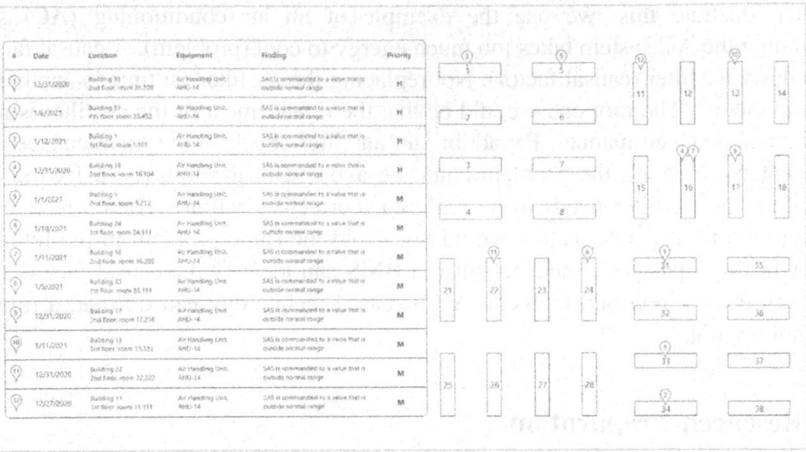

Fig. 2. Concept 1 (rule-based technology without uncertainty) – dashboard view (screen 1)

Concept 1 consists of two screens. The dashboard view (screen 1) consists of two parts. On the left, a list of incidents is displayed. Each incident has the following attributes: incident number (also shown on the map which is displayed on the right-hand side), a date when the incident occurred, the location of incident, the incident involved equipment, a finding description, and a priority. The priority reflects the severity of a finding. The right-hand side of the screen shows a map of the buildings. If an incident for one of the buildings were reported (on the left-hand side), a marker with the incident number is displayed associated with the building.

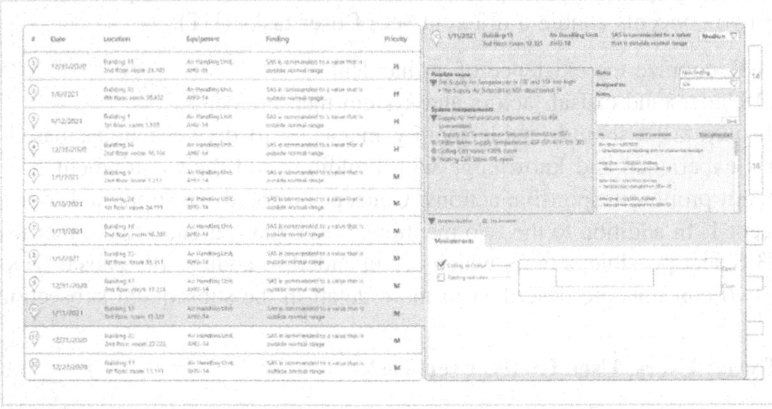

Fig. 3. Concept 1 (rule-based technology without uncertainty) – incident view (screen 2); note: The red triangle indicates that a measured value differentiates between the target (to-be) value and the actual value (as-is) which constitutes an unintended deviation. The green circle indicates that measured values are in line with the target value (no unintended deviation). The blue triangle indicates proposed action items. (Color figure online)

The second screen shows the content details for a selected incident. They include a possible cause, system measurements, status of incident, assigned to, notes and log file. At the bottom, additional incident related measurements are displayed. A red triangle indicates that a measured value differentiates between the target value and the actual value (deviation). A green circle indicates that a measured value is in line with the target value (no deviation).

The interaction concept of concept 1 is new and not available today in the market. The information displayed in the interaction concept can be realized with a rule-based technology.

4.3 Concept 2 (Using ML-Based Technology)

For the intended use of an ML-based technology, the information of concept 1 was extended with proposed actions (see concept 2 in Fig. 4).

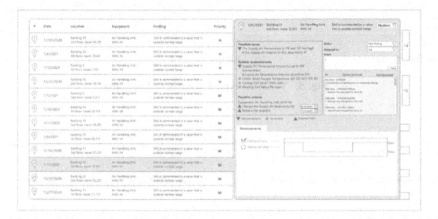

Fig. 4. Concept 2 – Baseline (ML-based technology with uncertainty) – incident view; note: The blue triangle indicates proposed action items which have been introduced in concept 2. (Color figure online)

We call the concept, displayed in Fig. 4, a baseline version. For the research with facility managers, we have added additional variations to this baseline version to understand different expectations when it comes to the use of ML-based technologies.

We have prepared three variation types. Each variation type has two to four variation instances:

- Variation type 1 (Number of options, see Fig. 5)
  - Variation 1a: Single option
  - Variation 1b: Several options ()
- Variation type 2 (Confidence level, see Fig. 6):
  - Variation 2a: No confidence level for single option
  - Variation 2b: With confidence level for single option

- Variation 2c: No confidence level for multiple options
- Variation 2d: With confidence level for multiple options
- Variation type 3 (Background data, see Fig. 7):
  - Variation 3a: No background data
  - Variation 3b: System background data
  - Variation 3c: Domain background data
  - Variation 3d: System and domain background data

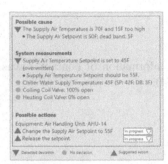 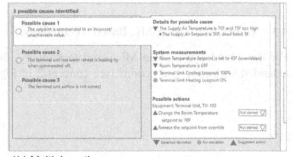

1a) Single option   1b) Multiple options

Fig. 5. Variation type 1 (Number of options)

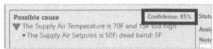

2a) Single option – no confidence level   2b) Single option – with confidence level

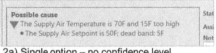 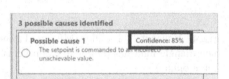

2c) Several options – no confidence level   2d) Several options – with confidence level

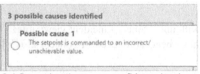

Fig. 6. Variation type 2 (confidence level)

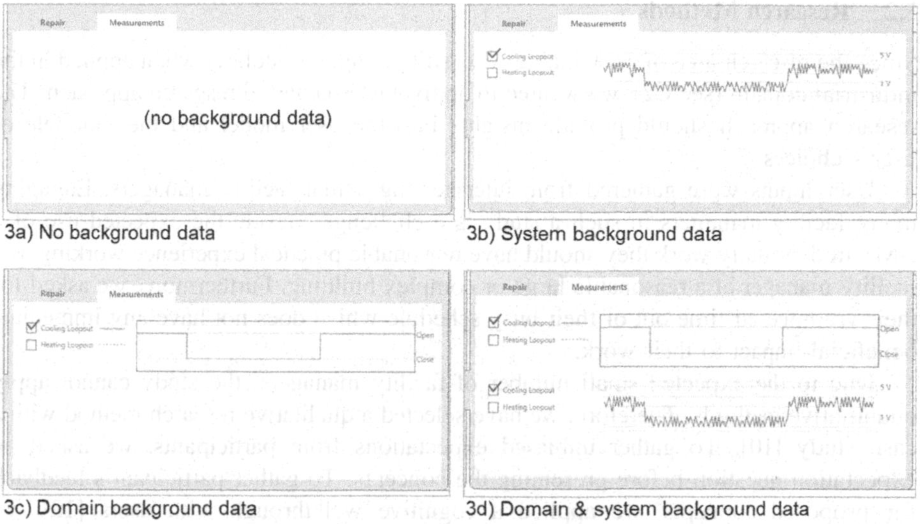

3a) No background data   3b) System background data

3c) Domain background data   3d) Domain & system background data

Fig. 7. Variation type 3 (background data)

When presenting instances of variation type 2 to the facility manager, the selection was dependent on the selected instance of variation 1. If a facility manager select instance 2 of variation type 1 (several options), only instances 2c and 2d were presented to the facility manager.

Variation type 3 displays different kind of system data. System background data (variation instance 3b) shows voltage values over a time of a cooling loopout. It was selected to represent inside-out content. Domain background data (variation instance 3c) shows the open and close state of a cooling loopout and was selected to represent outside-in content. It was expected that facility managers select variation type 3b (as outside-in content) and not variation type 3c (as inside-out content).

5 Research Approach

5.1 Research Goal

The research goal was to find answer to the two already introduced research questions in Sect. 1:

- RQ.1 Do outside-in users have different expectations for the use of a system, using an ML-based technology, compared to a system, using a traditional, rule-based technology?
- RQ.2 If RQ.1 is answered with no: Why not? If RQ.1 is answered with yes: What are such differences?

5.2   Research Methods

Since the research area of explainable AI is still young, particularly when applied in the industrial domain (see C2), we wanted to apply a user-centered research approach. The research approach should provide insights into the user model and the rationale of user's choices.

User inputs were gathered from interviewing actual facility managers. Engaging many facility managers in such a study is a challenge. Beside the expected use of a BMS in their daily work they should have reasonable practical experience working as a facility manager at a reasonable large or complex building. Furthermore, we asked for their volunteered time out of their busy schedule which does not have any immediate beneficial impact to their work.

Due to the expected small number of facility managers, the study cannot apply quantitative methods. Therefore, we have selected a qualitative research method with a case study [10]. To gather unbiased expectations from participants, we asked an expectation question before presenting the concepts. To gather participant's feedback for proposed concepts, we applied a cognitive walkthrough with users [12]. To understand which topics are more or less important for participants, we applied a conceptual content analysis to the participants' answers [24, 30]. To understand participant's preferences, we offered several options of variation types which we asked the participants to select from.

Selection of Participants - Plan
Remember that our target user role are facility managers. In most cases, they have a team which supports the facility manager in the daily work, e.g., addressing reported incidents. Commercial facility managers typically manage one or more buildings. In some cases, they can manage one or more campuses, consisting of several buildings each.

For our research, we approached the Siemens Smart Infrastructure sales team to identify facility managers for the research. We attempted to invite facility managers representing different industries, e.g., high-technology development, hotel, hospital, higher-education facility. Our goal was to interview six facility managers from different industries.

Selection of Participants - Execution
We have recruited and interviewed four facility managers from the following industries: high-technology development, hotel, and an event location. All facility managers are Siemens customers.

The facility managers did not receive any incentive for their participation.

Interview Session - Planned
The interview session was originally planned for 60 min with the following agenda:

- 1 Introduction, including participant's consent (5 min.)
- 2 Participant's profile (5 min.)
- 3 Concept 1 (with rule-based technology) (15 min.)

   3.1 Researcher explains the scope of an ideal smart building system

3.2 Question 1: Imaging you use the ideal smart building system which helps you to find and address facility management related findings and incidents in a timely manner. Which information/content or functions should a smart building system provide, ideally? (no concept was shown)

3.3 Participant expresses expectations

3.4 Researcher presents concept 1 and the intended user's goal (see Figs. 2 and 3)

3.5 Questions 2,3: What do you like? What would you change?

3.6 Participant provides feedback

- 4 Concept 2 (with ML-based technology, introducing uncertainty) (30 min.)

4.1 Researcher explains that AI is now used, and AI introduces uncertainty (we used AI instead of ML for simplification reasons under the assumption that facility managers are not aware of the difference between AI and ML).

4.2 Question 4: We now consider a smart building system which uses AI-based technology. One characteristic of AI-based technology is that it may identify anomalies/issues with a certainty less than 100%. Which information or functions should a smart building system with AI-based technology offer to you, introducing uncertainties? (Note: no concept was shown)

4.3 Participant expresses expectations

4.4 Researcher presents concept 2 and the intended user's goal (baseline) (see Fig. 4)

4.5 Question 5,6: What do you like? What would you change?

4.6 Participant provides feedback

4.7 Researcher presents three type of variations to participant (see Figs. 5, 6, and 7).

4.8 Question 7: Participant selects variations

4.9 Researcher presents concept 2 with variation types, selected by participant (not shown here)

4.10 Question 8, 9: What do you like? What would you change?

4.11 Participant provides feedback for concept 2 with selected variations

- 5 Wrap-up and thank you (5 min.)

To exclude bias due to the sequence of presented variations (see 4.7), the sequence of variations was changed. Variation sequence 1 was: Step 1: Background content was presented; step 2: number of options and confidence level was presented. Variation sequence 2 was: Step 1: Number of options and confidence level was presented; step 2: Background content was presented.

The number of options and the confidence level was not separated because the confidence levels depend on the number of options.

Interview Session - Execution

The interview sessions were performed remotely via Microsoft Teams. From Siemens, two product managers and three researchers participated in each session. After everybody has introduced himself or herself, one researcher facilitated the interview. One other researcher took notes while the third researcher kept track of following the interview plan. The role of the product managers was to clarify any domain under-standing where required. All questions and concepts were prepared on a PowerPoint slide and shared during each session.

Table 1. Interview sessions.

Facility manager's industry	Experience in facility management	Building space size in square footage	Interview duration	Variation sequence
High technology development	20+	About 16 million	30 min	1
Hotel	38	About 1 million	60 min	2
Healthcare	15	About 280 thousand	60 min	1
Conference center	7	About 147 thousand	60 min	2

During the introduction part of the interview, the participants were made aware of the purpose (research only) and the use of the elicited data (anonymous only). The participants were made aware that they could opt-out at any time during the session. The purpose and the opt-out option were presented on a slide to the participants. The participants gave their consent. The participants comments were documented during the session and analyzed afterwards.

We interviewed one facility manager per session. They support buildings or cam-puses for different types of industries. The experience as facility managers varies from 15 to 38 years in facility management, with a minimum of three years as a facility manager. They are responsible for buildings with a square footage from about 150,000 up to 16 million square foot. The interview lasted in three cases 60 min, in one case 30 min (see Table 1).

6   Research Results

A content analysis for the comments were performed. Each participant's comment was analyzed and mapped to one or more of the content types (see Table 2).

The intercoder agreement (reliability) with Cohen's Kappa is 0.73. The break-down of content mapping per concept (concept 1, concept 2 – baseline, concept 2 – selected) is displayed in Table 3.

Overall, we can see that the comment theme for concept 1 is about detecting issues (Monitoring and notifications: 14) and providing guidance how to resolve it (Mea-surements and control: 11; Causal factors and actions: 5).

The common theme for concept 2 - baseline shifts the focus more towards causal factors and actions (8). It reflects the need of facility managers to resolve a reported incident. Through conversational comments, it became obvious that the facility man-agers do not trust the system's results and want to verify the systems results themselves ("I won't trust the system for a year").

Table 2. Content categories and content types.

Content category	Content type
Notifications, display, status	• Ranking, urgency, prioritization • Monitor building status & notifications • Map, location, display status of buildings
Measurement and control	• Optimization of operations and costs • Dependent alarms, series of alarms with same root cause • Preventative measures, trends • Corrective measures, repairs, replacements • Self-healing, self-monitoring, and self-control
Causal factors and actions	• System context, equipment context • System components, building equipment, part numbers • System measurements & history, comparisons • Actual measurements
Action assignment and execution	• Integration with ticketing system • Action assignment to people, action status, action execution, action status • Part order & delivery • Call for assistance and help
Artificial intelligence	• User provides feedback for ML-based technology

Table 3. Concepts mentioned by facility managers.

Question topics	Notifications, display, status	Measurements and control	Causal factors and actions	Action assignment and execution	Artificial intelligence	Total
Concept 1 (rule-based)						
Question 1: Expectations	6	7	1	0	0	14
Question 2: Likes	4	0	1	1	0	6
Question 3: Changes	4	4	3	1	0	12
Concept 2 (ML-based, baseline)						
Question 4: Expectations	3	3	3	0	0	9
Question 5: Likes	2	1	2	0	0	5
Question 7: Changes	2	1	3	1	1	8
Concept 2 (ML-based, selected)						
Question 8: Likes	1	0	7	0	0	8
Question 9: Changes	0	0	4	0	0	4
Total	**22**	**16**	**24**	**3**	**1**	**66**

Reading example 1: for concept 1 (rule-based), question 1 (Expectations), the participants' answer statement contained six times a concept about notifications, display and or status. Reading example 2: For concept 1 (rule-based), the participants' answer statements for questions 1–3 contained fourteen times a concept about notifications, display, or status. Reading example 3: The participants' answer statements to questions 1–6 and 8–9 contained twenty-two times the concept of notifications, display, or status.

Several facility managers were concerned about prevention. Participant 1 (P1) wanted to see "analytics on premature failures to plan on events and those who do not need attention". Along the same lines, P2 mentioned that when a "device feels vibrations; air handler, air velocity are slowing down", the facility manager would like to see an alert, so that significant or more expensive damage can be avoided.

For concept 2 - baseline (with ML, introducing uncertainties), they expressed expectations towards the optimization of operation. They expect the ML-based system to help monitor and prevent major incidents. Also, they expect that the ML-based system to prioritize incidents.

For concept 2 – selected, the focus shifted towards trouble shooting. The liked the proposed list of actions which are explained with the system measurements and the possible causes. One participant mentioned that the system should initiate actions automatically, and still inform the facility manager. One participant said that he does "not trust the system for a year". However, the confidence level and the possible causes and actions help to develop trust, if the system comes to the same conclusion as the facility manager. In other words: the facility manager uses the explanations, provides by possible causes, system measurements and possible actions to validate the system-generated proposal.

Facility managers mentioned several benefits. It takes them up to a week to identify the causal factors of an incident. With the proposed concept, they'll see it within a few seconds. In addition, they mentioned that junior colleagues, less familiar with the building and the building equipment would be able to act on such system-generated causal factors and actions. They save significant time and require less skills and training.

From all sixteen possible variation combinations, the four facility managers selected for variation type 1 "multiple options" and for variation type 2 "with confidence level", and for variation type 4 "with system & domain data". The concept with the selected variations instances is depicted in Fig. 8.

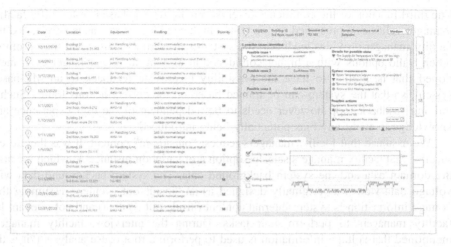

Fig. 8. Concept 2 with variation combination which was selected by all four facility managers

7   Conclusions and Future Work

In summary, our research shows that presented content should have the intent to enable outside-in users, in our case facility managers, to perform their work effectively and efficiently. Accordingly, the content needs to be outside-in content. This conclusion is independent whether a traditional, rule-based technology or ML-based technology is used. Also included in the conclusion is the content expressing the confidence level of ML-generated options which help users to select an option (e.g., the option with the highest confidence first).

We can distinguish between two types of explanations: One is about the incident, the causal factors, and the possible actions. The facility managers use them to validate the outside in content against the facility manager's experience and knowledge. This explanation is independent from the underlying technology. The second type of explanation is the confidence level. The confidence level per option helps the facility managers to focus their validation, i.e., which option they should check first. The more often the causal factors of the option with the highest confidence level is consistent with the root cause analysis of the facility manager the more and faster it helps to build trust into the system. Since the confidence level is used for selection, it can be considered as outside-in content.

The study indicates that facility managers find the confidence level which provides a hint about the self-reported quality of a ML-generated content (difference 2) useful. Three functions can be assigned to the self-reported confidence level. 1) For the facility manager, the confidence level helps to select an option. Most likely the option with the highest confidence level is selected first. 2) If the facility manager validates the option with the highest level as correct, the confidence level helps to build trust for the facility manager. In this case, the word "confidence" has two views. One view is the expression of *self-confidence* of the ML-based technology about the proposed options. The second view is the emerging confidence of the facility manager in the ML-based technology. 3)

The third function of the confidence level is to train the ML-based system. If a facility manager validates a presented option with a high confidence level as incorrect, and the facility manager provides feedback, the system will learn over time and may promote other, valid options with a higher confidence level. One facility manager even mentioned that he prefers to have the possibility to provide feedback to an ML-based system, so that the system can be trained based on the correct actions found. Such a training feedback loop however needs to be independent of the user experience and knowledge to avoid any bias potentially being introduced.

We assumed that facility managers request "outside-in" content. It was therefore a surprise that facility managers selected option 4 of variation instance 3d which includes the domain data and the system background data. The system background data with voltage data view was originally designed as an "inside-out" content, assuming that voltage information is system internal content (inside-out content) and not relevant for facility managers to perform their tasks. During the interview, facility managers mentioned that voltage information is used to perform a root cause analysis ("it is the first thing I look at"). Facility managers considered both proposed time series (domain and system view) as outside-in information. In this sense, our hypothesis of selecting outside-in content was supported. However, we have not received confirmation that facility managers do not want to use inside-out content.

The wrong assumption about the voltage information is unfortunate on one hand, since it was introduced to provide evidence that inside-out information is not useful. The fact that the assumption was wrong is a strong support that the identification of explainable outside-in content needs to be elicited with representatives of target user groups as part of a user-centered design approach.

None of the facility managers mentioned that they want to know details about the internal mechanisms of an ML technology, e.g., the structure or functions of neural networks. In other words: they did not request explicitly inside-out content.

The focus on outside-in content means that a solid user-centered design and development approach is needed to understand and identify which outside-in information enables facility managers to validate the ML-generated content. The identified out-side information should then become functional and interface requirements for the development of the ML-technology.

We can now answer the two research questions.

RQ.1: Do outside-in users have different expectations for the use of a system, using an ML-based technology, compared to a system, using a traditional, rule-based technology?

Yes. The interviewed facility managers have different expectations.

RQ.2: What are such differences?

The differences are that facility managers want to have several options (difference 1) with a confidence level (difference 2) and additional, out-side in system information (difference 3) which is associated with the reported incident. The identified information allows them to validate each option and select the most appropriate ones.

The finding about the usefulness of the self-reported confidence level is in line with the findings of [2].

The research result seems to be consistent with the findings from [23] about music recommendations. The found out that users prefer sound and complete recommendations (outside-in) which enable the users to validate the reason for song recommendations (why this song, why this artist) over what the computer knows or how it all works (inside-out information).

It is not clear whether our results are consistent with the results from [25]. They found out that thorough explanations are preferred over general explanations. It is worthwhile to mention that also contrastive explanations scored as high as thorough explanations. The target user groups of the research study are layman, not experts. Therefore, they may not be able to validate the content.

The research is not consistent with Miller's [28] findings that "explanations are *contrastive*" (p. 3, italic in original). There was no indication in this research that facility managers want to see positive *and* negative explanations (contrastive). Facility managers were looking for possible causes and actions which are in line with their understanding of the building. Our findings are not consistent with Miller's second finding that "probabilities probably don't matter" (p. 3). All four facility managers selected a confidence level as a variation option which expresses a probability. One of the facility managers expressed his expectations to see likelihood, before we presented our concepts. A potential explanation for the discrepancy between Miller's findings and ours is that Miller seem to focus on explanations for inside-out content, not so much on explanations for outside-in content.

The explanations used in this research belong to the explanation type *user benefits* [34].

If confirmed with extended research, a new proposition for explanations could be added to the list of propositions, expressed by [13]: "Explanations will be used to enable the user to validate the proposed content."

The presented study has certain limitations. One limitation is the sample size of four interviews. Although the study indicates a direction, it requires more interviews to reach a saturation point. Based on [14], six to twelve interviews would be desirable. The study should be extended to user roles and applications from other industrial domains.

Another limitation of the study is the use of a wire frame mockup and the cognitive walkthrough with user's technique. The study was performed as a non-behavioral study which is not reflecting user's behavior in the field. An interactive system should be built to allow a behavioral study, so that facility managers can be observed using the system in their context of use. It will provide additional insights which strengthen or weaken the made observations and conclusions.

Acknowledgement. We thank the Smart Building Intelligence team and the account managers for their support to recruit participants. We thank Stavroula Ntoa for valuable review comments.

References

1. Adadi, A., Berrada, M.: Peeking inside the black-box: a survey on Explainable Artificial Intelligence (XAI). IEEE Access **6**, 52138–52160 (2018). https://doi.org/10.1109/ACCESS. 2018.2870052
2. Antifakos, S., Kern, N., Schiele, B., Schwaninger, A.: Towards improving trust in context-aware systems by displaying system confidence. In Proceedings of the 7th International Conference on Human Computer Interaction with Mobile Devices & Services (MobileHCI 2005), pp. 9–14. Association for Computing Machinery, New York (2005). https://doi.org/ 10.1145/1085777.1085780
3. Arrieta, A.B., et al.: Explainable Artificial Intelligence (XAI): concepts, taxonomies, opportunities and challenges toward responsible AI. Inf. Fusion **58**, 82–115 (2020). https:// doi.org/10.1016/j.inffus.2019.12.012
4. Amershi, S., et al.: Guidelines for human-AI interaction. In: Proceedings of the 2019 CHI Conference on Human Factors in Computing Systems, pp. 1–13. Association for Computing Machinery, Glasgow (2019). https://doi.org/10.1145/3290605.3300233
5. Bird, E., et al.: The ethics of artificial intelligence: issues and initiatives. Panel for the Future of Science and Technology (STOA) European Parliament (2020). https://www.europarl. europa.eu/stoa/en/document/EPRS_STU(2020)634452. Accessed 27 Jan 2021
6. Chen, L., Yan, D., Wang, F.: User evaluations on sentiment-based recommendation explanations. ACM Trans. Interact. Intell. Syst. **9**(4), 1–38 (2019). https://doi.org/10.1145/ 3282878
7. Choo, J., Liu, S.: Visual analytics for explainable deep learning. IEEE Comput. Graphics Appl. **38**(4), 84–92 (2018). https://doi.org/10.1109/MCG.2018.042731661
8. Tsai, C.-H., Brusilovsky, P.: Evaluating visual explanations for similarity-based recommendations: user perception and performance. In: Proceedings of the 27th ACM Conference on User Modeling, Adaptation and Personalization (UMAP 2019), pp. 22–30. Association for Computing Machinery, New York (2019). https://doi.org/10.1145/3320435.3320465
9. Confalonieri, R., Coba, L., Wagner, B., Besold, T.R.: A historical perspective of explainable Artificial Intelligence. WIREs Data Min. Knowl. Discov. **11**, e1391 (2020). https://doi.org/ 10.1002/widm.1391
10. Men, H.: Research design. In: Vocabulary Increase and Collocation Learning, pp. 59–76. Springer, Singapore (2018). https://doi.org/10.1007/978-981-10-5822-6_4
11. Degen, H., Ntoa, S.: From a workshop to a framework for human-centered Artificial Intelligence. In: Degen, H., Ntoa, S. (eds.) HCII 2021. LNCS (LNAI), vol. 12797, pp. 166–184. Springer, Cham (2021). https://doi.org/10.1007/978-3-030-77772-2_11
12. Granollers, T., Lorés, J.: Incorporation of users in the Evaluation of Usability by Cognitive Walkthrough (2006). https://doi.org/10.1007/1-4020-4205-1_20
13. Gregor, S., Benbasat, I.: Explanations from intelligent systems: theoretical foundations and implications for practice. MIS Q. **23**(4), 497–530 (1999)
14. Guest, G., Bunce, A., Johnson, L.: How many interviews are enough?: An experiment with data saturation and variability. Field Methods **18**(1), 59–82 (2006). https://doi.org/10.1177/ 1525822X05279903
15. Google: People + AI Research. https://pair.withgoogle.com. Accessed 27 Jan 2021
16. Guidotti, R., Monreale, A., Ruggieri, S., Turini, F., Giannotti, F., Pedreschi, D.: A survey of methods for explaining black box models. ACM Comput. Surv. **51**(5), 1–42 (2019). https:// doi.org/10.1145/3236009
17. Hagerty, A., Rubinov, I.: Global AI ethics: a review of the social impacts and ethical implications of Artificial Intelligence (2019). https://arxiv.org/abs/1907.07892

18. Hind, M., et al.: TED: teaching AI to explain its decisions. In: Proceedings of the 2019 AAAI/ACM Conference on AI, Ethics, and Society (AIES 2019), pp. 123–129. Association for Computing Machinery, New York (2019). https://doi.org/10.1145/3306618.3314273

19. Holzinger, A., Carrington, A., Müller, H.: Measuring the quality of explanations: the system causability scale (SCS). KI - Künstliche Intelligenz **34**(2), 193–198 (2020). https://doi.org/10.1007/s13218-020-00636-z

20. IBM: IBM Design for AI. https://www.ibm.com/design/ai/. Accessed 27 Jan 2021

21. Janssen, C.P., Donker, S.F., Brumby, D.P., Kun, A.L.: History and future of human-automation interaction. Int. J. Hum. Comput. Stud. **131**, 99–107 (2019). https://doi.org/10.1016/j.ijhcs.2019.05.006

22. Jobin, A., Ienca, M., Vayena, E.: The global landscape of AI ethics guidelines. Nat. Mach. Intell. **1**, 389–399 (2019). https://doi.org/10.1038/s42256-019-0088-2

23. Kulesza, T., et al.: Too much, too little, or just right? Ways explanations impact end users' mental models. In: Proceedings of IEEE Symposium on Visual Languages and Human-Centric Computing, VL/HCC (2013). https://doi.org/10.1109/VLHCC.2013.6645235

24. Krippendorff, K.: Content Analysis. An Introduction to its Methodology, Fourth Edition. SAGE, Los Angeles (2018)

25. Larasati, R., de Liddo, A., Motta, E.: The effect of explanation styles on user's trust. ExSS-ATEC@IUI, 2020. http://ceur-ws.org/Vol-2582/

26. Lentzsch, T., Herrmann, T.: Intervention user interfaces for the smart home. Froehlich, P., et al (ed.). In: Proceedings of the Workshop on Automation Experience across Domains co-located with the ACM Conference on Human Factors in Computing Systems (CHI 2020), Honolulu, Hawaii, US, 26 April 2020. http://ceur-ws.org/Vol-2700/paper7.pdf

27. Margetis, G., Ntoa, S., Antona, M., Stephanidis, C.: Human-centered design of artificial intelligence. In: Salvendy, G., Karwowski, W. (Eds.) Handbook of Human Factors and Ergonomics, 5th Edition, Wiley. (2021, to appear)

28. Miller, T.: Explanation in Artificial Intelligence: Insights from the Social Sciences (2018). https://arxiv.org/abs/1706.07269

29. Mohseni, S., Zarei, N., Ragan, E.D.: A multidisciplinary survey and framework for design and evaluation of explainable AI systems. 2020. Human-Computer Interaction. https://arxiv.org/abs/1811.11839

30. Neuendorf, K.A.: The Content Analysis Guidebook, 2nd edition. SAGE, Los Angeles

31. Norman, D.: The Design of Everyday Things. Basic Books, New York (2013)

32. Nourani, M., King, J.T., Ragan, E.D.: The role of domain expertise in user trust and the impact of first impressions with intelligent systems (2020). https://www.semanticscholar.org/paper/The-Role-of-Domain-Expertise-in-User-Trust-and-the-Nourani-King/23c9685bbecaa187ea4d0d1f8aed8ca46f9bb996

33. OECD Principles on Artificial Intelligence - Organisation for Economic Co-operation and Development (2019). https://www.oecd.org/going-digital/ai/principles/. Accessed 27 Jan 2021

34. Phillips, P.J., Hahn, C.A., Fontana, P.C., Broniatowski, D.A., Przybocki, M.A.: Four Principles of Explainable Artificial 3 Intelligence. National Institute of Standards and Technology (NIST), Draft NISTIR 8312 (2020). https://nvlpubs.nist.gov/nistpubs/ir/2020/NIST.IR.8312-draft.pdf

35. Rana, A., Bridge, D.: Explanations that are intrinsic to recommendations. In: Proceedings of the 26th Conference on User Modeling, Adaptation and Personalization (UMAP 2018), pp. 187–195. Association for Computing Machinery, New York (2018). https://doi.org/10.1145/3209219.3209230

36. Riedl, M.O.: Human-centered artificial intelligence and machine learning. Hum. Behav. Emerg. Technol. **1**(1), 33–36 (2019). https://doi.org/10.1002/hbe2.117

37. Shin, D.: The effects of explainability and causability on perception, trust, and acceptance: implications for explainable AI. Int. J. Hum. Comput. Stud. **146**, 102551 (2021). https://doi.org/10.1016/j.ijhcs.2020.102551

38. Shneiderman, B.: Human-centered artificial intelligence: reliable, safe & trustworthy. Int. J. Hum. Comput. Interact. **36**, 495–504 (2020). https://doi.org/10.1080/10447318.2020.1741118

39. Thieme, A., Belgrave, D., Doherty, G.: Machine learning in mental health: a systematic review of the HCI literature to support the development of effective and implementable ML systems. ACM Trans. Comput. Hum. Interact. **27**(5), 1–53 (2020). https://doi.org/10.1145/3398069

40. Tjoa, E., Guan, C.: A Survey on Explainable Artificial Intelligence (XAI): Toward Medical XAI. IEEE Transactions on Neural Networks and Learning Systems (2020). https://doi.org/10.1109/TNNLS.2020.3027314

41. Vilone, G., Longo, L.: Explainable Artificial Intelligence. A Systematic Review (2020). https://www.researchgate.net/publication/341817113_Explainable_Artificial_Intelligence_a_Systematic_Review?_sg=4CYjXm5e8sNuFH0lGWPSYvE2-QB-eBgd4BrN07ImDmZDiit0k9zOOD_AlIZDzj-6piw8Z9titYdYreDW9jNBjibyPQHN7xzOvflGwF0F.LsYxQSmK-Zaw9en1XNnb2ImJVhbXSjogfd5hODIBwBr_zwmp_FPWt9DeFuhYexcY-YPvLvOU8t7W4M8G4XE7GQ

42. van der Waa, J., Nieuwburg, E., Cremers, A., Neerincx, M.: Evaluating XAI: a comparison of rule-based and example-based explanations. Artif. Intell. **291**, 103404 (2021). https://doi.org/10.1016/j.artint.2020.103404

43. Wilson, P.F., Dell, L.D., Anderson, G.F.: Root cause analysis: a tool for total quality management workbook. ASQC Quality Press, New York (1992)

44. Wei, X.: Toward human-centered AI: a perspective from human-computer interaction. Interactions **26**(4), 42–46 (2019). https://doi.org/10.1145/3328485

Toward AI-Based Scenario Management for Cyber Range Training

Jo Erskine Hannay[1]([⊠])(iD), Audun Stolpe[1], and Muhammad Mudassar Yamin[2]

[1] Department of ICT Research, Norwegian Computing Center (NR),
pb. 114 Blindern, 0314 Oslo, Norway
{jo.hannay,audun.stolpe}@nr.no
[2] Department of Information Security and Communication Technology,
Norwegian University of Science and Technology (NTNU),
pb. 191, 2802 Gjøvik, Norway
muhammad.m.yamin@ntnu.no

Abstract. There is an immediate need for a greater number of highly skilled cybersecurity personnel to meet intensified cyber attacks. We propose a cyber range exercise management architecture that employs machine reasoning to structure the design, execution and analysis of cyber range training scenarios. The scenarios are then used in simulation-based training in an emulated IT infrastructure environment. The machine reasoning is obtained by combining four AI methods: attack-defence trees, formal argumentation theory, answer set programming and multiagent systems. We argue that this type of advanced functionality that supports exercise managers in their design and analysis of scenarios is strictly necessary to improve current exercise management systems and build the required cybersecurity expertise.

1 Introduction

We are facing a pronounced cybersecurity workforce shortage and skills gap [11]. According to the recent European Network and Information Security Agency (ENISA) report[1] on cyber-security skills development, there is a 94% increase in cybersecurity job postings in Europe since 2013, and it takes 20% more time to fill those jobs compared to other IT jobs. For the present transformation to a massively digitalized society, this poses major concerns for both economic development and national security. The development of highly effective cybersecurity training frameworks that ensure appropriate cybersecurity skills is therefore a fundamental prerequisite for further safe digital transformation.

We outline a concept for enhancing cyber ranges with AI-based scenario design, execution and analysis tools to ensure an accountable skill-based focus throughout cybersecurity training programs. A cyber range is a training facility

---

[1] https://www.enisa.europa.eu/publications/the-status-of-cyber-security-education-in-the-european-union.

© Springer Nature Switzerland AG 2021
C. Stephanidis et al. (Eds.): HCII 2021, LNCS 13095, pp. 423–436, 2021.
https://doi.org/10.1007/978-3-030-90963-5_32

that comprises or emulates a variable number, sometimes thousands, of computers connected in multiple networks, where attackers, defenders, and benign users are, emulated, simulated or acted out by players [34]. Cyber ranges are key instruments in national cybersecurity strategies.[2] The aim for this research is to increase substantially the capability and capacity of cyber ranges to produce highly skilled cybersecurity professionals.

As an example, the Norwegian Cyber Range (NCR)[3] has a mission to provide cybersecurity training spanning three organizational levels: (1) the strategic level (societal level), where societal services are subject to cyber attacks, and decisions need to be taken at an executive level; (2) the tactical level (digital value chain level), where various parts of a national IT network are affected; (3) the operational level (the infrastructure level), where the focus is on one concrete system, such that technical attack and defence techniques are executed. It is crucial to enhance skills at each level and to coordinate training across levels [13].

It is extremely challenging to design scenarios of sufficient complexity and flexibility on and across organizational levels. The problems that are involved are instances of general challenges for simulation-based training [26] for crisis management, resulting in a lack of structured goal-based planning, a lack of subsequent longitudinal measurements and analyses of training effect and several other antipatterns for effective learning [15,24,30]. Exercise management systems and associated data tend to focus on *what objects and events* to put in a training scenario, with little explicit reference to *what skills* should be trained [16]. It follows that there is *a need to develop tool support for the explicit association between content in a scenario and its intended role in goal-oriented skill-building activities*, where state-of-the-art learning principles, such as *deliberate practice* [12] and *adaptive thinking* [27] are designed in from the start. Moreover, we will argue that the involved complexity calls for tools that utilize machine-reasoning in some form.

2 State of the Art and State of Practice

Substantial research has addressed the fact that configuring a cyber range for a particular training exercise is a tedious, inefficient and error-prone process [4].

2.1 Content Generation

Several solutions have been proposed for making the configuration of cyber ranges more efficient and reliable.

In [6], a method is proposed for automatically generating *capture the flag* (CTF) scenarios, in which participants use cybersecurity tools and techniques to find hidden clues or "flags". The flags represent digital resources over which red and blue teams compete. The red team attempts to capture flags while the blue team attempts to block them. A particular CTF game can be derived from

---

[2] See e.g., https://www.regjeringen.no/contentassets/c57a0733652f47688294934ffd93 fc53/list-of-measures--national-cyber-security-strategy-for-norway.pdf.

[3] https://www.ntnu.no/ncr/.

a template, once requirements have been inserted in the proper places, or it can be assembled from a random combination of well-defined sub-games. Although the latter procedure creates new and unique CTF competition scenarios automatically, the games are not very realistic as they do not support exercises with multiple steps and deeper attack paths.

CTF scenarios were extended in [33] to multi-host, multi-subnet environments with complex attack paths. These scenarios are deployed on the NTNU NCR infrastructure by an automatic orchestration procedure composed of a domain-specific description language connected with the Ansible automation tool.[4] One finding that emerges clearly from this work is that complex (multi-host, multi-subnet) CTF scenarios often do not have a model that is efficiently computable before execution of the game, since the real-time decision-making of the contestants makes the decision tree extremely complex. This hampers skill-oriented scenario design and precludes the *continuous evaluation of goal achievement* that is necessary for deliberate practice.

The *Alpaca* engine [10] is a software library for autogenerating cybersecurity exercises in the form of attack graphs. It is based on a vulnerability database that records pre- and post-exploit conditions for each vulnerability. Complex attack graphs can be composed by chaining these conditions. Of special interest is the use of techniques from AI-planning. However, Alpaca is currently limited to single-host environments. Whilst this can be useful in a limited classroom setting, it is too restrictive for the realistic cross-organizational cybersecurity training necessary for meeting oncoming cyberthreats.

In [32], a mathematical approach to scenario generation was explored, where attack trees—a graphical formalism used to represent the threats to a system in a particular scenario—are automatically inferred from process algebraic specifications. The authors explain how to compute the satisfying models of particular specification, i.e. particular cybersecurity scenarios, by encoding it into a satisfiability modulo theory. This work has a clear interface to AI-planning in Answer Set Programming (ASP). However, the generation procedure in [32] is static (i.e. performed ahead of play), and therefore not designed to support the flexibility needed in scenarios for incremental adaptive thinking.

In a similar vein, [7] proposed a theoretical approach to model *social-technical* attack trees that involve a human element within the information system such as insider threats. Using automated model checking and automata theory, the authors define an algorithm for autogenerating attack trees, and for checking properties that reveal details about the possible interaction between attacker and defender.

Taking stock, the general picture that emerges is one where support for designing cyberthreat scenarios exist for toy examples and mainly at the operational level. There is a focus on automatic configuration of the emulated IT infrastructure [4]. However, tool support for designing skill-targeted scenarios is lacking. Further, [13] states that there is a pressing need for cybersecurity training that spans different organizational levels. For example, [13] uncovered

---

[4] https://www.ansible.com/.

how different actors in an organization (CEO, CISO, CIO) interact with each other while following their own objectives under bounded rationality, manifested by somewhat myopic investment priorities on behalf of the CEO and CIO, and by cost-cutting on behalf of the CISO. As a consequence cybersecurity is very often relegated to supporting business operations, to the detriment of the overall cybersecurity of the organization as such.

2.2   Analysis and Metrics

Timely feedback is a requirement for successful skills development. This relies on gathering targeted information during training, and the generation of salient skill-relevant information has been extremely difficult in practice. Thus, metrics must be integrated with scenario design from the start with methods to generate information during training [9,16].

Some effort on expressing metrics for cybersecurity events has been made in the formalism of *attack-defence trees* (ADTrees) [19]. Quantitative analysis for such trees includes [3], who propose an extension of attack-defence trees in which temporal dependencies among contrary subgoals are expressed as stochastic two-player games. Strategies for attackers or defenders that guarantee or optimize some quantitative property are explored. In earlier work, [2] develop a method for computing the Pareto efficiency for trees with multiple conflicting parameters. Further, [17] explore how stochastic automata can be used to study attack-defence scenarios where timing plays a central role, similar to [7], and [5] develop methods to compute adversarial utility estimation by modelling attack-defence trees as games where attackers and defenders receive rewards or penalties in inversely proportional measures. Finally, [19] combine trees with Bayesian networks to identify probabilistic measures of attack-defence trees with dependent actions.

However, automated skill-based information handling seems to be uncharted territory. Several EU-projects are planning to develop models of skills and competencies, but we are not aware of work studying how qualitative descriptions of skills can steer the scenario generation process in the direction of explicit learning goals.

2.3   Other Relevant Initiatives

CONCORDIA, ECHO, SPARTA and CyberSec4Europe are the four pilot projects of the 2018 Horizon 2020 cybersecurity call and are expected to strengthen the EU's cybersecurity capacity and tackle future cybersecurity challenges for a safer European Digital Single Market.

The aim of the CONCORDIA project is to connect and assist academia and industry for collaboration on *cyber range* technology (definition pending), whence CONCORDIA is involved in the development of cyber ranges for mainly *operational* exercises in several European countries. The generation of learning content in the form of training exercises does not figure prominently.

The ECHO project aims to establish a cybersecurity competence network conceived mainly in terms of organizational and educational concepts. Of particular relevance is the ECHO Multi-sector Assessment Framework which aims to provide a structured method for analysis and development of management processes on all levels. Also of interest is the projected Cyber Skills Reference Model, as it may potentially be used as input to a formal representation of skills.

The CyberSec4Europe project shares with ECHO the emphasis on governance models and emphasizes the need for standardization across the European cybersecurity ecosystem. To that end, CyberSec4Europe is designing, testing and demonstrating potential governance structures for a future European Cybersecurity Competence Network using best practice examples derived from concepts like CERN as well the expertise and experience of partners. CyberSec4Europe is relevant, as its governance model can potentially inform a multilevel organizational perspective (operational, tactical, strategic).

The SPARTA project is in some ways a meta-project insofar as it aims to establish a research and innovation *roadmap* to stimulate the development and deployment of key cybersecurity technologies. Moreover, SPARTA aims to extrapolate a set of best practices from different European cybersecurity certification schemes, and to assess whether these practices are used by agents in the European digital marketplace. SPARTA WP9 is of interest, as it too is concerned with the development of a European Cybersecurity Skills Framework.

In addition, Cyberwiser addresses the educational needs for training at the operational and tactical levels and the ensuant requirements on training environments. Cyberwiser proposes a methodology for designing training exercises based on temporal-logic specifications of system states before and after an exploit. Complex probable attack graphs are formed by combining multiple formally represented vulnerabilities into a single structure. The Cyberwiser scenario design methodology, however, remains a largely manual process.

3   Call for Knowledge

In our view, the above state of affairs entail the following knowledge needs:

KN1: Understanding how to represent component and network configurations, threats, events and actions in design and analysis tools for exercise managers.[5]

---

[5] The term "Exercise Manager" encompasses several roles involved in exercise management that user-facing functionality must support. Cyberwiser (cyberwiser.eu) defines the following: Trainer (TR) – An individual responsible for the design of the scenario and the scenario configuration. Scenario Creator (SC) – An individual responsible for creating the scenario in the platform based on the design provided by trainer. Operator (OP) – An individual responsible for validating and instantiating the scenario. Asset Manager (AM) – An individual responsible for creation and modification Digital Library assets.

KN2: Understanding how such user-facing representations can be used to construct cyberthreat scenarios that are sufficiently complex and flexible for building the required cybersecurity skills.

KN3: Understanding how to translate the user-facing representations under KN1 to machine-processable representations.

KN4: Understanding how to employ machine reasoning for scenario design and analysis.

KN5: Understanding how to realize and execute digital scenarios in an emulated environment.

Together, KN1–KN5 express the need to understand how to map the intent of the exercise manager to a realistic emulation infrastructure.

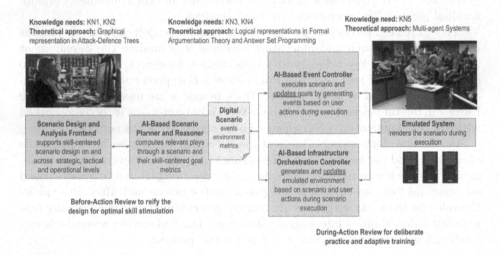

Fig. 1. Architecture for AI-Based Scenario Management for Cyber Range Training (ASCERT).

4   Main Idea

Our approach operationalizes the acquired knowledge in terms of a *reference architecture* for *AI-Based Scenario Management for Cyber Range Training* (ASCERT) depicted in Fig. 1: Activities in response to KN1 and KN2 must give actionable knowledge for constructing scenario design and analysis frontends that enable exercise managers to design and analyze skill-centered training scenarios on and across the three organizational levels. Activities in response to KN3 and KN4 must give actionable knowledge for constructing machine reasoning technology that supports the design and analysis of scenarios. Research to meet KN5 must give guidelines on how to generate content and events in an emulated environment from a digital scenario. The technological components are:

an *AI-based scenario planner and reasoner*, that maintains a digital scenario representation and computes the skill-building consequences of the exercise manager's design (before-action review)

an *AI-based event controller*, that executes the digital scenario, keeps track of partial goal achievement and recomputes new optimal goals according to actual plays through a scenario (during-action review)

an *AI-based infrastructure orchestration controller*, that generates and updates the emulated environment according to how the scenario is played out.

The ASCERT architecture consolidates a structured AI-based approach to cybersecurity training and outlines technical components to realize this approach. We plan to prototype the components using the core machine reasoning formalisms in the next section. Current exercise management systems typically offer a lot of functionality, but based on inadequate technology. In our experience, this demands on-site vendor support throughout an exercise; and in several cases, only the most basic functionality of the system is actually used (e.g., observation tracking, which could equally be done in excel.)

Several trends are changing the way one must think about cybersecurity, making cybersecurity more complex, and therefore, changing the way one must *train* cybersecurity. Continuous product development now demands that software developers, who used to focus on developing the system under development, now also maintain and deploy the parts of the system that they have developed. Increasingly popular, not least in public sector initiatives, this means that a substantially larger number of IT personnel need cybersecurity skills. Moreover, the "work from anywhere" trend, now boosted by the COVID-19 pandemic requires non-IT personnel to have cybersecurity skills with regards to their personal equipment. Further, both trends require cloud-based services for continuous rapid deployment and access, and cloud vulnerabilities are likely to be a target of future attacks. The recent attack on the SolarWinds Orion platform affected a large number of customers globally, including core governmental services and public service infrastructure.[6] In that attack, cybersecurity itself was targeted, in that the threat actors succeeded in manipulating the Orion software to digitally sign a malicious dynamic link library with a legitimate certificate.

Exercise managers who set out to design training scenarios for cloud and platform service vulnerabilities must focus on both organizational and technical complexity. When a specific organization is targeted, it will often try to contain the attack on its own before communicating the event to other organizations or national bodies. This wastes valuable time in platform-wide attacks such as in the SolarWinds Orion case. Training scenarios must therefore be designed to train cybersecurity personnel in the organization, which now include system developers in continuous product development, to recognize and report suspected attacks at the operational level immediately and securely to the organizational (tactical) level and national and international cybersecurity bodies (strategic level), and then to collaborate efficiently across levels in identifying the nature of the attack.

---

[6] https://www.cisecurity.org/solarwinds/.

Using the design and analysis frontend (Fig. 1), exercise managers must be able to set up various operational, tactical and strategic events that drive plays in a scenario forward, and where player actions affect the state of the play and sequence of events favourably or unfavourably, depending on the events and actions played so far. Planning such events, their sequencing and mutual effects and their relative adequacy in training the desired skills is highly complex. The AI-based scenario planner and reasoner computes all viable event sequences according to possible actions, complete with relative scores of adequacy. This analysis can be displayed compactly in, e.g., a sunburst diagram [25], and exercise managers can modify their design to optimize training, if, e.g., the scenario's event sequences are not seen to stimulate skill building sufficiently. Once the scenario has been decided, the infrastructure orchestration controller (Fig. 1) generates the required emulated environment to train in, and the event controller (Fig. 1) effectuates the appropriate scenario event sequences and action responses in the scenario. Both these components communicate action and effects from the emulated environment to the scenario planner and reasoner which recomputes event sequences and goal achievement continuously. In other words, it computes all viable plays and relative scores from that point onward. This generates dynamic scenarios where adaptive behaviour is fostered. This is essential for cybersecurity skill building, and is a substantial improvement on the more or less static exercise scripts that come out of exercise planning tools today.

5   Core Machine Reasoning Formalisms

Our technical approach is based on a triangle of concepts consisting of *attack-defence trees* (ADTrees) [19], *formal argumentation theory* [8] and *AI planning* [21]. The concept of an attack-defence tree is pivotal, since it serves as the principal conceptual and graphical model for training-scenarios in the cyber-security domain. Further, the integration of AI planning with emulated cybersecurity environments will be framed in terms of *multi-agent systems* [20,31]. Figure 1 indicates what part of the architecture each of these three concepts relate to: the human-readable representations is in terms of ADTrees, the machine-readable representations is in terms of Answer Set Programming (ASP), the translation between representations [14] is facilitated by argumentation theory, and the realization in emulated environments is effectuated in multi-agent systems.

5.1   Attack-Defence Trees

An ADTree is a node-labelled rooted tree describing the measures a perpetrator might take to attack the system and the countermeasures open to a defender [19]. The root of the tree represents a competing objective, which, intuitively, is successfully defended if the proponent has an arsenal that counters all the opponents actions. An example is given in Fig. 2. The root node represents the goal to secure (resp. crack) a login password. Dashed arrows represent attacks

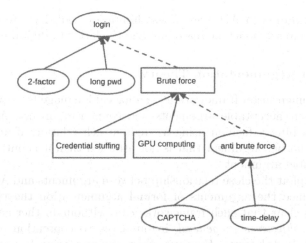

Fig. 2. A password-protection scenario.

and solid arrows represent defensive moves. The *login* node decomposes into two sub-goals, *long password* and *2-factor authentication* as ways of promoting the root goal. The dashed arrow from the *brute force* node indicates that an attacker may attempt to penetrate the system by repeated auto-generated login requests. This offensive move may be amplified by *GPU processing* and countered by e.g. a CAPTCHA. Whether the diagram in Fig. 2 represents an adequate regime for securing a login depends on the relationship between these basic offensive and defensive actions. Whereas a long password may not be enough to secure against a GPU-powered brute force attack, 2-factor authentication generally is. These relationships are specified by the *semantics* of the diagram which determines all successful attacks and defences that the constraints expressed by the diagram allow.

ADTrees function as a necessary convergence point between scientists and practitioners [18]. Scientist can explore the ramifications of a particular security model through the formal semantics of ADTrees, whereas the intuitive graphical nature of ADTrees enables stakeholders to bridge the gap between their diverse backgrounds.

Current Limitations. For our purposes, the theory of ADTrees currently has two limitations. Firstly, the established semantics for ADTrees [19] is an abstract semantics quite removed from logic programming in general and AI planning (see below) in particular. Hence it does not lend itself naturally to automation. Secondly, how to scale the concept of an ADTree to higher-level tactical and strategic scenarios is currently uncharted territory. For instance, when rehearsing tactical decision making, a trainee may be forced to prioritize sub-goals that are mutually exclusive due to *scarce resources*. However, there is currently no mechanism for incorporating resource considerations in a way that *influences the availability of moves* in ADTrees. These limitations will have to be addressed. The former relates to machine reasoning and the latter to digital representation.

5.2   Formal Argumentation Theory

A formal argumentation framework [8] is a logical language for representing and reasoning about acceptable arguments and counterarguments. Arguments are modelled in a binary fashion using a single attack relation: if an argument is attacked by another argument that is not attacked then it is out, hence cannot be an acceptable argument.

We will exploit the close relationship between arguments and ADTrees. More specifically, since the arguments of formal argumentation theory are entirely abstract, it is clear that such frameworks can, without further ado, be applied to *competing objectives in general*, in our case, to contention over computer resources and digital assets. However, most argumentation frameworks are not sufficiently expressive to capture the more general concept of an ADTree since they do not allow for notions such as joint attacks on arguments and explicitly modelled defensive moves. The former shortcoming was addressed in [23], and those results were later incorporated in [14], which also addresses the latter shortcoming. In fact, the stated aim of [14] is to show how ADTrees can be interpreted directly in terms of formal arguments, thus furnishing ADTrees with a argumentation-theoretic semantics.

From our vantage point, the benefits of using argumentation theory as a semantics for ADTrees arises from the fact that argumentation theory is studied as a form of *non-monotonic logic* with well-studied interfaces to logic programming. For instance, there is a known correspondence between acceptable arguments and *stable models* in ASP [8], which is a language that is well-suited for AI planning. Hence, formal argumentation theory has a well understood interface to *both* ADTrees and AI planning.

Current Limitations. There are two, both related to formal semantics: firstly, the semantics of [14] is itself abstract and does not yet have a translation into a particular logic programming formalism, although argumentation theory itself covers a bit of the distance. Secondly, the semantics of [14] is only *partly* declarative as it gives defensive moves an *algorithmic interpretation*. That does not square with the declarative nature of logic programming languages in general. We will therefore need to define the required translation from argumentation theory to ASP and to complete the declarative semantics.

5.3   Answer Set Programming

The basic idea behind ASP [21] is to describe a problem by means of a logic program and use a suitably modified *satisfiability solver* to compute all of its models. These models are called *answer sets* or *stable models*.

ASP has turned out to be a programming paradigm that is very well-suited for AI-planning, a branch of artificial intelligence that aims to compute strategies or action sequences that achieve a stipulated goal. Given a domain description in terms of basic actions and their effects together with a description of a goal-state, the answer set solver works backwards or *abductively* to generate models sequencing actions over time to yield a plan for realizing that goal. We intend to use AI-planning for three interrelated purposes: 1) to auto-generate training scenarios from a selection of goals or learning objectives, 2) to append quantitative information to basic actions in order to compute the performance of a trainee on a given exercise, and 3) to support the trainee during play by providing clues as to how to proceed, if requested, based on adaptive replanning and the heuristics from point 2.

Current Limitations. As yet, there is no study of how to represent and reason about the *skills* that a plan manifests for exercises. We will explore different ways to do this. Our tentative idea is to use a *formal conceptual model*, such as the JRC Cybersecurity Domains Taxonomy[7] or the NICE Framework Competencies,[8] to correlate actions, goals and subgoals with skills.

5.4 Multi-agent Systems

To understand the technical constraints and components needed to map high-level simulation scenarios into low-level realistic emulation infrastructures, the project will employ multi-agent systems simulation techniques [20]. Specifically, we will set out to use ADTrees and ASP as a formalism for modelling the multi-agent system that will be deployed in the technical infrastructure. Possible multiagent architectures include organizational systems empowered by autonomous agents with multifold purposes: Agents will play multiple exercise control roles in the scenario, for example, red team actors generating targeted attacks, media bots that populate media outlets, and benign users interacting with the existing systems and services. Second, the agents will collect required technical logs and events for automatic scoring of the operational teams. We will conduct research that will model and build multi-agent systems that enables the continuous translation of simulation scenarios into operational infrastructures.

Current Limitations. There are existing and standardized approaches to realizing digital plans in simulation environments.[9] For example, high-level digital plans expressing overall positions, movements and goals for entities (objects) can be written in the Coalition Battle Management Language (CBML) [29] and the Military Scenario Definition Language (MSDL) [28]. These plans can then be processed by multi-agent systems [22] to generate realistic movements of objects at lower levels of detail that are then communicated to a simulation environment using the Low-Level Battle Management Language (LBML) [1]. The focus of CBML and MSDL is to specify the entities of a scenario and then to specify

---

[7] https://www.cyberwiser.eu/news/jrc-proposal-european-cybersecurity-taxonomy.
[8] https://csrc.nist.gov/publications/detail/nistir/8355/draft.
[9] https://netn.mscoe.org/netn-modules/simc2.

what those entities should do in realistic manners. There is no way to specify causal relationships between objects or causal actions between objects, and thus no inherent support for machine reasoning. All machine reasoning is therefore relegated to the lower levels, where there is no goal-orientation. Our approach marks a substantial improvement on this. A key question is where to set the boundary between the machine reasoning of AI planning and that of multi-agent systems; in other words, to what extent the multi-agent system should be *passive, active* or *cognitive* [20].

6   Conclusion

The knowledge needs and the architecture presented in this article entail further development of the four formalisms (attack-defence trees, formal argumentation theory, answer set programming and multiagent systems) that we promote. We must investigate added expressiveness to capture both organizational and technical complexity. We must also ensure cohesiveness when designing scenarios across the three organizational levels and when integrating the organizational and technical elements of a scenario. Finally, further development of the formalisms is needed to represent and reason about the skills to be trained in a scenario; in other words, one must develop formal connections between events, actions and skill-driven goals.

Our design thus combines formalisms for AI reasoning and cybersecurity, with an emphasis on the value-chain from AI-supported user-facing support to AI-supported training functionality. This illustrates an integrative whole-product approach, which we argue is necessary to succeed in not only the cybersecurity domain, but also in other domains in which one should utilize cutting-edge AI techniques.

Acknowledgements. The authors are grateful to Bjarte Østvold at the Norwegian Computing Center, Basel Katt at the Norwegian Cyber Range and the referees for comments and insights that helped improve this article.

References

1. Alstad, A., et al.: Low-level battle management language. In: Proceedings of 2013 Spring Simulation Interoperability Workshop (SIW). Simulation Interoperability Standards Organization (2013)
2. Aslanyan, Z., Nielson, F.: Pareto efficient solutions of attack-defence trees. In: Focardi, R., Myers, A. (eds.) POST 2015. LNCS, vol. 9036, pp. 95–114. Springer, Heidelberg (2015). https://doi.org/10.1007/978-3-662-46666-7_6
3. Aslanyan, Z., Nielson, F., Parker, D.: Quantitative verification and synthesis of attack-defence scenarios conference. In: 29th IEEE Computer Security Foundations Symposium, CSF 2016, pp. 105–119. IEEE Computer Society (2016)
4. Beuran, R., Tang, D., Pham, C., Chinen, K.I., Tan, Y., Shinoda, Y.: Integrated framework for hands-on cybersecurity training: CyTrONE. Comput. Secur. **78**, 43–59 (2018)

5. Buldas, A., Lenin, A.: New efficient utility upper bounds for the fully adaptive model of attack trees. In: Das, S.K., Nita-Rotaru, C., Kantarcioglu, M. (eds.) GameSec 2013. LNCS, vol. 8252, pp. 192–205. Springer, Cham (2013). https://doi.org/10.1007/978-3-319-02786-9_12

6. Burket, J., Chapman, P., Becker, T., Ganas, C., Brumley, D.: Automatic problem generation for capture-the-flag competitions. In: 2015 USENIX Summit on Gaming, Games, and Gamification in Security Education (3GSE 2015) (2015)

7. David, N., et al.: Modelling social-technical attacks with timed automata. In: Proceedings of 7th ACN CCS International Workshop on Managing Insider Security Threats, pp. 21–28 (2015)

8. Dung, P.M.: On the acceptability of arguments and its fundamental role in non-monotonic reasoning, logic programming and n-person games. Artif. Intell. **77**(2), 321–357 (1995)

9. Durlach, P.J.: Can we talk? Semantic interoperability and the synthetic training environment. In: Proceedings of Interservice/Industry Training, Simulation, and Education Conference (I/ITSEC) 2006. National Training and Simulation Association (2018). Paper no. 18093

10. Eckroth, J., Chen, K., Gatewood, H., Belna, B.: ALPACA: building dynamic cyber ranges with procedurally-generated vulnerability lattices. In: Proceedings of 2019 ACM Southeast Conference, pp. 78–85 (2019)

11. Endicott-Popovsky, B.E., Popovsky, V.M.: Application of pedagogical fundamentals for the holistic development of cybersecurity professionals. ACM Inroads **5**(1), 57–68 (2014)

12. Ericsson, K.A.: An introduction to Cambridge Handbook of Expertise and Expert Performance: its development, organization, and content. In: Ericsson, K.A., Charness, N., Feltovich, P.J., Hoffman, R.R. (eds.) The Cambridge Handbook of Expertise and Expert Performance, chap. 1, pp. 3–20. Cambridge University Press (2006)

13. Fitzgerald, T.: Clarifying the roles of information security: 13 questions the CEO, CIO, and CISO must ask each other. Inf. Syst. Secur. **16**(5), 257–263 (2007)

14. Gabbay, D.M., Horne, R., Mauw, S., van der Torre, L.: Attack-defence frameworks: argumentation-based semantics for attack-defence trees. In: Eades III, H., Gadyatskaya, O. (eds.) GraMSec 2020. LNCS, vol. 12419, pp. 143–165. Springer, Cham (2020). https://doi.org/10.1007/978-3-030-62230-5_8

15. Grunnan, T., Fridheim, H.: Planning and conducting crisis management exercises for decision-making: the do's and don'ts. EURO J. Decis. Process. **5**, 79–95 (2017)

16. Hannay, J.E., Kikke, Y.: Structured crisis training with mixed reality simulations. In: Proceedings of 16th International Conference on Information Systems for Crisis Response and Management (ISCRAM), pp. 1310–1319 (2019)

17. Hermanns, H., Krämer, J., Krčál, J., Stoelinga, M.: The value of attack-defence diagrams. In: Piessens, F., Viganò, L. (eds.) POST 2016. LNCS, vol. 9635, pp. 163–185. Springer, Heidelberg (2016). https://doi.org/10.1007/978-3-662-49635-0_9

18. Hong, J.B., Kim, D.S., Chung, C.J., Huang, D.: A survey on the usability and practical applications of graphical security models. Comput. Sci. Rev. **26**, 1–16 (2017)

19. Kordy, B., Mauw, S., Radomirović, S., Schweitzer, P.: Attack-defense trees. J. Logic Comput. **24**(1), 55–87 (2014)

20. Kubera, Y., Mathieu, P., Picault, S.: Everything can be agent! In: Proceedings of Ninth International Joint Conference on Autonomous Agents and Multi-Agent Systems (AAMAS 2010), pp. 1547–1548 (2010)

21. Lifschitz, V.: What is answer set programming? In: Proceedings of 23rd National Conference on Artificial Intelligence, AAAI 2008, vol. 3, pp. 1594–1597. AAAI Press (2008)
22. Løvlid, R.A., Bruvoll, S., Brathen, K., Gonzalez, A.: Modeling the behavior of a hierarchy of command agents with context-based reasoning. J. Defense Model. Simul. Appl. Methodol. Technol. 15(4), 369–381 (2018)
23. Nielsen, S.H., Parsons, S.: A generalization of Dung's abstract framework for argumentation: arguing with sets of attacking arguments. In: Maudet, N., Parsons, S., Rahwan, I. (eds.) ArgMAS 2006. LNCS (LNAI), vol. 4766, pp. 54–73. Springer, Heidelberg (2007). https://doi.org/10.1007/978-3-540-75526-5_4
24. Pollestad, B., Steinnes, T.: Øvelse gjør mester? Master's thesis. University of Stavanger, Department of Media and Social Sciences (2012). In Norwegian
25. Rouwendal van Schijndel, D.K., Stolpe, A., Hannay, J.E.: Using block-based programming and sunburst branching to plan and generate crisis training simulations. In: Stephanidis, C., Antona, M. (eds.) HCII 2020. CCIS, vol. 1226, pp. 463–471. Springer, Cham (2020). https://doi.org/10.1007/978-3-030-50732-9_60
26. Salas, E., Wildman, J.L., Piccolo, R.F.: Using simulation-based training to enhance management education. Acad. Manage. Learn. Educ. 8(4), 559–573 (2009)
27. Shadrick, S.B., Lussier, J.W.: Training complex cognitive skills: a theme-based approach to the development of battlefield skills. In: Ericsson, K.A. (ed.) Development of Professional Expertise, chap. 13, pp. 286–311. Cambridge University Press (2009)
28. Simulation Interoperability Standards Organization: SISO-STD-007-2008 - Standard for Military Scenario Definition Language (MSDL) (2008)
29. Simulation Interoperability Standards Organization: SISO-STD-011-2014 - Standard for Coalition Battle Management Language (C-BML) Phase 1, Version 1.0 (2014)
30. Skarpaas, I., Kristiansen, S.T.: Simulatortrening for ny praksis: Hvordan simulatortrening kan brukes til å utvikle hærens operative evne. Technical report, Work Research Institute (2010). In Norwegian
31. Uhrmacher, A.M., Weyns, D.: Multi-Agent Systems: Simulation and Applications. CRC Press, Boca Raton (2009)
32. Vigo, R., Nielson, F., Nielson, H.R.: Automated generation of attack trees. In: Proceedings of 2014 IEEE 27th Computer Security Foundations Symposium, pp. 337–350. IEEE (2014)
33. Yamin, M.M., Katt, B.: Modeling attack and defense scenarios for cyber security exercises. In: Proceedings of 5th Interdisciplinary Cyber Research Conference, pp. 7–16 (2019)
34. Yamin, M.M., Katt, B., Gkioulos, V.: Cyber ranges and security testbeds: scenarios, functions, tools and architecture. Comput. Secur. 88, 101636 (2020)

A Situation Awareness Perspective on Human-Agent Collaboration: Tensions and Opportunities

Jinglu Jiang[1], Alexander J. Karran[2], Constantinos K. Coursaris[2(✉)],
Pierre-Majorique Léger[2], and Joerg Beringer[3]

[1] Binghampton University, Binghampton, NY, USA
jingluj@binghamton.edu
[2] HEC Montréal, Montréal, Canada
{alexander-john.karran, Constantinos.Coursaris,
pierre-majorique.leger}@hec.ca
[3] BlueYonder, Scottsdale, AZ, USA
Joerg.Beringer@blueyonder.com

Abstract. The rise of automation and artificial intelligence within the organization has come with many benefits. However, in conjunction with these benefits have come various concerns related to user empowerment (e.g., over-reliance, loss of human agency, lack of trust). Human-Computer Interaction researchers are seeking ways to address these concerns by informing user interface and task design. However, an overarching framework providing a holistic perspective is needed to guide such effort. We propose that for the intelligent agents to be utilized optimally within the organization, a contextual perspective is needed to capture various factors related to the user, task, technology, and environment, which can inform the value proposition of human-agent collaboration in the organization. To this end, we propose a situation awareness (SA) approach as a promising lens, which would in turn promote a human-centered artificial intelligence design and development perspective. This paper introduces the theoretical basis for SA and discusses three major tensions and the associated opportunities for developing SA in human-agent collaboration.

Keywords: Human-machine teaming · Human-agent collaboration · Situation awareness · Autonomy · Complexity · Automation · Confidence · Uncertainty · User empowerment

1 Introduction

Modern manufacturing, logistics, and high technology industries have evolved to become distributed computing platforms and information environments comprised of both human and intelligent computer agents. We present a working definition of intelligent agents (IAs) as "software entities varying in the level of autonomy within a larger socio-technical system" (hereafter, IA and agent are used interchangeably). The development of IAs has afforded a level of automation and rapid integration of artificial intelligence methods, which includes the ability for environmental sensemaking and

© Springer Nature Switzerland AG 2021
C. Stephanidis et al. (Eds.): HCII 2021, LNCS 13095, pp. 437–444, 2021.
https://doi.org/10.1007/978-3-030-90963-5_33

decision-making in the pursuit of a priori specified goals and sociality. Not surprisingly, individuals and organizations can benefit from such automation and gain a better understanding and projection of the task, processes, and environment (i.e., situation awareness). However, increasing reliance on IAs, perhaps ironically, may lead to reduced organizational and human situation awareness through a steep increase in uncertainty and system complexity, which is characterized by a lack of knowledge, agency (i.e., having the power to act and control), and trust (i.e., a positive use-relationship with a technology). Human-computer interaction researchers are seeking ways to reduce the potential negative impacts by informing task and user interface design [1].

We propose that for IAs to be utilized optimally within the organization, a contextual perspective is needed to provide the keys factors that may potentially impact the value proposition of IA for organizations concerning human-agent collaboration. This collaboration context may be characterized along four dimensions: (1) User: Human users' acceptance and utilization of the IA; (2) Task: Balancing the need for user control and IA automation; (3) Technology: Performance of the IA; and (4) Environment: Facilitating conditions for human-agent collaboration. Specifically, we propose a situation awareness (SA) approach [2] so that each of these factors should contribute to the development of SA for both system users and the organization at large. This paper discusses aspects of the theoretical basis for SA – using SA as a lens to explain human information processing during human-agent collaboration. We propose that SA is a promising theoretical angle to understand user empowerment and related contextual factors, including workload, engagement, and trust, in such collaborations. We further discuss the tensions and opportunities for developing SA in human-agent collaboration.

2   Theoretical Background: Endsley's Three-Tier Model of SA and Distributed SA

Defined as "the perception of the elements in the environment within a volume of time and space, the comprehension of their meaning, and the projection of their status in the near future" (p. 1, [2]), SA demonstrates how system operators process information and comprehend situations to achieve task goals. The state of SA reflects the extent of a user's perception, comprehension, and projection of elements related to the context that they aim to understand. To this end, SA as a state of knowledge is distinct from the processes required to achieve and maintain that state, which is referred to as situation assessment. Endsley's [2] SA model consists of three tiers, and each tier deals with the human factors associated with the current and future state of information within a dynamic system: *Level 1 SA*–perceiving the status, attributes, and dynamics of elements in the environment. *Level 2 SA*–synthesis of the attributes and elements identified within tier 1, emphasizing how the operator assigns significance to those elements to achieve their goals. *Level 3 SA*–the ability to project future actions of the elements by combining the knowledge of the situation gained from tiers 1 and 2. The three-tier model highlights the temporal nature of the knowledge embedded in the environment and systems – the elements in the environment are developing and changing over time and are not exclusively related to the current operation. Similarly, SA can be highly spatial and directly related to the operating environment (e.g., vehicular activities on land or in the sky).

It should be noted that SA referred solely to human situational awareness when it was originally defined, and SA has since become an essential factor when designing operator interfaces, automation concepts, and training programs [3]. However, considering the dynamics in human-machine collaboration, SA in individuals may not be sufficient to explain the new hierarchies brought by non-human agents. Concepts like team SA and shared SA have been proposed to explain group-level information processing and decision-making [4, 5]. While these concepts all focus on human teams, we posit that human-agent collaboration involves coordination and collaboration between human actors and non-human agents so that the agent performs like a collaborator and can have its own SA[1]. This view has been well echoed in the extant literature on distributed SA (DSA) [6], which views SA as an emergent property of a dynamic, collaborative system. SA emerges from the interaction and movement of information between elements of the system and not only within the perceptual and cognitive frameworks of individual human operators working within that system.

SA plays a significant role here to facilitate such a collaborative process. When IAs get involved in the process, a high level of automation and control might entitle these agents to become active collaborators of human users, and a common picture needs to be built to support joint operations and decision-making [7]. An SA-oriented design has been proposed to serve this purpose so that the information needs to be shared across domains and organized carefully to be compatible with members' goals [8]. Specifically, SA is expected to play a vital role in user empowerment through several conduits: first, empowerment grants users the motivation and right to adapt to various situations and roles, which can also bring extra responsibilities and task demands for users, hindering their task performance [9]. A successful SA-oriented design should alleviate such negative impacts by prioritizing the information, augmenting decision making, and thus reducing the mental demand [8]. Second, trust is critical for empowered users to perform collaboration. While the environment often involves uncertainty and vulnerability, which inhibits trust [10], an SA-oriented design emphasizes transparency, which reduces information uncertainty and enhances automation reliability to facilitate trust [11]. Third, SA contributes to task engagement and performance by allocating attention to the most relevant information and prioritized task goals. An SA-oriented design implements information filtering and alarming mechanisms to make critical cues more salient, which helps users pay more attention to the relevant information [8].

3 Developing SA in Human-Agent Collaboration

In a collaborative environment, the development of SA is influenced by various factors such as individual goals and skills, task complexity, and system design [12]. The extant literature has proposed various SA-oriented design principles to enhance SA development, which can be categorized into three major aspects: (1) interface design aiming

---

[1] We do not assume the level of automaticity of non-human agents. Non-human agents can simply be tools used by humans, and thus no active coordination is initiated by those agents. However, the agent can also be highly automated and perform active decision-making.

at a better visualization of the relevant information; (2) task representation design aiming at better integrating the task with the system procedure; and (3) implementation of various forms of automation [8]. Each aspect has its own challenges and opportunities. This section discusses three major tensions that we believe an SA-oriented design should consider for better human-agent collaboration.

3.1 Managing Uncertainty and Establishing Confidence

One of the significant tensions for complex socio-technical systems is how to efficiently present the information while allowing users to understand the situational uncertainty and build confidence in the information presented. Information uncertainty encompasses various aspects, such as ambiguity, low probability, and high complexity [13], which inhibits users' comprehension and projections of the situation. Although IAs have their technical mechanisms to perceive and integrate information to generate system knowledge, end-users rely on interface knowledge to build SA [14]. When converting system knowledge to interface knowledge, the agent and the user need to manage or reduce such uncertainties to establish confidence actively.

One of the most straightforward strategies for reducing uncertainty is to enhance agent transparency by providing more information, often with decision aids such as presenting thresholds, decision paths, and potential conflict resolutions [15]. Empirical evidence has shown that high agent transparency significantly improves SA at all three levels [16, 17]. Various types of agent transparency have been investigated, such as process transparency (i.e., display detailed process information), automation transparency (i.e., explain automation modes), reasoning transparency (i.e., explain the reasoning), and uncertainty transparency (i.e., display uncertainty information) [16, 18, 19]. The situation awareness-based agent transparency (SAT) model and its extensions provide an overarching guideline for improving transparency from the SA perspective [18]. However, the extent to which reducing uncertainty can help improve decision-making confidence in human-agent collaboration is largely unknown.

3.2 Balancing Real Complexity and Perceived Complexity

Task or process complexity is at the heart of human-agent collaboration. Complexity works against SA since it reduces users' ability to absorb relevant information among the various threads of information available in the system. Although complexity cannot be entirely avoided, an SA-oriented design has an inherent goal to better manage the complexity. The extant literature has investigated various elements that may contribute to different levels of *real* complexity. For example, system components, features, objects, the interdependence of these components, and predictability of the dynamics contribute to system complexity [20, 21]. Operational complexity (or process complexity) is often associated with users' tasks and goals since they determine the information flow [22]. Apparent complexity is often related to interface designs, which involves to what extent the interface can map the system function into a meaningful representation, the density of the information on the display, and the number of actions the user has to perform to fulfill the task goals [20, 23].

On the other hand, perceived complexity concerns how users deal with complexity through their mental model and experience with the system [24]. A good SA-oriented design should be consistent with users' mental models. However, in many situations, novice users may not have a mature mental model, and thus designing a system to fit existing mental models becomes practically impossible. Building a good mental model and reducing perceived complexity is more difficult when the intelligent agent is characterized by high system complexity, operational complexity, and apparent complexity because more components and interdependencies are involved. Hence, a tradeoff exists between choosing the extent of real complexity to present to users and managing the perceived complexity experienced by them. Empirical evidence has shown that presenting information regarding environment complexity to users can enhance SA; however, when the presented information is too dynamic, SA decreases [25]. Task complexity (e.g., more complex teleoperation tasks) also influences SA in a curvilinear way such that a tipping point exists for users to maintain SA and task performance [26, 27]. It is recommended that the system avoid feature creep and clearly map the system functions to users' goals and mental models [8]. By doing so, it becomes easier for users to understand how the system works and connect it to their task goals. Users can also build their mental models by grouping information based on SA requirements and task goals, which is helpful to reduce perceived complexity.

3.3 Merits and Pitfalls of Automation

Automation has significantly influenced how humans collaborate with intelligent agents [28]. Whereas many people believe that automation can enhance task performance and reduce the need for SA, the reality often shows the opposite. Automation may bring unexpected errors and degrade users' knowledge and skills, ultimately harming SA and task performance [29, 30] – it appears that automation may not always be beneficial. It is critical to note that automation can be applied to a broad range of initiatives. For example, [31] proposed that four types of tasks can be automated, including monitoring the information, generating options, selecting the option(s) to employ, and carrying out the actions. Different types of automation and the factors associated with their implementation may significantly impact SA and task performance. Moreover, since automation often adds complexity to the system, it becomes more difficult for users to understand what the system is doing and its rationale, which hinders level 2 and level 3 SA. As a result, users may not trust the system, and they may spend more effort to ensure system compliance, resulting in increased mental workload, perceived complexity, and system resistance [30, 32]. Consequently, when, where, and how to automate processes has become an issue of ever-increasing importance in research and industry. Despite the number of studies on this topic, the question of how best to apply automation in human-technology interaction tasks is still the subject of much theoretical research [33, 34].

4 Discussion and Conclusion

Given the ever-increasing interest in human-agent collaboration research in the era of artificial intelligence, we introduce the SA perspective as a promising approach to understand user empowerment and the contextual factors that may either impede or promote the optimal utilization of intelligent agents within an organization. We propose that developing SA is essential in effective human-agent collaboration to achieve organizational goals. However, considering the complexity and dynamics embedded in the socio-technical system where humans and agents interact, an SA-oriented design requires various tradeoffs regarding interface knowledge presentation, task representation, and automation implementation. We discussed three major tensions, highlighting the underexplored opportunities for future research in this area.

The three tensions – enhancing decision confidence under high uncertainty, reducing perceived complexity while real complexity is high, and mitigating the negative impacts when the system is increasingly automated – speak to the current debate regarding agent autonomy versus human agency. The rise of automation and AI within organizations has come with many benefits, such as the offloading of smaller, more repetitive tasks, quick decision making, and extended systems functions. However, in conjunction with these benefits has come a loss of human agency, such as reduced control, displacement, and impaired cognitive and social skills. The main driver of this loss is not automation *per se* but rather the nature of the automation that is being applied, how humans interact with the automated process [35], and the increased number and type of agents required to realize the goals of a system [36]. It has been argued that systems design that places humans in a supervisory role of the automated processes may not be sufficient. Humans suffer vigilance decrements over time, leading to signal detection errors [37], experience skill atrophy due to over-reliance [38], and become unaware of critical features of the systems they oversee [39], which leads to a lack of trust and underutilization of critical system resources. We consider SA to be a core mechanism that has the potential to address these issues. If SA can be developed during human-agent collaboration – which we consider a symbiotic gestalt characterized by a respective co-evolution – new ways of working may arise, which help increase human agency while reducing the concerns of agent automony, resulting in greater levels of trust and increased productivity.

Acknowledgments. The authors would like to thank Blue Yonder Inc for its collaboration and funding along with the NSERC-PROMPT Industrial Research Chair in UX.

References

1. Bennett, K.B., Flach, J.: Ecological interface design: thirty-plus years of refinement, progress, and potential. Hum. Factors **61**(4), 513–525 (2019)
2. Endsley, M.R.: Toward a theory of situation awareness in dynamic systems. Hum. Factors **37**, 32–64 (1995). https://doi.org/10.1518/001872095779049543
3. Endsley, M.R.: Theoretical underpinnings. Situation awareness analysis and measurement **1** (2000)

4. Salas, E., Prince, C., Baker, D.P., Shrestha, L.: Situation awareness in team performance: implications for measurement and training. Hum. Factors **37**(1), 123–136 (1995)
5. Saner, L.D., Bolstad, C.A., Gonzalez, C., Cuevas, H.M.: Measuring and predicting shared situation awareness in teams. J. Cognit. Eng. Decis. Mak. **3**(3), 280–308 (2009)
6. Stanton, N.A., et al.: Distributed situation awareness in dynamic systems: theoretical development and application of an ergonomics methodology. Ergonomics **49**(12–13), 1288–1311 (2006). https://doi.org/10.1080/00140130600612762
7. Panganiban, A.R., Matthews, G., Long, M.D.: Transparency in autonomous teammates: intention to support as teaming information. J. Cognit. Eng. Decis. Mak. **14**(2), 174–190 (2020). https://doi.org/10.1177/1555343419881563
8. Endsley, M.R.: Designing for situation awareness: an approach to user-centered design. CRC Press (2016)
9. Chan, K.W., Lam, W.: The trade-off of servicing empowerment on employees' service performance: examining the underlying motivation and workload mechanisms. J. Acad. Mark. Sci. **39**(4), 609–628 (2011)
10. Lee, J.D., See, K.A.: Trust in automation: designing for appropriate reliance. Hum. Factors **46**, 50–80 (2004). https://doi.org/10.1518/hfes.46.1.50_30392
11. Beller, J., Heesen, M., Vollrath, M.: Improving the driver-automation interaction: an approach using automation uncertainty. Hum. Factors **55**(6), 1130–1141 (2013). https://doi.org/10.1177/0018720813482327
12. Salmon, P.M., Stanton, N.A., Jenkins, D.P.: Distributed situation awareness: theory, measurement and application to teamwork (2017)
13. Dequech, D.: Uncertainty: a typology and refinements of existing concepts. J. Econ. Issues **45**(3), 621–640 (2011)
14. Endsley, M.R., Garland, D.J.: Situation awareness analysis and measurement. CRC Press (2000)
15. Bradac, J.J.: Theory comparison: uncertainty reduction, problematic integration, uncertainty management, and other curious constructs. J. Commun. **51**(3), 456–476 (2001)
16. Kunze, A., Summerskill, S.J., Marshall, R., Filtness, A.J.: Automation transparency: implications of uncertainty communication for human-automation interaction and interfaces. Ergonomics **62**(3), 345–360 (2019). https://doi.org/10.1080/00140139.2018.1547842
17. Rajabiyazdi, F., Jamieson, G.A.: A review of transparency (seeing-into) models. In: 2020 IEEE International Conference on Systems, Man, and Cybernetics (SMC), 11–14 Oct. 2020, pp. 302–308 (2020)
18. Chen, J.Y.C., Lakhmani, S.G., Stowers, K., Selkowitz, A.R., Wright, J.L., Barnes, M.: Situation awareness-based agent transparency and human-autonomy teaming effectiveness. Theor. Issues Ergon. Sci. **19**(3), 259–282 (2018). https://doi.org/10.1080/1463922X.2017.1315750
19. Stowers, K., Kasdaglis, N., Rupp, M.A., Newton, O.B., Chen, J.Y.C., Barnes, M.: The IMPACT of agent transparency on human performance. IEEE Trans. Hum. Mach. Syst. **50**(3), 245–253 (2020). https://doi.org/10.1109/thms.2020.2978041
20. Windt, K., Philipp, T., Böse, F.: Complexity cube for the characterization of complex production systems. Int. J. Comput. Integr. Manuf. **21**(2), 195–200 (2008)
21. Tegarden, D.P., Sheetz, S.D., Monarchi, D.E.: A software complexity model of object-oriented systems. Decis. Supp. Syst. **13**(3–4), 241–262 (1995)
22. Sivadasan, S., Efstathiou, J., Calinescu, A., Huatuco, L.H.: Advances on measuring the operational complexity of supplier–customer systems. Eur. J. Oper. Res. **171**(1), 208–226 (2006)
23. Liu, P., Li, Z.: Task complexity: a review and conceptualization framework. Int. J. Ind. Ergon. **42**(6), 553–568 (2012)

24. Li, K., Wieringa, P.A.: Understanding perceived complexity in human supervisory control. Cogn. Technol. Work **2**(2), 75–88 (2000)
25. Habib, L., Pacaux-Lemoine, M., Millot, P.: Human-robots team cooperation in crisis management mission. In: 2018 IEEE International Conference on Systems, Man, and Cybernetics (SMC), 7–10 Oct. 2018, pp. 3219–3224 (2018)
26. Cummings, M.L., Guerlain, S.: Developing operator capacity estimates for supervisory control of autonomous vehicles. Hum. Factors **49**(1), 1–15 (2007)
27. Mansikka, H., Virtanen, K., Harris, D.: Dissociation between mental workload, performance, and task awareness in pilots of high performance aircraft. IEEE Trans. Hum. Mach. Syst. **49** (1), 1–9 (2019). https://doi.org/10.1109/thms.2018.2874186
28. Prangnell, N., Wright, D.: The robots are coming. In: Deloitte Insight (2015)
29. Smith, P.J., Baumann, E.: Human-automation teaming: unintended consequences of automation on user performance. In: 2020 AIAA/IEEE 39th Digital Avionics Systems Conference (DASC), 11–15 Oct. 2020, pp. 1–9 (2020)
30. Miller, D., Sun, A., Ju, W.: Situation awareness with different levels of automation. In: 2014 IEEE International Conference on Systems, Man, and Cybernetics (SMC), 5–8 Oct. 2014, pp. 688–693 (2014)
31. Endsley, M.R., Kaber, D.B.: Level of automation effects on performance, situation awareness and workload in a dynamic control task. Ergonomics **42**(3), 462–492 (1999)
32. Hjälmdahl, M., Krupenia, S., Thorslund, B.: Driver behaviour and driver experience of partial and fully automated truck platooning – a simulator study. Eur. Transp. Res. Rev. **9**(1), 1–11 (2017). https://doi.org/10.1007/s12544-017-0222-3
33. Parasuraman, R., Sheridan, T.B., Wickens, C.D.: A model for types and levels of human interaction with automation. IEEE Trans. Syst. Man Cybernet. Part A: Syst. Hum. **30**, 286–297 (2000). https://doi.org/10.1109/3468.844354
34. Villaren, T., Madier, C., Legras, F., Leal, A., Kovacs, B., Coppin, G.: Towards a method for context-dependent allocation of functions. In: Proceedings of the 2nd Conference on Human Operating Unmanned Systems (HUMOUS 2010) (2010)
35. Berberian, B.: Man-machine teaming: a problem of agency. IFAC-PapersOnLine **51**(34), 118–123 (2019)
36. Kaber, D.B., Endsley, M.R.: The effects of level of automation and adaptive automation on human performance, situation awareness and workload in a dynamic control task. Theor. Issues Ergon. Sci. **5**(2), 113–153 (2004)
37. Molloy, R., Parasuraman, R.: Monitoring an automated system for a single failure: vigilance and task complexity effects. Hum. Factors **38**(2), 311–322 (1996)
38. Ruskin, K.J., Corvin, C., Rice, S.C., Winter, S.R.: Autopilots in the operating room: safe use of automated medical technology. Anesthesiology **133**(3), 653–665 (2020)
39. Endsley, M.R.: Automation and situation awareness. In: Automation and Human Performance: Theory and Applications, pp. 163–181. CRC Press (2018)

Roles of Artificial Intelligence and Extended Reality Development in the Post-COVID-19 Era

Chutisant Kerdvibulvech[1(✉)] and Zhao Yang Dong[2]

[1] Graduate School of Communication Arts and Management Innovation, National Institute of Development Administration, 118 SeriThai Rd., Klong-chan, Bangkapi, Bangkok 10240, Thailand
`chutisant.ker@nida.ac.th`
[2] School of Electrical Engineering and Telecommunications, University of New South Wales, High St. Kensington, Sydney, NSW 2052, Australia
`joe.dong@unsw.edu.au`

Abstract. This paper explores recent roles of artificial intelligence and extended reality development during the coronavirus pandemic and then predicts their significant roles in the post-COVID-19 era in an interdisciplinary manner. To begin with, we investigate roles of artificial intelligence in tackling coronavirus during the outbreak since 2020 until today. It has been effectively used for many ways, such as forecasting the spread of COVID-19 on multimodal data using data analytics, preliminary diagnosis the virus disease from specific symptoms using machine learning, and analyzing big data from social media platforms to accurately prevent the spread of virus. At the same time, due to rapid advancement in recent immersive technology and extended reality is a very popular research topic in computer science, we discuss roles of extended reality which has been extensively used during the virus outbreak for various purposes, such as supporting for businesses and education and helping the medical and health care workers. For instance, it can used for supporting psychological recovery from medical treatment for virus patients, reducing the face-to-face interactivity of physicians with the symptomatic patients, and helping people with the use of telemedicine. Next, we present a new summary of integrated roles of artificial intelligence and extended reality development in the post-COVID-19 era in an interdisciplinary perspective. Moreover, we suggest possible directions of artificial intelligence in extended reality which can be used to guide the design of the next-generation human-computer interaction applications in the future.

Keywords: Extended reality · Virtual reality · Augmented reality · Artificial intelligence · COVID-19 · Post-COVID-19 · Machine learning · Data analytics

1 Introduction

Since early 2020, the coronavirus disease 2019, usually and shortly called COVID-19, outbreak has become a critical impact on population human health, human wellbeing, and economic hardship worldwide. The world has been in pandemic mode for more

© Springer Nature Switzerland AG 2021
C. Stephanidis et al. (Eds.): HCII 2021, LNCS 13095, pp. 445–454, 2021.
https://doi.org/10.1007/978-3-030-90963-5_34

than a year. According to the Worldometers report as of March 2021, the world confirmed 123 million cases and 2.7 million of them passed away. USA, which is found to be the world's most impacted country, confirmed 30.4 million cases and 0.55 million of them were died. There are 11.8 million confirmed cases and 0.29 million deaths in Brazil which is the second most coronavirus-affected country on earth. Similarly, India is found to be the third worst impacted country at 11.5 million confirmed cases and 0.159 deaths. Because of the enormous impact of this outbreak around the world, medical research efforts have been globally underway to develop and discover vaccines to protect against infectious disease. At the same time in the multidisciplinary world, computer science-based research efforts have also been utilized to tackle this disease and help supporting medical works. In this paper, our main contribution is to explore recent roles of computer science development in the COVID-19 era and then predict their essential roles in the post-COVID-19 era in an interdisciplinary manner. We focus on two main computer science fields: artificial intelligence and extended reality, which are usually interconnected to each other. In fact, there was previously a work presented and discussed for the development of artificial intelligence and augmented reality technologies since the approximately beginning of coronavirus pandemic in 2020, as investigated by Kerdvibulvech and Chen [1]. Nevertheless, this paper focuses on recent roles of artificial intelligence and extended reality development for dealing with the COVID-19 from the beginning of coronavirus outbreak to now, and then predicts their essential roles in the post-COVID-19 era. This paper is divided into five sections as follows. Section 1 gives an overall introduction to this paper. Next, Sect. 2 discusses about artificial intelligence development for COVID-19. After this, Sect. 3 explores extended reality development for this coronavirus pandemic. Section 4 investigates the roles of artificial intelligence and extended reality together and attempts to forecast the future of these related-fields in the post-COVID-19 era. Ultimately, Sect. 5 gives a conclusion of this paper.

2   Artificial Intelligence Development for COVID-19

To begin with, artificial intelligence has been primarily considered as an important role in tackling COVID-19 during the early outbreak since 2020. It has been effectively used for many benefits. Their benefits are divided by us into three main categories in this paper: forecasting the spread of COVID-19, preliminary diagnosis the virus disease, and analyzing big data from social media platforms to prevent the spread of coronavirus.

First, artificial intelligence has been applied for forecasting the spread of coronavirus. For example, it has been used for predicting the spread of coronavirus on multimodal data using data analytics, as presented by Santosh in [2]. Machine learning algorithms are used for building a tool to analyze data and cognitive processes (decision-making). This tool has active learning-based cross-population test and train models which are based directly on multitudinal and multimodal data to examine if different types of data can help yield accurate results during the COVID-19 pandemic. They suggested that we do not have to necessarily wait for the total datasets for training, validating, and testing the models. But, in parallel with other processes, it is suggested that each artificial intelligence-driven tool can be used since the beginning of data collection. Also, a similar research for attempting to forecast the total number of COVID-19 infected cases was achieved by Al-qaness et al. [3]. In their work, a predictive model based on adaptive neuro-fuzzy inference method is built for calculating the number of coronavirus infected people in the next ten days using the past infected datasets. Similarly, Yahya et al. [4] also constructed a forecast model using three presented neural networks and a geographic information system (GIS) environment to predict coronavirus separation by using the public data reported by the Ministry of Health in Iraq. Their three artificial neural networks are nonlinear autoregressive-network with exogenous inputs (NARX), Fuzzy c-means (FCM), and radial basis-function (RBF). It is reported to be able to get a performance accuracy rate of 91.6%. They suggest improving the results by incessantly gathering confirmed cases and using more data from distance locations, such as suburbanized villages and remote districts in central the provinces of Iraq. Their aim is to help preparing suitable quarantine zones and selecting the appropriate medical needs based on the forecast of infected cases.

Second, artificial intelligence has been utilized for preliminary diagnosis the virus disease. For instance, it has been used for diagnosis the COVID-19 from cough samples using a smartphone application called AI4COVID-19 [5], built by Imran et al., that can send three seconds cough sounds to an artificial intelligence agent and give a quick prediction back within several minutes. Their research is challenging because cough can be a symptom of so many non-coronavirus related medical conditions, and therefore it is not easy to make the diagnosis of a coronavirus infection by this symptom alone. Their next challenge is about the cough training data shortage of coronavirus disease. In this way, they explore the clarity of pathomorphological changes in the ventilatory system caused by the coronavirus disease if measured against other ventilatory infections. To solve the cough training dataset inadequacy of coronavirus disease, they utilize transfer learning and then implement a multipronged mediator centered danger-averse architecture for supporting the artificial intelligence algorithm. A similar research for detecting and predicting of coronavirus diagnosis based on clinical signs and symptoms using machine learning was also presented by Zoabi et al. [6]. Their purpose is to help medical workers in prioritizing patients effectively, and therefore it can improve clinical priorities and facilitate optimized management of limited resources. They train from 51,831 tested individuals of 4,769 cases were confirmed for positive coronavirus results, while they use the test dataset containing from the following week which are 47,401 tested individuals of 3,624 cases were confirmed for positive coronavirus results by using the real infection data revealed by the Ministry of Health in Israel. A predictive method for detecting coronavirus cases by basic attributes is then built using basic questions gathered based on eight basic attributes: gender, age 60 years and/or older, revealed physical contact with a patient confirmed to have coronavirus, and the characteristic of five primary signs (i.e., cough, sore throat, shortness of breath, fever, and headache). Similarly, a method using artificial intelligence to use chest computed tomography detections with primary signs, exposure history screening, and testing in laboratory to quickly detect coronavirus diagnosis patients was also proposed by Mei et al. [7]. In their experiment, 46.3 percent tested positive for coronavirus by reverse transcriptase polymerase chain reaction

(RT-PCR) assay in real-time and next generation sequencing reverse transcriptase polymerase chain reaction based on a total of 905 tested patients. Among a test set of 279 cases, their artificial intelligence method is reported to be able to get an AUC of 0.92 which is sensitively similar to a medical expert in this field.

Third, artificial intelligence can be applied to analyze big data from social media platforms to prevent the spread of virus. This kind of technology can be used to seek the truths from the overabundance of disinformation in many popular social media sites (such as Twitter and Telegram) and even trusted sources, as described by Luengo-Oroz et al. [8]. More specifically, sentiment analysis, fact checking, and audience analysis for the coronavirus pandemic can be done and achieved by using machine learning algorithms. Arora et al. [9] gave a good review of artificial intelligence in curbing spread of distorted information from social media platforms during the coronavirus pandemic. There are several social media platforms that are usually used together for analysis with artificial intelligence, such as Twitter and Telegram. Here, we start with Twitter. Khan et al. [10] presented a system which analyzes the tweets automatically for sentiment analysis of Twitter coronavirus data. Their system can categorize the tweets into three different sets: neutral, negative, and positive. By using natural language processing and automata, they can accurately predict quantization and give the sentiment analysis about the reaction of people towards the decisions made if by the local authorities or the central government through this social media platform during the coronavirus outbreak. Because they can identify sentiment analysis and Twitter's trends, they can give correct information and help eliminating the distort information from this social media platform. A similar research about Twitter using machine learning for COVID-19 was also developed by Samuel et al. [11]. In their work, public sentiment in the United States using coronavirus tweets and R-computing software is identified. After that, the effectiveness in classifying tweets of modifying lengths about the virus are compared. For short tweets according to their experiments, it is reported to be able to get a high classification accuracy rate of 91 percent. Also, for Twitter about COVID-19, Gupta et al. [12] presented a machine learning-based labelled dataset on expressions and responses of 20 million users received from more than 132 million tweets publicly between 28 January 2020 and 1 January 2021. By using emotion analytic and natural language processing, each tweet is labelled with semantic attributes, such as the intensity of joy, of anger, of fear, and of sadness emotions. The temporal distributions and descriptive statistics of reactions to coronavirus worldwide about the latent topic, sentiment and emotion attributes are then reported. In addition, Pierri et al. [13] monitored conversations on Twitter in Italy about coronavirus vaccines from 1.8 million tweets online between the end of 2020 and the beginning of 2021 with a mean of 30 thousand tweets shared in each day. From their study, a regular amount of low-credibility information and/or misinformation about COVID-19 vaccines can be continuously found on Twitter. Next, another social media platform used for analysis with artificial intelligence during the coronavirus outbreak is Telegram. Franchini et al. [14] built a system, called Doing Risk sElf-assessment and Social health Support for COVID, quickly called Dress-COV, using Telegram instantly messaging robot on cloud that sends communications through cloud's servers securely. Their research purpose is to create a link between the tool and the user for modeling the dataset to evaluate potential danger of coronavirus infection and expanding complications to develop the personal empowerment of individual using this social media platform. Therefore, by analyzing big data from social media platforms both Twitter and Telegram, it is possible to identify the forceful escalation of verbal attacks which can finally lead to physical violence against some specific communities, such as Asian Americans in the United States, as described by Tessler et al.'s work [15]. Asian-Americans were targeted in the United States during the pandemic in almost 4,000 hate incidents in 2020. In early 2021, six Asian women among eight people were killed in shootings at three Georgia-area spas in the United States. Rather than analyzing big data from social media platforms during the coronavirus outbreak, artificial intelligence can help building smart warning systems by analyzing big data from social media platforms to prevent the spread of virus and then providing useful suggestions about the safety issues.

3 Extended Reality Development for COVID-19

Rather than artificial intelligence, another technology that is usually interconnected to artificial intelligence and is utilized to deal with the COVID-19 pandemic is extended reality. At the same time, due to rapid advancement in recent immersive technology, extended reality is a very popular research topic in computer science. This is because it allows human-machine interactions built by computer technology and wearable devices, even though people are in different locations or socially distant, as proposed by Kerdvibulvech and Guan [16]. It has been extensively used during the coronavirus outbreak for various purposes. Their benefits are divided by us into two main categories in this paper: supporting for businesses and education during COVID-19 and helping the medical and health care workers.

First, extended reality has been applied for supporting for businesses and education during the spread of COVID-19. For example, it has been utilizing for reviving tourism industry in a unique way using extended reality because this coronavirus has stopped people from travelling enormously for more than a year. Kwok and Koh [17] investigated how the coronavirus outbreak could possibly be the much-needed force for extended reality's significant direction in the tourism industry using Schumpeter's innovation theory. Their aim is to clarify how extended reality can change the tourism industry and generally give implications for related stakeholders. Sustainable competitive advantage is expected when applying this immersive technology in the tourism sector. Next, Mohanty et al. [18] gave a systematic exploration for understanding the importance of extended reality, focusing on augmented reality, for helping to reopen the tourism industry after the coronavirus outbreak. Thematic content analysis is used to find how extended reality can help dealing with the problems when reopening the tourism industry. Interestingly, their research suggests that current norms (lower mobility and social distancing) are still going to be kept, although the coronavirus will be fully contained in the future. Thus, web-based augmented reality and mobile augmented reality are needed to make sure that people in the tourism industry are safe, personalized, and accessible in memorably immersive experiences. Furthermore, this immersive technology has been applied to support education. Moreover, Bruschi et al. [19] explained a framework that uses a digital learning environment, called start@unito, to support online teaching in higher education during the coronavirus outbreak. Their aim is to understand how much teaching in higher education is eased through the start@unito model. Also, Nesenbergs et al. [20] gave a systematic umbrella review of using extended reality, both virtual reality and augmented reality, for remote higher education during the impact of coronavirus pandemic. In their study, they use papers explaining the utilization of extended reality in distant learning and their impact on learning outcomes for higher education in the Web of Science and Scopus databases. For supporting education in a different way, Puspasari et al. [21] also implemented an augmented reality-based system for supporting cultural education at the SMB II Museum in Indonesia during the coronavirus outbreak. Their system allows people to see the virtual collection in the museum, and at the same time understand the traditional details of each virtual collection remotely and safely.

Second, extended reality has been utilized for helping the medical and health care workers for dealing with the new virus disease. For instance, it has been utilizing for supporting psychological recovery from seriously medical treatment for virus patients using virtual reality. A COVID-19 intensive care unit-specific virtual reality, shortly called ICU-VR, is built by Vlake et al. [22] to cure coronavirus patients. In their work, they suggest that virtual reality can potentially improve mental rehabilitation, and then it should be determined by physicians for the medication of intensive care unit-related mental damage even after coronavirus. Next, it has been applied for reducing the physical face-to-face communication of physicians with the symptomatic patients and connecting people remotely, as proposed by Ponti et al. [23]. Also, this immersive technology can help people with the utilization of telemedicine and virtual care to minimize exposure to protect and support medical frontlines and/or patients, such as dealing with the burden of neurological diseases during the virus outbreak using virtual care explained by Appireddy et al. [24] and treatment of patients during the virus crisis remotely presented by Anthony Jnr. [25, 26].

4   Artificial Intelligence and Extended Reality in the Post-COVID-19

Since coronavirus vaccines, such as the Moderna vaccine, the Pfizer–BioNTech vaccine, and the Oxford–AstraZeneca vaccine, have been available in many countries in early 2021, the situation of coronavirus pandemic seems generally to be better compared to the active confirmed cases in 2020, especially in Israel, United States, and United Kingdom. For example, according to Rosen et al.'s work [27], Israel which has a population of slightly more than 9.32 million, had administered about 11.0 doses per 100 people as of the end of 2020. The vaccination deployment of the coronavirus vaccines has been successful quickly and highly in Israel. Then, the world starts to focus on recovering from the economic impact of the virus outbreak, connecting people virtually, inexpensively, and safely, and returning to the new normal. However, as stated in the previous section, Mohanty et al. [18] studies that current activities during the COVID-19 outbreak, such as lower mobility and social distancing, will continue in the future, even though the virus is vaccinated successfully and fully. Even though the coronavirus can be significantly contained, we predict that some current norms, including maintaining social distancing, wearing facial masks, and cleaning hands thoroughly with alcohol-based solutions, will never disappear. Because of these inconveniences, people will decide to use a tool applying artificial intelligence in extended reality to make their lives more convenient. Also, because of the economic impact of the virus outbreak, people will decide to use integrated technologies that can save money in their pockets. These possibly include online learning/meeting in education and telemedicine in hospital using artificial intelligence and extended reality which can save time and reduce some fixed costs, such as transportation fee. For this reason, we believe that the applications of artificial intelligence in extended reality are expected to become a great tool to deal with these challenges. While artificial intelligence methods are used for forecasting the spread of new disease, preliminary diagnosis the virus, and analyzing big data from social media platforms to prevent the spread of unknown disease, extended reality applications can help supporting for businesses and education and helping the medical and health care workers.

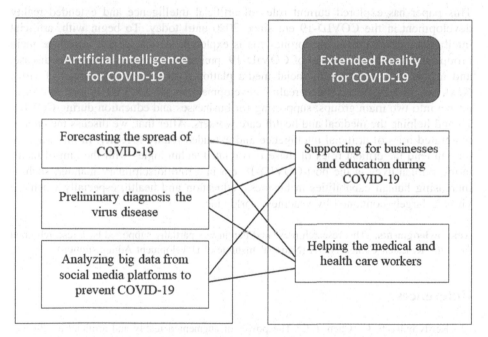

Fig. 1. Overall diagram of artificial intelligence and extended reality which each benefit is integrated crossly in the post-COVID-19

In the post-COVID-19 era, we believe that these two technologies should be crossly applied to solve some specific pain points or problem areas in common in a more interdisciplinary perspective. Figure 1 illustrates our crossly integrated overall diagram of artificial intelligence and extended reality in the post-COVID-19. On the one hand, a machine learning-based algorithm for forecasting the spread of new disease will be used in the extended reality-based application for supporting learning and teaching in lower and higher education, such as the strategic plan on distance learning and agility redesign of post-COVID-19 education described by Ahmad et al. in [28]. On the other hand, an artificial intelligence-based algorithm for preliminary diagnosis the unknown virus will be used in the virtual reality application for helping the medical and health care workers. Alternatively, a deep learning-based framework for analyzing big data from social media platforms to deal with the new disease can crossly be applied in the mobile augmented reality system for supporting small and medium-sized enterprises, such as in the hospitality business and industry. In other words, it has the potential to use the applications of artificial intelligence in extended reality can reduce cost of business virtually and remotely. Besides, we suggest using of big and thick data analytics to refine the challenges of the artificial intelligence-based applications in extended reality, such as their robustness and cost.

5   Conclusion

This paper has explored current roles of artificial intelligence and extended reality development in the COVID-19 era since 2020 until today. To begin with, artificial intelligence development for coronavirus is explored. We categorize into three main groups: forecasting the spread of COVID-19, preliminary diagnosis the virus disease, and analyzing big data from social media platforms to prevent the spread of virus. Next, we investigate extended reality development in the COVID-19 era. We categorize into two main groups: supporting for businesses and education during COVID-19 and helping the medical and health care workers. After that, we discuss the crossly integrated roles of artificial intelligence and extended reality together. In this way, we recommend the critical roles of these two related-technologies with the aim of facilitating human lives in the post-COVID-19 era in a multidisciplinary manner, such as increasing human capabilities in business, education and health, especially when the virus is largely contained by vaccines worldwide.

Acknowledgments. This research presented herein was partially supported by a research grant from the Research Center, NIDA (National Institute of Development Administration).

References

1. Kerdvibulvech, C., Chen, L.L.: The power of augmented reality and artificial intelligence during the Covid-19 Outbreak. In: Stephanidis, C., Kurosu, M., Degen, H., Reinerman-Jones, L. (eds.) HCII 2020. LNCS, vol. 12424, pp. 467–476. Springer, Cham (2020). https://doi.org/10.1007/978-3-030-60117-1_34
2. Santosh, K.C.: AI-driven tools for coronavirus outbreak: need of active learning and cross-population train/test models on multitudinal/multimodal data. J. Med. Syst. **44**(5), 1–5 (2020)
3. Al-qaness, M.A.A., Ewees, A.A., Fan, H., Abd El Aziz, M.: Optimization method for forecasting confirmed cases of COVID-19 in china J. Clin. Med. **9**(3), 674 (2020). https://doi.org/10.3390/jcm9030674

4. Yahya, B.M., Yahya, F.S., Thannoun, R.G.: COVID-19 prediction analysis using artificial intelligence procedures and GIS spatial analyst: a case study for Iraq. Appl. Geomatics **13**(3), 481–491 (2021). https://doi.org/10.1007/s12518-021-00365-4

5. Imran, A., Posokhova, I., Qureshi, H.N., et al.: AI4COVID-19: AI enabled preliminary diagnosis for COVID-19 from cough samples via an app. Inform. Med. Unlocked **100378**, 1–31 (2020)

6. Zoabi, Y., Deri-Rozov, S., Shomron, N.: Machine learning-based prediction of COVID-19 diagnosis based on symptoms. npj Digit. Med. **4**(3), 1–5 (2021). https://doi.org/10.1038/s41746-020-00372-6

7. Mei, X., et al.: Artificial intelligence-enabled rapid diagnosis of COVID-19 patients. medRxiv : the preprint server for health sciences (2020). https://doi.org/10.1101/2020.04.12.20062661

8. Luengo-Oroz, M., Hoffmann Pham, K., Bullock, J., et al.: Artificial intelligence cooperation to support the global response to COVID-19. Nat. Mach. Intell. **2**, 295–297 (2020)

9. Arora, N., Banerjee, A.K., Narasu, M.L.: The role of artificial intelligence in tackling COVID-19. Future Virology, vol. 15, no. 11, November 2020

10. Khan, R., Shrivastava, P., Kapoor, A., Tiwari, A., Mittal, A.: Social media analysis with AI: sentiment analysis techniques for the analysis of twitter covid-19 data. J. Critical Rev. **7**(9), 2761–2774 (2020)

11. Samuel, J., Ali, G.G., Rahman, M., Esawi, E., Samuel, Y.: Covid-19 public sentiment insights and machine learning for tweets classification. Information **11**(6), 314 (2020)

12. Gupta, R., Vishwanath, A., Yang, Y.: COVID-19 Twitter Dataset with Latent Topics, Sentiments and Emotions Attributes. Inter-university Consortium for Political and Social Research [distributor], Ann Arbor, MI (2020). https://doi.org/10.3886/E120321V5

13. Francesco, P., Silvio, P., Marco, B., Stefano, C.: VaccinItaly: monitoring Italian conversations around vaccines on Twitter. CoRR abs/2101.03757 (2021)

14. Franchini, M., et al.: Shifting the paradigm: the dress-cov telegram bot as a tool for participatory medicine. Int. J. Environ. Res. Public Health **17**(23), 8786 (2020)

15. Tessler, H., Choi, M., Kao, G.: The anxiety of being asian american: hate crimes and negative biases during the COVID-19 pandemic. Am. J. Crim. Justice **45**(4), 636–646 (2020). https://doi.org/10.1007/s12103-020-09541-5

16. Kerdvibulvech, C., Guan, S.-U.: Affective computing for enhancing affective touch-based communication through extended reality. In: Misra, S., et al. (eds.) ICCSA 2019. LNCS, vol. 11620, pp. 351–360. Springer, Cham (2019). https://doi.org/10.1007/978-3-030-24296-1_29

17. Kwok, A.O.J., Koh, S.G.M.: COVID-19 and Extended Reality (XR), Current Issues in Tourism, July 2020. https://doi.org/10.1080/13683500.2020.1798896

18. Mohanty, P., Hassan, A., Ekis, E.: Augmented reality for relaunching tourism post-COVID-19: socially distant, virtually connected. Worldwide Hospitality Tourism Themes **12**(6), 753–760 (2020)

19. Bruschi, B., Marchisio, M., Sacchet, M.: Online teaching in higher education with the support of Start@Unito during Covid-19 pandemic. In: Agrati, L.S., et al. (eds.) HELMeTO 2020. CCIS, vol. 1344, pp. 187–198. Springer, Cham (2021). https://doi.org/10.1007/978-3-030-67435-9_15

20. Nesenbergs, K., Abolins, V., Ormanis, J., Mednis, A.: Use of augmented and virtual reality in remote higher education: a systematic umbrella review. Educ. Sci. **11**(1), 8 (2021). https://doi.org/10.3390/educsci11010008

21. Puspasari, S., Suhandi, N., Iman, J.N.: Augmented reality development for supporting cultural education role in SMB II museum during Covid-19 pandemic. In: 2020 Fifth International Conference on Informatics and Computing (ICIC), Gorontalo, Indonesia, pp. 1–6 (2020). https://doi.org/10.1109/ICIC50835.2020.9288619

22. Vlake, J.H., van Bommel, J., Hellemons, M.E., Wils, E.J., Gommers, D., van Genderen, M. E.: Intensive Care Unit-Specific Virtual Reality for Psychological Recovery After ICU Treatment for COVID-19; A Brief Case Report. Front Med (Lausanne) (2021)

23. De Ponti, R., Marazzato, J., Maresca, A.M., Rovera, F., Carcano, G., Ferrario, M.M.: Pre-graduation medical training including virtual reality during COVID-19 pandemic: a report on students' perception. BMC Med. Educ. 20(1), 332 (2020). https://doi.org/10.1186/s12909-020-02245-8

24. Appireddy, R., Jalini, S., Shukla, G., Boissé, L.L.: Tackling the burden of neurological diseases in canada with virtual care during the COVID-19 pandemic and beyond. Can J. Neurol. Sci. 47(5), 594–597 (2020). https://doi.org/10.1017/cjn.2020.92

25. Anthony Jnr, B.: Use of telemedicine and virtual care for remote treatment in response to COVID-19 pandemic. J. Med. Syst. 44(7), 132 (2020). https://doi.org/10.1007/s10916-020-01596-5

26. Bokolo, A.J.: Exploring the adoption of telemedicine and virtual software for care of outpatients during and after COVID-19 pandemic. Irish J. Med. Sci. 190(1), 1 (2020). https://doi.org/10.1007/s11845-020-02299-z

27. Rosen, B., Waitzberg, R., Israeli, A.: Israel's rapid rollout of vaccinations for COVID-19. Isr J. Health Policy Res. 10, 6 (2021). https://doi.org/10.1186/s13584-021-00440-6

28. Ait Si Ahmad, H., El Kharki, K., Berrada, K.: Agility of the post COVID-19 strategic plan on distance learning at cadi ayyad university. An opportunity towards a total digital transformation of the university. In: Agrati, L.S., et al. (eds.) HELMeTO 2020. CCIS, vol. 1344, pp. 199–213. Springer, Cham (2021). https://doi.org/10.1007/978-3-030-67435-9_16

Digital Coaching System for Real Options Analysis with Multi-expert and Machine Learning Support

Jani Kinnunen[1], Mikael Collan[2,3], Irina Georgescu[4(✉)], and Zahra Hosseini[5]

[1] Åbo Akademi University, Turku, Finland
jani.kinnunen@abo.fi
[2] Lappeenranta-Lahti University of Technology, Lappeenranta, Finland
mikael.collan@lut.fi
[3] VATT Institute for Economic Research, Helsinki, Finland
[4] Bucharest University of Economics, Bucharest, Romania
irina.georgescu@csie.ase.ro
[5] Tampere University, Tampere, Finland
zahra.hosseini@tuni.fi

Abstract. Digitalization and artificial intelligence are growing in importance as parts of decision-support tools in various application domains. One of the important developments in this vein has been the creation of interactive tools for coaching users of complex decision-support systems to help them successfully and correctly use the said systems. This paper focuses on digital coaching in the context of strategic investment analysis, specifically connected to fuzzy real options analysis (ROA). We present some important and difficult choices connected to ROA and discuss how digital coaching may assist users in better using ROA tools. We illustrate the real-world use of digital coaching in the contexts of cash-flow evaluation with machine learning support and aggregation of cash-flows from multiple experts. The discussion and the cases illustrate well how digital coaching can make a difference, especially for an inexperienced user, in guiding users to use complex tools correctly and in creating better circumstances for credible analyses. The findings presented are new and contribute specifically to the literature on digital coaching and real options analysis.

Keywords: Digital coaching · Real options · Decision-support · Machine learning · Strategic investments

1 Introduction

With the growth of digitalization and access to the Internet in all areas of life, people's expectations toward learning and receiving information have changed, they expect to be serviced also in the digital environment in ways akin to what they are accustomed to in the physical realm. This issue is relevant also in education and coaching, where on-line education and digital coaching systems have emerged. Opposed to simply transmitting information, sophisticated digital learning- and digital coaching environments

C. Stephanidis et al. (Eds.): HCII 2021, LNCS 13095, pp. 455–473, 2021.
https://doi.org/10.1007/978-3-030-90963-5_35

aim to provide interactive services that both guide the user/learner in addition to informing her. This research concentrates on digital coaching and for the purposes of this research we define digital coaching as interactive services that guide or teach the user of digital systems to use the system better and to make better decisions based on the outputs from the system.

Klaassen et al. (2013, 2016) suggest some requirements for effective digital coaching system including understanding the user status, knowledge of relevant context information, teaching or assisting the user, and motivating the user. Mezei et al. (2020) define five important functions in the context of digital coaching including: mental support, exercise programs, goal setting, feedback, and social functionality. The researchers employ fuzzy-set qualitative comparative analysis for analyzing combinations of these five dimensions understand the users' opinions. They found exercise programs and goal setting functionality to be more important than feedback and social functionality.

One of the so far "strong" fields in which previous academic literature has described digital coaching to take place is the context of health and wellbeing (Klaassen et al. 2013, Kettunen et al. 2019, Harmelink et al. 2017, Stara et al. 2020). Topman et al. (2004) have developed the website titled Study Support to deal with students' procrastination, which mostly relates to anxiety, depression, or more severe forms of psychopathology in academic environment. They present several tools to offer consulting services to students. In another study, Kari and Rinne (2018) believe the potential and novelty of digital coaching in the context of sports and wellness technology and present digital coaching through numbers and graphs providing feedback from individuals. Digital coaching has further applied to assist diabetic Type I patients and Klaassen et al. (2013) present a digital coaching platform to increase self-management of their disease and suggested for helping patients with chronic condition.

Novic (2019) draws a future with artificial intelligence and digital coaching and believes that digital services are taking place in the market because of the growth of demand for psychotherapy & self-development. Artificial intelligence facilitates digital coaching through motivational and inspirational apps, develop social skills, nutrition coaching, psychotherapy coaching, and leadership coaching (Novic 2019).

Here we concentrate on how digital coaching can be used in the realm of corporate decision-making, to guide users of decision support systems (DSS) towards better use of the said systems and towards better understanding the results from the systems. Carlsson (2018a, 2018b, 2019a, 2019b) is among the first to discuss digital coaching in the context of DSS and observes that digital coaching is a way to help decision-makers better analyze options and to facilitate including option logic-based thinking in decision making under uncertainty and dynamic conditions. Kinnunen and Georgescu (2021) discussed the intuitive fuzzy real options models as a good modelling option to be integrated to a digital coaching system for strategic investments. They argued using examples with a center-of-gravity (CoG) fuzzy pay-off model that the fuzzy pay-off model family allows easy-to-learn modelling, which lowers the expertise requirements for a user, while also making coaching simpler. This research builds on the ideas of Carlsson (2018a, 2019a) and uses the most general CoG model discussed in Kinnunen and Georgescu (2021) and puts flesh on the bones of a digital coaching system by identifying some of the most important practical issues where coaching solutions add value. In this vein, this research concentrates on digital coaching connected to software-assisted real option valuation. To the best of our knowledge, this paper is the first to list various specific tasks, for which digital coaching systems can provide assistance in the context of real option valuation. As such we contribute to the grounds for further development of digital coaching systems in the context of investment analysis and specifically real option valuation. We also provide two illustrative examples of how digital coaching can assist a decision-maker/real option valuation system user in better using the system and in better understanding how real option valuation works. This research contributes both to literature on digital coaching and real option valuation and has also real-world practical relevance for designers of real option valuation systems.

The next section introduces real options analysis shortly and presents various "targets" for digital coaching in the context of real option valuation. Section three presents two digital coaching examples for real option valuation. Section four summarizes the findings and draws conclusions based on the research presented.

2   Real Options Analysis and Digital Coaching

Real options analysis (ROA) is using option logic in analyzing real-world situations that exhibit option-like characteristics, often called "managerial flexibility", such as the ability, but not the obligation, to wait before starting a project, the ability to change how a project functions (e.g., altering inputs/outputs), the ability to change the size of a project (expand/contract), and/or to abandon a project (walk away). Such opportunities or real options are valuable, because they may be used to alter the cash-flows from a project in a way that is beneficial to the holder of the said optionality, because of the inherent value real options are important in situations that carry uncertainty about the future. When real options are connected to or embedded in investments the value they have should be taken into consideration, when the value of the investments is analyzed – hence the answer to the question why real option valuation is of importance.

The origins of real option valuation (ROV) take us back to the 1970's, when Stuart Myers (Myers 1977) first coined the term real options in the context of growth opportunities and corporate liabilities. The idea back then was to use the Black-Scholes option pricing formula for valuation of real options (Black and Scholes 1970), something that we now know is not without challenges. Cox et al. (1979) discussed using binomial option valuation for real options already in 1979. Later on, real option valuation with simulation-based tools (Boyle 1977) and Datar and Mathews (2004) and based on fuzzy logic (Savolainen et al. 2017, 2016) have brought the valuation away from the valuation of financial options and relaxed many of the strict assumptions connected to the earlier used models. This development of the models used in valuation of real options and the changes in the types of situations in which valuation can credibly take place with the different models has not only been positive for users of real option valuation models but has also brought with it the problem of having to choose between many models – choice that may be decisive in determining the validity of the outputs from the analysis (Collan et al. 2016).

Moreover, there are multiple different types of real options that require different types of real option valuation methods, for example valuing the flexibility to wait before making the investment decision requires a different kind of model than making the choice between a technology that make it possible to mothball and then restart a mining operation and a technology that does not allow this flexibility. Understanding the different models and choosing a right model for the type of real option being valued is pivotal in being able to creates sensible analysis results. For more information about the various real option types, we refer the interested reader to see the books by Trigeorgis (1985), Brach (2003), and de Neufville and Scholtes (2011).

Furthermore, the different constructs of the various methods used in real option valuation, including the different variables and parameters used in the models, make for a rather hard to interpret landscape that certainly can look intimidating for a manager not well versed in the history of real options valuation, but with a will and a want to value real options in her organization. It is in this context that digital coaching has a potentially very high value in guiding the manager to make good choices on many levels of real option valuation – starting from selecting a suitable model for the task at hand up until the interpretation of the obtained results.

Next, we go through and describe some of the (difficult) choices and decisions that have to be made when starting from a scratch with real option valuation that may be facilitated by a digital coaching (system) designed for supporting ROV. The following list of nine choices is not exhaustive; we have rather lifted important "high level" issues that all contain many details that are left outside the scope of this research.

Choice 1. Identifying the type of uncertainty surrounding the real option:

- *Problem description:* What is the type of uncertainty that surrounds the valuation situation? The type of uncertainty that surrounds the valuation situation determines the models that can be used for valuation. If a model with a bad fit is chosen, the results may be irrelevant and lead to bad decisions.
- *Coaching solution:* Digital coach helps identify the type of uncertainty underlying the valuation-situation. Both help in correctly making observations that help identification and tool to help determining the type of uncertainty.

Choice 2. Identifying the type of real option to be valued:

- *Problem description:* What is the type of real option that is being valued? The type of real option determines the set of usable ROV methods. Using an incorrect method may cause results to be unusable. Types of real options include, for example, the option to wait or learn, the option to shut-down and restart, and the option to switch inputs or outputs – all of which require a different kind of logic to solve the valuation problem.
- *Coaching solution:* Digital coaching can be used to establish the type and subtype of real option under analysis and to select a suitable method.

Choice 3. Selection of ROV model to be used:

- *Problem description:* Which technically suitable ROV model to use to perform the valuation? Many models may be usable under a given type of uncertainty for a given type of real option. Which model is the most suitable for the type of valuation situation (e.g., deep analysis/quick and dirty)

- *Coaching solution:* The combination of real option type and underlying uncertainty limit the choice of suitable models. With specifying questions, a digital coaching system can help pinpoint the best method.

Choice 4. Cash-flow estimation:

- *Problem description:* How should the cash-flows be correctly estimated? Should a single stream of cash-flows be used, or does the use of two, three, four, or five cash-flow scenarios add value to the valuation?
- *Coaching solution:* By determining the actual valuation needs a digital coaching system may guide the user to choose a suitable number of cash-flows to be estimated

Choice 5. Estimation of single-period cash-flows:

- *Problem description:* How to estimate a single cash-flow and development over time? Composing cash-flows from sub-components, or by direct estimation and keeping the relationship between given single cash-flows within the borders of rationality determine the reliability and validity of valuations; estimating the development of future cash-flows assuming linear growth rate(s) or cyclical development (e.g. for 5 or 10 years period).
- *Coaching solution:* Digital coaching system can guide the user to "stay rational" in cash-flow estimation by checking cash-flows against other given estimates and, e.g., against cash-flows given for similar investments in the past; support can be given by suggesting the user to consider a cyclical development and/or using ranges instead of single estimates in a high-uncertainty situation.

Choice 6. Consolidating cash-flow estimates from multiple experts:

- *Problem description:* How to consolidate multiple cash-flow estimates for a single cash-flow from multiple experts? When multi-expert estimation is used to generate plausible cash-flow estimates, the way the estimates are aggregated is a non-trivial problem. Depending on the case, loss of minima / maxima may be an undesirable outcome, while other times the centroid value may be of most importance. Choosing the aggregation correctly directly affects the valuation results.
- *Coaching solution:* Digital coaching system can present the user with various aggregation methods and guide the user in choosing the aggregation that is the most relevant for the case at hand.

Choice 7. Cost-revenue cash-flow relationship (min-max):

- *Problem description:* How to correctly choose the relationship between cost and revenue cash-flows when multiple scenarios are used? When multiple cash-flow scenarios are used and cost and revenue cash-flows are separated it is important that the relationship between, e.g., minimum costs and maximum revenues is correctly considered, because the free cash-flows used in valuation depend on this relationship. Errors in judging the relationship may cause remarkable errors in valuation.

- *Coaching solution:* Digital coaching system can present the issue to the user and guide the user to choose the correct relationship between cost and revenue cash-flows. The corresponding changes in calculations can be automated or the user can be instructed on how they must be carried out.

Choice 8. Estimation of parameter values:

- *Problem description:* Estimation of parameter values How to choose correct parameter values for valuation? Some ROV methods have parameters that determine how the models work. Choosing the parameter values correctly helps create relevant and reliable results, while randomly or incorrectly selected parameter values deteriorate reliability and validity of results.
- *Coaching solution:* Digital coaching system can help the user understand what different parameter values mean in terms of their effect on the results, e.g., with examples and guide the user to set parameter values based on, e.g., historical parameter values derived from relevant data and/or from previously used parameter values.

Choice 9. Interpreting the results:

- *Problem description:* Interpreting the resultsWhat ROV results mean and what they do not mean in terms of actions? The answers from ROV follow a different from the well-known net present value logic, this may cause problems in understanding what they mean. Also, when using fuzzy logic based and simulation-based methods the results commonly include a distribution of outcomes that represent the risks involved. Interpreting the results correctly in terms of actions they point to is paramount in being able to reach desired results.
- *Coaching solution*: Digital coaching systems can extract "simple truths" from the results by using if-then rules built from option logic. A system can guide the user´s attention to relevant (critical) issues, such as the risks and the potential the value project has and the relationship between the single number net present value and the ROV. Importantly, the system can remind the user of the assumptions made that underlie the results.

As seen above, many rather difficult, but possible to solve choices come up in every real option valuation task and for each valuation case these choices must be made separately. Interestingly, one can observe that a certain learning or "machine learning" aspect exists for a digital coaching system that may be constructed around real option valuation – past valuations may be used in providing examples of how choices have been made previously in similar cases. One can take the choices made for a given valuation case as a "profile" of that case and match it with previous valuations for support. This obviously means having an archive of previous valuations for the purpose; such an archive may be constructed within an organization using a ROV system and a connected digital coaching system may utilize it. Other interesting aspects of research relevance arise from the above observations, such as the fact that an organization with a large archive that in effect serves as an organizational memory and captures the knowledge of the system users of an organization may even create some added advantages in terms of the organizational ability to better value real options and investments in general, as a consequence. These issues are however left outside the scope of this research.

In the next section we present two examples of digital coaching. The selected examples are based on a fuzzy real option valuation method and thus refer to a situation, where the choice of the model used has already been made.

3 Examples of Digital Coaching Support

We present two examples of how the digital coach supports fuzzy real option valuation of an investment. The key motivations for the digital coaching may be formulated as follows (cf. Kinnunen and Georgescu 2021):

1. a too complex and changing investment environment for an individual analyst to capture without some type of support tools and
2. the traditional role of support tools to help the agent get work done efficiently.

We will discuss the use of machine learning support to reduce the complexity (1) and to capture the user's abilities and preferences and do comparisons with past investments to help achieve the goals (2).

Table 1 shows the historical (simplified) choices/selections of nine past investment cases, Cases 1–9. These coincide with the choices 1.–6., which can be supported by the digital coaching system as discussed in Sect. 2. The bolded Case 0 of the last column represents the to-be-supported choices regarding the investment under analysis.

Table 1. Selection/choice data of ten historical analyses conducted by the coaching system.

Selection	Case 1	Case 2	Case 3	Case 4	Case 5	Case 6	Case 7	Case 8	Case 9	**Case 0**
1.	Prob	Fuz	Fuz	Fuz	Fuz	Prob	Fuz	Fuz	Fuz	**Fuz**
2.	Grow	Wait	Grow	Aban	Grow	Grow	Wait	Grow	Aban	**Grow**
3.	DM	FPOM	CoG	FPOM	CoG	DM	FPOM	CoG	CoG	**CoG**
4.	3	3	4	3	2	3	3	3	4	**3**
5.a	C	D	D	C	D	C	C	D	D	**D**
5.b	Cyc	Lin	Cyc	Lin	Cyc	Lin	Lin	Cyc	Lin	**Cyc**
6.a	2	1	5	1	4	1	10	5	3	**5**
6.b	Ran	Avg	Avg	Ran	Ran	Ran	Avg	Avg	Avg	**Avg**

The selections in Table 1 refer to: choice (1.) on Fuzzy (Fuz) or Probabilistic (Prob) uncertainty; choice (2.) on type of real option to wait and see (Wait), expend and grow (Grow) or abandon (Aban); choice (3.) on the pay-off model for real option valuation, i.e. center-of-gravity (GoG) model, possibilistic original fuzzy pay-off model (FPOM) or probabilistic Datar-Mathews (DM) model; choice (4.) on number of cash-flow scenarios (1–4); choice (5.a) on cash-flow estimation done by underlying more specific components (C) or direct analyst estimates (D) and (5.b) on forecasting the cash-flows growing linearly (Lin) or cyclically with a trend (Cyc); choice (6.a) on the number of expert analyzing the same investment (1–10) and (6.b) on preferring to obtain a centroid of the real option value, i.e. "mean" or "average" (Avg) or also a range (min-max) of ROV (which will support to select the aggregation method in subsequent Sect. 3.3). It must be noted that these are only the main choices with limited options for the sake of example, all choices also may have several sub-choices which may further be, e.g., industry-specific choices.

The following examples on valuation and coaching support are based on the recent center-of-gravity (CoG) fuzzy real option valuation method and thus refer to situations, where the choice of the model used has already been made together with previous choices (1.–4.). The CoG model is presented in Sect. 3.1. Then, the first example of cash-flow estimation (choices 4.–5. in Sect. 2) with machine learning support is discussed in Sect. 3.2. The second example of multiple-expert support is built on the cash-flow estimates of individual experts (like in Sect. 3.2 but allowing cash-flow estimates from several analysts). The aggregation of these estimates to obtain a single-valued real option value is discussed. The digital coach suggests aggregation methods of which the user will select one.

The examples will show how in the above cases a digital coaching system, during the making, can help the user perform the analysis to make good/correct choices.

3.1   Center-of-Gravity Fuzzy Pay-Off Model (CoG-FPOM)

The pre-selected model is center-of-gravity (CoG) real option model introduced by Borges et al. (2018) for triangular fuzzy numbers. The model is based on the real-option logic of fuzzy pay-off models (FPOMs), whose development started in 2009 from the introduction of the possibilistic FPOM by Collan et al. (2009) and the guidebook for its industrial applications (Collan 2012). The key idea of the fuzzy pay-off real option valuation (ROV) is to compute the value of an investment using cash-flow scenarios, which determine the (fuzzy) net-present-value (NPV) distribution from which ROV = Weight x Expected value of the positive side of the distribution is obtained:

$$ROV = \frac{\int_0^\infty A(x)dx}{\int_{-\infty}^\infty A(x)dx} \times E(A_+) \tag{1}$$

The integral part gives the ratio of area of the positive side of the NPV distribution and the total area of the distribution. The expected positive NPV value, $E(A_+)$, is weighted by this ratio. A is a fuzzy number which represents the NPV distribution and A_+ is the positive side of it, NPV > 0. Most typically A is either a triangular fuzzy number, which is determined by three NPV scenarios: pessimistic, base and optimistic scenarios, or a trapezoidal fuzzy number determined by four scenarios. It may further allow interval-valued fuzzy numbers in which case the pessimistic and optimistic scenarios are represented by a range of NPV values instead of a crisp number. We may note that the weight component is the same in different types of pay-off models, but the expectation part depends on the type of used uncertainty, e.g., possibilistic as in FPOM, credibilistic (Collan et al. 2012), or based on the center-of-gravity defuzzification (Borges et al. 2018).

Kinnunen et al. (2021) extended the original CoG model to interval-valued fuzzy numbers (IVFNs) and Kinnunen and Georgescu (2020b) extended it further, firstly, to trapezoidal fuzzy numbers and, secondly, to IVFNs. The last one is a general model of which the earlier ones are special cases. For this reason, the ROV algorithm for CoG models is built on the seven possible cases of the general model (cf. Appendix B in Kinnunen and Georgescu (2020b)):

Case 1. $0 \leq a - \alpha_1$, ROV:

$$\frac{1}{2}\left[\frac{\beta_1^2 - \alpha_1^2 + 3(a\alpha_1 + b\beta_1) + 3(b^2 - a^2)}{6(b-a) + 3(\alpha_1 + \beta_1)} + \frac{\beta_2^2 - \alpha_2^2 + 3(a\alpha_2 + b\beta_2) + 3(b^2 - a^2)}{6(b-a) + 3(\alpha_2 + \beta_2)}\right] \tag{2}$$

Case 2, $a - \alpha_1 \leq 0 \leq a - \alpha_2$, ROV:

$$\frac{\frac{-a^2}{2\alpha_1} + \frac{4b - 2a + \alpha_2 + \beta_1 + \beta_2}{2}}{2b - 2a + \frac{\alpha_1 + \alpha_2 + \beta_1 + \beta_2}{2}}$$

$$\times \frac{1}{2}\left[\frac{-a^3 + 3b^2\alpha_1 + 3b\beta_1\alpha_1 + \beta_1^2\alpha_1}{-3a^2 + 6b\alpha_1 + 3\beta_1\alpha_1} + \frac{\beta_2^2 - \alpha_2^2 + 3(a\alpha_2 + b\beta_2) + 3(b^2 - a^2)}{6(b-a) + 3(\alpha_2 + \beta_2)}\right] \tag{3}$$

Case 3, $a - \alpha_2 \leq 0 \leq a$, ROV:

$$\frac{2b + \frac{\beta_1 + \beta_2}{2} - \frac{a^2}{2}\left(\frac{1}{\alpha_1} + \frac{1}{\alpha_2}\right)}{2b - 2a + \frac{\alpha_1 + \alpha_2 + \beta_1 + \beta_2}{2}}$$

$$\times \frac{1}{2}\left[\frac{-a^3 + 3b^2\alpha_1 + 3b\beta_1\alpha_1 + \beta_1^2\alpha_1}{-3a^2 + 6b\alpha_1 + 3\beta_1\alpha_1} + \frac{-a^3 + 3b^2\alpha_2 + 3b\beta_2\alpha_2 + \beta_2^2\alpha_2}{-3a^2 + 6b\alpha_2 + 3\beta_2\alpha_2}\right] \tag{4}$$

Case 4, $a \leq 0 \leq b$, ROV:

$$\frac{2b + \frac{\beta_1 + \beta_2}{2}}{2b - 2a + \frac{\alpha_1 + \alpha_2 + \beta_1 + \beta_2}{2}} \times \frac{1}{2}\left[\frac{3b^2 + 3b\beta_1 + \beta_1^2}{6b + 3\beta_1} + \frac{3b^2 + 3b\beta_2 + \beta_2^2}{6b + 3\beta_2}\right] \tag{5}$$

Case 5, $b \leq 0 \leq b + \beta_2$, ROV:

$$\frac{\frac{\beta_1 + \beta_2}{2} + 2b + \frac{b^2}{2}\left(\frac{1}{\beta_1} + \frac{1}{\beta_2}\right)}{2b - 2a + \frac{\alpha_1 + \alpha_2 + \beta_1 + \beta_2}{2}} \times \frac{1}{2}\left[\frac{b + \beta_1}{3} + \frac{b + \beta_2}{3}\right] \tag{6}$$

Case 6, $b + \beta_2 \leq 0 \leq b + \beta_1$, ROV:

$$\frac{\frac{\beta_1}{2} + b + \frac{b^2}{2\beta_1}}{2b - 2a + \frac{\alpha_1 + \alpha_2 + \beta_1 + \beta_2}{2}} \times \frac{1}{2}\left[\frac{b + \beta_1}{3}\right] \tag{7}$$

Case 7, $b + \beta_1 \leq 0$: in this trivial case both the weight and expected value of the non-existing positive side of the distribution are zero, Thus, also ROV = 0.

Figure 1 shows the R code solving ROVs of Eqs. (2)–(7).

```
weight_2 = ((-a^2/(2*alpha1)+(4*b-2*a+alpha2+beta1+beta2)/2)/(2*b-2*a+(alpha1+alpha2+beta1+beta2)/2))
weight_3 = ((2*b+(beta1+beta2)/2-a^2/2*(1/alpha1+1/alpha2))/(2*b-2*a+(alpha1+alpha2+beta1+beta2)/2))
weight_4 = ((2*b+(beta1+beta2)/2)/(2*b-2*a+(alpha1+alpha2+beta1+beta2)/2))
weight_5 = (((beta1+beta2)/2+2*b+b^2/2*(1/beta1+1/beta2))/(2*b-2*a+(alpha1+alpha2+beta1+beta2)/2))
weight_6 = ((beta1/2+b+b^2/(2*beta1))/(2*b-2*a+(alpha1+alpha2+beta1+beta2)/2))

# IV-CoG-POM:
IV_CoGpomCalculator <- function(a, b, alpha1, alpha2, beta1, beta2){
  if(a-alpha1>=0){
    IV_ROVcog<- 0.5*((beta1^2-alpha1^2+3*(a*alpha1+b*beta1)+3*(b^2-a^2))/(6*(b-a)+3*(alpha1+beta1)))+0.5*((beta2^
2-alpha2^2+3*(a*alpha2+b*beta2)+3*(b^2-a^2))/(6*(b-a)+3*(alpha2+beta2)))}
  else if((a-alpha1<0)&(a-alpha2>=0)){
    IV_ROVcog <- ((0.5*(-a^3+3*b^2*alpha1+3*b*beta1*alpha1+beta1^2*alpha1)/(-3*a^2+6*b*alpha1+3*beta1*alpha1))+0.
5*((beta2^2-alpha2^2+3*(a*alpha2+b*beta2)+3*(b^2-a^2))/(6*(b-a)+3*(alpha2+beta2)))) * weight_2}
  else if((a-alpha2<0)&(a>0)){
    IV_ROVcog <- ((0.5*(-a^3+3*b^2*alpha1+3*b*beta1*alpha1+beta1^2*alpha1)/(-3*a^2+6*b*alpha1+3*beta1*alpha1))+(
0.5*(-a^3+3*b^2*alpha2+3*b*beta2*alpha2+beta2^2*alpha2)/(-3*a^2+6*b*alpha2+3*beta2*alpha2))) * weight_3}
  else if((a<=0)&(b>0)){
    IV_ROVcog <- ((0.5*(3*b^2+3*b*beta1+beta1^2)/(6*b+3*beta1))+0.5*(3*b^2+3*b*beta2+beta2^2)/(6*b+3*beta2)) * we
ight_4}
  else if((b<=0)&(b+beta2>0)){
    IV_ROVcog <- (0.5*(b+beta1)/3+0.5*(b+beta2)/3) * weight_5}
  else if((b+beta2<=0)&(b+beta1>0)){
    IV_ROVcog <- (0.5*(b+beta1)/3) * weight_6}
  else if((b+beta1)<=0){
    IV_ROVcog <- 0}
  print(IV_ROVcog)}
```

Fig. 1. R code for a callable IV-CoGpomCalculation function.

Figure 2 shows the above seven cases on the left side. The interval-valued trapezoidal fuzzy number is determined by the upper fuzzy number A^U and the lower fuzzy number A^L. These are defined by the base NPV from a to b and the pessimistic NPV (distance $-\alpha_1$ to $-\alpha_2$ from a) and the optimistic NPV (distance β_2 to β_1 from b).

The right side of Fig. 1 shows the simple triangular fuzzy number, which has only four possible cases: (1) fully positive NPV distribution (corresponding to case 1 on the left side of Fig. 1); (2) base NPV > 0, but pessimistic NPV < 0; (3) base NPV < 0 and only optimistic NPV > 0; and the fully negative (corresponding to case 7).

When value a replaces both a and b, value α similarly replaces both α_1 and α_2, and β replaces both β_1 and β_2 in Eqs. (2)–(7), then ROV of the simplified model of Borges et al. (2018) is obtained. The replacing values in Fig. 1 are shown for the sake of example; the three NVP scenario values may be different, but the general model still reduces in a way that the above presented equations solve the simplified case.

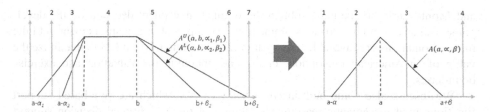

Fig. 2. General model with a trapezoidal interval-valued fuzzy NPV distribution with seven cases (left) reduces to simplified triangular fuzzy NPV distribution with 4 cases.

In the following examples, we use the simplified model (Borges et al. 2018) based only on three cash-flow scenarios, i.e., the triangular fuzzy number will represent the NPV distribution of an investment with four possible cases.

3.2 Machine Learning Support Built on Categorical Data

This example is related to choices 4 and 5 discussed in Sect. 2.

In the field of finance and economics, machine learning has been applied mainly to prediction in financial markets focusing on stock prices, especially neural networks. More recently, for stock price predictions, Long Short-Term Memory Networks (LSTM) are used in deep learning. LSTMs are a type of recurrent neural networks developed by Hochreiter and Schmidhuber (1997) used for learning long time dependencies. They consist of 4 layers, the second layer having two activation functions, sigmoid and tanh. Cho et al. in 2014 created a version of LSTM network, called Gated Recurrent Unit (GRU), also used in predictions. GRU is a simplified version of LSTM, which stores information from the previous moments and uses it for future predictions. Machine-learning algorithms have been utilized in lesser extent to real investments. Recently, machine learning techniques have been applied to support decisions in venture capital investments. The typical approaches are predicting two or more classes, such as being acquired by a company or offering shares to public, high returns or higher risk predictions (Arroyo et al. 2019). The paper by Arroyo et al. (2019) uses different ML classifiers: Support Vector Machines, Decision Trees, Random Forests to predict five possible events of the success of a start-up company. Applications are found, for example, in investments in renewable energy (Frey et al. 2019), in manufacturing (Dogan and Birant 2021) and for real options in oilfield development (Lazo et al. 2007) and (Pratikto et al. 2019) and in the context of abandoning options (reinforcement learning). These applications typically use large datasets. Frey et al. (2019) study investment decisions in renewable energy by comparing model quality for all years for Germany PV by 4 classifiers: generalized linear models, deep NNs, gradient boosting and random forests. Dogan and Birant (2021) underline the importance of supervised and unsupervised learning in manufacturing providing an overview of the use of these methods. They mention some advantages of ML applications in manufacturing such as: predictive maintenance, resource management, product design, quality control, diagnosis, decision support, optimizations, cycle-time reduction, etc. Lazo et al. (2007) simulate a real options model by genetic algorithms and Monte Carlo simulation to obtain the optimal investment decision on the development of an oilfield in two cases: immediate development or a postponement until the market conditions are favorable. Lawryshyn (2019) applied a deep NN to maximize the value of an American put option, in the end obtaining the valuation and exercise boundaries.

We discuss also some built-in *consistency checks*, which are rule-based support functions used in semantic reasoning systems and more traditional decision support systems, (Kinnunen and Collan 2009a, 2009b, Collan and Kinnunen 2008, 2009, Kinnunen 2010, Collan and Kinnunen 2011, Kinnunen and Georgescu 2019a, 2019b). They require limited data and also domain-specific knowledge from the designer of a digital coaching system. Machine learning support instead requires past case, i.e., mainly *in-house data* of past analyzed real investments of which, e.g., clustering algorithms require a relatively number of cases, while more advanced methods, such as reinforcement learning recommender algorithms (content learning, e.g., content-based filtering based on the attributes of the user and the specific investment at hand; or collaborative filtering based on the similar users' selections) may require a large database of past cases (Ricci et al. 2015, Aggarwal 2016). Machine learning support can also be designed for estimating cash-flows using *market data* on key underlying drivers of prices and business cycle of the relevant market or industrial sector (Lazo et al. 2007).

In the process of clustering categorical data there are three main clustering steps:

Step 1. Similarity matrix is computed to be able to compare two cases i and j with different characters (choices), k, and assigned score $s_{i,j,k}$ which is between [0, 1], zero when the cases are different and closer the unity, the higher the degree of similarity. In general, the similarity between cases i and j and can be defined as the average score over all possible choice comparisons (Gower 1971):

$$S_{i,j} = \frac{\sum_{k=1}^{v} s_{i,j,k}}{\sum_{k=1}^{v} \delta_{i,j,k}},$$

where quantity $\delta_{i,j,k}$ is equal to 1 when character k can be compared for i and j and 0 otherwise.

Step 2. Clustering method is chosen. We use hierarchical clustering with the agglomerative, complete linkage criteria between two observation sets A and B (cf. Székely and Rizzo 2005):

$$max\{d(a,b) : a \in B\},$$

where d is the chosen metric, here, Gower metric.

Step 3. Clusters and optimal cluster numbers are assessed. In our case both elbow method and silhouette method suggest optimal number of 3 clusters.

For the sake of example, we present Fig. 3 with clusters throughout the modelling choices 1–6. We further focus on categorical choices even if numerical ones could be presented.

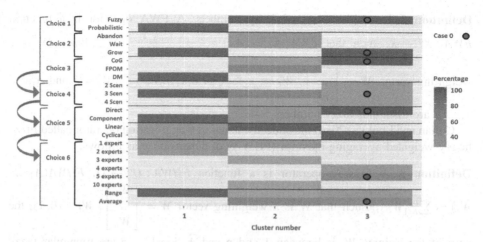

Fig. 3. Dynamic ML support for the current investment (Case 0) is built on percentage of historical choices across clusters.

The above discussed choices were categorical, but we may well have numerical sub-choices. Also, Choices 7–9 are mainly numerical. Thus, we have mixed data types and we may use various clustering methods (Kim et al. 2004, Jiang and Liu 2020) to include all past data otherwise analogously, or we may use typical clustering methods, along with machine laearning prediction algorithms separately for numerical choices like cost-revenue estimates (Choice 7), parameter estimates including also appropriate discount factors possibly separately for (possibly less uncertain) costs and (more uncertain) revenues (Choice 8), or related to interpretation of results (Choice 9), a wide range of risk metrics may be suggested by ML support. Some of the more advanced methods require large datasets, which may set restrictions, but while we have focused on in-house knowledge and data, for numerical ML support, market data can be extremely valuable, possibly even some crucial cost or revenue components allowing also the usage of more complex ML modelling.

3.3 Consolidating Cash-Flow Estimates with Multi-expert Support

This example is focused on choice 6 discussed in Sect. 2.

Yager (1988) introduced ordered weighted averaging operators (OWA), notion used in multiple decision-making problems.

Let $I \in [0, 1]$ and $F : I^n \to I$.

Definition 1 (Yager 1988). F is an OWA of dimension n if $F(a_1, ..., a_n) = W_1 b_1 + ... + W_n b_n$, where W is a weighting vector, $W = \begin{bmatrix} W_1 \\ ... \\ W_n \end{bmatrix}$, $W_i \in (0, 1), i = 1, ..., n$ and $\sum_{i=1}^n W_i = 1$ and b_i is the i-th greatest element in the set $\{a_1, ..., a_n\}$.

Collan and Luukka (2016) use the fuzzy weighted averaging operator (FWA) of dimension n as follows:

Definition 2. Let X be a set of fuzzy numbers. A FWA operator is a function $FWA : X^n \to X$, such that $FWA\left(\widehat{A}_1, ..., \widehat{A}_n\right) = \frac{\alpha_1 \widehat{A}_1 + ... + \alpha_n \widehat{A}_n}{\alpha_1 + ... + \alpha_n} = \sum_{i=1}^n W_i \widehat{A}_i$. W is a

weighting vector, $W = \begin{bmatrix} W_1 \\ ... \\ W_n \end{bmatrix}$, $W_i = \frac{\alpha_i}{\alpha_1 + ... + \alpha_n}, i = 1, ..., n$, $\sum_{i=1}^n W_i = 1$ and $\widehat{A}_i, i =$

$1, ..., n$ are triangular fuzzy numbers.

Collan and Luukka (2016) introduced a new fuzzy aggregation operator called fuzzy heavy weighted averaging operator (FHWA) of dimension n as follows.

Definition 3. A FHWA operator is a function $FHWA : U^n \to U$, $FHWA(\widehat{A}_1, ...,$

$\widehat{A}_n) = \sum_{i=1}^n W_i \widehat{A}_i$, such that W is a weighting vector $W = \begin{bmatrix} W_1 \\ ... \\ W_n \end{bmatrix}$, $W_i \in (0, 1)$, the

sum of the weights W_i is between 1 and n and $\widehat{A}_i, i = 1, ..., n$ are triangular fuzzy numbers.

FWA is a special case of FHWA operator. It was noticed that in risk management situations FWA operators do not aggregate optimally the relevant information, therefore Luukka et al. (2018) proposed the loosely fuzzy weighted average operator (LFWA).

Assume we have n decision makers for which n fuzzy numbers are provided. For each fuzzy number A_i, the decision makers give a credibility score $CS_i, i = 1, ..., n$. The credibility scores are converted into weights: $W_i = \frac{CS_i}{\sum_{i=1}^n CS_i}, i = 1, ..., n$.

Definition 4 (Luukka et al. 2018). A LFWA operator is a function $LFWA : X \to R$, $LFWA(x) = \sum_{i=1}^n W_i A_i(x)$, where $X = cl(supp(A_1 \cup ... \cup A_n))$.

(Recall that the support of a fuzzy set A is $supp(A) = \{x \in X | A(x) > 0\}$.)

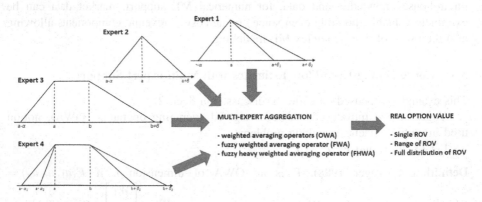

Fig. 4. Consolidation of multiple cash-flow estimates

If A = (a1, a2, a3) and B = (b1, b2, b3) are two triangular fuzzy numbers, then their sum is also a triangular fuzzy number: A + B = (a1 + b1, a2 + b2, a3 + b3). The multiplication between a positive scalar λ and the triangular fuzzy number A = (a1, a2, a3) is also a triangular fuzzy number: λA = (λa1, λa2, λa3) (Georgescu 2012).

According to Herrera-Viedma et al. (2008), fuzzy aggregation operators can evaluate the quality of a digital system by aggregating qualitative (fuzzy linguistic variables) and quantitative information (scores), aggregating criteria with different weights and adopting different scenarios from pessimistic to optimistic ones. In Fig. 4 one has fuzzy evaluations from four experts. They can be of any form, say, triangular or trapezoidal, and both also may be of interval-valued form for one or both tails.

The triangular fuzzy evaluation means triangular cash-flows expectations. Based on the available data, using fuzzy aggregation operators of the type enumerated above, one can build an intelligent multi-expert system for ranking Mergers and Acquisitions (M&As), R&D projects, or any strategic investments. Table 2 shows cumulative net present value (NPV) cash-flow estimates from one expert (A) for 5-years period from now. Assume these are cash-flows which may be achieved, by extending an existing production plant (growth option/option to scale) by managerial actions. It is seen that by year 5 the cash-flows can be $500.000 in the optimistic case, $300.000 most likely base case, and −$100.000 in the pessimistic case.

Table 2. Real option NPV cash-flow evaluation as a triangular fuzzy number

Expert A	Year 1	Year 1	Year 3	Year 4	Year 5
Optimistic scenario	300	350	400	450	500
Base scenario	100	150	200	250	300
Pessimistic scenario	60	−70	−80	90	100

By calling the IV-CoGpomCalculator function (Fig. 1) in our R application, i.e. computing the real option value (ROV) using Eq. (3), we obtain $234.722 as the value of option to scale up production. This is the value of managerial flexibility, the available growth option. Thus, we have the NPV estimates from expert A, which is a triangular number, where base scenario gives the centroid value of 300 (thousands USD) and difference from that to optimistic scenario gives the right width (alpha) and the difference to pessimistic scenario gives the left width (beta). The triangular fuzzy number becomes A = (300, alpha = 300 − (−100), beta = 500 − 300), i.e. A = (300, 400, 200). Now, assume, we have similar cumulative NPV estimates from three other experts (B, C and D): B = (300, 300, 300), C = (400, 500, 200) and D = (300, 400, 100). We also assume that the digital coach suggests equal weights assigned to these four triangular fuzzy numbers are equal: $w_1 = w_2 = w_3 = w_4 = 0.25$ and the use of the definition 2. Thus, we apply the FWA operator on A, B, C and D: FWA (A, B, C, D) = 0.25 (A + B + C + D) = 0.25 (1300, 1600, 800) = (325, 400, 200). By calling again the the IV-CoGpomCalculator, we obtain the consolidated real option value: ROV= 243.892.

4 Conclusions

In this paper we focus on how digital coaching can be used in corporate decision making and how DSS users can be guided towards a better use of their systems. We lay the grounds for further development of digital coaching systems in the context of investment analysis and specifically real option valuation. We also provide two illustrative examples of how digital coaching can assist a decision-maker/real option valuation system user in better using the system and in better understanding how real option valuation works. This research contributes both to literature on digital coaching and real option valuation and has also real-world practical relevance for designers of real option valuation systems.

Acknowledgements. This research is supported by the Finnish Strategic Research Council at the Academy of Finland project Manufacturing 4.0 grants 335980 and 335990.

References

Klaassen, R., op den Akker, R., Lavrysen, T., van Wissen, S.: User preferences for multi-device context-aware feedback in a digital coaching system. J. Multimodal User Interfaces **7**(3), 247–267 (2013). https://doi.org/10.1007/s12193-013-0125-0

Klaassen, R., Di Bitonto, P., van der Burg, G.J., Bul, K., Kato, P.: PERGAMON: a serious gaming and digital coaching platform supporting patients and healthcare professionals. CENTERIS/ProjMAN/HCist (2016)

Mezei, J., Sell, A., Walden, P.: Digital coaching - an exploratory study on potential motivators. In: Proceedings of the 53rd Hawaii International Conference on System Sciences (HICSS'53), pp. 1123–1132 (2020). https://aisel.aisnet.org/cgi/viewcontent.cgi?article=1168&context=hicss-53

Kettunen, E., Critchley, W., Kari, T.: Can digital coaching boost your performance? A qualitative study among physically active people. In: Proceedings of the 52nd Hawaii International Conference on System Sciences (HICSS'52) (2019)

Harmelink, K.E., Zeegers, A.V.C.M., Tönis, T.M., Hullegie, W., Staal, J.B.: The effectiveness of the use of a digital activity coaching system in addition to a two-week home-based exercise program in patients after total knee arthroplasty: study protocol for a randomized controlled trial. BMC Musculoskelet. Disord. **18**(1), 1–10 (2017). https://doi.org/10.1186/s12891-017-1647-5

Stara, V., Santini, S., Kropf, J., D'Amen, B.: Digital health coaching programs among older employees in transition to retirement: systematic literature review. J. Med. Internet Res. **22**(9), e17809 (2020)

Kari, T., Rinne, P.: Influence of digital coaching on physical activity: motivation and behaviour of physically inactive individuals. In: Bled eConference. University of Maribor Press (2018)

Topman, R.M., Kruise, D., Beijne, S.: Digital coaching of procrastinators in an academic setting. In: Schouwenburg, H.C., Lay, C.H., Pychyl, T.A., Ferrari, J.R. (eds.) Counseling the Procrastinator in Academic Settings, pp. 133–148. American Psychological Association, Washington D.C. (2004). https://doi.org/10.1037/10808-010

Novic, H.: The future with AI and automated digital coaching assistants (2019). https://medium.com/swlh/the-future-with-ai-and-automated-digital-coaching-assistants-e0ccf7072c54. Accessed 10 Mar 2021

Carlsson, C.: Digital coaching for real options support. In: Pelta, D., Cruz Corona, C. (eds.) Soft Computing Based Optimization and Decision Models. Studies in Fuzziness and Soft Computing, vol. 360, pp. 153–175, Springer, Cham (2018a). https://doi.org/10.1007/978-3-319-64286-4_9

Carlsson, C. Decision analytics mobilized with digital coaching. Intell. Syst. Account. Finance Manage. 25(1), 3–17 (2018b)

Carlsson, C.: Digital coaching to make fuzzy real options methods viable for investment decisions. In: 2019 IEEE International Conference on Fuzzy Systems (FUZZ-IEEE), New Orleans, LA, USA, pp. 1–6 (2019a). https://doi.org/10.1109/FUZZ-IEEE.2019.8858921. https://ieeexplore.ieee.org/abstract/document/8858921

Carlsson, C.: Combining ANFIS and digital coaching for good decisions in industrial processes. In: Kearfott R., Batyrshin I., Reformat M., Ceberio M., Kreinovich V. (eds.) Fuzzy Techniques: Theory and Applications. IFSA/NAFIPS 2019. Advances in Intelligent Systems and Computing, vol. 1000, pp. 190–200, Springer, Cham (2019b). https://doi.org/10.1007/978-3-030-21920-8_18

Myers, S.: Determinants of corporate borrowing. J. Financ. Econ. 5(2), 146–175 (1977). https://doi.org/10.1016/0304-405X(77)90015-0

Black, F., Scholes, M.: The pricing of options and corporate liabilities. J. Polit. Econ. 81(3), 637–654 (1970). https://doi.org/10.1086/260062

Cox, J., Ross, S.A., Rubinstein, M.: Option pricing: a simplified approach. J. Financ. Econ. 7(3), 229–263 (1979). https://doi.org/10.1016/0304-405X(79)90015-1

Boyle, P.: Options: a Monte Carlo approach. J. Financ. Econ. 4(3), 323–338 (1977). https://doi.org/10.1016/0304-405X(77)90005-8

Datar, V., Mathews, S.: European real options: an intuitive algorithm for the Black Scholes formula. J. Appl. Financ. 14(1), 7–13 (2004)

Savolainen, J., Collan, M., Kyläheiko, K., Luukka, P.: On the trade-off between the leverage effect and real options thinking: a simulation-based model on metal mining investment. Int. J. Prod. Econ. 194(1), 43–51 (2017). https://doi.org/10.1016/j.ijpe.2017.06.002

Savolainen, J., Collan, M., Luukka, P.: Analyzing operational real options in metal mining investments with a system dynamic model. Eng. Econ. 72(1), 54–72 (2016). https://doi.org/10.1080/0013791X.2016.1167988

Collan, M., Haahtela, T., Kyläheiko, K.: On the usability of real option valuation model types under different types of uncertainty. Int. J. Bus. Innov. Res. 11(1), 18–37 (2016). https://doi.org/10.1504/IJBIR.2016.077608

Trigeorgis, L. (ed.): Real Options in Capital Investment: Models, Strategies, and Applications. Praeger, Westport (1985)

Brach, M.: Real Options in Practice. Wiley, Hoboken (2003)

de Neufville, R., Scholtes, S.: Flexibility in Engineering Design. The MIT Press, Cambridge (2011). https://mitpress.mit.edu/books/flexibility-engineering-design

Borges, R.E.P., Dias, M.A.G., Dória Neto, A.D., Meier, A.: Fuzzy pay-off method for real options: the center of gravity approach with application in oilfield abandonment. Fuzzy Sets Syst. 353, 111–123 (2018). https://doi.org/10.1016/j.fss.2018.03.008

Collan, M., Fullér, R., Mézei, J.: Fuzzy pay-off method for real option valuation. J. Appl. Math. Decis. Syst. Article ID 238196, 14pp. (2009). https://doi.org/10.1155/2009/238196. http://www.hindawi.com/journals/ads/2009/238196/

Collan, M.: The Pay-Off Method: Re-Inventing Investment Analysis. CreateSpace Inc., Charleston (2012)

Collan, M., Fullér, R., Mezei, J.: Credibilistic approach to the fuzzy pay-off method for real option analysis. J. Appl. Oper. Res. 4(4), 174–182 (2012)

Kinnunen, J., Georgescu, I.: Intuitive fuzzy real options in digital coaching for strategic investment decisions. In: Dima, A.M., D'Ascenzo, F. (eds.) Business Revolution in a Digital Era. SPBE, pp. 191–206. Springer, Cham (2021). https://doi.org/10.1007/978-3-030-59972-0_14

Kinnunen, J., Georgescu, I.: Fuzzy Real options analysis based on interval-valued scenarios with a corporate acquisition application. Nordic J. Bus. **69**(1), 44–67 (2020b)

Kinnunen, J., Georgescu, I., Collan, M.: Center-of-gravity real options method based on interval-valued fuzzy numbers. In: Kahraman, C., Cevik Onar, S., Oztaysi, B., Sari, I.U., Cebi, S., Tolga, A.C. (eds.) INFUS 2020. AISC, vol. 1197, pp. 1292–1300. Springer, Cham (2021). https://doi.org/10.1007/978-3-030-51156-2_151

Collan, M., Kinnunen, J.: Acquisition strategy and real options. IUP J. Bus. Strategy **6**(3–4), 45–65 (2009)

Kinnunen, J., Collan, M.: Supporting the screening of corporate acquisition targets. In: Proceedings of the 42nd International Conference on System Sciences (HICSS 2009), Waikoloa, Hawaii, 5–8 January, pp. 1–7 (2009a)

Collan, M., Kinnunen, J.: A procedure for the rapid pre-acquisition screening of target companies using the pay-off method for real option valuation. J. Real Options Strategy **4**(1), 117–141 (2011)

Kinnunen, J., Georgescu, I.: Decision support system for evaluating synergy real options in M&A. In: Proceedings of the International Conference on Management and Information Systems (ICMIS-19), Bangkok, Thailand, 29–30 September, pp. 408–418 (2019a)

Collan, M., Luukka, P.: Strategic R&D project analysis: keeping it simple and smart. In: Collan, M., Fedrizzi, M., Kacprzyk, J. (eds.) Fuzzy Technology. SFSC, vol. 335, pp. 169–191. Springer, Cham (2016). https://doi.org/10.1007/978-3-319-26986-3_10

Luukka, P., Collan, M., Tam, F., Lawryshyn, Y.: Estimating one-off operational risk events with the lossless fuzzy weighted average method. In: Collan, M., Kacprzyk, J. (eds.) Soft Computing Applications for Group Decision-making and Consensus Modeling. SFSC, vol. 357, pp. 227–236. Springer, Cham (2018). https://doi.org/10.1007/978-3-319-60207-3_15

Yager, R.R.: On ordered weighted averaging aggregation operators in multicriteria decision-making. IEEE Trans. Syst. Man Cybern. **18**(1), 183–190 (1988). https://doi.org/10.1109/21.87068

Hockreiter, S., Schmidhuber, J.: Long short-term memory. Neural Comput. **9**(8), 1735–1790 (1997). https://doi.org/10.1162/neco.1997.9.8.1735

Arroyo, J., Corea, F., Jimenez-Diaz, G., Recio-Garcia, J.A.: Assessment of machine learning performance for decision support in venture capital investments. IEEE Access **7**, 124233–124243 (2019). https://doi.org/10.1109/ACCESS.2019.2938659

Frey, U.J., Klein, M., Deissenroth, M.: Modelling complex investment decisions in Germany for renewables with different machine learning algorithms. Environ. Model. Softw. **118**, 61–75 (2019). https://doi.org/10.1016/j.envsoft.2019.03.006

Dogan, A., Birant, D.: Machine learning and data mining in manufacturing. Expert Syst. Appl. **166**, 114060 (2021). https://doi.org/10.1016/j.eswa.2020.114060

Lazo, J.G.L., Pacheco, M.A.C., Vellasco, M.M.B.R.: Real options and genetic algorithms to approach of the optimal decision rule for oil field development under uncertainties. In: Castillo, O., Melin, P., Ross, O.M., Sepúlveda Cruz, R., Pedrycz, W., Kacprzyk, J. (eds.) Theoretical Advances and Applications of Fuzzy Logic and Soft Computing. Advances in Soft Computing, vol. 42. Springer, Heidelberg (2007). https://doi.org/10.1007/978-3-540-72434-6_44

Lawryshyn, Y.: Using boundary fitting and machine learning to value multi-stage real option investments. In: Proceedings of the NSAIS-ROW'19 Workshop on Adaptive and Intelligent Systems and Real Options 2019, LUT Scientific and Expertise Publications, Research Reports, vol. 97, pp. 38–41 (2019)

Kinnunen, J., Collan, M.: Supporting the screening of corporate acquisition targets. In: Proceedings of the 42nd International Conference on System Sciences (HICSS-09), Waikoloa, Hawaii, 5–8 January, pp. 1–8 (2009b)

Kinnunen, J., Georgescu, I.: Decision support system for evaluating synergy real options in M&A. In: Proceedings of the International Conference on Management and In-formation Systems (ICMIS-19), Bangkok, Thailand, 29–30 September, pp. 408–418 (2019b)

Ricci, F., Rokach, L., Shapira, B. (eds.): Recommender Systems Handbook, 2nd edn. Springer, Boston (2015). https://doi.org/10.1007/978-1-4899-7637-6

Aggarwal, C.C.: Recommender Systems: The Textbook. Springer, Cham (2016). https://doi.org/ 10.1007/978-3-319-29659-3

Georgescu, I.: Possibility Theory and the Risk. Springer, Heidelberg (2012). https://doi.org/10. 1007/978-3-642-24740-8

Herrera-Viedma, E., et al.: Applying aggregation operators for information access systems: an application in digital libraries. Int. J. Intell. Syst. 23(12), 1235–1250 (2008). https://doi.org/ 10.1002/int.20317

Gower, J.C.: A general coefficient of similarity and some of its properties. Biometrics 27(4), 857–871 (1971). https://doi.org/10.2307/2528823

Székely, G.J., Rizzo, M.L.: Hierarchical clustering via joint between-within distances: extending ward's minimum variance method. J. Classif. 22, 151–183 (2005). https://doi.org/10.1007/ s00357-005-0012-9

Kim, D.-W., Lee, K.H., Lee, D.: Fuzzy clustering of categorical data using fuzzy centroids. Pattern Recogn. Lett. 25(11), 1263–1271 (2004). https://doi.org/10.1016/j.patrec.2004.04.004

Jiang, Z., Liu, X.: A novel consensus fuzzy K-modes clustering using coupling DNA-chain-hypergraph P system for categorical data. Processes 8(10), 1326 (2020). https://doi.org/10. 3390/pr8101326

Pratikto, F., Indratno, S., Suryadi, K, Santoso, D.: Using machine learning to estimate reservoir parameters in real options valuation of an unexplored oilfield. In: SPE/IATMI Asia Pacific Oil & Gas Conference and Exhibition, Bali, Indonesia, pp. 1–18 (2019)

Collan, M., Kinnunen, J.: Strategic level real options in corporate acquisitions. In: Proceedings of the 1st International Conference of Applied Operational Research (ICAOR 2008), 15–17 Sept 2008 in Yerevan, Armenia. LNCS, vol. 1, pp. 168-177 (2008)

Kinnunen, J.: Valuing M&A synergies as (fuzzy) real options. In: Proceedings (CD) of the 14th Annual International Conference on Real Options (ROC 2010), Rome, Italy,16–19 June 2010

Applying Human Cognition to Assured Autonomy

Mónica López-González(✉) ⓘ

Institute for Human Intelligence, Baltimore, MD, USA
monica@ihintelligence.org

Abstract. The scaled deployment of semi- and fully autonomous systems undeniably depends on assured autonomy. This reality, however, has become far more complex than expected because it necessarily demands an integrated tripartite solution not yet achieved: consensus-based standards and compliance across industry, scientific innovation within artificial intelligence R&D of explainability, and robust end-user education. In this is paper I present my human-centered approach to the design, development, and deployment of autonomous systems and break down how human factors such as cognitive and behavioral insights into how we think, feel, act, plan, make decisions, and problem-solve are foundational to assuring autonomy.

Keywords: Assured autonomy · Artificial intelligence · Human factors · Trust · Explainability · Autonomous vehicles

1 Introduction

Artificial intelligence (AI)-based technologies, methods, and applications are increasingly entering all industries and domains, and their negative effect on individuals and society at large is no secret. From biased facial recognition algorithms [1] and medical AI devices [2] to the abuse of natural language processing systems [3] and resulting deaths from AI-enabled vehicles [4], to name a few, the promise of AI is not without risks and challenges. As a result, the concept of 'assured autonomy' –or 'trustworthy AI' as referred to by the European Commission– is capturing the ears of governments, international organizations, and industry alike [5–8]. While new autonomous systems are being built, trust in the new technology, however, is declining [9, 10]. Add the current COVID-19 pandemic, economic crisis, public outcry over systemic racism, and disintegration of democratic stability across the globe and trust is at a new low across a swath of sectors [11].

Notwithstanding, trust is a vital social process that helps us to cooperate with others and form a relationship [12]. Inherently risky due to the unpredictability of others' intentions, we nonetheless learn to accept vulnerability and depend on one another to produce positive, mutual advantages [13]. The success of this dependency relies on reciprocity and the gains perceived from such. For example, you offer me something with supposed 'x' characteristic to improve my life, I perceive or at least hope in your honesty, and I reciprocate your offer by engaging with that something because I expect 'x' to be true. In the context of assured autonomy, Company A offers me an AI-enabled

C. Stephanidis et al. (Eds.): HCII 2021, LNCS 13095, pp. 474–488, 2021.
https://doi.org/10.1007/978-3-030-90963-5_36

autonomous system 'a' with 'x, y, and z' characteristics, I believe in the integrity of the company, and I buy system 'a' because I expect 'x, y, and z' as true. Inherent in this business transaction example is my confidence in Company A providing me with the claimed system's performance capability. Problems arise when the system does not perform as intended, and explainability of such failure is left unanswered. The lack of explainability suggests a shortfall in Company A's standards of ethical behavior and accountability, and my trust in the company accordingly diminishes.

In this paper, an expansion of [14], I argue that we need a human-centered approach to the design, development, and deployment of AI-enabled autonomous systems if we are to fully trust the capabilities of these systems. Integrating essential human cognitive intelligence characteristics during design and development, and identifying potential negative impacts during deployment, along with mitigation strategies prior to the system's actual deployment in the field, can aid in setting a clear standard of ethical behavior and accountability from the onset. Using the autonomous vehicle industry as a backdrop, I delineate how assured autonomy –and the consequent regaining of the public's trust in AI– will depend on a united and cross-disciplinary effort in (a) setting consensus-based standards and compliance across industry, (b) fast-tracking scientific innovation within AI R&D of explainability, and (c) implementing robust end-user education. I end with recommendations for how to advance such a collaborative effort.

2   Case Study: Autonomous Vehicle (AV) Technology

Until April of this year, the auto industry (and all other industries intending to or already making use of AI-enabled technology) had arrived at a bifurcated road: competitively move forward business as usual, or collectively step on the brakes, critically evaluate the capabilities of current AV technology, and set ethical and sustainable long-term goals. Now, designing, developing, and deploying AI-enabled technology is no longer a free-for-all. The United States' Federal Trade Commission (FTC) and the European Commission have both separately voiced the potential harms of AI and proposed ways to govern AI through legal means [5, 6]. Crucially, the FTC has warned to go after unfair and deceptive practice within the AI industry in the United States, and the European Commission has proposed legislation that, if passed, would create significant obligations and limitations on the use of AI by the member states of the European Union. Specific to AVs, regulators in the United States now require manufacturers and operators to report incidents involving their driver-assistance and automated driving systems within one day of learning of a crash [15]. Leaving aside the FTC's and the European Commission's very different approaches to the governance of AI, the bottom line is clear: theoretical best practices are inadequate as the stakes are now higher than ever under the pressure of legal requirements to assure autonomy from these systems.

As with any technological change and the challenges that arise prior to its full-fledged adoption, these new demands can either hamper innovation or spur it. The first claim of this paper is that the science of assured autonomy is gathering unparalleled momentum outside of the engineering world for a new era of growth, and it crucially necessitates a human-centered approach. Assured autonomy is contingent on two factors: (1) the system can accomplish goals independently, or with minimal supervision from human operators in environments that are complex and unpredictable, and (2) the system's capability is guaranteed and thus safe, secure, predictable, and reliable. These two factors underscore, moreover, two essential requirements: (i) AI-based systems with human-like intelligence capacities to indeed navigate the world as efficiently as we humans do, and (ii) explainability, or transparency, in how automated decisions are made to provide a level of interpretability for actions similar to how we humans provide reasons behind our own actions. While much work is being done to provide solutions to these two requirements, the science is incomplete [16] and needs alternative AI methods that can combine accuracy with transparency and, further yet, privacy concerns and mitigation [17]. Despite such recognizable considerations, the roadway to automation has not fully addressed them.

2.1   Reality vs. Fiction

Between misleading statements of an AV takeover [18], report after report of real-life problems with AV technology [19–22], and calls for honest discussions on the reality of AV capabilities and AI at large [23–27], the entire ecosystem around designing, developing, and deploying AVs has ignored the very core of the entire enterprise: humanity.

The concept of 'humanity' may well be intuitive, but I define it here in this context for the sake of clarity: that which fundamentally characterizes and defines us as a human in comparison to a machine. Instinctively, this refers to our intelligent ability to merge past experiences and common sense knowledge to think, feel, act, plan, make decisions, and problem-solve as we adapt to changing environments. These cognitive behavioral activities are at play in the case of driving a vehicle, or being around a vehicle. For example, when moving from point A to point B we make micro decisions in accordance with what is occurring in real time and what we know about roadways and drivers more broadly to navigate the world as successfully as possible. Acknowledging that what is being developed, i.e. machines, is not independent of the environment and has societal consequences, AVs must be able to accurately identify us, predict our behavior, and interact with us with relative ease. More bluntly, we humans are part of the engineering design equation because we coexist with roadways as drivers, construction workers, cyclists, jaywalkers, pedestrians, traffic guards, vendors, etc. We reflect our desires and goals through actions, and those actions are an integral part of what roadways entail and how they work, both through successes and failures. Any machine that enters today's roadways will face a plethora of contexts. Remove us and create a 100% interconnected robotized world –immune from hacking included– and we are not part of the engineering design equation.

Imagine the following scenario:

A maze of concrete, steel, and glass dominated. Gates opened and closed in synchrony: opening just one second before a fully automated driverless level 5 pod-like structure arrived, and remaining open for exactly the time it took to enter into the pod before locking into place as the pod smoothly pulled away. Gone were the speed limit signs; gone were the speed bumps; gone were the traffic lights; gone were the bicycle lanes; gone were the pedestrian walkways; gone were the parking spaces; gone were all the penalties for violating traffic laws. Living beings were prohibited from entering "the vehicle zone," as it was legally known.

Bridges were erected at every block to connect one side of the street to the other, every new bridge painstakingly merged to the previous one. In fact, so many bridges had been built and so many merged with swaths of steel and concrete that an entire floor exclusively for humans and animals had been created. The climate controlled and noiseless vehicle zone was a world of its own, an ever-growing cocoon impervious to unknowns. What the metro was to the humid underground, connected fully automated driverless level 5 vehicles were to the ground floor, and all living organic beings were to the scorching second floor.

You paid to enter an elevator or use the flights of stairs to move downwards for public transit or upwards for freedom...

Thus begins a short science fiction story I wrote as I read bombastic announcements of imminent deployment of AVs as early as 2019 [26, 27] and narrated to an audience of AV engineers and company executives during a keynote address in 2020 [14]. I re-share this fictionalized account of a future possibility to not only underscore the fantastical nature of a roadway devoid of humans, but to pose again the more fundamental question the AV industry needs to address: what do we as a society want to create with AVs? I ask in earnest as the industry must finally prioritize the unexpected complexities and challenges of real-life human behaviors and the ethical weight of human lives at stake over fast profits.

For conceptual clarity, the question can be broken down further: Do we want to create a machine that thinks and acts like us? Or do we want a machine that thinks and acts like us but in a better way in order to replace us? And what does 'better' even mean? Safer? How do we define safety? Do we want to replace our ambiguous, biased, distracted, emotional, error-prone, rule-breaking, and unpredictable behaviors? Is elimination of all human cognitive behavioral characteristics, or some of them, equivalent to engineering safety? Or do we want to create an entirely other thing? Would this other thing be not to replace us per se but to complement us in some way? And complement us in what way exactly? As a real-time guide that monitors our thoughts and behaviors moment-by-moment? Like a moral barometer that decides with or for us what is right or wrong? Or maybe we want the fictional world above where robo-vehicles coexist with each other in unwavering connected synchrony, free of interference from organic beings like ourselves? Or perhaps what we need most imminently is to create something that can interface with us much in the same way as we interface with our fellow human beings...

Whether addressing the external or internal environment of the vehicle, or both, the reality is that animals, the weather, and we humans are not going anywhere any time soon. Moreover, the physical infrastructure described in the story above is nowhere near actualization. We humans are, in effect, at the center of the problem. And all the above questions are not answerable by any one individual. Multiple stakeholders must address them collaboratively. Interdisciplinary and cross-disciplinary solutions are required because the problem is an interconnected human-machine-society issue with its resulting web of intertwined implications the science of engineering alone is not tackling. The characteristic 'make x to yield y' mindset of engineering systems to solve a 'single' problem is insufficient because context can neither be removed nor simply ignored. In the case of AVs, where the human sits in regards to the machine's perspective –as a driver, passive occupant, or pattern of pixelated points in its path– is critical to designing a predictable and thus reliable system to be used by, for, and around humans. The second claim of this paper is that AI has not been contextualized as belonging to the greater socio-technical ecosystem that science, technology, and society as a concept of dynamic interrelationships embody. The result has been a gap between paying heed to the values and choices of the people for which these AI-enabled systems are to be used by and the designing, developing, and deploying of AVs under the aura of vibrant change and innovation.

2.2   The Human-Centered Argument Distilled

Addressing the design of AVs from a human-centered perspective brings to the forefront two themes: (i) function allocation and (ii) human brain-inspired computing. Function allocation refers to the division of responsibility between humans and machines. In other words, who/what can and/or should do what and when and why. This is a decades old question, taking flight in the 1950s with the founding of the discipline of Human Factors as a way to directly address human problems within air navigation and traffic control. Specifically, it was "…a way of formulating a long-range integrated plan for human engineering research to parallel and support long range planning for equipment and systems design." [28, p. iii] Understanding the abilities, possibilities, and responsibilities of humans and/vs. machines, and translating that understanding into the design of machines ensures smooth interaction between users and the technology [25].

As performance demand rises for more intelligent and human-like artificial systems – most significantly with speech recognition and image classification capacity– human cognition-inspired models are becoming more and more invaluable. Human brain-inspired computing refers to the building of algorithms and architectures that mimic the natural forms of human cognition and the physiology of the human brain. This approach offers benefit for both the advancement of AI and the enlightenment of our understanding of human behavior. This method, like function allocation, is also decades old. Principally heralded by the creation of the first AI program in 1956 [29], the Logic Theorist was specifically built to resemble the problem-solving and decision-making skills of a human; it was capable of proving theorems in symbolic logic. Fast-forward to today and the need to surpass domain specificity and a reliance on vast numbers of high quality labeled training data is growing. The human mind/brain stands as a powerful example of maximal efficiency (i.e. domain generality/knowledge transference/inferential learning capability) within a finite space. Robots engineered in this way have illustrated improved performance [e.g. 30] and suggest promise for applications requiring power efficiency and cognitive abilities similar to that of humans.

Identifying and integrating the role of the human is inevitable for AV advancement. If the argument is to remove the human altogether and/or not replicate human cognition and behavior in the name of safety, e.g. to reduce the number of fatalities because of traffic accidents caused by human error, contrastive empirical support is needed on both sides regarding when and why humans succeed and fail, as well as when and why machines succeed and fail. Crash data between conventional vehicles and AVs, for example, are a stark reminder that minimization of error as an optimization objective for machine learning models is not a clear-cut metric for safety [25, 31]. On the other hand, if the argument is to replicate human cognition and behavior in the name of safety, e.g. to increase the potential for seamless integration of human-machine interaction, a new empirical challenge needs to be prioritized over the traditional optimization objective of most machine learning models that are trained on data sets and deployed into the real world [See 24 for a unique cognitive behavioral parallelism between creative thinking and doing in the arts with driving a car in the city].

This assertion informs the third claim of this paper: insights from human perception and cognition as they relate to learning and adapting to ever-changing environments have an essential role in creating machine learning problem formations that are perfectly matched to the complex real-world tasks they will need to solve. In short, innovative AI R&D methods are urgently needed.

2.3 Explainability

Function allocation and human brain-inspired computing are not only critical to improving, for example, seamless interaction between humans and machines and accuracy of image classification systems [25], but they have further utility in the area of explainability. Explainability, explicability, interpretability, or transparency –all terms with varying definitions and periodic interchangeable usage [16, 32]– "deals with the capability to provide the human with understandable and relevant information on how an AI/[machine learning] ML application is coming to its results." [16, p. 52] Again, human perception and cognition is our model for how we expect relationships in our world to function and how we test and explain the black box that is our mind/brain. The reasons we provide behind decision-making matter in our every day interactions; they serve as answers to agree or contest with on why a particular action or set of actions was made under a given situation. When presented with 'why did you do x?' we explain by breaking down what we believe to be the logic behind our decision(s). In the AI context where models are making predictions from orders of magnitude more data than any human being, the rationale behind the system's output behavior also needs to be provided. Biases, abuses, and failures of these systems need explanation. Transparency of actions through explanation is important because it can strengthen the perception of honesty and improve trust.

In effect, we are at a pivotal moment in the history of AI-enabled technology and the development of legal constraints where the possible claim 'the neural network we don't understand is at fault' by a manufacturer's AV that crashed while on autopilot, for example, is insufficient. Moreover, explanations provided need to be understandable by a range of stakeholders that may include regulators, system engineers, system operators, and accident investigators with varying degrees of knowledge about data, machine learning, computations, algorithms, and the like. The following in Table 1 is a summary of the three types of explanations with increasing specificity for an AI-enabled system proposed by [16]. I include a sample of questions the three types could be utilized to answer.

While such types of explanations are a helpful starting point to setting standards for explainability, they have elicited varying degrees of transparency (e.g. different or

Table 1. Three proposed types of AI systems' explanations.

Type	Definition	Sample questions to answer
Simulatability	System/model	How does the system work?
Decomposability	System's components (e.g. model parameters, inputs, computations)	Where is the system's bias coming from? What is determining the system's safety criteria?
Algorithmic transparency	System's training algorithm	How is the system using the input data?

conflicting definitions between research groups; techniques are unique to specific architectures and thus non-generalizable) and incomplete adherence to the suggested types (e.g. some techniques explain the data but not the model and vice versa) across the board [16]. Moreover, even a battery of qualitative and quantitative tests on system-level methods targeted at the composition of the utilized neural network model do not necessarily provide insights on how the model functions and only inspire a false sense of confidence [16]. These observations underscore the current problems with explainability and the due diligence of such: (1) there is no academic and/or industry-wide unity on the various elements of explainability, and (2) the science behind machine learning must be supplemented by other techniques if any significant advancement with AI is to be made. Identification of principles and priorities such as 'transparency and explainability of AI systems' and 'accountability and responsibility' underpinning proposed legal frameworks [33] will be deficient without prioritizing and reframing the goals of the above two problems. The fourth claim of this paper is that consensus-based standards and compliance checks across industry and academic research labs are needed to significantly move forward with the potential of explainability as a means for assuring autonomy.

2.4 AV Automation Levels

In the meantime, revisiting SAE's levels of driving automation in Table 2 and narrowing in on agent responsibility underscores the indispensable requirement of keeping the human in the loop as the role of control gradually shifts from the human to the machine. Fundamental to this role shift is the diminishing (yet still expected) cognitive behavioral capacity required of the human as the machine takes over at level 3 and beyond [34]. Although level 3 is a turning point in the machine's monitoring capacity, there is still a noted reliance on critical human input. This is no easy feat when research reveals that human operator alertness and overall understanding of the traffic context and the system's functional limitations, among other things, are critical for successful decision-making and task takeover in emergencies [28], [35–36]. It is unfair to assume a human, dozing off in their automated driverless pod, for example, would have to be awakened and forced to intervene in a split-second emergency because the AV's sensors were unable to correctly classify and predict the behavioral trajectory of whatever was the cause of the resulting collision.

Not included in the table is the hypothesized number of vehicles from each level to be simultaneously on the road. The real world is not cleanly divided into strict cate-

Table 2. SAE levels of driving automation and their respective human-machine relationship.

Availability[a]	Level	Automation	Agent responsibility
On public roadways	0	None	Human driver (fully engaged)
On public roadways	1	Assisted	Human driver (fully engaged) with feet off; machine handles a function or two
On public roadways	2	Partial	Human driver (fully engaged) with feet and hands off; machine handles several functions
In closed course testing and on limited roadways	3	Conditional	Human (fully engaged enough to take control with notice) with feet, hands, and eyes off; machine handles most functions and monitors the environment under certain circumstances
In closed course testing and on limited roadways	4	High	Human (unengaged) with the option to take control; machine handles all functions and monitors the environment in certain circumstances
In closed course testing	5	Full	Machine handles all functions and monitors the environment; human is only a passenger and has no option to take control

[a]Availability of particular AV automation levels is a dynamic variable that varies across states here in the United States (and internationally) [37].

gories and boundaries. This is essential to consider and thus test because the very premise of the humanity argument presented here and in [25] is founded on a reality most likely before us: conventional vehicles (level 0), advanced driver assisted systems (ADAS) (levels 1 and 2), automated driving systems (ADS) (levels 3, 4, and 5), and everything else common to roadways will be eventually sharing roadways. Again, if the goal is to create a version of the fictional account presented earlier or simply a human-less roadway, then humanity takes on a distinct role than the one presented at length in [25] and discussed here. But if the goal is yet unclear as particular levels of AVs enter roadways beyond closed-course sunny areas with low speed limits, and a genuinely coordinated understanding and integration of the science among all stakeholders is pursued, let alone regaining trust from the general public, we have a moral obligation to keep humanity at the center of our AI building actions.

Fragile human-machine automation architectures need to be made robust. Without the general public's knowledge of what AVs realistically can and cannot do, the expectation is that 'if the car is on autopilot, it drives on its own.' The information feeding this expectation needs to be honest and deceptive tactics are not the answer. Possible claims of 'the user of the system was being inattentive' or 'the user didn't read the fine print in the car manual' by a manufacturer's AV that crashed while on autopilot, for example, are insufficient. The fifth claim of this paper is that proper training and education for the end-user must be mandatory for any deployment of AI-enabled technology into the public domain.

2.5   The Trolley Problem is a Factor but not the Only Factor

Earlier I mentioned the indispensable role of trust in supporting cooperative relationships between humans. I then highlighted the importance of internal explainability as a tool for transparency of a system's outward actions. Linking trust and explainability is decision-making. We form opinions and choose actions via mental processes that are influenced by biases, reason, emotions, and memories. If assured autonomy is ultimately about guaranteeing a system's safety, security, predictability, and reliability, unpacking the logic behind the decision-making of all tasks performed by the system will be inevitable.

A decision-making situation that receives much attention is the classic Trolley Problem. The gruesome hypothetical is designed to test our moral intuitions in regards to choice making and the value we put on our decisions and the worth we give to others' lives. The problem generally states: a trolley is moving along in its tracks. Not too far ahead there are five workers lying in its direct path. On an alternate track there is only one worker. By chance, you happen to be next to a switch that can change the trolley's fate. If you pull the switch, the trolley will veer onto the alternative track and kill the one worker in its path. Question: do you pull the switch for the trolley to kill one person or do you leave as is and allow the trolley to kill five? There is no satisfactory right or wrong answer. The answer depends on a multitude of factors and conditions influenced by not only the environmental context per se of the moment and whether there is realistically any time to react with full awareness and judgment capacity, but by beliefs of self as a determiner of outcomes and the worth of others' lives. That is, who is to judge whose life is more valuable than another's? Such belief systems are not uniform across people and vary significantly across cultures [38].

This thought experiment, and subsequent transformations, calls urgent attention to the fact that we human drivers are routinely faced with a range of different moral decisions relating to our behavior in respect to other road users. Moreover, there is no one definitive answer to which decisions we want to delegate, and why, to AVs. I point out this decision-making situation among a host of possible decision-making situations AVs have to perform, let alone AI-enabled technologies more broadly, because it accentuates the very human intelligence reality we must contend with and it leads to the sixth claim of this paper: explaining automated decision-making may well remain a black box issue until we definitely answer the black box of how our own mind/brain learns, adapts, and executes new tasks effectively.

3   Our Ethical Responsibility Moving Forward

From where is our moral obligation borne to keep humanity at the center of our actions as it concerns AI? Two interrelated elements, one grander in its appeal and the other specific to the physical production of AI-enabled systems: human rights and business optics. Every human being possesses basic rights and freedoms that need to be respected, protected, and fulfilled, and the longevity of businesses in democratic societies arguably depends on providing products and services that uphold our basic human rights and freedoms. The problem of assured autonomy is the 21st century's ethical and legal quandary as a result of the innovations from the fourth industrial revolution we are currently living.

2020 was coincidentally a year of clarity amongst the eruption of many entrenched problems within society, and the disintegration of trust was one of many consequences to boil to the surface. Publicly acknowledged perils of AI-enabled technologies fueled the already burning fire.

Whether considering intelligent adaptive capacities, human-to-machine takeover, and/or the ethical context of who, what, when, and why behind actions and outcomes, the Human is the core model from which to build a fruitful AI-enabled future. Table 3 summarizes the claims made throughout this paper as they were informed by a human-centered approach. These claims reveal the imperative role such an approach has on

Table 3. Summary of claims as informed by a human-centered approach.

Claim	Statement
1	The science of assured autonomy is entering a new era of growth
2	AI has not been contextualized as a socio-technical innovation
3	Alternative AI R&D methods that integrate insights from human perception and cognition must be prioritized
4	Industry and academic research labs must unify across standards and compliance measures of explainability
5	Training and education for the end-user are critical
6	Explaining the black box of automated decision-making rests on definitely answering the black box of our own mind/brain

building a sustainable foundation for the long-term development of assured autonomy because they endorse an interdependent and dynamic relationship whereby standards and compliance measures are collaboratively set, empirical paradigms within AI R&D of explainability are reframed, and the requirements of end-user education are shifted accordingly. Technology policy does not have to lag behind technology development.

3.1 Recommendations

Science does not exist in a vacuum; it is a social journey of inquiry where experiments are built and data acquired from the very multitude of experiences that shape our lives. As we humans are the major deterrent to the operational advancement of AVs and other AI-enabled technologies that require human-like intelligence to efficiently function within our human-centered world, productive solutions for assuring autonomy must be formulated via interdisciplinary, collaborative means. I propose the following recommendations by claim.

Claim 1: As mentioned, the science of assured autonomy will not significantly advance under an exclusive 'build x to do y' mindset. AI-enabled technologies are complex and evolving, dynamic systems entering into a complex and evolving, dynamic world. The successful building of 'x' to do 'y' requires recognizing that a range of interconnected factors and an array of possible consequences surround 'x' and 'y'. To not recognize and act upon the interconnected factors and consequences AI-enabled (and non-AI-enabled) systems have beyond their individual physical and computational parts is to remain bound to intellectual confines no longer tenable by today's changing legal landscape, let alone the justifiable uproar of voices demanding societal reforms. Safety, security, predictability, and reliability are real-world requirements not necessarily critical within static, closed-course laboratory environments. Furthermore, they are simply not answerable through purely mathematical means. This argues forcefully that a paradigm shift is needed within STEM education and STEM workforce industry culture to prepare and support our AI builders of today and tomorrow. Specifically, an interdisciplinary approach to learning and making must be instituted that connects multiple disciplines outside of traditional STEM fields and incentivizes their integration [e.g. 39]. Higher education learning institutions with AI programs can start by boldly reorienting their curricular options and evaluation metrics. Industry and government research sponsors can also start by requiring researchers to consider the societal ramifications of their work and provide real-time mitigation strategies.

Claim 2: The above can be extended to AI more broadly. In effect, this claim calls for an even broader overhaul across education and workforce culture that not only impacts the STEM fields and their respective industries, but the social sciences, humanities, and arts as well. Again, AI is not just an engineering problem; it's a societal matter that intersects with communities and all the unique individuals that define those communities. Everyone needs to thoroughly understand what AI is so that engagement with the technology can be meaningful, purposeful, and equitable across the entire AI lifecycle of design, development, and deployment. Foundational knowledge of data, machine learning, computations, and algorithms is just as important as foundational knowledge of legal frameworks, ethics, and storytelling techniques. Companies need to spend more aggressively in workforce development both in training their own employees and evaluating their progress, and in attracting new talent through pre-college and college internships and mid-career training fellowships and other work opportunities. Research funding agencies could also create targeted programs for the development of cross-disciplinary AI talent.

Claim 3: Typical train-then-deploy machine learning systems are increasingly failing to improve the intelligence capacities of AI-enabled systems. Risky, outside-of-the-box research proposals can no longer fall under the curiosity-driven funding category; they need to be the mainstream. We need computational models that accurately mimic our capacity to constantly compare, contrast, and collate new information from actions performed by us and by those of others and innovative, cross-disciplinary research projects have the best chance at discovering a holistic solution. The United States needs a science and technology strategy for AI R&D that is unabashedly risk favorable.

Claim 4: Industry needs greater cooperation among its peers. At the macro level, this is a national security issue with transnational implications. Who decides the narrative of what AI is, can, and should be, pursues a specific science and technology strategy, and accomplishes goals will be the leading influencer. Given the reality of how globally networked scientific and engineering capabilities and innovation processes are today, a collaborative approach is requisite. This is where a robust network of international organizations with clearly defined standards and regulations that uphold democratic values and universal rights become paramount in pressuring companies to adhere for competitive advantage: the OECD Principles on AI [40], RAI Certification [41], the Global Partnership on AI (GPAI) [42], and others.

Claim 5: Following from the above and moving to the micro level, the end-user needs to be well informed, not oblivious to the realities of today's AI capacities. While all the above recommendations apply here as well, industry peers can unite now around end-user education policies in the form, for example, of uniform educational campaigns, and the compliance of such. This type of transparency even simplifies oversight and offers clear entrance points for revision, if and when needed.

Claim 6: We humans are the elephant in the room and our mind/brain holds the key to what we have the potential to build, both from a metacognitive sense and a technical sense. Priority must lie in reverse engineering the human mind/brain and pausing to reflect as a human species on what we want with AI in this next phase in our evolutionary history.

3.2   Beyond AVs

While I have used AVs to contextualize the claims made and summarized in Table 3, they are by no means the end-all of AI-enabled technologies. In effect, AVs are but one example of many established and burgeoning AI-enabled systems resulting from the advancement of sensors, software, and emerging technologies that constitute the Internet of Things (IoT). From empathetic AI and companion robots to drones and urban air mobility, the list is long. Assured autonomy becomes an even more critical issue by the minute as AI-enabled use cases amplify, increasing the network of connected smart systems and thus the number of interdependent factors involved and possible outcomes of failure. But whether we build one AI-enabled technology or $N \geq 1$ AI-enabled technologies the problem remains: it or they will be used by, for, and around humans.

The question now is: can we succeed in uniting efficiently and understanding ourselves better enough to create smarter machines not yet fathomable by our own intelligence?

Acknowledgements. Thanks to Dr. I. Gonzalez for her insightful comments and to the Institute for Human Intelligence for providing the required resources for this research.

References

1. Leslie, D.: Understanding bias in facial recognition technologies: an explainer. The Alan Turing Institute (2020). https://doi.org/10.5281/zenodo
2. Wu, E., Wu, K., Daneshjou, R., Ouyang, D., Ho, D.E., Zou, J.: How medical AI devices are evaluated: limitations and recommendations from an analysis of FDA approvals. Nat. Med. 27(4), 582–584 (2021)
3. Lee, P.: Learning from Tay's introduction. Microsoft – Official Microsoft Blog, 25 March 2016. https://blogs.microsoft.com/blog/2016/03/25/learning-tays-introduction/
4. Tesla Deaths: https://www.tesladeaths.com/. Accessed 24 June 2021
5. Jillson, E.: Aiming for truth, fairness, and equity in your company's use of AI. Federal Trade Commission – Business Blog, 19 April 2021. https://www.ftc.gov/news-events/blogs/business-blog/2021/04/aiming-truth-fairness-equity-your-companys-use-ai
6. Proposal for a regulation of the European Parliament and of the Council laying down harmonised rules on artificial intelligence (Artificial Intelligence Act) and amending certain union legislative acts. European Commission, April 2021. https://eur-lex.europa.eu/legal-content/EN/TXT/?qid=1623335154975&uri=CELEX%3A52021PC0206
7. Ethics and governance of artificial intelligence for health: WHO guidance. Geneva: World Health Organization, June 2021. Licence: CC BY-NC-SA 3.0 IGO. https://www.who.int/publications/i/item/9789240029200?utm_source=newsletter&utm_medium=email&utm_campaign=newsletter_axioswhatsnext&stream=science
8. The Association for Unmanned Vehicle Systems International (AUVSI) Industry News Webpage. https://www.auvsi.org/news. Accessed 24 June 2021
9. Trust in tech is wavering and companies must act. Edelman Research, April 2019. https://www.edelman.com/research/2019-trust-tech-wavering-companies-must-act
10. Rainie, L., Anderson, J., Vogels, E.A.: Experts doubt ethical AI design will be broadly adopted as the norm within the next decade. Pew Research Center, June 2021. https://www.pewresearch.org/internet/2021/06/16/experts-doubt-ethical-ai-design-will-be-broadly-adopted-as-the-norm-within-the-next-decade/
11. 2021 Edelman Trust Barometer. Edelman Research, January 2021. https://www.edelman.com/trust/2021-trust-barometer
12. Erikson, E.: Childhood and Society. Norton & Company Inc, New York (1950)
13. Rousseau, D.M., Sitkin, S.B., Burt, R.S., Camerer, C.: Not so different after all: a cross-discipline view of trust. Acad. Manag. Rev. 23(3), 393–404 (1998)
14. López-González, M.: Regaining sight of humanity on the roadway to automation. In: IS&T International Symposium on Electronic Imaging: Autonomous Vehicles and Machines, IS&T. Springfield, Virginia (2020). https://doi.org/10.2352/ISSN.2470-1173.2020.16.AVM-088.
15. National Highway Traffic Safety Administration (NHTSA): NHTSA orders crash reporting for vehicles equipped with advanced driver assistance systems and automated driving systems. NHTSA Press Release, 29 June 2021. https://www.nhtsa.gov/press-releases/nhtsa-orders-crash-reporting-vehicles-equipped-advanced-driver-assistance-systems
16. EASA and Daedalean: Concepts of design assurance for neural networks (CoDANN) II, May 2021. https://daedalean.ai/tpost/kg4j07xlx1-daedalean-and-easa-conclude-second-proje
17. General Data Protection Regulation (GDPR). https://gdpr.eu/tag/gdpr/. Accessed 13 July 2021
18. Waldrop, M.M.: Autonomous vehicles: no drivers required. Nat. News 518(7537), 21–22 (2015)

19. Miller, R.: Closing the curtains on safety theater, Medium, 18 April 2019. https://medium.com/pronto-ai/closing-the-curtains-on-safety-theater-f442b70645a4
20. Boudette, N.E.: Despite high hopes, self-driving cars are 'way in the future'. The New York Times, 17 July 2019. https://www.nytimes.com/2019/07/17/business/self-driving-autonomous-cars.html
21. Taub, E.A.: How jaywalking could jam up the era of self-driving cars. The New York Times, 1 August 2019. https://www.nytimes.com/2019/08/01/business/self-driving-cars-jaywalking.html
22. Edmonds, E.: AAA warns pedestrian detection systems don't work when needed most, AAA NewsRoom, 3 October 2019. https://newsroom.aaa.com/2019/10/aaa-warns-pedestrian-detection-systems-dont-work-when-needed-most/
23. Young, S.: The moral algorithm: how to set the moral compass for autonomous vehicles. Report produced by Gowling WLG (UK), LLC, December 2016
24. López-González, M.: Theoretically automated conversations: collaborative artistic creativity for autonomous machines. In: IS&T International Symposium on Electronic Imaging: Human Vision and Electronic Imaging, IS&T. Springfield, Virginia (2018). https://doi.org/10.2352/ISSN.2470-1173.2018.14.HVEI-531
25. López-González, M.: Today is to see and know: an argument and proposal for integrating human cognitive intelligence into autonomous vehicle perception. In: IS&T International Symposium on Electronic Imaging: Autonomous Vehicles and Machines, IS&T. Springfield, Virginia (2019). https://doi.org/10.2352/ISSN.2470-1173.2019.15.AVM-054
26. Naughton, N.: GM moves to deploy driverless car fleet in 2019, The Detroit News, 12 January 2018. https://www.detroitnews.com/story/business/autos/general-motors/2018/01/12/gm-driverless-car-fleet-cruise-av/109381232/
27. Walker, J.: The self-driving car timeline – predictions from the top 11 global automakers, Emerj, 21 December 2018. https://emerj.com/ai-adoption-timelines/self-driving-car-timeline-themselves-top-11-automakers/
28. Fitts, P.M. (ed.): Human engineering for an effective air-navigation and traffic-control system. In: Report prepared for the Air Navigation Development Board. National Research Council, Washington, D.C., March 1951
29. Stefferud, E.: The logic theory machine: a model heuristic program. Memorandum RM-3731-CC, The Rand Corporation, Santa Monica, CA, June 1963
30. Lázaro-Gredilla, M., Lin, D., Guntupalli, J.S., George, D.: Beyond imitation: zero-shot task transfer on robots by learning concepts as cognitive programs. Sci. Rob. 4(26), eaav3150 (2019)
31. Favarò, F.M., Nader, N., Eurich, S.O., Tripp, M., Varadaraju, N.: Examining accident reports involving autonomous vehicles in California. PLoS ONE 12(9), e0184952 (2017)
32. Lipton, Z.C.: The mythos of model interpretability: in machine learning, the concept of interpretability is both important and slippery. Queue 16(3), 31–57 (2018)
33. Leslie, D., Burr, C., Aitken, M., Cowls, J., Katell, M., Briggs, M.: Artificial intelligence, human rights, democracy, and the rule of law: a primer. The Council of Europe (2021)
34. National Highway Traffic Safety Administration, United States Department of Transportation, Automated Vehicles for Safety. https://www.nhtsa.gov/technology-innovation/automated-vehicles-safety
35. Safety Alert for Operators (SAFO - 13002): Manual flight operations. U.S. Department of Transportation Federal Aviation Administration, 4 January 2013. https://www.faa.gov/other_visit/aviation_industry/airline_operators/airline_safety/safo/all_safos/media/2013/SAFO13002.pdf

36. National Transportation Safety Board: Collision between vehicle controlled by developmental automated driving system and pedestrian. Public Meeting of 19 November 2019. https://www.ntsb.gov/news/events/Documents/2019-HWY18MH010-BMG-abstract.pdf
37. AutoInsurance.org: Which states allow self-driving cars? (2021 Update), 26 February 2021. https://www.autoinsurance.org/which-states-allow-automated-vehicles-to-drive-on-the-road/. Accessed 30 June 2021
38. Awad, E., et al.: The moral machine experiment. Nature **563**(7729), 59–64 (2018)
39. López-González, M.: For female leaders of tomorrow: cultivate an interdisciplinary mindset. In Women in Engineering (WIE) Forum USA East. IEEE (2017). https://doi.org/10.1109/WIE.2017.8285606
40. Oecd.org: OECD Principles on Artificial Intelligence. https://www.oecd.org/going-digital/ai/principles/. Accessed 13 July 2021
41. Responsible AI Institute: RAI Certification. https://www.responsible.ai/certification. Accessed 13 July 2021
42. Gpai.org: The Global Partnership on Artificial Intelligence. https://www.gpai.ai/. Accessed 13 July 2021

A Quantum Leap for Fairness: Quantum Bayesian Approach for Fair Decision Making

Ece Mutlu and Ozlem Ozmen Garibay[✉]

Department of Industrial Engineering and Management Systems,
University of Central Florida, Orlando, FL 32816, USA
{ece.mutlu,ozlem}@ucf.edu

Abstract. With the increasing demand for using artificial intelligence algorithms, the need for a fairness-oriented design in automated decision-making systems emerges as a major concern. Since poorly designed algorithms that ignore the fairness criterion in sensitive attributes (e.g., age, race, and gender) may generate or strengthen bias towards specific groups, researchers try to improve the fairness of AI algorithms without compromising their accuracy. Although many studies focused on the optimization of the trade-off between fairness and accuracy in recent years, understanding the sources of unfairness in decision-making is an essential challenge. To tackle this problem, researchers proposed fair causal learning approaches, which enable us to model cause and effects knowledge structure, to discover the sources of the bias, and to prevent unfair decision-making by amplifying transparency and explainability of AI algorithms. These studies consider fair causal learning problems based on the assumption that the underlying probabilistic model of the world is known; whereas, it is well-known that humans do not obey the classical probability rules in making decisions due to emotional changes, subconscious feelings, and subjective biases, and this yields uncertainty in underlying probabilistic models. In this study, we aim to introduce quantum Bayesian approach as a candidate for fair decision-making in causal learning, motivated by the human decision-making literature in cognitive science. We demonstrated that quantum Bayesian perspective creates well-performing fair decision rules under high uncertainty on the well-known COMPAS (Correctional Offender Management Profiling for Alternative Sanctions) data set.

Keywords: Algorithmic bias · Algorithmic fairness · Bayesian decision making · Fair decision making · Quantum Bayesian method

1 Introduction

Artificial intelligence (AI) algorithms are proving increasingly useful in numerous situations since they can perform more complex computations by handling bigger data sets than humans may comprehend. Nowadays, AI-centered technologies are utilized for a wide range of activities including optimization of healthcare

© Springer Nature Switzerland AG 2021
C. Stephanidis et al. (Eds.): HCII 2021, LNCS 13095, pp. 489–499, 2021.
https://doi.org/10.1007/978-3-030-90963-5_37

systems, medical diagnosis, robot controls, automated trading systems [19]. Furthermore, automated algorithms are not only used for prediction purposes but also considered as a decision-maker because it is believed that these algorithms may simulate decision-making processes more objectively. However, data used to train AI algorithms for learning may include biased measurements or historically biased human systematic errors. Missing data values or selection biases may also result in biased learning outcomes. Moreover, the prediction method might be biased against the minority groups by itself since it aims to optimize the aggregate error which is mainly more favored to majority groups.

Nowadays, AI algorithms rank job candidates in receiving jobs, rate students in college admissions, predict the likelihood of criminality of individuals and/or estimates the risk in giving loans. With the increasing demand for using artificial intelligence algorithms in making decisions that affect people's lives, the need for a fairness-oriented design in automated decision-making systems emerges as a major concern. These concerns about algorithmic fairness have also caused a lot of controversy in recent years. One of the most remarkable examples is that recent studies showed that the United States criminal justice system is falsely biased against the likelihood of criminality of African-American people compared to that of white people [7]. Surprisingly, some big tech companies are also showed to have gender discrimination in their automated decision-making systems. For example, Amazon's AI hiring system is more likely to hire males than females in hiring job candidates for software development and technical positions [21]. Also, Google's ad-targeting algorithms make recommendations of executive jobs positions more to male compared to female users [8]. [19] also discusses some real-world examples of algorithmic biases in AI chatbots, employment matching, flight routing, and automated legal aid for immigration algorithms, and search and advertising placement algorithms.

Since these automated systems may affect people's lives in almost everything, there is great importance in assessing and improving the ethics of the decisions made by these automated systems. Therefore, researchers have introduced various tools to measure fairness in an algorithm or system. For example, Aequitas offers a toolkit that measures the fairness of models used for making estimations for different population subgroups. Additionally, IBM launched AI Fairness 360 (AIF360) toolkit to help industrial applications of algorithmic fairness research studies. In all these examples, fairness metrics are calculated either for different groups or individuals. The most common measures of algorithmic fairness classification tasks are disparate impact, demographic parity, and equalized odds. Disparate impact [11] and demographic parity [10] aims to quantify the legal notion of disparate impact by considering true positive rates for different groups. Equalized odds [12], on the other hand, is designed to measure differences between predictions for different groups by considering both false-positive rates and true positive rates of the two groups.

Although there is a great interest in algorithmic fairness among machine learning and deep learning researchers, and their studies focused on the optimization of the trade-off between fairness and accuracy in recent years [2,5,15,16,18, 22,24]; whereas, understanding the sources of unfairness in decision-making is an essential challenge. To tackle this problem, researchers proposed fair causal learning approaches, which enable us to model cause and effects knowledge structure, to discover the sources of the bias, and to prevent unfair decision-making by amplifying transparency and explainability of AI algorithms. Loftus et al. discuss the importance of causal graphs in designing fair algorithms in detail [18]. They argue that mitigation of bias is only possible when the causal sources are examined thoroughly. Thus, they review extant fairness notions and show a methodology to combine these with causal techniques such as counterfactual fairness. Additionally, these causal interventions are carried out to address contrastive fairness in algorithmic decision-making [4]. [23] developed a novel methodology to get a fair classifier when the causal model is not complete by linking causal inference to multiple dependencies. Despite using traditional fairness measures in causal algorithms, [13] brought new definitions, i.e. fair on average causal effect (FACE), and fair on average causal effect on the treated (FACT) for more robust estimation in fair causal learning.

These studies consider fair causal learning problems based on the assumption that the underlying probabilistic model of the world is known; whereas, it is well-known that humans do not obey the classical probability rules in making decisions due to emotional changes, subconscious feelings, and subjective biases, and this yields uncertainty in underlying probabilistic models. In this study, we draw from quantum theory and convert classical probability rules to more generalized concept of quantum probability rules. The reason behind this attempt can be explained as follows: In quantum theory, the uncertainty principle states that one cannot assign the exact position and momentum of a physical system at the same time. Therefore, these quantities are determined with some characteristic uncertainties. There are a lot of examples of quantum decision making modeling in cognitive science due to the same reasons [3,14]. In this study, we aim to employ quantum-like approach to classical Bayesian framework to generate more fair causal learning framework because we argue that transforming classical probability values as complex quantum amplitudes allow us to model the uncertainties in the underlying probabilistic model of the world is more efficiently.

2   Methodology

We study a Bayesian setting in which decision-maker (DM) tries to maximize its expected utility, and consider the fairness of the decision simultaneously. A Bayesian framework for the decision-making problem can be seen in Fig. 2. Here, x, y and z represents observations, the outcome, and sensitive variable(s), respectively. The joint probability distributions of x, y and z are depend on an unknown parameter θ. The conditional probability distribution of action a given x is also conditioned by the selected policy π. With the given belief β, the DM tries to maximize its objective function that comprises expected utility u and fairness f. In this Bayesian framework, we consider the same strategy as in [9]: At each discrete time step t, the DM's policy acknowledge the current action $a_t \in \mathcal{A}$,

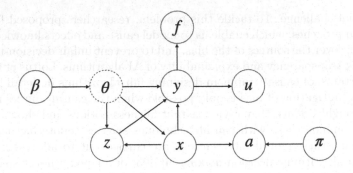

Fig. 1. A decision problem with observations x, the outcome y, and sensitive variable(s) z. The joint probability distributions of x, y and z are depend on an unknown parameter θ. The conditional probability distribution of action a given x is also conditioned by the selected policy π. With the given belief β, the DM tries to maximize its objective function that comprises expected utility u and fairness f.

by observing some data $x_t \in \mathcal{X}$ depending on its current belief β_t and makes a decision $\pi(a_t|\beta_t, x_t)$. Therefore, the stochasticity of the model parameters in β will influence the outcomes in each time step and yield a stochastic outcome in the case of higher uncertainty. Here, we assume that β has a probability distribution $\mathcal{P} \triangleq \{P_\theta | \theta \in \Theta\}$ that contains the actual law of $P_\theta^* = P$ for some θ^*. The trade-off between utility and fairness is satisfied with the following criteria (Fig. 1):

$$\max_{\pi}(1 - \lambda)\mathbb{E}_P^\pi u - \lambda\mathbb{E}_P^\pi f \qquad (1)$$

Here, P denotes the underlying probability distribution and λ is a multiplier used to adjust trade-off between fairness and utility, i.e. $\lambda = 0$ has no emphasis on fairness, while $\lambda = 1$ considers maximizing fairness only. The fairness is measured with disparate impact as in [7], and the decision rule is assumed to be fair if the decision rule is independent for all sensitive variables, i.e., $y \perp\!\!\!\perp z$.

For the same decision problem, [9] introduces two balance models that considers model uncertainty by taking all possible decisions into account to maximize DM's objective. In Bayesian balance model, the deviation from balance of policy π is measured with respect to each possible parameter θ, and the outcomes are weighed to prevent extreme unfairness and lowest utility.

Definition 1. *A decision rule $\lambda(.)$ is (α, p)-Bayes balanced with respect to β if $\forall a, y, z$:*

$$f(\pi) \triangleq \int_\Theta \leq \sum_{a,y,z} \left| \sum_x \pi(a|x)[\mathbb{P}_\theta(x, z|y) - \mathbb{P}_\theta(x|y)\mathbb{P}_\theta(z|y)] \right|^p d\beta(\theta) \leq \alpha^p \qquad (2)$$

In marginal balance approach, on the other hand, a single point estimate for the model is considered instead of using a fully Bayesian approach, i.e., $\mathbb{P}_\beta \triangleq \int_\Theta P_\theta d\beta(\theta)$.

Definition 2. *A decision rule* $\lambda(.)$ *is* (α, p)*-marginal balanced with respect to* β *if* $\forall a, y, z$:

$$\sum_{a,y,z} \left| \sum_x \pi(a|x)[\mathbb{P}_\beta(x, z|y) - \mathbb{P}_\beta(x|y)\mathbb{P}_\beta(z|y)] \right|^p \leq \alpha \quad (3)$$

2.1   Quantum Bayesian Balance Framework

Since quantum theory is very comprehensive in its representations, computations, and inferences; their explanation and applications require a very detailed description. For the sake of simplicity, we will focus on finite-state systems, although quantum approaches can facilitate modeling continuous state systems due to their more advanced representation compared to classical approaches. The differences in classical and quantum sample space representations mainly stem from the assumptions that are used in these approaches. The classic probabilistic theory assumes a sample space in which the outcome of the events are mutually exclusive. In quantum probabilistic theory, on the other hand, events are modeled as subspaces of a Hilbert space in which each orthogonal basis vector corresponds to an elementary outcome. To employ quantum-like probabilistic approach, we represent probabilistic entities as complex probability amplitudes by employing Inverse Born Problem (IBP). This transition using Born's rule can be seen in this expression:

$$Pr(A) \propto \left| e^{i\theta_A} \psi_A \right|^2 \quad (4)$$

As we mentioned before, we assumed that β has a probability distribution $\mathcal{P} \triangleq \{P_\theta | \theta \in \Theta\}$ that contains the actual law of $P_\theta^* = P$ for some θ^*. Therefore, for the application of balance gradient descent, we need to focus on the following expression as in Eq. 5:

$$f(\pi) \triangleq \int_\Theta \leq \sum_{a,y,z} \left| \sum_x \pi(a|x)\Delta_\theta(x, y, z) \right|^p d\beta(\theta) \leq \alpha^p \quad (5)$$

where $\Delta_\theta(x, y, z) = [\mathbb{P}_\theta(x, z|y) - \mathbb{P}_\theta(x|y)\mathbb{P}_\theta(z|y)]$ in Bayes balanced approach. Identifying delta expression with its quantum counterpart is possible with integrating Eq. 4 in Eq. 5.

$$\left| e^{i\theta_{x,z|y}}\Psi_\theta(x,z|y) - e^{i\theta_{x|y}}\Psi_\theta(x|y)e^{i\theta_{z|y}}\Psi_\theta(z|y) \right|^2$$

$$= \left| e^{i\theta_{x,z|y}}\Psi_\theta(x,z|y) - e^{i\theta_{x|y}}\Psi_\theta(x|y)e^{i\theta_{z|y}}\Psi_\theta(z|y) \right|$$

$$\cdot \left| e^{i\theta_{x,z|y}}\Psi_\theta(x,z|y) - e^{i\theta_{x|y}}\Psi_\theta(x|y)e^{i\theta_{z|y}}\Psi_\theta(z|y) \right|^*$$

$$= e^{i\theta_{x,z|y}}\Psi_\theta(x,z|y).e^{-i\theta_{x,z|y}}\Psi_\theta(x,z|y) + e^{i\theta_{x,z|y}}\Psi_\theta(x,z|y).e^{-i\theta_{x|y}}\Psi_\theta(x|y)e^{i\theta_{z|y}}\Psi_\theta(z|y) \tag{6}$$

$$+ e^{-i\theta_{x,z|y}}\Psi_\theta(x,z|y).e^{i\theta_{x|y}}\Psi_\theta(x|y)e^{i\theta_{z|y}}\Psi_\theta(z|y)$$

$$+ e^{i\theta_{x|y}}\Psi_\theta(x|y)e^{i\theta_{z|y}}\Psi_\theta(z|y).e^{-i\theta_{x|y}}\Psi_\theta(x|y)e^{i\theta_{z|y}}\Psi_\theta(z|y)$$

$$= |\Psi_\theta(x,z|y)|^2 + |\Psi_\theta(x|y)\Psi_\theta(z|y)|^2 + |\Psi_\theta(x,z|y)|.|\Psi_\theta(x|y)\Psi_\theta(z|y)|e^{i(\theta_{x,z|y} - \theta_{x|y}\theta_{z|y})}$$

$$+ |\Psi_\theta(x|y)\Psi_\theta(z|y)|^2 + |\Psi_\theta(x,z|y)|.|\Psi_\theta(x|y)\Psi_\theta(z|y)|e^{i(\theta_{x|y}\theta_{z|y} - \theta_{x,z|y})}$$

Knowing that

$$cos(\theta_1 - \theta_2) = \frac{e^{i(\theta_1-\theta_2)}e^{i(\theta_2-\theta_1)}}{2} \tag{7}$$

Then Eq. 6 can be rewritten as:

$$|\Psi_\theta(x,z|y)|^2 + |\Psi_\theta(x|y)\Psi_\theta(z|y)|^2$$
$$\pm 2|\Psi_\theta(x,z|y)|.|\Psi_\theta(x|y)\Psi_\theta(z|y)|cos(\theta_{x,z|y} - \theta_{x|y}\theta_{z|y}) \tag{8}$$

Therefore, we can redefine delta expression in quantum counterpart of Bayes balanced approach as in Eq. 8.

Definition 3. *A decision rule* $\lambda(.)$ *is* (α, p)-*Quantum Bayes balanced with respect to* β *if* $\forall a, y, z$:

$$f(\pi) \triangleq \int_\Theta \leq \sum_{a,y,z} \left| \sum_x \pi(a|x) \left[|\Psi_\theta(x,z|y) - \Psi_\theta(x|y)\Psi_\theta(z|y)|^2 \right] \right|^p d\beta(\theta) \leq \alpha^p \tag{9}$$

which satisfies

$$f(\pi) \triangleq \int_\Theta \leq \sum_{a,y,z} \left| \sum_x \pi(a|x) \left[\mathbb{P}_\theta(x,z|y) + \mathbb{P}_\theta(x|y)\mathbb{P}_\theta(z|y) - 2cos\theta\sqrt{\mathbb{M}} \right] \right|^p d\beta(\theta) \leq \alpha^p \tag{10}$$

where

$$\mathbb{M} = \mathbb{P}_\theta(x,z|y)\mathbb{P}_\theta(x|y)\mathbb{P}_\theta(z|y) \tag{11}$$

3 Results

The aim of this study is to compare and contrast performances of our Quantum Bayes balanced framework with the extant approaches of marginal and Bayes balanced approaches given in [9] when the underlying probabilistic model of the world is not known. For this purpose, we have used ProPublica COMPAS (Correctional Offender Management Profiling for Alternative Sanctions) data set [1,17,20]. ProPublica risk assessment data set includes a number of previous felonies, charge degree, age, race, and gender of 7214 individuals as features and a binary outcome variable that shows whether an inmate recidivated within two years after release from prison. We assigned race and gender as sensitive attributes, while the remaining attributes are used as observations for policy. For the non-binary features, we applied discretization by assigning the average value as a threshold, and the values higher than the threshold are assigned as 1, while the rest is assigned as 0. Randomly selected 6000 observations are used for training, whereas, remaining 1214 are tested for validation purposes.

3.1   When $\lambda < 0.5$

Figure 2 shows the results of the optimization criteria given in Eq. 1 by using marginal-balanced (black bar), Bayes-balanced (red bar) and quantum Bayes balanced (blue bars) with varying interference values ($cos\theta$). Since the aim is to maximize the utility and minimize the deviation from the fairness criterion, the higher values are more favorable.

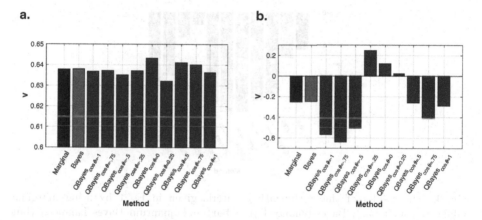

Fig. 2. The results of the optimization criteria given in Eq. 1 by using marginal-balanced (black bar), Bayes-balanced (red bar) and quantum Bayes balanced (blue bars) with varying interference values when **a.** $\lambda = 0$, **a.** $\lambda = 0.25$. (Color figure online)

In Fig. 2.a, $\lambda = 0$, that means fairness is not taken into account and the gradient descent algorithm tries to maximize utility only. We realized that the Bayesian approach performs slightly better than the classical marginal approach. The superiority of the performance of the quantum Bayesian approach varies with respect to the specified interference effect. When $cos\theta = 0$, a higher score is obtained, i.e. A higher utility is obtained in the decision-making process. When we assign more importance to fairness in the objective function as $\lambda = 0.25$ in

Fig. 2.b, we could not observe a significant difference in the results obtained via marginal and Bayesian approaches. However, in some definite interference values $(-0.25 \lesssim cos\theta \lesssim 0.25)$, the quantum Bayes balanced approach gives significantly better results with satisfying higher utility and less deviation from fairness.

3.2   When $\lambda = 0.5$

Figure 3 shows the results of the optimization criteria given in Eq. 1 by using marginal-balanced (black bar), Bayes-balanced (red bar) and quantum Bayes balanced (blue bars) with varying interference values $(cos\theta)$ when equal importance is given to utility and fairness ($\lambda = 0.5$). Here, we observed that the Bayesian balanced approach decreases the objective function compared to the marginal balanced approach, and quantum Bayesian balanced with interference term $-1 \lesssim cos\theta \lesssim 0$ yields even smaller values. However, results demonstrated that the quantum Bayesian approach performs better when the range of interference term between ∼0.25 to ∼0.5.

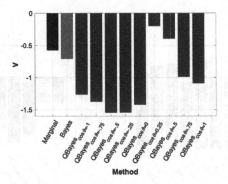

Fig. 3. The results of the optimization criteria given in Eq. 1 by using marginal-balanced (black bar), Bayes-balanced (red bar) and quantum Bayes balanced (blue bars) with varying interference values when $\lambda = 0.5$. (Color figure online)

3.3   When $\lambda > 0.5$

Figure 4 shows the results of the optimization criteria given in Eq. 1 by using marginal-balanced (black bar), Bayes-balanced (red bar) and quantum Bayes balanced (blue bars) with varying interference values $(cos\theta)$ when the optimization function weight more on fairness than utility.

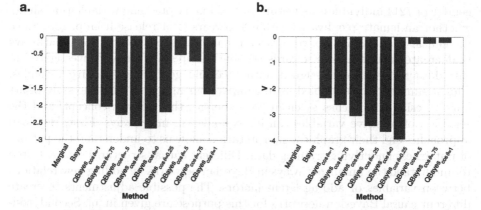

Fig. 4. The results of the optimization criteria given in Eq. 1 by using marginal-balanced (black bar), Bayes-balanced (red bar) and quantum Bayes balanced (blue bars) with varying interference values when **a.** $\lambda = 0.75$, **a.** $\lambda = 1$. (Color figure online)

Although the quantum Bayes balanced approach may show relatively similar results when $cos\theta = 0.5$ compared to the Bayesian approach, the marginal approach performs better than both. When the optimization of the decision making is only keep the deviation on fairness as low as possible, the quantum Bayesian approach falls short regardless of the interference value. It should be noted that, better results in the quantum Bayesian approach are observed when interference is $0.5 \lesssim cos\theta \leq 1$.

4 Conclusions

Despite the impressive performances of AI algorithms, recent studies showed that these algorithms might be biased and may generate unfair outcomes for some minority groups. To prevent this unfairness in AI algorithms, researchers proposed fair causal learning approaches, which enable us to model cause and effects knowledge structure, to discover the sources of the bias, and to prevent unfair decision-making by amplifying transparency and explainability of AI algorithms. However, these studies consider fair causal learning problems based on the assumption that the underlying probabilistic model of the world is known. In this study, we focused on the fairness of decision-making when there is uncertainty in the underlying probabilistic model of the world. This concern is mainly addressed in [9], and the Bayesian balanced approach has been proposed as a fair causal learning alternative to the classical marginal balanced approach. Here, we introduced the quantum Bayesian approach as a candidate for fair decision-making in causal learning, motivated by the human decision-making literature in cognitive science. For this purpose, we have used COMPAS (Correctional Offender Management Profiling for Alternative Sanctions) data set which includes a number of previous felonies, charge degree, age, race, and gender of 7214 individuals as features and a binary outcome variable that shows whether an inmate recidivated within two years after release from prison. Since the causal relationships between variables and the specific conditional pathways that create an unfair bias towards specific features are already investigated in this data set, we have assigned both race and gender as sensitive variables. This assumption also enabled us to compare our approach with the state-of-art fair Bayesian approaches given in [9]. Whereas, this fairness concept, and the selection of sensitive variables can be expanded in many ways. First, Bayesian approaches and their graphical interpretation allow us to understand the pattern of unfairness underlying training data. Different causal structures can be tested to understand the unfair pathways in Bayesian networks by adding new relations between variables or adding latent factors. The possible adjustments to create different causal Bayesian networks for this purpose are given in [6]. Second, contrastive and counterfactual inferences to make predictions fair across different subgroups also enables us to make fair predictions with respect to multiple possible causal models at the same time. More discussions on this approach can be found in [22].

Here, we introduced the quantum Bayesian approach as a candidate for fair decision-making in causal learning, motivated by the human decision-making literature in cognitive science. We demonstrated that the quantum Bayesian perspective creates well-performing fair decision rules under high uncertainty on the well-known COMPAS data set when the optimization function aims to maximize the utility and minimize the deviation from the fairness at the same time. Whereas, when the aim of the DM to make a fair decision only, marginal and Bayes balanced approaches perform better than their quantum counterpart. Although our approach yields very promising results, it should be noted that computational complexity of Bayesian methods are raised significantly with the increasing number of data points and features. This complexity increase is much more higher when quantum Bayesian approaches are employed, since these methods bring extra interference terms. The most efficient way to tackle this problem is to discover heuristics that predict the interference terms. Then, our method will be as fast as classical Bayesian approaches in the existence of larger data sets. Future studies may aim to find a heuristic to predict optimum interference value in the quantum approach, and adapting the quantum framework to different AI methodologies.

References

1. Angwin, J., Larson, J., Mattu, S., Kirchner, L.: Machine bias. ProPublica, pp. 139–159, May 2016
2. Barabas, C., Virza, M., Dinakar, K., Ito, J., Zittrain, J.: Interventions over predictions: reframing the ethical debate for actuarial risk assessment. In: Conference on Fairness, Accountability and Transparency, pp. 62–76. PMLR (2018)
3. Bruza, P.D., Wang, Z., Busemeyer, J.R.: Quantum cognition: a new theoretical approach to psychology. Trends Cogn. Sci. 19(7), 383–393 (2015)

4. Chakraborti, T., Patra, A., Noble, J.A.: Contrastive fairness in machine learning. IEEE Lett. Comput. Soc. **3**(2), 38–41 (2020)
5. Chiappa, S.: Path-specific counterfactual fairness. In: Proceedings of the AAAI Conference on Artificial Intelligence, vol. 33, pp. 7801–7808 (2019)
6. Chiappa, S., Isaac, W.S.: A causal Bayesian networks viewpoint on fairness. In: Kosta, E., Pierson, J., Slamanig, D., Fischer-Hübner, S., Krenn, S. (eds.) Privacy and Identity 2018. IAICT, vol. 547, pp. 3–20. Springer, Cham (2019). https://doi.org/10.1007/978-3-030-16744-8_1
7. Chouldechova, A.: Fair prediction with disparate impact: a study of bias in recidivism prediction instruments. Big Data **5**(2), 153–163 (2017)
8. Datta, A., Tschantz, M.C., Datta, A.: Automated experiments on ad privacy settings: a tale of opacity, choice, and discrimination. In: Proceedings on Privacy Enhancing Technologies, vol. 2015, no. 1, pp. 92–112 (2015)
9. Dimitrakakis, C., Liu, Y., Parkes, D.C., Radanovic, G.: Bayesian fairness. In: Proceedings of the AAAI Conference on Artificial Intelligence, vol. 33, pp. 509–516 (2019)
10. Dwork, C., Hardt, M., Pitassi, T., Reingold, O., Zemel, R.: Fairness through awareness. In: Proceedings of the 3rd Innovations in Theoretical Computer Science Conference, pp. 214–226 (2012)
11. Feldman, M., Friedler, S.A., Moeller, J., Scheidegger, C., Venkatasubramanian, S.: Certifying and removing disparate impact. In: Proceedings of the 21th ACM SIGKDD International Conference on Knowledge Discovery and Data Mining, pp. 259–268 (2015)
12. Hardt, M., Price, E., Srebro, N.: Equality of opportunity in supervised learning. arXiv preprint arXiv:1610.02413 (2016)
13. Khademi, A., Lee, S., Foley, D., Honavar, V.: Fairness in algorithmic decision making: an excursion through the lens of causality. In: The World Wide Web Conference, pp. 2907–2914 (2019)
14. Khrennikov, A.: Quantum-like modeling of cognition. Front. Phys. **3**, 77 (2015)
15. Kilbertus, N., Rojas-Carulla, M., Parascandolo, G., Hardt, M., Janzing, D., Schölkopf, B.: Avoiding discrimination through causal reasoning. arXiv preprint arXiv:1706.02744 (2017)
16. Kusner, M.J., Loftus, J.R., Russell, C., Silva, R.: Counterfactual fairness. arXiv preprint arXiv:1703.06856 (2017)
17. Larson, J., Mattu, S., Kirchner, L., Angwin, J.: How we analyzed the COMPAS recidivism algorithm. ProPublica, vol. 9, no. 1, May 2016
18. Loftus, J.R., Russell, C., Kusner, M.J., Silva, R.: Causal reasoning for algorithmic fairness. arXiv preprint arXiv:1805.05859 (2018)
19. Mehrabi, N., Morstatter, F., Saxena, N., Lerman, K., Galstyan, A.: A survey on bias and fairness in machine learning. arXiv preprint arXiv:1908.09635 (2019)
20. Northpointe, I.: Practitioner's Guide to COMPAS Core (2015)
21. Pessach, D., Shmueli, E.: Algorithmic fairness. arXiv preprint arXiv:2001.09784 (2020)
22. Russell, C., Kusner, M., Loftus, C., Silva, R.: When worlds collide: integrating different counterfactual assumptions in fairness. In: Advances in Neural Information Processing Systems, vol. 30. NIPS Proceedings (2017)
23. Salimi, B., Rodriguez, L., Howe, B., Suciu, D.: Interventional fairness: causal database repair for algorithmic fairness. In: Proceedings of the 2019 International Conference on Management of Data, pp. 793–810 (2019)
24. Zhang, J., Bareinboim, E.: Fairness in decision-making-the causal explanation formula. In: Thirty-Second AAAI Conference on Artificial Intelligence (2018)

Cultural Understanding Using In-context Learning and Masked Language Modeling

Ming Qian[1]([✉]), Charles Newton[1], and Davis Qian[2]

[1] Soar Technology, Orlando, FL, USA
{ming.qian, charles.newton}@soartech.com
[2] University of North Carolina at Chapel Hill, Chapel Hill, NC, USA
davisq@live.unc.edu

Abstract. With the rapid advancement of natural language processing (NLP) as a sub-field of artificial intelligence (AI), a number of unsupervised pre-trained language models trained on large corpus have become available (e.g. BERT and GPT-3). While these models have tremendous linguistic knowledge, a lot of other types of knowledge are embedded in them as well. We perform cross-culture analysis experiments using AI-based Masked Language Modeling (MLM) and GPT-based Generative Language Modeling (In-context learning modeling). The designed approach is to set up a cultural context in sentences with masked words (for MLM) or in a human-prompted text segment (for GPT-based NLG). Consequently, the predicted masked words or the machine generated stories will reflect measurable intercultural differences because language models are trained on different corpus in different languages, and on English corpus containing a significant amount of knowledge on foreign cultures. We show a variety of examples: geopolitical knowledge, holidays, gestures, customs, social norms, emotion schema, role schema, procedure schema, and emotion change detection based on a diplomatic speech. The deep learning neural network model encodes its knowledge in the weights of a neural network instead of as organized semantic concepts. The model can reflect biases brought in by the training data and can give us inaccurate or faulty answers. Overall, with the rapid advancement of language technology, pre-trained language models have grown more powerful, and have great potential to serve as a culturalization tool.

Keywords: Cultural understanding · Language modeling · Masked language modeling · Generative language modeling · Cross-lingual writing assistance · Culturalization · Localization · Cross-lingual · Inter-culture

1 Introduction

Culturalization is how one can adapt content for other cultures and other geographies beyond just normal localization. Culturalization looks beyond the language component, focusing on every other aspect of the content that can be potentially sensitive to a particular cultural environment. After culturalization, the contents become both culturally appropriate and have a much higher chance of connecting with the target audience.

© Springer Nature Switzerland AG 2021
C. Stephanidis et al. (Eds.): HCII 2021, LNCS 13095, pp. 500–508, 2021.
https://doi.org/10.1007/978-3-030-90963-5_38

Cultural understanding is firmly grounded in a group-level cognition that emerges from the interactions between the members of a cultural group. The group-level cognition of a cultural group is constantly negotiated and renegotiated through generations of members across time and space. Humans acquire inferred knowledge of diverse and varied cultural understandings through a lifetime of learning and interaction.

We are interested in automatic discovery of cultural knowledge, something that would allow digital assistants equipped with the automatic mechanism to help a user to discover culture-sensitive knowledge, avoid cultural miscommunication, and prevent negative and unintended consequences. Cultural schemas are a generalized collection of knowledge of past experiences that are organized into knowledge groups and guide human behaviors in familiar situations.

Humans can learn quickly based on a brief instruction or after seeing only a few examples. Using in-context learning, machines can learn just as efficiently as humans with no data (zero-shot) or very little data (few-shot) [1, 2]. Compared with multi-task learners such as GPT-2 [7] that require fine-tuning, in-context learners such as GPT-3 do not require a large amount of training data for a specific task and are much easier to scale. The reason for this is that the language model develops a broad set of skills and pattern recognition abilities during training time, which it then uses at inference time to rapidly adapt to or recognize the desired task based on the prompted text.

In this paper, we used GPT-3 generative language modeling and AI-based Masked Language Modeling (MLM) as a tool for cultural knowledge discovery. The approach is a human-machine teaming approach because a human user builds a masked task by giving a detailed description on the context and sets up the query as a mask or multiple masks. Then the MLM solves the puzzle by applying its linguistic and cultural knowledge learned from a huge training corpus (e.g. BERT model trained on Wikipedia and Book Corpus, a dataset containing + 10,000 books of different genres). In the same vein, a human user can establish a context by preparing a prompt text for the GPT-3 model, and the GPT-3 model can generate synthetic text containing culture intelligence related to the described context.

2 Methodologies and Simple Examples

2.1 GPT-3

GPT-3 is a transformer-based language model [1] that takes input and generates text from it. GPT-3 takes any text prompt like several phrases or sentences and returns a text completion in natural language. Users can also program GPT-3 by showing just a few examples (few shots) [2]. A full-version of GPT-3 model has 175 billion machine learning parameters.

Table 1 shows several examples of cross-cultural knowledge discovery. The first example is related to geopolitical knowledge: both the United Kingdom and Argentina claim sovereignty over a certain group of islands located in the south-west Atlantic Ocean. The UK calls these the Falkland Islands whilst Argentina calls these Islas Malvinas. The second example shows that the language model can discover different federal holidays in different countries. The third example shows that the language model can detect culture specific gestures.

Table 1. Cross-cultural Knowledge generated by GPT-3 Model (the bold part is the prompted text, and the regular text is the generated text).

Geopolitical knowledge	**The islands were called the Falkland Islands by the British, and in Argentina it was called** Islas Malvinas
Holidays	**In US, the October federal holidays are: Oct 12, Columbus Day. In China, the October federal holidays are:** Oct 1, National Day (public holiday)
Gesture	**The Greek equivalent of a middle finger in the US is** the Moutza, where you fling your hand out, fingers pushed apart, and yell "Moutza!"

2.2   Masked Language Modeling

The objective of masked language modeling (MLM) is to mask one or more words in a sentence and have the Natural Language Processing (NLP) model identify those masked words given the other words (representing context) in a sentence [3]. By training the model with this objective, it can learn certain statistical properties of word sequences embedded in a training corpus. BERT is the first large transformer architecture to be trained using this masked language modeling task [4, 5].

MLM can provide cross-cultural knowledge as illustrated by the examples listed in Table 2 below. The first two examples showed social norms in the US: family and friends exchange gifts on Christmas Eve; and door etiquette of entering and exiting with others. The third example is in Chinese, and it illustrates the Chinese tradition that during a funeral, people throw specially made papers into the sky (撒紙) to "bribe" the ghosts so they do not bother the dead.

Table 2. Cross-cultural knowledge generated by MLM Model.

Inputs	Model Prediction
We give each other [MASK] on Christmas evening	Gifts 25.5%
	Presents 23.1%
This guy walked into the building right in front of me. He was very nice to [MASK] the door for me	Open 75.3%
	Hold 9.3%
他家老人去世了，在地上[MASK]紙。	撒 13%
	寫 6.8%
Translation	燒 5.7%

3 Cultural Schema Examples

Cultural schemas are generalized collections of knowledge of past experiences that are organized into related knowledge groups. They guide human behaviors in familiar situations [8]. In this section, we showcase more cultural schema related examples of using MLM and GPT-3.

3.1 Emotion Schema (MLM Example)

Emotion schemas contain information about effect and evaluation stored in long-term memory [8]. It develops through social interactions throughout a person's life. Social interactions are usually shared by certain cultural groups.

A Chinese emotion (sadness) schema, listed in Table 3, can be elaborated as: X experiences sadness when he/she senses a gap or lacking ability, because of a lack of exposure, awareness, and sufficient knowledge, when he/she compares himself/herself to others. This Chinese cultural sadness schema indexes inferiority, self-pity, and helplessness [6].

Table 3 shows the MLM task helps to find the interpretation in the Western culture. The top emotions found are 'awkward', 'inferior', and 'embarrassed'.

Table 3. The emotion of 'sadness' is unique to Chinese culture when a person senses a gap or lacking ability. Therefore, a proper emotion for Western culture needs to be identified.

Original Chinese	我的英语词汇量太小了, 每次跟英语母语的美国人比我都觉得伤心。
English translation generated by Google Translator	My English vocabulary is too small, and I feel sad every time I compare myself to a native English speaker
My English vocabulary is too small, and I feel [MASK] every time I compare myself to a native English speaker	Awkward 10.3%
	Inferior 5.3%
	Embarrassed 4.4%

3.2 Role Schema (MLM Example)

Role schemas are knowledge about social roles that denote expected sets of behaviors of people in certain social position and relations [8].

Table 4 shows the results of English and Chinese MLM tasks for the same context: whether a college student will listen to their parents or grandparents opinions about finding a boyfriend. While in the English versions, the student refuses to listen to both parents and grandparents, in the Chinese versions, the student refuses to listen to the parents, but is actually willing to listen to the grandparents' opinion. This shows the difference of social roles played by grandparents across the two cultures.

Table 4. Role Schema Example. A Chinese college student is willing to listen to grandparents' opinions.

Regarding finding a boyfriend, this college student **[MASK]** to listen to the opinion of her parents	关于找男朋友的事，这个大学生 [MASK]听她父母的意见。
Regarding finding a boyfriend, this college student **refuses** to listen to the opinion of her parents. 15.8%	关于找男朋友的事，这个大学生不 听她父母的意见。 26.1% [translation: do not want to]
Regarding finding a boyfriend, this college student **has** to listen to the opinion of her parents. 10.9%	关于找男朋友的事，这个大学生没 听她父母的意见。 12.8%
Regarding finding a boyfriend, this college student **[MASK]** to listen to the opinion of her parents	关于找男朋友的事，这个大学生 [MASK]听她爷爷奶奶的意见。
Regarding finding a boyfriend, this college student **refuses** to listen to the opinion of her grandparents. 14.7%	关于找男朋友的事，这个大学生想 听她爷爷奶奶的意见。 14.1% [translation: want to]
Regarding finding a boyfriend, this college student **has** to listen to the opinion of her grandparents. 8.4%	关于找男朋友的事，这个大学生不 听她爷爷奶奶的意见。 10%

3.3   Procedure Schema (GPT-3 Example)

Procedure schemas are knowledge about the appropriate sequence of events in common situations. This includes the specific steps to take and the appropriate behavioral rules for the events [8]. Figure 2 shows an example in which a guest uses the position of a teapot lid to signal the need to refill the teapot. The GPT-3 generated synthetic text contains the answer and a lot of other relevant information. Figure 2 shows that we can use a BERT-based Question & Answer (Q&A) to extract the correct answer from the synthetic text (Fig. 1, Fig. 3).

Prompt:
When drinking tea in a Dim Sum restaurant, the tea guest lifted the lid of the teapot and placed it on top of the mouth of the teapot. What is the guest trying to signal?

Generated synthetic text:
The guest is letting the host know that the tea is good an that they would like more. In the Chinese culture, when drinking tea with someone, the host always pours the tea for the guest. A guest can only drink when the host has poured for them. This is a way to show respect to the host and indicate that you are enjoying the tea. When a guest wants more tea, they do not pour it themselves. They lift the lid of the teapot and place it on top of the mouth of the teapot. This is a signal to the host that the guest...

Fig. 1. GPT-3 example on tea culture.

What is the guest trying to signal?
The guest is letting the host know that the tea is good and
they would like more
Why the lid of the teapot was lifted?
When a guest wants more tea, they do not pour it themselves.
What should the host do?
Pours the tea for the guest.

Fig. 2. Q&A based on GPT-3 synthetic text (https://www.pragnakalp.com/demos/BERT-NLP-QnA-Demo).

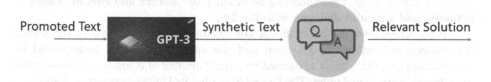

Fig. 3. Combine GPT-3 synthetic text generation and Q&A system.

4   Change Detection on Diplomatic Speech (GPT-3 Example)

Humans can perceive crucial shifts in norms and emotions in discourse. We experimented to detect changes of emotion for a lengthy diplomatic speech by querying the generative language model on the emotions being detected on the fly.

The example we chose was the ill-tempered high-level talks in Anchorage on March 19th 2021 involving Secretary of State Antony Blinken and National Security Adviser Jake Sullivan on the US side facing off with China's most senior foreign policy official Yang Jiechi and foreign minister Wang Yi. The US side claimed that the Chinese delegation had broken an agreement to keep opening statements to two minutes. Instead, the speech from Mr Yang Jiechi lasted 16 min without being interpreted. So, during the time interval, the US delegates were actually not able to track what was going on. So now, our question is whether an AI mechanism supported by the GPT-3 model can monitor the changes of emotion. Below are five paragraphs extracted from Mr. Yang's speech, and the emotion detected using GPT-3 model. The bolded words were generated by GPT-3 as synthetic texts related to emotion.

"Secretary Blinken and Mr. Sullivan, the State Councilor and Foreign Minister Wang Yi and I have come to Anchorage, the United States, to have this strategic dialogue with the United States. We hope that this dialogue will be a sincere and candid one. Both China and the United States are major countries in the world, and together we shoulder important responsibilities to the peace, stability and development of the world and the region. In China, we have just concluded the Lianghui, or the two sessions of the National People's Congress and the Chinese People's Political Consultative Conference. During the sessions, we adopted the outline for the 14th five-year economic and social development plan and the long-range objectives through the year 2035. For China, we are now in a historic year where we will move from finishing the first centenary goal to the second centenary goal, and by the year 2035 China will surely achieve basic modernization. And by the year 2050, China will achieve full modernization. China has made decisive achievements and important strategic gains in fighting COVID-19, and we have achieved a full victory in ending absolute poverty in China. China's per-capita GDP is only one-fifth of that of the United States, but we have managed to end absolute poverty for all people in China. And we hope that other countries, especially the advanced countries, will make similar efforts in this regard. And China has also made historic achievements in building the country into a moderately prosperous one in all respects. The Chinese people are wholly rallying around the Communist Party of China. Our values are the same as the common values of humanity. Those are: peace, development, fairness, justice, freedom and democracy. "

The Chinese speaker is expressing an emotion of **"sincere and candid" desire to actually hold a candid dialogue with the US.**

"What China and the international community follow or uphold is the United Nations-centered international system and the international order underpinned by international law, not what is advocated by a small number of countries of the so-called rules-based international order. The United States has its United States-style democracy and China has Chinese-style democracy. It is not just up to the American people, but also the people of the world, to evaluate how the United States has done in advancing its own democracy. In China's case, after decades of reform and opening up, we have come a long way in various fields. In particular, we have engaged in tireless efforts to contribute to the peace and development of the world, and to upholding the purposes and principles of the U.N. Charter. The wars in this world are launched by some other countries, which have resulted in massive casualties. But for China, what we have asked for, for other countries, is to follow a path of peaceful development, and this is the purpose of our foreign policy. We do not believe in invading through the use of force, or to topple other regimes through various means, or to massacre the people of other countries, because all of those would only cause turmoil and instability in this world. And at the end of the day, all of those would not serve the United States well. "

The Chinese speaker is expressing an emotion of **"determined" resolve to follow its own path.**

So we believe that it is important for the United States to change its own image and to stop advancing its own democracy in the rest of the world. Many people within the United States actually have little confidence in the democracy of the United States, and they have various views regarding the Government of the United States. In China, according to opinion polls, the leaders of China have the wide support of the Chinese people. So no attempt to – the opinion polls conducted in the United States show that the leaders of China have the support of the Chinese people. No attempt to smear China's social system would get anywhere. Facts have shown that such practices would only lead the Chinese people to rally more closely around the Communist Party of China and work steadily towards the goals that we have set for ourselves.

The Chinese speaker is expressing an emotion of **"anger".**

So what we need to do is to abandon the Cold War mentality and the zero-sum game approach. We must change the way we think and make sure that in this century, the 21st century, countries big or small, particularly the big countries, should come united together to contribute to the future of humanity and build a community with a shared future for humankind. It's also important for all of us to come together to build a new type of international relations, ensuring fairness, justice, and mutual respect. And on some regional issues, I think the problem is that the United States has exercised long-arm jurisdiction and suppression and overstretched the national security through the use of force or financial hegemony, and this has created obstacles for normal trade activities, and the United States has also been persuading some countries to launch attacks on China.

The Chinese speaker is expressing an emotion of **"anger"**.

The United States itself does not represent international public opinion, and neither does the Western world. Whether judged by population scale or the trend of the world, the Western world does not represent the global public opinion. So we hope that when talking about universal values or international public opinion on the part of the United States, we hope the U.S. side will think about whether it feels reassured in saying those things, because the U.S. does not represent the world. It only represents the Government of the United States. I don't think the overwhelming majority of countries in the world would recognize that the universal values advocated by the United States or that the opinion of the United States could represent international public opinion, and those countries would not recognize that the rules made by a small number of people would serve as the basis for the international order.

The Chinese speaker is expressing an emotion of **"anger"**.

The example shows that the GPT-3 model can track emotional changes over time. Based on the GPT-3 results, Mr. Yang's speech started with an emotion of "sincere and candid" desire for a dialogue, which was then followed with an emotion of "determined" resolve for China to follow its own path. And then after a while, the emotions become anger, anger, and more anger.

The results match with the human perception very well, and shows the potential for in-context learning language models to serve as a communicative change detection tool. Working with a machine translation system, such a tool can monitor the diplomatic discourse and warn delegates about potential changes for crucial events/dynamics.

5 Conclusion

With the rapid advancement of natural language processing (NLP) as a sub-field of artificial intelligence (AI), a number of unsupervised pre-trained language models trained on large corpus have become available (e.g. BERT and GPT-3). While these models have tremendous linguistic knowledge, a lot of other types of knowledge are embedded in them as well. We perform cross-culture analysis experiments using AI-based Masked Language Modeling (MLM) and GPT-based Generative Language Modeling. The designed approach is to set up a cultural context in sentences with masked words (for MLM) or in a human-prompted text segment (for GPT-based NLG). Consequently, the predicted masked words or the machine generated stories will reflect measurable intercultural differences because language models are trained on different corpus in different languages, and on English corpus containing a significant amount of knowledge on foreign cultures. We show a variety of examples: geopolitical knowledge, holidays, gestures, customs, social norms, emotion schema, role schema, procedure schema, and emotion change detection based on a diplomatic speech. The deep learning neural network model encodes its knowledge in the weights of a neural network instead of as organized semantic concepts. The model can reflect biases brought in by the training data and can give us inaccurate or faulty answers. Overall, with the rapid advancement of language technology, pre-trained language models have grown more powerful, and have great potential to serve as a culturalization tool.

References

1. Vaswani, A., et al.: Attention is all you need. arXiv preprint arXiv:1706.03762 (2017)
2. Brown, T.B., et al.: Language models are few-shot learners. arXiv preprint arXiv:2005.14165 (2020)
3. Wang, C., Li, M., Smola, A.J.: Language Models with Transformers. https://arxiv.org/pdf/1904.09408.pdf (October 2019)
4. Devlin, J., Chang, M.W., Lee, K., Toutanova, K.: BERT: Pre-training of Deep Bidirectional Transformers for Language Understanding. https://arxiv.org/abs/1810.04805 (October 2018)
5. Masked language modeling demo, AllenNLP, Allen Institute for AI. https://demo.allennlp.org/
6. Zhichang, X., Sharifian, F.: Unpacking cultural conceptualizations in Chinese English. J. Asian Pac. Commun. 27(1), 65–84 (2017)
7. Radford, A., Wu, J., Child, R., Luan, D., Amodei, D., Sutskever, I.: Language models are unsupervised multitask learners. OpenAI blog 1(8), 9 (2019)
8. Cultural Schema Theory. https://en.wikipedia.org/wiki/Cultural_schema_theory

Towards Fairness in AI: Addressing Bias in Data Using GANs

Amirarsalan Rajabi[1] and Ozlem O. Garibay[2]([✉])

[1] Department of Computer Science, University of Central Florida,
Orlando, FL 32816, USA
amirarsalan@knights.ucf.edu
[2] Department of Industrial Engineering and Management Systems,
University of Central Florida, Orlando, FL 32816, USA
ozlem@ucf.edu

Abstract. Can we trust machine learning models to make fair decisions? This question becomes more relevant as these algorithms become more pervasive in many aspects of our lives and our society. While the main objective of artificial intelligence (AI) algorithms is traditionally to increase accuracy, the AI community is gradually focusing more on evaluating and developing algorithms to ensure fairness. This work explores the usefulness of adversarial learning, explicitly generative adversarial networks (GAN), in addressing the problem of fairness. We show that the proposed model is able to produce synthetic tabular data to augment the original dataset in order to improve demographic parity, while maintaining data utility. In doing so, our work increases algorithmic fairness while maintaining accuracy.

Keywords: Fairness · Bias · Generative adversarial network · Artificial intelligence

1 Introduction

Recently the application of AI algorithms in automated decision making has increased dramatically. Spanning across many diverse industries such as healthcare, finance, human resources, legal, transportation, etc., these systems are used to make treatment decisions by the healthcare providers, risk assessment by insurance companies, load decision by financial institutions, and recruitment decisions, with the objective of more precise and efficient decisions being made with lower cost. Although accuracy of AI models have improved, there is plenty of evidence that the bias in these models remain an issue [24].

The unbiasedness of the models involved in automated decision making has critical importance as the outcome of these decisions can have profound impacts on individuals and society in general. One example of such systems is Correlational Offender Management Profiling for Alternative Sanctions (COMPAS) that is used by the US criminal justice system to predict the likelihood of recidivism. Studies

© Springer Nature Switzerland AG 2021
C. Stephanidis et al. (Eds.): HCII 2021, LNCS 13095, pp. 509–518, 2021.
https://doi.org/10.1007/978-3-030-90963-5_39

show that the COMPAS system predictions are biased against African Americans [8]. These biased predictions are used to make decisions in the courts and can result in favoring certain groups unfairly. Another example of bias manifested by AI models is the case of an algorithm that showed advertisement to promote jobs in STEM fields to potential applicants. Although the algorithm was designed to deliver the advertisement in a gender-neutral manner, it has been shown that the model delivers the advertisement to women in a lower rate [21].

1.1   Background

Recent studies in algorithmic bias aims to identify, evaluate, and improve fairness in AI as well as understand the underlying factors that causes bias in AI systems [3,9,14,25]. Most of the underlying factors causing unfairness in AI models are attributed to the datasets on which the models are trained, including bias existing in data attributed to biased device measurement, historically biased human decision making, bias caused by missing and unbalanced data, bias caused by proxy non-sensitive attributes, etc. [28]. The biases caused by the model algorithms are attributed to their objective function which aim to minimize overall aggregated prediction errors and therefore benefiting the majority groups rather than the minority groups [28].

There are multiple fairness metrics and definitions introduced which could be divided into different categories, including *group fairness*, *Individual Fairness*, and *subgroup fairness*. Let a $D = \{X, S, Y\}$ be a dataset where $X \in \mathbb{R}^n$ shows the unprotected attributes, S is the protected attributes which determines the unprivileged groups, e.g. gender or race, and $Y \in 0, 1$ is the label or decisions, where we assume $Y = 0$ is the undesired label, e.g. an individual being predicted to commit a crime, and $Y = 1$ being the desired label. The property of *demographic parity* [7] in the labeled dataset is defined as $P(Y = 1|S = 1) - P(Y = 1|S \neq 0)$, for which a lower value indicates a more similar desirable prediction rate conditioned on the protected attribute. There are other measures of fairness proposed including *disparate impact* [13], *equal opportunity*, and *equal odds* [17].

In addition to the proposed fairness measures and concepts noted, there are other emerging sub-fields of algorithmic fairness research that don't necessarily lie within the boundaries of the above mentioned definitions. One such important and interesting field is fair word embeddings. While there are a couple of algorithms proposed to construct representations of words and map them to vectors, it has been shown that the produced embeddings inherently contain biases (e.g. [5]). To address the bias in word embeddings, a couple of processes are suggested [4]. This line of research is important in combating bias in AI systems since word embeddings are broadly used in many natural language processing systems such as machine translation, search engines, job recommender systems, etc. Another emerging research line is the fair visual descriptions. Buolamwini and Timnit show that the under-representation of female dark-skinned faces in most datasets would result in high misclassification rates for those groups [6].

A simple method to enforce fairness could be neglecting sensitive attributes and training machine learning models without using the sensitive attributes.

However, there are a couple of technical problems attributed to this approach [12]. The excluded attributes could still have implicit effect in non-sensitive attributes [27]. For example, simply removing "race" attribute from data does not address the bias in loan decision making because the corresponding effect could still be present in the "zipcode" attribute of an individual as a proxy for race [22,30]. There could also be proportionally less appropriate loans for a certain race that may impact the loan decision outcome even if the sensitive attribute is removed. More advanced fairness enforcement methods are divided into three categories. The first is **Pre-processing** in which the training dataset is modified before being fed to the machine learning algorithm. There are various pre-processing methods proposed, ranging from changing the labels of data points (Y), reweighing them before training [19], to more advanced proposed mechanisms including modifying feature representations [13]. **In-processing** methods attempt to enforce fairness during the training of the algorithm [1,20]. Finally, **Post-processing** methods attempt to enforce fairness by accessing a holdout set which was not involved during the training of the model [10].

Recently some studies have attempted to address fairness problem using adversarial learning. In their study Wadsworth et al. developed an adversarially-trained neural network that besides prediction, is trained to mitigate racial bias in the classifier [31]. In another study a generative adversarial network (GAN) was used to generate a synthetic dataset similar to the real dataset, preserving salient statistical properties while reducing bias [32].

In this paper we will explore the capacity of GANs to be incorporated into fairness research. The fairness measure we focus in this study is *demographic parity*. In Sect. 2 we discuss generative adversarial networks value functions. In Sect. 3 we explain the proposed network architecture, data transformations and the algorithm for accuracy and fairness training, and in Sect. 4 we show some preliminary results of an experiment conducted on UCI Adult Dataset [11]. We show that the model is able to produce synthetic data such that the demographic parity in the generated dataset is decreased, while an acceptable trade-off between fairness and accuracy is maintained in the augmented data consisting of the original dataset with the synthetically generated data added to it.

2   Model Description

2.1   Generative Adversarial Networks

The original GAN is based on a mini-max game being played between two competing networks called the *generator* and the *discriminator* [15]. The generator takes samples from a random noise latent vector. By passing the noise from its layers it tries to generate a vector that is similar to the real data distribution. Generator tries to fool the discriminator into recognizing the produced data as coming from the real data distribution, while the discriminator tries to classify generated data as fake and real data as real. The following is the minimax objective function of a GAN as described in [15].

$$\min_{G} \max_{D} \mathop{\mathbb{E}}_{\mathbf{x} \sim P_{data}(\mathbf{x})} [log D(\mathbf{x})] + \mathop{\mathbb{E}}_{\mathbf{z} \sim P_z(\mathbf{z})} [log(1 - D(G(\mathbf{z})))] \qquad (1)$$

where P_{data} is the real data distribution, P_z is the distribution of noise input to the generator, and $G(z)$ is the produced data by the generator. [15] shows that training the discriminator to optimality is equivalent to minimizing Jensen-Shannon divergence [23]. GANs are attributed with some common training problems, namely: requirement to maintain a careful balance in training of the discriminator and the generator and the mode dropping phenomenon (the case when the model only generates a limited subset of possible outcomes). To address these issues, Arjovky et al. [2] develops Wasserstein GAN, where a *critic* replaces discriminator, and Earth-Mover's distance [29] replaces Jensen-Shannon divergence. The new value function is then constructed by the Kantorovich-Rubinstein duality:

$$\min_{G} \max_{D \in \mathcal{D}} \mathop{\mathbb{E}}_{\mathbf{x} \sim P_{data}(\mathbf{x})} [D(\mathbf{x})] - \mathop{\mathbb{E}}_{\mathbf{z} \sim P_z(\mathbf{z})} [D(G(z))] \qquad (2)$$

where $\mathcal{D}$ is the set of 1-Lipschitz functions. Under an optimal critic, minimizing the value function with respect to generator minimizes Earth-Mover's distance. In this work, we propose a WGAN network in which the 1-Lipschitz constraint is enforced using gradient clipping [16].

3   Model Architecture

In this subsection we explain the architecture of the designed GAN model. This network generates tabular data while maintaining a joint probability distribution of variables similar to the original data. The proposed model is a WGAN. In their study Xu et al. [32] use a GAN network and implement two discriminators. While the generator produces fake data conditioned on the protected attribute, one discriminator updates the generator for accuracy, and the second discriminator updates the generator for fairness. In our model we implement a WGAN using one critic with different loss functions between the two phases of training.

3.1   Data Transformation

A tabular dataset consists of m continuous variables and n discrete variables. Prior to feeding the data to the model, each continuous variable is transformed using a quantile transformer with a uniform output distribution, and discrete columns are converted to one-hot vectors. For each categorical variable, the dimensions of one-hot encoded vectors are $L_{D_1}, L_{D_2}, ... L_{D_n}$, where L_{D_1} captures the dimension of the one-hot encoded vector of the first categorical variable, e.g. "occupation" (based on how many different values the variable "occupation" possesses in the dataset), L_{D_2} captures the dimension of the one-hot encoded vector of the second categorical variable, and so on. All continuous variables are represented with an L_C dimensional vector. The transformed continuous and discrete variables are then concatenated and the dimension of the resultant vector is recorded as *input dim*.

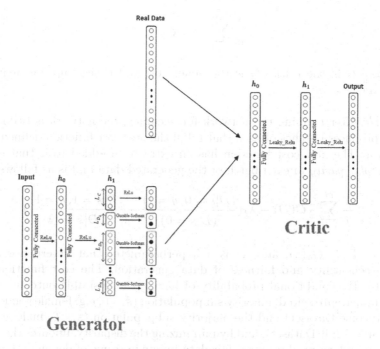

Fig. 1. Model architecture

3.2   Generator and Critic

The generator network receives a sample from a standard multivariate normal distribution (MVN). As shown in Fig. 1, the first and the second hidden layers of the network are fully connected layers with ReLu activation function. After two fully connected layers, the nodes are partitioned as follows: the first L_C nodes are each passed through a ReLu activation function, the next L_{D_1} nodes are together passed through a Gumble-Softmax activation function, the next L_{D_2} nodes are together passed through a Gumble-Softmax activation function, and this is done for all node groups representing categorical variables. By using Gumble-Softmax activation function, the model is able to sample discrete random variables in a way that is differentiable [18], and therefore enabling the model to generate one-hot vectors.

The critic network also consists of two fully connected hidden layers with Leaky ReLu activation functions.

3.3   Training for Accuracy and Fairness

There are two phases of training for the network. *Phase I:* the network is trained for accuracy and the goal is to train the generator's parameters such that it could produce data having a similar joint probability to that of the reference tabular data. The cost function of the generator in the first phase of training is as follows:

$$\frac{1}{m}\sum_{i=1}^{m} -(C(G_\theta(z))) \tag{3}$$

Where C is the critic, G is the generator, and θ accounts for generator's parameters.

Phase II: After training the network for accuracy, the network is trained such that it produces batches of data that fulfill the new cost function defined for the generator. The new cost function has an extra term added to it that enforces *demographic parity* in each batch of the generated data and is as follows:

$$\frac{1}{m}\sum_{i=1}^{m} -C(\hat{D}) - \lambda_f(\frac{(\hat{D}|\hat{s}=0, \hat{y}=1)}{(\hat{D}|\hat{s}=0)} - \frac{(\hat{D}|\hat{s}=1, \hat{y}=1)}{(\hat{D}|\hat{s}=1)}) \tag{4}$$

where $\hat{D} = G_\theta(z)$, and λ_f is a hyperparameter that determines a trade off between utility and fairness of data generation. The cost function above calculates the conditional probability of having the desirable outcome ($\hat{y} = 1$) for the underrepresented minority subpopulation ($\hat{s} = 0$, e.g. female gender in the Adult Income Dataset) and the majority subpopulation ($\hat{s} = 0$, male gender in the Income Adult Dataset), and by minimizing the disparity, updates the weights of the network to produce more fair data points in terms of demographic parity.

4 Experiment

In this section, we show the effectiveness of our proposed model for the task of generating a dataset that is similar to the reference dataset and also satisfies the fairness definition of demographic parity.

4.1 Data

The dataset used in this section is the UCI Adult Income Dataset [11][1], also known as "Census Income" dataset. This dataset contains information extracted from the 1994 census data about people with features including age, occupation, education, sex, race, marital-status, etc. and the target variable is whether each individual has an income of above 50K or below 50K. We have considered the protected attribute in this data to be sex. This dataset has been used broadly in fairness related studies. Figure 2 shows the disparity in probability of having an income > 50K between females and males. The demographic parity in the original dataset is calculated as follows:

Demographic Parity = P(income > 50K | Male) − P(income > 50K | Female) = 0.196 (5)

---

[1] http://archive.ics.uci.edu/ml/datasets/adult.

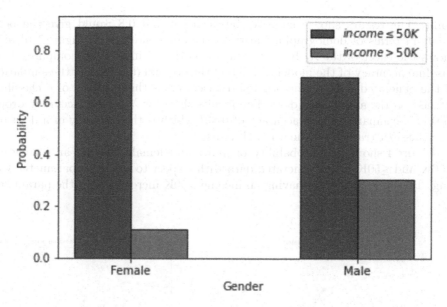

Fig. 2. Disparity in probability of having an income > 50K between females and males in adult dataset.

4.2 Results

To evaluate the effectiveness of the proposed model, the model is implemented and the performance of the GAN is reported. The GAN model aims to generate synthetic samples that have the same joint probability distribution as the real data, while constrained to produce samples that are fair with respect to the demographic parity penalty term implemented in the cost function. In every run, after training the model, 20,000 synthetic data samples are generated. Next, the 20,000 synthetic data is augmented to the 32,561 original data points, and together they form 52,561 data points.

To measure the quality of the synthetic data points, first, we use a Decision Tree Classifier with the default parameter setting [26]. We train the model on the original training data and then test on the testing set. This is the baseline accuracy and it is 0.821. Then, the network is trained five times, each time with a different $\lambda_f \in [0.2, 0.4, 0.6, 0.8, 1.0]$. In each run, the network is trained 100 epochs for accuracy and 20 epochs for fairness, with batchsize of 256 and Adam optimizer with learning_rate = 0.0002, $\beta_1 = 0.5$ and $\beta_2 = 0.999$.

Figure 3 shows the effect of λ_f hyper parameter on demographic parity of the generated data. As λ_f increases, demographic parity in the generated data decreases, meaning that the odds of a female having an income of ">50K" is getting closer to that of a male. Figure 3 a) shows three lines, the demographic parity of the original dataset which is 0.196, demographic parity of the synthetic generated dataset, and demographic parity of the augmented data which consists of adding the 20,000 synthetic generated data points to the 32,561 original data point. The results show that a λ_f between 0.6 and 0.8 would give the best result in terms of demographic parity in the augmented data. Figure 3 b) also shows the effect of the λ_f hyperparameter on the accuracy, and compares it to baseline accuracy of the model trained on the original dataset, i.e. the similarity of the generated data to the original dataset versus the accuracy of a classifier trained on the augmented data. The results show for $\lambda_f = 0.8$, accuracy drops to 0.775, comparing to an accuracy of 0.821 which is the accuracy of a decision tree classifier trained on the original dataset.

Figure 4 shows the probability of males and females having an income of >50K and ≤50K in the generated data with respect to the hyperparameter setting. The odds of females having an income >50K increases with the parameter λ_f.

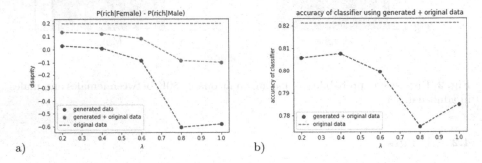

Fig. 3. Comparing disparity (demographic parity) in the original data with disparity in the synthetic data and the augmented data (original + synthetic).

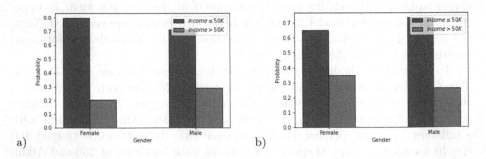

Fig. 4. Comparing disparity in probability of having an income > 50K in the augmented dataset with a) $\lambda_f = 0.6$ and b) $\lambda_f = 0.8$.

5   Conclusions

In this work we presented a framework to address the problem of fairness. As discussed, one main reason for bias in AI is the bias present in the data. The proposed Wasserstein generative adversarial network in this work is able to produce data with a similar joint probability distribution as the original dataset. The enforced penalty term for demographic parity in the cost function, removes demographic parity from the generated data. Augmenting the original data with the data generated using our model preserves utility while improving fairness in tabular datasets. Future work includes investigating other measures of fairness such as equality of odds and testing the proposed network on other datasets such as COMPAS.

References

1. Agarwal, A., Dudik, M., Wu, Z.S.: Fair regression: quantitative definitions and reduction-based algorithms. In: International Conference on Machine Learning, pp. 120–129. PMLR (2019)
2. Arjovsky, M., Chintala, S., Bottou, L.: Wasserstein generative adversarial networks. In: International Conference on Machine Learning, pp. 214–223. PMLR (2017)
3. Barocas, S., Hardt, M., Narayanan, A.: Fairness in machine learning. In: NIPS Tutorial, vol. 1, p. 2 (2017)
4. Bolukbasi, T., Chang, K.W., Zou, J., Saligrama, V., Kalai, A.: Man is to computer programmer as woman is to homemaker? Debiasing word embeddings. arXiv preprint arXiv:1607.06520 (2016)
5. Brunet, M.E., Alkalay-Houlihan, C., Anderson, A., Zemel, R.: Understanding the origins of bias in word embeddings. In: International Conference on Machine Learning, pp. 803–811. PMLR (2019)
6. Buolamwini, J., Gebru, T.: Gender shades: intersectional accuracy disparities in commercial gender classification. In: Conference on Fairness, Accountability and Transparency, pp. 77–91. PMLR (2018)
7. Calders, T., Verwer, S.: Three Naive Bayes approaches for discrimination-free classification. Data Mini. Knowl. Discov. **21**(2), 277–292 (2010). https://doi.org/10. 1007/s10618-010-0190-x
8. Chouldechova, A.: Fair prediction with disparate impact: a study of bias in recidivism prediction instruments. Big Data **5**(2), 153–163 (2017)
9. Chouldechova, A., Roth, A.: The frontiers of fairness in machine learning. arXiv preprint arXiv:1810.08810 (2018)
10. d'Alessandro, B., O'Neil, C., LaGatta, T.: Conscientious classification: a data scientist's guide to discrimination-aware classification. Big Data **5**(2), 120–134 (2017)
11. Dua, D., Graff, C.: UCI machine learning repository (2017)
12. Dwork, C., Hardt, M., Pitassi, T., Reingold, O., Zemel, R.: Fairness through awareness. In: Proceedings of the 3rd Innovations in Theoretical Computer Science Conference, pp. 214–226 (2012)
13. Feldman, M., Friedler, S.A., Moeller, J., Scheidegger, C., Venkatasubramanian, S.: Certifying and removing disparate impact. In: Proceedings of the 21th ACM SIGKDD International Conference on Knowledge Discovery and Data Mining, pp. 259–268 (2015)
14. Friedler, S.A., Scheidegger, C., Venkatasubramanian, S., Choudhary, S., Hamilton, E.P., Roth, D.: A comparative study of fairness-enhancing interventions in machine learning. In: Proceedings of the Conference on Fairness, Accountability, and Transparency, pp. 329–338 (2019)

15. Goodfellow, I.J., et al.: Generative adversarial networks. arXiv preprint arXiv:1406.2661 (2014)
16. Gulrajani, I., Ahmed, F., Arjovsky, M., Dumoulin, V., Courville, A.: Improved training of wasserstein GANs. arXiv preprint arXiv:1704.00028 (2017)
17. Hardt, M., Price, E., Srebro, N.: Equality of opportunity in supervised learning. arXiv preprint arXiv:1610.02413 (2016)
18. Jang, E., Gu, S., Poole, B.: Categorical reparameterization with Gumbel-softmax. arXiv preprint arXiv:1611.01144 (2016)
19. Kamiran, F., Calders, T.: Data preprocessing techniques for classification without discrimination. Knowl. Inf. Syst. **33**(1), 1–33 (2012)
20. Kamishima, T., Akaho, S., Asoh, H., Sakuma, J.: Fairness-aware classifier with prejudice remover regularizer. In: Flach, P.A., De Bie, T., Cristianini, N. (eds.) ECML PKDD 2012. LNCS (LNAI), vol. 7524, pp. 35–50. Springer, Heidelberg (2012). https://doi.org/10.1007/978-3-642-33486-3_3
21. Lambrecht, A., Tucker, C.: Algorithmic bias? An empirical study of apparent gender-based discrimination in the display of stem career ads. Manage. Sci. **65**(7), 2966–2981 (2019)
22. Lepri, B., Oliver, N., Letouzé, E., Pentland, A., Vinck, P.: Fair, transparent, and accountable algorithmic decision-making processes. Philos. Technol. **31**(4), 611–627 (2018)
23. Menéndez, M.L., Pardo, J.A., Pardo, L., Pardo, M.C.: The Jensen-Shannon divergence. J. Franklin Inst. **334**(2), 307–318 (1997)
24. O'neil, C.: Weapons of math destruction: how big data increases inequality and threatens democracy. Crown (2016)
25. Oneto, L., Chiappa, S.: Fairness in machine learning. In: Oneto, L., Navarin, N., Sperduti, A., Anguita, D. (eds.) Recent Trends in Learning From Data. SCI, vol. 896, pp. 155–196. Springer, Cham (2020). https://doi.org/10.1007/978-3-030-43883-8_7
26. Pedregosa, F., et al.: Scikit-learn: machine learning in Python. J. Mach. Learn. Res. **12**, 2825–2830 (2011)
27. Pedreshi, D., Ruggieri, S., Turini, F.: Discrimination-aware data mining. In: Proceedings of the 14th ACM SIGKDD International Conference on Knowledge Discovery and Data Mining, pp. 560–568 (2008)
28. Pessach, D., Shmueli, E.: Algorithmic fairness. arXiv preprint arXiv:2001.09784 (2020)
29. Rubner, Y., Tomasi, C., Guibas, L.J.: The earth mover's distance as a metric for image retrieval. Int. J. Comput. Vis. **40**(2), 99–121 (2000)
30. Schermer, B.W.: The limits of privacy in automated profiling and data mining. Comput. Law Secur. Rev. **27**(1), 45–52 (2011)
31. Wadsworth, C., Vera, F., Piech, C.: Achieving fairness through adversarial learning: an application to recidivism prediction. arXiv preprint arXiv:1807.00199 (2018)
32. Xu, D., Yuan, S., Zhang, L., Wu, X.: FairGAN: fairness-aware generative adversarial networks. In: 2018 IEEE International Conference on Big Data (Big Data), pp. 570–575. IEEE (2018)

Genetic Algorithm to Plan Routes. Case: Waste Collectors - Huanuco, Peru. 2020

Julissa Elizabeth Reyna-González[1]([envelope]) [iD],
Alberto Gómez Fuertes[2] [iD], Moisés David Reyes Pérez[2] [iD],
Gilberto Carrión-Barco[3] [iD], and César Augusto Piscoya Vargas[3] [iD]

[1] Hermilio Valdizan National University, Huanuco, Peru
[2] Cesar Vallejo University, Pimentel Km 3.5, Chiclayo, Peru
[3] Pedro Ruiz Gallo National University, Lambayeque, Peru

Abstract. The management of solid waste is of great importance to avoid floods, infections and respiratory diseases, for this reason the present research aimed to develop a route planner for the collection of solid waste in the city of Huánuco, using general algorithms. Ethics. In addition, the study was of a quantitative-experimental approach. The following techniques and instruments were used to collect the information: scientific observation because we will examine the external reality in order to obtain the data in advance, observation guide to record evidence of solid waste collection, which was validated using the expert technique, who evidenced the existing relationship between the proposed objectives, categories, indicators, items and response options considering their coherence, relevance and writing The population was made up of 192,627 inhabitants of the city de Huánuco, The results of the tests show the effectiveness of the genetic algorithm with a population of 4 vehicles, in which lower cost values were obtained, and with respect to the execution time, a greater number of destinations. The graph was constructed by gathering information from the streets and/or avenues of the Huánuco district such as addresses, coordinates, and street intersections, through the Google Maps map provider through an Adjacency matrix, to then run the Genetic Algorithm.

Keywords: Genetic algorithms · Route planner · Waste collectors

1 Introduction

In Latin America and the Caribbean, households continue to form the primary source of production and composition of urban solid waste, so real communication about production and composition is essential for their management, because they often lack the necessary infrastructure for the correct treatment of these.

The generation of garbage in Peru and the world is linked to practically anything we do, and it is only in Peru that more than 18 thousand tons of garbage are generated every day; This garbage produced must be collected and properly treated by the municipalities and institutions in charge of it. In Peru, the collection of household solid waste has been the work of the municipalities, which are in charge of assigning routes

C. Stephanidis et al. (Eds.): HCII 2021, LNCS 13095, pp. 519–535, 2021.
https://doi.org/10.1007/978-3-030-90963-5_40

for the collection of waste, these being empirically designated without a formal optimization study. (Manrique 2020, p. 5).

The figures are not encouraging at all. If humans do not change our habits, it is estimated that by 2050 there will be more plastic than fish in the ocean and that 99% of marine animals will have ingested it, according to the United Nations Environment Program.

In 2018, the city of Huánuco reported to the National Institute of Statistics and Informatics that per day it collected 282,181 kg of garbage, this collection represents, according to data from the Ministry of the Environment, 70% of the garbage produced daily, that is, approximately 120 934 kg of garbage remains on the streets, this is due to different factors, the main cause being the poor distribution of solid waste collectors.

The city of Huánuco collects solid waste constantly and through defined routes, although it is true at first glance this method seems to work without problems, the reality is that it does not, this because there are places in the city. city where there is a greater concentration of people, which leads to a greater generation of waste in the main areas of the city, such as the popular markets (Mercado Modelo de Huánuco), parks and squares (Plaza Mayor and Plaza de Armas), among other areas.

The degree of awareness achieved in society on the issue of ecology requires that solid waste management take care of the environmental environment; Therefore, citizens demand superior and important controls and regulations. On the other hand, Hermitaño (2019), argues that The VRP (Vehicle Routing Problem, in English) is one of the best known problems, as well as captivating and challenging of the integer combinatorial optimization, it is placed in the category of problems Called NP - Complete, it is a large set of problem variants and customizations. From those that are simpler to some that today are still a matter of research (p. 13).

In turn, the New Law of Integral Solid Waste in Peru Legislative Decree No. 1278, establishes that solid waste is an input for other industries where it is no longer considered as garbage and is now considered as raw material in other industries that can give value to waste. Another contribution of the new Comprehensive Solid Waste Law is that it lays the foundations for the development of a large recycling industry at the international level, in such a way that Peru could become a regional solid waste treatment hub, generating higher income, investment, higher employment and high standards of environmental management. However, this law has not yet been applied in the city of Huanuco, where a reality different from that supported by the Law is reflected, main streets with excess garbage and uncontrolled traffic that does not meet planning standards.

Finding the shortest route from a certain source to a certain destination is a well-known and widely applicable problem. Most of the work done in the area has used static route planning algorithms such as A*, Dijkstra, the Bellman-Ford algorithm. Although these might be optimal algorithms, they are not capable of dealing with certain real-life scenarios. (Nanayakkara et al. (2007)).

In turn, Li et al. (2006). Argues that algorithms allow various acceptable solutions that will depend on the problem treated, operations such as encoding, crossing and mutation are adapted to adapt to the optimal route planning. The simulation results show that the specific genetic algorithm has advantages such as a fast calculation speed and a high probability of an optimal solution, however each of the methods to be applied has its own advantages and disadvantages. (Li et al. 2006).

2   Theoretical Framework

2.1   Genetic Algorithm

The so-called evolutionary genetic algorithms (GA) work with a population of individuals, who represent possible solutions to a problem. This population undergoes certain transformations and subsequently a selection process, which favors the best individuals. (Petriv 2012, p.7). In turn, genetic algorithms (GA) address a wide range of concepts, and are thus a useful tool for the detection of optimized solutions. They are inspired by biological evolution and its genetic basis, evidenced in the evolutionary traits of a population.

These individuals are subjected to random actions similar to those that act in nature (genetic recombinations and mutations), developing through iterations called generations. (Petriv 2012, p.7).

For Goldberg (1989), he argues that a genetic algorithm consists of a population of solutions encoded in a similar way to chromosomes. Each of these chromium-somes will have an associated adjustment, goodness or fitness value, which quantifies its validity as a solution to the problem.

Genetic algorithms require that solutions to the problem can be represented in some binary format, that two or more of these solutions can be significantly combined, and that an objective function value can be evaluated for each of these solutions.

2.2   Structure of the Genetic Algorithm

A genetic algorithm requires the following structures: a genetic representation and an objective function.

Genetic representation refers to the way to represent individuals or solutions, in genetic representation information on the characteristics of individuals must be included.

The objective function is used to determine how fit an individual is based on what you want to achieve in the final solution. The objective function evaluates the performance of individuals and this is how the fittest can be determined. (Castillo 2018, p. 18).

2.3   Characteristics of the Genetic Algorithm

The characteristics of the proposed AG were taken as a reference from (Nanayakkara et al. 2007), (Moratilla et al., 2014) and (Ikeda & Inoue, 2016) since they demonstrated optimal results in their investigations of vehicular routing problems.

The simplest meta description for a genetic sequence.

The algorithm has the following steps:

1) Coding
2) Initial population generation
3) Repeat until completion criteria are met
a) Evaluation
b) Crossing

c) Mutation
4) Decoding

More detailed description of genetic and evolutionary algorithmic approaches, and applications of such approaches can be found in Mitchell M. (1998) in (Nanayakkara et al. 2007).

2.4   Stages of a Genetic Algorithm

The stages of a GA, defined by Schmitt (2001), are:

Initialization: Form the initial population of possible solutions.

Selection: The selection process consists of executing the objective function in each one of the individuals to determine their level of aptitude.

Genetic operations: It is the stage in which the subset of the population selected in the previous stage is altered to obtain a new population, it may be by the Crossover or Mutation methods.

Termination: It is defined when a solution is obtained that satisfies certain criteria, a certain number of iterations is reached, or when the iterations no longer produce better results.

2.5   Graph Theory

The theory of graphs is used in the treatment of various problems, the graphs constitute a useful abstraction to model various real situations such as the problem of vehicle routes, and its greatest importance is manifested in the theory of networks, in the computer science and telecommunications, among others. (Hermitaño 2019, p. 8).

A graph G = (V, E) is an ordered pair in which V is a nonempty set of elements called vertices and E is a set of elements called edges, consisting of unordered pairs of vertices, such that yes {x, y ⊂ E}, then we say that x and y are adjacent vertices; it is represented by an unoriented line that joins these vertices. (Hermitaño 2019, p. 8).

-   Given a graph G = (V, E), then it is said that:
-   It is a lasso or loop to all edges of the form with ($v \in V$)
-   The edges are multiple when the edges that appear repeated in E.
-   Vertices are adjacent if they are joined by an edge.
-   Edges are adjacent if they have a common vertex.
-   An edge and a vertex are incidents if the vertex is extreme of the edge.
-   A vertex is isolated if it is not adjacent to any other vertex.
-   A graph is simple if it has no loops or multiple edges. (Hermitaño 2019, p. 9).

2.6   Metaheuristics

Metaheuristics is a kind of special method or strategy that performs an intensive exploration of the solution space. (Hermitaño 2019, p. 9).

Metaheuristic Techniques

The best known metaheuristic methods are:

- Simulated Annealing (Simulated Annealing, 1993)
- Genetic algorithms (Holland, 1960)
- Taboo search (Glover, 1986)
- Greedy random adaptive search procedure (Horowitz, 1978)
- Ant colony algorithms (Dorigo, 1999)
- Guided local search (1999)
- Search for the neighborhood of a variable (2003)

Route Planning

It is the procedure of creating the most profitable route possible, minimizing the distance or travel time we need to get to our set of planned stops.

Planning is a critical process within logistics both due to the existing competition and the reduction of margins of action in the market. A high expenditure on vehicles, boats or any type of transport along with fuel and maintenance of the same to which we must add labor (Saminef 2020).

Route Programming

The main objective of the programming of a route is to reduce expenses as well as the time factor, intervening stops, arrivals and destination. However, route optimization includes factors such as schedules, time constraints, road restrictions, weight capacity among others (Saminef 2020).

2.7 Objecives

General Objecives

Develop a route planner for the collection of solid waste in the district of Huanuco using Genetic algorithms.

Specific Objectives

- Determine the problem of solid waste collection in the Huanuco district.
- Design the genetic algorithm.
- Design the optimal route plan for the Huanuco district.
- Conduct tests of the planner for the collection of solid waste in the district of Huanuco.

3 Methodology

The study carried out is of a complementary type because it uses qualitative techniques (Observation Guide) and quantitative techniques (Development of an algorithm to define an optimal route plan). Therefore the approach is complementary.

In itself, the design is experimental of the quasi-experimental subtype, because a stimulus is used through the route planner and determines the optimal route, in a set of routes established by the researchers.

The technique for collecting the information was the observation guide in order to obtain the data that, in advance, have been defined as of interest for the investigation. According to Sampieri, the population defines it as: "A set of all cases that meet certain specifications", which is equivalent to 12 vehicle units in charge of collecting garbage in the study area.

The sample "Subgroup of the universe or population from which the data are collected and which must be representative of it". For the study the sample is made up of 4 vehicle units in charge of collecting garbage in the city.

The study sampling was established as a non-probability sampling for the convenience of the researchers.

4   Results

The main results obtained are defined according to the objectives indicated in this study:

According to the objective of Determining the problem of solid waste collection in the Huanuco district, the problem was defined through an Observation Guide, whose objective was to collect information on the routes of solid waste collection in the city of Huánuco, The problem found was the inadequate solid waste collection management in the Huánuco district, the observation area was carried out in the streets of the city of Huánuco and strategic places, the observation time was carried out in 3 h a day for 3 days, the observation guide was structured according to 5 dimensions of web platform analysis, operation, test, restrictions and planning, through a nominal scale with a yes and no answer, reporting through the instrument used, that the management of the authorities is terrible, residents accumulate their waste next to their houses or in places accumulated by neighbors, recent accumulations were observed in The places where waste accumulates, uniformed collectors were also observed carrying safety tools (helmet and gloves), few places were observed to deposit their waste, garbage bags were located around the places where the collection trucks pass.

According to the objective of Designing the genetic algorithm, it was established that genetic algorithms are particularly appropriate to solve real route optimization problems due to their robustness and flexibility to adapt to changing environments, and complies with a structure defined as:

- Genetic architecture.
- Populations and their size.
- Initial population.
- Evaluation.
- Selection.
- Crossing.
- Mutation.

The operation of the genetic algorithm follows the following process:

1. Initialization of the population.
2. Repair function.

3. Fitness assessment.
4. Repeat the process.
5. Selection of survival, elitist strategy.
6. Cross operation.
7. Selection of parents, selection by tournament.
8. Mutation operation.
9. Repair function.
10. Assessment of aptitude.
11. Until meeting a convergence criterion.
12. Decode the best solution.

Genetic Algorithm Application Model

The case study presented in this section corresponds to the cleaning and collection of solid waste needs in the city of Huánuco.

For which the model was then started, with a set of classes (initial population, route and final vertex), which have associated their distances from vertex to vertex and costs, divided, the routes are divided into vertices, usually the distance -from one vertex to another is different, we have 4 trucks available, 2 trucks for garbage collection during the day shift hours and 2 trucks for garbage collection during the night shift hours, for this, 4 optimal routes were generated.

We define then: A route of 4 assignments, one for each collection truck. The routes were subjected to multiple restrictions, greater number of vertices and the schedule, no route was accepted if it did not comply with all the established restrictions.

Variables Involved

a) Path length: The maximum size of an individual
b) Start vertex: The beginning of the route
c) Final vertex: It is the end of the tour
d) Maximum length
e) Generation: Initialization of the Initial population
f) Temporary population
g) Population size
h) Elitism: 2 Individuals
i) Selection operation: Selection by tournament
j) Crossing Operator: 1 point
k) Crossover rate: 0.80%
l) Mutation rate: 0.1%

According to the objective of designing the optimal route plan for the Huanuco district, the most suitable route plan was established.

Graphic Representation of a Route

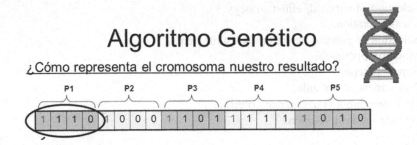

Fig. 1. Representation of the assigned vertices.

It must be taken into account that the vertices assigned in a chromosome are generated randomly, "but not so random", this because it can randomly repeat the vertices; therefore, it is considered invalid vertex, which is considered in the creation of valid chromosome. Authors' elaboration.

And it fulfills the following structure: Chromosome = [$vertex_1$, $vertex_2$, $vertex_3$, $vertex_4$,... $vertex_n$].

ó chromosome = [$route_1$, $route_2$, $route_3$, $route_4$, ... $route_n$] (Fig. 1).

Analyzing the structure of the chromosome, it is indicated that one of the possible optimal pathways is the *vertex* 1, followed by $vertex_2$... until the *vertex n*. This reflects the distance of the $vertex_1$ a $vertex_2$, plus the distance of $vertex_2$ a $vertex_3$, so keep adding up to the distance of $vertex_{n-1}$ until $vertex_n$.

Fitness: It is the adaptation value of each chromosome, which allows to corroborate which chromosome is more suitable among the population. This is reflected by the following equation:

Fitness = 1−distance/maximum distance * tam Chromosome).

Coding an Individual According to the Structure Described

Fig. 2. Coding an individual according to the structure described

The figure shows the representation of the route of the collection trucks, represented by the location points of the area under study and its vertices. Obtained through the online server Google Maps (Fig. 2).

Representation of a Vertex

The code for a vertex consists of (3) characters. The vertex codes can be coded from V1 to V99 (See Fig. 3).

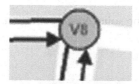

Fig. 3. Representation of a vertex.

The figure shows the representation of a vertex. Example V8.

Representation of a Route. The most optimal route for the collection trucks is represented (See Fig. 4).

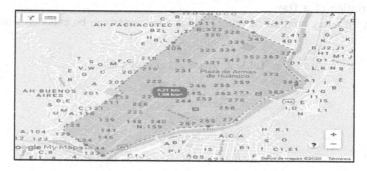

Fig. 4. Representation of a route, image obtained through the online server Google Maps.

Representation of a Collection Truck

They are made up of (4) alphanumeric characters that are the first two characters of the truck and the last two of the truck schedule. Characters can be from C1D1 to C4D2 (Table 1).

Table 1. Representation of a collection truck

Truck name	Truck code
Truck 1 Morning	C1D1
Truck 2 Afternoon	C2D2
Truck 3 Morning	C3D1
Truck 4 Afternoon	C4D2

Note. The table shows the way a collection truck will be represented, the name of the truck and the collection truck code

Distance Representation

It is formed by two vertices, the distance codes can be alphanumeric of (3) digits. The distance codes can be from D01 to D99.

– Conduct tests of the planner for the collection of solid waste in the district of Huanuco.
– Develop a route planner for solid waste collection in the Huanuco district using Genetic algorithms (Fig. 5).

Fig. 5. Distance representation.

The figure shows how to represent the distance between two vertices. Image obtained through the online server Google Maps.

Representation of a Day

The code for a day consists of one (1) digit. Day codes can be encoded from 1 to 3.

Table 2. Representation of a day

Día	Código
Tuesday	1
Thursday	2
Saturday	3

Nota. The table shows the way of the representation of a day, where the collection truck only passes through the route three times a week. The days of the week will be Tuesday, Thursday and Saturday.

Data Set Preparation

To obtain the georeferential points, it begins with obtaining the georeferenced points (latitude and longitude) by the "Google Maps" map application server, on the map of the city of Huánuco, to later convert those points into a weighted directed graph. The georeferenced points to take into account will be obtained at random. The georeferenced points are obtained in this manual way according to the investigations of (Zhang, Chen, & Li, 2015).

Based on the information obtained from the map server Google Maps, we obtain the summary of the data of each simulated route.

VERTICE	LATITUD, LONGITUD	LUGAR
V1	9°56'24.44"S , 76°14'56.47"O	Jr. Dos de Mayo con jr. Tarma
V2	9°56'21.11"S , 76°14'54.83"O	Prol. Abtao
V3	9°56'19 41"S , 76°15'1 10"O	Jr Tarma con prol San Martin
V4	9°56'12.28"S , 76°15'7.91"O	Jr. Tarma con jr. Independencia
V5	9°56'7.95"S , 76°14'58.82"O	Jr. Leoncio Prado con jr. Seichi Izumi
V6	9°56'10.14"S , 76°14'56.40"O	Prol. San Martin con jr. Seichi Izumi
V7	9°56'13.76"S , 76°14'52.27"O	Calle Huallaga con jr. Seichi Izumi
V8	9°56'17.63"S , 76°14'48.12"O	Jr. Dos de Mayo con jr. Seichi Izumi
V9	9°56'12.50"S , 76°14'39.34"O	Jr. 28 de Julio con jr. Junín
V10	9°56'10.27"S , 76°14'32.26"O	Jr. Hermilio Valdizán con Malecón Alomia Robles
V11	9°56'5.47"S , 76°14'33.89"O	Jr. 28 de Julio con jr. Mayro
V12	9°56'7.53"S , 76°14'44.86"O	Jr. Abtao con jr. Junín
V13	9°56'3.01"S , 76°14'51.20"O	Jr. San Martin con jr. Junín
V14	9°56'9.67"S , 76°14'49.31"O	Psje. Dos Aguas con jr. Libertad
V15	9°56'0.91"S , 76°14'40.28"O	Jr. Abtao con jr. Mayro
V16	9°55'56.46"S , 76°14'46.50"O	Jr. San Martin con jr. Mayro
V17	9°55'59.17"S , 76°14'56.80"O	Jr. Independencia con jr. Junín
V18	9°55'53.08"S , 76°14'51.37"O	Jr. Independencia con jr. Mayro
V19	9°56'8.55"S , 76°14'22.59"O	Malecón Alomia Robles con jr. Tarapacá
V20	9°56'3.08"S , 76°14'22.67"O	Jr. Bolívar con jr. Aguilar
V21	9°55'58.68"S , 76°14'29.22"O	Jr. 28 de Julio con jr. Aguilar
V22	9°55'54.35"S , 76°14'35.71"O	Jr. Abtao con jr. Aguilar
V23	9°55'50.06"S , 76°14'42.11"O	Jr. San Martin con jr. Aguilar
V24	9°55'45.51"S , 76°14'48.99"O	Jr. Independencia con jr. Aguilar
V25	9°56'1.76"S , 76°14'18.10"O	Malecón Alomia Robles con jr. Ayacucho
V26	9°55'55.57"S , 76°14'12.74"O	Malecón Alomia Robles con jr. General Prado
V27	9°55'57.75"S , 76°14'16.58"O	Jr. Huánuco
V28	9°55'56.20"S , 76°14'23.01"O	Jr. Hermilio Valdizán con psje. La Merced
V29	9°55'52.15"S , 76°14'24.86"O	Jr. 28 de Julio con jr. Huánuco
V30	9°55'47.72"S , 76°14'31.21"O	Jr. Abtao con jr. Huánuco
V31	9°55'43.32"S , 76°14'37.61"O	Jr. San Martin con jr. Huánuco
V32	9°55'38.60"S , 76°14'44.47"O	Jr. Independencia con jr. Huánuco
V33	9°55'53.53"S , 76°14'8.52"O	Malecón Leoncio Prado con jr. Dámaso Beraun
V34	9°55'47.82"S , 76°14'17.08"O	Jr. Hermilio Valdizán con jr. Dámaso Beraun
V35	9°55'41.34"S , 76°14'26.95"O	Jr. Abtao con jr. Dámaso Beraun
V36	9°55'36.95"S , 76°14'33.52"O	Jr. San Martin con jr. Dámaso Beraun
V37	9°55'32.65"S , 76°14'40.14"O	Jr. Independencia con jr. Dámaso Beraun
V38	9°55'44.77"S , 76°14'5.51"O	Psje. San Cristóbal con Malecón Leoncio Prado
V39	9°55'39.41"S , 76°14'8.23"O	Malecón Leoncio Prado con jr. Progreso
V40	9°55'39.19"S , 76°14'15.96"O	Jr. 28 de Julio con jr. Constitución
V41	9°55'34.84"S , 76°14'22.69"O	Jr. Abtao con jr. Constitución
V42	9°55'30.45"S , 76°14'29.27"O	Jr. San Martin con jr. Constitución
V43	9°55'25.97"S , 76°14'36.08"O	Jr. Independencia con jr. Constitución
V44	9°55'35.56"S , 76°14'6.97"O	Malecón Leoncio Prado con jr. Pedro Puelles
V45	9°55'32.70"S , 76°14'11.59"O	Jr. 28 de Julio con jr. Pedro Puelles
V46	9°55'28.42"S , 76°14'18.17"O	Jr. Abtao con jr. Pedro Puelles
V47	9°55'23.94"S , 76°14'25.05"O	Jr. San Martin con jr. Pedro Puelles
V48	9°55'23.16"S , 76°14'33.72"O	Jr. Independencia con jr. Progreso
V49	9°55'19.73"S , 76°14'31.33"O	Jr. Independencia con jr. Pedro Puelles
V50	9°55'32.25"S , 76°14'5.70"O	Malecón Leoncio P. con Alameda de la Republica
V51	9°55'29.63"S , 76°14'9.54"O	Jr. 28 de Julio con Alameda de la Republica
V52	9°55'27.23"S , 76°14'12.79"O	Jr. Dos de Mayo con Alameda de la Republica
V53	9°55'24.96"S , 76°14'16.07"O	Jr. Abtao con Alameda de la Republica
V54	9°55'21.68"S , 76°14'18.52"O	Jr. Huallayco con Alameda de la Republica
V55	9°55'20.15"S , 76°14'20.79"O	Jr. San Martin con Alameda de la Republica
V56	9°55'16.84"S , 76°14'25.30"O	Jr. Leoncio Prado con Alameda de la Republica
V57	9°55'16.48"S , 76°14'29.00"O	Jr. Independencia

Fig. 6. Simulated routes.

The figure represents the vertices, latitude, longitude and place of the Huanu-co district, which have been considered in the simulation with Google Maps.

The data previously produced in Fig. 6 were obtained from the representation of the map of the city of Huánuco, making use of the "Google earth" map application server as indicated in the following figure (Fig. 7).

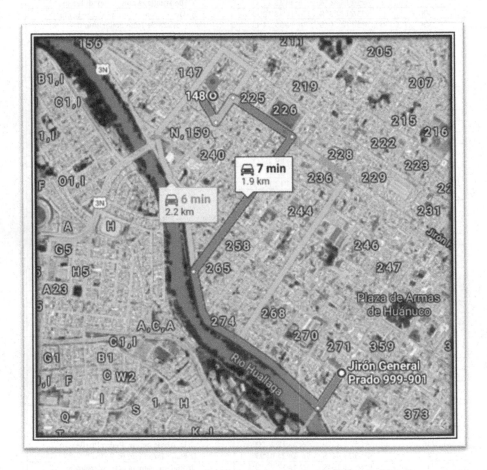

Fig. 7. Simulated routes obtained on the map server "Google Maps".

It is important to mention that in Fig. 4 the projected trajectory is not the optimal route, but is the trajectory automatically produced by the "Google Maps" application when placing various points on the map.

Convert Georeferenced Points to Graphs

Launch the Problema

The solid waste collection truck must travel at the infectious focus points set by the user, so how to determine an optimal path for the solid waste collection truck so that the length traveled is the shortest, taking into account the direction of the streets.

Modeling the Problem

From the point where the truck is to the points of infectious foci, a graph must be originated, now both the truck and the infectious foci from now on will be called vertices. Where the starting vertex of the truck will be called *v 0*, the rest of the vertices are the infectious foci, which will be "*v1,2*", and the routes between them will be called edges. The modeling is carried out in this way because the map application server "Google earth", although it can save the information of a part of the map that the user selects automatically, the format of that information is a list of coordinates (latitude and longitude), which does not show the relationship of a coordinate with another coordinate (adjacent vertices), nor the direction of the streets, nor the value of the distance (cost) of a coordinate with another coordinate The graph presents a Starting Point: V1 End Point: V57 (Fig. 8)

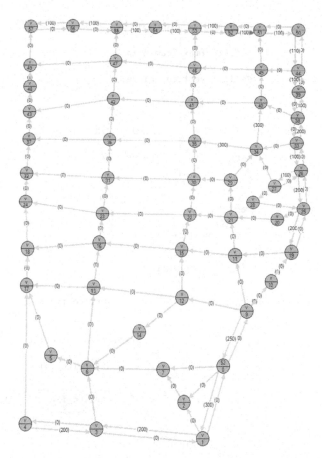

Fig. 8. Weighted directed graph of the solid waste collection network. Obtained from Google Earth. Authors' elaboration.

Problem Solution

The solid waste collection network is abstracted as follows, "v0" the vertex where the truck is located, and the other vertices are the infectious foci, the weight of the edge between the vertices is the length of the route interpreted in meters (m).

The procedure to carry out the adjacency matrix is summarized in abstracting the distance between a pair of vertices that are associated and in turn accessible, from the directed graph of Fig. 14, see Table 2.

It is necessary to refer to some conclusions in the development of the planning of routes established in this aspect, under the evolutionary model, the shortest route of n vertices can be found and it does not present complications due to the number of vertices to be evaluated, considering that it was tested with "n" nodes and we predict that it will be in seconds.

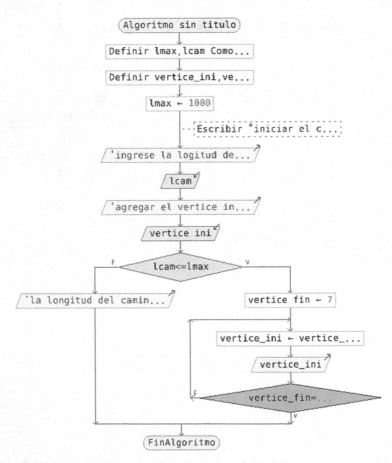

Fig. 9. Flow diagram of the algorithm for route planning, designed in the PsInt tool. Prepared by the authors.

The genetic algorithm that is developed calculates optimal routes based on distance, time, taking into account random events such as distances, vertices and the time of, while the GoogleMaps algorithm has an average error of 24%, therefore, With the proposed genetic algorithm, the accuracy of route calculation is improved compared to GoogleMaps.

From the tests it is necessary to highlight the importance of the initial vertex of the route because any additional deviation affects the trajectory considerably (Fig. 9).

Application of the Genetic Algorithm on the Graph
Flow Chart Design

5 Discussion

Having concluded with the results of the present investigation, in this chapter it is intended to approach the discussion of results, considering the results obtained, the theories that support the investigation and the antecedents, as José Jaime Ruz says, the application that helps to obtain the most optimal, it reduces costs for our entities, which is a good option. You use genetic programming to carry out these types of projects. On the other hand, Jorge Andrés Quintero tells us that the world of transport has very serious problems causing many losses and for this, using technology is a good option to combat these deficiencies, he also tells us that the most important thing for this type of implementation is the Planning is for this reason that in our project we first saw the part of the guide in order to see the deficiencies that transport has for waste collectors, after that we plan the type of language that we will use and how we intend to solve this problem, for this we use a page that is known to all or the vast majority called Google Maps. This page helped to collect real data for our project; Medina tells us that there are eight basic elements to design genetic algorithms.This heuristic technique originally developed to solve TSP has been modified to satisfactorily solve CVRP and SCVRP and this helped us to design the genetic algorithm of the routes for waste collection. And finally we designed this genetic algorithm in a small city called Huánuco, because we saw that the management of the garbage collectors' routes was not good and with all the data collected we started to implement this project, the An explanation of our project is in the annexes, in more detail but here we will explain in a summarized way, it is an app where it will ask you for the number of streets, the transition if it is a lot or this street is empty and then ask if they are two-way or No, and with all these data our algorithm will identify which is the most optimal route, but first we have to make some adjustments because we know, or at least those who live in Huánuco, that the streets of Huánuco are not square, for this are the adjustments before of the search, and the result will come out of a nomenclature elaborated by us, the first letter identifies the column and the first number the number of the column then it will find another l This will be the row and the row number in order to arrive at the optimal route.

Conclusions

The graph was constructed by gathering information from the streets and/or avenues of the Huánuco district such as addresses, coordinates, street intersections, through the Google Maps map provider through an Adjacency matrix, to later execute the Genetic Algorithm.

The procedure to find the best route between several infectious foci causes the genetic algorithm to be used twice to find the best solution. The first place, when entering the initial point and the infectious foci, evaluates the most optimal route in the order from which the collection truck should pick up, and secondly, constructing the shortest route between each pair of vertices to arrive from the truck to the first infectious focus, and from the infectious focus to the next if there is one, and so on progressively.

The execution time of the genetic algorithm to find an optimal solution can be decreased, reducing the population size, but it is observed that, for complex routes, the precision of the genetic algorithm decreases as the population size is reduced.

Recommendations

Municipalities or public or private companies in the town of Huánuco are recommended to implement a route planning software using the genetic algorithm, since it provides you with a more optimal solution to find a route from an initial point to an end point.

Future researchers are recommended to modify the genetic algorithm developed to a multiobjective algorithm, where it can take into account information on traffic, route through main roads, etc. Converting the proposed genetic or algorithm into an intelligent route planning system.

References

Bernays, E.L.: Public Relations Idea book. Printers In Pub. Co, USA (1958)

Botto, M.: La comunicación en las instituciones educativas de nivel (2011)

Goldberg D.: Genetic Algorithms in Search, Optimization and Machine Learning, 1st. edn.). Addison-Wesley Longman Publishing Co., Inc., Boston (1989). ISBN:978–0–201–15767Digital Library, https://dl.acm.org/doi/book/https://doi.org/10.5555/534133

Hermitaño, M.: Optimización de rutas para la recolección de residuos sólidos con uso de contenedores aplicando el algoritmo colonia de hormigas en la ciudad de Huaraz. Universidad Nacional Santiago Antunez de Mayola. Repositorio Institucional NASAM (2019). http://repositorio.unasam.edu.pe/handle/UNASAM/4056

Manrique, F.: Sistema de recojo de residuos sólidos domiciliarios y sus efectos ambientales y económicos en el distrito de Pocollay. Universidad Privada de Tacna. Repositorio Institucional UPT (2020). http://repositorio.upt.edu.pe/handle/UPT/1660

MINAM: Nueva ley de residuos sólidos (2020). https://www.minam.gob.pe/gestion-de-residuos-solidos/nueva-ley-de-residuos-solidos/

Arkhipov D., Wu, D., Wu, T., Regan, A.C.: Un marco de algoritmo genético paralelo para la planificación del transporte y la gestión logística. IEEE Access **8**, 106506–106515 (2020). 10.1109 / ACCESS.2020.2997812

Petriv, C.: Algoritmos genéticos aplicados a soluciones logísticas de sanidad. Centri Educativo de las Fuerzas Armadas de Argentina. Trabajos Finales Integradores de Especialización Repositorio Digital CEFA (2012). http://cefadigital.edu.ar/handle/1847939/285

Nanayakkara, S., Srinivasan, D., Wei, L., German, X., Taylor, E., Yong, S.H.: Planificador de rutas basado en algoritmos genéticos para grandes redes de calles urbanas. In: Congreso IEEE sobre Computación Evolutiva, pp. 4469–4474. Repositorio institucional IEEE (2007). 10.1109 / CEC.2007.4425056, https://ieeexplore.ieee.org/document/4425056

Li, Q., Liu, G., Zhang, W., Zhao, C., Yin, Y., Wang, Z.: A specific genetic algorithm for optimum path planning in intelligent transportation system.In: 6th International Conference on its Telecommunications, pp. 140–143 (2006). 10.1109 / ITST.2006.288799

Saminef: Planificación y estudio de rutas. LOCOEX (ASCOEL S.A.L.) LOGÍSTICA Y COMERCIO (2020). https://logisticaascoel.com/planificacion-estudio-rutas/

Schmitt, M.: Theory of genetic algorithms. Theoretical Computer Science (2001)

Castillo, J.: Implementación de un algoritmo genético para elaborar un conjunto de rutas óptimas para el transporte de la comunidad universitaria desde y hacia el campus principal. Pontificia Universidad Catolica del Perú. Repositorio Institucional PUCP (2018). https://tesis.pucp.edu.pe/repositorio/handle/20.500.12404/13047

Moratilla, A., Fernández, E., Sánchez, J.J., Borja, V.: Selection optimal number of operators for the treatment of VRP problems withGenetic algorithms (2014)

Ikeda, Y., Inoue, M.: An Evacuation Route Planning for Safety Route Guidance System after Natural Disaster Using Multi-Objective Genetic Algorithm. Procedia Comput. Sci. **96**, 1323–1331 (2016). https://doi.org/10.1016/j.procs.2016.08.177

Zhang, X., Chen, Y., Li, T.: Optimization of logistics route based on Dijkstra. In: Proceedings of the IEEE International Conference on SoftwareEngineering and Service Sciences, ICSESS, 2015–Novem(1), pp. 313–316 (2015).https://doi.org/10.1109/ICSESS.2015.7339063

A Toolkit to Enable the Design
of Trustworthy AI

Stefan Schmager[1] and Sonia Sousa[2(✉)]

[1] Cyprus University of Technology,
Archiepiskopou Kyprianou 30, 3036 Limassol, Cyprus
stefan.schmager@idmaster.eu
[2] Tallinn University, Narva mnt 25, 10120 Tallinn, Estonia
scs@tlu.ee

Abstract. Technological progress in artificial intelligence (AI) and machine learning (ML) has an enormous impact on our society, economy and environment. And although the urgent need for creating sustainable and ethical AI technology is admitted, there exists a lack of design tools and expertise to facilitate this advancement. This study investigates how to help designers design for the value of trust in AI systems. A literature review unveiled a myriad of ethical AI principles as well as gathered existing tools addressing the research area. Iterative reviews together with an expert on trust in technology evaluated these guidelines and a first iteration of the toolkit containing 28 design principles had been created. Through multiple participatory design workshops the next iteration of the toolkit was co-designed in collaboration with design professionals. The result is an iterated toolkit comprising 16 principles relevant in the design for trust in AI systems, and providing tool suggestions for each principle.

Keywords: Trustworthy AI · Human-centered AI · AI guidelines · Ethical AI

1 Introduction

Technological progress has a tremendous impact on society, the environment and the wider economical context, especially in the fields of artificial intelligence (AI), machine learning (ML) and autonomous systems. But it's also acknowledged amongst experts that although there is an urgent need for finding ways and concepts to develop sustainable AI, the topic is vastly underrepresented [1]. Unfortunately, design as a profession, and as a craft, follows this trend and is underutilized and misunderstood in the creation of modern technologies. The traditional view is that design is a technical and value-neutral task of developing artifacts that meet functional requirements formulated by clients and users [2]. And design should be looked at as a tool that services humanity. Yet AI systems will impact all dimensions of our lives, from commercial and social interactions to relationships with the state, including dramatic structural transformations in the public sphere. Hence the design of such technologies can't be value-neutral. The theories, tools and methods need to integrate societal, legal and moral values into the development process of these systems at all stages of the design and development process to ensure human flourishing and wellbeing in a sustainable world [3].

© Springer Nature Switzerland AG 2021
C. Stephanidis et al. (Eds.): HCII 2021, LNCS 13095, pp. 536–555, 2021.
https://doi.org/10.1007/978-3-030-90963-5_41

However, it seems that design practices aren't keeping pace and struggle to incorporate human values and algorithmic logic together into socially, economically and politically sustainable models. There is a lack of knowledge, skills and roles in the field of design to support and enable the creation of beneficial, human-centered products, services and systems.

1.1 Research Problem

Guidelines on how to build technology in ethical and sustainable ways are nothing new. For the field of artificial intelligence alone, recent studies have demonstrated that there exists an abundance of guidelines, created by research institutes, private companies and the public sector [4–6]. But although such ethical principles and guidelines ought to shape the development and implementation of ethical technologies, their existence is not without criticism. Morley et al. found that the tools and guidelines being developed and provided to address AI ethics are often difficult to map in regard to the categories or principles they could help to address [7]. According to McNamara et al., studies suggest that guidelines have little impact on the practices surrounding AI development as they lack real implementation mechanics and assessment practices that would turn guidelines into more ethically aware development [8]. This indicates that existing guidelines on ethical, explainable and trustworthy AI are too abstract and difficult to put into practice. In consequence, it's difficult for designers and developers of AI technologies to determine which ethical concerns they should be aware of, how these can present themselves and how they may be addressed [9]. In addition, existing guidelines are often difficult to understand as they tend to be written for technical users who constitute only one key user group. More often than not it is argued that ethical problems can be addressed with technical fixes. Yet this perspective would position advanced modern technology, and AI in particular, as something outside of the social-relational structure and obscure the larger, often socio-technical problems. To make AI policies work, it is important to build a bridge between abstract high-level ethical principles and the practices of technology development and use in their particular contexts [10]. To overcome this misconception, humans need to be involved in the process to incorporate human values into the developed products, services and systems [11].

1.2 Research Goal

The goal of this research was to develop a design toolkit which has the objective of enabling the design of trustworthy AI. The aim is to provide assistance during the design process, helping designers to define the appropriate design for a given use case. By co-designing the toolkit with experienced designers the most useful and beneficial toolkit for its later users is ensured. Based on the research goal, one main research question, as well as three sub-research questions can be defined. Main research question: *"How to help designers design for trustworthy AI?"*, with the sub-research questions (SRQ): SRQ1: *"What current design practices exist to support the translation of existing trustworthy AI guidelines into practice?"*, SRQ2: *"How to create a toolkit that will enable designers to design for the formation of trustworthy AI systems?"* and SRQ3: *"How does the toolkit enable the design of trustworthy AI systems in the dimensions of "usefulness", "satisfaction" and "efficiency?".*

2 Research Strategy

As the methodological foundation for this study, a Research through design approach was followed. It focuses on the contribution to the field of Human-Computer Interaction (HCI) and the creation of new knowledge. According to Zimmermann et al., by following Research through design methodology, designers produce novel integrations of HCI research with the goal of creating a product that transforms the world from its current state to a preferred state [12]. Or as Pärnpuu describes it, "Research through design aims to produce artifacts that become design examples, providing an appropriate conduit for research findings to easily transfer to the HCI community" [13].

The structure of this research process consists of three pillars, which are based on each other. A literature review, an expert evaluation to create the first iteration of the toolkit and a participatory co-design workshop to evaluate and iterate on the toolkit. Each of these process elements has a defined set of goals, a specified research method and expected outcomes. The outcome of each pillar builds the foundation for the next step in the process (Table 1).

Table 1. Research process

Pillar	1. Literature review	2. First iteration	3. Evaluation & iteration
Input	Sub-research question 1	Sub-research question 2	Sub-research question 2 Sub-research question 3
Goals	Identifying key concepts Identifying research gaps Collecting existing tools & methods	Identifying relevant principles for the design of trustworthy AI Shortlisting principles to include in prototype	Co-designing next iteration of the toolkit with practitioners Evaluating toolkit
Methods	Scoping Review Web Search	Expert Evaluation	Participatory Design Workshop
Participants	Researcher	Trust expert Design expert	Researcher Design professionals
Outcomes	Theoretical foundation Collection of existing tools	First iteration of the toolkit	Iterated toolkit Toolkit evaluation

3 Literature Review

To contribute novel knowledge, methodology and tools to the field of designing for trustworthy artificial intelligence, a thorough literature review is pertinent. The literature review in this work served two purposes: First, it examined the extent, range and nature of existing research activity, to identify and define key concepts. Particular attention was directed towards identifying common principles for the design and development of trustworthy AI in the literature. The second goal was to assemble a collection of existing tools and methodologies for the translation of ethical AI guidelines into practice. This collection was supplemented with a dedicated search for available tools and methods, also outside of the academic spectrum and the narrow topic of trustworthy AI. The literature review was conducted as a scoping study, using the suggested framework from Arksey and O'Malley [14]. Colquhoun [15] states that the "scoping review constitutes a knowledge synthesis which addresses an exploratory research question by mapping key concepts, types of evidence and gaps in research by systematically searching, selecting and synthesizing knowledge". The defining search strings were *"design for trust"*, *"design for trust toolkit"*, *"design for trustworthy AI"*, *"designing for trust tool"*, *"ethical design tool"*, *"ethical design toolkit"*, *"human-centered AI"*, *"trust in AI"*, *"trust sensitive design"*, *"trust toolkit"*, *"trust-centered design"* and *"trustworthy AI AND ethics guidelines"*. A pilot search for studies was performed on the Google Scholar platform (scholar.google.com). A refined search has been repeated on the ACM Digital Library (dl.acm.org). The initial list of 312 sources underwent multiple screening and assessment stages, eliminating 97 sources as they were addressing very specific and sensitive sub-fields for which artificial intelligence is becoming increasingly relevant, such as health, education, military use and robotics. But as designing for those specific contexts also requires specific domain knowledge, studies from these fields were excluded. Also, 156 studies had been excluded as they didn't fulfill the eligibility criteria of contributing to answering the research questions and whether they'd describe an existing tool or method to put theoretical AI guidelines into practice. A total of 66 eligible, non-duplicate documents related to the topics were identified and went into the literature review. The literature review provided an overview of the existing advancements in the field of ethical AI, Human-centered AI, and how to induce trust into AI systems by design.

3.1 Ethical AI

The rapid advancement of AI technology is recognizable in various fields, thus also in the appraisal of the importance of ethical considerations in the development and use of AI. In 2014, Bostrom [16] concluded that AI offers only a few new ethical issues, which are not already present in the design of other technologies. No more than a few years later, this assessment seems outdated. The literature review revealed a strong body of research on ethical AI and indicates a growing awareness and acknowledgment of the need for ethical and moral thoughts into the design and development of AI technologies. The concept of AI ethics has emerged as a response to the abundance of societal and individual perils caused by the abuse, misuse, poor design, or unintended consequences of AI systems. In their 2019 report "Understanding artificial intelligence ethics and safety", the Alan Turing Institute has provided an overview of the most common potential harms caused by AI systems [17]. Mark Coekelbergh [10] warns that if the project of ethical AI fails, we risk ethical, social and economic disaster with unpredictable human, non-human and environmental costs. But in contrast to the sensational image of a dystopian future, AI already has a huge positive impact on the life of many of us. AI systems are used in healthcare, public safety and transportation to support humans in their work, ensure security and reliefs in a myriad of contexts [18]. But it is important that future systems must be introduced in ways that build trust and understanding and further respect human and civil rights [3]. The need for ethical considerations in the development of intelligent interactive systems is becoming one of the main influential areas of research. Coekelbergh [10] describes that the recent spectacular breakthroughs in AI have created a sense of urgency on the part of ethicists and policymakers. Gamberlin [19] describes a new role that has been appearing more and more often in the latest discussions: the role of the AI ethicist. Bietti [20] argues that the concepts of ethics and morality in relation to technology are more and more at risk of being exploited, either by the industry in the form of "ethics washing", or by scholars and policy-makers in the form of "ethics bashing". She states that "[...] the more ethics is used in tech circles as a performative façade, the more it is instrumentalized and voided of its intrinsic value" (p.218). Consequently, in their paper "Ethicist as Designer", van Wynsberghe and Robbins [21] state that ethical considerations need to be integrated at an earlier stage into the design process before a product or service is getting developed or even introduced. In their perspective, ethics ought to be pragmatic and the ethicist should be considered a designer in the process of technology development, who subscribes to a pragmatic view of ethics in order to bring ethics into the research and design of artifacts. Another issue that needs to be recognized is described by Hagerty and Rubinov [22], who identified that the current analyses of AI in a global context are biased towards western perspectives and that there is a lack of research, especially outside the U.S. and Western Europe. But to approach AI ethics seriously, they need to be addressed with a cross-cultural understanding.

3.2   Human-Centered AI

Human-centered AI provides a new perspective on the design and development of AI systems. The Ethics Guidelines of the High-Level Expert Group of the European Commission state that a human-centric approach "in which the human being enjoys a unique and inalienable moral status of primacy in the civil, political, economic and social fields" [23]. It is the evolution of bringing human-centered design (HCD) into the field of AI as it aims to bridge the gap between ethics and practical application by providing specific recommendations to create products and services that augment, amplify, empower, and enhance humans. Human-centered AI research strategies emphasize that the next frontier of AI is not just technological but also humanistic and ethical. According to Ben Shneiderman [24], the concept of human-centered AI reverses the current emphasis on algorithms and AI methods, by putting humans at the center of systems design thinking. It emphasizes the user experience and measuring human performance, aiming to empower people, rather than to emulate them. This mental shift could result in a safer, more understandable, and more manageable future, mitigating existing fears of AI's existential threats and raise people's belief that they will be able to use technology for their daily needs and creative explorations [24]. According to Auernhammer [25], there seems to be a strong commitment that high-lights the need and the potential of designing human-centered and ethical AI systems to play a pivotal role in the development and use of AI technology for the well-being of people.

3.3 Ethical AI Guidelines

One of the measures taken to address the nascent concerns about malicious, uncontrollable or hostile technology has been the development of ethical guidelines on the development of artificial intelligence. Various organizations, private companies as well as research institutions, have produced guidelines for the ethical development and use of AI systems. These guidelines comprise normative principles and recommendations aimed to harness the "disruptive" potentials of new AI technologies [4]. The comprehensive analysis of a corpus of 84 existing AI ethics guidelines, conducted by Jobin, Ienca and Vayena [5] reveals a convergence of five prevalent ethical principles, namely transparency, justice and fairness, non-maleficence, responsibility and privacy, which appear in more than half of the analyzed guidelines. However, the analysis also shows a substantive divergence in relation to how these principles are interpreted, why they are deemed important, what issue, domain or actors they pertain to and how they should be implemented [5]. Fjeld et al. [6] have identified eight themes, 47 principles within a body of 36 sources. But their value for practical implementation is often half-baked. The term "ethics washing" is used in this context, meaning polishing your public image on false grounds, says Anna-Mari Rusanen, one of the driving forces behind the "Ethics of AI" online course, developed and provided by the University of Helsinki [26]. AI ethics is failing in many cases as it lacks reinforcement mechanisms as well as practical recommendations for actions [4]. And in cases where ethics is integrated into institutions, it currently mainly serves as a marketing strategy. Empirical experiments even show that the mere reading of ethics guidelines has currently no significant influence on the decision-making of software developers. To make AI policies work, it would be imperative to build a bridge between abstract high-level ethical principles defined by research institutes, companies or nation-states and the practices of technology development and use in particular contexts [10].

3.4 Applying Guidelines in Practice

As the AI guideline analyses by Fjeld et al. [6], Hagendorff [4] and Jobin, Ienca & Vayena [5] illustrate, nearly all of the formulated guidelines consider similar values to be crucial requirements for the development of "ethically sound" AI applications. Yet, how the development of ethical AI technology should work and how to implement these precepts is currently still uncertain and fuzzy. The lack of specific and verifiable principles endangers the effectiveness and enforceability of ethics guidelines. The AI Ethics Impact Group [27], a joint research initiative, has developed a framework that offers concrete guidance to decision-makers in organizations developing and using AI. The framework offers directives on how to incorporate values into algorithmic systems, and how to measure the fulfillment of values using criteria, observables and indicators combined with a context-dependent risk assessment. It introduces different tools and methods to operationalize abstract principles and to classify application contexts, e.g. through a risk matrix [27]. The risk matrix tool developed by Krafft and Zweig [28] is a schematic visualization for identifying categories - classes - of an algorithmic decision-making system according to its risk potential. In his paper "Bridging the Gap Between Ethics and Practice: Guidelines for Reliable, Safe, and Trustworthy Human-centered AI Systems" [29], Ben Shneiderman proposes a set of recommendations, divided by levels of governance – team, organization and industry, which aim to increase the reliability, safety and trustworthiness of Human-centered AI systems. Floridi et al. [30] have defined an ethical framework for a good AI society, presenting a synthesis of five ethical principles and a list of 20 concrete recommendations to assess, develop, incentivize and support the concept of "good" AI. The authors state that in order to create a "Good AI Society", the ethical principles they described need to be embedded in the default practices of AI.

3.5   Trust in AI

In their comprehensive literature review "Human Trust In Artificial Intelligence: Review Of Empirical Research", Glikson and Wooley [31] state that success of integrating AI into the organizational context critically depends on workers' trust in AI technology. They define Trust as particularly relevant to the human-AI relationships because of the perceived risk embedded in them, due to the complexity and nondeterminism of AI behaviours. The European Commission's High-level Expert Group on AI (AI-HLEG) has adopted the position that we should establish a relationship of trust with AI and should cultivate trustworthy AI [23]. According to Xu [32], especially the so-called "black-box phenomenon", common for deep learning technologies, can result in users questioning decisions from the system. Such reflexive skepticism can affect users' trust and decision-making efficiency, which in turn will also affect the adoption of AI solutions. Ferrario et al. (2019) also see the current advancements in the field of Trust in AI critical, as they argue that the overall level of awareness in society on topics like AI is still quite low. According to their analysis, most users of AI-powered products and services are not aware of the presence of AIs. In their paper "In AI We Trust Incrementally: a Multi-layer Model of Trust to Analyze Human-Artificial Intelligence Interactions" (2019), Ferrario et al. propose an incremental model of trust that can be applied to both human-human and human-AI interactions [33].

3.6   Trustworthy AI

Trustworthy AI (TAI) is grounded on the concept that trust is a fundamental prerequisite to create societies, economies, and sustainable development. Thiebes, et al. [34] derive that individuals, organizations, and societies will only be able to realize the full potential of AI, if trust can be established in its development, deployment, and use. Francesca Rossi, a member of the AI-HLEG concludes in her work, that to fully gauge its potential benefits, a system of trust needs to be established, both in the technology itself as well as in those who produce it. The development of several high-level principles has laid the foundation to guide AI towards a positive impact. The necessary next step is to put such principles to work and create robust implementation mechanisms [35]. By analyzing how the involved parties interact with each other during the development and co-creation process of AI, Thiebes et al. [35] identify tensions between the current state of AI development, deployment, and use and the five proposed TAI principles. Shneiderman [24] proposes a two-dimensional framework of Human-Centered Artificial Intelligence (HCAI) to seek high levels of human control AND high levels of automation. The framework separates the levels of automation and autonomy from the levels of human control. The author claims that by applying the new guideline, it is more likely to produce computer applications that are reliable, safe and trustworthy. Mark Ryan on the other hand states that the concept of trustworthy AI is not accurate. He suggests either changing the term "trustworthy AI" to "reliable AI" or removing it altogether, as trust can only occur between trusted parties, whereas he describes AI as a systematic group of techniques [36].

3.7 A Collection of Existing Tools and Methods

The second goal of the literature review was to collect already existing tools and methods and to evaluate their suitability and adaptability for the specific use-case of designing for trustworthy AI and to provide hands-on assistance. However, the scope of the collection was deliberately kept broad, to capture a variety of tools and methods. Despite focusing only on those which already address the specific topic of "design for trustworthy AI", the search also considered adjacent and related fields, like "Design for Trust", or "Ethical Design", without a specific focus on AI. Further, the collection also considered data ethics tools, as they could also be relevant in addressing some of the aspects when designing for trustworthy AI. During the literature review a collection of 34 existing tools, techniques and frameworks have been identified to create a collection of available practices.

4 First Iteration of the Toolkit

One of the fundamental values for the development of artificial intelligence is the value of trust. Trust is an essential principle for interpersonal interactions and it constitutes a prerequisite for a society to work. It is therefore indisputable that trust needs to be acknowledged as a key requirement for the ethical deployment and use of AI [9]. The High-Level Expert Group on Artificial Intelligence even uses trustworthiness as the overarching paradigm for their ethical AI guidelines [23]. However, there aren't many details, specifics or instructions available on how the design and development of "trustworthy AI" should be approached from a design perspective. Sutrop [37] states that, "If it is important that people trust AI systems, it is not enough to establish and articulate the purpose of achieving trustworthy AI. It is imperative that we also think about how to build trust in AI". To fill this gap between theoretical principles and the practical application of existing tools and methods embodies the underlying research objective of this work. To advance the current state of knowledge and tooling for designers working with AI systems, a Research through design constitutes its conceptual foundation. According to Zimmermann et al. [12], the target output is a concrete problem framing and artifacts like prototypes and design process documentations.

Besides the literature reviews, the research process was composed of two main iterative parts. In the first part, the most common ethical principles from a wide body of ethical AI guidelines were identified based on the literature review and synthesized into a comprehensive list of agreed-upon principles. Furthermore, the list of principles is assessed for the first time by a professional designer (author 2) in collaboration with an expert in the field of trust in technology (author 1). Each principle was assessed whether it qualifies to be understood and addressed as a design problem for the value of trust. In the second part of the research process, the qualified principles were evaluated by design professionals in participatory design workshops. Within the workshops, the design professionals were tasked to assess if a principle relates to one or more phases in a design process. Furthermore, the principles are assessed whether they contribute to one of three trust-inducing qualities from the Human-Computer Trust Model [39] namely "Benevolence", "Competence" and "Risk perception". Additionally, the design professionals were asked to highlight if a principle is already addressed in other user interface or human-computer interaction guidelines, to avoid redundancy. And lastly, the participants are also encouraged to share any tools and methods they think could be useful to address a specific principle.

4.1   Identifying Design Principles for Trustworthiness

To determine the relevant principles for the emergence of trust, a multi-phase framework was developed. As a result of the conducted literature review it became apparent that there exists an abundance of guidelines on the ethical and moral design, development and use of AI systems. But a comparative study, let alone deeper analysis of all currently AI ethics guidelines would go beyond the scope of this study. Therefore, this work draws upon existing, reviewed studies of such nature. In 2019, Jobin et al. undertook the ambitious endeavor to create a comprehensive overview of the available AI ethics guidelines at the time [5]. Altogether, 84 documents had been reviewed, their content described and convergence as well as common themes across these guidelines had been identified. In 2020, Ryan and Stahl built upon the robust categorization of ethical principles from Jobin et al. [5], analyzing 91 sources in total, including the 84 guidelines from the Jobin et al. study, plus 7 additional sources [9]. Their goal was to move beyond the high-level ethical principles that are common across the AI ethics guidance literature and provide a description of the content that is covered by these principles [9]. They created a categorization system of eleven principles, with 61 sub-principles. In the same year, the Berkman Klein Center for Internet & Society at Harvard University, led by Jessica Fjeld et al. [6], published a report called "Principled Artificial Intelligence: Mapping Consensus in Ethical and Rights-based Approaches to Principles for AI". The report states that guidelines for ethical, rights-respecting, and socially beneficial AI develop in tandem with the underlying technology. Therefore an urgent need to understand these guidelines is obligatory. The report analyzed 36 prominent AI guideline documents, discovering eight themes which suggest an emergence of sectoral norms, and outlines 47 principles elicited from these documents.

Another relevant study had been conducted by Morley et al. [7], building upon the work by Hagendorff [4] and Floridi [40], connecting five high-level ethical principles and 23 identified tangible system requirements. In summary, the starting point for the analysis of relevant ethical guidelines was composed by a corpus of 131 guidelines.

As the body of ethical guidelines was a composition of multiple sources, the collection needed to be synthesized, deduplicated and cleaned up to achieve a coherent list of principles. For the synthesis, the principles had been compared by name, description and semantic meaning, to mitigate misunderstanding and redundancy. The same process has been applied across all 131 principles from the collection, to standardize naming, content and meaning. However it's relevant to mention, that the descriptions and definitions provided in the different studies aren't written by the authors of the comparative studies, but they are the descriptions from the original sources. This means that multiple descriptions existed for each of the principles. Although the selection of the most suitable description for a principle has been conducted with rigor and diligence, there hasn't been any extended analysis on the coherence of the gathered definitions within the scope of this work. The synthesis has been conducted based on the assumption of scientific accuracy from the authors of the comparative studies. After the synthesis process of the three sources, the list of ethical AI principles was reduced to a total number of 80 principles.

To focus the toolkit specifically on the concept of designing for trustworthy AI, the list of 80 general ethical AI principles needed to be scrutinized with regard to which of the principles would qualify to be understood as general design principles contributing to the emergence of trust. However, this endeavor wasn't straight-forward, as aptly described by Blackler et al. in their latest paper analyzing 20 years of discussion on how to define "design". In the article it's stated that "Ever since the industrial revolution, a solid, common understanding of what design is and does has proven nearly impossible to establish" [41]. As there was no commonly agreed upon definition available, which could be applied to decide which of the ethical AI principles would qualify as design principles for trust, multiple non-structured filters have been deployed. The identifications were the result of multiple extended expert evaluations and iterations between a professional designer (author 2) and a subject matter expert on the topic of trust in technology (author 1). During the process of elimination each principle was reviewed whether it would be approachable from a different perspective than design, and how more or less suitable this perspective would fit the principle in comparison to the design discipline. Further, there was an initial assessment of the relevance for the value of trust, assessing whether it could contribute to the emergence of trust when designing an AI system. If a principle was considered to be not, or only marginally influenceable by the broader responsibility of a designer, or was found to not relate to a trust quality, a principle had been discarded from the list.

These evaluation filters have been applied for all of the remaining 80 principles to further reduce and specify the list of principles into a concise and relevant list. As with every subjective, less formalized process, the decisions haven't been clear and precise for each of the principles. There have been vague and ambiguous cases, where a distinct definition and decision weren't straightforward. For these cases, the heuristic of keeping the list of principles as lean as possible has been defined and applied. This means that in cases where a decision couldn't be made unambiguously, the principle was also eliminated from the list. By this multi-layer elimination process, the list had been further reduced to 28 principles, which constitutes the first iteration of the toolkit.

5 Evaluation and Iteration

In the next stage, the first iteration of the toolkit was evaluated together with design professionals in several participatory design workshops. Design workshops are a variant of the participatory design concept which consolidates creative co-design methods into organized sessions for several participants to work with designers [42]. The objective of conducting participatory workshops together with experienced designers was to ensure continuous involvement of the envisioned "users" of the toolkit already during the toolkit development. The goal of the workshops was to assess the identified principles and to co-design the next iteration of the toolkit. According to Sanders and Stappers [43], co-design is understood as a collective creativity which is applied across the whole span of the design process and refers to the collective creativity of collaborating designers.

Design workshops encompass methods with the unifying philosophy to allow face-to-face involvement of users via co-design engagements [42]. Co-Design as a concept can be used in conjunction with many other tools, as they can be adapted for a co-creative setting [44]. According to Sanders and Stappers [43], Co-Design carries the notion that "The person who will eventually be served through the design process is given the position of 'expert of his/her experience', and plays a large role in knowledge development, idea generation and concept development". This is especially relevant in the context of developing a toolkit for designers as it allows the craftswoman and craftsman to shape their own tools. The workshops were organized as one-on-one online sessions, using appointment scheduling (calendar.google.com), video conferencing (meet.google.com) and collaborative work applications (sheets.google.com) Prior to the workshops, there was a pilot study conducted to run through the planned session and test the associated materials. The pilot study yielded feedback on the timeframe of the workshops, the clarity of the instructions as well as the composition of the worksheets. Furthermore, it also provided practice in running the workshop and increased confidence in the research design from the author [45].

For the participatory design workshops, three professionals from the field of designer had been recruited. The profiles ranged from a Product Design Lead to a Master student in Human-Computer Interaction (HCI) to a Usability Testing Expert and Digital Business Expert in User Experience and Service Design. The professional tenure varied between the participants, but all had multiple years of experience working in the design field. The product design lead brought around nine years of experience in various product and user experience (UX) design roles. The Usability Testing and Service Design Expert had a decade of experience working in different UX research roles in software companies as well as multinational corporations. The Master's student had multiple years of experience working as a web designer in different roles.

5.1 Workshop Activities

The workshops began with a short introduction to the participants, explaining the research goal, the structure of the workshop, the provided material and the tasks they were supposed to perform during the different activities. Further, the participants were asked whether they would consent to have the session recorded, under the premise that the recordings will be deleted after the research has been completed. Also, some basic information about the participants has been collected, namely their current role as well as their number of years of experience as a design professional. Lastly, any questions the participants had before the activities were addressed.

After the introduction, the participants left the video conferencing call to work on the individual activity by themselves. As the goal of the activity was to better understand and capture unique individual perspectives, it's recommended to ask participants to work individually [46]. The individual activity consisted of a mapping exercise, which was an adaptation of the Card Sorting method. Card Sorting is a participatory design technique to explore how participants relate concepts to each other [42]. Furthermore, according to the participatory design framework defined by Sanders et al. [46], activities involving card-based artifacts are useful for the purpose of understanding the perception and experience of participants. For this research, the traditional card-sorting method was adapted to fit the need and purpose of the research goal. During the individual activity, the participants needed to decide if a design principle could be related to at least one phase of a predefined design process, if it would contribute to one of three trust qualities and if they could suggest an existing tool which would be useful to address the principle. To ensure comparability of the results of the workshops, a formalized design process model, the "Double-Diamond" process model was predetermined for the participants [38]. To allow for this kind of multi-dimensional mapping, the participants didn't have to organize "principle-cards" into different categories, but the mapping happened in a more formalized process by selecting from predefined options in the worksheet. The worksheet was created in Google Sheets, containing an introduction sheet, two task sheets and three material sheets. The worksheet was shared with the participants so that they could interact with the spreadsheet on their own devices. In addition to the mapping exercise, the individual activity also included a short evaluation task, in which the participants should rate the toolkit prototype on a Likert scale in the dimensions of "usefulness", "satisfaction" and "efficiency". This rating was implemented to elicit a perception and evaluation of the idea of the toolkit, as well as its current state.

The final stage of the workshop was a collaborative activity, together with the researcher, with the goal of evaluating the toolkit prototype and co-creating the next iteration together. The collaborative generative research session built upon the results from the individual activity. According to Sanders et al. [46] the individual expressions set the stage for successful collaboration in later activities, as it's often in the collaborative act of making, telling or enacting that innovation occurs. A key feature of running generative sessions is to combine the participatory activities with verbal discussions [42]. In preparation for the collaborative activity, the author had also completed the mapping exercise separately. The first iteration of the toolkit served as an artifact to trigger an engaged and comfortable conversation between the participant and the researcher with the goal of trying to find a consensus for the next iteration of the toolkit. For these conversations, the laddering technique allowed deep introspection and contemplation on fundamental values as well as potential considerations about consequences and the elicitation of underlying values [47].

The first thread of the collaborative activity was the evaluation of each principle in regard to its relevance as a design principle. As mentioned above, the mechanism to identify and assess the relevance of a principle consisted of the general design process mapping. The mapping exercise should prompt the participants to perform a critical analysis of the principle. If it would not be possible to attribute a principle to one or multiple design process phases, the relevance of a principle would be put into question and a principle removed from the toolkit. Another thread in the collaborative activity was the mitigation of redundancies with already available frameworks, norms or guidelines. This section in the research design aimed to keep the design principles as relevant as possible to avoid the repetition of common and established practices. The participants were prompted, if they would think that a design principle from the toolkit prototype was already addressed, or at least affected, in an existing guideline or recommendation they know from their professional practice. To initiate the thought process, the participants were given examples of such guidelines, like the "Usability Heuristics" defined by Jakob Nielsen [48] or the ISO 9241-210 norm, which provides requirements and recommendations for human-centered design principles [49].

The final thread of the evaluation of the principles from the toolkit prototype was to consolidate principles where possible, with the intention to reduce semantic overlap within the toolkit. Again, the laddering technique allowed for specific probing into considerations about consequences as well as relevant and underlying values within the participants. This helped to better comprehend how participants understood particular principles and how they would foresee their application. This was the most sensitive part of the activity, as it was important to not dilute the importance and relevance of a specific principle when merging it with another, similar principle.

6 Results

The next iteration of the toolkit consists of 16 design principles, their respective descriptions as well as suggested tools when working with these principles (see appendix). The ultimate list of principles is the result of an extensive literature review, during which common themes and guidelines for the development of ethical AI systems have been identified. Based on the most common ethical AI guidelines, the specifically relevant principles for the design towards the value of trust have been elicited. The toolkit has been co-developed and co-designed in collaboration with several design practitioners from the field as well as a subject matter expert in the area of trust in technology. The principles have been validated in multiple participatory workshops and underwent extensive scrutiny during the co-design sessions.

6.1   Limitations

During the research process, a couple of limitations have been identified. The first potential limitation can be delineated by the lack of a formalized theoretical framework during the initial phase of principle selection. It's possible that a different set of experiences and backgrounds of the authors could have yielded different results. Another potential deficiency within the research structure could be found in the selection of the descriptions for the toolkit prototype. Although the descriptions had been chosen to the best of the knowledge and belief of the authors, it could have happened that in cases where multiple descriptions were mentioned in the original list, this pre-selection might have influenced the understanding of the principles in the participants. Another issue identified during the participatory design workshops was the varying understanding of the selected design process and its particular phases. Even though the "Double-Diamond" process is a well-known and documented process and an explicit process description had been provided to the participants, some misunderstandings and confusions occurred. This rendered the comparison additionally complex. It also raises the more fundamental question, if a human-centered design process is the best approach when approaching complex systems like AI or ML? Does an HCD approach maybe ignore or neglect other perspectives like environmental sustainability? Could a "More-Than-Human Design" approach, as discussed by Giaccardi and Redström [50] be the more inclusive maxim?

6.2   Further Research

One of the most apparent suggestions for continuing this research would be to conduct another evaluation on the latest iteration of the toolkit in regard to the dimensions of "usefulness", "satisfaction" and "efficiency". For now, the evaluation happened on the first iteration, without any usage of the toolkit, but only the crude list of principles and the general concept. The latest iteration has implemented the feedback from the workshops, which would also provide a good opportunity to link the evaluation with a real-world task, in which designers could field-test the toolkit in their own projects. Another opportunity would be to conduct more and slightly variant workshops. As Hair Jr et al. state, "When the aim of the study is to contribute to scale development, nonsignificant attributes from initial studies cannot simply be discarded without testing them in different ways and in different contexts to ensure proper construct validity and reliability" [51]. Another direction for continuing this research would be to turn the toolkit into a more actionable and practical format to be suitable for field implementation. A possible manifestation could be in the format of physical cards, which are considered playful and creative in their usage and that they can be applied in collaborative sessions [52]. Pärnpuu describes several implementations where design cards have proven their usefulness [13]. They help to spark discussion and support reflection by being tangible and accessible. Lucero et al. describe them as "tangible idea containers" [53].

7   Conclusion

This research project began with a gargantuan task, hidden in the main research question of *"How to help designers design for trustworthy AI?"*. This objective demanded to first understand what designing for trustworthiness means in the context of artificial intelligence. In an extensive literature review it has been recognized that the current culprit in designing for trustworthy AI, isn't a lack of theoretical suggestions or recommendations. It's rather even the sheer volume of available ethical guidelines which can result in paralysis and obstruct their practical application. It was identified that a practice-oriented compilation containing only trust-relevant principles with some helpful tool suggestions could be a potential remedy. In collaboration with design professionals as well as experts in the field of trust in technology, relevant design principles have been identified, compiled and iterated on. Furthermore, a list of useful methods and tools has been composed to undergird the theoretical framework with hands-on suggestions to apply in practice. This developed toolkit provides a small advancement in the field of designing for trustworthy AI, as it addresses the afore-mentioned lack of knowledge, skills and roles in the field of design for beneficial technologies.

Acknowledgment. This research was supported by AI-Mind "Intelligent digital tools for screening of brainconnectivity and dementia risk estimation in people affected by mild cognitive impairment". Sónia Sousa. H2020 CORDIS No: 964220.

Appendix

Table 2: Toolkit to enable the design of trustworthy AI

Principle	Description	Tool
Autonomy	AI organisations should ensure that end users are informed, not deceived or manipulated by AI and should be allowed to exercise their autonomy [9]	[53]
Consent	The use of personal data must be clearly articulated and agreed upon before its use [9]	[54]
Dignity	AI should be developed and used in a way that respects, serves and protects humans physical and mental integrity, personal and cultural sense of identity, and satisfaction of their essential needs [9]	[55]
Explainability	The translation of technical concepts and decision outputs into intelligible, comprehensible formats suitable for evaluation [6]	[56, 57]
Fairness	There should be steps in place to ensure that data being used by AI is not unfair, or contains errors and inaccuracies, that will corrupt the response and decisions taken by the AI [9]	[58, 59]

(continued)

Table 2: *(continued)*

Principle	Description	Tool
Human oversight	The "ability to opt out of automated decision" principle is defined, as affording individuals the opportunity and choice not to be subject to AI systems where they are implemented [6]	[56, 60, 61]
Impact assessment	The objectives and expected impact of AI must be assessed, reviewed and documented on an ongoing basis [9]	[61, 63, 64]
Inclusion	Attention should be given to under-represented and vulnerable groups and communities, such as those with disabilities, ethnic minorities, children and those in the developing world. Data that is being used should be representative of the target population and should be as inclusive as possible [9]	[55, 65, 66]
Non-Bias	Developers should examine unfair biases at every stage of the development process and should eliminate those found [9]	[53, 66]
Non-discrimination	AI should be designed for universal usage and not discriminate against people, or groups of people, based on gender, race, culture, religion, age or ethnicity [9]	[59, 66]
Privacy	Users should have control and access to data stored about them [9]	[53, 56, 65, 67]
Purpose	The purpose for building the system must be clear and linked to a clear benefit —system's should not be built for the sake of it [7]	[56, 66, 68]
Reversibility	It is important to clearly articulate if the outcomes of AI decisions are reversible. The ability to undo the last action or a sequence of actions allows users to undo undesired actions and get back to the 'good' stage of their work [9]	[61]
Showing	It should be clear to the end user that they are interacting with an AI system, rather than a human. Further, where an AI has been employed, the person to whom it was subject should know [9]	[69, 70]
Stakeholder participation	To develop systems that are trustworthy and support human flourishing, those who will be affected by the system should be consulted [7]	[58, 64, 65]
Transparency	The principle of "transparency" is the assertion that AI systems should be designed and implemented in such a way that oversight of their operations are possible [6]	[65, 66]

References

1. Pooley, L., Metcalfe, M.: We need to talk about A.I [Motion picture]. GFC Films (2020)
2. van den Hoven, J., Vermaas, P.E., van de Poel, I.: Design for values: an introduction. In: van den Hoven, J., Vermaas, P.E., van de Poel, I. (eds.) Handbook of Ethics, Values, and Technological Design, pp. 1–7. Springer, Dordrecht (2015). https://doi.org/10.1007/978-94-007-6970-0_40

3. Dignum, V.: Ethics in artificial intelligence: introduction to the special issue. Ethics Inf. Technol. **20**(1), 1–3 (2018). https://doi.org/10.1007/s10676-018-9450-z
4. Hagendorff, T.: The ethics of ai ethics: an evaluation of guidelines. Mind. Mach. **30**(1), 99–120 (2020). https://doi.org/10.1007/s11023-020-09517-8
5. Jobin, A., Ienca, M., Vayena, E.: Artificial Intelligence: the global landscape of ethics guidelines. ETH Zürich: Health Ethics & Policy Lab (2019)
6. Fjeld, J., Achten, N., Hilligoss, H., Nagy, A., Srikumar, M.: Principled artificial intelligence: mapping consensus in ethical and rights-based approaches to principles for AI. SSRN Electron. J. 1–68 (2020). https://doi.org/10.2139/ssrn.3518482
7. Morley, J., Floridi, L., Kinsey, L., Elhalal, A.: From what to how: an initial review of publicly available AI ethics tools, methods and research to translate principles into practices. Sci. Eng. Ethics **26**(4), 2141–2168 (2019). https://doi.org/10.1007/s11948-019-00165-5
8. McNamara, A., Smith, J., Murphy-Hill, E.: Does ACM's code of ethics change ethical decision making in software development? In: Proceedings of the 2018 26th ACM Joint Meeting on European Software Engineering Conference and Symposium on the Foundations of Software Engineering, pp. 729–733 (2018). https://doi.org/10.1145/3236024.3264833
9. Ryan, M., Stahl, B.C.: Artificial intelligence ethics guidelines for developers and users: clarifying their content and normative implications. J. Inf. Commun. Ethics Soc. 1–26 (2020). https://doi.org/10.1108/jices-12-2019-0138
10. Coeckelbergh, M.: AI Ethics. MIT Press, Cambridge (2020)
11. Boden, M.A.: Ai: Its Nature and Future. Oxford University Press. ProQuest Ebook Central (2016). http://ebookcentral.proquest.com/lib/cut-ebooks/detail.action?docID=4545415
12. Zimmerman, J., Forlizzi, J., Evenson, S.: Research through design as a method for interaction design research in HCI. In: Proceedings of the SIGCHI Conference on Human Factors in Computing Systems, pp. 493–502 (2007). https://doi.org/10.1145/1240624.1240704
13. Pärnpuu, M.: Designing for values: value elicitation toolkit (thesis). Tallinn University (2020).   https://www.etis.ee/Portal/Mentorships/Display/f1774a45-1cd1-4712-853a-f7a10d3fd315
14. Arksey, H., O'Malley, L.: Scoping studies: towards a methodological framework. Int. J. Soc. Res. Methodol. **8**(1), 19–32 (2005)
15. Colquhoun, H.L., et al.: Scoping reviews: time for clarity in definition, methods, and reporting. J. Clin. Epidemiol. **67**(12), 1291–1294 (2014). https://doi.org/10.1016/j.jclinepi.2014.03.013
16. Bostrom, N.: The ethics of artificial intelligence. In: Yudkowsky, E. (ed.) The Cambridge Handbook of Artificial Intelligence, pp. 316–334. Machine Intelligence Research Institute (2014). https://www.cambridge.org/core/product/identifier/CBO9781139046855A027/type/book_part
17. Leslie, D.: Understanding artificial intelligence ethics and safety: a guide for the responsible design and implementation of AI systems in the public sector. The Alan Turing Institute (2019). https://doi.org/10.5281/zenodo.3240529
18. Stone, P., et al.: Artificial Intelligence and Life in 2030. Stanford University, Stanford, CA (2016). http://ai100.stanford.edu/2016-report
19. Gambelin, O.: Brave: what it means to be an AI Ethicist. AI Ethics **1**(1), 87–91 (2020). https://doi.org/10.1007/s43681-020-00020-5
20. Bietti, E.: From ethics washing to ethics bashing: a view on tech ethics from within moral philosophy. In: FAT* 2020: Proceedings of the 2020 Conference on Fairness, Accountability, and Transparency, pp. 210–219 (2020). https://doi.org/10.1145/3351095.3372860
21. van Wynsberghe, A., Robbins, S.: Ethicist as designer: a pragmatic approach to ethics in the lab. Sci. Eng. Ethics **20**(4), 947–961 (2013). https://doi.org/10.1007/s11948-013-9498-4

22. Hagerty, A., Rubinov, I.: Global AI ethics: a review of the social impacts and ethical implications of artificial intelligence, pp. 1–27 (2019). https://arxiv.org/abs/1907.07892
23. High-Level Expert Group on Artificial Intelligence (AI-HLEG). Ethics Guidelines for Trustworthy AI. Brussels: European Commission (2019). https://ec.europa.eu/futurium/en/ai-alliance-consultation/
24. Shneiderman, B.: Human-centered artificial intelligence: three fresh ideas. AIS Trans. Hum.-Comput. Interact. 109–124 (2020). https://doi.org/10.17705/1thci.00131
25. Auernhammer, J.: Human-centered AI: the role of human-centered design research in the development of AI. In: DRS2020: Synergy, pp. 1–19 (2020). https://doi.org/10.21606/drs.2020.282
26. Helsinki.fi. The Ethics of AI online course urges us to consider what technology should be used for. University of Helsinki (2020). https://www.helsinki.fi/en/news/data-science-news/the-ethics-of-ai-online-course-urges-us-to-consider-what-technology-should-be-used-for. Accessed 27 Nov 2020
27. AI Ethics Impact Group. From Principles to Practice - An interdisciplinary framework to operationalise AI ethics. VDE Association for Electrical Electronic & Information Technologies e.V., Bertelsmann Stiftung, pp. 1–56 (2020)
28. Krafft, T.D., Zweig, K.A., König, P.D.: How to regulate algorithmic decision-making: a framework of regulatory requirements for different applications. Regulat. Govern. 1–18 (2020). https://doi.org/10.1111/rego.12369
29. Shneiderman, B.: Bridging the gap between ethics and practice: guidelines for reliable, safe, and trustworthy human-centered AI systems. ACM Trans. Interact. Intell. Syst. 10(4), 1–31 (2020). Article 26. https://doi.org/10.1145/3419764
30. Floridi, L., et al.: AI4People—an ethical framework for a good AI society: opportunities, risks, principles, and recommendations. Mind. Mach. 28(4), 689–707 (2018). https://doi.org/10.1007/s11023-018-9482-5
31. Glikson, E., Woolley, A.: Human trust in artificial intelligence: Review of empirical research. Academy of Management Annals (in press). The Academy of Management Annals (2020)
32. Xu, W.: Toward human-centered AI. Interactions 26(4), 42–46 (2019). https://doi.org/10.1145/3328485
33. Ferrario, A., Loi, M., Viganò, E.: In AI we trust incrementally: a multi-layer model of trust to analyze human-artificial intelligence interactions. Philos. Technol. 33(3), 523–539 (2019). https://doi.org/10.1007/s13347-019-00378-3
34. Thiebes, S., Lins, S., Sunyaev, A.: Trustworthy artificial intelligence. Electron. Mark. 31(2), 447–464 (2020). https://doi.org/10.1007/s12525-020-00441-4
35. Rossi, F.: Building trust in artificial intelligence. J. Int. Aff. 72(127), 127–133 (2018)
36. Ryan, M.: In AI we trust: ethics, artificial intelligence, and reliability. Sci. Eng. Ethics 26(5), 2749–2767 (2020). https://doi.org/10.1007/s11948-020-00228-y
37. Sutrop, M.: Should we trust artificial intelligence? TRAMES XXIII(4), 499–522 (2019). https://kirj.ee/public/trames_pdf/2019/issue_4/Trames-4-2019-499-522.pdf
38. Design Council. The Design Process (2005). http://www.designcouncil.org.uk/designprocess
39. Gulati, S., Sousa, S., Lamas, D.: Design, development and evaluation of a human-computer trust scale. Behav. Inf. Technol. 38(10), 1004–1015 (2019). https://doi.org/10.1080/0144929x.2019.1656779
40. Floridi, L.: Translating principles into practices of digital ethics: five risks of being unethical. Philosophy & Technology 32(2), 185–193 (2019). https://doi.org/10.1007/s13347-019-00354-x

41. Blackler, A., Swann, L., Chamorro-Koc, M., Mohotti, W.A., Balasubramaniam, T., Nayak, R.: Can we define design? Analyzing twenty years of debate on a large email discussion list. She Ji: J. Design Econ. Innov. **7**(1), 41–70 (2021). https://doi.org/10.1016/j.sheji.2020.11. 004

42. Martin, B., Hanington, B.M.: Universal Methods of Design:100 Ways to Research Complex Problems, Develop Innovative Ideas, and Design Effective Solutions. Rockport Publishers, Beverly (2012)

43. Sanders, E.B.N., Stappers, P.J.: Co-creation and the new landscapes of design. CoDesign **4** (1), 5–18 (2008). https://doi.org/10.1080/15710880701875068

44. Stickdorn, M., Schneider, J.: This is Service Design Thinking: Basics, Tools, Cases. 1st edn. BIS Publishers Amsterdam (2012)

45. Sanders, E.B.N., Stappers, P.J.: Convivial Toolbox: Generative Research for the Front End of Design. BIS Publishers, Amsterdam (2016)

46. Sanders, E.B.N., Brandt, E., Binder, T.: A framework for organizing the tools and techniques of participatory design. In: Proceedings of the 11th Biennial Participatory Design Conference, pp. 195–198 (2010)

47. Gutman, J.: A means-end chain model based on consumer categorization processes. J. Mark. **46**(2), 60–72 (1982). https://doi.org/10.1177/002224298204600207

48. Nielsen, J.: Enhancing the explanatory power of usability heuristics. In: Proceedings of ACM CHI 1994 Conference, Boston, MA, 24–28 April 1994, pp. 152–158 (1994)

49. International Organization for Standardization. (2019). Ergonomics of human-system interaction—Part 210: Human-centred design for interactive systems (ISO Standard No. 9241-210). Retrieved from https://www.iso.org/obp/ui/#iso:std:iso:9241:-210:ed-2:v1: en

50. Giaccardi, E., Redström, J.: Technology and more-than-human design. Des. Issues **36**(4), 33–44 (2020). https://doi.org/10.1162/desi_a_00612

51. Hair, J.F., Jr., Hult, G.T.M., Ringle, C., Sarstedt, M.: A Primer on Partial Least Squares Structural Equation Modeling (PLS-SEM). Sage Publications, Los Angeles (2016)

52. Lucero, A., Dalsgaard, P., Halskov, K., Buur, J.: Designing with cards. In: Markopoulos, P., Martens, J.-B., Malins, J., Coninx, K., Liapis, A. (eds.) Collaboration in Creative Design, pp. 75–95. Springer, Cham (2016). https://doi.org/10.1007/978-3-319-29155-0_5

53. Ideo.Com: AI & Ethics: Collaborative Activities for Designers, July 2019. https://www.ideo. com/post/ai-ethics-collaborative-activities-for-designers

54. Hesketh, P.: Ethics kit in 2019 - ethics kit. Medium (2019). https://medium.com/ethics-kit/ ethics-kit-in-2019-ba1bf483663

55. Santa Clara University: An Ethical Toolkit for Engineering/Design Practice. Markkula Center for Applied Ethics (2018). https://www.scu.edu/ethics-in-technology-practice/ethical-toolkit/

56. People + AI Research: People + AI Research (2017). https://pair.withgoogle.com/

57. Ribeiro, M. T., Singh, S., Guestrin, C.: Why should i trust you? In: Proceedings of the 22nd ACM SIGKDD International Conference on Knowledge Discovery and Data Mining (2016). https://doi.org/10.1145/2939672.2939778

58. Gipson, J.: Ethics for designers—the toolkit. ethics for designers (2017). https://www. ethicsfordesigners.com/tools

59. Lane, G., Angus, A., Murdoch, A.: UnBias fairness toolkit (version 1). Zenodo (2018). https://doi.org/10.5281/zenodo.2667808

60. High-Level Expert Group on Artificial Intelligence (AI-HLEG). Assessment List for Trustworthy Artificial Intelligence (ALTAI) for self-assessment. European Commission (2020)

61. Smith, C.J.: Designing trustworthy AI: a human-machine teaming framework to guide development, pp. 1–6 (2019). http://arxiv.org/abs/1910.03515
62. Zhou, K.: DESIGN ETHICALLY (2021). https://www.designethically.com/toolkit
63. Fleetwood, A., Unsworth, G., Tobia, T.: Product development with consequence scanning. TechTransformed, April 2019
64. Friedman, B., Hendry, D.G.: Value Sensitive Design: Shaping Technology with Moral Imagination. The MIT Press, Cambridge (2019). (Illustrated ed.)
65. Ballard, S., Chappell, K.M., Kennedy, K.: Judgment call the game. In: Proceedings of the 2019 on Designing Interactive Systems Conference, pp. 421–433 (2019). https://doi.org/10.1145/3322276.3323697
66. The Open Data Institute: The Data Ethics Canvas – The ODI (2019)
67. Reijers, W., Lewis, D., Levacher, K., Calvo, A., Burburan, A., Mohri, F.: The ethics canvas. The Ethics Canvas (2017)
68. SRI International: Design for trust (2020)
69. The IEEE Global Initiative on Ethics of Autonomous and Intelligent Systems. Ethically Aligned Design: A Vision for Prioritizing Human Well-being with Autonomous and Intelligent Systems, First Edition. IEEE (2019)
70. Lockton, D., Harrison, D., Stanton, N.A.: Design with intent. Equifine (2010)

Acceptance of Artificial Intelligence in Cars: A Survey Approach

Christina Strobel[1]([✉])[iD] and Jason Dana[2][iD]

[1] Institute for Digital Economics, Hamburg University of Technology,
21079 Hamburg, Germany
christina.strobel@tuhh.de

[2] School of Management, Yale University, New Haven, CT 06511, USA
jason.dana@yale.edu

Abstract. This exploratory descriptive survey analyzes the acceptance of different automated systems used in partly and fully autonomous cars, and whether there is a difference between the level of acceptance for someone's own use and desire for others to use them. The survey reports answers from 199 respondents to an online questionnaire run on Amazon Mechanical Turk (Amazon MTurk). The majority of respondents express high or very high acceptance of partly automated systems; however, when it comes to full automation, the acceptance rate drops significantly. Moreover, the acceptance rate for roughly half of the systems does not differ significantly for the respondent's own use and use by others.

Keywords: Autonomous driving · Survey · Acceptability

1 Introduction

The rapid technological progress made by automotive and tech companies has brought automation technologies to the forefront of public interest. Self-driving cars – also known as autonomous cars, personal automated vehicles, or robotic cars – that guide themselves to a specific target autonomously without any human intervention, are by far the most discussed autonomous technology. The ongoing discussion reveals that the expectations about self-driving cars are immense. For example, the European Commission [15] expects self-driving cars to make driving cheaper, to reduce pollution, and to lower congestion rates. The National Highway Traffic Safety Administration (NHTSA) [36] even sees the technology as the greatest safety innovation in automotive history, as it eliminates from the road the leading cause of motor vehicle accidents: the human driver.

To achieve the environmental, congestion, and safety improvements mentioned above, widespread acceptance of autonomous systems is necessary. The

This document has been generated on November 6, 2021, with R version 3.4.1 (2017-06-30), on x86_64-w64-mingw32. We thank the Yale School of Management for financial support.

C. Stephanidis et al. (Eds.): HCII 2021, LNCS 13095, pp. 556–573, 2021.
https://doi.org/10.1007/978-3-030-90963-5_42

current debate focuses very strongly on ethical issues. Issues about how self-driving cars should react in case of an impending accident. To this end, nearly every discussion considers some version of the so-called *Trolley Problem* by Foot [16] – a thought experiment about whether to act or not to sacrifice or save certain people in the event of a runaway trolley.

The *Moral Machine* experiment by Awad et al. [2], an experiment that empirically investigates different versions of the trolley problem in the context of self-driving cars, gained worldwide attention. Awad et al. [2] asked 2.5 million people from 233 countries who to spare in 13 accident scenarios inspired by the trolley problem. The survey revealed that there is no global preference when it comes to whether young or old, rich or poor, more or fewer people should be sacrificed in an accident but the study identified clusters of countries with similar preference patterns. The so called Western cluster contains North America as well as many European and Scandinavian countries, the Eastern cluster contains countries such as Japan, Taiwan, Indonesia, Pakistan and Saudi Arabia, and the Southern cluster consists mainly of Latin American countries. The clusters differ in the weight they give to certain preferences. For example, the preference for sparing higher status people rather than older people is much more pronounced for countries in the Southern cluster than in the Eastern cluster. The Southern cluster also shows a stronger preference for sparing fit characters and women. The preference to spare more lives (versus fewer lives) is more pronounced in the Western and the Southern cluster than in the Eastern cluster. The study also revealed an ethical paradox: participants prefer an autonomous vehicle to sacrifice the passengers to protect pedestrians, but stated that they would not purchase such a car. Bonnefon et al. [6], however, point out that the trolley problem is mainly a single discrete case of a statistical problem and, thus, is technically irrelevant to solve the problem about how an autonomous car should be programmed to behave in the event of an accident.

As investments in the new technology are mainly influenced by the (expected) demand for partly and fully autonomous cars, end users' attitudes toward and acceptance of self-driving systems will actually determine the success of the technology on the market. Thus, it is not only important to research the moral challenges caused by self-driving cars but also to assess acceptance of various types of autonomous driving systems.

Today, a growing number of vehicles are already equipped with more-or-less autonomous systems that assist the human driver. The consultancy company McKinsey, for example, estimates that 24% of the total vehicle sold worldwide in 2020 contained Level 2 entry or advanced autonomous driving features and expect a growth by +16% per annum in the next few years [13].

Former research has shown that acceptance highly depends on the level of trust in the automated driving systems [3, 22, 23, 31, 41]. Given that self-driving cars are not single devices but rather a collection of different technologies applied in a novel way [1] it is important to not only investigate the acceptance of different levels of automation as a whole but take a close look at which systems users are reluctant to use. Thus, it is not only important to distinguish between the acceptance of a range of cars, from fully to non-autonomous, but to take a close look at what technologies people are hesitant to use. In spite of the lack of studies dealing with acceptance of different self-driving car systems we examine people's willingness to accept varying levels of automation in cars. We also study whether people show different levels of acceptance when thinking about using the systems on their own, compared to when they consider if they would like other people to use specific systems.

We organize the remainder of the paper as follows. Section 2 provides a literature review focusing on studies about the general acceptance of self-driving cars, as well as about people's major concerns about them, and about separate autonomous systems. In Sect. 3, we describe the survey design. We present the results in Sect. 4. Section 5 concludes the paper by summarizing the main findings and discussing their implications, as well as further research ideas.

2   Related Literature

In this section, we first present studies on general acceptance of self-driving cars and then turn to studies examining acceptance of different autonomous systems used in self-driving cars.

2.1   Acceptance of Different Levels of Self-driving Cars

As automation in cars increased, so did the reluctance to embrace autonomous functions and self-driving cars. A study by Schoettle and Sivak [45] shows, people hesitate to use highly or fully automated systems, and reveals main concerns people have when it comes to self-driving cars. The reasons for hesitation are concerns about an error or system failure, concerns about interaction, concerns about system security, privacy, liability, and usability. In addition, reports of incidents involving autonomous vehicles attracted attention for prediction errors and failures in predicting human behavior, thus reinforcing the perception of self-driving cars as complex networked systems, as stated by Liu et al. [32].

A study by Epprecht et al. [14] indicates that experts do not assume that user acceptance of novel technologies can be ensured only by the maturity of the technologies. Customer reluctance to embrace self-driving car technologies may therefore not automatically recede over time. According to the technology acceptance model by Davis [11], one's feelings and attitudes toward a new technology are crucial for its actual use.

---

[1] For example, self-driving cars sense their environment by using a number of different sensor sets and localization techniques, as well as validation and verification systems. An advanced control system then interprets the information from those systems to identify the appropriate driving behavior of the car.

Much research has been done on the various factors that influence acceptance. There is a vast literature on the moral implications of self-driving cars [12, 17–19, 28, 33], on acceptance models for advanced driver assistance systems [9, 34, 43] as well as on what determines [25, 29, 38] and drives [8, 21, 47, 49] people to accept self-driving. Several literature reviews shed light on the willingness to actually use different levels of automation in cars [5, 7, 20, 37]. The majority of studies focus on examining acceptance of autonomous vehicles as a whole using the NHTSA automation levels.[2]

Hewitt et al. [24] conducted a 26-item survey (n = 187) about expectations, attitudes, and intended uses along the 6 levels of autonomy and find that the behavioral intention to use decreases if the autonomy level increases. Payre et al. [39] conducted a paper and pencil survey of 421 drivers, describing features of a fully automated car along with use-cases. The results show that 68.1% of the participants a priori accepted fully autonomous driving. Zmud et al. [50] surveyed 556 respondents and conducted 44 qualitative interviews to find out how likely people are to use self - driving vehicles. According to the results, 14% of respondents stated that they would be extremely likely to use self-driving vehicles; however, the majority of the respondents seem to be in a wait-and-see position, as 36% reported being only somewhat likely to use them. Schoettle and Sivak [46] investigated what levels of vehicle automation people preferred by asking 505 licensed drivers in the United States of America. The results show that completely autonomous vehicles are the least preferred choice and respondents prefer no self-driving capabilities over partially self-driving vehicles. Rödel et al. [44] focus on users' acceptance of different levels of vehicle autonomy in their online survey of 336 respondents. Respondents were confronted with non-autonomous to fully autonomous car scenarios. The results show that acceptance and user experience are highest for cars that people are used to; highly autonomous cars are not as accepted as currently deployed cars. J.D. Power [26] conducted a survey of 17,400 vehicle owners about their interest in emerging automotive technologies. 37% of the respondents stated that they would purchase an automated driving system. In this study, respondents were nearly as likely to select fully autonomous driving systems as they were to select semi-autonomous driving systems. The results from a repeated online survey by J.D. Power [27], however, show that all respondents except those from Generation Y were becoming more critical of self-driving technologies compared to previous elicitations.

---

[2] The NHTSA [35] defines different levels of autonomy from non-autonomous to fully autonomous cars. In level 0 to level 2 cars, drivers are fully in control of driving. Level 2 cars, however, already include marginally autonomous systems, such as adaptive cruise control, lane departure warning and traffic sign recognition. In level 3 cars, drivers do not need to monitor the road but have to intervene occasionally. For level 4 and level 5 cars, human interventions are not necessary. Driving decision processes are carried out independently by the car, which makes decisions on the basis of various sensory data and predetermined and self-learning algorithms.

2.2   Acceptance of Separate Autonomous Systems

Less research exists that breaks down the acceptance of self-driving cars into acceptance of different features of self-driving cars. The automotive supplier Continental [10] asked people in Germany, China, Japan, and the United States of America whether they would welcome different advanced driver assistance systems and autonomous driving. The results revealed that 79% of respondents are generally open to automated driving systems. In particular, cruise control, parking sensors, and rear-view systems received high appreciation rates in all four countries.

Abraham et al. [1] elicited the maximum level of automation that respondents would be comfortable with by having 2,976 individuals living in the United States of America answer an online questionnaire. The results show that the majority of the respondents would be comfortable with features that actively help the driver while the driver remains in control. In particular, while 88% of the respondents feel comfortable with a feature that reduce the potential for or severity of a collision, only around 64% of the respondents would feel comfortable with a feature that helped with speed control or steering and only 38% of the respondents stated that they would be comfortable with a feature that periodically took control of driving.

Bansal and Kockelman [4] surveyed 2,176 respondents across the United States of America regarding their preferences for specific connected and automated vehicle systems. According to the results, respondents are very interested in blind spot monitoring technology, as well as in emergency automatic braking systems. More than half of the respondents (50.4%) were also comfortable with transmitting information to other vehicles, and 42.9% were comfortable sending information to the vehicle manufacturer. However, only 19.5% of respondents stated that they would be comfortable sending an autonomous vehicle driving on its own.

Li et al. [30] conducted an online survey (n = 650) to research drivers' attitudes towards two connected vehicle technologies - lane speed monitoring and high speed differential warning. The results reveal a high acceptance rate for the two applications but the willingness to use those systems strongly correlates with age, gender, education level and income. The level of acceptance was higher for older, male, higher-educated, or higher-income respondents.

Payre and Diels [40] took a slightly different approach by using a driving simulator to study the acceptance of four connected vehicle features, i.e. emergency electronic brake lights, emergency vehicle warning, roadworks warning and traffic condition warning. As a first step, 36 drivers where confronted with various driving situations and had to assess the acceptance of the automated features in a survey later. The results show a high level of hesitation when it comes to using these connected vehicle features.

The surveys by mentioned above are most similar to our study as they investigate participants' openness to the automation of specific functions. However, the studies mainly focus on a small number of features and do not follow a structured approach. We study attitudes toward single key technologies for self-driving cars used along the six levels of autonomy classification by the NHTSA.

3 Survey Design

We conducted a survey to identify attitudes toward key technologies for self-driving cars. Our goal was to study acceptance of different technologies used along the entire range of automation.

3.1 Questions

The survey consisted of 25 questions about different systems used in partially to fully automated cars.[3] In the questions, we asked the participants about their attitude toward technologies that enable the car to autonomously conduct longitudinal and lateral control, perception and object analysis, vehicle-to-vehicle communication, cloud learning, and actuation.

Each question contained a short description of the technology to control for differences in background knowledge. We chose the systems and compiled the descriptions based on publicly available information from car manufacturers, as well as governmental and non-governmental institutions. All systems are currently available, but their use on the road varies according to individual state and country regulations. The order of the questions was randomly varied for each participant, to control for potential order effects. We also asked the participants about socio-demographic and mobility-related characteristics.

3.2 Treatments

We conducted two different treatments. In treatment *You*, participants were confronted with the statement *"I would like other drivers to use this system."* In treatment *Me*, participants were confronted with the statement *"I would like to use this system."* In both treatments, participants had to state whether they *"Strongly agree"*, *"Agree"*, *"Somewhat agree"*, *"Somewhat disagree"*, *"Disagree"*, or *"Strongly disagree"* to use a specific system. An even number of categories for the rating was used to encourage more thoughtful responses and to avoid possible misinterpretations of the mid-point. We used a between-subjects design so that observations for all statistical tests are independent for the two treatments.

4 Results[4]

We conducted the survey in March 2018 via Amazon MTurk, using workers within the United States of America. The workers had to have completed at least 100 so-called Human Intelligence Tasks (HITs) on Amazon MTurk and had to have an approval rate of 99% for their completed HITs to be able to take part in the experiment. The entire experiment was computerized using Qualtrics [42]. A total of 199 participants (52.8% female) participated in the survey. In

---

[3] Data, methods and questions are available upon request.

[4] We use R version 3.4.1 (2017-06-30) for graphs and statistical analysis in all chapters.

total, 109 participants (54.1% female) participated in treatment *Me*, 90 participants (51.1% female) participated in treatment *You*. The participants were on average 40 years old (treatment *Me*: 41, treatment *You*: 39). Around one-third of the participants held a bachelor's degree (35.7%).[5] A large proportion of the participants also claimed to be moderately technology-aware (37.2%). The majority of the participants (86.9%) stated that they owned a car. The owned cars were on average 9 years old. We tested for differences between the two treatments and found no significant difference between the treatment groups regarding the aforementioned demographics, technology-awareness and car ownership. Subjects who completed the questionnaire were paid, on average, $1.20 for 5 min.

4.1   System Acceptances

In this section, we present the results of the acceptance of different systems for own (treatment *Me*) and other (treatment *You*) use. Agreement is shown as a stacked bar to the left, disagreement as a stacked bar to the right in Fig. 1–6.

Warning Systems: As Fig. 1 shows, most warning systems reached higher than 90% acceptance rates, with the exception of the High Speed Alert system. Thus, warning systems are widely accepted in both treatments. Interestingly, participants supported the use of a High Speed Alert system, a Lane Departure Warning system, and a Forward Collision Warning system for other drivers significantly more than for themselves.

Assisted Driving Systems: As Fig. 2 shows, assisted driving systems are widely accepted. Most of the assisted driving systems reached an acceptance rate of more than 80%. Participants, however, supported the use of a Lane Keeping Support and an Imminent Braking system for other drivers significantly more than for themselves.

Occasional Autonomous Driving Systems: As Fig. 3 shows, occasional autonomous driving systems are not as accepted as assisted driving systems but still reach acceptance rates between 74% and 86% with the exception of the Cyclist Gesture system and the Shape Recognition system. The desired use by others does not differ significantly from the participants' stated willingness to use the system themselves.

Autonomous Driving Systems: As Fig. 4 shows, the acceptance rate drops when it comes to fully autonomous driving systems. While the majority of participants supported the other systems, they disliked autonomous driving systems. Unlike the warning systems, assisted driving systems, and occasional autonomous systems, participants stated that they would be happier to use most

---

[5] The number of participants holding a bachelor's degree corresponds closely to the number reported for the population in the United States of America. According to the U.S. Census Bureau [48] Current Population Survey, about 35.0% of people 25 years and older have a bachelor's degree.

of the autonomous driving systems themselves than they would be for others to use them. However, the difference is only significant for the Car on Call system.

Cloud Using Systems: As Fig. 5 shows, cloud-based systems were widely accepted by participants, not only for their own use but also for use by others.

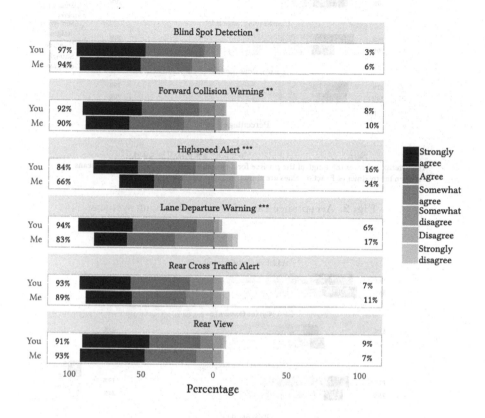

Note: *p < 0.1; **p < 0.05; ***p < 0.01.
The asterisk indicates the range of the p-value for a two-sided t-test on the equality of means between the treatments. Exact p-values are shown in Table 2 in Section 4.3.

Fig. 1. Acceptance rates for warning systems.

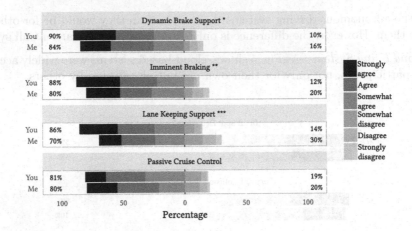

Note: *p < 0.1; **p < 0.05; ***p < 0.01
The asterisk indicates the range of the p-value for a two-sided t-test on the equality of means
between the treatments. Exact p-values are shown in Table 2 in Section 4.3.

Fig. 2. Acceptance rates for assisted driving systems.

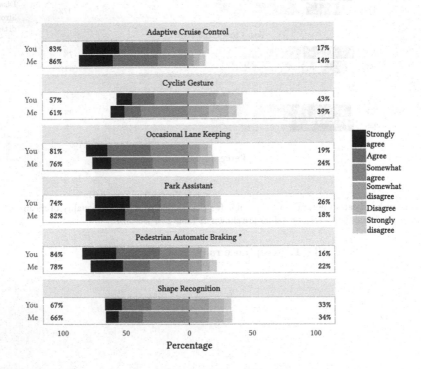

Note: *p < 0.1; **p < 0.05; ***p < 0.01
The asterisk indicates the range of the p-value for a two-sided t-test on the equality of means
between the treatments. Exact p-values are shown in Table 2 in Section 4.3.

Fig. 3. Acceptance rates for occasional autonomous driving systems.

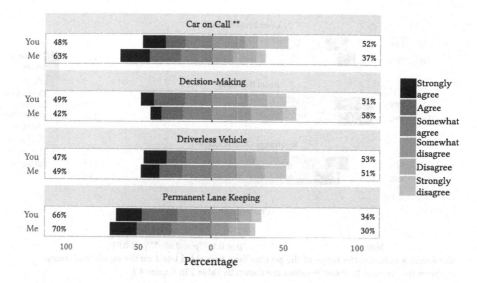

Note: *$p < 0.1$; **$p < 0.05$; ***$p < 0.01$
The asterisk indicates the range of the p-value for a two-sided t-test on the equality of means
between the treatments. Exact p-values are shown in Table 2 in Section 4.3.

Fig. 4. Acceptance rates for autonomous driving systems.

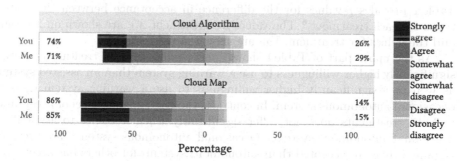

Note: *$p < 0.1$; **$p < 0.05$; ***$p < 0.01$
The asterisk indicates the range of the p-value for a two-sided t-test on the equality of means
between the treatments. Exact p-values are shown in Table 2 in Section 4.3.

Fig. 5. Acceptance rates for cloud-based systems.

Perception and Vehicle-to-Vehicle Communication Systems: As Fig. 6 shows,
perception systems and communication systems are widely accepted. The perception technologies, however, have higher approval rates than the Short-Range
Communication system.

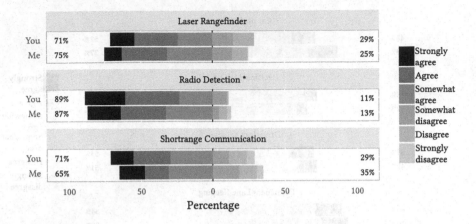

Note: *$p < 0.1$; **$p < 0.05$; ***$p < 0.01$

The asterisk indicates the range of the p-value for a two-sided t-test on the equality of means between the treatments. Exact p-values are shown in Table 2 in Section 4.3.

Fig. 6. Acceptance rates for perception and vehicle-to-vehicle communication systems.

4.2   Comparison Between Systems

Table 1 provides p-values for the difference in acceptance between the system types for each treatment.[6] The values for treatment *Me* are shown on the right and the values for treatment *You* are shown in the middle.

As the upper part of Table 1 shows, participants in both treatments state a significantly higher willingness to use a warning system than an assisted system, as well as a significantly higher willingness to use a warning system than an occasional autonomous system. In contrast, the participants' level of acceptance in both treatments does not differ significantly when it comes to assisted vs. occasional autonomous systems. Occasional autonomous systems, however, are significantly more accepted than autonomous systems for others but acceptance of each system does not differ significantly for own use. Furthermore, we compare the participants' level of acceptance for additional autonomous systems. As shown in the lower part of Table 1, participants in both treatments are just as willing to use a Shape Recognition system as a Cyclist Gesture system. The level of acceptance in both treatments also does not differ significantly for using

---

[6] We refrain from assigning the individual systems to the NHTSA automation levels. Categorizing the systems used in the survey according to specific levels of automation, is only of limited value as the level of automation of a vehicle depends on the combination of and collaboration between the systems. For example, a car classified as Level 1 by the NHTSA takes over either longitudinal or lateral control while a car classified as Level 2 takes over longitudinal and lateral control in specific use cases at the same time.

a Laser Rangefinder system compared to a Short-Range Communication system. Acceptance of a Cloud Algorithm, however, is significantly lower than acceptance of a Cloud Map system in both treatments. Furthermore, participants in both treatments are also less accepting of a Radio Detection system compared to a Laser Rangefinder system or a Short-Range Communication system.

Table 1. Comparison of acceptance of different systems.

Systems	You		Me	
Warning vs. assisted driving				
Lane Departure Warning vs. Lane Keeping Support	$\Delta = 0.4222$	$p = 0.0005^{***}$	$\Delta = 0.3762$	$p = 0.0006^{***}$
Warning vs. occasional autonomous				
Forward Collision Warning vs. Pedestrian Automatic Braking	$\Delta = 0.4889$	$p = 0.0002^{***}$	$\Delta = 0.4771$	$p = 0.0000^{***}$
Assisted vs. occasional autonomous				
Imminent vs. Pedestrian Automatic Braking	$\Delta = 0.1778$	$p = 0.0881^{*}$	$\Delta = 0.0917$	$p = 0.3637$
Passive vs. Adaptive Cruise Control	$\Delta = -0.2556$	$p = 0.0626^{*}$	$\Delta = -0.0826$	$p = 0.5399$
Occasional autonomous vs. autonomous				
Occasional vs. Permanent Lane Keeping	$\Delta = 0.3223$	$p = 0.0071^{***}$	$\Delta = 0.1009$	$p = 0.3885$
Communication and detection				
Shape Recognition vs. Cyclist Gesture	$\Delta = 0.2666$	$p = 0.0718^{*}$	$\Delta = 0.1284$	$p = 0.2102$
Cloud Map vs. Cloud Algorithm	$\Delta = 0.4556$	$p = 0.0001^{***}$	$\Delta = 0.5779$	$p = 0.0000^{***}$
Radio Detection vs. Laser Rangefinder	$\Delta = 0.6111$	$p = 0.0000^{***}$	$\Delta = 0.6111$	$p = 0.0005^{***}$
Radio Detection vs. Short-Range Communication	$\Delta = 0.7667$	$p = 0.0000^{***}$	$\Delta = 0.5782$	$p = 0.0000^{***}$
Laser Rangefinder vs. Short-Range Communication	$\Delta = -0.6111$	$p = 0.2214$	$\Delta = -0.3486$	$p = 0.0526^{*}$

Note: $^{*}p < 0.1$; $^{**}p < 0.05$; $^{***}p < 0.01$

The table shows differences in the average acceptance of different systems ($\Delta = \ldots$) and p-values for a two-sided paired-samples t-test where this difference could be zero.

4.3   Comparison Between Treatments

Table 2. Treatment difference in the level of acceptance.

System	You-Me	
Warning systems		
Blind Spot Detection	$\Delta = 1.9470$	$p = 0.0530^*$
Forward Collision Warning	$\Delta = 2.2099$	$p = 0.0283^{**}$
High Speed Alert	$\Delta = 3.6667$	$p = 0.0003^{***}$
Lane Departure Warning	$\Delta = 3.9632$	$p = 0.0001^{***}$
Rear Cross Traffic Alert	$\Delta = 1.5057$	$p = 0.1338$
Rear View	$\Delta = 0.0734$	$p = 0.9415$
Assisted driving systems		
Dynamic Brake Support	$\Delta = 1.8665$	$p = 0.0635^*$
Imminent Braking	$\Delta = 2.1511$	$p = 0.0327^{**}$
Lane Keeping Support	$\Delta = 3.0160$	$p = 0.0029^{***}$
Passive Cruise Control	$\Delta = -0.7806$	$p = 0.4360$
Occasional autonomous driving systems		
Adaptive Cruise Control	$\Delta = 0.2237$	$p = 0.8232$
Cyclist Gesture	$\Delta = -0.0601$	$p = 0.9521$
Occasional Lane Keeping	$\Delta = 0.9334$	$p = 0.3518$
Park Assistant	$\Delta = -1.0821$	$p = 0.2806$
Pedestrian Automatic Braking	$\Delta = 1.6935$	$p = 0.0919^*$
Shape Recognition	$\Delta = 0.6479$	$p = 0.5178$
Autonomous driving systems		
Car on Call	$\Delta = -2.3242$	$p = 0.0212^{**}$
Decision-Making	$\Delta = 0.7954$	$p = 0.4274$
Driverless Vehicle	$\Delta = -0.4202$	$p = 0.6748$
Permanent Lane Keeping	$\Delta = -0.2399$	$p = 0.8107$
Cloud using systems		
Cloud Algorithm	$\Delta = 0.3833$	$p = 0.7020$
Cloud Map	$\Delta = -0.2535$	$p = 0.8002$
Perception and vehicle-to-vehicle communication systems		
Laser Rangefinder	$\Delta = 0.0933$	$p = 0.9257$
Radio Detection	$\Delta = 1.7833$	$p = 0.0761^*$
Short-Range Communication	$\Delta = 0.4510$	$p = 0.6525$

Note: $^*p < 0.1; ^{**}p < 0.05; ^{***}p < 0.01$

The table shows differences in the average acceptance between treatments ($\Delta = \ldots$) and p-values for a two-sided independent-samples t-test where this difference could be zero. T-test results are in accordance with results from nonparametric Wilcoxon signed-rank tests.

As Table 2 shows, participants support the use of certain systems for other drivers more than for themselves. Participants especially prefer others to use warning systems and most of the assisted driving systems more than to use them themselves. However, when it comes to occasional and fully autonomous driving systems, there seems to be no difference between the respondents' own intention to use those systems and the desire that those systems be used by others.

5 Conclusion

In our exploratory descriptive survey, we study the level of acceptance of automated technologies for peoples' own use as well their desire for others to use those systems. Reports suggest that drivers are eager to use self-driving cars. The majority of these reports ask about the general openness and readiness for self-driving cars and advanced driver assistance systems. We ask about the acceptance of individual automated systems used in self-driving cars which allows a more granular analysis of the question to what extent self-driving cars are accepted.

Our results show that the distribution of acceptance levels for different systems varies significantly. Automated driving systems are not yet as accepted as advanced driver assistance systems. More specifically, while the vast majority welcomes warning systems and assisted driving systems (acceptance rates between 66% and 97%), occasional and fully autonomous driving systems are met with skepticism (acceptance rates between 42% and 86%). Participants accepted the automation of non-self-driving capabilities the most, followed by partially self-driving vehicles, with completely self-driving vehicles being the least accepted choice. Furthermore, participants' desire for others to use the systems is higher for many of the autonomous systems than their acceptance for own use. The difference between acceptance for own use and preferred use by others could be interpreted as an indication that participants are most likely to know about the benefits of autonomous systems but are not yet willing to use them themselves. Another explanation could be that participants trust their own driving skills more than the other drivers. We leave it to further research to disentangle the motives behind the divergent results for the preferred own use and the preferred use by others. Participants' willingness to use fully automated systems such as the Car on Call service, the Driverless Vehicle system and the Permanent Lane Keeping system, however, is higher than their stated preference about the use of those systems by others. It is particularly noteworthy that a driverless vehicle is a desirable option for just under half of the respondents (49%) but only 42% of the participants stated that they would use a decision-making system.

Some points should be kept in mind when interpreting the results. Due to the prerequisites to participate in the experiment and the fact that it was conducted online via Amazon MTurk, participants might be more familiar with technology and related topics in general. In addition, all participants in this study were residents of the United States of America and thus represent a regionally homogeneous group. A follow-up study with an increased sample size and a more heterogeneous pool of participants in terms of technology affinity and geolocation, would enhance the reliability and representativeness of our results and might allow for the detection of clusters of similar acceptance patterns between geolocations and cultural groups. Furthermore, since highly and fully automated cars have not yet been fully commercialized, study results depend on people's imagination about the functionality of the systems. We controlled for differences in knowledge by offering a short explanation of each autonomous system. Nevertheless, a repeat of the study could provide clarity on the extent to which the reservations toward autonomous systems are caused by unfamiliarity or fundamental concerns.

Our results can provide insights into the existing reservations about self-driving technologies. Based on our findings, people are reluctant to hand over control of their cars to technology, especially when it comes to complex automated systems with a wide range of actions, but are less afraid of using automated systems for specific tasks. People do not seem to have an aversion to automated systems in cars in general, but rather hesitate to use systems whose actions are not directly predictable and whose functionality is not easy to explain. In other words, people seem to shy away from uncertainty when it comes to automated systems. For example, our results show that systems that reproduce an easily comprehensible function, such as "seeing", "warning", "supporting" or "alerting", are generally more accepted than systems that reproduce a complex task, such as evaluating gestures and recognizing shapes, where it is not even clear how the human mind handles the task. One idea to reduce the reluctance to use highly automated systems might be to provide step-by-step explanations about the functions of these systems.

References

1. Abraham, H., Reimer, B., Seppelt, B., Fitzgerald, C., Mehler, B., Coughlin, J.F.: Consumer interest in automation: preliminary observations exploring a year's change (2017)
2. Awad, E., et al.: The moral machine experiment. Nature **563**(7729), 59–64 (2018)
3. Azevedo-Sa, H., Jayaraman, S.K., Yang, X.J., Robert, L.P., Tilbury, D.M.: Context-adaptive management of drivers' trust in automated vehicles. IEEE Rob. Autom. Lett. **5**(4), 6908–6915 (2020)
4. Bansal, P., Kockelman, K.M.: Forecasting Americans' long-term adoption of connected and autonomous vehicle technologies. Transp. Res. Part A, 49–63 (2017)
5. Becker, F., Axhausen, K.W.: Literature review on surveys investigating the acceptance of automated vehicles. Transportation **44**, 1293–1306 (2017)
6. Bonnefon, J.F., Shariff, A., Rahwan, I.: The trolley, the bull bar, and why engineers should care about the ethics of autonomous cars. Proc. IEEE **107**(3), 502–504 (2019)
7. Bornholt, J., Heidt, M.: To drive or not to drive-a critical review regarding the acceptance of autonomous vehicles. In: International Conference on Information Systems (ICIS) 2019 Proceedings, p. 5. AIS eLibrary (2019)
8. Chen, H.K., Yan, D.W.: Interrelationships between influential factors and behavioral intention with regard to autonomous vehicles. Int. J. Sustain. Transp. **13**(7), 511–527 (2019)

9. Cho, Y., Park, J., Park, S., Jung, E.S.: Technology acceptance modeling based on user experience for autonomous vehicles. J. Ergon. Soc. Korea **36**(2), 87–108 (2017)
10. Continental: German motorists want automated freeway driving (2013). https://www.continental-corporation.com/en/press/german-motorists-want-automated-freeway-driving-7398. Accessed 18 Oct 2018
11. Davis, F.D.: A technology acceptance model for empirically testing new end-user information systems: theory and results. Ph.D. thesis, Massachusetts Institute of Technology (1986)
12. De Moura, N., Chatila, R., Evans, K., Chauvier, S., Dogan, E.: Ethical decision making for autonomous vehicles. In: 2020 IEEE Intelligent Vehicles Symposium (IV), pp. 2006–2013. IEEE (2020)
13. Doll, G., Kellner, M., Wiemuth, C., Ebel, E., Heineke, K.: Private autonomous vehicles: the other side of the Robo-taxi story. McKinsey & Company (2020)
14. Epprecht, N., Von Wirth, T., Stünzi, C., Blumer, Y.B.: Anticipating transitions beyond the current mobility regimes: how acceptability matters. Futures **60**, 30–40 (2014)
15. European Commission: Roadmap to a single European transport area-towards a competitive and resource efficient transport system (2011)
16. Foot, P.: The problem of abortion and the doctrine of double effect. Oxford Rev. **5**, 5–15 (1967)
17. Frank, D.A., Chrysochou, P., Mitkidis, P., Ariely, D.: Human decision-making biases in the moral dilemmas of autonomous vehicles. Sci. Rep. **9**(1), 1–19 (2019)
18. Gill, T.: Blame it on the self-driving car: how autonomous vehicles can alter consumer morality. J. Consum. Res. **47**(2), 272–291 (2020)
19. Gill, T.: Ethical dilemmas are really important to potential adopters of autonomous vehicles. Ethics Inf. Technol., 1–17 (2021)
20. Gkartzonikas, C., Gkritza, K.: What have we learned? A review of stated preference and choice studies on autonomous vehicles. Transp. Res. Part C: Emerg. Technol. **98**, 323–337 (2019)
21. Golbabaei, F., Yigitcanlar, T., Paz, A., Bunker, J.: Individual predictors of autonomous vehicle public acceptance and intention to use: a systematic review of the literature. J. Open Innov. Technol. Market Complex. **6**(4), 106 (2020)
22. Haspiel, J., et al.: Explanations and expectations: trust building in automated vehicles. In: Companion of the 2018 ACM/IEEE International Conference on Human-Robot Interaction, pp. 119–120 (2018)
23. Hegner, S.M., Beldad, A.D., Brunswick, G.J.: In automatic we trust: Investigating the impact of trust, control, personality characteristics, and extrinsic and intrinsic motivations on the acceptance of autonomous vehicles. Int. J. Hum.-Comput. Interact. **35**(19), 1769–1780 (2019)
24. Hewitt, C., Politis, I., Amanatidis, T., Sarkar, A.: Assessing public perception of self-driving cars: the autonomous vehicle acceptance model. In: Proceedings of the 24th International Conference on Intelligent User Interfaces, pp. 518–527 (2019)
25. Hohenberger, C., Spörrle, M., Welpe, I.M.: How and why do men and women differ in their willingness to use automated cars? the influence of emotions across different age groups. Transp. Res. Part A Policy Pract. **94**, 374–385 (2016)
26. J D Power and Associates Reports: Vehicle owners show willingness to spend on automotive infotainment features (2012). https://www.prnewswire.com/news-releases/jd-power-and-associates-reports-vehicle-owners-show-willingness-to-spend-on-automotive-infotainment-features-149088105.html. Accessed 18 Oct. 2018

27. J D Power: Hands off? not quite. Consumers fear technology failures with autonomous vehicles (2017). https://www.prnewswire.com/news-releases/hands-off-not-quite-consumers-fear-technology-failures-with-autonomous-vehicles-300441106.html. Accessed 21 Oct 2018

28. Karnouskos, S.: Self-driving car acceptance and the role of ethics. IEEE Trans. Eng. Manage. **67**(2), 252–265 (2018)

29. Lee, C., Ward, C., Raue, M., D'Ambrosio, L., Coughlin, J.F.: Age differences in acceptance of self-driving cars: a survey of perceptions and attitudes. In: Zhou, J., Salvendy, G. (eds.) ITAP 2017. LNCS, vol. 10297, pp. 3–13. Springer, Cham (2017). https://doi.org/10.1007/978-3-319-58530-7_1

30. Li, W., Wu, G., Yao, D., Zhang, Y., Barth, M.J., Boriboonsomsin, K.: Stated acceptance and behavioral responses of drivers towards innovative connected vehicle applications. Accid. Anal. Prev. **155**, 106095 (2021)

31. Liu, H., Yang, R., Wang, L., Liu, P.: Evaluating initial public acceptance of highly and fully autonomous vehicles. Int. J. Hum. Comput. Interact. **35**(11), 919–931 (2019)

32. Liu, L., et al.: Computing systems for autonomous driving: state of the art and challenges. IEEE Internet Things J. **8**(8), 6469–6486 (2020)

33. Martinho, A., Herber, N., Kroesen, M., Chorus, C.: Ethical issues in focus by the autonomous vehicles industry. Transp. Rev., 1–22 (2021)

34. Nastjuk, I., Herrenkind, B., Marrone, M., Brendel, A.B., Kolbe, L.M.: What drives the acceptance of autonomous driving? An investigation of acceptance factors from an end-user's perspective. Technol. Forecast. Soc. Change **161**, 120319 (2020)

35. National Highway Traffic Safety Administration (NHTSA): Preliminary statement of policy concerning automated vehicles (2013)

36. National Highway Traffic Safety Administration (NHTSA): Federal automated vehicles policy: Accelerating the next revolution in roadway safety (2016)

37. Othman, K.: Public acceptance and perception of autonomous vehicles: a comprehensive review. AI Ethics **1**(3), 355–387 (2021). https://doi.org/10.1007/s43681-021-00041-8

38. Panagiotopoulos, I., Dimitrakopoulos, G.: An empirical investigation on consumers' intentions towards autonomous driving. Transp. Res. Part C Emerg. Technol. **95**, 773–784 (2018)

39. Payre, W., Cestac, J., Delhomme, P.: Intention to use a fully automated car: attitudes and a priori acceptability. Transp. Res. Part F **27**(B), 252–263 (2014)

40. Payre, W., Cestac, J.: I want to brake free: effect of connected vehicle features on driver behaviour, usability and acceptance. Appli. Ergon. **82**, 102932 (2020)

41. Petersen, L., Robert, L., Yang, J., Tilbury, D.: Situational awareness, driver's trust in automated driving systems and secondary task performance. SAE Int. J. Connected Auton. Veh. (2019, forthcoming)

42. Qualtrics: Online survey software tools and solutions: Qualtrics (2014). https://www.qualtrics.com/pt-br/research-suite/. Accessed 21 Sept 2017

43. Ribeiro, M.A., Gursoy, D., Chi, O.H.: Customer acceptance of autonomous vehicles in travel and tourism. J. Travel Res., 0047287521993578 (2021)

44. Rödel, C., Stadler, S., Meschtscherjakov, A., Tscheligi, M.: Towards autonomous cars: the effect of autonomy levels on acceptance and user experience. In: Miller, E., Wu, Y. (eds.) Proceedings of the 6th International Conference on Automotive User Interfaces and Interactive Vehicular Applications, pp. 1–8, Association for Computing Machinery, Seattle (2014)

45. Schoettle, B., Sivak, M.: A survey of public opinion about autonomous and self-driving vehicles in the U.S., the U.K., and Australia (2014)

46. Schoettle, B., Sivak, M.: Motorists' preferences for different levels of vehicle automation (2015)
47. Spurlock, C.A., et al.: Describing the users: Understanding adoption of and interest in shared, electrified, and automated transportation in the san Francisco bay area. Transp. Res. Part D: Transp. Environ. **71**, 283–301 (2019)
48. U.S. Census Bureau: Current populations survey: Annual social and economic supplement to the current population survey (2018). https://www.census.gov/library/stories/2019/02/number-of-people-with-masters-and-phd-degrees-double-since-2000.html
49. Xu, Z., Zhang, K., Min, H., Wang, Z., Zhao, X., Liu, P.: What drives people to accept automated vehicles? Findings from a field experiment. Transp. Res. Part C Emerg. Technol. **95**, 320–334 (2018)
50. Zmud, J., Sener, I.N., Wagner, J.: Consumer acceptance and travel behavior impacts of automated vehicles. Texas A&M Transp. Institute PRC, 15–49 (2016)

Mental Models and Interpretability in AI Fairness Tools and Code Environments

Jana Thompson[✉]

Maryland Institute College of Art, Baltimore, MD 21217, USA
jthompson05@mica.edu

Abstract. The real-world impacts of social biases in artificial intelligence technologies has come increasingly to the fore in the last several years. Basic comprehensions and translations for how biases are represented in data is seen as a key step forward in mitigating harms in AI products and services. This paper examines the core issues of mental models with users and developers working with AI models, metrics, and interpretability in AI. With the assumption that users of tools such as IBM's AI Fairness 360 and Google's What-if Tool work within the environment of computational notebooks, such as those developed by Project Jupyter or Google Colab, this paper looks at the use of notebooks for visualization, collaboration, and narrative. In examining the design implications for these tools and environments, new directions are proposed for the development of more critical interactive tools to empower data science and aI teams to build more equitable AI models in the future.

Keywords: Explainable AI · Human-centered AI tools · AI evaluation

1 Introduction

Problematic issues in artificial intelligence (henceforth AI) have drawn increasing attention in the media and from scholars in the last few years. In response, technology companies have created libraries in the Python and R programming languages to allow data scientists and ML practitioners to address social biases in the data and machine learning models, notably IBM's *AI Fairness 360* (henceforth AIF360) library and Google's *What-if Tool* (henceforth WIT). AIF360 was designed explicitly to address the issues with social biases and fairness and to serve as a common library and basis of a common programmatic language for fairness for practitioners. WIT was designed as a more general tool for interpreting AI models with a strong emphasis on visualization that had fairness and social bias metrics as part of the design. This paper will make the assumption that data scientists will make use of these libraries within the environment of a computational notebook, such as a Jupyter notebook or Google's own online Colab notebook.

In addressing the effective use of these tools by data scientists and ML practitioners, some questions of usability must be addressed:

C. Stephanidis et al. (Eds.): HCII 2021, LNCS 13095, pp. 574–585, 2021.
https://doi.org/10.1007/978-3-030-90963-5_43

- Do the mental models of data scientists/AI practitioners match the models' behavior as shown in output from these tools?
- Do the tools and notebooks provide an adequate environment to produce readable output for the data scientists/ML practitioners to interpret the metrics?
- In response to recommendations on multi-disciplinary collaboration for development for ML models (Schiff et al. 2020; Rakova et al. 2020) do the notebooks provide an adequate collaborative environment for cross-functional teams?

First, this paper will examine the core issues of mental models with users and developers in working with AI models, metrics, and interpretability in AI. Following this, we will probe the use of notebooks for visualization, collaboration, and narrative. In the final section, the design implications for the tools and environments will be explained, with a look at the strengths of these frameworks and where they fall short.

2 Core Findings

Building machine learning models, whether statistical or deep learning, is by its very nature a demanding and detail-oriented process that requires a substantial amount of training in mathematics and computer science before one can typically have a successful run of working in the field. The work of determining bias impacts and fairness are yet another set of difficulty in creating and ultimately deploying models in production environments, with a high number of metrics that can be applied to both datasets and to machine learning models throughout a pipeline from pre-to-post processing (Raji 2021). These metrics each take their own form of understanding that must be adapted into the model of understanding for a practitioner. From a user's standpoint, this makes for a high cognitive load that means much data and metadata be held in the user's own memory throughout the machine learning process. This then leads to a constant high cognitive demand for the developer for several mental models to work in tandem. Tools that support this high amount of short and long term memory needed to create good models are necessary for a successful outcome.

Non-practitioners in the AI space tend to anthropomorphize AI models (Bos et al. 2019) and imbue systems with reasoning capabilities as can often be seen in the behavior of people interacting with personal assistants such as Siri and Alexa (Lemaignan et al. 2014; Yip et al. 2019). Data scientists and ML practitioners, on the other hand, tend to view machine learning models in terms of mathematical formulas and algorithmic procedure. This type of work when viewed from the "bottom-up" (Dourish 2016) with patterns as emergent from the gathered data is divorced from the potentially necessary state of understanding the models as both an artifact of human behavior and an actor in human society.

Computational notebooks, as define by Lau et al. (2020) are:

> *"... a system that supports literate programming using a text-based programming language while interweaving expository text and program outputs into a single document." (Lau et al. 2020: 3)*

These notebooks are the environment in which much of the model exploration and evaluation of metrics for AI models are computed in data science and machine learning projects. Currently used notebooks are not necessarily the best environments for the non-linear narrative, iterative, and interactive nature of the processes of AI anti-biasing and fairness work, although the potential for visualization within currently used notebooks is often adequate.

3 Supported Findings

3.1 Machine Learning Models are Hard to Interpret

Human interpretability of machine learning is an ongoing cause of concern (Hong et al. 2020; Kaur et al. 2020). While *functional*, or shallow, mental models of systems are fine for end users of AI, *structural* (deep) mental models, where there is a "detailed understanding of why and how it works" (Kulesza et al. 2012: 2) must be sound and "many instances of unsound mental models guiding erroneous behavior have been observed (Kulesza et al. 2012: 2). This paper will follow the definition of interpretability as given by Hong et al. (2020): "the alignment between a human user's mental model of how a system will behave and the system's actual behavior" (Hong et al. 2020: 2). In examining ML models for social bias and fairness, there is a two-fold difficulty for interpretability: the developer's mental models for social bias and fairness and their own mental model for the ML models themselves create intersecting layers of mental models the practitioners themselves are unaware of and don't know how to account for.

Much research has been done on the interpretability of ML models by practitioners in the last couple of years (Hong et al. 2020; Kaur et al. 2020; Hohman et al. 2019). Researchers have looked at tools developed to effectively examine interpretability. The investigations of Kaur et al. (2020) revealed that users did not develop in-depth structural mental models for the tools they examined (in this study, the authors used the SHAP – SHapley Additive exPlantations – library and GAMs – generative additive models) as several of the users they interviewed simply trusted the tools without fully grasping their meaning. As the users did not have the structural mental models required to effectively wield the tools, the systems were failing the rule of *Closeness of mapping* in Green's Cognitive Dimensions of Notation (Blackwell et al. 2001). The lack of close mapping between the model interpretation tools in SHAP and GAM leads the users to not correctly interpret the model metrics. These interpretability issues have implications for both AIF360 and WIT as will be seen in Sect. 4 below.

Additionally, these tools also fall under another of Green's Dimensions of Notation, that of *hard mental operations* (Blackwell et al. 2001: 4). If notations, or more generally, systems do not allow for interpretability, the data scientist or ML practitioner cannot determine or build a system for how a model "reasons" (Hong et al. 2020: 12). As Hong et al. (2020) note: "When a mismatch between the two models [ML model and user's mental model] occurs, without explanation, it can also lead to frustration and progressive mistrust towards the ML system." The research from Hong et al. (2020) also discusses the in-depth issues that can occur with data scientists and end users when the ML models that are built fail to meet human expectations. They further discuss how interpretability is cooperative, a process, and context-dependent: from their summary: "Our results lead us to characterize interpretability as inherently social and negotiated, aimed at fostering trust both in people and in models, context-dependent and arising from careful comparisons of human mental models." (Hong et al. 2020: 22).

Kaur et al. (2020) notes that tools must be designed for deliberative reasoning. The visualization of tools can cause quick judgements that engage what Kahneman (2011) refers to as System 1 decisions that are quickly made based on heuristics, versus System 2 which engages more in-depth before making a decision. When practitioners, according to Kaur et al. (2020: 9), have a better mental model, the better they are able to use the tools available to them.

3.2 Metrics for Bias

Again, referring to Green's work on Cognitive Dimensions of Notation (Blackwell et al. 2001; Blackwell and Green 2003), one key issue a notation should help resolve is that of *hard mental operations*. Machine learning metrics can be difficult to interpret (see Sect. 3.1 above) and most metrics included in libraries for interpretability take specific expertise to use effectively. Bansal et al. (2019) suggests two useful dimensions for presentations of metrics that allow for better understanding and interpretability for ML model metrics (although the dichotomy between System 1 and System 2 thinking is noted here); they suggest that parsimony and non-stochastic presentations of metrics would enable human to learn better model metrics for AI (Bansal et al. 2019: 2). As per this work, a metric is described as *parsimonious* if it simple to represent and is *non-stochastic* if it can be modeled with a small set of features that "reliably and cleanly distinguishes successes from errors without uncertainty." (Bansal et al. 2019: 3) The paper additionally found in their work that such metrics improved the development of mental models for users with an AI system. Similarly, Kocielnik et al. (2019) found that simplicity and the combination of visualization and text lead to greater structural understandings of the AI system the user testers they worked with developed over the course of their study.

3.3 Notebooks are Mixed for Visualizing

Visualizations are often one of the first ways in which data scientists and ML practitioners view metrics and work on interpretability for their ML models. Visualizations, as noted above in Sect. 3.1, can lead to System 1 thinking dominating over System 2 thinking for evaluation of ML models, while in Sect. 3.2, it is noted that visualization can help improve mental models and interpretations for users. Within the context of the notebook environment, in particular Jupyter notebooks and Google Colab, visualizations can sometimes be limited within the confines of a notebook, and outside tools such as Tableau are employed instead. However, many visualizations, such as line graphs representing curves, or bar charts are rendered well within the notebook environment. Chattopadhyay et al. (2020: 9) note that many data scientists find visualization straightforward and easy to implement in the notebook environment, but also say (2020: 4) that creating effective visualizations can be challenging for some.

However, as noted in many weaknesses of the notebook, one strong possible advantage for the notebook environment is what Wood et al. (2019) terms *literate visualization*, defined as "a form of storytelling where the designers of some visualization specify not only its implementation, but also the rationale behind the design of the implementation. This is likely a form of design as Wood et al. (2019) employed in the creation of their tool, *litvis*, discussed throughout their paper to evoke System 2 aka deliberative reasoning in development of code. This type of notebook would solve for issues of exploration with *branching narrative* and would link narrative and interpretation, and the development of an integrated notebook that uses visualization, description, and schemas that would allow for the discovery of garden paths in looking at interpretability of ML models in greater detail than the linearity of commonly used notebooks as we will discuss in Sect. 3.4 below.

3.4   Notebooks are Poor for Non-linear Narratives and Collaboration

Wang et al. (2019) discuss that data scientists often create *computational narratives*, which combine data, code to process that data, and natural language explanations to form a narrative. Increasingly, notebooks are used to share narratives and to collaborate. However, there were many significant challenges for these types of uses. First, developers could interfere with each other's notations in choosing conflicting variable names for data structures that could lead to breakdowns with the code. While Google Colab does allow for synchronous editing by multiple users (similar to Google Docs), there is a lack of ability to see editing and changes made by others, indicating a need for version control and change tracking. In addition, and compounded due to these editing and version issues, the linear structure of cells within most computational notebooks means that one error in a cell that is previous in the chain of cells in the notebook means that collaborators often have to guess and search extensively for the error. These issues could be alleviated with a history of how the cells should be executed or a history of where changes were made. Currently, to make such issues clear, users must document extensively in notebooks without a pre-created structure or a design to help facilitate collaboration. Rule et al. (2018) found that data analysts at the IMF found data artefacts more incomprehensible as more judgments and work were performed on the artefact. As noted by Hong et al. (2020) and Schiff et al. (2020, interpretability for machine learning requires cross-team functionality and multi-disciplinary know-how, meaning that data scientists and ML model creation teams will increasingly rely on collaboration in the future for bias analyses in the machine learning process (Fig. 1).

```
In [2]: # Get the dataset and split into train and test
        dataset_orig = load_preproc_data_adult()

        privileged_groups = [{'sex': 1}]
        unprivileged_groups = [{'sex': 0}]

        dataset_orig_train, dataset_orig_test = dataset_orig.split([0.7], shuffle=True)
```

```
In [3]: # print out some labels, names, etc.
        display(Markdown("#### Training Dataset shape"))
        print(dataset_orig_train.features.shape)
        display(Markdown("#### Favorable and unfavorable labels"))
        print(dataset_orig_train.favorable_label, dataset_orig_train.unfavorable_label)
        display(Markdown("#### Protected attribute names"))
        print(dataset_orig_train.protected_attribute_names)
        display(Markdown("#### Privileged and unprivileged protected attribute values"))
        print(dataset_orig_train.privileged_protected_attributes,
              dataset_orig_train.unprivileged_protected_attributes)
        display(Markdown("#### Dataset feature names"))
        print(dataset_orig_train.feature_names)
```

Training Dataset shape
(34189, 18)

Favorable and unfavorable labels
(1.0, 0.0)

Protected attribute names
['sex', 'race']

Privileged and unprivileged protected attribute values
([array([1.]), array([1.])], [array([0.]), array([0.])])

Fig. 1. Jupyter notebook with AIF360

As also noted above in Sect. 3.3, visualization is central to fully explore and attempt to undertake a deliberative reasoning approach as is necessary for successful model metrics exploration. In exploratory processes with code, or *exploratory programming* (Kery and Myers 2017: 1), Kery and Myers note that in relating to Green's (Blackwell et al. 2001; Blackwell and Green 2003) cognitive dimension of *hard mental operations*, programmers must keep track of many explorations and variations over time. In having to engage in deliberative reasoning, the tools that ML practitioners use must allow for clear readability and designs so that the comments, code, and other aids in remembering past thought processes to be fully understood. Rule et al. (2018) note that people are often embarrassed by the messiness of their notebooks and future designs could take this into account, just as the reality of technical debt must be acknowledged and designed for, rather than held as a state that will eventually disappear. The authors suggest the development of a "clean up" tool for notebooks to help with legibility and maintainability. Additionally, as algorithmic and pipeline auditing become a more common practice within companies, such tools enable better documentation for determining the process by which impactful AI models are created before deployment.

4 Implications for Design

4.1 Tools Under Consideration

The tools under consideration here are IBM's AI Fairness 360 (AIF360), Google's What-if Tool (WIT) used in the environments of Jupyter notebooks and Google Colab. For more details on these tools, please see the Appendix.

4.2   Mental Models

While these tools provide the raw materials for an ML developer and data scientist to work on the problems of bias, they do not inherently give a framework by which a developer can learn and develop expertise in the challenging mental models required to address bias in machine learning models. Like most research areas in ML, there are many papers that document metrics for bias and fairness (see https://aif360.mybluemix. net/resources for an example), but perhaps a more constructive approach would be to build a more comprehensive framework for these tools that help novice learners develop the mental models and understanding necessary to use these systems well as done in Bansal et al. (2019).

Additionally, these systems could use *more friction* so as to force users to reason more and engage System 2 type thinking. AIF 360 lacks such a framework, but WIT's is built to engage the users in more deliberative reasoning. AIF 360's strengths lie in the greater number of metrics included, but it lacks explanation and built-in visualization. WIT's interactive tool includes three tabs. One tab is a Datapoint Editor, which allows for a user to play with changing and examining data as it would impact model development. Another tab is a Features tab that shows summary statistics in a dashboard configuration. The third tab in WIT's interactive tool is a unique partial-dependence plot view that allows for users to explore the interaction of how different data fields and thus their potential intersectional impact on data models (Crenshaw 1989). While the WIT configuration tool gives a great deal of exploratory space to help developers with reasoning, for novice users, it could perhaps additionally benefit from having a tutorial developed inline with the tool. More in-depth explanations available quickly within the tool (such as exist within the *ground truth* and *slicing* options within the Performance and Fairness tab of the WIT interactive tool) could serve as prompts for developers to explore the possibilities and improve upon their mental representations for what social biases can exist in data.

In contrast, the WIT tool does not engage users to strongly investigate the downstream effects in modeling that result in unfair AI systems. The common misperception/mental misalignment (Raji 2021) is that all social biases in AI result purely from the data. The AIF360 library, on the other hand, with its range of metrics that address fairness and social bias throughout the machine learning process, reinforces the actual paradigm that testing for these issues through *every step of the process* is crucial. AIF360 fails at not have a more substantial framework to support the mental models and instead relies on the developer themselves to develop the expertise to be aware of how and when to use their tools in an ML pipeline.

Within the larger role of having to examine metrics for AI ethics concerns, practitioners and ethicists (Jeffrey Gleason personal communication 7th December 2020, Bogdana Rakova personal communication 10th December 2019, 21st March 20212020/21, Alka Roy personal communication November 2020) that many people who use these tools approach the process as something to check off of a checklist, a finding supported by Kaur et al. (2020) and thus fail to engage in the deeper reasoning necessary due to a lack of appropriate mental models for the process. In Kaur et al. (2020), users would simply trust visualizations without a more in-depth investigation. Introducing greater friction through dialogues, prompting a user to not necessarily trust a model, perhaps even introducing an element of distrust, could lead to greater deliberative reasoning and more effective usage of these tools as suggested by the work of Kocielnik et al. (2019).

4.3 Interpretability and Visualization

Following the work of Chattopadhyay et al. (2020), Kocielnik et al. (2019), Bansal et al. (2019), Wood et al. (2019), and Rule et al. (2018), there is no standard visualization and interpretation given in either AIF360 or WIT. While there are visualizations built into WIT, there are no such visual tools in AIF360. Instead, users must construct visualizations via the *Plotly, matplotlib*, and *seaborn* libraries in Python and *Shiny* and *ggplot* in R. There is no standard way in which these metrics are represented and no readability standard (in this case, readability is referring to such things as labeling what units measurements are given in, what they represent, or what the scaling is). This in turn leads anyone using these tools to rely on their memory if they are the creator of the visualization, or on educated guess work (especially if there is no documentation given by the creator) for another person looking at a notebook from a colleague or collaborator (see Sect. 4.3 below for more on impacts on collaboration). While these issues could possibly be rectified by a standard training or framework that fosters knowledge discovery, such as that of Apache's UIMA project. However, many users discuss in Wang et al. (2020) and Chattopadhyay et al. (2020) that they typically have messy notebooks as they work, and it is not clear that such frameworks will easily help remedy these issues. Perhaps a better approach would be to create features that enforce certain readability standards by having visualizations fail to execute properly if not used. These standards are used within other aspects of cells within computational notebooks: Markdown will not display correctly if hashtags and spaces are not used correctly, and code will fail to execute if there are errors in the syntax of the language. Forcing greater visualization standards for examination of metrics is possibly the only path forward to enforce readable visualizations.

WIT's interactive tool gives visualizations that are clearly readable in terms of color and data points: the colors are distinct enough by default to be interpretable by division of data categories, following the *parsimony* rule as defined by Bansal et al. (2019). In terms of scaling and interpretability, it is limited on some fronts as it is adapted purely from data field. An additional step of helping consider what data is actually present would prod the practitioner to more carefully probe what data exists in their data set and its meaning within larger social contexts. Also, these setups could lead to the use of visualization to be more carefully applied as a tool for interpretability of data and model outputs. As stated above in Sect. 3.4, interpretability is defined by Hong et al. (2020) as both contextual and team-driven. It is to this we now examine as the final aspect of design implications in this paper.

4.4 Interactivity and Collaboration

Given the emphasis placed on collaboration and multi-disciplinary teams in Schiff et al. (2020), Rakova et al. (2020) and the conclusions of Hong et al. (2020) of model interpretability as essentially a team sport driven by the experience and communication within a data science team, the ability for collaboration using notebooks and social bias/fairness libraries is at a premium. One challenge noted in Hong et al. (2020: 13) – "model builders often had difficulties in identifying what other stakeholders don't know. Even if they did grasp stakeholders' knowledge level, determining how to deliver the insights seemed difficult, even with the help of visualizations".

General suggestions are given by Wang et al. (2019) for improving collaborations in notebook design – ways to increase awareness for what a collaborator has done, access control, and enabling discussion within the notebook format – imply clear design change that could happen to notebooks rather than the linear structure and single version system that both Jupyter notebooks and Google Colab employ. As per Hong et al. (2020), interpretability is a process and the interpretability work takes different forms through the machine learning process, implying that social bias and fairness work does as well. By being able to clearly link notebooks and cells within notebooks, this could enable the cross-functional teams necessary for social bias and fairness work to have the usable tools they need. By perhaps integrating some form of comment structure and communication flow into a truly collaborative environment, this could improve the use of multi-disciplinary teams and multitude of stakeholder perspectives into the development of fair and equitable AI models.

5   Conclusion

HCI tools in machine learning and interpretability are a field in rapid flux and development currently. There is increasing and on-going interest in developing tools for non-technical specialists to develop models and deploy them. Adjacent to this work is the need for understanding the impacts these models will have in the real world and social contexts they will live in. Readability for visualizations, collaborative environments, and mental models for understanding AI generally and social biases/fairness within data and ML models remains a challenge that current tools need to address more fully.

Hong et al. (2020: 18) discusses the need for interpretability to align with what expectations and outcomes teams creating the models expect. Fairness and bias depend upon the interpretability of models by their creators. WIT shows a path forward beyond merely methods in libraries, giving an interactive tool for users to explore datasets visually with some limitations. Perhaps by developing a truly speculative tool – one that would allow different stakeholders and perspectives – business perspectives, impacted users, social scientists, and ML practitioners – to combine their mental models, develop visualizations and explanations to build the understanding that is necessary for a truly human-centered AI, is the key to explainable and equitable AI. Such a tool could allow for all stakeholders to map what a model should actually output, and how it performs to build greater interpretability and collaboration across the AI lifecycle. While some speculative tools (to explore their usability and mental models is beyond the scope of this paper) – Poieto, the AI meets Design toolkit – but these tools have not been integrated into a larger workflow. By tying the speculative approaches of designers with the metrics and exploration with developer tools and bridging mental models, incorporating interpretability of models from the very start of the machine learning process, can such approaches be integrated and used to their full potential.

Appendix

AI Fairness 360: Originally released by IBM researchers in 2018, this tool consists of programmatic libraries in the Python and R programming languages that have computational methods for looking at metrics for examining bias in datasets, and in pre-processing, in-process, and post-processing steps of the machine learning pipeline. It is designed for Python to fit into the "standard" machine learning pipeline that includes use of the commonly used scikit-learn library for machine learning. It does not include visualization tools.

What-if Tool: Released by Google's PAIR (People + AI Research) group in 2019. The What-if Tool also is designed for use in the Python programming language, as well as the ability to be used directly in the TensorBoard tool (visualization library for the TensorFlow deep learning framework also developed by Google) and to be used in Google's own Colab notebooks. WIT contains multiple metrics as does AIF360, but also includes a configuration tool that reflects mental models of the designers in addressing such things as intersectional bias and allows for multiple interactive visualizations on a dataset or model.

Jupyter notebooks: A computational notebook that grew out of the iPython notebooks and began as an independent project in 2015. Designed so that each "cell" in a notebook can contain Markdown (a way to create styles and visual hierarchy in a text-like document), or code in each cell that can be run with output displayed as in a terminal or interpreter environment, but also can have visualizations inline. Hosted locally on machines.

Google Colab: A notebook environment similar to Jupyter notebooks, developed by Google. Unlike Jupyter notebooks, Colab notebooks can easily hide code for demonstration purposes and are hosted online using Google's cloud infrastructure for running processes in the notebook.

References

Bansal, G., Nushi, B., Kamar, E., Lasecki, W.S., Weld, D.S., Horvitz, E.: Beyond accuracy: the role of mental models in human-AI team performance. In: Proceedings of the AAAI Conference on Human Computation and Crowdsourcing, vol. 7, no. 1, pp. 2–11 (2019)

Bellamy, R., et al.: AI Fairness 360: an extensible toolkit for detecting, understanding, and mitigating unwanted algorithmic bias. arXiv preprint: arXiv:1801.01943 (2018)

Blackwell, A.F., et al.: Cognitive dimensions of notations: design tools for cognitive technology. In: Beynon, M., Nehaniv, C.L., Dautenhahn, K. (eds.) CT 2001. LNCS (LNAI), vol. 2117, pp. 325–341. Springer, Heidelberg (2001). https://doi.org/10.1007/3-540-44617-6_31

Blackwell, A.F., Green, T.R.G.: Notational system – the cognitive dimensions of notations framework. In: Carroll, J.M. (ed.) HCI Models, Theories, and Frameworks: Toward a Multidisciplinary Science, pp. 103–134. Morgan Kaufmann, San Francisco. (2003)

Bos, N., Glasgow, K., Gersh, J., Harbison, I., Paul, C.L.: Mental models of AI-based systems: user predictions and explanations of image classification results. In: Proceedings of the Human Factors and Ergonomics Society Annual Meeting, pp. 183–188. (2019). http://dx.doi.org/10.1177/81319631392

Chattopadhyay, S., Prasad, I., Henley, A.Z., Sarma, A., Barik, T.: What's wrong with computational notebooks? Pain points, needs, and design opportunities. In: Proceedings of the 2020 CHI Conference on Human Factors in Computing Systems (CHI 20), 12 p. Association for Computing Machinery (2020). http://dx.doi.org/10.1145/3313831.3376729

Crenshaw, K.: Demarginalizing the intersection of race and sex: a black feminist critique of antidiscrimination doctrine, feminist theory, and antiracist policies. Univ. Chicago Legal Forum **1989**(1), 139–167 (1989)

Dourish, P.: Algorithms and Their others: algorithmic culture in context. Big Data Soc. (2016). http://dx.doi.org/10.1177/2053951716665128

Hohman, F., Head, A., Caruana, R., Deline, R., Drucker, S.M.: GAMUT: a design probe to understand how data scientists understand machine learning models. In: Proceedings of the 2019 CHI Conference on Human Factors in Computing Systems (CHI 19), Paper 579, 13 p. Association for Computing Machinery (2019). http://dx.doi.org/10.1145/3290605.3300809

Hong, S.R., Hullman, J., Bertini, E.: Human factors in model interpretability: industry practices, challenges, and needs. In: Proceedings of the ACM on Human Computer Interaction 4. CSCW 1, Article 68, 26 p. (2020). http://dx.doi.org/10.1145/3392878

Kahneman, D.: Thinking Fast and Slow. Farrar Straus, and Giroux, New York (2011)

Kaur, H., Nori, H., Jenkins, S., Caruana, R., Wallach, H., Worthman Vaughan, J.: Interpreting interpretability: understanding data scientists' use of interpretability tools for machine learning. In: Proceedings of the 202 CHI Conference on Human Factors in Computing Systems (CHI 20).14 p. Association for Computing Machinery (2020). http://dx.doi.org/10.1145/3313831.3376219

Kery, M.B., Myers, B.A.: Exploring exploratory programming. In: 2017 IEEE Symposium on Visual Languages and Human-Centric Computing (VL/HCC), pp. 25–29 (2017). http://dx.doi.org/10.1109/VLHCC.2017.0103446

Kocielnik, R., Amershi, S., Bennett, P.N.: Will you accept an imperfect AI? Exploring designs for adjusting end-user expectations of AI systems. In: Proceedings of the 2019 CHI Conference on Human Factors in Computing Systems (CHI 19). Association for Computing Machinery, Paper 411, 14 p. (2019). http://dx.doi.org/10.1145/3290605.3300641

Kulesza, T., Strumpf, S., Burnett, M. Kwan, I.: Tell me more? The effects of mental model soundness on personalizing an intelligent agent. In: Proceedings of the SIGCHI Conference on Human Factors in Computing Systems (CHI 2012), 10 p. Association for Computing Machinery (2012). http://dx.doi.org/10.1145/2207676.2207678

Lau, S., Drosos, I., Markel, J.M., Guo, P.J.: The deisgn space of computational notebook: an analysis of 60 systems in academia and industry. In: 2020 IEEE Symposium on Visual Languages and Human-Centric Computing (VL/HCC), pp. 1–11. (2020). http://dx.doi.org/10.1109/VLHCC.2020.9127201

Lemaignan, S., Fink, J., Dillenbourg, P., Braboszcz, C.: The cognitive correlates of anthropomorphism. In: Proceedings of the 2014 Human-Robot Interaction Conference, Workshop on Neurosciences and Robotics (2014)

Nielsen, J.: Usability Engineering. Academic Press, San Diego (1993)

Raji, I.D., et al.: These are the four most popular misconceptions people have about race & gender bias in algorithms..., 27 March 2021. https://twitter.com/rajiinio/status/1375957284061376516

Rakova, B., Chowdhury, R., Yang, J.: Assessing the intersection of organizational structure and FAT* efforts within industry: implications tutorial. In: Proceedings of the 2020 Conference on Fairness, Accountability, and Transparency (2020)

Rule, A., Tabard, A., Hollan, J.: Exploration and explanation in computational notebooks. In: Proceedings of the 2018 CHI Conference on Human Factors in Computing Systems (CHI), Article 32, 12 p. Association for Computing Machinery (2018). http://dx.doi.org/10.1145/3173574.2173606

Schiff, D., Rakova, B., Ayesh, A., Fanti, A., Lennon, M.: Principles to practices for responsible AI: closing the gap. Presented at 2020 European Conference on AI (ECAI) Workshop on "Advancing Towards the SDGs: AI For a Fair, Just, and Equitable World (AI 4EQ)" (2020). https://arxiv.org/abs/2005.04707

Yin, M., Wortman Vaughn, J., Wallach, H.: Understanding the effect of accuracy on trust in machine learning models. In: Proceedings of the 2019 CHI Conference on Human Factors in Computing Systems (CHI 19), Paper 279, pp. 1–12. Association for Computing Machinery New York (2019). http://dx.doi.org/10.1145/3290605.3300509

Yip, J.C., et al.: Laughter is scary, but farting is cute: a conceptual model of children's perspectives of creepy technologies. In: Proceedings of the 2019 CHI Conference on Human Factors in Computing Systems (CHI 2019), Paper 73, pp. 1–15. Association for Computing Machinery, New York (2019). http://dx.doi.org/10.1145/3290605.3300303

Wang, A.Y., Mittal, A., Brooks, C., Oney, S.: How data scientists use computational notebooks for real-life collaboration. In: Proceedings of the ACM on Human-Computer Interaction 3. CSCW, Article 39, 30 p. (2019). http://dx.doi.org/10.11453359141

Wexler, J., Pushkarna, M., Balukbasi, T., Wattenberg, M., Viégas, F., Wilson, J.: The what-if tool: interactive probing of machine learning models. IEEE Trans. vis. Comput. Graph. 26(1), 56–65 (2020). https://doi.org/10.1109/TVCG.2019.2934619

Wood, J., Kachkaev, A., Dykes, J.: Design exposition with literate visualization. IEEE Trans. Vis. Comput. Graph. 25(1), 759–768 (2019). http://dx.doi.org/10.1109/TVCG.2018.285436

Related Websites

Project Jupyter. https://jupyter.org/
Google Colab. https://colab.research.google.com/
AI meets Design toolkit. http://aimeets.design/
Poieto. https://aidesigntool.com/
Apache UIMA. https://uima.apache.org/

Identification of Hate Tweets:
Which Words Matter the Most?

Kezheng Xiang, Zixing Zhang, Yuwen Yu, Luis San Lucas,
Mohammad Ruhul Amin$^{(\boxtimes)}$, and Yanjun Li

Department of Computer and Information Science,
Fordham University, New York, USA
{kxiang1,zzhang366,yyu149,lsanlucas,mamin17,yli}@fordham.edu

Abstract. For years, social media platforms have been used to incite
violence towards minority groups using hate speech or writing that
express pejorative or discriminatory language undermining gender, ethnicity, religion, or nationality. In this article, we assembled a multi-class
dataset of 83,360 tweets, which include four hate classes and one non-
hate class. We adopted three popular machine learning and deep learning
models, such as SVM, long short-term memory model extended with an
attention mechanism (LSTM-Attention), and BERT model for the classification of those hate tweets. Our experiments show that for the identification of religious-hate tweets, LSTM-Attention model consistently
produced the best performance, while for other two types of hate tweets,
such as sexist and racist, we observed that on average BERT produces
the best result. Both the LSTM-Attention and BERT reached an overall F1-score of 90% and 91% respectively for multi-label classification.
Our detail analysis reveals that since sexist or racist tweets make use
of more hate or slang words than that of religious-hate tweets, BERT
performs better in detecting the first two classes. However, since many
of religious-hate tweets not necessarily include any disparaging words,
BERT failed to identify those hate speeches. Thus, LSTM-Attention was
used to extract the words with higher attention weights to identify which
words matter the most for the classification of hate speech. We show that
words that carry more predictive information for the hate tweets classification are not necessarily high frequency or hateful words.

Keywords: Abusive language detection · Hate tweets detection · Deep
learning model interpretability

1 Introduction

Nowadays, more and more people express their own opinions on social media
platforms. However, some online postings contain unpleasant, even hate content, which are considered as hate speech. As described in [1], hate speech is
commonly defined as any communication that disparages a person or a group
on the basis of some characteristic such as race, color, ethnicity, gender, sexual
orientation, nationality, religion, or other characteristics. According to the New

© Springer Nature Switzerland AG 2021
C. Stephanidis et al. (Eds.): HCII 2021, LNCS 13095, pp. 586–598, 2021.
https://doi.org/10.1007/978-3-030-90963-5_44

York Times [2], personal attacks motivated by bias or prejudice reached a 16-year high in 2018, with a significant upswing in violence against Latinos outpacing a drop-in assault targeting Muslims and Arab-Americans. Since Tweeter is a very popular social network, certain group of people use the network to spread hatred by posting tweets attacking ethnic or minority groups using religious-hate, sexist, racist, and offensive. Hence in 2019, Twitter launched a program to promote research work to improve the overall health of the network by censoring the abusive tweets [3]. Although, researchers have been working on hate tweet detection for a long time, the effort was folded following Twitter's announcement.

Related Work. For the classification of hate tweets, traditional natural language processing techniques, such as unigrams and larger n-grams were reported as predictive features [4], and character n-gram were studied to be more predictive than token n-grams [5]. It was investigated that features other than words, such as URL frequency, special symbols not found in English, could improve the performance [4]. Later, a multi-lingual and multi-aspect annotation schema was proposed to identify hate tweets [6]. Various other sentiment analysis models were also used for this task assuming that hate tweets might generally contain negative sentiment; but it did not perform well [7]. Among other attempts, lexicons of hate words were considered for abusive tweets detection. Two of the most well-regarded examples are Hatebase [8] and VADER [9]. They both contain extensive lexicons validated by humans. For each word in its lexicon, Hatebase includes definitions, provides offensiveness scores as well as Boolean values for whether the word is usually used as racist, a religious offense, homophobic, etc. VADER, on the other hand, includes positive words in its lexicon as well. It is also very good at determining overall sentiment of phrases. It achieves this by applying weights to the overall scores of each word in a phrase. The weights consider negations, emoticons, and punctuation.

Contribution. Using the largest dataset on abusive tweets, we applied three popular models, namely SVM, LSTM-Attention and BERT model for the classification of hate tweets. In this paper, we present the following research contributions:

1. We assembled the largest dataset, a total of 83,360 tweets labeled in five classes, such as religious-hate, sexist, racist, offensive, and non-hate for the hate tweet classification.
2. We show that LSTM-Attention model produces the best performance for religious-hate tweet classification, while BERT performs best for both racist and sexist tweets classification.
3. We studied the distribution of hateful words, high frequency words, and words with high attention weight assigned among the classified tweets by the LSTM-Attention model. Our experiments show that words with higher attention carry more predictive information regarding hate tweets detection.

2   Datasets

The combined dataset includes a total of 83,360 tweets as shown in Table 1, collected from four different sources:

- Hate speech identification dataset by Thomas et al. [10]
- Hate speech dataset by Hurmet et al. [11]
- Stanford sentiment dataset by Kazanove et al. [12]
- Hate speech detection in multimodal publication by Raul et al. [13]

Table 1. Number of tweets, vocabulary size and unique tokens in each of the tweet datasets.

Class	# of tweets	# of tokens	Vocabulary size
Racist	20,000	160,312	22,784
Sexist	16,243	158,747	21,654
Religious-Hate	3,857	60,493	9,912
Non-Hate	19,986	164,154	29,465
Offensive	20,620	201,980	23,324

Table 2. Details of training datasets. We created 7 different datasets using combinations of abusive classes.

Dataset	Classes	Class names
A	4	Non-Hate, Racist, Sexist, Religious-Hate
B	2	Non-Hate, Hate (Racist, Sexist, and Religious-Hate)
C	2	Non-Hate, Offensive
D	3	Racist, Sexist, Religious-Hate
E	2	Non-Religious-Hate, Religious-Hate
F	2	Non-Racist-Hate, Racist
G	2	Non-Sexist-Hate, Sexist

In the Hate Speech Identification dataset [10], 24,802 tweets were manually labeled as Hate Speech, Offensive, or neither Offensive nor Hate Speech by CrowdFlower workers. A tweet was labeled as hate speech not just if it contains hate words from Hatebase.org but also if its context carries hateful meaning. The dataset contains a total of 24,783 tweets, comprising of 1,430 tweets of hate speech, 19,190 tweets of offensive speech, and 4,163 tweets of non-abusive tweets. Hate speech and offensive speech were combined to create the offensive class (20,620 tweets) for this study.

In the Hate Speech dataset [11], each tweet contains the word *religion*. Preprocessing includes removing username, hashtags, URLs, numbers, punctuation, and special characters (@, &, #, %, etc.), short words (less than three characters). Then the collection words like religion or religious were removed. Tweets with less than 3 tokens were also removed. For this dataset, SONAR algorithm [14] was adopted to perform hate speech detection and tweets were labeled as hate, offensive, or neither. We combined 248 hate-speech and 3,609 offensive tweets and created religion-hate class with 3,857 tweets.

In the Stanford Sentiment dataset [12], 1,600,000 tweets with emoticons were extracted using the Twitter Application Programming Interface (API). Tweets containing five positive emoticons [:) , :=), :), :D, =)] were annotated as positive and tweets with negative emoticons [:(, :-(, : ( ] were annotated as negative. These emoticons were stripped off to reduce biases in modeling task. After processing, there are 800,000 positive and 800,000 negative tweets. 19,986 positive tweets were sampled as non-hate tweets for our study.

In the Hate Speech Detection in Multimodal Publication dataset [13], the original tweets containing both text and images were annotated by Amazon Mechanical Turk workers into six categories (no attacks to any racist, sexist, homophobic, religion based attacks, including attacks to ethnic communities). If a tweet had only sexist annotations, it was labeled as sexist tweet; and if a tweet had only racist annotations, it was labeled as racist tweet. We processed the downloaded dataset and performed some cleaning. In this study, we kept only the text tweets and removed images. We collected 16,243 sexist tweets, and 20,000 racist tweets which were randomly sampled from 47,246 racist labeled tweets.

Finally, the combined dataset includes a total of 83,360 tweets as shown in Tables 1 and 2. Some examples of each class can be seen in Table 3.

Table 3. Data sample for each twitter hate class.

Tweet class	Tweet example
Non-hate	- I'm back Twitterville! and good morniiiiing! - On fanfictions, the greatest retort when one says -F*ck you!- is -Didn't know you want to..– WIN
Racist-hate	- This nigga cried camera got rich scamming niggas got exposed racist dipped - white trash smh
Sexist-hate	- I fucking hate internet dating... Seriously what in the actual fuck... What a bigot cunt - gays be so mean for no reason like yall dont have a hobby?? other than being a cunt??
Religious-hate	- Everyone is going to hell according to someone else's religion - Religion is for people Who are afraid of hell Spirituality is for people Who have already been there
Offensive	- Having a 'new boyfriend' every month doesn't mean you're gorgeous.... It means you're easy, and retarded - what a retard lol

We created a total of 7 different datasets to perform various experiments (Table 2). Dataset A include four classes of tweets, namely non-hate vs three hate classes (racist, sexist and religious-hate). We also have one dataset (D) that includes three different hate classes to show whether a model can differentiate among different types of hate tweets. We did not compare the offensive tweet class to the other three hate tweet classes, as almost all the offensive words can be found in the three other hate classes. Datasets B, C, E, F, and G combine the subset of all the five tweet classes for experimenting with binary classification task. In dataset B, there are two classes, one is hate class (which has three hate subclasses combined with only one label), and the other one is non-hate class. In dataset C, there are two classes, one is non-hate class, and the other one is offensive class. In dataset E, there are two classes, one is non-religion-hate (combining racist, and sexist) and the other one is religious-hate. Similarly, dataset F has two classes such as non-racist hate tweets combining other two hate classes and racist hate tweets; while dataset G contains non-sexist hate tweets (i.e., racist, and religious-hate tweets) and sexist hate class.

3   Methodologies

To understand which words matter the most for the identification of the hate tweets, we experimented with several models. We discuss each of them below.

3.1   Vader-SVM Model

We applied an SVM model on Vader-tokenized words for the classification task. To do so, we followed the following steps.

1. We retrieved the sentiment score in Vader's lexicon for each word in our 83,360 tweet database. Forming a vector for each tweet which was then padded to achieve equal-length vectors.
2. We split the data in 80:20 ratio to create train and test datasets. We fit the SVM model to the train dataset and obtained results of predictions on the test set.

The model didn't perform as well as the others in the classification task. Even though Vader takes into account various speech modifiers like negations and punctuation it is not designed specifically for classification. By testing this model we learned that it is not the most effective way to classify hate speech by taking single words into account without considering other factors like context or type of hate.

3.2   SVM Model on Word Tokenization

In previous work [15], the authors presented that text classification problem can be solved using the support vector machine (SVM) delivering state-of-the-art performance. So we decided to include SVM modeling to perform the classification task. The modeling was performed as follows:

1. We used Sklearn's CountVectorizer which builds a dictionary of features and transforms vocabularies, i.e., unigrams to feature vectors. For this task, CountVectorizer was performed on the word N-grams for each tweet.

2. Then, the dataset was split following the 80:20 rules for training and testing of each class. Since, we have enough data for each class, we did not perform any cross validation.
3. Training was performed for each of the seven datasets. Once the dataset was fitted in the SVM model, the CountVectorizer for the test data was fed to the trained model for performance evaluation.
4. Later, we extracted the SVM coefficient for each word following its index in the CountVectorizer. These weights were analyzed to interpret the results of the SVM.

3.3   LSTM-Attention Model

In a feed forward neural network, neurons of one layer take the input and apply matrix transformation to produce the output, which is taken as the input of next layer of the network model. In a recurrent neural network (RNN), the output of current layer is taken as the input of the same layer through the loop structure. In this way, information of previous step could be passed to next step, which is ideal for processing the sequence input, such as text data. However, when a sequence input is processed, not all previous parts of the input are relevant to current state, which is defined as the long term dependency problem [16,17]. LSTM models [18], a special kind of RNN, is designed to solve this problem. This model can learn how to process the sequence of input retaining the sequential dependency during the training process.

LSTM networks have been shown to learn long-term dependencies more easily than the simple recurrent architectures. Still, the final state of this kind of RNN architecture is not capable to include the significance of different parts of the input - thus impacting the classification performance. To solve this problem, attention mechanism [19] was proposed to assign significance to different parts of the input.

Intuitively, people would identify a hate tweet by matching certain keywords, such as hateful words. The observations show that basic word filtering does not work well since not all hate tweets contain hateful words, and the meaning of words could be interpreted in different ways within their context [20]. Considering tweets as sequences of terms, and terms contributing to the sentiment of tweets in different ways within different context, the LSTM-Attention model can be considered as a better choice for hate tweets detection. The model summary is presented in Fig. 1.

LSTM-CNN model with an attention layer were implemented in Python in our project. The vocabulary size of input is 20,000. As the average length of tweets are around 15 words, we set the maximum length of input sequences as 20 words. The dropout rate of the model is 0.5, and the loss function is spare categorical cross-entropy. This same architecture was used to perform both the multi-label and binary classification tasks.

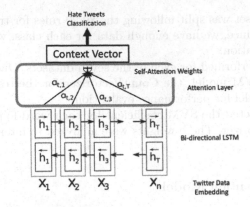

Fig. 1. LSTM-Attention model architecture used in experiment.

3.4   BERT Model

BERT stands for Bidirectional Encoder Representations from Transformers. The BERT model is a popular state-of-the-art machine learning model that is able to cope with multiple NLP tasks such as supervised text classification without human supervision [21]. BERT performs well since it uses the encoder of the transformer to model the left and right contexts of the word. In our experiment, we used the contextual sentence representation from pre-trained BERT-base uncased followed by a dense layer to perform classification task.

As the BERT works with fixed-length sequences, we set max length of input sentence as 20 for our experiment. Each of the input token is represented with an embedding vector of size 768 in BERT. So for a given input set, we used BertTokenizer function to vectorize tokens for the entire set into a shape of [Number-of-Tweets X Max-Length-of-Tweet X Embedding-Vector-Size]. Then, we retrieve the pooled-out layer from pre-trained BERT model as vector representation of the input content having a vector size of 768 for each tweet. Finally, we use a dense layer as classifier to perform classification task.

4   Results

In this section, we describe the results obtained by our models in the classification task as well as interpret the models' results with respect to which words get the most attention.

4.1   High Frequency Words Observed in Hate Tweets Classes

We combined four classes with hate content as one hate class and compared its high frequency words with that of non-hate class (dataset B). The word clouds of top 100 frequent words for the combined hate, and non-hate classes are shown in Fig. 2. The size of each word is equivalent to its frequency. Among top 100 frequent words from each class, 42 words are shared; among top 50 frequent words, 20 words are shared; and among top 20 frequent words, only 5 words are shared - such as 'get', 'got', 'know', 'like', 'u'. We investigated further by comparing top 50 high frequent words among three hate classes (racist, sexist, and religious-hate tweets). The overlapping among them is displayed in Fig. 3. It is observed that 48% of high frequent words of religious-hate tweet class are shared with other classes, and more than 60% of high frequent words of racist and sexist classes are shared with other classes.

(a)   (b)

Fig. 2. Word clouds of top 100 high frequent words in the (a) Combined hate tweet class and (b) Non-hate class.

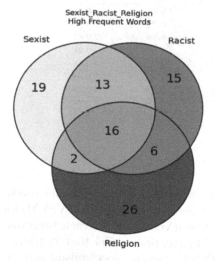

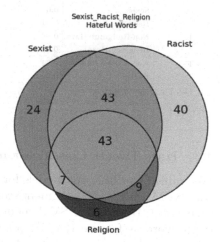

Fig. 3. Venn diagram showing set inclusion of high frequency words from three hate classes.

Fig. 4. Venn diagram representing the set inclusion of hateful words and three other hate tweet classes.

4.2   Share of Hate Words Observed in Different Tweets Classes

Hatebase.org is the largest hateful words repository available online. By accessing its API, we collected 1,533 English words to create a list. There are 33 hateful words appearing in all classes including hate classes and non-hate class, and 40 hateful words appearing in all hate classes (offensive, religious-hate, racist and sexist). We investigated further by comparing the overlapping of hateful words among sexist, racist and religious-hate classes (Fig. 4). Total 172 hateful words are found in these three classes, 25% of them are shared by all classes. 86% of hateful words in religious-hate class, 80% in racist class, and 70% in sexist class are shared with other classes.

Table 4. F1-score for each classification task as produced by each predictive model: Vader-SVM (VSVM), SVM, LSTM and BERT.

Dataset	Class names	VSVM F1-score	SVM F1-score	LSTM F1-score	BERT F1-score
A	Non-Hate	0.62	**0.99**	0.96	**0.99**
	Racist	0.43	0.84	0.85	**0.88**
	Religious-Hate	0.64	0.96	**0.99**	0.80
	Sexist	0.37	0.79	0.79	**0.84**
B	Non-Hate	0.85	**0.99**	**0.99**	**0.99**
	Hate	0.60	**0.99**	0.9	**0.99**
C	Non-Hate	0.84	0.98	**0.99**	0.98
	Offensive	0.80	0.98	**0.99**	0.98
D	Racist	0.62	0.84	0.85	**0.89**
	Sexist	0.65	0.78	**0.79**	0.72
	Religious-Hate	0.41	0.98	**0.99**	0.97
E	Non-Religious-Hate	0.96	0.99	1	0.99
	Religious-Hate	0.38	0.98	1	0.98
F	Non-Racist-Hate	0.71	0.83	0.83	**0.89**
	Racist	0.62	0.84	**0.85**	0.78
G	Non-Sexist-Hate	0.67	0.87	**0.88**	0.79
	Sexist	0.63	0.79	0.78	**0.87**

4.3   Hate Tweets Classification

We trained four different models for the classification task: (a) a baseline model with SVM using Vader sentiment score of each tweet word as feature (VSVM) for each tweet; (b) another SVM model using CountVectorizer for each tokenized tweet word as feature (SVM); (c) an LSTM-Attention model that is trained over the embedding of each tweet word with self-attention mechanism; and (d) a deep learning classifier that use contextual sentence representation from the pre-trained BERT-base uncased followed by a dense layer. The F1-score of each model is shown in Table 4. For training each of these models, we used 80% of each dataset, and tested with rest of the 20% data. Furthermore, we present the weighted F1-score of all the seven datasets for each model in the Table 5. The results show that with an exception for the religious-hate tweets classification BERT performs best in all other tasks.

Table 5. Overall F1-score for each of the seven datasets as produced by each predictive model.

Dataset	VSVM F1-score	SVM F1-score	LSTM F1-score	BERT F1-score
A	0.52	0.89	0.90	**0.91**
B	0.73	**0.99**	**0.99**	**0.99**
C	0.82	0.98	**0.99**	0.98
D	0.56	0.84	0.84	**0.88**
E	0.67	0.99	1	0.99
F	0.67	0.84	0.84	**0.85**
G	0.65	0.84	0.84	**0.85**

4.4 Attention Words Detected by LSTM-Attention Model

When LSTM model predicts the label of a tweet, the attention layer assigns each word of a given tweet an attention weight, and words with higher weights contribute more to the prediction result. To investigate words that are getting more attention in the LSTM model, we studied a trained multi-class model with dataset A. This model predicts hate tweets for the four classes as mentioned above, such as non-hate, racist, sexist, and religious-hate. We run the trained model to predict class labels for all tweets in each class of the training dataset. If a prediction is correct, the word being assigned the maximum attention weight is considered as the *Attention Word*. Our experimental results show that overlapping of higher attention words with high frequency words for the three hate classes are quite high. On the other hand, the overlapping of higher attention words with hateful words for each class is relatively low (Table 6).

4.5 Words with Highest Weights from SVM Model and BERT Model

We extracted the positional weights of each word corresponding to the CountVectorizer to interpret the classification performance of SVM model. We observed that the top weighted word list for each hate class include wrong, misspelled, twitter usernames and even hashtags. Our analysis produced only a few common words (such as annoying, nigga, etc.) among these three lists and the hateful words from Hatabase.org.

As BERT attention mechanism lets each input token to focus all of its surrounding tokens in 12 separate attention layers, it is hard to interpret how BERT leverage on individual words. One could argue to extract the keywords from the tweets using BERT and pick the most weighted keywords. But then according to our background study on transformer models, we concluded that it could mislead the analysis of abusive words in hate tweets as the BERT transformer model was never really trained based on the similar objective as ours. So, we consider this analysis as out of the scope of this paper.

Table 6. Overlap of attention words from LSTM model with high frequency and hateful words. We also included the higher attention words for the non-hate class at the end of the table.

Class	Overlap of higher attention words from LSTM model and high frequency words	Overlap of higher attention words from LSTM model and fateful words
Religious-Hate	'muslim', 'hell', 'sex', 'shit', 'ass', 'church', 'bullshit', 'religion', 'christian', 'islam', 'belief', 'fuck', 'women'	'trash', 'dyke', 'nigga', 'gay', 'cunt', 'faggot', 'twat', 'bitch'
Sexist	'cock', 'cunt', 'retard', 'babe', 'dick', 'faggot', 'cum', 'feminazi', 'milf', 'ass', 'sjw', 'fat', 'dyke', 'twat', 'bitch', 'slut', 'nigga', 'fuck'	'whore', 'fag', 'dyke', 'spic', 'slut', 'nigga', 'cunt', 'retard', 'faggot', 'feminazi', 'bint', 'twat', 'bitch'
Racist	'race', 'retard', 'faggot', 'trash', 'card', 'shit', 'ass', 'redneck', 'racist', 'dyke', 'nigger', 'bitch', 'nigga', 'white', 'realdonaldtrump', 'fuck'	'trash', 'wigger', 'redneck', 'fag', 'dyke', 'spic', 'rube', 'nigga', 'retard', 'faggot', 'wetback', 'nigger', 'bitch'
Non-Hate	'new', 'twitter', 'song', 'work', 'fun', 'great', 'haha', 'weekend', 'though', 'tweet', 'wait', 'night', 'home', 'cool', 'bed', 'hey', 'tomorrow', 'good', 'time', 'see', 'best', 'quot', 'thank', 'yay', 'well', 'today', 'soon', 'day', 'lol', 'tonight', 'love', 'back', 'hope', 'nice', 'week', 'sleep', 'better', 'amp'	

5 Discussion

In our analysis, we relied on the LSTM-Attention model for its interpretable outcomes. For each class of dataset A, we ranked all collected attention words based on their frequencies and created a set of top 100 attention words. The set of attention words of non-hate class overlaps with only a small number of words of religious-hate, racist and sexist classes - the numbers of shared words are (3, 4, 4) respectively. The overlapping of attention words in three hate classes are shown in Fig. 5. It is observed that 29% of attention words of religious-hate class are shared with other classes, while 39% of both the racist and sexist classes are shared with other classes.

Figure 6 shows that in the religious-hate class, 8% of attention words overlap with hateful words, and 13% overlap with high frequency words. However, there is no overlapping between hateful words and high frequency words in religious-hate class. This observation indicates that simple hateful words filtering does not work well for religion related hate tweet detection. The high performance of LSTM-Attention model on predicting religious-hate class became possible due to the model's capacity to capture the context of religious-hate tweets.

To understand the relationship among high frequency words, hateful words, and attention words of non-hate class, we performed comparisons among them. Figure 7 shows that attention words and high frequency words of non-hate class have 40% overlapping. It is understandable that hateful words in tweets of non-hate class are not high frequency words or attention words. The high performance of LSTM-Attention model on predicting non-hate class is thus contributed by capturing words which are neither high frequent nor hateful words.

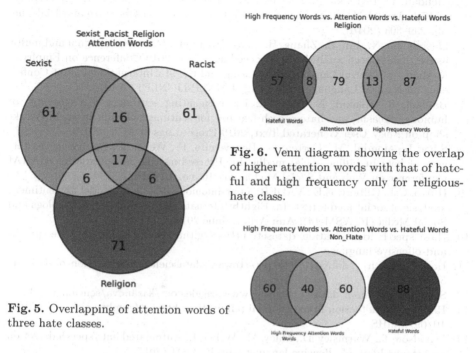

Fig. 5. Overlapping of attention words of three hate classes.

Fig. 6. Venn diagram showing the overlap of higher attention words with that of hateful and high frequency only for religious-hate class.

Fig. 7. Comparison of different word lists for non-hate class.

6 Conclusions

Experiments show that great amount of attention words captured by the self-attention layers are not hateful words or high frequent words in each class. The high performance of the LSTM-Attention model on predicting both non-hate and hate classes, especially religious-hate class indicates that attention words could be considered as the useful predictive words for hate tweets detection.

References

1. Nockleby, J.T.: Hate speech. In: Encyclopedia of the American Constitution, 2nd edn., pp. 1277–1279. Macmil- lan (2000)
2. Hate Crime Reports on NYTIMES, vol. 12, 2–19, November 2019. Link: https://www.nytimes.com/2019/11/12/us/hate-crimes-fbi-report.html
3. A Healthier Twitter: progress and more to do. https://blog.twitter.com/en_us/topics/company/2019/health-update.html

4. Bobata, C., Tetreault, J., Thomas, A., Mehdad, Y., Chang, Y.: Abusive language detection in online user content. In: Proceedings of the 25th International Conference on World Wide Web, pp. 145–153 (2016)
5. Mehdad, Y., Tetreault, J.: Do Characters abuse more than words? In: Proceedings of 17th Annual Meeting of the Special Interest Group on Discourse and Dialogue, pp. 299–303 (2016)
6. Ousidhoum, N., Lin, Z., Zhang, H., Song, Y., Yeung, D.Y.: Multilingual and multi-aspect hate speech analysis. In: Proceedings of the 2019 Conference on Empirical Methods in Natural Language Processing and the 9th International Joint Conference on Natural Language Processing (EMNLP-IJCNLP) (2019)
7. Badlani, R., Asnani, N., Rai, M.: Disambiguating sentiment: An ensemble of humour, sarcasm, and hate speech features for sentiment classification. In: Workshop on Noisy User Generated Text, 2019 Proceedings of ACL (2019)
8. Silva, L., Mondal, M., Correa, D., Benevenuto, F., Weber, I.: Analyzing the targets of hate in online social media. In: Proceedings of the International AAAI Conference on Web and Social Media, vol. 10, no. 1 (2016)
9. Hutto, C.J., Gilbert, E.E.: VADER: a parsimonious rule-based model for sentiment analysis of social media text. In: Eighth International Conference on Weblogs and Social Media (ICWSM-14). Ann Arbor, June 2014
10. Hate speech identification dataset. https://github.com/t-davidson/hate-speech-and-offensive-language
11. Hate speech dataset. https://towardsdatascience.com/religion-on-twitter-5f7b84062304
12. Stanford sentiment dataset. https://www.kaggle.com/kazanova/sentiment140
13. Hate speech detection in multimodal publication. https://gombru.github.io/2019/10/09/MMHS/
14. Davidson, T., Warmsley, D., Macy, M., Weber, I.: Automated hate speech detection and the problem of offensive language. In: ICWSM (2017)
15. Joachims, T.: A statistical learning learning model of text classification for support vector machines. In: Proceedings of the 24th Annual International ACM SIGIR Conference on Research and Development in Information Retrieval (2001)
16. Bengio, Y., Simard, P., Frasconi, P.: Learning long-term dependencies with gradient descent is difficult. IEEE Trans. Neural Netw. 5(2), 157–166 (1994)
17. Hochreiter, J.: Untersuchungen zu dynamischen neuronalen Netzen Diploma Thesis, Institut fur Informatik. Brauer, Technische Universitat Munchen, Lehrstul Prof (1991)
18. Hochreiter, S., Schmidhuber, J.: Long short-term memory technical report FKI-207-95. Technische Universitat Munchen, Fakultat fur Informatik (1995)
19. Bahdanau, D., Cho, K., Bengio, Y.: Neural machine translation by jointly learning to align and translate. In: Proceedings of the International Conference on Learning Representations (2014). arXiv:1409.0473
20. Schmidt, A., Wiegand, M.: A survey on hate speech detection using natural language processing. In: Proceedings of the Fifth International Workshop on Natural Language Processing for Social Media, pp. 1–10 (2017)
21. Meena, S.: BERT text classification using keras (2020). https://swatimeena989.medium.com/bert-text-classification-using-keras-903671e0207d

Author Index